THE BOOK OF MUSICAL KNOWLEDGE

WAGNER

THE BOOK OF
MUSICAL KNOWLEDGE

The History, Technique, and Appreciation of Music, together with Lives of the Great Composers

FOR MUSIC-LOVERS, STUDENTS AND TEACHERS

By ARTHUR ELSON

With Illustrations

NEW AND ENLARGED EDITION

BOSTON AND NEW YORK
HOUGHTON MIFFLIN COMPANY
The Riverside Press Cambridge

The Riverside Press
CAMBRIDGE . MASSACHUSETTS
PRINTED IN THE U.S.A.

PREFACE

THIS book was planned with a view to placing before the general reader the main facts that would enable him to appreciate music intelligently. Many people have made the remark, "I'm fond of music, but I don't understand it." It was felt that a work of this sort would go far toward remedying any such lack of knowledge, and enlightening the non-musician as well as the more or less experienced concert-goer. By perusing these pages the reader could make himself familiar with the various historical schools of music, the lives of the great composers, the qualities that made their works become known and stay in the repertoire, the use of the instruments, the various musical forms, and a number of special subjects.

In the years that have elapsed since this book was first issued, much progress has taken place in music, and many changes have come about, whether for better or worse. So it has been deemed advisable to add a chapter covering this period, and discussing the modernist tendencies of the day as well as the recent composers and their work.

During these twelve years, also, the advent of the radio has brought music before a much larger public than concert or operatic audiences, which were necessarily limited. With such a greatly increased number of people paying attention to good music, it is felt that this work, which offers a thorough musical education from the auditor's point of view, will be of increased use and service to those who listen to music with a wish to know something about it.

October, 1927

CONTENTS

PART I. — THE EVOLUTION OF MUSIC

PART II. — THE GREAT COMPOSERS

CONTENTS

ILLUSTRATIONS

THE BOOK OF MUSICAL KNOWLEDGE

PART I

THE EVOLUTION OF MUSIC

THE BOOK OF MUSICAL KNOWLEDGE

I

PRIMITIVE AND SAVAGE MUSIC

FÉTIS defines music as the art of moving the emotions by combinations of sound. This statement would give to the tonal art a very early origin, and would even allow it a pre-human existence in the songs of birds. The beginning of human music must have been vocal in character. Herbert Spencer considers song as a form of expression arising from the reflex action of the vocal organs under stress of emotion, just as a cry follows pain. This would reverse the definition of Fétis, and make music a result of emotion rather than a cause.

It seems probable that the early songs developed from hunting-calls, or other vocal signals employed in primitive life. As soon as such calls were used for the pleasure expressed or imparted, apart from any useful purpose, they became music in the strict sense of the term. Melody would thus arise easily from the amplification of a single call or the union of several. Some authorities think that song was first an accompaniment to the muscular expression that led to dancing; but the hunting-signals probably antedated the rudimentary tangos of the primitive races.

The origin of different scales may be traced with more detail, even if some of it is legendary. Our own scale is "founded on fact," for Pythagoras brought its mathematical relations from Egypt, and made them the basis of the Greek scales. In this system the pitches of the notes corresponded to definite fractional parts of a stretched string. The Greek system became the basis of the Ambrosian and Gregorian modes, described in detail in a later chapter; and the same pitches were employed in the diatonic mode that replaced these. For the last two centuries the intervals, by common consent, have been altered slightly, to make our twelve equal semitones that permit of modulation from one key to any other.

Not all people, however, use our scale. In Siam and some neighboring countries the octave is divided into five, six, or seven equal parts to form a scale. The Hindus, on the other hand, used smaller scale-parts than ours, having third- and quarter-tones. The legends tell us that when the god Krishna came to earth, he was met by no less than sixteen thousand nymphs, each of whom sang to him in a mode different from that of the others. If they all sang at once, the hearer would certainly have needed more than human patience; but the account does not deal with that point. From this event came the numerous modes, or *Raagnis*, that were found in the native Indian music. These were often of great power; and some were held even too potent for mortal use. Thus it is related that the Emperor Akbar commanded the famous singer Naik Gobaul to sing the Mode of Fire. That performer, after finding all refusal vain, started his fatal task, but took the precaution of plunging up to his neck in the waters of the Djumna. Before his song was over, the water around him began to boil. Even then the Emperor would not let him stop; so he resumed the fiery strain, only to burst into flames and be consumed as he finished it. The story seems apocryphal, though many later singers have been known to be persuaded into attempting things that they cannot manage safely.

China uses the so-called pentatonic scale, consisting of intervals similar to those of the black keys on our pianos. That this scale may give pleasing effects is shown by the Scotch folk-music, in which many of the most beautiful songs, such as "Auld Lang Syne" or "Bonnie Doon," are wholly in the five-note scale. Turning again to legend, we find that the Chinese evidently preferred this scale to our diatonic mode. Long ago the sage Ling-Lun, in search of knowledge, came to the banks of the sacred river. Here he found the immortal bird of China, the Foang-Hoang, with its mate. The female bird sang the notes of our diatonic scale, while the male bird limited his outpourings to the pentatonic scale. At that time everything feminine was held of little account in China, so the female's notes were rejected, and those of the male bird chosen. A little judicious cutting among the bamboo reeds on the river-bank enabled Ling-Lun to perpetuate this scale. At present the Chinese often sing with a piercing intonation; but their music itself is not at all unpleasing, as the song in praise of the Mu-Li flower will show.

(A Chinese song praising a branch of Mu-Li flowers thrown into a maiden's door.)

Among ancient instruments, those of the Chinese are best described. Their invention is ascribed to Kai-Tien-Chi, the ninth emperor of the spiritual dynasty mentioned in Chinese mythology. They are classified according to their material, and form the following eight groups: (1) The sound of skin; (2) the sound of stone; (3) that of metal; (4) of baked clay; (5) of silk strings; (6) of wood; (7) of bamboo; (8) of calabash.

The skin of animals, suitably tanned, is used in the eight varieties of Chinese drum. Most of these are barrel-shaped, but two of the smaller ones are more flat, and often partly filled with rice-grains. Musical stones, to the number of sixteen, form what is known as the *king*, the stones being shaped much like a carpenter's square and hung in a row. These are very valuable when perfect. They date from early times, a set of them having been received as tribute in the year 2250 B.C. The sound of metal is heard in the many bells and gongs, which are highly esteemed in China. Baked clay forms the material of the *hiuen*, a whistle with from five to seven apertures. Silk strings are employed on the *kin* and the *che*, which are widely used. The former has seven strings, giving only the five tones of the pentatonic scale. The latter is much larger, having twenty-five strings. These strings are plucked to produce the tone, which is unusually soft and agreeable. Wooden instruments are devoted altogether to noise. The chief forms are a hollow box struck by a hammer, and a tiger-image with wooden pegs in its back, the pegs being swept at a stroke in much the same fashion that a small boy will use in running a stick along a picket fence. Bamboo forms the *siao* and the flutes. The former is a set of sixteen Pan-pipes. The latter have only three finger-holes, and therefore demand much skill in playing. Still more difficult was the obsolete form with the mouthpiece in the centre, three holes on each side, and the ends stopped up. The calabash, or gourd, serves as the air-chamber of the *cheng*, which has gold-tipped reeds stuck into it to form a primitive organ. In recent years the Chinese have adopted foreign instruments of the banjo and trumpet type.

Musical instruments were probably copied from natural models. The wind whistling in a hollow reed would suggest the flute; a branch bumping against a hollow tree may well have led to drums; while the twanging bowstring develops naturally into a rudimentary harp. In Egyptian mythology the invention of the lyre, ascribed to Thoth (the Greek Hermes), took place when that god's foot came in contact with the tendons of a dead tortoise, which had dried and tightened on the animal's shell.

According to the evidence of prehistoric relics, the most ancient instrument is of the flute type. Thus, a primitive flute, rudely fashioned from the bone of an Irish elk, was found among remains near Desmond Castle; a whistle of reindeer bone formed one of the relics found among troglodyte remains in the Dordogne Valley; a bone pierced with several holes was found with flint implements at Gourdan; and a stag-horn flute was discovered near Poitiers. Flutes of the bronze age, discovered in Belgium and Schleswig, were more advanced; while the early Egyptian flutes were well-developed instruments.

The conditions existing among the early races may be judged from those which obtain among savages of more recent times. The Caribs of Guiana, for instance, employed jaguar bones for their flutes; and when these grew scarce, they fell back upon human bones. The Surinam tribes have the pleasing custom of making flutes from the bones of slain enemies. In a country as distant as New Zealand flutes made of human bone were also used. The most practicable material, however, was a hollow reed. The Greeks said of the reed that it was useful in subjugating nations by furnishing arrows, in softening men's manners by the charm of music, and in educating them by affording the means for tracing letters. Its use for making flutes has been widespread. Thus Humboldt describes the skill of the American Indians in making and tuning their flutes; Schweinfurth praises the African Bongos for similar ability; and Cook does the same for the natives of Tahiti. The last-named could tune a flute by surrounding it with a leaf, in the form of a scroll which could be lengthened or shortened at will. In some cases double flutes were used, consisting of two tubes branching from one mouthpiece. Still other flutes were arranged to fit the nostrils, and played by blowing through the nose. The syrinx, or Pan-pipe, was usually made from a set of reed tubes, though an old Peruvian instrument shows eight pipes cut from a piece of soft stone. As a rule, the savage performer was not a great virtuoso. Thus the Kaffirs employed flutes chiefly to call cattle; the Caribs used the instrument as a signal to show approach; and the Iroquois braves reserved it for love-calls. The finger-holes were usually few in number, making it difficult for the performer to get any but the simplest effects.

Instruments of the horn and trumpet type also are found among primitive peoples. African horns have been made of ivory, wood, or even large seashells. Just as Siegfried, in Wagner's Nibelungen Trilogy, has his own horn call, so many African chiefs had special horn signals of their own, for use in battle or to indicate approach. Sometimes nearly every member of a tribe would have such a signal. The Maoris of New Zealand had wooden war-trumpets seven feet long, which were audible for several miles. The Indians on the upper Rio Negro had something between a trumpet and a bassoon, made in eight different sizes for use in their so-called devils' music. On these they played good melodies, with full accompaniment. Women were barred from this ceremony on pain of death, and even forbidden to look at the instruments; and it is said that the poison used as a penalty for breaking this rule was given by fathers to their own daughters, and by husbands to their own wives.

The gong is very popular among savages. Gong-like sounds are obtained in Borneo from small pieces of iron, and even from chains thrown into the air. Skilful African players can get many effects from the gong. Its chief use, however, has been to arouse its hearers to warlike frenzy, — a condition that sometimes results from gong music in more civilized nations. Bells were adopted by the East Indian Pegus, who united twenty of them into one instrument, played by hammer-strokes. The Javanese bells, or *gammelong*, sounded like a string orchestra when heard from a distance by the Challenger expedition.

Primitive drums come in all sizes, from the skin-covered bowls of the Hottentots to the large hollow tree-trunks of the Ashantis. In Africa the drum has several uses beside that of accompanying music or dancing. It is employed to announce the arrival or departure of a stranger, to give the marching time for native carriers, or even for a code of signals. The Dwalla tribes have such signals, which they read with as much skill as a telegraph operator will use in receiving messages on his sounder.

The *marimba* is a set of flat sticks on gourds of different sizes, the sticks being struck by a hammer. Some have claimed this as the origin of the piano, but it would be far more correct to call it the precursor of the xylophone.

Plucked-string instruments are well represented by the guitar of the Ashantis, known as the *lanku*. This has a long neck joined to a hollow, skin-covered wooden box. It has eight strings, supported in two rows by a bridge. The Africans have zithers also, with strings of bamboo fibres or twisted rattan threads.

Most widespread among stringed instruments is the harp. It undoubtedly developed from the twang of the bowstring, although the New Zealanders do not have bows, and yet do possess a form of the lyre. The harp of the Kaffirs is a simple bow, on which the string may be tightened or loosened at will by means of a sliding ring. For resonance, a hollow gourd is lashed to the bow near one end. Other African tribes have harps varying in size, and with the strings ranging in number from seven to eighteen. In Guinea the natives make an æolian harp from the leaf-stalk of the æta palm, by separating its parallel fibres and putting a bridge under them. Lutes have been found on the lower Congo, with strings of palm fibres. Dahomey has a primitive mandolin, while New Britain and the York Islands possess a rudimentary banjo.

The use of friction in tone-production seems to have originated in Africa. The negro habit of rubbing two sticks together produces fearful and wonderful results, but it is a principle easy to apply to other materials. Thus the Damaras stroked their bowstrings, and produced practically a violin tone. The M'Balunda negroes evolved a crude violin with three strings of plant fibre. The Malays have a two-stringed violin, while East Java offers a sort of flattened violoncello, with horsehair strings on a frame of a rare variety of cocoanut. The Arabian *rebab*, often considered the origin of our violin, had two strings which were plucked at first, and only bowed in later times. Other Arabian instruments were the lute (*al ud*), the tabor (tambourine), the single-stringed monochord, the kettledrum, the *zamar* (an oboe), the *nefyr* (trumpet), several flutes, and the dulcimer, with its hammer-struck strings tuned in sets of three. The last-named is the real prototype of the harpsichords and spinets that led to the modern piano. The Arabian music, like that of Mohammedans in general, has a seven-toned scale, derived from a theoretical system of seventeen fractional tones. The scale, however, is not uniform, its intervals differing according to the number of fractional parts used in each tone. The music is rhythmical in character and striking in effect. It is well echoed in Félicien David's symphonic ode "The Desert," and in Saint-Saëns' song "La Brise."

Babylonia and Assyria possessed harps, dulcimers, lyres, lutes, pipes, trumpets, and drums. The lyres were much like those of Greece, — instruments with an enlargement or resonance chamber at the bottom, nearly vertical sides, and cross-bar at the top, from which the vertical strings ran down. Some of the Babylonian instruments mentioned in the third chapter of Daniel have Greek names. A dulcimer-like affair, with strings plucked instead of struck, was known as the psaltery.

Among the Hebrews, music was cherished by the prophets as early as the time of Samuel, or about 1000 B.C. In the second temple, built about 520 B.C., singing with instrumental accompaniment was customary, and the psalms were collected for such use. This early music is lost, even the old Hebrew tunes of to-day, such as "Kol Nidrei," being comparatively modern. The Hebrew instruments were almost wholly borrowed from other nations. The *kinnor*, or harp, was probably small enough to be a lyre. The *nebel* was a psaltery, sometimes hung on the player's neck. The *asor*, which David mentioned as an instrument of ten strings, was a lyre played with a plectrum. The timbrel, or tabor, or taboret, was a small hand-drum, or tambourine, probably made in different sizes. Cymbals were known, and trumpets and flutes; while probably some use was made of the Egyptian sistrum, as well as guitars and pipes. The organ in the temple was probably a set of very large Pan-pipes. The Talmud asserts that when this organ was played, the people in the streets of Jerusalem could not hear one another talk. But the name used, *magrepha*, meant fire-shovel also, and may have referred to the large shovel that was thrown down after the sacrificial fires were built. Some authorities even hold it to be a drum. All this shows our lack of knowledge on the subject, and the inaccuracy of the early writers. Another striking story comes from Josephus, who mentions a concert of two hundred thousand singers, forty thousand sistra, forty thousand harps, and two hundred thousand trumpets.

Ancient Egypt, that land of much forgotten civilization, had a well-developed system of music. The flutes in the old tombs, as already mentioned, are found to be excellent instruments. There were three varieties of harp, — a small, bow-shaped affair to be carried on the shoulders, a larger, bow-shaped instrument that was held upright, and the more massive, loop-shaped affair, often triangular in form. None of these, however, had the pillar beyond the strings that completes the triangle in modern harps and keeps the instrument in perfect tune. For this reason the Egyptian harps could not have stood very great tension, and must have been comparatively low in tone. The strings varied in number from three to twenty or more. The Egyptian lyres, shaped like the letter U with a cross-bar above, had five or more strings. The lyres were usually set upright on a table or pedestal, but could be held horizontally instead. They were played either by a plectrum or by the fingers. The later lutes were provided with frets along the neck, in quite modern fashion. There were oboes with straw reeds in the mouth-pieces, and sometimes double tubes. Trumpets were made of copper or bronze, and used chiefly for military purposes. The syrinx existed in various sizes. Percussion instruments included bone or ivory clappers, cymbals, tambourines, and at least two kinds of drum, besides the sistrum. The last was a set of metal bars hanging loosely in a frame, and giving a jingle when shaken. It is thought that this instrument was used to give signals for workmen to pull and haul together, just as one of a group of sailors tugging at a rope will sing a "chantey" to guide the men in pulling together rhythmically. Apparently Egypt had no bells or gongs, and nothing of the violin or dulcimer type.

The Egyptians employed music as a social diversion, a courtly luxury, and an adjunct of religious ceremonies. It was united with poetry and dancing. Professional singers, players, and dancers received careful training at large institutions, and some of the picture-relics show this in great detail. The existing instruments indicate that the ancient Egyptian scale was probably diatonic, and some of the pictures suggest the use of harmony in instrumental combinations.

In the seventh century B.C., Egypt was opened to the Greeks, and this international intercourse grew very rapidly. The Greek music is derived largely from the Egyptian, many of the Greek works on music having been written in Egypt. This being so, the Egyptian music, as well as the Greek, becomes the source from which our own tonal art developed. We know little of the Egyptian scale, and nothing of the notation; but apparently it could not have been greatly different from that of Greece, which has been described in detail by many writers. The so-called Ptolemaic scale system became a later model for Greece.

Enough has been set down here to show that music is by no means a recent development. The known antiquity of the Chinese instruments (of which, in passing, we may note that the Japanese are mostly copies) is so great that it makes our earliest musical classics blush for their extreme youth. The widespread employment of comparatively advanced instruments shows us that music might well have developed into a great art elsewhere than in Europe. Music, after all, is largely a matter of taste; the Chinese, on hearing European music under the auspices of Father Amiot, said that it was no doubt very learned, but that it did not touch the heart like their own music. But the old motto offers "to each his own," and for Occidental nations the history of music, except for the earliest Egyptian suggestions, is wholly confined to Europe. The postscript of the last century shows us a development in America too; but that has been largely a reflection of European standards and models.

II

GREECE AND ROME

WHEN the poet Collins called upon some party or parties unknown to "revive the just designs of Greece," at the expense of
"Cecilia's mingled world of sound," it is doubtful if he knew just
what those designs were. Certainly it was disloyal to the memory of
Purcell and the great Elizabethan composers who had gone before
him. But subsequent discoveries have given us a better insight into
the subject of ancient Greek music, and we now have several actual
specimens of that music to supplement the many historical trea-
tises.

In Greece, poetry and music were at first treated as one art. In
the Mythical or Heroic Age, the wandering minstrel flourished. He
would travel about from place to place reciting his epic fragments
or shorter poems with a certain style of chanting, or cantillation,
for each kind of poetry. The music, therefore, was not definite, the
vocal chanting and lyre accompaniment varying on repetition even
though the style remained constant. The poets were received with
sufficient honor in their peripatetic vocation. We read that

> "Seven cities claimed the birth of Homer dead,
> Through which the living Homer begged his bread."

But this was written some twenty-seven centuries after the event;
and it is probable that geniuses of the Homer or Hesiod type would
not often go hungry.

Shorter lyrics began to appear in the seventh and sixth centuries
B.C. Ionic iambics and elegiacs were composed by Archilochus and
Tyrtæus, to be succeeded by the lyrics and odes of Sappho, Alcæus,
and Anacreon, to say nothing of Pindar, and the later poetesses
Myrtis and Corinna. These were still sung with improvisational
accompaniment. They must have had a strong effect, for Solon, on
hearing a work of Sappho, expressed the hope that he might not die
before he had learned such a beautiful song.

Music was given a scientific basis by Pythagoras. Born in Samos in the year 582 B.C., he travelled extensively, and brought back from Egypt the knowledge of systematic music. He gave to the scale the mathematical proportions explained in the later chapter on acoustics, — a scale which was employed almost intact until 1700 A.D., and then changed only slightly to form our present scale. From his work and that of his successors came the well-developed system of Greek modes.

The basis of the modes was the tetrachord, or group of four adjacent notes. The diatonic tetrachord consisted of intervals represented by E, D, C, and B in our notation. The chromatic tetrachord had the intervals of E, C-sharp, C, and B; while the enharmonic tetrachord had still smaller intervals in its lower part. The diatonic tetrachord was varied by the use of C-sharp instead of C, and D-sharp also instead of D. The original tetrachord was called Dorian, that with one sharp Phrygian, and that with two sharps Lydian. These tetrachords were made into scales by the addition of tetrachords below. If the tetrachords were added above, the scales became Hypodorian, Hypophrygian, and Hypolydian, with an extra one, the Mixolydian, to complete the series. Their intervals, when tuned on the octave lyre, were as follows: —

Dorian...............	E	D	C	B	A	G	F	E
Phrygian..............	E	D	C♯	B	A	G	F♯	E
Lydian................	E	D♯	C♯	B	A	G♯	F♯	E
Mixolydian............	E	D	C	B♭	A	G	F	E
Hypodorian...........	E	D	C	B	A	G	F♯	E
Hypophrygian.........	E	D	C♯	B	A	G♯	F♯	E
Hypolydian...........	E	D♯	C♯	B	A♯	G♯	F♯	E

These, it will be seen, correspond in size of intervals with white-key scales on our pianos starting on each degree of our diatonic scale. Thus the Dorian has E to E intervals, the Phrygian D to D intervals, and so on. The Lydian mode corresponds to our diatonic scales; so that when Collins wrote, "Wrap me in soft Lydian measures," he was calling for nothing new to modern ears. Each mode was supposed to have its own special qualities, the Dorian being decidedly strong and martial. The "Hymn to Calliope," one of the few bits of old Greek music still extant, is Dorian in effect, its chief note being what we would call the third scale degree. The impressive power of this mode may be seen also in the older Scotch setting of "Auld Robin Gray," which begins and ends on the third scale degree.

HYMN TO CALLIOPE.

Palimpsest from the Library of Cardinal St. Angelo, Rome ; harmonized by Macfarren.

The Greeks combined all their scales into one large two-octave affair, composed of four Dorian tetrachords with the necessary alterations. These notes were named from the strings on the large two-octave lyre. The names, and further details, may be found in Waldo Selden Pratt's excellent book "The History of Music." The music was notated by letters. The Greeks used few letters, but gave them new meanings when written sidewise or upside down. The Romans did not understand the principle of the octave; and in adopting the Greek system they continued the letters through the alphabet, and even added other characters.

The Greek drama made use of music. Its declamation, half epic and half lyric, resembled in some degree the cantillation of the early minstrels, but was used by the chorus as well as by single performers. Instruments of the wood-wind class (flutes, oboes, clarinets, etc.) were gradually introduced also.

Most common among Grecian instruments was the lyre. This had a resonance box (often tortoise-shell), a U-shaped frame, and a cross-bar, with from four to eighteen strings. Larger than the lyre was the *kithara,* or *phorminx,* in which the strings were carried partly over the side of the resonance box instead of being attached to the top. It is held by Greilsamer, an authority on the violin, that later *kitharas* with enlarged side-frames behind the strings may have suggested the viols that led to the modern violin. The *magadis* was an Oriental harp of varying shape, with about twenty strings. From this came the term "magadizing," which meant playing in octaves instead of unison. Other harps were known under the names of *barbitos* and *trigon,* according to their shape. All these were played with the plectrum or plucked by the fingers.

Among the wind instruments, the most popular was the *aulos,* or direct flute of cane or bored wood. This had a detachable mouthpiece, and from two to eight finger-holes. There were double flutes, in which two tubes extended from one mouthpiece. The player often wore a strap around his cheeks, enabling him to get greater power. Sometimes a bellows was attached, making the flute a bagpipe. The syrinx was a set of tubes bound together, and played by blowing over the open ends. The *salpinx* was a natural trumpet of bronze, somewhat tapering in shape. The term "flute" probably included also instruments of the clarinet or oboe type, with single or double bits of vibrating reed in the mouthpiece. The deeper flutes were probably like our bassoon. Thus the sombre and impressive character of the "Nome of Kradias," a death-march played on the journey to an execution, must have drawn much of its effect from some tone-color similar to that of the bassoon.

Among the wind instruments is also the rather mysterious water-organ, invented by Ktesibios at Alexandria in the year 150 B.C. In Roman times this consisted of two or three sets of pipes mounted on a wind-chest, a keyboard of valve levers, and a pair of partly filled pumps causing air-pressure by hydraulic means.

Many of these instruments were played at private or semi-public occasions; but they became a prominent feature in the public games. The Olympic Games, occurring once every four years at Elis, dated back to the ninth century B.C. At these games there was often a contest of trumpeters, which became a regular event in 396 B.C. Most famous among the Greek trumpeters was Herodorus of Megara, who won the prize ten times in succession, and in one year was victorious in all four of the great festivals, the Olympic, the Pythian, the Nemean, and the Isthmian. Many anecdotes are told of this musician(?). He would sleep on a bearskin, in imitation of Hercules and the lion's skin. His music was so loud that at times some of his auditors were stunned by the concussion. He could play upon two trumpets at the same time, and when he did so the audience had to sit farther away than usual, to avoid the bad effects of the noise. Once at the siege of Argos, when the troops were giving way, he began to sound his two trumpets, which so inspired the warriors that they returned to the fight and won the victory. The trumpet was used for military signals rather than for really musical purposes. It was blown on the march, or to usher in a proclamation, or even to arouse the animals in horse-races.

In the musical contests the prize seems to have gone to loudness rather than to what we should call expression. Trumpeters would often injure themselves in their efforts, and sometimes even burst a blood-vessel. Harmonides, wishing to astonish his auditors, is said to have killed himself thus while playing the flute.

Flute contests took place in the Pythian games, held in honor of Apollo's victory over the Python. One of the contestants once won the prize in a rather singular manner. While he was playing on a straight flute (held directly before the face, like a trumpet), he found the mouthpiece suddenly clogged. Instantly changing the position of his instrument, he continued by playing it as a side-flute, in the manner of our present-day performers. His presence of mind was rewarded by the victor's crown.

It was natural that music should play a large part in any festival dedicated to Apollo; and in later years these events became ambitious enough. Thus in the year 250 B.C., shortly after Athens had won a temporary freedom from Macedonia, a musical festival took place that would have delighted the hearts of Richard Strauss and other modern wholesalers. The work performed was a representation of the combat between Apollo and the Python, in five movements. The composer is unknown, and it is probable that the music took shape gradually under many hands; but the details of the scoring are recorded with some fulness.

The first movement represented Apollo coming to Pytho, and joining other celestial beings in their pastimes. This included a dance of the Horæ, with the Graces and Muses presiding. The movement opened with thirty *simikions*, or hand-played harps; and these may have given some harmony, for the playing of chords on the harp (instead of unison) had already been taught by Stratonicus. Twelve of the harps were of the enlarged form known as *epigoneion*, with forty strings instead of thirty-five. After a time ninety-five woodwind players were heard, using the *plagiaulos* (side flute) and *bombyx* (a sort of clarinet). This was all in the Æolian or Phrygian mode. At the dance were heard the *krotala*, or clappers, commonly used to accompany the dances of Bacchantes and others.

The second movement portrayed the descent of Apollo to the fray. It was in the Mixolydian mode, a scale that even in our music suggests hesitation and suspense. The low notes of twenty-seven deep *bombos* pipes, somewhat like our bass clarinets, gave a portentous and funereal effect to the end of the movement.

The third movement pictured the actual combat, in the martial Dorian mode, and with a rapid iambic rhythm. Forty-three clarinets were struck on the outside, to represent the sound emitted by the monster gnashing his teeth. Fifty players on the syrinx imitated the Python's groans. A hundred lyre players handled the *polyphthongos* and *barbitos*, large instruments with comparatively few strings. The complete forces were now in action, and numbered over five hundred, including the loud *kumbaloi*, or cymbals, with the smaller varieties known as *lekidoi* and *oxubaphoi*. At the height of the tumult, major thirds (considered the most discordant interval) rang out from forty-five trumpets.

The fourth movement showed the monster's dying struggles. Fifty-five shrill fifes gave a portrayal of his angry hisses. The earlier strings, with the forms of the lyre known as *atropos*, *phoinix*, and *sambuca*, gave striking quarter-tone accompaniments to represent the Python's last gasps. With his death, a solemn spondaic rhythm ended the movement.

The final movement was an ovation to Apollo, in the Hypolydian mode.

Such a festival consisted of what is known as programme music, which tries to tell a story or portray some event or scene that necessitates explanation on the programme. In contradistinction is the school known as pure, or absolute, music, in which the music is to be enjoyed for its beauty without the aid of any written story or description of what it might mean. The programme school was well developed in ancient Greece, and has even given us a modern phrase. When a musician attempted to give on his lyre a picture of a storm, the wit Dorian, who was present, remarked, "I have heard a better tempest in a pot of boiling water." This has come down to us, in altered form, as "A tempest in a teapot."

The Nemean games, celebrating the slaying of the Nemean lion by Hercules, contained no definite musical contest; but flute-playing was allowed for the purpose of stimulating the athletes, and probably prizes were awarded for it.

A stone discovered at Chios bears on its face the names of many musical victors. It shows that prizes were awarded for reading music at sight, for rhapsodizing, for accompanying with a small harp played by hand, and for accompanying on the *kithara* played partly by the left hand and partly by a plectrum held in the right. Many lesser festivals, such as the Panathenæa, had their musical contests. Pericles gave much encouragement to music, and erected the Odeon for musical events. This building had a dome-shaped roof, which gave it excellent acoustic properties.

The power of music among the ancient Greeks was most marked.

We read of Terpander singing away the Spartan dissensions; Tyrtæus arousing that same people to martial glory; or Solon inspiring the defeated Athenians to retake Salamis. In these songs the words were naturally of very pointed significance; but there was a reverence for the compelling power of music that does not exist to-day. Even though our music may be far more involved and developed than that of Greece, modern auditors are not swayed by music as were the Greeks and a few other primitive races. Orpheus and the Sirens could have been evolved only among a people strongly influenced by the tonal art.

That music was cherished in many ways is shown by the example of Polycrates, who kept a boy choir at his court in Samos to sing sweet Lydian melodies during his meals. But the most pleasing picture in Greek music was perhaps the spectacle of Sappho at Mitylene, training her school of fair young Grecians in the mysterious power of poetry, song, and instrumental music.

Rome adopted Grecian cultivation, and was only slightly original in music. Trumpets were more varied in form, as befitted a martial people. The hydraulic organ has been mentioned already. With the Romans, the *tibia*, or flute (often with reed mouthpiece like a clarinet), usurped the prominent position that the lyre held in Greece. The *tibia* was used in all religious ceremonies except those of Bacchus, which demanded the *kithara;* so Mendelssohn showed historical accuracy in using flutes prominently for the chorus "O be gracious, ye Immortals," in "St. Paul." Flute-players were used at Roman funerals, and in such ostentatious numbers that a sumptuary law was passed limiting their number to ten.

The flute-players formed a guild, or union; and Valerius Maximus gives an anecdote showing their power. When the musicians were once excluded from the temple of Jupiter, where they had previously been allowed to take their meals, the whole guild left Rome in protest, and went to the neighboring locality of Tibur. Without them it was almost impossible to carry on many of the religious and public ceremonies. The Senate therefore sent messengers to ask their return. When the strikers remained inflexible, the wily messengers persuaded the people of Tibur to give a feast in honor of their visitors; and before the musicians could "sober up" from the effects of this feast, they were bundled into chariots and brought back to

Rome. They received all their former privileges, with new ones in addition; but at certain public performances after this event they always masked themselves, to show their shame at their inglorious return.

Rome had her games, but at these, as in the military triumphs, the musical effects were striking and colossal rather than artistic. The music of private establishments was probably better in quality; and Apuleius, after hearing some of this, gave high praise to the combination of flutes, *kitharas*, and voices. The Roman plays were accompanied by gently flowing flute music, which was pleasing enough; but in later times this too grew more devoted to effects of display. In the later days of the Empire, there was a great demand for Gaditanian singers or dancers. These came from the neighborhood of the modern Cadiz, which still supplies tenor vocalists. Many of the theatrical performers were slaves, and were subjected to the most stringent rules to prevent them from spoiling their voices by excesses.

The dance, especially in pantomime form, reached a high state of perfection in ancient Rome. A certain dancer was once told by Demetrius the Cynic that his art was merely an adjunct to music; whereupon the dancer made the instruments stop, and enacted the subject of Mars and Venus with such skill that Demetrius was forced to withdraw his reproach. On another occasion a prince of Pontus was entertained by Nero. The prince could not understand Latin, and did not enjoy the plays given for him. But he admired the pantomimes greatly. When Nero wished him to name a parting gift, he asked for the dancer who had appeared in these spectacles, explaining that an artist so gifted in physical expression would make an invaluable interpreter.

Nero himself cultivated music with marked assiduity, even practising breathing in a recumbent position with weights placed upon him. In his own estimation he was a great artist, though in reality his voice was rather thin and husky. He used to contrive to have his friends ask him to sing, and would accept princely fees for his appearance. When a soothsayer once told him that he would sometime find himself deserted by all his friends, he replied, "An artist can earn his living in any country." When he appeared publicly, his soldiers prevented the audience from leaving; though some jumped from windows, and others feigned death in order to be carried out.

Inattention was severely punished; and when Vespasian was caught asleep at such an event, his friends had hard work to save his life. Nero once made a tour of the Grecian games. There he bribed better artists to withdraw; and one of these, proving obdurate, was forced aside and killed by his soldiers. Naturally under such conditions he was always awarded the prize. He did not fiddle while Rome burned, because the ancients had no violins; but he ascended a tower, and was moved to sing "The Destruction of Troy," accompanying himself on the lyre. When his enemies revolted, he considered winning back their allegiance by singing pathetic songs to them. When Rome rebelled, he tried to placate it by offering to appear in many musical events in the approaching public games; but somehow the city declined his offer. When he fled, he was much rankled by being called "that pitiful harper"; and he kept asking his few comrades if anyone could play better than he could. Before his suicide, he exclaimed, "What an artist the world will now lose!"

There was undoubtedly some beauty in the Roman music; but on the whole, this feature was overshadowed by the display of the games and triumphs. When Ambrose arranged the church modes, he took them from Grecian rather than from Roman sources.

III

EARLY CHRISTIAN MUSIC

WHILE Roman music went on its way from simplicity to bombast and then to decay, a new force arose in music — the worship of the Christian Church.

In the earliest days of the Church, the music was of a simple but effective character. Most of the converts were of the humbler classes, and so not well versed in the intricacies of the Greek modes. The music they adopted for their chanting and singing was therefore simple and expressive rather than involved. It is probable that the hymns which echoed in the days of services in the catacombs were not greatly different in style from those in our modern hymnals.

According to a report of the Proconsul Pliny, made for the Emperor Trajan, the singing was at first individual. Pliny wrote of the Christians, "They claim that their only fault or error consists of this, — they convene at stated days, before sunrise, and sing, each in turn, a song to Christ as to a God." But it is possible that the word *invicem*, or "in turn," referred only to responsive chanting of the Scriptures; for in the time of Origen, in the second century, the whole congregation sang together. St. John Chrysostom describes this practice in the words: "The psalms which we sing unite all the voices in one, and the canticles arise harmoniously in unison. Young and old, rich and poor, women, men, slaves, and citizens, all of us have formed but one melody together." The custom of allowing women to sing with men in the psalms lasted until the Synod of Antioch abolished it, in the year 379. At least one woman became publicly identified with music before that; for a noble Roman convert named Cecilia, afterwards made a saint, is described by writers of the second century, when she lived, as having "lifted up her voice in praise of the Lord." Some accounts state that she became a martyr to her faith under the Prefect Almacus; but that gentleman's name is not to be found in any historical narrative.

The rise of choir-singing came about somewhat as in the case of the Puritans in Massachusetts. Some of the congregation would naturally sing better than others, and the experts would gradually gather in one spot, where their voices would lead while others followed or became silent altogether. Paid singers existed as early as the second century. Gradually they came to disregard the simple and expressive style, and to indulge in brilliancy to arouse admiration. It was probably to remedy this state of affairs that Pope Sylvester I founded a singing-school at Rome in the year 320. At that time, too, a special place was assigned to the choir. In A.D. 481, the Council of Laodicea decreed that none but clerks (called canonical singers) should be allowed to sing during the service. At this period the churches were ambitious in architecture, and the arts of painting and sculpture combined their attractions with those of music. At first no instruments were employed in the service, but gradually the organ was adopted, and by the year 450 it was commonly used in Spain.

Toward the end of the fourth century, Ambrose, Bishop of Milan, tried to establish music on a definite system. He adopted from his idea of the Greek modes four scales, or "tones." These, called "authentic," had intervals like white-key scales on our pianos beginning with the notes D, E, F, and G. In the authentic modes the keynote was at the bottom, and the dominant (chief note) usually a fifth above it. From each of these four authentic modes Pope Gregory the Great derived a plagal (oblique) mode, having the same keynote, but with the scale now reaching from a fourth below the keynote to a fifth above it, and with the dominant less than a fifth above the keynote. As the compass of the average voice is not much over an octave, the interval from the lowest plagal note to the highest authentic note was large enough to satisfy the demands of the singers. After the sixth century, four more modes were added, two authentic and two plagal, on the intervals of white-key scales beginning with C and with A. The music of the Catholic service has been based largely on these modes ever since that time.

Other branches of the Church had their music. The Greek Church used much ornamentation, for example, and sometimes employed the Byzantine scale (intervals like C, D-flat, E, F, G, A-flat, B, and C); the Syrian Church had its own hymns, especially those by Ephraem Syrus, who was called "The Harp of the Holy Spirit";

while the Coptic Church adopted melodies that were intricate and full of modulation. But the Gregorian was the only system that influenced Europe. It was tabulated later into a set of hexachords, or six-note groups, with a semitone in the middle of each. The scale was diatonic except for the fact that some of these hexachords caused a change from B to B-flat. B-natural was called *durum*, or hard, and B-flat *molle*, or soft — words which gave rise to the German terms *Dur* for major and *Moll* for minor. In the eighth century we find Charlemagne sending emissaries to Rome to get full and accurate details on the methods of Gregorian singing.

The music at this time was sung wholly in unison or octaves. Hucbald, a monk of St. Amand living at the beginning of the tenth century, is said to have been the first to systematize part-singing. He allowed some voices to sing the melody, while others took the same melody a fifth higher or a fourth lower. This procedure, called "parallel" motion, would seem horribly harsh to modern ears. Probably it was not greatly enjoyed even at first; for in the next century we find Guido of Arezzo discarding the fifths, and modifying the fourths somewhat. Guido, who died about 1050, was a noted singer and teacher. He had a famous boy choir, which sang, among other numbers, a hymn to St. John running thus: —

"Ut queant laxis
Resonare fibris
Mira gestorum
Famuli tuorum,
Solve polluti
Labii reatum,
Sancte Johannes."

In the hymn melody it happened that each line except the last began a degree higher than the preceding line. Guido therefore adopted the syllables at the beginning of the first six lines as names for the notes of the scale, — *Ut, Re, Mi, Fa, Sol, La*. These names have lasted until the present, with *Si* (or *Ti*) added later, and *Ut* replaced by *Do*, except in French instrumental music. Thus Guido was the inventor of what is called *solfeggio* (singing by note-names instead of words). By its means he trained his choir very thoroughly; and he took this choir with him when called to Rome in 1026 to explain his system to the Pope.

From this time on, for more than four centuries, England took the lead in the musical advance. The length of this period may be appreciated when we consider that the German classics, which form the most important part of modern music, were all created during the last two centuries. The Netherlands were supreme in the fifteenth and sixteenth centuries, and Italy's sway lasted only into the eighteenth, even then overlapping the work of Bach and Handel.

Guido had lessened the effect of constantly recurring fourths in part-singing by allowing two voices to come together, when near either end of their compass, one part then diverging gradually from the other, which remained stationary until the interval between the two had reached the requisite size. Thus was introduced what is now known as "oblique" motion. Between the date of his death and the end of the century, England had developed the principle of contrary motion, in which voices or parts could proceed in opposite directions, and had also made it allowable for voices to proceed in the same direction by varying intervals. Thus there came about a sort of musical declaration of independence, asserting that all voices in part-music were to be considered free and equal. This took place before the year 1100, and is made clear by a relic known as the "Winchester Troper," which dates from that year. In addition to the old fourths and fifths, thirds and sixths were now used. Hucbald had given his system the name of *organum*, while the newer intervals were known under the title of *fauxbourdon*.

In the mean while, musical notation grew from its crude beginnings in the Dark Ages to something not unlike its modern form. Notation has been a most conservative affair. Every now and then some one proposes a wholly new system of writing music; and most of these systems would be an improvement, as our present method is rather cumbersome. But the innovations do not gain ground, for the present system has the inertia of many centuries behind it.

Before the tenth century no one had any idea of the principle of the staff. Music was at first learned orally, and sung to words in the uncial characters that preceded the black-letter. Gradually the monkish teachers and pupils began to invent and use little signs to aid their memory. The chief principle of these signs rested in the fact that a horizontal line above a word meant stationary pitch, a rising line or curve meant rising pitch, and a downward line falling pitch. These signs were supplemented by others representing trills,

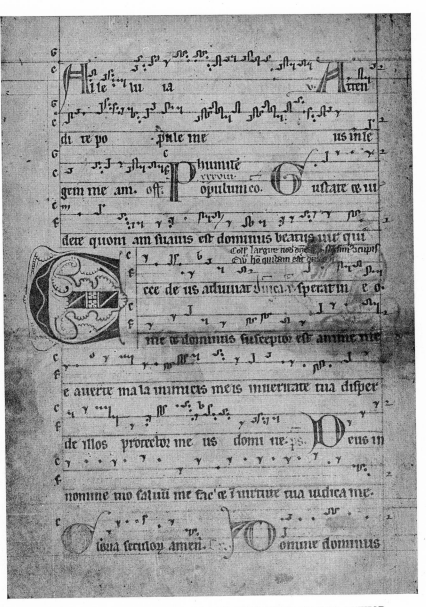

FROM AN OLD MANUSCRIPT IN THE POSSESSION OF THE AUTHOR

turns, and the various component parts of melody; and our trill and turn signs, among other bits of notation, come directly from such early experiments. These primitive marks were known as the "neumes," and flourished from before the seventh century until well beyond the tenth. There were different systems, the Byzantine neumes being unlike those used in western Europe. One variety was known as the "fly-track" notation (*pedes muscarum*), because its thickly spread signs looked like the marks that a fly would make if it crawled over the parchment after a sojourn in the ink-bottle.

It will be seen from the above description that the neumes were not an exact notation. They served as a guide to the memory; they also showed if the voice should go up or down; but they did not state how far up or down it should go. Thus a specimen of neume notation did not give any accurate suggestion to the person seeing it for the first time. Yet modern investigation is tireless, and men of the Riemann type have shown that patient research enables them to solve almost all the signs used in this ancient system of notation.

Some time between the year 925 and 950, an unknown musician became dissatisfied with the indefiniteness of the neumes. With some red ink, or pigment, and a ruler, he made musical progress possible by drawing a single line. This line extended through the neumes horizontally, and represented the pitch of the F below middle C. Now all the notes above F could be represented by signs above the line, and lower notes by signs below it. The principle worked so well that another line was added soon after, perhaps by the same man. The second line, green or yellow in color, represented the C above the F, and was marked, like the earlier line, with its proper letter. This F and C are still with us to-day, having changed their form only slightly to become the F and C clefs of the present, which are put on the beginning of a staff to show the position of the notes F or C. Two other lines were then added, making a four-lined staff.

Other attempts at staff-notation had been made, either independently or as a result of the lines through the neumes. The chief one was perhaps the work of Hucbald, who died in 932. It employed the principle of a staff of many lines, but in this staff only the spaces were used. These spaces, too, did not contain notes, but actual words, each syllable being written in the space showing the pitch at which it was to be sung. The spaces of Hucbald's staff were marked by the old but clumsy method of using four Greek letters, the pitch varying when they were placed sidewise or upside down. In this system the words had to be rewritten in their proper position for each added part; and we can trace Hucbald's fourths and fifths by following the lines of syllables along his pages.

The first use of the four-lined staff, which lasted through the Middle Ages, has been ascribed to Guido, though probably it took place before his day. The third line of this staff represented A, and was between F and C, while the fourth line was either above or below the other three, specimens of old missals showing both cases, and usually having the F and C marked on each staff. Thus both lines and spaces were used; and the gradual adoption of a fifth line gave us the staff of to-day. For the non-musician, it may be stated that while the F and the later G are marked in definite places on our staff, by clefs which grew from the old forms of those letters, we have also a relic of the movable letters in the C clef, which may be put on almost any line of the staff.

At first the lines, and even the staff, were used with the neumes. But gradually the latter gave way to notes, and we find Franco of Cologne giving these notes a definite value in his thirteenth-century treatise on measured music. The early plain-song (Gregorian chanting) showed little variety of rhythm. But gradually, as music was more widely used, the need for the notation of rhythm resulted, and attempts to represent it were made. After the adoption of measured notes, there came a division of music into triple or double rhythms. The former, being typical of the holy Trinity, was called "perfect rhythm," and marked by a circle. The latter, being only two thirds of the triple rhythm, was marked by two thirds of the circle; and this broken circle has been mistakenly transformed into the letter C, which is now used as a time-signature for four-quarter rhythm. It is not really a C, and therefore cannot be the initial of what is known as "common time." There was a further division of each beat into triple or double rhythm, this subdivision being called the "prolation." The major, or triple, prolation was accepted if no sign was present, while the minor, or duple, prolation, was called for by a dot placed in the middle of the perfect or broken circle. Thus the circle practically called for $\frac{9}{8}$ time; the broken circle for $\frac{6}{8}$; the circle with a dot in it meant a rhythm corresponding to 3/4 time with six eighth notes in a measure; while the broken circle with the dot was the same as our 4/4 time. There was no bar-line then; it did not come into use until after the Middle Ages, and no one knows who introduced it. But the bar was, of course, needless if the notes were fairly equal in value, and the melodies not too disjointed.

The notes adopted by Franco, and also by the English musician named Walter Odington, were in part derived from the neumes. The latter offered the *virga* and the *punctum*, which were now changed into the *longa* and *brevis*. The *maxima* was made a double *longa*, and the *semibrevis* half the *brevis*. The *minima, semiminima, fusa,* and *semifusa* were adopted gradually after the year 1300. In major prolation a *longa* was equal to three *breves* instead of two.

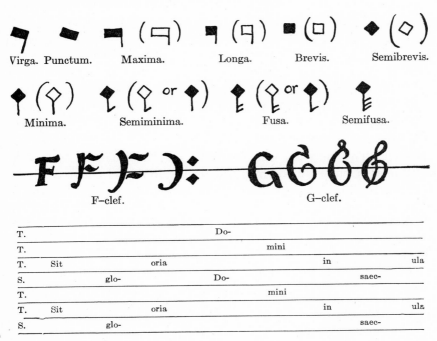

Virga. Punctum.　　Maxima.　　　　Longa.　　　Brevis.　　Semibrevis.

Minima.　　　Semiminima.　　　　Fusa.　　　Semifusa.

F–clef.　　　　　　　　　　　G–clef.

T.			Do-			
T.				mini		
T.	Sit	oria			in	ula
S.		glo-	Do-		saec-	
T.				mini		
T.	Sit	oria			in	ula
S.		glo-			saec-	

Music at the end of the eleventh and beginning of the twelfth century was in a rather mixed state. Some composers kept to the strict rules of the *organum* for the most part; while others began to work in a freer style, as if obeying the old rule of Aristoxenus, that "whatever sounds good, is good." In the Ambrosian Library at Milan there is an old treatise, called "Ad Organum faciendum," which dates from about the year 1100. This contains examples of very free part-writing, the voices at times making bold skips, or crossing each other, even when the harmony is only two-part.

The growth of the principle of imitation marked a great step forward toward the contrapuntal forms. The charm of such imitation gradually led to canonic writing, in which the parts follow one another; and that was almost surely the first form of artistic composition. An early suggestion of imitation is found in an old French manuscript, the work being probably composed in the twelfth century. It consists of a low voice singing the words, apparently an old hymn, "Custodi nos," while the two upper voices that are set against it give clear imitation, approaching the canonic style. As will be shown in a later section, the canon consists of a melody used as its own accompaniment in other voices, the theme entering at different times in each voice. The simplest examples of this style are the familiar part-songs known as "rounds."

In the thirteenth century certain composers began to appreciate what we call "double counterpoint," in which two voices change their relative positions and repeat their themes in a new relative location. But the first contrapuntal form to develop fully was the canon. This may be seen from the old English *rota*, or round, "Sumer is icumen in," which is described in a later chapter.

Further development of notation caused the rounded *b* (at first meaning our B-flat) to be used as a sign for any flat. The Germans still speak of our B-flat as B; and as they mistook the square B for an H, they use the latter letter to designate our B-natural. The square B gave rise to the sign for any natural. The sharp was at first a cross, and is still called so in Germany. Originally it merely neutralized a flat, but soon it assumed its present significance. The bar-line was introduced early in the seventeenth century, and the grouping of notes just before the eighteenth.

IV

THE MINSTREL KNIGHTS

THE Minnesingers (love-poets) of Germany are said to have begun their career under Frederick Barbarossa, in the last half of the twelfth century. But the first of their number, Henry of Veldig, is the author of a poem lamenting the decadence of the Minnesinger's art; so we are forced to consider its real origin as of an earlier date.

The Minnesingers were minstrel knights, such as Wagner pictured in his opera "Tannhäuser." There is said to have been an actual tournament of song on the Wartburg, as in Wagner's opera; and the names that he used were real. The Suabian Court was the centre of the Minnesinger's art, and the Suabian language was used, though the minstrel poets came from all parts of the empire. So highly was their position rated that nobles and princes were proud to be known as Minnesingers.

As may be judged from the name, many of the poems of these knightly minstrels were love-songs. Some of them were ideal in their purity of sentiment, while others were less lofty in style. Examples of the former class are found in the works of Henry of Meissen, considered the last of the Minnesingers. He became so noted for his homage to the nobler qualities of womanhood that he was given the name of "Frauenlob," or "Praise-of-Women"; and when his funeral took place, numbers of high-born ladies followed to his open grave, and each cast a flower into it until it was overflowing with blossoms.

In their more personal love-songs, the Germans did not usually go to the same lengths as the more ardent Troubadours of France. Yet there must have been some degree of amorous adventure, and the latter is reflected in the so-called *Wachtlieder* (watch-songs). In these a knight may plead with a watchman for secret admittance to a castle; or the watchman may warn the knight of impending danger or discovery.

Such songs were all set to music, and sung by the knights, who would accompany themselves on a small harp.

The school of epic poetry, corresponding with that of the Trouvères in France, is represented by such works as the "Nibelungen-Lied," or the "Parsifal" of Wolfram von Eschenbach.

From this period also come many short proverbs and epigrams. Among these were couplets; such as

"The king must die,
And so must I."

There were also sage bits of advice; such as "Never borrow trouble," or "Don't set the wolf to guard the sheep."

The art of the Minnesingers displayed itself also in fables and brief allegorical stories. There were many historical tales too.

A short bit of verse is quoted here (ascribed to Frederick II) to show what was considered of excellence at the time. It runs thus: —

"I like a cavalier Frances,
And a Catalonian dame;
The courtesy of the Genoese,
And Castilian dignity;
The Provence songs, my ears to please,
And the dance of the Trevisan;
The graceful form of the Arragonese,
And the pearl of the Julian;
An English face and hands to see,
And a page of Tuscany."

The freedom of thought and speech permitted by the House of Suabia did much to encourage poetry and music. But with the downfall of that house, in the year 1256, the Church regained power, and the current of free thought became diverted into an art whose chief aim was to make paraphrases of the Scriptures, in bad German or worse Latin.

The Meistersingers (master-singers), who followed the Minnesingers, were not the equal of their predecessors in poetic inspiration. Their name may have come from the fact that a Minnesinger who was not of noble birth was called a Meister; but it is also similar to the name given to the leaders in all the guilds. The Meistersingers flourished in the great and growing cities, and were tradespeople rather than nobles. Again we find Wagner giving a wonderfully faithful picture of early times in his opera (music-drama, he called it) "Die Meistersinger von Nürnberg." Nuremberg was an important centre for these humble but earnest poet-musicians, and was also the home of Hans Sachs, whose excellent plays and farces represent the best work of this period. The characters in Wagner's libretto (which he wrote himself, and which is now a textbook in German schools) were real in their day, and their names may be found in the old records. The picture of petty rules is also entirely correct, for the Meistersingers classified their poetic and musical methods in a very strict and detailed fashion. This adherence to rules interfered seriously with free inspiration, for in their trials of skill there was always a hidden "marker" (as in the opera), to keep a record of any technical mistakes. So far as we know, the Meistersinger movement originated soon after the year 1300, at Mayence. It flourished until 1600, after which it became unimportant. The last Meistersinger society, that of Ulm, was not disbanded until 1839, and its last surviving member lived until 1876. The Meistersinger music had little real effect. It may have influenced the chorales of the Reformation, but these were far stronger in character. Except for a few of the tunes, or "tones," which Wagner used so wonderfully in his opera, it is wholly out of date.

The Troubadours, and in some sense the Trouvères (both words meaning "finders" or "inventors"), are considered to have developed their art from Moorish models as found in Spain, or at the Crusades, or in various other ways. Some Celtic and ancient Roman influences may have played their part, but if so it was a subordinate one. The styles of song, the instruments, and even some of the names, show a Moorish origin.

The first of the Troubadours is held to have been William IX, Count of Poitou and Duke of Acquitaine. He had some influence on England as well as on France, for his war-cry of "St. George" was adopted by England, as well as his granddaughter Eleanor of Acquitaine, who married Henry II. The leopard crest of the early English kings was another legacy from William of Poitou. This pioneer died in 1127.

The poetry of the Troubadours was written in the so-called "Langue d'oc," in which the word "oc," meaning "yes," distinguished it from the northern French "Langue d'oïl," and the Italian "Lingua di si." The poems were of various forms, though in general those of the Provençal Troubadours were short, while those of the northern Trouvères were long stories similar to epics.

The Verse was a short form of free style, though it might consist of seven couplets. The Chanson also was free in style, but usually divided into stanzas. The Sonnet, too, was free, the term signifying lyric, or song, without any of the later division into rhymed lines. The Couplet, or Stanza, was a general class of verse, signifying love-songs in contrast to other subjects. The Planh was a dirge, with ten or twelve syllables in a line; usually it mourned a lost friend or lover, though sometimes it treated of more public calamities. The Tenson, or Contention, was a dialogue in verse, in which the two parties alternated their stanzas, using the same rhymes that occurred in the first one. The Tournament consisted of stanzas given in turn by more than two participants. The Sirvente, or Pasquinade, free in metre, was a war-song, or else an outburst of satire against some enemy. The Sixtine had six stanzas of six lines each, with no rhymes in the first one, but with each of the later stanzas using the end-words of the lines in the first, but in different order. The Discord was a free poem in irregular form, often using several languages in succession. The Pastorelle, or pastoral poem, usually with short lines, consisted of a dialogue between the Troubadour and a shepherdess or shepherd; it often began with a description of the scene, and generally displayed a charming simplicity of style. The Serenade, from *sera*, or evening, was an evening love-song, while the Aubade, from *alba*, meaning dawn, was a morning song of the same character, often resembling in sentiment Shakespeare's "Hark, hark, the lark." The Ballad was a somewhat longer form, telling a story; and many of the Trouvère epics are evidently sets of ballads joined together. The Novel was a short poem in free style recounting some amorous adventure. The Romance was the name given to the larger epic narratives in which the northern French poets excelled; and many of these are still in existence. The custom of adding an *envoi* at the close of a poem arose from the fact that the Troubadours did not always sing their own songs, so that they sometimes needed an *envoi* to show their retainers and minstrels for whom the poem was intended, or even how it should be sung.

The Troubadour was usually of noble blood, and sometimes even of royal station, as with Richard Cœur-de-Lion. Only a very few musicians of ordinary birth were able to lift themselves from the ranks of the Jongleurs, or minstrels, and be recognized as Troubadours. The Troubadour needed resources to enable him to entertain and to keep a sufficient number of minstrels. When spring came, after a winter varied by martial exercises and musical composition, he would issue forth at the head of his retainers, perhaps to visit some neighboring castle. There he would be entertained sumptuously, while his followers played and sang his new songs. Occasionally he would take a harp from one of them and give a rendering of some song himself; but this was usually in a small gathering, and not often in a crowded hall.

The music of the Troubadours and Trouvères was sufficiently refined in style, and at the same time popular in spirit. Best known now as a composer is Adam de la Hale, called the Hunchback of Arras, who lived from 1240 to 1287. He produced, among other musical plays, the "Jeu de Robin et Marion," which is nothing less than an early comic opera. Robin is a boastful shepherd suitor who tells the shepherdess Marion he is afraid of nothing; but when a nobleman comes to pay her unwelcome attentions, Robin turns out to be a coward, and is received back only on sufferance. The music to this little farce is pleasingly fluent in style. But most of the poet-composers were content to produce the words and music of single songs.

As the Troubadours always chose a lady as the object of their devotions, their poetry was often more personal than that of their German brethren; and as the lady was often a married woman, there was much more chance for jealousy and tragedy.

Thus William Cabestaing, brought up in the castle of Roussillon, on receiving encouragement from Margherita, the wife of its lord, began to pay poetic and other attentions to her. When some of their secret meetings aroused the suspicion of the castle's lord, Baron Raymond, he taxed Cabestaing with being in love. The latter's poems proved this, but Cabestaing pretended that it was Lady Agnes, sister of Margherita, who had given him her love. As Agnes was keen enough to see the truth, she calmed Raymond's suspicions for a time by pretending that Cabestaing's statement was correct. But the real lovers grew more imprudent in their actions, until finally Margherita was rash enough to have her idol write a poem asserting his love for her alone. The baron's suspicions of certain gossip being thus confirmed, he led Cabestaing outside the castle and stabbed him to death. Tearing the heart out of the body, he took it to the castle cook, ordering him to prepare it and serve it to Margherita. The cook did so, thinking the heart was that of a deer; and the lady ate it with the same idea, and praised its delicious flavor. Raymond then explained to her what her meal had been, and showed her the head of the man whose heart she had just eaten. She fainted away; but on recovering, she said, "Yes, barbarian, I have found that meat so delicate and beautiful that, for fear I may ever lose the taste of it, I will eat no more as long as I live." Raymond drew his sword and rushed at her in anger; whereupon she fled, and jumped to death from the castle walls rather than let herself be killed by him.

But not all ladies were so imprudent. Thus Marie de Ventadour, noted for her wisdom and good character as well as her beauty, once found herself the target of too pronounced attention from the adventurous Gaucelm Faidit, who was staying at her castle. As she feared his evil and sarcastic tongue, she resorted to stratagem to get rid of him. She took counsel with a friend, Madame de Malamort, who agreed to act as directed. Then she refused Gaucelm's attentions definitely. He departed in anger, but had gone only a little way when a messenger overtook him and asked whether he preferred a little bird in the hand or a crane flying high in the air. His curiosity was so much aroused that he let himself be led back, and was taken to Madame de Malamort. This lady explained that she was the bird in hand, while Marie, who would not respond to him, was the unattainable crane flying high in air. Gaucelm then agreed to transfer his devotion, and was asked in return to take formal leave of Marie's affections. This he did in a dignified poem, far gentler than might otherwise have been expected. But when the poem was made known, he found that Madame de Malamort grew suddenly cold to his devotion, and withdrew all semblance of encouragement. But much as he was chagrined, it was too late for him to indulge in any sarcasm at Marie's expense. Incidentally, Faidit was well known as a poet, and was patronized by King Richard of England, for whose death he wrote a most touching Planh, or dirge.

But true love sometimes ran smoothly. Rambaud de Vaqueiras, who was brought up in the home of the Marquis of Montferrat, soon became devoted to his master's sister Beatrix del Carat. She was an athletic beauty; and once, when her brother accidentally left a sword in her room, she threw off her dress, donned a buckler, and began to wield the weapon with much delight. She thought herself unobserved, but a partly open door had enabled Rambaud to see the entire performance. Thereafter he celebrated her in many beautiful poems as "Le bel Cavalier." When unable to keep his love for her silent, he spoke to her as if asking for advice. "Madame," he began, "vouchsafe to give me your opinion. I love a lady of superlative charms. I converse with her continually without letting her know the state of my feelings. Tell me, ought I to die of love, for fear of revealing myself to her?" Beatrix then answered, "By no means. I advise you to declare your love, and to request the lady to retain you as her lover and her troubadour. If she is wise, she will certainly not take it amiss, but will think herself honored; for, believe me, you are so lovable and noble in yourself that there is no lady in the world who ought not freely to receive you as her knight."

"Then, madame," said Rambaud, "you are the lady."

"Then, Rambaud," said Beatrix, "you are my knight."

Before returning to the musical side of this period, it may be pardonable to add that the devotion of the Troubadours often took fantastic forms. Thus Geoffrey Rudel, who is the subject of one of Browning's poems, did actually die of love. Hearing of the beauty and virtues of the Countess of Tripoli, he decided to devote himself to her, although he had never seen her. He wrote poems in her praise, and questioned returning travellers about her. After a long time he decided to embark and sail to her home, intending to throw himself at her feet. Whether his health was poor, or whether the excitement was too much for him, it is a fact that on landing he fell down as if near death, and was carried to a neighboring house. Meanwhile his companions had told the countess of his devotion, and brought her to him. He was actually dying, but he managed to take her hand and say, "Most illustrious princess, I will not complain of death. I have seen you, and thus achieved the sole object, the sole desire of my life." Then he expired in her arms; and she afterwards had a magnificent tomb prepared for him.

Pierre Vidal, apparently a Don Quixote among the Troubadours, fell in love with a girl named Louve de Penautier. As Louve was the feminine for wolf, he at once adopted the word "Loup," or he-wolf, as his name. In order to prove his earnestness in the matter, he

dressed himself in a wolf's hide and had his friends and retainers
bring dogs to hunt him. The hunt was by no means a farce, for he
kept on running until the dogs caught him and fastened their teeth
in him. He was rescued in time, and no doubt cured by his lady-
love, to whose honor he probably considered his wounds a great
tribute.

More touching is the story of William de la Tour. He married a
girl of low degree because of her charms, and loved her dearly. After
her untimely death, he gave orders that her tomb should be so built
that it could be opened at will. When this was done, he would open
the tomb every night and converse with her body, imagining that it
was alive. Later on he came to know that she was dead, but believed
that she would rise again if he said prayers enough, which he gal-
lantly undertook to do.

The so-called "Courts of Love" were presided over by ladies of
rank, such as Queen Eleanor, or the Countess of Champagne. These
courts, in which a number of women aided in discussion, decided
upon questions of amorous etiquette. Thus a certain knight had
loved a lady from girlhood; and during her younger days she had
extracted the promise that the knight should kiss her every time he
came to see her. When grown up she denied him the privilege, saying that she had been too young to understand what the promise
would involve. He then brought the matter before a court of love,
which decided in his favor.

Another case, tried before Queen Eleanor, had to do with a lady
who accepted a knight's gifts but rebuffed his attentions. Eleanor
gave the verdict for the knight, and said that the lady should have
refused his gifts or given him back something of equal value.

Of much interest also are the so-called "Essenhamens," or poems
on manners and customs, intended for training in etiquette. One
such is by Amaneius des Escas. It begins by telling how a lady of
position, at some great court, sought out the poet for advice. He
told her at first that she must know ten times as much as he did; but
apparently he overcame his scruples, for he launched into a long
discourse of "What-to-dos" and "Don'ts." He treated such personal subjects as washing, care of teeth, care of nails, and dressing,
as well as modest personal bearing and courtly discourse. Incidentally, women's accomplishments were then held to be cooking, sewing,

surgery, and chess, the first two helping her to oversee and administer a household of retainers, while the last two were for the care and amusement of noble visitors. A German etiquette book of this time asserts that when a man enters a room, the women should rise, and remain standing until he sits down.

With a description of the Jongleurs we are brought back from a long digression to the subject of musical progress. While the Troubadours confined themselves chiefly to composition, the Jongleurs became proficient on all the instruments of their time. These were fairly numerous; and we find one minstrel claiming (in the Bodleian manuscript), "I can play the lute, the violin, the pipe, the bagpipe, the syrinx, the harp, the gigue, the gittern, the symphony, the psaltery, the organistrum, the regals, the tabour, and the rote." Of these the gigue was a small, high-pitched viol, called after its German name "Geige"; the gittern was a guitar strung with catgut; the symphony (Italian, *zumpogna*) was a form of bagpipe; the regals was a tiny folding organ, the tabor a tambourine, and the rote (old Celtic, *crwth*) a small square harp. The organistrum, from its descriptions, seems to be the prototype of the modern hand-organ. The player turned a wheel, and could depress by keys any of the strings on the instrument, thus making them sound by bringing them against the revolving wheel. Certain so-called mechanical violins use the same idea to-day. Other instruments of the time were the flute, trumpet, flageolet, sackbut (trombone), shalm or shawm (clarinet), rebeck (a bowed mandolin derived from the Arabian Rebab), and marine trumpet (having merely a single long string, much like that of a violoncello). On all these, the Jongleurs were possessed of much skill.

At first the Jongleurs were the paid musical retainers of the Troubadours. Girard Calanson, for example, gave to his Jongleurs the following instructions.: "Learn to act well, to speak well, and to extemporise rhymes well. Learn to invent clever and amusing games to please people. Learn to play on the tabour, the cymbals, and the bagpipe. Learn to throw and catch little apples on the point of knives. Learn to imitate the song of birds with your voices, to pretend to make an attack on a castle as if besieging it, to jump through four hoops, to play on the citall and mandore, to perform on the cloncorde and the guitar, for they are delightful to all. Learn how to string the viol with seventeen chords, to sound the bells, to play the harp, and to compose a jig that shall enliven the sound of the psaltery." From this it will be seen that the modern juggler is the old Jongleur with only a partial change of occupation. The citall (citole) was a box-like form of the psaltery, and the mandore a variety of guitar.

The Troubadours were practically destroyed in the war of the Albigenses — a war preceded by many pasquinades, that exposed faults both in the pleasure-loving adherents of the new creed and the absolution-peddling authorities at Rome. The war itself was a constant triumph for Rome, under the leadership of Simon de Montfort; and many of the captured cities witnessed the burning of their citizens alive by hundreds. Even Pedro of Aragon met defeat when he came to aid his Provençal friends.

But whatever the rights and wrongs were, the killing-off of so many Troubadours was a serious set-back to cultivation in its allied forms of literature and music. They had been the composers, while their performing retainers were merely the publishers of their compositions, as Petrarch said. The art of the Jongleurs, when no longer backed by the inspiration of their masters, soon began to deteriorate. Their status and their entertainments grew to be such that they attracted only the coarsest audiences. They became wandering minstrels, earning a precarious living by amusing people in the market-places. Yet girls and women sometimes became Jongleuses, as the term was. We read that William the Conqueror rewarded his Jongleuse Adeline with an estate. In later times these feminine performers led a wandering life, and were known as "glee-maidens." But at first they held honored positions and showed themselves gifted enough. For example, the many Romances of Marie de France, Jongleuse of William Longsword (son of Henry III), are now held to have rare value, and kept as much-prized treasures in the British Museum. They include versions of the Arthurian legends, as well as others of prime importance. But on the whole, the Jongleurs, male and female, were persons of no respectable position.

The change from well-born poets to paid entertainers took place in Germany also. There was no violent war in that country, but the alteration came just as surely if more gradually. There were evidently German musicians of the Jongleur type in the Suabian times; for there exists an old song, which runs, —

> "King Rudolph is a worthy king;
> All praise to him be brought!
> He likes to hear the minstrels play and sing,
> But after that he gives them naught."

Thus in Germany, too, the nobler composer gave way to the paid musician; and for many years, even extending down to the nineteenth century, the musician was regarded and treated as a hired underling, if not an actual outlaw.

V

THE SCHOOLS OF COUNTERPOINT

IT has already been stated that England held the lead in music for many centuries. The famous song "Sumer is icumen in," which sounds remarkably fresh and beautiful even to modern ears, probably dates back to the year 1215, if not earlier. This was a "six men's song," but two of the voices sang a drone bass. The other four, however, command interest; for they follow in one another's footsteps with the strict canonic imitation that is found in the songs known as "rounds."

Soon after the earliest English development came a French school. This must have been in the thirteenth century, for by 1325 we find Jean de Muris, in his "Speculum Musicæ," lamenting the departure of the good old times, and regretting that the composers had lost the inspiration shown in the preceding generation. This seems to be a common complaint; and it has a familiar ring even to-day.

These early schools were in part an outcome of the chanson — not that of the Troubadours, but the people's song, that was popular through all of western Europe. Sometimes these part-songs were in the strict form shown by "Sumer is icumen in"; but more often they were fairly free in their part-writing. While the Troubadour music, when not in unison, has its melody in the upper part, in accordance with modern ideas, there grew up in early days the custom, already mentioned, of having the melody held by the tenor voice. The word "tenor" comes from the Latin *tenere*, to hold. The chief melody, taken by the tenor, was called the *cantus firmus* (fixed song), or often simply the *cantus*. A second part, added above this melody and sung with it, was called the *discant*. Other parts were added above or below these two, and called from their position either *bass* or *alto* — words that meant "low" or "high." The term "treble," signifying a third part, was sometimes used for a voice above the discant. The word "soprano," meaning "above," was introduced later on, when the melody was given to the upper part.

CANON, from an ancient MS. in the British Museum.

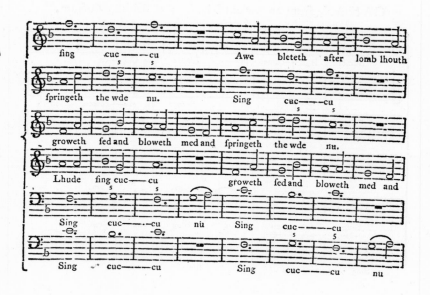

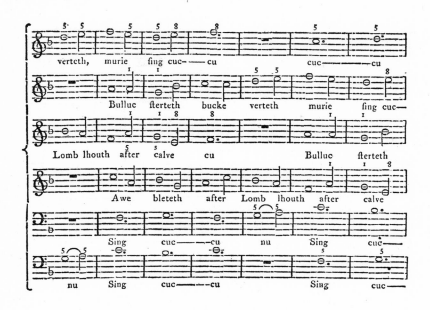

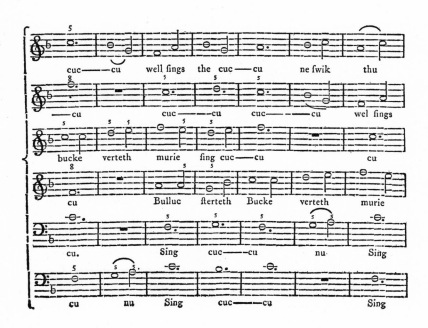

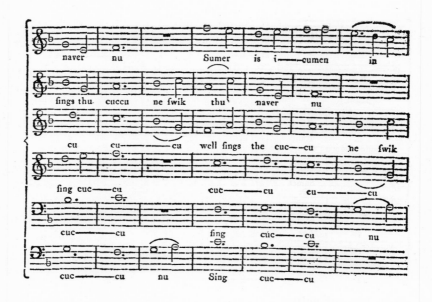

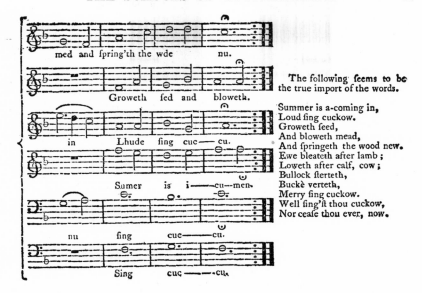

The following seems to be the true import of the words.

Summer is a-coming in,
Loud fing cuckow.
Groweth feed,
And bloweth mead,
And fpringeth the wood new.
Ewe bleateth after lamb ;
Loweth after calf, cow ;
Bullock fterteth,
Buckè verteth,
Merry fing cuckow.
Well fing'ft thou cuckow,
Nor ceafe thou ever, now.

Paris was still active in the fourteenth century; and the part-song style was gradually developed by Jehannot Lescurel and Guillaume de Machau, as well as by Cesaris, Tapissier, Carmen, and Henricus de Zeelandia in a later generation. These names carry little import now; but such composers, probably with others living in the Netherlands, brought about a gradual change from the popular style to polyphony.

The term "polyphony" refers to music written definitely in various parts, or voices. Homophony, which arose in the seventeenth century, denotes a melody supported by chords and harmony. Counterpoint, meaning much the same as polyphony, was derived from the phrase *punctum contra punctum*, the *punctum* being an old note-name, and the phrase meaning note against note. The contrapuntal forms are treated in a later chapter.

The strength of the popular influence is shown by the common use of secular melodies for the *cantus* in various parts of the mass. These melodies were used by the composers because the people knew the tunes, and the work could be more readily comprehended by them, or more easily performed. So customary did this become that the tenors often sang the words of the original song instead of the mass. We should be decidedly surprised if our church tenors should troll forth, "We won't go home till morning," with the rest of the choir wreathing sacred words around that tune; but custom sanctions everything, and such use of popular melodies lasted for over a century in the early Netherland days.

Certain songs became favorites for use in sacred works. Thus it seemed to be a point of honor for each composer to write at least one mass using the tune called "L'Homme Armé"; while "Se la face ay pale" was not far behind it in popularity. Sometimes old plain-song (Gregorian) tunes were used; and as these were sacred originally, they seem appropriate enough.

The chief forms used were the mass, the motet, the madrigal, and the canon, to which Italy added the *frottola*, or ballad. The mass is described in the chapter on vocal forms. The motet was a sacred part-song of contrapuntal character, the name being derived either from *mot*, referring to the sacred word, or from *motus*, meaning movement, as the parts all moved contrapuntally. The madrigal was much the same in style, usually with from three to six parts, and always unaccompanied; but very often the melody did not stay wholly in one voice, being distributed in separate phrases among various parts. The derivation of the name is doubtful. Some ascribe it to *madre*, referring to the Virgin Mary, but the words of the madrigal were often secular. This was one of the earliest forms used by the contrapuntal composers, though sporadic canons of earlier date have been found. The canon, as already implied, is a piece in which the same melody is used in each voice, but the voices enter in succession, so that the melody is made to serve as its own accompaniment. Thus, a round is a canon, though there are many canons that are not rounds. Various canons are illustrated in the section on musical form, in this work. These pieces were all sung without accompaniment at first, though the organ gradually came into use with the mass. Certain of the early canons were known as "fugas" (fugues), but they were not real examples of the later fugue, which is analyzed in connection with musical form.

The Netherland school shows as its first great exponent William Dufay. Like many of the early composers, he began as a choir-boy, and grew up to hold important church positions. He wrote polyphonic songs for Italian weddings, and studied at the Papal Chapel. Returning to church work in Belgium, he became known and honored throughout Europe. His existing works include masses, motets, and chansons — crude enough by our standards, but containing the germ of future growth.

Another composer of this period was Gilles Binchois, who died at Lille in 1460. The writer Tinctor said Binchois's name would "endure forever," but very few of his works remain in existence. Still others of this period were Petrus de Domart, Philippe Caron, Vincent Faugues, Anthony Busnois, Eloy, and Van Ghizeghem.

The real leader, however, appeared in England, in the person of John Dunstable. Born at Dunstable, living in England, and dying at London in 1453, he is quoted by the French poet Martin le Franc as the model upon which Dufay and Binchois based their music. By 1440 he was known as far away as the Tyrol. His motets and madrigals are now to be found in many Continental libraries, where works of historic value are too often left to languish in hidden manuscripts. Many writers call him the first contrapuntist; and there is no doubt that he led the way for the school that arose in the Netherlands. As England and North France were politically united, it is possible that Dunstable borrowed something from the French composers; but the freshness of his style bears witness to his own genius, and makes it seem probable that English music had developed steadily from the days of "Sumer is icumen in."

The next development in the Netherlands came in the shape of increased skill. Under the lead of Jean de Okeghem and Jacob Obrecht (or Hobrecht) it became customary for composers to use the utmost skill in writing puzzle canons. The so-called "crab-canon" consisted of a melody in one voice, while another voice sang the same melody backwards for accompaniment. Sometimes one voice would sing the melody from the beginning, while others started in the middle and went both ways. For such work, the melody was sometimes written only once, and a few words put with it to show what the different voices should do. A favorite catch-phrase was "out of light, darkness," or *vice versa*, referring to the outlined notes (introduced by Dufay) as light, and the solidly-written notes as dark. This would be equivalent to our directing a singer to use quarter-notes instead of halves, or halves instead of quarters. There were many such directing phrases used which are now wholly obscure in meaning.

This set of composers covered a wide range of territory. Okeghem was born at Antwerp, and became active in Paris, where three kings in succession were glad to employ his services. His masses, motets, and chansons show great skill and mastery of technique, and caused him to be called the "Prince of Music." Obrecht worked in Antwerp, as did also Jacques Barbireau, Antonius Wyngaerde, Jean Regis, Philippon de Bourges, and others. The Netherlands musicians working in Italy included Guillaume Guarneri, Gaspar Weerbecke, and Alexander Agricola. Germany had her own composers, such as Traugott Eugenius and Heinrich Finck; while Spain produced Francisco de Peñalosa.

This second Netherlands group devoted itself too much to the technical side of music. Yet it rendered great service to the cause of music by its development and mastery of certain technical methods. Its music was not what we should call pleasing. The attention paid to intricacies often caused beauty and expressive power to be lost in curious feats of polyphony. The texts were frequently treated with little respect; single words were sometimes spun out till they lost their sense, and little attention was paid to making the music as a whole suit the words. But some of the works of this time are important enough.

Immediately following this set of composers is another group, that carried music over into the sixteenth century. The new leader was Josquin des Près; and under his guidance music was again given real expressive beauty. Yet he was not lacking in technique or control of resources, for we find Luther saying of him, "Josquin rules the notes, while others are ruled by them." The archaic styles of the preceding century were now replaced by a more fluent manner, much better able to express emotion.

Josquin was born about 1445, in Hainault, and died in 1521. He held several important court posts, at Florence and elsewhere, and became a leader in the Papal Chapel. The year 1500 found him in Paris as a choirmaster. Very many of his works are still in existence, and they show not only technical skill, but real tonal beauty and a delicate fitness to their text. Josquin exercised a great influence upon his successors.

Others of this period were Pierre de la Rue, of Picardy, whose manuscripts were treasured highly; Antoine Brumel, of Flanders, a master of technique; Loyset Compère, a Flemish composer of romantic gifts; and the less known men named Jehan Cousin, Guillaume Crespel, Jean Prioris, Jean Verbonnet, and Noel Baulduin.

At this time the cause of music received great aid from the art of printing. Before 1500, musical manuscripts were usually drafted and illuminated by hand, in the monasteries or other centres of learning. The formation of the first book-printing firm, Gutenberg and Faust, took place in 1451. In 1476, Ulrich Hahn tried to print music at Rome, and five years later Jörg Resier, of Würzburg, and Ottavio Scotto, of Venice, made similar efforts. But in these cases only the comparatively simple plain-song was attempted, and separate impressions were made for the staff and the notes. Petrucci, of Fossombrone, working at Venice, was the first to print all varieties of music, no matter how intricate. In 1498, he secured a monopoly of the music-printing in that city, and from 1501 onward he published many valuable collections. Oeglin began publishing at Augsburg in 1507, and Scheffer did the same at Mayence before 1512. The first to invent a one-impression method printing both staff and notes was Pierre Haultin, in 1525, whose types were used by Attaignant, of Paris, in 1527. Another change came in 1530, when Briard, of Avignon, replaced the diamond-headed notes with the rounded forms that we use to-day. Music-printing by types soon became an important industry. At present, however, its use is limited; for by far the larger part of our music is printed from engraved plates.

The presence of certain Netherlands masters in Italy led to the formation of two distinct schools there — that of Venice and that of Rome. The prominence of Venice was due to Adrian Willaert, who was chorus-master at St. Mark's until after 1550. Born at Bruges before 1490, he studied with Josquin, to such effect that when he went to Rome he heard one of his own motets sung and ascribed to his master. He showed a tendency to extend still further the style of his teacher, while keeping up all the skill in technique. Thus, besides masses, motets, and madrigals by Willaert, we have also some freer part-songs and instrumental *ricercari*. The latter term signifies "research," and was used to designate pieces in which the composer sought to show his mastery over intricacies.

The Venetian school included many famous names. Jachet de

Buus was evidently a Netherlandian visitor. Another Netherlander, Ciprian de Rore, wrote music of rich charm, and began to use chromatic and harmonic effects freely. Gioseffo Zarlino is now best known by his books. Annibale Padovano represented the growing tendency toward organ pieces — a field which was well exploited by Claudio Merulo, Andrea Gabrieli, and Giovanni Gabrieli. There were other Venetian masters, and not a few in neighboring cities, a famous name being Animuccia. Under these, music began to take on those characteristics that made the Italian composers preëminent through two centuries.

The school of Venetian contrapuntists naturally did not think of harmony as a branch of study. All through the contrapuntal period, music was regarded as consisting of parts, or voices, that flowed on together. Under Okeghem these voices were allowed to flow in the most discordant fashion if the desired form demanded it. But from Josquin on, we find a constantly increasing attention paid to the expressive qualities of the music. Although the later contrapuntal composers still considered music as consisting of parts, they gradually approached a melodic style, with harmonies not radically different from our own. The introduction of the harmonic idea as a principle dates from the end of the fifteenth century, when Peri, Caccini, and others used it in the earliest operas. But it would not have taken such a firm hold as it did if the times had not been ripe for it. While the masses, motets, madrigals, and canons were kept as part-music, the *ricercari* and chansons were often freely harmonic in style. With the advent of opera, the contrapuntal style gradually disappeared; and chords began to be studied for their formation, independently of their occurrence in part-music. This gave rise to the saying that "Of old, music was horizontal; now it is vertical." The old idea of interwoven parts certainly gave music a horizontal aspect.

In Germany, there was a development parallel to that of the Venetian school, exemplified in part by Heinrich Isaac. But Saxony supplemented the Protestant Reformation by developing a new school of music in the Lutheran chorales. The style of these is shown by "Ein feste Burg," ascribed to Luther, but probably written by one of his friends. The rugged vitality of these chorales led to a further expansion of German music long after the Italian contrapuntists had passed away. Such men as Dietrich, Ammerbach, Schroeter,

Rosth, or Gesius are not often treated at any length in the histories, while Prætorius is known chiefly by his writings. But among the early chorale composers are Hans Bach and his son Veit, ancestors of the great John Sebastian Bach, who was to unite the vigor of this school with the most amazing contrapuntal skill, in a way which places his works among the very best that we have to-day. A famous organ composer of the seventeenth century was Samuel Scheidt.

France numbered among her early composers Jean Mouton, pupil of Josquin and teacher of Willaert. More original was Clément Jannequin, whose many chansons illustrate their pictorial titles, such as "La Bataille," "L'Alouette," "Le Caquet des Femmes," "La Chasse au Cerf," or "Les Cris de Paris." Claudio Goudimel was identified in some degree with the Huguenot and Calvinistic music. The Netherlands continued its activity with such men as Waelrant and Sweelinck. Spain, under the tuition of the Netherlander Gombert, had a school of composers represented by Antonio de Cabezon (called "the Spanish Bach") and Francisco Guerrero; while Portugal offered Damiao de Goes, and at a later date Duarte Lobo.

The English music, kept alive by Robert Fayrfax and others, culminated in a worthy school under Elizabeth. Christopher Tye and Thomas Tallis were the leaders, with Richard Farrant, William Byrd, and John Bull following them. The secular side was represented by Thomas Morley, Ford, and the lutenist John Dowland. The changing conditions of music at the time are well shown by this school. While Tye and Tallis favored the earlier contrapuntal forms, Morley wrote free madrigals, and Dowland produced lute music, as well as "madrigals and ayres" and a set of early dances, chiefly pavanes. In addition, many of these composers wrote for the virginals, a boxlike predecessor of the spinet and harpsichord. The old virginal music, collected by Fitzwilliam, shows a most remarkable trend toward the broad effects of modern piano music.

The music of Rome was given a strong sacred tendency by the Papal Chapel of singers. The Roman school contained such names as Giovanni Nanino, Felice Anerio, his nephew Giovanni, the Spaniard Vittoria, and the madrigal composer Luca Marenzio. But the chief name was that of Giovanni Pierluigi da Palestrina. With him is often mentioned Orlando di Lasso, of the Netherlands. Each of these two formed a culmination of his school; and the death of both in the same year, 1594, is held to mark the close of the contrapuntal epoch. As a matter of fact, motets and madrigals were composed freely until fifty years afterward; but opera and instrumental music drew public attention away from the older schools, so the statement is fair enough.

Orlando di Lasso was born at Mons in 1530 or 1532, though some give the date as 1520. The old Netherlandian name was sometimes written Lassus, while his native city knew him as Roland Delattre. He sang in a church choir at Mons when eight years old; and his voice was so attractive that it is said he was twice kidnapped for other institutions. It is sure that he was taken to Italy, for he spent much of his youth there. His earliest existing work is a set of madrigals published at Venice in 1552. In his younger years he seems to have devoted himself largely to secular music; but by 1563 we find him publishing a sacred collection, and continuing in that field. His secular music shows the most freedom and ease of construction. In this he avoided the so-called "Flemish tricks," or devices of ingenuity, adopting instead a style of simplicity and directness.

In 1556 or 1557, Di Lasso accepted a post with Duke Albert V of Bavaria; and for the rest of his life he made Munich his permanent home. But he travelled considerably, being the recipient of many honors and attentions from high dignitaries, including the French King and the Pope. In Munich he still produced some pieces of secular, and even humorous, character; but his sacred works were of greater importance. Most prominent among them was a set of "Seven Penitential Psalms," which are still to be found in the Royal State Library at Munich, in full glory of morocco and silver, with illuminated text. This set contains the composer's portrait, and was prepared for him by the Duke's order, as a mark of respect. These psalms were written before 1565; and that date disproves the claim that they were composed to soothe the remorse of Charles IX after the Massacre of St. Bartholomew. But they were important enough to have come to that monarch's attention. The historian Ambros considered that these psalms, and Palestrina's "Mass of Pope Marcellus," were the two most important musical productions of the sixteenth century.

Di Lasso was a very prolific composer, producing about two thou-

DI LASSO

PALESTRINA

sand works. These showed great versatility, for they included madrigals, love-songs, humorous songs, and even drinking-songs, as well as sacred works of several sorts. A statue of him, in Mons, testifies to his fame. After his burial in Munich he was given an epitaph consisting of a bright pun on his name: —

" Hic ille est Lassus, lassum qui recreat orbem."

This may be translated, "Here lies, weary, he who a weary world refreshed"; but the Latin for the first "weary" coincides with the composer's name.

In Italy, the sacred standard was upheld by Palestrina. Giovanni Pierluigi da Palestrina received his last name from the village where he was born, the date being probably 1524. He came to Rome in 1540, where he is said to have won favor by his voice. After returning to his native town, where he married and lived as organist, he appeared again at Rome in 1551, as master of the boys in the Vatican Chapel. At this time he became known as a composer by publishing a set of four- and five-voiced masses.

These were very welcome, because up to their appearance the Church had been forced to depend almost wholly upon Flemish composers. Pope Julius III then made Palestrina a singer in the Papal Choir — an exceptional honor, since its members were supposed to be celibates. Under Paul IV, Palestrina was ruled out; but he afterwards received the post of musical director at the Lateran, which enabled him to live and to support his family. During six years at the Lateran, Palestrina wrote some four-voiced lamentations, a notable eight-voiced "Crux Fidelis," and the famous "Improperia," or reproaches of Christ to his enemies — the composer's best work, according to Mendelssohn.

In 1561, Palestrina became director at the church of Santa Maria Maggiore. While there, it is stated, an event happened that made him known and respected by all Catholics. Haberl, his best biographer, does not give the story; but Baini does. It seems, according to Baini, that the Council of Trent, disgusted with the secular songs and words woven into the Flemish masses, thought of excluding music from the service. A commission of cardinals took up the matter with some of the papal singers; and as a result Palestrina was commissioned to write a mass that should show whether music could be made dignified enough for sacred use. Unwilling to trust the issue to one work, Palestrina wrote three; and one of these, the "Mass of Pope Marcellus," was so beautiful that the Council at once decided in favor of retaining music. This story, however, is doubted by many.

Palestrina now received frequent honors, but little profit. The papal copyist wrote the notes of the successful mass in a larger size than usual; Pope Pius IV exclaimed that such must be the music of the angels; while Philip II, on receiving a copy of these masses and finding them dedicated to him, sent in return nothing but his thanks. Yet Palestrina was not without friends among the cardinals, who may have helped him in many ways. The success of his mass won him a new post — that of composer to the Papal Chapel. He had his moments of popular triumph, too. In 1575, no less than fifteen hundred of his fellow townsmen entered Rome in three groups, and sang the works of their beloved composer while he himself marched at the head and directed the proceedings.

Palestrina was also choir-leader at St. Peter's, and teacher in the important music school of his friend Nanini. He continued active until shortly before his death, which occurred in 1594, four months before that of Di Lasso.

Palestrina's music has been divided into three periods. In the first, he led the voices independently, without much attention to harmony. In the second, he paid more attention to good harmonic effects, but in consequence led the voices awkwardly. In the third period, he showed excellence in both details. Naturally his later works are his best; but the "Improperia," falling in the second period, shows a chorale-like strength that is very impressive.

Palestrina brought the old school of pure counterpoint to its culmination. He discarded chromatics, and kept to the strict Gregorian modes as a tenet of religion. He took care also to make his music emphasize the words properly. His compositions may be less popular in style than those of his great Flemish contemporary, but they are more lofty in conception. There is a certain lack of rhythm in Palestrina's works, which makes them sound strange to modern ears; but the devotee of Bach will soon learn to appreciate the simplicity and nobility of the earlier master. Among other things, Palestrina has been called "the Homer of music"; and there is a stateliness of style in his works which makes the title very appropriate.

The year 1594 was marked also by the composition of the first Florentine opera, "Dafne." The new work was definitely in the harmonic style; and from that date onward, counterpoint was gradually replaced by a simpler and more dramatic utterance.

VI

THE HARMONIC STYLE

THE textbooks usually dwell on the year 1600 as the date of the beginning of opera. In that year a set of Florentine musicians, consisting of Jacopo Peri, Giulio Caccini, and others, brought out Peri's "Euridice," embodying dramatic principles as they understood them after studying the old Greek drama. Sometimes Peri's earlier work, "Dafne," is called the first opera. But as a matter of fact, Italy had witnessed what was practically an opera over a century earlier than that date, and had seen the development of a tentative operatic school.

Mediæval drama consisted of mystery plays, miracle plays, and moralities. The mysteries were plays representing Biblical stories. The miracle plays treated the lives of the saints, and may be said to have included the passion play, dealing with the life and crucifixion of Christ. The moralities were allegories of a moral or religious sort, such as the play of "Everyman," recently revived by an English company. In South France the "Fête de l'Âne" introduced an element of comedy.

Italy, however, developed the secular drama, which flourished first at Mantua. In 1472, when the Cardinal Francesco Gonzaga returned to Mantua from Bologna, we find the former place witnessing what may fairly be considered the first opera — "La Favola di Orfeo," by Angelo Poliziani. The plot begins among shepherds. When Orpheus enters, he is told of Euridice's death, and determines to seek her among the shades, as in the mythical story. He wins her from Pluto, loses her by looking back in defiance of his agreement, and is stopped by Tisiphone from trying to find her again. His railings then incense the mænads, who drive him off the stage and slay him. This is set to music, consisting of solos, dialogues, and choruses which suggest the *frottola*, the carnival songs, and the old *ballata*, or dance-song. The solo parts were arranged in the manner developed by the lute-players, who would sing one part of a polyphonic composition and play the others as accompaniment. In this manner melodic music was made to take its place in the contrapuntal world as early as the fifteenth century. The *frottola*, as already indicated, was a popular song, set in polyphonic style, to be sure, but simple and singable in effect, like the earlier English "Sumer is icumen in." It was not meant to be canonic, or otherwise intricate. Cerone wrote, in 1613, "He who puts into a *frottola* fugues, imitations, etc., is like one who sets a worthless stone in gold. A *frottola* thus ennobled would become a madrigal, while a madrigal, all too scantily treated, would sink to a *frottola*." The *frottola* afterwards developed into the still less involved *villanelle*, which was often a simple pastoral song.

There were at least two solo instruments in Poliziano's work. One was the shepherd's pipe, and the other the lyre of Orpheus. There was also, almost surely, a general accompaniment given by several instruments. While works for instruments alone did not exist in Italy until organ pieces were composed by Merulo, nearly a century later, orchestral accompaniment to voices was employed constantly at this time. Old reliefs and illuminations show viols of various sizes, harps, lutes, dulcimers, flutes, pipes, oboes, trombones, and the portable folding organ known as the regals. It is probable that the early orchestras were somewhat haphazard, consisting of those instruments that could be obtained at a particular court or city; and they were small in size, perhaps having less than a dozen players. In Italy the *chitarrone*, or large guitar, was much used.

With the coming of Willaert to Venice, and his impressive use of double choruses for the two organs in St. Mark's, the madrigal began to flourish. In spite of the fact that Poliziano showed the power of solo music for operatic purposes, the lyric drama drew away from this, and adopted the madrigal as its means of expression. A part of the cause for such a backward step may be found in the lack of artistic taste in the nobles, who began to care more and more for spectacular rather than artistic effects. As the musical plays were written for festival occasions at their courts, their ideas were naturally respected. This tendency can be traced through various works. Bergonzo Botto (1488), and Nicolo de Corregio Visconti (1487), produced plays on mythical subjects that continued the lyric style; but in the next century the madrigal ruled without a rival.

In 1539, at the marriage of Cosmo I, two plays were given, one containing a solo madrigal, but both, with that exception, consisting of music sung in all the parts. On this occasion a song by Aurora was accompanied by *gravicembalo* (primitive precursor of the piano), organ, flute, harp, and a large viol; while the Song of Night was set with four trombones to produce a grave and melancholy effect.

In 1554, Beccari, of Ferrara, brought out " Il Sagrificio," a pastoral play, which had for one character a high priest who sang to his lyre, but did not in other ways adopt the lyric form. The choruses in this, as in Lollio's "Aretusa" (1571) and Argenti's "Sfortunato," were treated contrapuntally.

Among other occasions, the marriage of Grand Duke Ferdinand at Florence in 1589 seems of interest, because the members of the Florentine coterie above mentioned took part in producing musical *intermezzi* given between the acts of a play. The first, "The Harmony of the Spheres," was by Emilio del Cavaliere, who afterwards produced the first oratorio. Next, by Luca Marenzio, came the contest between the Muses and the Pierides, the singers accompanied by lutes and viols while the judges had harps and lyres in addition for support. Next came a picture of Apollo slaying the Python, — with some features of a ballet-pantomime, — a success as great as the others, but a rather tame affair when compared with the old Greek tone-picture of the same event. Another of these playlets showed Arion's adventures, and included a solo sung by him with harp accompaniment. A picture of heaven and hell by Caccini offered some strong instrumental effects. Last came an antiphonal bit between three groups of Muses, with dances interspersed.

The varied character of these short works shows that reform was impending. The madrigal plays seemed dominant, but had the inherent weakness that they did not present the text clearly. Ingenious attempts were made to remedy this trouble, Striggio writing excellent operatic comedies, and Orazio Vecchi even having the dialogue spoken while singers behind the scenes kept up a background of madrigals. But it remained for the Florentine coterie to establish the true principle of opera — the solo style of singing, with the music aimed to reflect the emotions of the text, instead of being merely a skilled but irrelevant piece of contrapuntal composition.

The reformers found a little trouble awaiting them in another shape. Where at first the spirit of opera was sacrificed to the composer's ingenuity, now it met with another obstacle in the shape of the singer's desire for display. The early works of the Florentine group, in 1600 and later, were declamatory in style, and almost like what is now known as "melos," or melodic recitative. The instrumental music was now definitely harmonic, and subordinate to the sense of the words; in a primitive fashion, to be sure, but with as much of artistic ideal as Gluck and Wagner showed in later times when bringing opera back to its true mission. Yet even in the first of the Florentine works now extant ("Euridice," produced in 1600), the singer Vittoria Archilei is said to have enlivened the occasion by introducing *"lunghi giri e gruppi"* — long roulades and embellishments, such as Rossini and his school used in later days, which obscure the dramatic effect in order to let the singer display her powers. Thus began a disagreement that has not been settled, even in the present. Artistic ideas should rule, but the public too often demands mere vocal display; and the singers know it, from Patti and Melba down.

Opera soon broadened its scope, and in the hands of Monteverde became a public amusement. In 1637, a public opera-house was built in Venice, in which his later works were produced. One of his earliest operas ("Orfeo," produced at Mantua in 1608) shows an orchestra far beyond that of his predecessors. It consisted of two harpsichords, two bass viols, ten tenor viols, one double harp, two small French violins, two large guitars, two wooden organs, three *viole da gamba*, four trombones, one regal, two *cornetti* (wooden pipes), one treble flute, one clarion, and three trumpets with mutes. It will thus be seen that Monteverde was an instrumental pioneer — the Richard Strauss of his time. Like Strauss, he was fond of experimenting with new orchestral colors; and he originated the viol and violin *pizzicato*, or plucking of the string, and the *tremolo*, or rapid repetition of a tone. Monteverde's career, with that of his successors Rossi, Cesti, and Cavalli, brought opera down to the year 1675.

Spectacular effects were much sought after. For Cesti's "Il Pomo d' Oro," given at Vienna in 1666, a special theatre, with room for fifteen hundred, was constructed in the courtyard of the castle. According to Pratt,[1] "the scenery included landscapes and a harbor view, the open sea with tritons, the nether world, and the Olympian

[1] *The History of Music.*

heaven, each with its respective divinities; and the number of characters was bewildering. In the prologue appeared the personified divisions of the Empire, Spain, Austria, Hungary, Bohemia, Germany, Italy — even America! There were five acts and sixty-seven scenes. The cost of production was said to be 100,000 thalers."

Venice remained an opera centre for some time, the names of Ferrari, Sartorio, and Legrenzi being only a few of its many celebrities. But before the end of the century, the sceptre passed to Naples, owing to the work of Alessandro Scarlatti. He was a Sicilian, having been born at Trapani in 1659. He composed an immense number of sacred works, including two hundred masses. But he became better known by his operas, which numbered over a hundred. About one third of these are still in existence. His orchestral writing was excellent, and his themes full of vigor and charm. He did much to establish the *da capo* aria, in which the first part returns to close the piece. His overtures, consisting of a slow section between two quick ones, became very popular. He also wrote harpsichord or spinet works that are still performed by pianists.

Oratorio arose from St. Philip Neri's practice of having music given in the oratory of his church. The transition from other sacred works to oratorio was probably gradual. In 1600 came Cavaliere's "Rappresentazione di anima e di corpo," which is considered the first oratorio, though it may have been one of a set of similar works. It shows the influence of the morality plays. It has about ninety numbers, including recitatives, solos, choruses, part-songs, and an instrumental intermezzo. The accompaniment is for *gravicembalo*, large lute, double lyre, and two flutes, with a violin to aid the soprano.

Carissimi did away with the old procedure of having oratorio given in costume. He replaced the sacred opera or play idea by oratorio as we know it in its concert form. He also adhered strictly to Biblical subjects, treating others in what were practically cantatas. Nearly all the Italian composers who came just after Carissimi tried their hand at oratorio; but their work was not very distinctive. Most prominent among them were Alessandro Scarlatti and Stradella, but even their oratorios did not have the permanent value that Handel was soon to give to the form.

Stradella may be cited as an instance of the way in which false anecdotes thrive in the musical world. There is a well-known and expressive song that has been known as "Stradella's Prayer." The story-tellers asserted that Stradella was in love with a noble Roman lady, who returned his love; that her brother was incensed, and hired assassins to kill the aspiring musician; and that these assassins, waiting outside Stradella's church to murder him, were so moved when he sang the "Prayer" that instead of attacking him they warned him and gave him money to get away. The story sounds a little excessive as it stands; but research has shown that the "Prayer" in question was not by Stradella at all, and was not written until after his death.

In France, opera developed from the ballet. In 1581, Baltazarini's "Ballet comique de la reine" attracted much notice. Under Henry IV, about eighty ballets were given at the court. Cambert started producing operas in 1659, but he was soon overshadowed by Lully.

Jean Baptiste Lully, born at Florence in 1633, was taken to Paris by the Duc de Guise. At first a kitchen scullion, Lully rapidly bettered his position by his violin-playing. Entering the private band of Louis XIV, he soon became its leader, and made it very efficient. From 1653 he was court composer, producing many successful ballets. Nearly twenty years later he began the series of about fifteen operas that made him famous. He had a hand in developing the French overture form, which consists of a slow movement followed by a quick one, and sometimes ending with another slow section.

In Germany the so-called *Singspiel* was of rather elastic character. It included the solos and part-songs that were so popular with the German people, along with a certain minimum of spoken dialogue. Not far different from this type were the first German operas, — Schütz's "Dafne," in 1627, and Staden's "Seelewig," in 1644. The real advance came with the opening of the Hamburg Opera-House, in 1678. Reinhard Keiser soon became the leader of this enterprise, writing over one hundred and sixteen operas. Other composers of the school were Kusser, the violinist Strungk, and Johann Theile. The operas tended toward display, and sometimes became very spectacular through intricate stage appliances.

England had something in the nature of opera in 1656, when "The Siege of Rhodes" was composed by five native musicians. But the chief English form of that time was the masque. This was taken from Italian models in the sixteenth century, but made into something more original by the great Elizabethan poets. The masque was practically a private theatrical representation, in which members of cultivated society enacted some mythological or fanciful plot, with poetic words interspersed with dancing, singing, and even incidental pieces. The actors were more or less disguised, as the name of such musical plays would indicate. Masques were forbidden by the Puritans, but revived after the restoration of Charles II. Yet the Commonwealth could not have been violently opposed to the form, as the Puritan poet Milton included it in his works.

The music to these poetic affairs was written by the most gifted composers of the time. Among these were Campion, Lanier, Lawes, Banister, and Pelham Humfrey; but greater than all was Henry Purcell. Humfrey had investigated Lully's work at Paris, and brought back ideas about opera. Purcell made use of these, and wrote a number of real operas in addition to the customary masques. Purcell is reckoned by many as England's greatest composer. Doubtless this title is fair enough, though Dunstable was more widely known in his day. Purcell was one of the short-lived geniuses, for he died at the age of thirty-seven, in 1674. It is said that his death was caused in part by his being locked out of his house in the cold after a rather riotous night with boon companions; but he was probably as steady-going as was expected at that time. His masques and operas together number about forty. Of the latter, "King Arthur," with Dryden's words, is considered the greatest. These operas are not now given, although "The Faëry Queen" was recently revived in London as a curiosity.

The name of Purcell brings into notice also the development of instrumental music. The Italians were the pioneers in this field. All through the seventeenth century there was a constantly increasing repertoire of such music. The perfecting of the violin and the development of the harpsichord, spinet, and clavichord did much to bring this about. The widespread adoption of the harmonic style was a second important factor. The growth of the old dances was another incentive to the composers.

The English virginal school, previously mentioned, seemed not to develop into anything definite, in spite of the strikingly modern effects of some of its music. But it may have had an influence on Purcell. Whether he followed this or his cherished Italian models, it is certain that he produced instrumental music of the most valuable character. His sonatas for various combinations of instruments are not often heard at present, but they are none the less wonderfully attractive. In recent years Arnold Dolmetsch and others have given concerts of old music on the old instruments. In these the variety of harpsichord effects (due to the many pedals) combines most excellently with the quiet, plaintive sweetness of the viols and early wood-wind instruments. Under such conditions the seventeenth-century music shows a combination of earnestness and grace, and seems to have a "sweet reasonableness" that is of the utmost charm. Many of the early instrumental composers are deemed hardly worthy of mention except in the largest histories; but the musical antiquary knows the worth of their productions. In listening to these works the student does not have to learn any forgotten or obsolete methods of expression. He will acknowledge, too, that such unforced and spontaneous music is really more pleasing to the auditor than many of the contemporary experiments in abstruse harmony.

Germany was perhaps a little backward in instrumental development; but it had some masters, especially in the domain of the organ. Froberger, Kerll, Muffat, and Pachelbel are good examples, the last three coming near the end of the seventeenth century. Froberger was for a time imperial organist and clavecinist at Vienna. On a trip to England he was wrecked and robbed, and had a hard time persuading any one of his identity. Finally he managed to get a chance at an organ. Here he was overheard by a lady who had studied with him on the Continent; and she recognized him by the brilliance of his performance. Charles II then took him into favor. He put his reminiscences of all this into a comical little tone-picture of a Channel trip, even introducing suggestions of seasickness. His works consist of br'lliant *toccatas, capriccios,* and secular suites. Kerll also wrote for harpsichord as well as organ; and his solid style is said to foreshadow that of Bach.

The student who wishes to go more minutely into the early epochs will find many other composers of this period described in Pratt's "History"; while the "Oxford History" and Ambros are the great authorities for the contrapuntal masters. After 1700 the development of music came through individuals rather than schools, and the story of music becomes largely an account of the great composers.

PART II
THE GREAT COMPOSERS

VII

BACH

SOON after the end of the Middle Ages, and at least as early as 1550, we may find mention of a Thuringian family of musicians named Bach. Hans Bach, of Wechmar, the first prominent musician in a long line, lived in the sixteenth century. His son Veit died in 1619. Of Veit's two sons, Hans, called "The Player," died in 1626. Hans had three sons, of whom Christoph was the second. Christoph's second son, Johann Ambrosius, who lived at Eisenach, had three sons in his turn; and the youngest of these was the great Johann Sebastian Bach. There were many other Bachs, the descendants of the original Hans numbering about four hundred in three centuries. But among them all, Johann Sebastian stands preëminent as a world-genius, far above even his most gifted sons.

Johann (or John) Sebastian Bach was born at Eisenach in 1685. His parents died soon after his birth, and he was brought up by his brother Johann Christoph, an organist in a little village near Weimar. The youngster soon displayed musical ability. The elder brother, somewhat of a martinet, forbade his protégé's using certain manuscripts; whereupon the young enthusiast copied them secretly by moonlight, thereby laying at least a partial foundation for the blindness with which he was afflicted in later life. A choir position in Lüneburg enabled him to have access to a large musical library. His violin-playing won him a post at Weimar, but in 1704 he began his real career by becoming town organist at Arnstadt.

In earlier years he had heard Reinken play, and from Arnstadt he went to Lübeck to listen to Buxtehude. Bach was much influenced by them, and became a devotee of all that was best in the old contrapuntal style. This, as already described, is a system of writing in parts that flow along side by side, instead of using a melody supported by chords. Sometimes these parts are comparatively free; in certain cases, however (described in the section on musical form), they must obey very strict and intricate rules. Bach not only made his music conform to the rules, but did it with a freedom and skill that allowed him to keep his music astonishingly fresh and interesting. The organ was the scene of many an improvisation by him, in which masterly command of musical structure and design was united with remarkable expressive power. It is said that he could improvise an intricate fugue with more ease than many lesser composers would show in extemporising a simple fantasie.

At Mühlhausen, Bach met and married his cousin Maria Barbara. He was a man who held family life in the highest reverence, like some noble patriarch of old. After his first wife's death he married the singer Anna Wülken. He had twenty children in all; and as most of them were trained by him, we may be sure that there was much concerted music in the Bach household. With such a large family, it was almost inevitable that Bach should suffer poverty. He often had to see much less gifted musicians chosen over his head to fill lucrative posts; but he bore all his troubles with a cheerful optimism that gave way to anger only when any one spoke slightingly of music in his hearing.

Bach's next position was that of court organist to the Duke of Weimar. In that place he developed his powers by still further practice, and the study of more music, including the early Italian compositions. He became known as a teacher, and began to write some of the fugues, suites, and Lutheran cantatas that have made his name immortal.

Under the Prince of Anhalt-Cöthen (from 1717 to 1723), he had no good organ within reach, but devoted himself to other instruments, including the clavichord and harpsichord. Here he composed the first part of his famous "Well-Tempered Clavichord," a set of wonderful fugues. These introduced the system of twelve equal semitones, to replace the so-called "scale of nature," which had been used up to 1700. Here, too, he wrote concertos and other instrumental music.

Bach's next position took him to Leipsic, as organist of the Thomas Church and musical director in the Thomas School. Here he remained until his death in 1750. His Leipsic years brought him honor and glory, even if wealth seemed far away. He composed, taught, played, and lived out his admirable domestic career in a way that must have won him some happiness, even if his life was uneventful for the most part.

In 1747, his fame induced Frederick the Great to send him an invitation to come to Potsdam. His son Carl Philipp Emanuel Bach held a permanent musical post at Frederick's court, and at last the old man consented to go. When he arrived, Frederick sprang up from supper, saying, "Old Bach is here," and hastened to receive the distinguished visitor. Bach played on the King's new pianos, but said that he preferred the clavichord, and held the piano fitted only for light rondos or variations. Then he improvised a four-voiced (four-part) fugue on a subject given by the King, and he afterwards elaborated it into a six-voiced work for his "Art of Fugue." After he left, Frederick sent him a sum of money; but it was embezzled before it reached its destination.

This trip may have hastened Bach's last illnesses. His eyes, none too strong, were overtasked by his engraving the plates for the "Art of Fugue," which poverty forced him to do for himself. Operations were succeeded by blindness; and a sudden return of sight was only a prelude to the fit of apoplexy that killed him.

The number of Bach's works is enormous. The large recent edition by the Bach Society includes over fifty sizable volumes. His commanding genius was not fully realized during his life, and for more than a century after his death most of his works remained in manuscript. When Mendelssohn and others began to unearth them, a number of these manuscripts were lost. But among those that remain are examples of many forms, from the short choral to the great orchestral suite or the large vocal-orchestral Passion.

Among the organ works are nearly a score of long preludes and fugues; a few *toccatas;* and many choral-preludes and fantasias.

For clavichord alone, and now suitable for the piano, are the forty-eight preludes and fugues of the "Well-Tempered Clavichord." Each of its two volumes has one prelude and fugue in each one of the twenty-four possible keys, twelve major and twelve minor. The old Greek scale of Pythagoras, the "scale of nature," based on mathematical intervals, did not have twelve equal semitones, but included tones of two different sizes, and kept the flats and sharps much nearer to their notes than at present. In the old system, for example, C-sharp was lower than D-flat. This scale did not allow much modulation, so it was altered slightly to what was known in the seventeenth century as "mean temperament." But by 1691, Werckmeister and others advocated the equal-semitone system; and Bach's great collection of fugues, of which the first volume was completed in 1722, gave it permanence. Bach's other clavier works include twelve suites, many inventions and smaller works, "The Musical Offering" (1747) and "The Art of Fugue" (1749), while he wrote also about a dozen concertos for one or more claviers (keyboard instruments) with orchestra.

The hearer who is unfamiliar with music will usually find himself unenlightened when listening to his first Bach fugue. But if he perseveres, and learns to understand the beauties of the contrapuntal style, he will open for himself a vast treasure-house of musical enjoyment. The Bach fugues are farthest away from the student's natural bent, and more unlike popular music, than any other works now in the repertoire. In developing a taste for most of the classics, the student learns that tinkling tunes are not a necessity, and that the general pervading tunefulness of a classical piece may be treated in better ways, and with far more variety, than a hard-and-fast tune in conventional sections of monotonously equal length. But the student still seeks for bits of melodious work, supported by chords, such as he is accustomed to.

In the fugue, the listener must take a still more radical step. He must give up hunting for melody supported by chords, and in place of that he must imagine a musical method in which there are various parts (called "voices") proceeding together. In harmonic writing, the chords support the melody just as the piers of a bridge uphold its superstructure. But in counterpoint, the different parts are interwoven to form a whole, more in the way that strands are wound to make up a rope, or colored threads interwoven to form a delicate tapestry.

The chief possibility of importance in counterpoint is that of imitation. A phrase, or theme, or figure, which is used in one voice, may be repeated in another, in such a way as to give balance and contrast to the work in which it occurs. By repeating the motive judiciously, the composer evolves an actual musical design. To those who are trained to appreciate the contrapuntal works, this sense of design, or perception of graceful structure, is a matter of keen delight. The fugue is the most intricate of all the contrapuntal designs. In it the whole work is practically developed out of a single theme, called the subject. Such a subject should always be short and striking, so that the hearer may grasp it at once. At first the subject is echoed and reëchoed by the different voices, in well-balanced and orderly succession. Then follow various passages built out of the subject. In some of these it is used in part as an accompaniment for itself, while in others certain figures or fragments taken from it are employed to build up apparently new effects.

As an instance of the way in which Bach could rearrange and develop the briefest of themes, the reader is referred to the fifth fugue in volume II of the "Clavichord" set. In this the first nine notes form the subject. The figure of the last four notes in the subject is used to build up episodes; and the reader may amuse himself by taking a pencil and seeing how many appearances of this figure he can mark or pick out in the entire fugue. Further details of this and other fugues will be found in the last chapter on musical form.

Bach's chamber works include concerted pieces for various combinations of solo instruments. He wrote also sonatas and other works for violin, flute, or *viola da gamba* (large 'cello-like viol), with clavier, as well as similar pieces for violin, *viola pomposa* (large viola), or 'cello alone. One of the most famous violin pieces in the repertoire is the *chaconne*, for the solo instrument, taken from one of the Bach sonatas. This *chaconne* has become a sort of test piece for great players.

Bach's orchestral works include suites, overtures, and various concertos. Among the latter, the so-called Brandenburg concertos are still favorites with the public. These and the suites are very strong and direct in their effect, and clearly melodious in spite of their somewhat contrapuntal structure. The D-major suite has a wonderfully fine overture, full of beautiful harmonies; a broadly effective air; and a striking gavotte. The gem of the B-minor suite, which comes next in popularity, is the exquisite "Badinerie," in which a solo flute is made to carry on an inimitably delightful dialogue with the orchestra. But it is hardly fair to make special citations, for Bach's orchestral works are almost all highly interesting. They do not aim to be strongly dramatic, but they flow along with calm dignity, or easy grace, or compelling enthusiasm.

Bach wrote a great many secular cantatas, serenades, and other vocal works. Among the former are two humorous ones — a "Peasants' Cantata," showing some of the trials of country life, and a "Coffee Cantata," in which a wilful girl is held back from afternoon coffee-parties, with their attendant gossip, only by the promise of having a husband given to her.

Among the vocal works are many motets, cantatas, etc., for use in the Lutheran service. These comprise about two thirds of five complete sets of works for the entire church year.

Bach composed also five large masses, a number of smaller ones, and two *Magnificats*. More important than these, however, are the five Passions (of which two are lost and one doubtful), the long six-part "Christmas Oratorio," and similar works for Easter and Ascension. The "St. Matthew Passion," the most famous of the sacred works, is still performed with some frequency. It contains many great touches, such as the shouts of the crowd to free Barabbas, the picture of the trampling footsteps of the mob, and the great final chorus of sorrow. Of the other works, the "Christmas Oratorio" is best known by its pastorale, which figures on many orchestral programmes when Christmas is approaching.

In spite of the great variety of forms used by Bach, there are certain very definite qualities common to all his music.

First of all, as already stated, his works are built wholly or partly on the contrapuntal system. Even in his most clearly melodious compositions, such as the orchestral suites, there is some contrapuntal imitation; and there is almost always part-writing, which constitutes counterpoint in its simplest form.

Bach was a master of rhythm. All his pieces appeal to us by their clearness of accent and steadiness of flow. This is one of the points that make his fugues so great, for their straightforward rhythm allows the various parts to come clearly to the auditor's ear. There is no monotony about it, no lack of variety in rhythm; but the style is always clean-cut, and never confused.

The third quality to be noted in Bach's music is the beauty and originality of his harmonies. They do not glow with the impressionism of the modern score-masters; but they, too, are clear and clean-cut, or blended into one another with the most exquisite delicacy. Bach did not try to "tear passion to tatters," in the exaggerated fashion of certain later composers; but he could show an emotional

HANDEL

BACH

power that has proved to be deeply effective, even if somewhat repressed and quiet.

Incidentally, it must not be claimed from the last paragraph that Bach strove for the harmonic style. As a matter of fact, he always held to counterpoint. He summed up and perfected the style of his predecessors. His improvisations grew famous because of their wonderful contrapuntal intricacy. When he played for Reinken, the latter, then an old man, grew devoutly thankful that the art of the past was thus nobly cherished, in defiance of conditions which were even then changing.

Of Bach's sons, the eldest, Wilhelm Friedemann, was an erratic but highly gifted composer, whose orchestral works show a wild power that was remarkable for a time so long before Beethoven. Carl Philipp Emanuel found time, when not composing sonatas or accompanying the flute of Frederick the Great, to write a notable work on "The True Art of Piano-Playing." Johann Christian became famous in London, wrote symphonies, and helped to popularize the early pianos, besides composing curious little tone-pictures, such as "The Battle of Rossbach." Battle-pieces have been popular with the composers, and in this one we see the usual devices — marching of troops, trumpet fanfares, the rattle of musketry, deep notes giving the booming of cannon, and so on. In this piece the cries of the wounded are present, being misprinted into "Les l'Amendations des Blessés." All this may have earned money. It was infinitely below the lofty earnestness of his father's work; but after the father's death, poverty made his family separate in their search for sustenance. Descendants of the great Bach kept the line in existence until 1846, when the family became extinct.

Among the pioneers in the sonata, which became important as a form underlying many modern works, Domenico Scarlatti was one of the earliest. The sonata form is described in a chapter of its own, in the musical-form section. Here it may be stated that one of the chief ideas of the form in classical times was its adaptability for good contrast in styles of themes. The sonatas of Scarlatti are little more than dance-fantasias, and they were frequently written in one movement, where the later sonata had three or four. Scarlatti's piano work is mentioned in the article on famous pianists, in this volume. He composed operas, but was best known in connection with the harpsichord. It was he who wrote the so-called "cat fugue," using as his subject the notes played by a pet cat as it stalked along his keyboard. But he is best known for his harmonic work, his primitive sonatas helping to perpetuate the homophonic style.

Paradisi and Galuppi were two Italians who produced somewhat more ambitious sonatas. In their works the sonata had more than one movement. The chief movement had two contrasted themes, then a so-called development that began with the chief theme, and a recapitulation beginning with the second theme. But the form had not yet become wholly definite in shape. Another Italian deserving mention is Sammartini, who wrote sonatas and symphonies that foreshadowed those of Haydn.

Bach's sonatas showed a grasp of the possibilities of thematic contrast. But his devotion to contrapuntal expression prevented these works from becoming models for the harmonic composers, in spite of Bach's greatness. His contemporary Kuhnau was more in line with the subsequent developments. But if Bach's sonatas took no part in the evolution of the form, those of his son Carl Philipp Emanuel were decidedly more productive of results. It was the latter composer who led the way to the real beginning of the sonata; and one of his works, coming to Haydn's attention, showed the later genius the possibilities of the new form.

Bach had no great successor in the field of actual church-service music. Karl Heinrich Graun was the leader of a German group. He is known by his oratorio, "The Death of Jesus," certain numbers of which are still occasionally heard in concert. In Italy Padre Martini, Pergolesi, and Jommelli deserve mention for their church works; but nearly all the early Italian opera composers tried their hand at sacred music also.

In the clavier field, François Couperin and Jean Philippe Rameau developed an attractive French school of harpsichord (or spinet) works. Where the Italians had produced sonatas and suites, these two and their followers wrote many light but pleasing tone-pictures.

VIII

HANDEL

GEORG FRIEDRICH HÄNDEL (whose last name was afterwards anglicized to Handel) was born at Halle, in 1685. As this was the year of Bach's birth, these two pioneers have sometimes been called the "Siamese Twins of Music." But the resemblance between them is not close enough to justify the title. Both were composers, and both wrote in a more or less contrapuntal style; but Handel strove for dramatic effect, and emphasized harmony. Where Bach summed up the glories of the past, Handel foreshadowed those of the future.

During childhood, Handel showed an early devotion to music. Finding himself discouraged, he is said to have used a clavichord in the garret of his house, upon which he could practise in secret. When seven years old, he asked to be taken with his father on a visit which the latter was paying to the Duke of Saxe-Weissenfels. This the father refused altogether. But when the carriage had gone a little way, it was found that the youngster had run after it, and was clinging on behind. His persistence caused him to be taken along, with perhaps decisive results upon his career; for the Duke, on hearing him play, advised his father earnestly to let the boy devote himself to the music that he loved so irresistibly. Handel was therefore put under a good teacher, by name Zachau; and four years later he was taken to Berlin as a prodigy.

After a university course, with organist work, at Halle, Handel entered upon an important phase of his career by becoming a violinist in Keiser's orchestra at the Hamburg Opera-House. Here he became intimate with Mattheson.

The first incident in this friendship was a trip to Lübeck. The pair went thither in search of the post of city organist. The old Buxtehude, who had held the post for many years, was about to retire; but he had made it a condition that his successor should marry his daughter. After looking over the situation (and the lady in the case), the two young aspirants withdrew from the contest.

Handel soon became known as a composer, starting his operatic career in 1704, with "Almira," and producing a Passion in the same year. He also attained a higher rank in the orchestra; for when Keiser was once unexpectedly absent, Handel stepped into the vacant place, and became the conductor. This position he held with firm control; but it brought him into another episode with Mattheson, which might have proved fatal. Handel refused to let Mattheson lead parts of an opera which the latter had written; and after the performance the composer was so angered that he boxed the arbitrary conductor's ears. The two drew swords at once, and began a duel. Mattheson broke through Handel's guard, but, fortunately for the world, his weapon snapped against a large button on Handel's coat.

After three years or so at Hamburg, Handel betook himself to Italy. There he had the keyboard duel with Scarlatti that is mentioned in the chapter on famous pianists, in this book. He travelled about, receiving honors in Florence, Venice, Rome, and Naples. He made his operas conform to Italian standards, which were even then becoming conventional.

On returning to Germany, Handel accepted a post with the Elector of Hanover. He had leave to travel, and went to London, where his "Rinaldo" made a hit in 1711. He liked London so well that on a second visit he decided to stay, in spite of the fact that his leave of absence had expired. It was, therefore, a decided surprise to him when his former electoral master was called to London to succeed Queen Anne as George I of England. Handel kept in hiding for a time. At length a friend gave him a chance of reinstating himself in favor, and he summoned his musical genius to his aid. The King was to give a water-party upon the Thames. As the procession floated along the river, an unknown boat drew near to the royal barge. The occupants of the strange boat played some new and very beautiful music. This, in accordance with the plan formed, caught the King's attention, and caused him to investigate. When he found that this attractive surprise was the work of his old servant Handel, he at once asked the composer aboard the royal boat, and pardoned him. The composition, known as the "Water Music," is still heard occasionally in orchestral concerts.

Handel then received royal pensions. For some years, too, he was in the pay of the rich Duke of Chandos, under whom he composed his first oratorio, "Esther," in 1720.

In that year an opera company was formed, with Handel and the Italian Bononcini as directors. This company lasted for eight years, but in all except the first of these there was bitter strife between the two directors. Many partisans took sides, and the political parties even became involved, to say nothing of the fierce rivalry among the singers. It was this bickering which brought the sopranos Cuzzoni and Faustina to blows. It also led Dean Swift to write the rhymes,—

> "Some say, compared to Bononcini,
> That Mynheer Handel's but a ninny;
> Others aver, that he to Handel
> Is scarcely fit to hold a candle;
> Strange all this difference should be
> 'Twixt Tweedledum and Tweedledee."

The rivalry continued after the company had broken up in riotous dispute; for Handel considered it right to start a company of his own, and produce his own operas, which immediately caused his opponents to start another company. Bononcini failed to please, in spite of the backing of the Marlboroughs; but after his relapse into obscurity, Porpora, Hasse, and others were called to replace him. As a result, both companies lost money, and finally failed.

But this failure proved a blessing to music, for it made Handel turn definitely to the oratorio form. After producing "Saul," "Israel in Egypt," and similar works, he brought out his masterpiece, "The Messiah," in 1742. This is a work that still stands at the head of the repertoire, nearly two centuries after it was written. It shows most admirably its composer's sure touch, varied power of utterance, and control of strong dramatic effect. This work alone was enough to win Handel a lasting renown. For ten years after producing it he continued writing oratorios, but he never quite equalled it again. Like Bach, Handel became blind in his last years; but he bore the affliction with equanimity, and continued his activity in music. He died in 1759.

Handel was a hard and quick worker. His great "Messiah" took him only about three weeks to write. The inspiring nature of the subject must have helped him to compose rapidly, for he stated that when he began the "Hallelujah" chorus, it seemed as if "all Heaven

and Earth were lying open to his gaze." Handel sometimes adopted
the themes of others, and some critics have christened him "the
great robber"; but the percentage of plagiarized work is so infinitely
small, in comparison with the composer's own achievements, that
it cannot count against him. Yet it is true that he did sometimes
adopt a theme from other composers, much as he transferred themes
from his own early works into later ones. His song "Lascia ch' io
pianga" figures originally as a *sarabande* in his first opera, "Almira."
When reproached with stealing a melody from a certain composer,
Handel once replied, "That pig does n't know what to do with such
a tune." This gives a clue to the fact that while a short melody
might be borrowed, its treatment and development were the composer's own; and he beautified whatever he appropriated.

Handel was bluff and hearty in character — rather arbitrary, as
was necessary for an opera manager, but always honest, and even
generous. He had a tremendous appetite, and is shown in caricature
with a hog's head, sitting before an organ decorated with sausages,
ham, and other solid foods. He never married. Once he aspired to
win a young lady's hand; but her father resented the attentions of a
"mere fiddler." Later, when Handel grew famous, the father intimated that he would withdraw his opposition; but by that time the
composer's ardor had cooled.

Handel's operas soon dropped out of the repertoire. They were
cast in the conventional mould of the time, and grew moribund even
before Gluck's reforms introduced higher artistic ideals. The Han-
delian operas were nearly all based on legendary subjects, usually
mythological. There were always three acts. The number of characters was prescribed, six or seven of a certain kind being always
expected. Each of these characters had to have a fixed number of
appearances in concerted or solo work, and the latter consisted of
arias of prescribed character. These operas were tremendously popular in their day, the heroine's costume in "Rodelinda" being
adopted as a national uniform of youth and beauty. But the system
was too conventional to last.

Yet if Handel did not try to be a reformer in opera, he at least
imbued his works with the strength of his own genius. Many single
numbers from these operas are very much alive to-day, even though
the operas themselves are buried. His dramatic power of expression

was strikingly great, and it is shown in dozens of these selections which are still heard. Thus the famous Largo, so familiar in its piano or violin shape, was originally a number in "Xerxes," in which the Persian monarch praised the grateful shade of the plane tree under which he encamped.

Handel's secular cantatas offer a similar group of famous solos. A very few examples may well include "O ruddier than the cherry," from "Acis and Galatea"; the brilliant soprano aria "Sweet bird," from "Il Penseroso," full of warblings that imitate the nightingale; the strong "Revenge, Timotheus cries," from "Alexander's Feast"; or the expressive "Angels ever bright and fair," from the more ambitious "Theodora."

The oratorios offer a still larger selection; and this is especially true of the "Messiah," in which great songs are as thick as blackberries in August. The very first two vocal numbers, the recitative "Comfort ye" and the air "Ev'ry valley," are famous solos for the tenor, while "Thou shalt break them" is another *tour-de-force*. The contralto has the bright air "O thou that tellest good tidings," and the expressive "He was despised." For soprano there are the brilliant solo "Rejoice greatly," and the wonderful air "I know that my Redeemer liveth." The bass has the vigorous "Why do the nations so furiously rage," and "The trumpet shall sound," which is a duet between the singer and the instrument. The choruses, too, though less apt to be given as single numbers, are of the most glorious sort. Best among them are the characteristic "All we, like sheep," the powerful "Unto us a Son is born," the tremendously broad "Hallelujah" chorus, and the finale of the work.

Handel wrote some orchestral works, chiefly overtures. These, however, are not often heard, except when attached to an oratorio. They are mostly in what is known as the French form, consisting of a slow movement followed by a rapid section, the latter usually a fugue. His orchestral concertos are still performed.

Handel's anthems were written mostly while he was choirmaster for the Duke of Chandos. At the same time he wrote a number of harpsichord pieces, including fugues. These are good, though they are below the Bach fugues in value and interest.

Handel's music is often surprisingly modern in character. In the harmonic work of his oratorios he foreshadowed the classical period that came many decades after his death. Oratorio, unlike opera, was not fettered by traditional or conventional rules, so Handel could make of it all that his genius permitted. His success in this form led to an English cult of oratorio and cantata that is still in a flourishing state, even if it has not produced master-works. Handel wrote for immediate success. If his works lack the deeper qualities and the more involved intellectuality of Bach, they were far more directly effective in their day; and they deserve all their renown.

Handel experimented with the orchestra, trying out lutes, harps, and early clarinets. His introduction of horns aroused much criticism. As conductor, the composer often led his work by playing at the harpsichord or organ. He thus filled out harmonies which were left in a more rudimentary state in the written score. It has therefore been found necessary for later musicians to fill in the scoring of certain works by Handel, the chief examples being two versions of the "Messiah," one arranged by Mozart and the other by Robert Franz.

Of the Hamburg school of opera, both Mattheson and Telemann outlived Handel. The former wrote few works with much effort, while the latter composed freely, but rather superficially. Other German cities soon followed Hamburg's lead; and operas by Graupner, Stölzel, Graun, and their kind were heard in Darmstadt, Breslau, Prague, Berlin, and other places. Frederick the Great, famous as a patron of music, was also a composer, writing the opera, "Il Re Pastore."

Italian opera, brought to its climax of popularity by Alessandro Scarlatti, was carried on by many composers. Antonio Lotti won success in many fields at Venice. Domenico Scarlatti wrote several dramatic works; while Mancini, Sarri, and Fago kept the school in activity. Porpora wrote nearly fifty operas, but was best known as a singing teacher. The names of Feo, Durante, Leo, and the artist Da Vinci are somewhat more important, and bring opera to the middle of the eighteenth century; but none of their stage works survived for long. The old operas were comparatively simple in structure, and as a result they were produced by hundreds.

Two composers of a later generation who became known in opera were Nicola Jommelli, in Italy, and Johann Adolph Hasse, in Germany.

A school of light opera had its rise in Naples. Pergolesi, known by expressive church works, won a tremendous success with the comedy "La Serva Padrona." Logroscino, who followed him, developed grand *ensembles* at the ends of his acts. Galuppi, who is apostrophized in one of Browning's poems, wrote the "Toccata" that Browning describes, and other organ works, but was better known by his many operas, the light ones earning him the title of "the father of *opera buffa*."

French opera offered Campra and Destouches, but was more ably represented by Jean Philippe Rameau. His works gradually replaced those of Lully, from which they did not differ radically, although he was more gifted musically. Rameau became known by an early treatise on harmony. It was this composer who once said, "Music is dead," meaning that about all possible combinations of tone had been worked out, and nothing new could be found. But since then music has been pretty lively for a corpse, as the long list of subsequent masters will show.

Jean Jacques Rousseau, the philosopher, was another well-known opera composer of the time. His "Devin du Village" made a great success, while his later "Pygmalion" laid the foundations of melodrama. Rousseau championed the Italian company that came to Paris with Italian singers and operas. The resulting dispute between the upholders of French and of Italian standards was known as the "Guerre des Buffons." After an acrimonious struggle, French *opéra comique* won the ascendancy.

It must not be supposed that forgotten operas are necessarily weak or unmusical. Rousseau's works are very tuneful. Revivals of dramatic works by Rameau, Purcell, and others show that these composers wrote good music, even if their operas are cast in an archaic mould. The same is true of the Italians, of whom Lotti and the Scarlattis were really gifted musicians. If the Scarlatti operas are on the shelf, the piano repertoire still contains a number of pieces by both the elder and younger Scarlatti. Those who heard Paderewski's early programmes will remember that they almost always began with a selection from these compositions. In the violin field, Kreisler and Ysaye have won remarkable successes with the works of such early composers as Couperin, Vitali, Pugnani, Vivaldi, and others of the sort; while the compositions of Tartini are often played. Musical changes are sometimes an affair of manner rather than matter; and the music of the late sixteenth and early seventeenth centuries often shows the rarest beauty, when it has once been unearthed from the dust of ages.

England did not follow Handel's lead in opera, but even during his life developed a school resembling the German *Singspiel*, and known as the ballad-opera. In this a number of songs were strung together on a thread of dialogue, to make an amusing or satirical work. The first example of this form was the "Beggar's Opera," the music composed and arranged by Pepusch. The work had a great success. As Gay wrote the words and Rich produced the affair (in 1728), it was said to have made Gay rich and Rich gay.

Henry Carey, sometimes considered the composer of "God save the King," was another writer of ballad-operas. He ridiculed the bombastic style of certain Italian operas, and satirized it very effectively.

Of a later date was Thomas Augustine Arne, now known by his dainty settings of certain lyrics from Shakespeare's plays. Arne wrote oratorios, operas, masques, and other dramatic works. He was the composer of the popular English song "Rule, Britannia."

In spite of the genius of Purcell and Handel, which kept English opera abreast of that in other countries during their lives, England did not influence the development of opera. The ballad-opera was not high enough in aim to inspire imitation in other countries. Moreover, it soon changed its character, and grew into the over-sentimental affair that retarded musical progress in England until quite recently.

IX

CRISTOPH WILLIBALD GLUCK was born at Weidenwang, in Bohemia, in 1714. He studied in a Jesuit school at Komotau, where
he learned something of the clavier, the organ, the violin, the 'cello,
and singing. At the age of eighteen he went to Prague, where he
gave lessons and played at rustic gatherings. Four years later he
came to the notice of Prince Lobkowitz in Vienna, and through that
prince he became known to Count Melzi, who took him to Milan for
lessons with Sammartini.

Gluck's first opera was brought out at Milan in 1741. Although
in the conventional style, or perhaps because of that fact, it was
popular enough, and resulted in his obtaining many commissions.
A London trip in 1745 was not successful, because Handel held the
public notice. Visits to Hamburg and Dresden brought Gluck at
last to Vienna, which he made his home. Yet he continued to make
trips, which ranged from Copenhagen to Naples. At Rome the
Pope made him a Chevalier of the Golden Spur; and for this reason
he became known as "Ritter von Gluck."

Many of his works at this period were on texts by Metastasio.
These were poetic enough at times, but always cast in the conventional mould of the day. Even in setting these, however, Gluck
began to show a gradual departure from ordinary models and a vein
of originality. Such works as his "Telemacco" and "Il Re Pastore"
contained hints of growing individual genius, and the overture of
the latter proved especially effective. Gluck was also successful in
light comedies, such as "La Rencontre Imprevue." But now he
turned to more serious paths, with Calzabigi as librettist.

The first example of Gluck's new style was "Orfeo ed Euridice,"
which appeared in 1762. There was still some degree of conventional
melodic utterance, which may be seen even in the famous solo "I
have lost my Eurydice." This is so smooth in character that it
might equally well have been set to the words, "I have found my

Eurydice." But there were many dramatic touches in the opera, such as the barking of Cerberus, the threatening refusal of the Furies to aid Orpheus, or the final loss of Eurydice. Gluck was developing the idea that operatic music should not be a set of meaningless melodies, but should bring out the dramatic possibilities of the text. The Viennese public were somewhat bewildered at first, but finally accepted the new work.

Gluck continued with "Alceste," on another of the Calzabigi librettos. This work, brought out in 1767, was not a popular success, because of the gloomy nature of its subject.

"Paride ed Elena," with another Calzabigi text, appeared in 1770. It showed a remarkable control of romantic lyricism, and contained many strong bits of solo work. By this time Gluck had built up a considerable appreciation of his works at Vienna, though there were adverse critics also. Later, he met with the same experience in Paris.

It was not until 1774 that his first Parisian work was brought out. This opera, "Iphigénie en Aulide" (Racine), was not one of the best in the new style, although it has an effective overture. The incompetence of the performers and the machinations of enemies delayed the production considerably; and in the end its appearance was due largely to the efforts of Marie Antoinette. That unfortunate queen had known Gluck during her girlhood at Vienna, and in Paris she became an enthusiastic patroness of his works. Jean Jacques Rousseau, himself a gifted composer, was another ardent supporter of Gluck. But there were many opponents, who were not only ready to use caricature and paragraph, but would actually fight duels over the merits of the new operas.

Gluck's next work was "Armide," which was given in 1777. It was based on an old Quinault text which had been set by Lully. This opera showed much romantic beauty, though it did not succeed at once.

In the mean time, Gluck's opponents had rallied around the Italian Piccini, who represented the old school of mellifluous but meaningless tunes. Finally it was suggested that the rival composers should set the same libretto, "Iphigénie en Tauride"; and this they agreed to do. Gluck finished his setting very quickly, but had to wait some time for that of Piccini. The two were finally performed

GLUCK HAYDN

THE MOZART FAMILY

in 1781. Gluck's work, given first, made a tremendous impression, while Piccini's production fell flat. The latter's singers, knowing that failure lay ahead, had attempted to drown some of their sorrows in copious libations. The prima donna's condition was especially noticeable; and a Parisian wit was moved to cry out, "This is not Iphigenia in Tauris, but Iphigenia in Champagne." Such sarcasms gave the final blow to Gluck's rivals, and his greatness was acknowledged by the musical public.

Gluck died at Vienna in 1787, after some years of failing health.

Gluck's earlier years have been held by some critics as wasted; but this is too harsh a verdict. His earlier operas, to be sure, are never heard, and contain nothing of real artistic originality. But their very composition must have been of value to the composer as so much technical training. His close acquaintance with existing styles led him gradually to see their weakness, just as Wagner's early conducting of Italian opera caused him to notice its hopeless conventionality.

The main idea of Gluck in reforming opera was to bring back to it the dramatic truth and significance that really belonged to it. When Peri and Caccini founded opera by trying to revive the ancient Greek dramatic ideals, they based their work on principles that were much like those of Gluck. Their melody and instrumentation was much more primitive, but they were striving, nevertheless, to let the music echo the ideas of the text.

Gradually opera began to take shape as a singing-concert, which grew to have wholly conventional structure in the days of Handel. Such a musical form can certainly display charm of a vocally melodic sort; and the great arias of Handel are still favorite concert numbers. But until the principle was definitely formulated that operatic music should support its text, no real progress toward a dramatic school was possible. Individual composers could work toward the truth, but a reformer was needed to show how much of the older conventionality should be discarded. That reformer was Gluck.

Even in his early works, Gluck did not adopt the florid style of Handel. The latter, on hearing a Gluck opera in London, said of its composer, "He knows no more of counterpoint than my cook." But as Handel's cook, Waltz, was something of a musician, the comment was not so adverse as it might appear at first sight.

Gluck dropped the old French overture form, and adopted that of the prelude, or introduction leading directly into the play. While his later overtures were worthy classical compositions, the descriptive nature of their themes was made to conform with the scenes that would follow. The old rules about the necessary kinds and numbers of arias were entirely discarded. This meant that the poet had a freer hand to produce something of literary and dramatic merit. The music was considered as following the text, and emphasizing the emotion brought out by the dramatic situation.

The orchestra, too, was given more important work than merely supporting the voices or indulging in occasional short passages. It became an integral part of the dramatic scheme. The touches mentioned above in "Orpheus" (the barking of Cerberus and the gruff anger of the Furies) are only a few of many that may be found in the score. In "Iphigénie en Tauride" are found wild tone-pictures of barbarous Scythian revelry, or gloomy mutterings to accompany the exhaustion of Orestes. The other operas in the "great six" show equally skilful instrumental touches.

Works of this sort were far more important than the conventional strings of melody that earlier writers had thrown off by the hundred. The composer could not toss them off with the slight attention demanded by works of the former school; instead, he had to study his text and characters, and put into the music real expressive power and dramatic force. The performers, too, had to understand the aims of the new system before they could do their work properly. The public had to be educated up to entirely new standards, as was the case with Wagner's music in later years. Opera was changed from an entertaining variety-concert to a true art-work; and it was inevitable that some who understood the former should be unable to learn to appreciate the latter. The progress made by Gluck in the direction of dramatic strength is shown by the fact that his later works are occasionally given even to-day, almost a century and a half after their creation. Gluck did not discard lyricism, but used it as a means for dramatic expression, instead of an excuse for the display of singers. His reforms cleared the way for modern opera, in spite of the fact that Rossini reverted to the type of florid and meaningless vocalism.

Nicolo Piccini, who sometimes misspelled his own name as Niccolo

Piccinni, was one of a flourishing school that had its headquarters at Naples. He was not without his meed of deserved fame; for he entered into competition with Logroscino, and supplanted the latter in the field of comic opera. His command of melody was great, and he showed an admirable mastery of concerted finales. He was really an unwilling rival of Gluck. He fulfilled the commissions given to him, but finally acknowledged his rival's greatness with absolute frankness. After the latter's death, Piccini even tried to collect funds for an annual concert of Gluck's works. Piccini wrote over one hundred and thirty operas, some of which served as models for Mozart in the latter's earlier years.

Antonio Sacchini was a fisher-boy, whose gifts were discovered by Durante. He wrote comic operas for Naples, and showed a popular freshness of style that made him a rival of Piccini. He composed also for orchestra and for clavier.

Tommaso Traetta saw his operas produced in such various cities as Vienna, Parma, Venice, London, and St. Petersburg. He was first known as a church composer. He had good ideas of dramatic values, and even foreshadowed some of Gluck's reforms.

Other opera composers of this time were Pietro Guglielmi, who was able to rival Cimarosa and Paisiello; Johann Christian Bach, who wrote operas in Milan and London; and Johann Gottlieb Naumann, who won fame in Germany, Denmark, and Sweden.

Giovanni Paisiello (1741–1816) wrote many symphonies and quartets, but was best known by his operas. His works showed much spontaneous melody, and his accompaniments were often original and ingenious. His operas are sometimes strongly dramatic, but more often piquant and charming in style. He composed at the Russian Court for eight years, and afterwards became a favorite of Napoleon at Paris. His "Barber of Seville" was very popular, and for some time prevented Rossini's work on the same subject from becoming well known.

Domenico Cimarosa (1749–1801) was almost as gifted as Mozart in opera. He soon became a competitor of Paisiello, and afterwards succeeded the latter at St. Petersburg. This period was followed by further successes in Vienna and Italy. Cimarosa was very popular, and received high salaries. His best work is "Il Matrimonio Segreto," produced at Vienna in 1792; but many of his other works were almost as great. The dainty lightness of Mozart's operas had its rise in the works of Piccini, Paisiello, and Cimarosa.

Giuseppe Sarti worked in Italy, Denmark, and St. Petersburg. In the last-named place he wrote much sacred music. He was the author of an extraordinary attack on Mozart's quartets.

Karl Ditters von Dittersdorf (1739–1799) composed many quartets, some concertos, and over a hundred symphonies. He wrote oratorios too, but was best known by his comic operas, of which "Doktor und Apotheker" still holds the boards in Germany.

In Paris, Pierre Montan Berton produced a few operas of his own before becoming a Gluck partisan.

François Danican-Philidor, the chess expert, was another Parisian opera-composer. He was best known in comic opera, and won much success with his concerted numbers — trios, quartets, etc.

Pierre Alexandre Monsigny (1729–1817) devoted himself to comic opera when forty years old. He showed some dramatic instinct, but lacked technical skill.

André Ernest Modeste Grétry (1741–1813) was a contemporary and successor of Monsigny, whom he eclipsed in fame. Grétry showed a marked ability to handle musical declamation, a certain gift of melody, and an excellent dramatic success. He became known by such comedies as "Zemire et Azor," "Le Tableau Parlant," and "L'Amant Jalouse," and entered the serious field with "Richard Cœur-de-Lion." An aria from the last-named, entitled "O Richard, O mon roi," is still a popular solo number. Grétry's operas were orchestrated very thinly, so that the later composers have sometimes found it advisable to enrich their accompaniment. These works are not now given, except as curiosities; but many individual songs taken from them are still effective numbers in the concert singer's repertoire. The operas as a whole lack the variety and dramatic force that contemporary audiences demand; but that is no bar to the enjoyment of short selections from their pages.

X

HAYDN

FRANZ JOSEF HAYDN was born on March 31, 1732, at the little Austrian village of Rohrau. His parents were peasants, and his home was a one-story farmhouse. He showed musical inclinations at a very early age, and was trained to some extent by a cousin named Frankh. At length he was heard by Reutter, choir-director in the Vienna Cathedral, who persuaded the lad's parents to let him sing in the choir of St. Stephen's.

While Frankh was severe but earnest, Reutter was neither, and neglected his protégé altogether; so that while Haydn came to feel grateful to Frankh, he could remember only two lessons given to him by Reutter. But the young Franz kept on at the church singing, until his voice broke, and he was replaced by his brother Michael. Misfortune was now upon him. The Empress of Austria had said of him, "Young Haydn sings like a crow"; and perhaps this remark, as much as a prank played on a fellow student, caused his dismissal. At any rate, Haydn found himself discharged, after a flogging, when seventeen years old.

As a return home might have involved the giving-up of music, Haydn determined to stay in Vienna. He lived largely on the charity of friends, taught whenever he got a chance, and played violin for dances. Meanwhile he continued his studies. He used as models Fux's "Gradus ad Parnassum," Mattheson's works, and a set of six sonatas by Carl Philipp Emanuel Bach.

An unexpected loan from a kindly tradesman named Buchholtz enabled Haydn to hire a garret of his own. Through this he met Metastasio, who not only brought him fashionable pupils, but introduced him to Porpora. Haydn became the latter's valet in exchange for lessons; and he has been sometimes nicknamed "Porpora's boot-black." But Porpora helped Haydn greatly, by letting him accompany or sit by at the lessons of richer pupils. Here Haydn learned composition as well as singing.

At twenty, Haydn had written his first mass, and one of the comic operas that have been lost since that time. Three years later he produced his first string quartet. Soon his early sonatas gained the notice of aristocracy. Countess Thun brought him a set of fashionable pupils, and induced Count Morzin to engage him as private orchestral director. In that position he composed many string quartets, and at last tried his hand at a symphony, in 1759.

A year later Haydn married, with unfortunate results. He had been in love with the younger daughter of a wig-maker named Keller, and had tried to win her hand; but she was deeply religious, and at last disappointed him by becoming a nun. The father then suggested that Haydn should marry her elder sister; and the composer finally did so. The result was most unhappy for the obliging Haydn; his wife became selfishly extravagant, and proved to be a consummate virago.

In 1761, Haydn was appointed second conductor to Prince Anton Esterhazy. When that patron of music died, his successor, Prince Nicholas, made Haydn first conductor, with a reasonable salary; and Haydn stayed in this position until his master's death, in 1790.

The first contract, with Prince Anton, showed that musicians in those days were practically servants. The composer was directed to be strictly temperate, and to avoid any coarseness in eating, dress, or manners; while he was addressed as "Er," in the contemptuous third person reserved for underlings.

But in spite of all this, the composer "lived happily ever after." He was master of a band of sixteen musicians, to say nothing of singers in addition; he had time to compose as much as he wished; and he began to receive money for the sale of his works, which were constantly growing in public appreciation. He remained in seclusion mostly, writing the many symphonies and string quartets that have made him famous, and that earned him medals, rings, and other testimonials during his life. He might have finished his career in this fashion; but in 1790 his patron died, and his orchestra was disbanded.

Haydn was now able to travel freely; and an English manager named Salomon induced him to visit London. In that capital he received the highest honors. The six symphonies that he had com-

posed for British performance met with an enthusiastic reception;
the Prince of Wales entertained him for three days; Oxford gave
him an honorary doctor's degree; and fashionable pupils flocked to
him at high prices.

By 1792 he was back in Vienna, where the entire city delighted to
honor him. At that time a young man named Beethoven came
to take lessons of him, at the rate of twenty cents an hour. Haydn
rather neglected the young man at first, perhaps because he was
used to higher rates. After a time Beethoven grew so independent,
in demeanor as well as composition, that Haydn christened him
"the Great Mogul."

Haydn took six more symphonies to London in 1794. On this
trip he was invited to stay at Windsor Castle; but he preferred to
return to Vienna.

The English enthusiasm for "God save the King" caused Haydn
to decide upon writing the Austrian National Hymn. Such deliberate attempts to produce national music are almost always failures;
but in this case the song proved a great success.

London influenced him still further by its oratorio music, especially that of Handel; and Haydn determined to enter this field also.
His first effort, "The Creation," met with much success at Vienna
and elsewhere, and is still a favorite with oratorio societies. Haydn,
like Handel, felt that his gifts were the result of divine inspiration;
and this was shown at a performance of "The Creation," which
took place shortly before his death. At the words, "'Let there be
light,' — and there was light," a striking change from minor to
major occurs. On that day nature aided the effect; for while the
day had been overcast, the sun burst forth at these words. The
auditors were thrilled by this coincidence; and the aged composer
arose in excitement, and exclaimed, pointing to heaven, "It all
came from there."

"The Creation" was followed by "The Seasons"; but the drudgery of composition, united to the fervor of creative work, weakened
the composer considerably. He spent his last years in comparative
inactivity, and died at Vienna in 1809. While he was on his deathbed, Napoleon's forces were bombarding the city. His servants were
terrified, but he reassured them by saying, "You are safe with
Haydn." During the same bombardment, Beethoven took to a

cellar — not from any lack of bravery, but because of fear that the noise of the guns would ruin his already impaired hearing. When the city was taken, some of the French officers bore testimony to Haydn's fame by visiting him on his deathbed, and attending his funeral.

Haydn is now known by his symphonies, his sonatas, and the two works in oratorio form. But he was very versatile, and attempted almost everything except organ pieces. His vocal works include masses, operas, and songs. The operas are practically all lost, though remnants of some are discovered now and then. Once Haydn thought that his chief mission would be the composing of operas; but he grew into orchestral work. Among his songs, such a dainty lyric as "My mother bids me bind my hair" proves that he could write vocal music with the most charming grace. Brahms resuscitated a chorale theme by Haydn as a subject for variations; but too many of the earlier composer's vocal works have been allowed to lapse into undeserved oblivion.

The orchestra of Haydn was somewhat variable. It consisted of the usual string parts, with the variation occurring in the wind instruments. The former were divided into first and second violins, violas, 'cellos, and contrabasses, as at present. The latter ranged from oboes and horns up to a fairly full list of wood-wind and brass instruments, though mostly without clarinets. The later classical orchestra, as developed from the Haydn model by Beethoven, had four wood-wind parts and three brass parts, the former being flutes, oboes, clarinets, and bassoons, while the latter were horns, trumpets, and at the last, trombones. The kettledrums completed the list; and Haydn's naïve use of a loud kettledrum stroke in the "Surprise" symphony was very effective in its day.

Haydn's several hundred instrumental works include about one hundred and twenty-five symphonies, thirty trios, seventy-seven string quartets, about one hundred pieces for various chamber combinations, thirty-one concertos for various instruments, and about fifty sonatas or other works for clavier. In Haydn's time the clavier (keyed instrument) still referred to the clavichord or harpsichord. The piano had been invented in 1711, but it did not become really popular until Beethoven turned the scale in its favor by writing music that was too powerful for the earlier instruments. The best

of Haydn's clavier works are found in the volume of "Ten Celebrated Sonatas" by him, while his most famous symphonies have
been gathered into a similar group of ten, and a larger set of twenty-
four. Haydn wrote also nearly two hundred solos for the baryton,
the so-called *viola di bordone* that had sympathetic strings like the
viola d' amore. These pieces were for his princely master, who found
much pleasure in playing them himself.

With Haydn the sonata took shape at last. The form was no
longer experimental, as in the hands of Galuppi, Paradisi, or Bach's
sons. It had at last crystallized into something definite, which Haydn
and Mozart used, and which Beethoven brought to a grand culmination. This form is described in the section on "Musical Form,"
in this work; but one may state here that its excellence depended
on the two artistic principles of balance and contrast. The three
or four movements forming the sonata or symphony or other work
in sonata form were in contrasted style, and in so far were an outgrowth of the old suite movements. The *sonata allegro* form, upon
which so many movements or portions of orchestral works are built,
shows three main divisions, — themes, development of a new musical
structure from the thematic material, and a return of the themes.
The first and second of these themes were usually well contrasted,
the former being bold, while the latter was often tender and lyrical;
and a short closing theme followed them. While the *sonata allegro*
had its recognizable divisions, its chief strength lay in the fact that
it did not hamper composers. The great sonata writers, especially
Beethoven, could create the most powerful and dramatic music
while keeping strictly to the prescribed outlines of the form.

Haydn's style was not that of a Beethoven. The earlier composer
did not scale Olympus, nor talk in the accents of the gods. His
utterances consisted rather of unaffected bits of cheerfulness. Some
of his symphonies seem rather artless and naïve when judged by
modern standards; but they still hold our interest. They have sufficient vigor and virility to prevent their directness from becoming
too simple in effect. There is strength as well as optimism in Haydn's
music. It has its own beauty, too, though its charms are those of a
simpler harmonic system than that used by the more recent orchestral colorists. For a time it was customary to call him "Papa
Haydn," and sneer at his simplicity; but his works still show the

charm of refreshing directness. At the time of their composition, they were of value as pioneer work in the orchestral field. Even Beethoven followed the Haydn models at first.

If Haydn's symphonies are still heard on their own merits, the same is doubly true of his string quartets. In these his clear style and calm serenity are very much in place; so that they still remain models of their school. The slow movements are, perhaps, a little too dragging for modern standards, but apart from that point these quartets hold their own easily against nearly all later works in the same form.

Haydn's brother Michael became noted as a church composer, but he was a good orchestral writer also. He composed over two dozen symphonies, and several chamber works; but he kept most of these in manuscript, and thus failed to have any great influence.

The symphony received an early development at the hands of the Mannheim group of violinists. Johann Stamitz was the pioneer of this group, writing nearly fifty symphonies before his early death in 1757. These symphonies figured frequently on early programmes in the United States, which are admirably described by Oscar G. Sonneck in his "Early Concert Life in America." Other symphonists of the Mannheim group included Franz Xaver Richter, Anton Filtz, Christian Cannabich, Ignaz Holzbauer, Eichner, Toeschi, Beck, Karl Stamitz, and Anton Stamitz. All these men composed symphonies, and made the growing form known in many different places. Others, from different cities, were Schwindl, Wagenseil, Wanhal, Pichl, Roessler, Wranitzky, Pleyel, and Wolf. Many of their works were known and heard in the eighteenth-century programmes of our own country, and "the celebrated Wranitzky," as he was called, was at one time held as a rival of Haydn.

More important in symphonic development was François Joseph Gossec, who was known at Paris as an opera composer. His symphonies and string quartets showed real value.

Luigi Boccherini was an Italian symphonist — rather a lonely figure, for Italy soon reverted wholly to opera of a popular variety, and let Germany develop the classical school unaided. He composed some symphonies and very many chamber works.

Dittersdorf worked in this field also, producing about fifty symphonies.

Leopold Hoffmann wrote church music in Vienna, and at the same time composed such clever orchestral works that he is said to have delayed the recognition of Haydn's genius for some time. Haydn, however, showed more virility than many of his contemporaries, so that their works are now little known.

XI

MOZART

WOLFGANG AMADEUS MOZART, "composer by the grace of God," was born at Salzburg on January 27, 1756. His full name was Johann Chrysostom Wolfgang Theophilus Mozart. His father, Leopold, was a musician of some standing, in the service of the local archbishop. Wolfgang's sister Maria Anna was given piano lessons at home when seven years old, and afterwards became a famous performer. At her early lessons her little brother was greatly captivated by the beauty of the clavier tones, and tried to reach up to the keyboard. His extreme musical sensitiveness was shown also by the small size and unusual shape of his aural passages. His ears were so delicately built that the sound of a trumpet would send him into spasms of terror.

The boy began to compose little pieces when only four years old; and at the age of six he was discovered hard at work over the much-blotted manuscript of a clavier concerto. His father, happy at finding the son so gifted, began to train him carefully from his earliest years. Soon Wolfgang became proficient at the keyboard, and was taken on tours with his sister. The two child-prodigies won much attention, even from the Empress Maria Theresa. On a later trip to London, the boy performed at sight some difficult pieces by Bach, and gained renown by improvising. He soon became still further noted by playing his own pieces.

Returning to Salzburg at twelve years of age, he wrote the opera "Bastien et Bastienne." At Vienna he composed "La Finta Semplice," but his youth prevented its performance. A trip to Italy, however, proved more successful. Mozart's Italian travels (between 1770 and 1773) resulted in constant ovations.[1] His new operas, "Mitridate" and "Lucio Silla," were applauded to the echo by Milan audiences. The Pope gave him the same order of knight-.

[1] For an account of one of his display performances, see the chapter "Some Famous Pianists," in this volume.

hood that Gluck had received. The people called him "Il Cavaliere Filarmonico," while the nobles made him an honored guest. Padre Martini, composer and historian, was amazed at Mozart's ease in improvising fugues; and Hasse exclaimed, "This boy will throw us all in the shade some day."

After his return from Italy, Mozart brought out "La Finta Giardiniera" at the Munich Carnival of 1775. This caused the poet Schubart to exclaim that Mozart would become "the greatest operatic composer who ever lived."

Unfortunately, the Archbishop of Salzburg, in whose orchestra he was employed, did not appreciate the young composer. When Mozart asked for decent pay, the Archbishop declined to raise his wages above his former stipend, which was merely nominal. Mozart tried again to earn a better position, this time by composing "Il Re Pastore"; but his efforts went for nothing. The little Salzburg Court listened to his works readily enough; but whenever he sought a financial return for them, he was told that they were valueless, and advised to learn composition in an Italian conservatory. The Archbishop even began to oppose Mozart's piano tours, and said, "I don't approve of such beggary from town to town."

Forced to try for an official position elsewhere, Mozart again met with a series of disappointments. At Munich he was kept dangling with no results. At Mannheim, where he met Abt Vogler, he fared little better. Abt Vogler deserves mention as the musician whom Browning immortalized in his noble poem of that name. Vogler was a teacher of much originality. Mozart called him a charlatan, but his teaching formed both Weber and Meyerbeer. He boasted that he could make his pupils composers in six months.

At Mannheim Mozart met also a family named Weber. He fell in love with the second daughter, Aloysia, who was both beautiful and musical. She seemed to like him well enough; but his father, hearing of the reason for Mozart's delay, ordered him to proceed at once to Paris. Aloysia was piqued at his departure; and whether because of this or for some other reason, she declined Mozart, and afterwards married an actor named Lange.

At Augsburg, Mozart tried the new pianos of Stein, and recognized their value; but he never really gave up the harpsichord.

In Paris Mozart did not attract much notice, partly because

the Gluck-Piccini contest held public attention. He declined a small position in the royal orchestra, saying that "whoever entered the royal service was forgotten at Paris." He might have worked up in the French capital as Lully did a century earlier; but apparently he did not approve of Parisian standards. After the death of his mother, who had been with him, he returned to Salzburg, where the miserly prelate, Hieronymus, had at last begun to give a grudging appreciation. There he became concert-master, with a salary of five hundred florins — still a meagre amount, though at that time money had more purchasing power than at present. Of his Paris stay, Mozart had written home, "If I were where people had ears to hear, hearts to feel, and even a small degree of perception and taste, I could laugh at everything; but really, as far as music is concerned, I am living among mere brute beasts." Mozart's greater compositions were still in the future, so Paris was not to be wholly condemned.

In 1781, Mozart composed "Idomeneo" for the Munich Carnival. This work was an advance over its predecessors, and an improvement over the Cimarosa-Piccini style. Its success made Mozart devote himself largely to opera, though he composed church music and instrumental works also. "Idomeneo" was no longer an imitation, but displayed fully the melodic fluency, dramatic grasp, and power in handling voices that became so marked in his later operas.

In the ensuing year, Vienna heard his "Abduction from the Seraglio," which brought opera in German to a high state of excellence. The old *Singspiel* was a rather elastic affair. Reichardt had made it a spoken drama with music in the unimportant parts, while Benda changed it into a melodrama, with words spoken against an accompaniment. Mozart revived the old idea, and let the important parts be sung, while only the most unimportant episodes were spoken. The Emperor thought the work contained "too many notes"; but Mozart retorted that there were "just enough for the subject."

Meanwhile Mozart's position in the Archbishop's *entourage* was that of an absolute underling. Dining with the servants, he was subjected to all sorts of indignities by his strangely hostile master, and was often branded with such insulting titles as "Lump," "Lausbube," or "Gassenbube" — words that are hard to translate, but are about on a par with our "churl," "varlet," or "guttersnipe."

At last the situation became unbearable, and Mozart presented his resignation; whereupon the Archbishop ordered his steward to kick the composer downstairs — which was done.

Though Mozart suffered enough from poverty after that event, he was never again subjected to contumely.

Having lost Aloysia Weber, he turned to her sister Constance, whom he married in 1782. The two loved each other truly enough, but he earned little money, while she was a poor manager. Yet their cheerfulness was unfailing; and a visitor once found the couple dancing to keep warm when they had no fuel and no cash to buy it. Constance outlived her husband by more than fifty years, dying in 1842.

Mozart's poverty seemed as much a matter of loyalty as anything else. He might have done well if he had stayed in Paris; London, which welcomed Haydn, would pretty surely have enriched Mozart also; while he declined a liberal offer of the King of Prussia, to stay in the ill-paid service of the Emperor of Austria.

He continued his operatic work with several comedies, such as "L' Oca del Cairo," "Lo Sposo Deluso," and the German "Schauspieldirektor." But these were soon forgotten, for his later masterworks were at hand.

"The Marriage of Figaro," produced in 1786, contains little of the political suggestion of the comedy by Beaumarchais, but is rather an intensely exhilarating bit of dramatic and musical humor. The plot deals with the love of Figaro, valet and factotum of count Almaviva, for Suzanna, the maid of the countess. The count's pronounced admiration for Suzanna is made into a means of discomfiting him. The others start to trick him by dressing the page Cherubino in Suzanna's clothes, and afterwards the masquerade is made more effective by having Suzanna and the countess exchange dresses. The count then makes exaggerated declarations to a supposed Suzanna who is really his own wife. The count is also tormented by Figaro's attentions to the supposed countess. The final unveiling brings about the count's discomfiture, Figaro's marriage, and a general reconciliation.

The music to this vivacious comedy is superlatively delightful, and contains many of Mozart's very best vocal numbers. Some of the most attractive selections are Figaro's bright duet with Suzanna, his half-humorous defiance to the count ("Se vuol ballare"), his inimitably comic lesson in soldiery to Cherubino, who is to be sent off to the army in disgrace, Cherubino's love-song ("Voi che sapete"), the beautiful air of regret sung by the countess ("Dove sono"), and Suzanna's captivating encouragement of the count ("Deh vieni, non tardar"). But it is a thankless task to cite single numbers, for the complete score is overflowing with delightful musical humor. The overture, too, is a gem of tonal brightness.

"Don Giovanni," produced in 1787, achieved another great success. It deals with the career of a totally wild and licentious nobleman, who invades the room of a certain Donna Anna, is discovered by her father, Don Pedro, and kills him to escape unrecognized. He continues his amorous career by laying siege to Zerlina, a peasant girl who is about to marry Masetto. Don Giovanni captivates her, but is thwarted by Donna Anna and her betrothed, Don Ottavio, who come with Elvira, a former conquest of the adventurer's. Don Giovanni next exchanges costumes with his servant Leporello, and pays court to Elvira's maid while Leporello gets a beating from Masetto, who thinks him Don Giovanni. Then the dissolute nobleman sneers at Don Pedro's statue. He is surprised to find the statue answering his invitation to sup together; and the climax comes when the statue does actually enter the banquet-room and drag the criminal down to perdition.

Here, as in "Figaro," there is a profusion of melody. Leporello's famous "catalogue aria" is a rollicking list of his master's conquests. Zerlina's "Batti, batti" and "Vedrai carino" are gems of lyricism. Don Giovanni's duet with Zerlina, "Reach me thy hand," is another of many famous selections from this work. The *ensembles* are admirable; and Gounod said of the trio between Don Giovanni, Leporello, and Donna Elvira, that if all compositions but this were destroyed, our music could be evolved again from it. While such praise is exaggerated, there is no doubt that Mozart showed a wonderful grasp of the situation in this and other concerted selections. The overture, it is said, was written during the night before the performance. Mozart worked at the score while Constance regaled him with home-made punch, or told him stories while he rested.

"Don Giovanni" has been upheld by the classicists as the quintessence of everything worthy. One fairly recent writer said of it,

"Whether we regard the mixture of passions in its concerted music, the profound expression of melancholy, the variety of its situations, the beauty of its accompaniment, or the grandeur of its heightening and protracted scene of terror, 'Don Giovanni' stands alone in dramatic eminence." But one may question such unmixed praise, when modern standards are considered. Even in comparison with Gluck, Mozart was none too powerful. The trombone chords that go with the statue's dread awakening are highly dramatic in effect; but for the most part Mozart's music was almost too fluent. It is that quality, combined with the simplicity of the early harmonic effects, that makes some modern composers consider Haydn less monotonous. At the same time, Mozart's work has held its place in the repertoire until the present, and its merits deserve full recognition. It seems lacking to-day because of its slow motion and comparative monotony of style; but in its time it was held dramatic enough, and its harmonies seemed the height of expressive beauty.

Even after these works, Mozart remained poor. The Emperor made him court dance-composer at about four hundred dollars a year, but this was done merely to prevent Mozart from going to London.

Mozart's next operas were the light "Cosi fan Tutti" and the conventional "Clemenza di Tito." Neither of these proved supremely important; but his last opera, "The Magic Flute," met with a better fate. It has a rather mixed libretto. The absurdities of the text have been explained by the statement that they have Masonic significance; but that fact does not make them interesting or dramatically effective. Its plot deals with the High Priest Sarastro, who has rescued Pamina from her wicked mother, the "Queen of the Night." The queen's retinue save Tamino, a foreign prince, who is then given a magic flute and told to bring back Pamina. He starts with the bird-catcher Papageno; but instead of doing any rescue work, he becomes a disciple with Pamina. After a long and spectacular probation he is admitted to be worthy, and marries Pamina; while Papageno also finds a mate.

The music of this jumbled work is fully up to the best Mozart standard. The queen's brilliant solos, the deep bass numbers of Sarastro, and the bright selections of Papageno, are all effective in their way. But the libretto has been too great a handicap, and the opera received few performances in comparison with "Don Giovanni."

Of the three dozen songs that Mozart wrote, apart from his operas, the most famous is the tender "Violet." Mozart composed fifteen masses, though he probably wrote very little of the one known as his twelfth. Such mistakes have often arisen, from the carelessness of composers or publishers. Thus Schubert's "Adieu" is probably not by him; Weber's "Last Thought," or "Last Waltz," was not his at all, but sent to him by Reissiger; while Beethoven's "Farewell to the Piano" (a publisher's title) was written before he composed some of his greatest piano sonatas.

In addition to masses, Mozart wrote motets and cantatas for voices.

His piano music is best represented by his two-hand sonatas. These, which are seventeen in number, show a clearness of form that makes them valuable to the teacher. Some of them are dramatic enough, the "Fantasia and sonata" being especially powerful. Mozart composed also five four-hand sonatas, and seventeen organ sonatas.

His chamber music, which is still prized for its union of clearness with fluency and a proper amount of expression, is headed by twenty-six string quartets. These are supplemented by quintets, many violin-and-piano sonatas, and concertos for piano and various other single or multiple instruments. A concerto is a concert-piece, usually in three movements, to display one or more instruments; and it may have either piano or orchestral accompaniment. Modern composers have made it a three-movement symphony with a thread of solo work running through it.

The example of Haydn and others led Mozart into the symphonic field also. Of his symphonies, which number nearly fifty, the last three, which he wrote in 1788, toward the close of his life, are decidedly the greatest. These consist of the so-called "Jupiter Symphony," the "Clarinet Symphony," in which that instrument was first brought into the symphonic orchestra, and the tenderly beautiful symphony in G Minor.

Mozart, like Haydn, echoed the style of his time by making his symphonies clear and fluent. Where Haydn showed vivacity, however, Mozart relied more on smoothness. Yet in his three last symphonies, Mozart showed a surprising vigor.

In 1791, the year of Mozart's death, he wrote his famous "Requiem." His illness was upon him, and he had a presentiment that he was composing for his own funeral. There were other unusual details about the work, too. A mysterious stranger, clothed in black, visited him to give him the commission for the work, and to name a date when he would come for the finished composition. He returned on time, but Mozart had been busy with other things, the work was unfinished, and the stranger extended the time to still another date. Mozart, it is said, began to brood over the matter. Ultimately he grew to consider the stranger a messenger from the other world, sent to announce his death. He had what was called a miliary fever; but he began to believe also that some one had poisoned him. He died before completing the "Requiem," and directed his pupil Süssmayer to finish the work for him; so that now it is not definitely known which parts of the composition were Süssmayer's additions.

The mystery of the stranger in black was afterwards explained. He was a certain Leutgeb, steward of Count von Wallsegg, and was sent in secrecy because his master wished to get hold of the "Requiem" and publish it as his own.

Mozart was a most delightful personality, being lively, fascinating, and a versatile talker. He was full of droll humor, but at the same time gifted with keen and accurate judgment. If he was rather too easy-going to achieve wealth, he at least bore poverty with cheerfulness. He was fond of various amusements, and often thought out his themes while playing billiards.

His burial-place is not even known. The day of his funeral was stormy, and his coffin was hurried into a public grave. Some years later his admirers wished to give him a monument; but as the grave had been emptied and used over again, the composer's remains are not beneath the memorial that was finally erected to his memory in the large central cemetery of Vienna.

The *Singspiel*, which influenced Mozart to some extent, was carried on by such men as Johann Adam Hiller, Johann André, Johann Abram Peter Schulz, Johann Schenk, Ferdinand Kauer, and others. Owing to the loose structure of their musical plays, many of their songs became popular as separate numbers, and earned them reputations as song-composers. Schulz became famous for his collection of "Lieder im Volkston." Johann Häffner, who lived until 1833, wrote in a style resembling Gluck's, and exerted a great influence in Sweden.

Antonio Salieri was a pupil of Gluck, and made a Parisian success with the opera "Les Danaïdes." He wrote afterwards for Vienna, where he was in some sense a rival of Mozart. It is said that he prevented the proper recognition of Mozart at the imperial court; and those who accepted Mozart's idea that he was poisoned held Salieri responsible. But that idea has absolutely no evidence to support it.

There were many pianist-composers in Mozart's day. In Vienna were Franz Duschek, Anton Eberl, and Johann Nepomuk Hummel, the last being Mozart's pupil for a time. The school that followed the famous Muzio Clementi included Beethoven in its ranks; while others of this group were Dussek, Mueller, Cramer, Woelfl, and Prince Louis Ferdinand. Hüllmandel, Louis Adam, and Steibelt were identified with Paris. Nearly all of these men composed something for their instrument.

English song-plays were written by Samuel Arnold and William Jackson; but Charles Dibdin became much greater than either. Dibdin's many musical plays were often on maritime subjects, or at least contained his famous sea-songs, such as "The Token," "Tom Bowling," etc. They were most inspiring to their auditors; and it is said that Dibdin's songs were worth ten thousand men to the English navy.

Among other English composers, Michael Arne, son of Thomas A. Arne, produced nine operas. Thomas Linley composed a dozen of these song-plays, and wrote also many graceful songs. His son was a personal friend of Mozart. Others who worked in the vocal field were William Shield, James Hook, Thomas Carter, Michael Kelly, and William Reeve. Stephen Storace, the violinist, was another *Singspiel* composer, and a close friend of Mozart.

English music of that time came to include catches and glees. The glee was simply a part-song, often unaccompanied, and in spite of its name it was not necessarily lively or mirthful. The catch was a song that depended for its point upon some comicality in the use of words. Thus in one of Bishop's catches, the questioning phrase, "Ah, how, Sophia," becomes "A house afire" when sung quickly in the chorus; and other similar alterations of sense follow in due course. Madrigals were also composed, and a madrigal club existed; but this form was rather indefinite at the time.

Italian opera was continued by such men as Vittorio Trento, Giuseppe Mosca, Vincenzo Lavigna, and others. Greater than these, however, was Ferdinand Paër. Writing at first in a conventional style, Paër afterward learned much by hearing Mozart's operas at Vienna. His works include a setting of the subject used later by Beethoven in "Fidelio." Another composer of the same epoch was Simon Mayer, a Bavarian who worked in Italy. His "Lodoiska" and "Medea" anticipated Cherubini's works on the same subjects. Mayer taught Donizetti, and so may serve as a link between the Gluck-Mozart period and the Donizetti-Rossini school.

XII

BEETHOVEN

LUDWIG VAN BEETHOVEN was born at Bonn, probably on December 16, 1770. There is some doubt about the day, while Beethoven himself used to assert that his birth-year was 1772. He was of Belgian descent, his grandfather having come from Antwerp to the Electoral Chapel at Bonn in 1733. His father was a singer in the chapel. His mother was of low degree, being the daughter of a cook; but she was much more useful in the household than her shiftless husband.

Mozart's precocity and childish success served as an example which other fathers desired to see their sons emulate. This was the case in the Beethoven family, as well as in Weber's. But Beethoven was scarcely a child-prodigy; and his father was certainly not the man to develop one. The father was dissipated and worthless, and his efforts to train the child were irregular and severe. With a boon companion named Pfeiffer, he would rout out the youngster at all hours of the day or night, and force him roughly to the keyboard. Visitors sometimes saw him shedding tears at the piano; and it is a wonder that his father's harshness did not drive him to hate music. He did play in public when eight years old, and he composed at ten; but he was not the money-making prodigy that his indigent father desired.

At twelve Beethoven began taking lessons of his first good teacher, the court organist, Neefe. That worthy pedagogue gave his pupil an excellent training in Bach's works, and inspired him with a real love of good music. At this time he composed some early sonatas, and an admirable two-voiced fugue. In the next year the young Beethoven became cembalist at the theatre, leading the orchestra from the keyboard in the usual fashion of the time. A year later he was made assistant organist.

In 1787 the Elector sent Beethoven to Vienna for a time. There he met Mozart, who was astounded at his power of improvisation,

BEETHOVEN

and exclaimed, "Watch this young man; he will yet make a noise in the world."

Returning to Bonn, Beethoven played viola in the reorganized orchestra. This work, like his theatre conducting, may have seemed unimportant drudgery in a way, but it gave him that thorough comprehension of the instruments that is shown in all his larger works.

When Beethoven's mother died, the Elector arranged to pay a part of the father's salary to the young man, so that it would not evaporate too quickly in drink. In 1792 the father died — an event which was reported to the Elector as "a great loss to the tax on liquors."

Receiving leave to settle at Vienna, Beethoven began his long course of lessons with Haydn. One day, however, he showed an exercise to a musician named Schenk, and learned that Haydn had left a number of mistakes uncorrected. From that time on, he took lessons with Schenk also. He received some training from Salieri, and studied a good deal with the great contrapuntal teacher Albrechtsberger. Beethoven was so radical in his work that the latter advised his other pupils to avoid the newcomer, and not be misled by his bad example. But soon Beethoven began upon the compositions that were to make him famous, and then he could afford to disregard his mentors. When he dedicated his three sonatas, Op. 2, to Haydn, the latter inquired why Beethoven had not printed "Pupil of Haydn" after his name; whereupon Beethoven replied, "Because I never learned anything from you." But this retort, though just enough, should be supplemented by the fact that even if Haydn was careless in the lessons, his music influenced Beethoven greatly, and served as a model for the younger man's earlier works.

In person, Beethoven was short and stocky, like a stunted giant. His face seems intensely expressive and powerful, but as a whole he was said to have had a picturesque ugliness. His manners were often brusque and uncouth. His lack of order was noticeable, both in his costume and in his way of living. He would work amid a litter of old papers and other relics, sometimes stopping to declaim about order with Ciceronian fulness. He was careless about notifying landlords when he moved, and often got into lawsuits on that account. He had a habit of cooling his wrists by pouring water over them — a proceeding none too beneficial to the ceilings in the rooms below his.

Yet in spite of all these eccentricities, he made many friends among the nobility, and kept them through life. They must have recognized not only his commanding genius, but the innate nobility of his character. Though practically uneducated except in music, he built for himself a natural religion, and had broad ideals of human brotherhood.

First among these friends came Count Waldstein and the Breunings, at Bonn. He taught music to Eleonora von Breuning, and at the same time his contact with her and her cultivated family remedied some of the defects of his education. In Vienna he was known and liked by such people as the Lichnowskys, Prince Lobkowitz, Van Swieten, Prince Kinsky, the Russian ambassador Rasumowsky, and even many members of the royal families.

Beethoven was continually falling in love, though somehow he never got as far as marriage. Perhaps it would have been better for him if he had tied the Gordian knot of matrimony; for he would have been looked after, and possibly kept alive some extra years, to give the world more master-works. His first idol (or ideal) was Eleonora von Breuning. Following her came a long list, including Countess Erdödy, Babette de Keglevics, Baroness Ertmann, Bettina von Brentano, Countess Giulietta Guicciardi, and Amalia Seebald. When Beethoven died, three letters were found in his desk, written by him, and containing the most impassioned devotion. It is not absolutely sure which lady was the "Immortal Beloved" that they mentioned; but Countess Guicciardi was almost certainly the person for whom they were meant. She was a pupil of Beethoven, and at times he grew irritable enough over her playing, in spite of his love. She afterwards married Count Gallenberg.

The three periods of Beethoven's work extended approximately from 1795 to 1802, from then to 1814, and from that year to his death, in 1827. It was in 1795 that he began his actual list of published works. He was one of the first to label his compositions with opus numbers. An opus is simply a work or a group of works published together. If a composer issues a piece without any opus number it is usually a sign that he considers this work unimportant. Beethoven's early compositions are left without numbers, his Op. 1 being three piano trios published in 1795, while his Op. 2 consisted of his first three piano sonatas.

After a trip to Nuremberg, Prague, and Berlin, Beethoven settled down to composition as his life-work. Other productions of his first period consisted of the *scena* "Adelaïde," a septet, six string quartets, fifteen sonatas in all, the First Symphony, the music to the ballet "Prometheus," and the oratorio "The Mount of Olives." After these works were written he felt deafness growing upon him. By 1802 this worried him so much that he feared for his sanity. He described his condition in a letter to his brothers that is known as his will; yet even in that despairing document he showed a determination to defy the blows of fate.

It is in the music of his first period that Beethoven shows the influence of Haydn. But where Haydn and Mozart had sometimes made music a matter of passing entertainment to their auditors, Beethoven let it echo the noble sentiments and aspirations that seethed within his own intense nature. Even in the first period, Beethoven's music showed a power and intensity of expression that was far above anything that his contemporaries could bring forth. The first of his piano sonatas is based on the Haydn form, though having four movements; yet Haydn could never in the world have equaled its tremendous strength, which suggests a young giant tugging at his fetters. There are many reminiscences of Haydn in some of the other works — sometimes in parts of the string quartets, but especially in the brisk and lively finale of the First Symphony. On the whole, though, Beethoven showed a vigor and a dramatic intensity that must have seemed like a revelation after the light geniality of Haydn and the smoothness of Mozart.

The second period was astonishingly brilliant, and during its twelve years Beethoven poured forth a constant stream of great masterpieces. The dozen piano sonatas of this time included the intense "Waldstein" and "Appassionata" sonatas. The noble "Kreutzer Sonata" for violin, and the famous sonata in A for 'cello, came early in this period. The "Kreutzer Sonata," dedicated to the violinist of that name, may be cited especially as a wonderful example of pure beauty in music; for Tolstoy saw fit to read into it certain debased meanings, that could only have existed in his own mind. The string quartets of this period include the three that are dedicated to Rasumowsky. The so-called triple concerto, with piano, appeared in 1804. The fourth piano concerto (with orchestra.

of course) came out in 1805, and the fifth in 1809. While the latter was being given once in Vienna, the French soldiers under Napoleon were in the city; and an officer, on hearing it, called it "the Emperor among concertos" — a name that has clung to it since. In this period came the overtures entitled "Coriolanus," "Egmont," "The Ruins of Athens," and "King Stephen." The chief vocal works were the mass in C, the cantata "Der Glorreiche Augenblick," and the opera "Fidelio." The Second Symphony belongs to the first period in style, its suave, hymn-like, slow movement again suggesting Haydn. But with the Third Symphony (1804) Beethoven found a freer and more virile utterance. The Fourth Symphony came two years later, the Fifth and Sixth in 1808, and the Seventh and Eighth in 1812.

In speaking of Beethoven's symphonies, one may exhaust all the adjectives in the dictionary and scarcely do justice to these great works. They are minutely described in Sir George Grove's book entitled "Beethoven's Nine Symphonies." They are not all of equal value. The story goes that a pupil, asked how many symphonies Beethoven wrote, answered, "Three." "What were they?" inquired the surprised teacher; whereupon the pupil responded, "The Third, the Fifth, and the Ninth." Those three are certainly the greatest, but the Sixth and Seventh are hardly below them in value. When Wilhelm Gericke, former leader of the Boston Symphony Orchestra, was asked which one of Beethoven's symphonies he preferred, he replied, "Always the one I have played last."

To describe them at length would demand a book; and their glories can only be briefly outlined here.

No. 1. 1st movement. Starts with an *adagio* introduction which aroused criticism by not beginning in the tonic key. The *sonata allegro* has a first theme built of a rhythmic three-noted figure, the accent coming on the third note; a melodious tributary and second theme, in Haydn's style; and an expressive closing theme with little downward drops after apparent cadences. Development and recapitulation of themes follow, as is proper in the *sonata-allegro* movement.

2d movement. An *andante* with expressive song-like themes.

3d movement. A tremendously virile minuet, with trio full of rhythmic iteration.

4th movement. A bright rondo in Haydn's cheerful style.

No. 2. 1st movement. An ornate introduction leads to the sonata form. The first theme is brisk, lively, and full of chatter because of repeated notes; the second theme is of similar character, with fanfare-like effects; while the closing theme brings minor modulations.

2d movement. A song-like *larghetto*, the first theme of which has been used as a hymn.

3d movement. Has the minuet shape, but is marked *scherzo*. Beethoven afterwards made the *scherzo* into a much freer form.

4th movement. A rapid, brilliant movement, with more vigor than the finale of the First Symphony. It has a broad coda. Beethoven often put very important climaxes into his codas.

No. 3. Eroica Symphony. Was planned to glorify Napoleon, but title changed when he seized the imperial throne.

1st movement. Themes now more pregnantly expressive. The first, in triple rhythm, moving with a slow, majestic swing; the second a three-noted figure echoed about among the instruments; and a long double closing theme, the first part contemplative, the second triumphant.

2d movement. A long and tremendously expressive funeral march, interspersed with phrases of tenderest regret, and contrasted with a major section of consolatory character.

3d movement. A *scherzo*, still showing minuet divisions, but much freer than that of the Second Symphony. Rapid, chattering style, now and then suddenly showing forth into bold relief; quarter-notes in swift $\frac{3}{4}$ rhythm. The trio contains broadly noble horn passages.

4th movement. Variation form. Effective enough, though hardly equal to the earlier movements, and not so "heroic" a finale as that of the Fifth Symphony.

No. 4. 1st movement. An impressive minor and modulatory introduction. A first theme of simple but pleasing harmonic structure; a tributary passage increasing in power; a second theme of chattering, imitative character, except for some unison string work; and a syncopated closing theme.

2d movement. A song-like *adagio*, embroidered with many rapid notes of very small denominations. Highly praised by Berlioz.

3d movement. A reversion to the minuet form, but very free. Notably beautiful horn passages in the trio.

4th movement. Bold themes of lively and vigorous character. Important contrabass passages.

No. 5. A classic among symphonies, notable for its tremendous vigor, and the simple means by which this strength is obtained.

1st movement. In minor except where the sonata form permits major. Themes, development, recapitulation, and coda built almost wholly from the first four-noted figure, treated in various ways. This rhythm (three eighth-notes followed by an accented note) was said to have been suggested by a nocturnal reveller pounding on a door for admission; but Beethoven gave it a better significance by saying, "Thus Fate knocks at the door." The coda in this movement especially powerful. The whole movement intensely effective.

2d movement. An *andante*, built out of two short themes, the first being song-like, while the second has a fanfare character. The consummate art of Beethoven is shown by the skill and beauty with which he handles these themes, making their simple harmonies seem as perfectly balanced and as inevitably right as if they were the very "music of the spheres."

3d movement. A mysteriously effective *scherzo*, in which the heavy four-note rhythm of the first movement recurs. The trio, in rapid, rushing style, forms a good contrast. Much contrabass work. A soft but impressive transition passage leads directly into the finale.

4th movement. A grandly triumphant *allegro*, with reminiscences of the mysterious *scherzo* for a middle part.

No. 6. Pastoral Symphony. The first great programme work in musical history. Tone-picture of life in the country.

1st movement. Cheerful impressions on going to the country. The first sixteen bars give a theme from parts of which the rest of the movement is built. All rhythmic, lively, and cheerful in character.

2d movement. Andante, entitled "By the Brook." A tone-picture of gently rippling water, varied by bird-calls.

3d movement. Joyous gathering of the peasants. Themes of lively rustic character. A peasants' dance, in which an old bassoonist joins in with battered instrument (see chapter on the bassoon). Recurrence of opening theme. Approach and breaking of a storm, with instrumental suggestions of rising wind, thunder, etc. Thanksgiving after the end of the storm. Practically a five-movement symphony with the last three joined together.

No. 7. Very rhythmic. Sometimes called the apotheosis of the dance.

1st movement. A slow introduction, with runs and broad chords. The *allegro* begins with a waltz-like theme of most pleasing character; the same rhythm being carried through the second theme and the closing theme.

2d movement. Marked *allegretto*, but really the slow movement of the symphony. A most wonderful use of the rhythm shown by a quarter-note, two eighths, and two more quarters. This rhythm is carried entirely through the movement. The chords at first correspond to this rhythm, and a bipartite theme (with second half repeated) in minor is worked up to a great climax. A side-section, in major, brings into the upper part an infinitely melodious theme with triplet accompaniment, while the bass continues the former rhythm. The first theme returns, worked out in very elaborated and effective counterpoint. The side-section and a suggestion of the original theme then end the movement.

3d movement. *Scherzo* is here replaced by *presto*, though the form is kept the same. Mysterious, chattering themes are alternated with a simple but rhythmic trio.

4th movement. A tremendously rapid rondo, of brusque and lively character.

No. 8. Light and short in comparison with the three preceding ones, but very humorous, bright, and pleasant. This and the Seventh Symphony were inspired partly by the enlivening influence exerted on Beethoven by Amalia Seebald.

1st movement. No introduction. Themes cheerful, having almost the character of a slow waltz.

2d movement. A light, dainty *allegretto scherzando*, with themes tossed about and mimicked in humorous fashion.

3d movement. *Tempo di menuetto.* Like a playful minuet in style.

4th movement. *Allegretto vivace.* Lively, chattering themes in even rhythm.

No. 9. The *Choral Symphony*, introducing voices in the finale. A tonal picture of world-struggles followed by human brotherhood.

1st movement. Empty fifths and fourths, serving as an introduction, lead directly into the wildly strong first theme. The second theme is more tender in character, and in the contrasting major mode; while the closing theme is short. After development and recapitulation, the coda, ending in a grand climax, lets the sombre mood of the first theme prevail.

2d movement. *Molto vivace.* A gracefully melodious theme in minor, said to resemble a certain Russian folk-dance. This is varied and continued through the movement, which ends tranquilly in major.

3d movement. An *adagio* of very expressive character meant to typify the best sentiments of humanity. Its two contrasted sections, however, are scarcely so striking as the slow movement of the Fifth Symphony.

4th movement. At first in some sense a review of preceding movements. Wild themes from the first and second movement are rebuked by stern passages on the contrabass; a suggestion of the *adagio* dies away plaintively; then the contrabass breaks into the impressive theme that is sung afterward, to the words of Schiller's

"Ode to Joy." The inner meaning of all this is that human striving (the first three movements) is to be replaced by universal brotherhood, shown by the sentiments of the song.

The Ninth Symphony belongs to Beethoven's third period, in which he gave up piano performances because he was entirely deaf. Other works of this period were the great "Missa Solemnis," the last five piano sonatas, and the last of his string quartets. These show a discarding of the forms that he used in such powerful style in his second period. The sonatas are more like free rhapsodies, and the Ninth Symphony an approach toward the modern tone-picture idea. Toward the end, Beethoven said that all he had written was as nothing beside what he was planning; and we may conclude that if he had lived he would have given us great orchestral canvases, as broadly outlined as those of Liszt, with perhaps even more valuable thematic material.

In 1815, Beethoven's brother Caspar died, leaving the composer with the charge of a nephew. Lawsuits with the boy's mother followed; and the boy himself gave Beethoven much trouble. The young ward of the composer has usually been rated as a black sheep, because of some escapades that troubled his uncle; but the nephew finally went into the army, and afterward settled down as a good citizen. Beethoven's arbitrary ways no doubt caused at least a part of whatever friction arose. He lavished affection on the nephew, but perhaps showed too little self-control for a really good guardian.

Beethoven loved the open air, and used to walk about frequently. On these walks he would often stop to note down themes in some one of his many sketch-books. The difference between the themes of the notebooks and their final form in his published works is often remarkable, and proved that Beethoven possessed the capacity for taking pains that Carlyle calls genius. But he had inspiration also. Sometimes he would become so absorbed in his themes as to block traffic, or cut his friends. At times, when he wandered far afield, the authorities would look with suspicion on such an eccentric stranger; and once he was arrested as a vagrant. But he was safe from trouble in one favorite spot — a tree in Schönbrunn, whose forked branches formed a natural seat.

Beethoven had no fixed position. Once he thought of becoming a *Kapellmeister* under Jerome Bonaparte; but his friends subscribed for an annuity to keep him in Vienna. In spite of later currency depreciation and many lawsuits, the composer was never driven into bankruptcy. He was always able to sell his works, and had many influential friends upon whom he could rely. The respect in which he was held was shown at his first performance of the Ninth Symphony, at Vienna. Beethoven, being totally deaf, did not hear the wild applause at the end, but stood gazing at the orchestra. At last one of the performers turned him around; and the audience, recognizing his inability to hear their clapping, began to wave hats and handkerchiefs at him.

Beethoven's illness, a tendency to dropsy, was complicated by lung trouble. The latter may have resulted from a visit to a surviving brother at Gneixendorf; for he had to sleep in a draughty room while there, and he returned in very bad weather.

On his deathbed (in 1827) he came to know and appreciate Schubert. He also saw a picture of Haydn's birthplace and remarked, "Strange that such a great man should have been born in such a hovel." His irritability remained with him, and he even quarrelled with his doctors. The very manner of his death was unusual and dramatic. A great storm had come over the city; and after a loud clap of thunder Beethoven raised himself, shook his fist at the elements, and fell back dead.

Beethoven's works may be listed as follows: —

For piano, thirty-two sonatas, one four-hand sonata, and over one hundred smaller pieces, including variations, dances, rondos, bagatelles, etc.

For voice, with piano or orchestra mostly, the opera "Fidelio," one oratorio, two masses, ten cantatas of various sorts, one chorale fantasia, a number of concert-solos, eighteen canons, and about two hundred and forty songs, nearly two thirds of the songs being written for the publisher Thomson, of Edinburgh.

For orchestra, nine symphonies, eleven overtures, incidental music, about ten minor works (including the tone-picture "The Battle of Vittoria"), five concertos for piano, and one concerto for violin.

For various instrumental combinations, eight piano trios, three piano quartets, one piano quintet, one triple concerto, ten violin sonatas, five 'cello sonatas, one horn sonata, five trios, sixteen string quartets, two quintets, two sextets, one septet, and two octets.

His compositions are nearly all alive to-day, but the symphonies, overtures, piano sonatas, and string quartets receive more performances at present than his other works. Of the overtures, that to "Egmont" is perhaps the most intensely powerful, with "Coriolanus" a good second; but the three "Leonora" overtures, especially the third, are also strongly dramatic. The early string quartets are great, while the last few show the utter breadth of Beethoven's final style. The piano sonatas are nearly all famous solo selections. Best among the early ones are the first three and the "Pathétique," the latter being full of tremendously strong contrasts and great possibilities. The well-beloved "Moonlight Sonata" is not really a moonlight affair. One of the weird stories that are sometimes saddled upon an innocent work states that Beethoven, wandering in a forest, came upon a house, entered to find it filled by a social gathering, and improvised this work with the moonlight streaming over the keyboard. In reality, he composed the work in his study, and entitled it "Sonata quasi una fantasia." Another false story arises from the name of the piece entitled "Farewell to the Piano." This piece was not Beethoven's last for the piano, and his own title for it was "Thoughts on Departure." Of the later sonatas, the "Waldstein" and "Appassionata" are great, while the last five are freer in form, but grandly effective.

The opera "Fidelio" deals with the misfortunes of Florestan, a Spanish nobleman who has been supplanted and imprisoned by Pizarro. Florestan's wife Leonora disguises herself as a youth, under the name of Fidelio, and enters Pizarro's employment as assistant to Rocco, his jailer. Pizarro, learning of the governor Ferdinand's approach, decides to kill Florestan; but at the crucial moment Leonora prevents him from stabbing his victim by flourishing a pistol. Just at this moment the governor's trumpet-call is heard from without; and when that official learns the truth, he banishes Pizarro and restores Florestan to all he had lost. The music is somewhat symphonic according to modern standards, but strongly dramatic. Fidelio's outburst of indignation ("Abscheulicher"), followed by the smooth aria "Komm, Hoffnung," is a favorite concert selection; while the second act as a whole is a marvel of intensity.

But the purely orchestral Beethoven was the greatest, after all. In treating the instruments, Beethoven brought out their capabilities in the fullest measure. Those that earlier composers had held unimportant were often raised by him to a position of prominence. He thought orchestrally, and his last five sonatas seem like symphonic rhapsodies for piano.

His themes were almost always fraught with the most intense feeling and significance. Their vigor is unexampled, and their depth of musical expression remarkable. When the works of several different composers are practised constantly, some of them seem to wear threadbare after a short time; but Beethoven's works never grow stale. They arouse constant admiration for their strength, and mark their composer as *primus inter pares* — a leader among the musical Titans who have tried to scale Olympus.

XIII

SCHUBERT

FRANZ PETER SCHUBERT was undoubtedly the most spontaneous of composers. Melodies occurred to him with the most amazing rapidity, and his short life was one continual outpouring of compositions. He seldom revised his work, being in this respect the opposite of Beethoven. But he gave forth his "native wood-notes wild" in an inexhaustible stream. Even Mozart, his only rival in this respect, was certainly behind him in melodic and harmonic expressiveness.

Schubert was born on January 31, 1797, in the large family of a poor schoolmaster at Lichtenthal, a suburb of Vienna. His home life was restricted by poverty, but his father and his elder brothers Ignaz and Ferdinand were devoted to music, which Franz soon found to be a congenial atmosphere. He received his earliest instruction at home, with the addition of some lessons from Holzer, the local choir-leader. Schubert's natural genius had evidently begun to make itself manifest; for Holzer said, "He seems to have known instinctively whatever I tried to teach him."

Soon after he reached the age of eleven he was transferred to the choir-school (*Konvikt-Schule*) of the imperial chapel in Vienna, where he stayed until 1813. There he had some chances to develop himself, such as hearing occasional operas, or playing in the school orchestra, of which he became first violin and assistant conductor. The playing at home, too, grew to a larger scale, and the domestic performances sometimes included symphonies as well as quartets. He began to compose also. In that branch he was handicapped at first by an unusual situation — the lack of money to buy music-paper. Fortunately the situation was discovered by an older and richer student, who generously bought the needed supplies. Schubert's poverty was shown in another way; for the students were none too well fed, receiving only two meals a day, and a letter exists in which Franz begged his brother for extra *Kreutzers* (pennies) to buy more food.

Schubert received a few lessons from Ruzicka, who taught thoroughbass at the school. This was supplemented by occasional advice from Salieri. But on the whole, as with Holzer in the earlier days, he was practically self-taught. He felt the greatest admiration for the works of Mozart and Beethoven, though they do not seem to have served as models for his own vein of emotional expression. He might have obtained imperial aid if he had worked harder at certain general subjects in the school course; but he did not do this, and when his voice broke he was thrown on his own resources.

For a time he taught in the primary grades of his father's school, to escape military conscription. During this period he worked as much as possible at composition; and when the school-teaching was given up he devoted himself wholly to music. Even before this time he had composed large works. At seventeen he had written his first mass, which pleased his devout father so greatly that the latter presented the youth with a new piano. An early opera is now only a fragment, for it was left as a pledge in care of a friend named Hüttenbrenner, at whose house a servant used the first act and part of the second to light the fires. Schubert wrote so much that many of his works were lost through carelessness of various kinds; and even at his death his manuscripts were rated as a "pile of old music, worth ten florins." Schumann, Sir George Grove, and others did much valuable work in recovering various Schubert manuscripts; and it is possible even now that some of his lost works may be rediscovered.

At eighteen, Schubert wrote one of his most powerful songs, "The Erl-King," producing it in a single day. Goethe, the author of the poem, did not appreciate this setting, and seems to have been somewhat lacking in good musical taste; but the public and the critics now rate it as one of the most dramatic songs ever written.

From this time on Schubert came face to face with poverty, and was often saved from actual want only by the aid of his friends. Most helpful among these was the Swedish poet-musician Franz von Schober. This "friend in need," who was fairly well off, had admired some Schubert songs before meeting their composer; and when the two became acquainted, Von Schober suggested that they share lodgings, and took advantage of this plan to shoulder almost the entire financial burden. Von Schober was a valuable friend to Schubert, for he understood the composer's moods and made due allowance for them. He was also able to introduce Schubert to certain valuable friends, such as the baritone Vogl. With Vogl or Von Schober the composer made several very pleasant vacation trips. Another friend of this little group was the poet Mayrhofer, whose melancholy disposition must have been cheered by Schubert's geniality. From this beginning there came ultimately a fairly large circle of poets, painters, and musicians, including Lachner, Schwind, Spaun, and other notables. They were a somewhat Bohemian lot, leading a rather shiftless life; but they made it a life of at least some happiness. In its way the circle was almost communistic. If one had money, all shared it with him, and drank champagne until a renewed financial deficit forced them back to simpler potations. Once, when Schubert sold a group of songs to a publisher, he took the coterie to hear the great violinist Paganini, at over two dollars a ticket. Hats, coats, and other articles of clothing were appropriated whenever needed, and any one making a visit arrayed himself in the best of this borrowed plumage. During a week of poverty, Schubert once missed his wooden spectacle case. After a hunt, he found that Schwind, too poor at the time to buy a pipe, had filled the case with tobacco, bored a hole in it, and inserted a stem, at which he was puffing contentedly.

Schubert was recognized as the leader of the Bohemian gatherings; and they were called "Schubertiades," in his honor. All the members of the clique were active in some phase of artistic work. When a newcomer was introduced, Schubert invariably asked, "Kann er was?" This question, which meant "Can he do anything," finally became Schubert's own nickname.

In 1818, a change came, in the shape of a chance to teach at the Hungarian estate of Count Johann Esterhazy. There he must have become acquainted with the gypsy music, which is echoed in so many of his own great works. Unlike Beethoven, he did not impress the aristocracy. He felt ill at ease when with them, and more at home among the servants. But this did not prevent him from falling in love with the Count's younger daughter, Caroline, on a later visit. His passion was sincere, if hopeless. It has been stated that once, when Caroline asked why he dedicated nothing to her, he replied, "All that I ever did is dedicated to you."

Schubert's remarkable rapidity in composition is attested by

WEBER   SCHUBERT

MENDELSSOHN

many anecdotes. If a musical idea came to him at night, he would often arise to write it down. In this way he composed his song "Die Forelle." But when he reached for the bottle of sand, then used for blotting purposes, he was so sleepy that he seized the bottle of ink instead, and poured its contents over half the manuscript before he discovered his mistake. Too tired to rewrite the work, he took no further pains with it for many days.

Still more suggestive of his speed in creative work was his composition of "Hark, hark, the lark." On a summer morning in 1826, he was returning with a party of friends from an early walk. At the restaurant "Zum Biersack," in Währing, Schubert saw his friend Tieze at one of the tables; and the party joined the latter at breakfast. While they were waiting to be served, Schubert began to look over a translation of Shakespeare that Tieze had brought. Always hunting for poems that could be set to music, Schubert soon noticed "Hark, hark, the lark," the beautiful morning song in "Cymbeline." In a moment he exclaimed, "If I only had paper here, I have just the right setting for this poem." At these words Doppler, who was one of the party, started ruling staff-lines on the back of a bill of fare, and soon handed the improvised music-paper to the composer. Schubert then wrote his exquisitely beautiful setting of the poem, completing it with full harmony in the space of twenty minutes.

If Schubert composed quickly, he also forgot quickly. Once he sent Vogl a song, which the latter found too high, and directed a copyist to transpose down to the desired key. A week or two afterward, Schubert saw the song, now in a strange handwriting, and looked it over. "That's not bad," he said; "who composed it?"

As a pianist, Schubert was expressive enough, but too lazy to gain any real mastery over technique. On one occasion he broke down while trying to play one of his own works, the "Fantasie," op. 15. Continuing, he found himself in difficulty for a second time; whereat he jumped up from the piano-stool in a rage, and exclaimed to the friends who were present, "That stuff is only fit for the devil to play!" ("*Das Zeug mag der Teufel spielen!*").

Schubert's retiring manners really stood in the way of his career. He refused a post as court organist, probably through a distaste for the formalities required. He met Beethoven and Weber in 1822, but did not get into close touch with them; and Beethoven did not recognize Schubert's greatness until he examined some of the younger man's works while on his own deathbed. In similar fashion, Schubert found it hard to treat of business matters, and became a prey to the avarice of his publishers. Thus Diabelli bought a large number of Schubert songs for about ten florins apiece; while he made over twenty-seven thousand florins from a single one of these, "The Wanderer." In 1826, when the supply seemed to exceed the demand, Schubert sold some of the songs in the famous "Winterreise" set for twenty cents apiece.

After attending Beethoven's funeral in 1827, Schubert proposed a toast to the next great composer who would die, not knowing that it was to be himself.

Schubert's friends often reproached him with carelessness in composition; and toward the close of his life their words took effect. He showed more than usual care in writing his great symphony in C, and revised the manuscript considerably. After that he even decided to take lessons in counterpoint, feeling that the skilful handling of voices (parts) and figure treatment would give added strength to his works. He had planned the course with Sechter, but he died before he could start it. Toward the end of the year 1828 he was attacked by a sudden distaste for food, which soon changed into a fever of the typhus sort, similar to the one that carried off Mozart. Schubert's friends did not at first realize the serious nature of his illness; but even if they had known, their best efforts would probably have been insufficient to save a constitution worn out by irregular living. Schubert died on November 19, 1828, when less than thirty-two years old.

The epitaph on Schubert, by the poet Grillparzer, states, very justly, —

> "Fate has buried here
> A rich possession, but yet greater promise."

Schubert was by nature a song-composer, and all his works, even the orchestral ones, charm us by their wealth of spontaneous melody; but if he had carried out his plans of study, and united the solid value of contrapuntal knowledge with the melodic beauty of his works, there is no telling to what heights he might or might not have risen. As it was, he earned a place among the world's masters at thirty-one — an age at which Beethoven had not yet finished the first period in his activity, and Wagner had written only one of the operas that were destined to make him famous. In person, Schubert was short, stout, and round-shouldered, with a chubby face, a pasty complexion (due to poor food), thick black hair, and alert eyes, which were unfortunately near-sighted. He spent his mornings in composition, which with him was little more than the copying of works already completed in mental vision.

Schubert's operas are now forgotten for the most part. He wrote quite a number of them, but the librettos were often poor, and his style was lyrical rather than strongly dramatic. Best known among his operatic compositions are the overture and *entr'actes* of "Rosamunde."

Two of Schubert's ten symphonies have survived in the repertoire of the present — the "Unfinished" Symphony, and the one in C. The former consists of two remarkably emotional and expressive movements, the opening one being in the *sonata-allegro* form of a first movement, while the second is a calm but richly expressive slow movement. The warm feeling of the first movement and the rich harmonies of the second make this work absolutely *sui generis* — a veritable lyric among symphonies. The C-major work is based on larger proportions. The broadly developed themes of its first movement, the fiery gypsy character of its second, the lyric brightness of its *scherzo*, and the triumphant glory of its finale are familiar to many concert-goers. This work may not have the astonishing depth of expression that Beethoven showed, say in the finely wrought slow movement of his Seventh Symphony; but the Schubert composition charms us none the less by its wealth of melody and the changing beauty of its harmonies.

Schubert's other works include twenty expressive string quartets, and chamber music for various combinations. His two dozen piano sonatas are rather long and diffuse for a form that should be powerful rather than lyrical. His many shorter piano pieces, avoiding this defect, are often very successful. They consist of dances, marches, impromptus, *moments musicals*, and so on. His sacred productions consist of six masses, two sacred cantatas (including "Miriam's Song of Victory"), and a number of motets and hymns, some quite elaborate. For voice he wrote also about sixty part-songs; but he is best known by his solo songs, which number between six and seven hundred.

Schubert's songs brought into existence the highly poetic and expressive style of lyric known as the German *Lied*. The *Lied* is a complete work that contains the maximum of artistic creation in the minimum of space. The *Lied* may be compared to a gem in music, while the longer symphony or overture resembles rather a large decorative fresco. Such songs as Schubert's "Erl-King," or "The Wanderer," contain vivid bits of the most widely different styles, welded into an artistic whole with the utmost skill and delicacy. The same variety is shown in the other songs when they are taken as a whole, though often a single song may be devoted to a special style. Thus the "Schöne Müllerin" cycle, depicting the love of a rustic swain for the miller's daughter, and his jealousy of the green-clad hunter who supplants him in her affections, is pervaded by suggestions of mill-stream and forest, although its various numbers differ among themselves in character. Songs like "Die Allmacht" or "Aufenthalt" demand breadth or power. Others again, like "Die Post," or "Das Fischermädchen," are lyric melodies of swingy enthusiasm or compelling charm. Some numbers in the "Winterreise" and elsewhere are settings of apparently unmusical subjects, done in such a clever way that the accompaniment proves effective after all. In setting emotional subjects, Schubert did not quite reach to the depth of Schumann; but he showed the way for the latter, and surpassed him in the variety of uses to which he put his lyric ability.

There had been song-composers before Schubert, such as Schulz, Zelter, and others. But where their work was primitive or experimental, Schubert's represents a full artistic fruition.

With Schubert as a song-composer two other men have been classed — Robert Schumann, and Robert Franz.[1] The former will be treated under his own name; but Franz's work may well be described here.

Robert Franz was born in 1815, at Halle, where he lived, with short exceptions, until his death in 1892. Gifted with musical taste at an early age, he enjoyed greatly the choral singing that took

---

[1] The family name was Knauth, but his father changed it to Franz, by royal permission.

place at his home. In school he added alto parts to the songs, and nearly earned a flogging from the teacher, who did not understand such deviations from the printed notes. After some study at Dessau, Franz returned to his native place, where he gradually became known as a song-composer, and was made a chorus-director. Poverty and deafness came upon him, but Liszt came to his aid, and gave a series of "Franz concerts" that put him beyond the reach of want.

Franz thought that after Beethoven it was sacrilege to attempt symphonies; and he limited himself to song-composition. In a letter to Louis C. Elson, Franz claimed that "music began with the lyric form, and will end with it — a process of development that is true of poetry also." Whether one agrees with the prediction or not, he must admit that Franz's songs did much to justify it. They show something of the lyric charm that was Schubert's and the melodic strength that was Schumann's; but with these they unite a delicacy of artistic workmanship that deserves the highest praise. They are often of such an intimate nature that they lose effect in large concert-halls. Some of them, like "Mit schwarzen Segeln," show power enough; but most of them are more quietly contemplative. This quality may be found in such widely different lyrics as the rhapsodical "An die bretterne Schiffswand" and the infinitely tender "Slumber-Song." Franz wrote some choral music, but avoided the instrumental field.

Karl Loewe, born near Halle in 1796, attempted the larger forms. After a youth of performance that was finally stopped by apoplexy, he devoted himself to composition. His works include operas, oratorios, orchestral, chamber, and piano pieces; but he became best known by his dramatic ballads. Undoubtedly Schubert's "Erl-King" and "Wanderer" pointed out the way for these; but Loewe carried the form to much greater length, and made it extremely dramatic. Such ballads as "Sir Olaf," "Archibald Douglas," "Odins Meeresritt," "Edward," "Heinrich, der Vogler," and others of the sort are really little dramas for solo voice and piano. He practically founded the ballad form.

XIV

WEBER AND ROMANTICISM

CARL MARIA VON WEBER was born at Eutin in 1786. He was a cousin of the Constance Weber who married Mozart. His father had been the local choirmaster and conductor for some years, and had hoped for a child-prodigy among his offspring. The children of his first wife showed only a meagre amount of talent; so that when the young Carl brought forth a juvenile composition, the father began to think that his hopes might be realized. He did not hesitate to falsify his son's age, wishing thus to draw attention to a new child-prodigy. But he was not such a well-equipped teacher as Leopold Mozart, and his son was not nearly so precocious as the young Mozart.

Weber's father was restless as well as versatile. The family began a long period of wandering when Carl was only a year old. Vienna, Cassel, Meiningen, Nuremberg, and many other places were visited in search of theatrical or other employment; and it is only a slight exaggeration to say that Weber grew up behind the scenes.

Weber's training was desultory, though he had some lessons from Michael Haydn at Salzburg. At Munich, under Kalcher, the boy produced his first opera, "Die Macht der Liebe." Weber's father grew interested at this time in the lithographic work of his friend Senefelder, and thought of giving up music; but he did not carry out his design. In Freiburg, Weber produced "Das Waldmädchen," which was afterwards rewritten as "Sylvana." Next came "Peter Schmoll," which was still immature, and had little more success than its two predecessors.

After study with Abt Vogler, who helped him much, Weber became *Kapellmeister* at Breslau. There he wrote the opera "Rübezahl," now unfortunately lost. There, too, he accidentally ruined his attractive voice by sipping at a glass of his father's nitric acid, which he mistook for wine. Unlike the Irishman in the anecdote, who merely stated that he "had never tasted that brand before," Weber fell to the floor unconscious, and did not recover his health for a long time.

At Stuttgart, Weber entered into the fast court life that flourished under Duke Ludwig of Würtemberg. There he was drawn into various kinds of gayety and dissipation, and became one of a coterie known by the pleasing title of "Faust's Descent into Hell." As secretary to the Duke, Weber received some of the wrath that his ducal master had aroused in King Frederick; and he made the breach irreparable by directing to the chamber of that royal gossip an old lady who was asking for the court washerwoman. As a result, Weber was banished when one of his servants secretly negotiated a loan by promising a court appointment in return for it — an act of which the composer was wholly ignorant.

But this banishment was of good influence, for a more orderly life was coming. At Darmstadt there was renewed work with Abt Vogler, who said of Weber and Meyerbeer that they would express his artistic principles for him. At this time came Weber's first real success in opera — the one-act comedy "Abu Hassan."

Still more conducive to good effects was Weber's marriage with Caroline Brandt. She made him give up the wild associates and habits of his Stuttgart days, and lead a more orderly and industrious life, before she would consent to the marriage. In after life she continued to be his good angel.

It was during his stay as conductor in Dresden that he started composing the works that have made him most famous. His opera "Preciosa" belongs to this period, but his fame rests chiefly on three great stage works — "Der Freischütz," "Euryanthe," and "Oberon."

The plot of "Der Freischütz" is based on the old legend of a demon who gives huntsmen magic bullets in exchange for their souls. The demon's name is Zamiel, and the huntsman Kaspar is in his power. Kaspar, who must furnish a new victim to prolong his own lease of life, beguiles to Zamiel's glen a young huntsman named Max, who loves Agatha, daughter of the chief huntsman Kuno. As Kuno is about to retire, Max wishes to succeed him, for Agatha's sake. Max is made to shoot badly in the preliminary contest, which impels him to get the magic bullets. With these he shoots perfectly, but the last one, which was to do Zamiel's bidding, aims itself at Agatha. Deflected by a sacred wreath, it kills Kaspar instead. Zamiel is satisfied with this victim, whereupon Max confesses and is forgiven.

This work is justly considered as the foundation of the romantic school in German opera. The school derived its name partly from its subjects, and partly from its methods of treating them. The classic mythological texts of the Metastasio sort were now replaced by legendary lore, or historical pageantry. The music was based largely on the folk-song style.

Weber's opera contains many examples of the simple beauty that pervades the German *Volkslied*. Artificialities were banished in a smooth flow of music that made a strong popular appeal. Such numbers as the horn quartet in the overture, or the close of Agatha's prayer, are exactly in the style of the German folk-music. Such music as this, in connection with the brisk hunting-choruses and the impressive incantations, must have exerted a strong appeal when contrasted with some of the conventionalities that had preceded it. The entire German nation went wild over the work. After a Vienna performance, Weber wrote, "Greater enthusiasm there cannot be, and . . . it is scarcely possible to rise higher than this. To God alone the praise!"

"Preciosa" was based on a Spanish gypsy subject, and had no national import. "Die Drei Pintos," a comedy written at this time, was left unfinished, and not performed until after the composer's death.

"Euryanthe," Weber's second great success, was handicapped by a mixed and poor libretto. Count Adolar, praising the virtue of Euryanthe, his betrothed, is told by Lysiart, a rejected suitor, that she can be made faithless. Lysiart, aided by Euryanthe's maid Eglantine, obtains a ring and learns a secret about Adolar's sister Emma, both of which seem to compromise Euryanthe by showing her to be on confidential terms with him. Adolar, incensed, drags her to the wilderness to kill her, and leaves her alive only because she saves him from a serpent. Returning, Adolar is told by Eglantine that she compromised Euryanthe out of jealousy. Lysiart stabs Eglantine and is led off to punishment; while Euryanthe, who has been found and saved by the king, is restored to the repentant Adolar. The music of this work was again of high rank; and

Beethoven, on hearing it, wrote, "I am glad; for this is the way that the Germans must get the upper hand of the Italian sing-song."

"Oberon," the prototype of much fairy music, is founded on the old romance of Sir Huon of Bordeaux. Oberon has quarrelled with Titania, and will not be reconciled until he finds two lovers who are constant through everything. Puck brings news of Sir Huon's pilgrimage to Bagdad, a penalty imposed because he had killed Charlemagne's son. As one of his tasks, Huon rescues the Caliph's daughter Rezia, with whom he falls in love. The pair are persecuted by fate, enduring shipwreck and slavery; but they remain faithful, so that Oberon is reconciled to Titania at last. Huon is ultimately pardoned by Charlemagne.

This work has in it many possibilities, and there is a strong contrast between the delicate fairy music and the powerful climaxes in other parts of the opera. One of the scenes, "Ocean, thou mighty monster," is still a favorite display piece for concert sopranos.

Weber is best known by his operas, but he composed many other works. He wrote three detached overtures and two symphonies. He produced a number of orchestral concertos, the two for piano and the "Concertstück" being best known. He composed several cantatas, of which "Kampf und Sieg" is the most famous. He was a great pianist, and wrote many solos for his instrument, including four sonatas, a number of rondos, some very effective polonaises, and so on. His dances include the well-known "Invitation to the Dance." His "Last Waltz," as already stated, was not his, but Reissiger's. It was found among his papers after his death, but Reissiger was able to prove that he had given Weber the manuscript. Weber died at London in 1826. His "Oberon" was composed for London, and in spite of his consumption he went to the British capital, on what proved to be his last trip. "Oberon" was a great success, and added one more proof to the fact that its composer was remembered best for his operas.

Ludwig Spohr, who was born in 1784, is sometimes named as the real founder of the romantic school. But in spite of Spohr's many claims to fame, he hardly deserves that title. His best operas included "Faust," "Zemire and Azor," "Jessonda," "Der Berggeist," and "Der Alchymist." The first of these (not on Goethe's drama, incidentally) was produced in 1818. But while it antedated "Der

Freischütz" by three years, it did not cause any national feeling, or serve to found a school.

Spohr studied the violin during boyhood, and won some attention by writing a concerto at the age of fourteen. By further study, and the hearing of great artists, he developed himself into a leading violinist, of a broad and solid school that superseded the Parisian coterie of Rode and Kreutzer. He was active also as an opera conductor, and Weber helped him to become court choirmaster at Cassel, where he remained for many years. He married the harpist Dorette Scheidler, and composed many harp-and-violin duets for her and himself.

Spohr's works consist of nine symphonies, including the famous "Consecration of Tones"; fifteen violin concertos, and other works of the sort; much chamber music; ten operas in all; and several oratorios, such as "Calvary" and "The Last Judgment." Many of these works have retained their popularity; but they are almost all marked by Spohr's peculiar mannerisms. He wrote in a very modulatory style, sometimes so chromatic as to seem artificial. He has been likened to a man who, on wishing to enter a house, will not walk through the front door, but dodges around the corners, and finally jumps in through some unexpected window. Yet much of his music is effective, for he was a good contrapuntist and a fair master of orchestration.

Peter von Winter and Joseph Weigl antedated the romantic school, at least by their operas. They form a link between the Mozart-Salieri period and the school that followed Weber. Winter's "Unterbrochene Opferfest" and Weigl's "Schweizerfamilie" were their best works. Others of this intermediate period were Friedrich Himmel and Ignaz von Seyfried. Himmel became known as a pianist, but wrote several operas, treating romantic subjects in "Die Sylphen" and "Der Kobold." Seyfried, a pupil of Mozart, Haydn, and Winter, treated such effective topics as "Die Druiden" and "Der Wundermann am Rheinfall." Ernst Theodor Hoffmann, the famous writer, produced a number of operas, of which "Undine," his best work, was given in 1816. From all this it may be seen that various German composers were working toward the romantic school; but Weber was the first to give the school a conscious existence, and a firm foundation on German folk-music.

The chief successor of Weber in the romantic school was Heinrich Marschner (1795–1861). After some years as a boy-prodigy, he met Beethoven, and began to settle down to composition. He became associated with Weber at Dresden. Of his fifteen operas, the most famous were "The Vampire," "Hans Heiling," and "Templar and Jewess," the last being based on the story of "Ivanhoe." Marschner became known also by his chamber works, piano music, and songs. His success in treating scenes of homely simplicity or supernatural weirdness was not far behind that of Weber himself. Both men influenced Wagner.

Adalbert von Gyrowetz is almost forgotten to-day, though he lived from the time of Mozart to the middle of the nineteenth century. He produced stage works after Weber, but his chief successes came with "Der Augenarzt" in 1811 and "Robert" in 1813. He composed symphonies, chamber works, and sonatas with great facility.

Peter Joseph von Lindpaintner, another pupil of Winter, became known by "The Vampire," produced in 1829, and the later "Lichtenstein." With him may be mentioned Poissl, Blum, Kuhlau the flutist, and Schnyder von Wartensee.

Karl Gottlieb Reissiger won fame by his "Yelva," "Die Felsenmühle," and "Turandot," which were given soon after Weber's death. He wrote ten masses, and the oratorio "David," as well as chamber works and light piano pieces.

Konradin Kreutzer composed songs, piano pieces, and chamber works, but was best known by his operas. Most successful among the latter were "The Spendthrift" and "The Camp before Granada," both of which are still performed in Germany.

Gustav Albert Lortzing had a rather unsettled youth, much as Weber did. Lortzing was a tenor of some renown, and his operas show a very practical and easy leading of the voices. Most successful among them were "Die beiden Schützen," the humorous "Czar und Zimmermann," "Hans Sachs," "Der Wildschütz," "Undine," and "Der Waffenschmied." A posthumous work, "Regina," was given in 1899 with fair success.

Other names deserving mention are Reuling, Titl, Netzer, and Nicolai.

The work of all these men is now largely relegated to the past.

Even the Weber operas are not often heard outside of Germany. Their merits were such as to win them immense popularity in their day; but the standards of the present demand more advanced librettos and more spicily dramatic music. But if the romantic operas are mostly off the stage, they still contain much that is of value for the concert platform. In many cases their composers were gifted enough; but they cast their material in a form that is now held antiquated. Works by Weber and Spohr are still to be found on the dramatic stage, and are fairly familiar on concert programmes. Weber is especially remembered for the excellence of the overtures to his three great operas. But apart from them the school is little known now. Popular taste, however, is not necessarily a safe guide; and the work that was done by the romantic school should not be forgotten or underestimated.

XV

MENDELSSOHN

FELIX MENDELSSOHN-BARTHOLDY, born in 1809, came of a wealthy and cultivated family, originally Jewish, but adopting Christianity. His grandfather was the famous philosopher and scholar Moses Mendelssohn. His father, the banker Abraham Mendelssohn, used to say, after Felix became known, "Formerly I was rated as the son of my father; now I am considered the father of my son."

There were four children in the family, the eldest, Fanny, being gifted musically. Both she and Felix showed an early aptitude for music, and both possessed what their mother called "Bach-fugue fingers." Both displayed talent in composing, though at that time, for some unknown reason, such gifts were looked at askance in girls. Mendelssohn afterward printed some of his sister's pieces as his own, rather than let them lie in obscurity. But he met with retribution for this on at least one occasion. When he was presented to Queen Victoria, she tried to please him by praising his song "Italy"; but he had to admit, with shame, that this was one of his sister's compositions.

Mendelssohn studied under various good teachers, and even received help from Cherubini while on a Paris trip. By the age of twelve the boy was already a good composer for voice, piano, and other instruments. He admired Beethoven, and especially Bach. Weber influenced him, and Moscheles helped him. The result of all this was that when he was seventeen years old he produced some remarkable compositions. These included a string quartet in B minor, an octet for strings, and the short opera "Camacho's Wedding." But more important than all of the above was the overture to "A Midsummer Night's Dream," — a work of such maturity and dainty charm that no other composer of seventeen years has come anywhere near equalling it.

In 1828, Mendelssohn began the earnest study of Bach's great

"St. Matthew Passion," and soon he organized a performance of the work, which took place at Leipsic. This did much toward bringing all of Bach's music into renewed attention. Mendelssohn was a zealous devotee of Bach; and his own music shows the earlier master's influence.

Soon after this, Mendelssohn made his first trip to the British Isles. His journey to Scotland was especially productive of results; and its effects are seen in many of his compositions, both large and small. He composed many songs in the Scotch style, which he seemed able to assimilate with more success than other Continental composers; while his "Hebrides" Overture (sometimes called "Fingal's Cave") and the Scotch Symphony show the influence of that Northern land on his larger works. When he first visited Fingal's Cave, and saw the sea swishing against the majestic basalt columns under a gray sky, he was so impressed that the scene translated itself into tones for him. On the back of an old envelope he scrawled a theme of twenty measures, which he sent back to his sister as a description of the place; and this theme was afterward used as the opening of his "Hebrides" Overture. Its minor lilt gives a wonderful picture of the waves, echoing the rhythm of the wavelets over the deeper bass of the larger surges in truly inimitable fashion.

Back in Germany, Mendelssohn tried for positions in Berlin, and conducted festivals in Düsseldorf and elsewhere. But his real home was Leipsic. There he became conductor of the Gewandhaus Orchestra, and lived in the most pleasant and useful activity. It was during this period that he performed for the first time Schubert's great symphony in C, which Schumann had discovered at Vienna.

Mendelssohn's charming personality was now winning him many friends. He was full of magnetism and liveliness, besides being kind and tactful. He was eager to do favors for others, and constantly active in their behalf. In his domestic circle he was full of gayety, and this sometimes showed itself in a musical way. After his sister married the painter Hensel, Mendelssohn composed the cantata "Son and Stranger" for a domestic festival. Hensel was very unmusical, so Mendelssohn "tempered the wind to the shorn lamb" by giving him a part consisting of a single note, repeated whenever necessary. Even then, Hensel failed to hit the note correctly; and the little party burst into a storm of merriment at his expense.

Mendelssohn himself married Cecile Jeanrenaud, whom he met at Frankfurt. She was the daughter of a Swiss clergyman. Five children resulted from this union.

A trip to Italy was followed by the composition of the Italian Symphony; but this was not so characteristic as the Scotch work.

As a conductor, Mendelssohn was sunny and cheerful in his readings, but not deep. His style may be shown by his statement that "too slow a tempo was infernal." The bright, rapid character of his own works shows that he was most at home in that vein, and not successful in handling dramatic passages. In his compositions for orchestra he avoided the dramatic vein for the most part. His chief work in that field, the "Ruy Blas" Overture, is not rated as a great success. This overture was the occasion of a rapid piece of work on his part. It was wanted for a certain concert, but he delayed writing it until only a short time was left. Then he completed the work in two days, filling in each measure for all the instrumental parts before proceeding to the next. Composers usually make it a practice to write out the string parts first, with only the most important melodies in the other instruments. The missing parts are filled in last. This method is much easier than the one Mendelssohn adopted for the occasion.

At Leipsic, Mendelssohn composed a long series of important works. There were piano pieces of much value; the oratorio "St. Paul," given in England as well as Germany; the violin concerto, which is still one of the few great examples of its kind; and the effective symphonic cantata known as the "Hymn of Praise." His activity in behalf of teaching resulted in the founding of the great Leipsic Conservatory.

His last large work, the oratorio "Elijah," was conducted by him at Birmingham in 1846, and won a tremendous success.

In connection with this work, Mendelssohn had a narrow escape from plagiarism. When he first wrote the solo, "O rest in the Lord," he set it, note for note, to Leeves' tune of the Scotch song known as "Auld Robin Gray." Composers always have many themes in mind, and in Beethoven's case these themes were transferred to note-books. Mendelssohn had evidently heard the Scotch song, but had forgotten its identity, and he came to regard it as one of his own melodies. When the work was shown to his English friend Horsley, the latter sent Mendelssohn a copy of the song in question; whereupon the composer altered the number by writing the beautiful melody now used.

The work of writing "Elijah" was somewhat wearing to Mendelssohn. He planned a complete revision of the oratorio, while hunting up suitable text for another work, "Christus." In the midst of this task he received word that his sister Fanny had died. There had always been the closest relationship between them; and when Mendelssohn heard the news, he fell in a faint. This shock, in combination with the extra work that he was doing, proved too much for his delicate constitution; and he never recovered his health. He died in 1847.

Mendelssohn was by all odds the most unequal of the great composers. His works seem to show that it is but a step from the sublime to the commonplace, if not the ridiculous. Some of his compositions arouse the liveliest admiration and wonder, while others disappoint all really musical hearers by their trite simplicity.

This strange condition of things may be explained by the fact that Mendelssohn wrote too much. He adopted as his motto the phrase, *Nulla dies sine linea*, meaning that no day should pass without its line, at least, of music. While such constant activity was praiseworthy in its way, the composer could not count upon the presence of his highest inspiration. If genius were only a capacity for taking pains, then Mendelssohn surely earned the title. But in music one expects more than mere work; it must be work of an inspired sort, revealing great ideas and broadening the hearer's mental or emotional vision, before we admit that its composer is a genius. Some of Mendelssohn's music stands the test; but not all.

The so-called "Songs without Words," for piano, show traces of the weaker and more conventional Mendelssohn. These are short piano pieces of much daintiness and charm in their way. They also show a most skilful handling of comparatively simple forms, so that the student will find them of much interest and value. But here and there is a trace of conventionality in their melodies, which makes them seem too simple and sugary. The same defect is found more frequently among the composer's shorter vocal works. Many of his songs are daintily graceful, or sweetly melodious; but some of them are merely fluent without being great.

On the other hand, certain piano works by Mendelssohn are of the utmost excellence. Examples of these are the preludes and fugues, especially the great one in E minor, and the famous "Variations Sérieuses." Both of these works display Mendelssohn's strong points, and are tremendously effective. They show a leaning toward counterpoint that makes their composer a true disciple of Bach. There is not only strength in them, but balance, contrast, and skill. The appeal of such music is in part intellectual. There is something of the idea of design to be grasped, something of formal beauty as well as forceful expression. Mendelssohn was a consummate master of the skill that makes form serve as a potent factor in the sum total of musical greatness. Thus Wagner, whom many critics consider the very antithesis of Mendelssohn, admired the "Hebrides" Overture greatly for these qualities.

Of Mendelssohn's orchestral works, the "Reformation" Symphony contains a great climax on "Ein feste Burg." The Italian Symphony has a fairly conventional first movement, a scherzo with charming horn passages in the trio, a sombre but strong slow movement, and a dashing saltarello close. The Scotch Symphony has a first movement consisting of rapid work in minor, sometimes lightly chattering, but often broadly powerful; it ends with a tone-picture of a storm. Its second movement is the daintiest of light, charming scherzos, with a marked Scotch flavor to its themes. The third movement is more conventionally melodic. The finale, again in minor, shows almost savage power, and certainly suggests the wildness of the Scotch scenery. The interweaving of two clarinet parts just before its coda gives a wonderful touch of brooding loneliness. The coda itself is a broad but rather conventional ending, in major.

Mendelssohn was the first to give importance to the concert overture, making it a more or less definite programme piece apart from any opera or incidental music, such as followed the older overtures. The style of the "Hebrides" Overture, as already intimated, is a union of grace, strength, and skill that is highly artistic. The daintiness of the "Midsummer Night's Dream" Overture cannot be exaggerated. Mendelssohn afterward wrote other music for this play, including the richly beautiful nocturne and the widely known "Wedding March." "Calm Sea and Prosperous Voyage" was another of his overtures that enjoyed great vogue for a time, though

its picture of monotony, followed by favoring winds and a triumphant reception in port, is rather tame in contrast with recent works.

Mendelssohn wrote much chamber music, including string quartets and piano trios of great value. In such pieces he showed all the
requisite skill in balancing and interweaving the parts.

His choral works, however, have made Mendelssohn most widely
known. The two oratorios and the "Hymn of Praise" meet with a
constant welcome. Fragments of an opera, "Die Lorelei," show
some beauty; but his cantatas are far more effective. Of these, such
works as the music to Sophocles' "Antigone" and "Œdipus at
Colonus" show a most solid and strong handling of the voices. In
the sacred field Mendelssohn composed also the cantata "Lauda
Sion," settings of eight psalms, and many motets and anthems.

The chief of those who came under Mendelssohn's influence was
Niels Wilhelm Gade, the Danish composer. Born in 1817, Gade
achieved his first great success in 1840, with the "Ossian" Overture.
He spent five years at Leipsic, and became so devoted to the Mendelssohn style and standard that some critics have nicknamed him
"Mrs. Mendelssohn." Yet his works have enough originality in
them. Even if not so characteristic as Grieg, Gade still shows some
Scandinavian traits in his music, allied to a poetic romanticism. He
became known by his attractive cantatas, such as "The Crusaders,"
"Comala," "Psyche," "The Message of Spring," etc. He composed
also symphonies, overtures, a violin concerto, chamber music, piano
pieces, and songs. But outside of his own country his works are
not often heard.

Hartmann, whose daughter Gade married, deserves mention as a
pioneer in Danish music. Hartmann was much influenced by Spohr
at first. The Hartmann symphonies and overtures are practically
on the shelf. He achieved more success with his four operas, and
smaller works for voice or piano.

Another member of this Danish coterie was Erik Siboni, whose
symphonies, choral works, and chamber music show Mendelssohn's
influence.

Ferdinand Hiller (1811–85) was known in various fields. He composed operas, oratorios, orchestral works, chamber music, piano
pieces, etc. These were marked by technical skill, and had a fair
share of expressive power. But as a whole they lack the vigor of

deep originality. They are in part what is known as "Kapellmeister-musik," — that is, music of only the average routine excellence that an orchestral leader would be expected to show.

William Sterndale Bennett (1816–75) was an intimate friend of Mendelssohn who became famous as a pianist. His works were chiefly for his instrument. They display some skill, and a few analo-gies with Chopin, but they lack a deep appeal. Bennett composed also an oratorio, "The Woman of Samaria," and a pastoral, "The May Queen."

Moritz Hauptmann was a Mendelssohn protégé who was best known by his writings. The same is true of Ernst Richter, though the latter composed instrumental works and the oratorio "The Redeemer."

Ignaz Moscheles, the pianist, became another of the Leipsic group. His compositions are piano solos or concertos.

Ferdinand David, the violinist, who was made concert-master of the Gewandhaus Orchestra, composed much for violin, but wrote also in the larger forms.

Julius Rietz was a 'cellist who assisted Mendelssohn at Düssel-dorf. He composed overtures, symphonies, and smaller works.

Karl Reinecke was a Mendelssohn pupil who became well known to many Americans as a teacher of composition. He conducted the Leipsic Orchestra for thirty-five years, following Mendelssohn's standards. As composer he wrote symphonies, overtures, concertos, chamber works, and many smaller pieces. His "Nut-cracker and Mouse-King" music is a charming example of mock-heroic fairy music.

Salomon Jadassohn, whose works on harmony and counterpoint have caused hard labor for many music students, was another versa-tile composer. He wrote orchestral and chamber works, but his most interesting productions are his sets of canons and other contrapuntal pieces. His skill in writing canons earned him the nickname of "the musical Krupp."

Franz Lachner (1803–90) was of more importance in his day. He knew Beethoven, and was a prominent member of the "Schubert-iades." He was active as a conductor at Vienna and Munich. He wrote symphonies, chamber music, oratorios, and operas, including "Catarina Cornaro" and "Benvenuto Cellini." But he is best known because of his orchestral suites. The old suites of Bach's day were sets of dances. In Lachner's hands the suite became a set of movements not unlike those of the symphony, but somewhat more informal in style. One of these suites contains a well-known march and an admirable orchestral fugue.

Wilhelm Taubert was another Mendelssohn disciple. His compositions include symphonies, overtures, chamber works, and incidental music to various plays.

With the exception of Lachner, all of these men were more or less directly influenced by Mendelssohn. Lachner was a conservative whose works placed him in line with the others. Lachner was so opposed to the freedom of the growing Wagnerian movement that he gradually withdrew from composition after 1865. All these men worked along the lines of fairly strict form. They did not always display deep inspiration; but they possessed the learning and skill demanded by the classical style, and in many instances their works were sufficiently great to win and hold public esteem.

XVI

SCHUMANN

ROBERT SCHUMANN was born in 1810 at Zwickau, in Saxony. The son of a bookseller and a doctor's daughter, he inherited literary taste from his father and a vein of deep sentiment from his mother. His early education was rather desultory, though he showed an aptitude for music, becoming a pianist and organizing a school orchestra. When he was sixteen his father died, and his mother decided to make him a lawyer. But at this time he acquired a vein of dreaminess, and a devotion to the mystic writings of Jean Paul, that did not exactly promise legal success. He was sent to Leipsic to study law; but he showed much more interest in the piano lessons that he took from Friedrich Wieck. He was greatly devoted to Schubert's works, and became known himself for his power in improvising. He was finally sent off to Heidelberg, and after that to Italy. But at last what he called the "twenty-years' war" ended in his favor, and he was allowed to devote himself to music.

At this time Schumann was rather opposed to theoretical studies. He held that a composer could write well by instinct. While he had to alter his opinion of the value of such studies, he never thoroughly mastered orchestration, and the instrumental colors of his orchestral works are often very muddy. At this time Schumann was practising to be a great pianist; and all his musical ideas occurred to him in a pianistic form, even later in life. While Schubert thought vocally, and Beethoven orchestrally, Schumann unconsciously fitted everything to the piano keyboard. The result is shown in the fact that his symphonies show less loss of effect than almost any others when transcribed for piano.

Schumann tried to strengthen the weak fourth fingers of his hands by means of a pulley-and-weight device. As a result, he lamed one of his fingers so badly that he had to give up all thoughts of becoming a great performer. But his loss, as he considered it, was the world's gain; for the accident turned him to composition, and led him into bringing forth many beautiful works. Schumann then began the theoretical studies that he had previously held in such contempt; and the mistakes in his early harmony exercises prove that he was in need of training.

Soon after these events Schumann entered the critical field, founding the paper known as the "Neue Zeitschrift für Musik." This "New Paper on Music" is still flourishing. At first it fulfilled a valuable mission; for the fetters of classicism were being discarded by the freer school of romanticists, of which Schumann himself was a leader. The greatness of the classical masters remained undimmed; but Schumann and his comrades were ready to give due appreciation to new styles, and prevent the old forms from becoming a clog on originality. Thus while Mendelssohn composed with one eye on the past, Schumann looked more to the future. Of Chopin he wrote, "Hats off, gentlemen! A genius!" He spoke of the piano sonatas of Brahms as "veiled symphonies," — a term that has been used to describe the last five sonatas of Beethoven. He also knew and encouraged Wagner.

He had already begun composing, and was getting known as a writer of piano pieces. These ranged from his variations in honor of Fräulein Abegg, which used the letters of her name as a musical theme, to the varied and attractive group of little tone-pictures known as the "Carnival." The latter, written in 1835, was dedicated to Ernestine von Fricken, a fellow pupil of his to whom he was much devoted at the time. Her native village of Asch was hinted at again and again in the work, by the use of the notes A, Es (E-flat), C, and H (our B-natural). The pieces consist of little ballroom pictures, such as the "Promenade," "Valse," "Aveu," or "Reconnaissance"; hints at masqueraders, such as Arlequin, Pierrot, or Colombine; and even tonal descriptions of real characters, such as Chopin or Chiarina, the latter being Clara Wieck, who afterwards became his wife.

Schumann's courtship of Clara Wieck, and their subsequent devotion to each other, have been so minutely described that many people believe she was his only love. But his thoughts were evidently elsewhere when he wrote the "Carnival." His admiration was so pronounced that Ernestine von Fricken afterwards complained of his desertion, and acted as though a breach-of-promise suit would be in order.

SCHUMANN

One of the false stories in musical history has woven itself about the Schumann piece known as "Warum" ("Why"), which is one of a set of eight great fantasy-pieces. This "Why," with its questioning upward cadence, was considered an inquiry as to why Friedrich Wieck should oppose Schumann's love for his daughter Clara, which began to show itself in 1836. Whoever made up the story claimed also that this piece moved Wieck to withdraw his opposition. But the story seems to exhibit a total disregard for facts.

In the first place, the piece was dedicated to another fellow student, the Scotch pianist Anna Robena Laidlaw; and Schumann wrote to her concerning the music, and various other matters. In the second place, Wieck did not withdraw his opposition to the match, and opposed it until Schumann brought a successful lawsuit against him, restraining him from further opposition without cause.

As a matter of fact, there is romance enough in Schumann's love and marriage without importing any falsehoods or exaggerations.

Clara Wieck was born in 1819. She grew up to be a famous pianist, and at first was something of a child prodigy. When she was seventeen, Schumann's intimacy with her began to ripen into love, and the two came to an understanding. Since her youth and his poverty made it necessary for them to wait, he set about making a career in earnest. He went to Vienna to seek a better opening, but that gay capital did not appreciate the dreamy, poetic composer. He gave some lectures which resulted in a doctor's degree from a university. Also he worked at his periodical until it became reasonably successful. After all this he had to resort to law to make Wieck consent; but he was successful, and the marriage took place in 1840.

Clara Schumann was a faithful helpmeet, inspiring her husband to do his best work, and making his piano pieces known to the public by frequent performances. She outlived him for many years; but she always considered it a sacred duty to bring his compositions into popular notice. During his life she was more of a public figure than the composer himself. When the pair once visited a certain court, where she played, one of the noble auditors, after praising her execution, turned to her husband, and asked, "Are you, too, musical?"

The year after Schumann's marriage was marked by great activity on his part. At this time he translated his happiness into the beautiful song-cycles entitled "Poet's Love" and "Woman's Love and

Life." He wrote also his joyous First Symphony, a triumphant work of much beauty.

In 1842 he was busy at his chamber music, and in the next year he began his larger vocal compositions. After this he suffered a nervous breakdown from overwork. Moving from Leipsic to Dresden, where he gradually recovered, he became intimate with Hiller, and grew to know Wagner. He gradually resumed his own work, finishing the opera "Genoveva" and his "Faust" Cantata. A trip to Düsseldorf resulted in his beautiful Rhine Symphony, the third of his four, though perhaps the manuscript of the fourth was completed at an earlier date.

In 1853 the composer's mental malady took fresh hold upon him. He attended spiritualist meetings, and insisted that Beethoven was trying to communicate with him by knocks in the rhythm of the figure that begins the Fifth Symphony. He continually heard the note A sounding in his ears; and he thought that certain themes were brought to him by spirits. One of these themes, which he wrote down, was used by Brahms in the variations that end with a funeral march. Feeling that his reason was going, Schumann tried to drown himself. The last two years of his life were passed in an asylum at Endenich. He died in 1856.

The romance and poetry of Schumann's nature showed themselves most admirably in his music. But in place of the excessive emotion of Chopin, Schumann's works usually show a hearty, healthy enthusiasm that carries all their auditors by storm. Less skilled in technique than Mendelssohn, and much less gifted in counterpoint, he showed a far deeper and more vital inspiration. His works seem to combine earnest thoughtfulness and depth of feeling with a joyous strength. In his reviews, and in the "Carnival," Schumann distinguished two sides of his character, the dreamy and poetic nature being named Eusebius, while his more impatient and fiery side was called Florestan. A judicial blend of the two he christened Meister Raro. The distinction is one that does not apply to Schumann's works except in a few cases.

The depth and power of Schumann's music was not at first appreciated. Liszt, to be sure, called him "the greatest music thinker since Beethoven." Wagner, however, said patronizingly that Schumann "had a tendency toward greatness." Mendelssohn did not appreciate Schumann properly, though the two were associated for a time in Leipsic. The public, especially the English public, understood Mendelssohn's grace and skill, but was slow in comprehending the expressive warmth of Schumann. Chorley was noticeably bitter against Schumann, speaking of his music as "the broken-crockery school." Mendelssohn himself must be held somewhat to blame for Chorley's abuse. A word would have stopped it, but Mendelssohn did not utter that word.

Among the best of Schumann's piano works are the "Papillons," a toccata, the "Carnival," the "Fantasiestücke," three sonatas, a set of "Novelettes," and the great variations known as the "Études symphoniques." He wrote many short pieces, such as the "Kinderscenen," containing the familiar "Träumerei." His chamber music includes a great piano quartet and quintet, three trios, two violin sonatas, and many other pieces for solo instrument with piano. His longer vocal works include the opera "Genoveva" (with a beautiful overture), the cantata "Faust," "Paradise and the Peri," "The Pilgrimage of the Rose," etc. In this field also is his charming "Manfred," which is partly melodramatic. A melodrama, as already explained, consists of spoken words against a musical background. In this case there is only one reader, who recites many of the selections chosen from Byron's poem. But it is possible to have various characters, and to give actual spoken plays in this form.

Schumann's songs are in many cases the most enthusiastic outpouring of emotional warmth. Less varied in style than Schubert's, they strike a fuller note of feeling. There are almost two hundred and fifty of them, varying from the melting lyricism of "Woman's Love and Life" to the more narrative vein of such ballads as "Blondel's Song," or "The Two Grenadiers." So intense is their emotion that in many cases they seem to pulsate with the warmth of life itself.

The Schumann symphonies, though not always well orchestrated, are gloriously spirited works. The first of them has a rushing, rhythmic first movement, a contemplative, slow movement, a strong, brusque scherzo, and a finale that alternates with strong chords a rapid, chattering theme of rare brightness. The Second Symphony has a slow, broad introduction, followed by rapid chord-themes; a quiet slow movement; a strongly rushing scherzo; and a finale full of grand chord effects. The Third, or Rhenish, Symphony has a triumphantly joyous first movement; a scherzo-like movement that is redolent of half-humorous Rhine-wine songs; a slow movement of expressive charm; a church service suggesting Cologne Cathedral; and a varied, animated chord-finale, representing the pleasant intercourse of the people after the service. The Fourth Symphony strikes a new note for Schumann, varying strong minor effects with exotic orientalism. Its first movement, after a striking introduction, has minor themes of almost wild power, with a contrasted middle part in major, and a gloriously triumphant coda; the slow movement seems Oriental in its odd harmonies and languorous style; the third movement is again a brusque scherzo; while the finale, in spite of some conventional moments, brings renewed suggestions of power.

Schumann's influence has been very great. While Mendelssohn excelled him in popularity during their lives, time has brought an appreciation of Schumann's strength of expression. His music has been an inspiration to many composers, not only in his own country, but in Scandinavia and Russia also. He has come in for some abuse at the hands of the extreme French modernists; but as they rely too much on an ultra-refined delicacy of effect, it is evident that they do not understand the value of his music, and do not appreciate the qualities of emotional breadth and vigor that pervade it.

The most prominent name associated with Schumann's is that of Robert Volkmann (1815–93), who came to Leipsic in 1836, and studied with Schumann. Volkmann taught at Prague and Pesth, the atmosphere of the latter place giving some of his works a Hungarian gypsy flavor. He composed symphonies, overtures, string-serenades, chamber music, and various vocal works. His overture to "Richard III" has enjoyed a fair amount of popularity. But it contains a decided anachronism, in the shape of the tune "The Campbells are comin'." A Scotch tune hardly fits an English battle-field; but when one remembers that the tune in question was composed a hundred years or so after the battle of Bosworth Field, the melody begins to seem decidedly out of place. But this blunder does not detract from the dramatic power of the work.

Friedrich Kiel (1821–85) lived in Berlin, but followed the leadership of the Leipsic coterie. He composed an oratorio, "Christus," and many other sacred works. He also wrote much chamber music. In style he was conservative, following Mendelssohn as much as Schumann.

Théodore Gouvy was of French birth, and lived much at Paris. His works, however, belong with those of the romanticists, and were appreciated most in Germany. He composed seven symphonies, two overtures, a number of chamber works, an opera, and other vocal productions.

Karl Graedener (1812–83) was a 'cellist at Kiel and Vienna. He composed two symphonies, a piano concerto, and much chamber music, including admirable violin sonatas and 'cello sonatas. He was best known by his songs, choral works, and piano pieces, which were Schumannesque in style. He showed a keen sense of form, and a good command of harmonic richness.

Woldemar Bargiel (1828–97) was another composer who showed the Schumann influence plainly, though he did not have much personal contact with the Leipsic master. Bargiel's works include a symphony, three overtures, some chamber works, and many shorter pieces. Bargiel was a stepbrother of Clara Schumann. Incidentally, Madame Schumann fits into this list because of her piano works.

Other orchestral composers who belong with Schumann as disciples or imitators are Julius Otto Grimm, who wrote symphonies and canons for strings at Münster; Albert Dietrich, whose symphony and cantatas were produced at Oldenburg; Richard Wuerst, who produced orchestral, chamber, and operatic works in Berlin; and Ludwig Meinardus, who wrote symphonies, but was best known by his choral works.

Heinrich Dorn was a Berlin composer who wrote orchestral pieces, but was best known by his operas. These were a belated offshoot of the Weber school. Dorn, however, did not approve of the Wagnerian movement, though in many ways it was an outgrowth of the Weber school.

Theodor Kirchner was a protégé of Schumann who became known by his short piano pieces. He composed also some chamber music, and a number of songs.

Schumann's chief disciple in the song field was undoubtedly Adolf Jensen (1837–79). Studying in Russia and with Gade, he planned to take lessons of Schumann, but was prevented by ill health. He was always poor, and was troubled by consumption, which finally carried him off. Jensen was an enthusiast who could hardly stop when he started to play over the world's masterpieces for himself. As a result, he paid for long sessions of Wagner's music by many hours of pain. Jensen composed large works, such as the posthumous opera "Turandot," the cantata "Jephtha's Daughter," and a "Gaudeamus" set to Scheffel's words. His songs are gems of the *Lied* school, and show a warmth of feeling much like that of Schumann. His piano works are very beautiful and fluent, though not vigorous. The charming "Bride-Song," one of his best-known pieces, is one of a set of four-hand music, which includes also a wedding march, a dance-like "Reigen," and a nocturne.

Carl Banck was another song composer who followed Schumann. Banck's works are unassuming in style, but their grace and charm is well shown by such a lyric gem as his "Abendreigen."

Franz Abt, though not belonging to the Schumann school, deserves mention as being a composer of more popular vein. His songs do not reach the highest level, but they show a fluent smoothness that makes them widely known.

Other song composers who should be named here are Edward August Grell, Karl Curschmann, Friedrich Kücken, Karl Eckert, and Joseph Dessauer.

XVII

CHOPIN

IT is not every composer who can have two centennials of his birth celebrated, in two successive years; but Frederic Chopin achieved this seemingly impossible feat. Many authorities give the date of his birth as March 1, 1809. Some, however, including one or two who ought to have known about it, place the event in 1810. The latter date is probably right.

Chopin was born at Zelazowa Wola, near Warsaw. His father was French, and his mother Polish. From them he seemed to inherit a combination of Parisian grace and elegance with Polish intensity and patriotism. He was one of four children, two of his sisters becoming well-known writers. His father was a successful private school teacher, who imparted an atmosphere of cultivation to the family life.

Chopin at first showed an aversion to the piano. After a time, however, he took lessons under a Bohemian teacher named Zywny. These lessons must have been excellent, for they cured him of his distaste, and enabled him to appear in public when nine years old. Poland idolized him, and Warsaw called him "the new Mozart." Catalani heard his playing when he was ten, and gave him a watch; while the Czar of Russia supplemented this gift with a diamond ring.

Entering the Lyceum, where he became known for high spirits and dramatic talent, he studied composition with Joseph Elsner, and profited greatly by the lessons. In 1826 he issued his first published work, which he had preceded by several dances in manuscript. In the next year he finished his studies, and entered an active musical career.

At this time he was a great admirer of the beautiful Warsaw soprano named Constantia Gladkowska. He dedicated some of his works to her, and stated that she had inspired the adagio of his F minor concerto. But in spite of his feelings, the couple parted quietly enough, with conventional phrases, when he set off to strange lands.

He had played in Vienna with some success; and in 1830, after three great farewell concerts at Warsaw, he started on a longer tour. He spoke of this trip as "going to the United States via Paris." But when we consider how primitive the American conditions were at that time, it was no doubt fortunate for the composer that he never got beyond the French capital. He travelled slowly through various German cities. At Stuttgart he learned that the rebellion of his countrymen had failed, and Warsaw had been taken by the Russians.

At Paris his artistic gifts and aristocratic ways soon brought him into contact with the best circles. He was welcomed by all the great musicians, from the aged Cherubini to the young Liszt. He became very fashionable as a teacher, and charged high prices for his lessons. As he met with some rivalry on the part of Kalkbrenner, he decided to smooth it over by taking some lessons of the latter artist. But when he gave a concert, early in 1832, Mendelssohn said of him, "Chopin is worth twenty Kalkbrenners." But he did not continue his public appearances for long. In a few years his growing weakness interfered with them; and the cool reception accorded to his second concerto made him take a dislike to the concert room.

As a pianist, Chopin showed all the delicacy that one would have expected from a man of his temperament. His fortissimos were far less powerful than those of the average player, to say nothing of Liszt. His gradations of power were thus kept in a fairly limited range. He was not entirely successful as an interpreter of other men's works. But when it came to playing his own, he was unrivalled. His delicate *nuances* of expression gave to his performances the utmost charm. He was an absolute master of *rubato*, — the giving of character to a melody by prolonging some notes at the expense of others, without disturbing the rhythm as a whole. Sometimes, for amusement, Chopin would sit down at the keyboard and rattle off a piece mechanically, as a sort of burlesque; but this procedure was reserved for his intimates.

Late in 1836 Chopin met the authoress George Sand (Madame Dudevant), with whom he lived in close connection for over ten years. Two years after their meeting they passed a winter at Majorca, described in one of Madame Dudevant's books. After that they stayed either at Paris or at Nohant. In Majorca Chopin

CHOPIN

fell ill, and laid the foundations of the consumption that carried him off in after years. Madame Dudevant was rather arbitrary, while he was sensitive and irritable; so it is a wonder that their intimacy lasted for so long. When it was finally ended by her, in 1847, she put him into one of her novels, "Lucrezia Floriani," where he figures as Prince Karol.

Chopin returned alone to his Paris quarters. Back in his old rooms, he began to improvise at the piano. The excitement and frenzy to which he was a prey led him to think that he saw visions. The nobility of his native Poland seemed to march before him in review, as if going into battle. He grew so afraid of his own mental state that he rushed from the room, and was found later wandering about the Paris streets. But the themes that echoed his vision remained in his mind. It is said that they were shaped by him into the great A-flat Polonaise; but probably it was the A-major Polonaise.

The revolution of 1848 found him in England, where he made several private appearances. Returning to Paris, he died there in 1849. He was given an impressive funeral at the Madeleine. Following the Polish military custom of being buried in uniform, he was interred in his concert clothes.

Chopin's music is mostly for piano. Unlike the other great masters, he confined his efforts almost wholly to this single branch of music. His concertos and dances with orchestra are practically piano works with an instrumental accompaniment. His piano trio and 'cello sonata are not among his best works. His songs are sometimes lightly joyous, like "Were I a birdling," but in some instances they are tinged with wild power. Anything connected with his native land moved Chopin to the depths of his heart. An example is found in the song "Poland's Dirge," which is a gloomy threnody of the strongest intensity.

In his piano works as a whole, Chopin introduced the idea of embellishments and refinements, not in their seventeenth-century forms, but as episodes or connecting links in the melodic structure. Little runs, or passages of several grace-notes together, take their place in the design of the piece, and give it an exquisite charm. With Chopin everything must be made poetic and full of feeling. This result is attained in part by the proper use of *rubato* and pedals, and for the rest by interpreting and expressing the sentiment that glows in the music itself. Chopin has been called with justice "the poet of the piano."

With Chopin, music was a matter of emotion almost wholly. He did not devote himself to the learned elaboration of figures or balancing of the stricter forms. With him music was always to be free, plastic, and expressive. Emotion was the chief thing with him, whether it proved to be dreamy and languorous or fiery and heroic. Field, noting this excess of emotion, spoke of Chopin as "a talent for the sick-room." But Chopin is not usually morbid. His sentiment is not sentimentality, his feminine qualities not effeminate. His pathos and intensity are Polish, his ethereal delicacy French in style.

Perhaps the most splendid of Chopin's works is the great A-flat Polonaise. The title marks it as one of the stately dances of Poland, originating when the nobles paraded before John Sobieski after his victory over the Turks. Chopin's work, which is his Op. 53, is known as the "Heroic Polonaise," and demands a pianist of the first rank for its interpretation. The work is both impassioned and majestic, and its broad sweeps of expressive power make the musical auditor lose himself in admiration. Of the dozen or more polonaises by Chopin, that in F-sharp minor, Op. 44, is another great work; while the "Military Polonaise," in A, is shorter, but impetuously enthusiastic.

Comparable with the polonaise for excellence is the sonata, Op. 35, in B-flat minor. The work consists of four movements, — an opening allegro, a scherzo, the well-known funeral march, and a short but rapid finale. In the true sense of the word the work is not a good sonata; it does not aim to employ figure treatment and development as its chief resource. But it is wonderfully beautiful. The melodic and expressive themes of the first two movements form an admirable foil to the sombre gloom of the funeral march. The latter is even more widely known than the sonata as a whole; though the prim and formal Mendelssohn said of the march, "I abhor it." The unrest of the finale is a fitting close for the work.

In point of numbers, the mazurka seems to have been Chopin's favorite form. He wrote over fifty of these dances. The mazurka, or masurek, is a popular Polish dance, which Chopin must have seen often in the country. It was in $\frac{3}{4}$ time, and was often accented by a little kick on the second beat of the measure. Chopin brought to the form an infinite variety of expression. So full of nuance and suggestiveness were his mazurkas that he himself, it is said, never played them twice alike. These were the works that he would sometimes parody by giving them with exaggerated mechanical exactness.

Chopin's nineteen nocturnes are for the most part musical gems of the first water. He did not invent the form, but he perfected it, and brought to it an intensity of passionate feeling that remains unequalled. There is a sadness about them that is sometimes morbid; but often there is also the rarest beauty. In the nocturnes the feminine note of Chopin's nature is sometimes over-emphasized; but usually it lies with the performer to prevent them from becoming too sentimental. Probably the most popular of them all is the one in G-major, Op. 37, no. 2. The melodic character of this work is so rich as to be almost too sensuous.

Highly varied and very expressive also are Chopin's twenty-five preludes, which form a set except for the last one. These are nearly all of the smallest dimensions; but their contents are pregnant with meaning.

The two dozen or more études are another mine of tonal richness. They are more than their title implies; for they are not only technical works, but studies in expression as well. Huneker calls them a "series of palpitating music-pictures"; while Kullak says that in these pieces Chopin "pours forth the entire fulness of his transporting poesy."

With the ballades, four in number, we come again to a larger and freer form. The one dedicated to Schumann is especially melodious, and full of strong contrasts.

Chopin, like Kullak, made the scherzo a separate piano form. Chopin wrote four works of this sort.

Among Chopin's other compositions the beautiful "Berceuse" deserves high rank. He composed also impromptus, fantasies, and a barcarolle. His fifteen valses are full of the most captivating grace. Avoiding conventionality, they are too expressively varied to be suitable for actual dancing.

Associated with Chopin for a time was Stephen Heller (1815–88), who was known for many years as a pianist. Like Chopin, he had a very sensitive temperament, that made concert appearances something of a trial for him. He wrote several hundred short piano pieces of various sorts, — ballades, nocturnes, études, and so on.

John Field, who sneered at Chopin, did not differ so greatly in style from the Polish master. He wrote several concertos, and a number of solo pieces, but is best known now by his nocturnes for piano. These are full of delicate sentiment, and seemed to foreshadow the more passionate outpourings of Chopin.

Kalkbrenner's use of a guide bar to support the wrist is mentioned in the chapter on "Famous Pianists," in this volume. His conceit was somewhat excessive, and Chopin's taking lessons of him resulted from his rather brazen offer to teach the Polish performer. Kalkbrenner wrote fluent concertos, sonatas, and other works, and played with smoothness. These men, with Czerny, Moscheles, Tomaschek, and other masters of still earlier date, brought piano playing to a high level. But the works of Chopin were the first that showed the full capabilities of the instrument in emotional expression.

The pianists who flourished in the middle of last century (see chapter on "Famous Pianists") included such famous names as Henselt, Herz, Thalberg, and Dreyschock. Henselt practised for large stretches, and devised exercises for that purpose. He composed a concerto, a number of études, and other solos. Thalberg had great technique, but devoted himself largely to salon music. Dreyschock played his own pieces for the most part, and they were showy rather than deep. Herz, too, wrote and played works that were brilliant, but shallow.

The term salon music, in its strict sense, implies music suited for the drawing-room. It signifies also music that is not of the highest type, requiring serious attention, but is aimed merely to please in a more or less superficial manner. This is not equivalent to saying that salon music is necessarily trashy. It does, however, lack the depth and earnestness of the master works. Salon pieces are not necessarily easy to compose; and in many cases they show much skill and dexterity, or real expressive power. A number of salon music composers are now mentioned.

Albeniz, who died in 1855, was active at Madrid for many years. Leybach, who was an organist at Toulouse, became known by his nocturnes, of which the fifth is still widely popular. Litolff, the well-known publisher, wrote some salon music, but attempted also concertos and other large forms. Bovy, sometimes writing as Lysberg, became famous at Geneva. Alkan (Morhanges) became known at Paris by his études and other works. Jacques Blumenthal was pianist to Queen Victoria. Gobbaerts composed many light, short pieces at Brussels. Eugene Ketterer became known by his popular dances.

In our own country, Louis Moreau Gottschalk deserves mention. Born at New Orleans in 1829, he probably inherited musical taste from his Creole mother. Studying in Paris and elsewhere, he soon became known as a pianist. But his fame rests chiefly on his compositions, which are light in a way, but very characteristic and effective in suggesting their titles. His "Bamboula" reproduces the turmoil of that Negro dance. His "Bananier" and "Savane" have an inimitable southern flavor. His "Banjo" echoes the sounds of the plantation darkies very daintily. "Ojos Creolas" displays a romantic style. "The Last Hope" is a pathetic picture inspired by a mother's death just before the desired return of an absent son. "Ossian" consists of two richly poetic bits of bardic utterance. These may well serve as a type of salon music. There is here none of the development of the sonata, or the studied intricacy of the fugue. Instead, there are light, but pleasing melodies, and harp-like sweeps of rich harmony.

On the whole, however, salon music covers a multitude of sins. While it may include works of interest and value, it offers room also to the tawdry effects of many commonplace pieces, or the conventional triviality of popular dances. Strictly speaking, many of the great composers have written salon pieces. The shorter bits of Beethoven, such as the "Six Bagatelles," or the "Träumerei" of Schumann, or some of the melodic bits of Schubert, show the simplicity of style and the popular appeal that is a characteristic of salon music. Yet if a composer uses nothing higher than that style, he can hardly be reckoned as a master.

XVIII

ITALIAN OPERA

WHILE Germany had added to the earlier names of Bach and Handel the more recent ones of Haydn, Mozart, Beethoven, Schubert, and Weber, Italy produced no genius of the first rank. A certain decadence had begun to show itself in Italian music. The works of the Scarlattis, Lotti, or even Cimarosa, no longer appealed to the people of Italy, and public taste in that country began to be satisfied with something far simpler in style. It was this decadence of Italian taste that led Von Bülow to remark, "Italy was the cradle of music, — and remained the cradle." Instead of keeping abreast of German classical development, Italy shut her ears to the geniuses of the north, and turned her attention to a school of bright but rather trivial melody. This musical isolation lasted until within a few decades.

Gioachino Antonio Rossini, who led the movement toward this popular style of opera, was born at Pesaro in 1792. His father was town trumpeter, and his mother a baker's daughter. He studied singing and horn-playing at home. Entering the conservatory at 15, he took up counterpoint under Mattei; but he had no patience with such serious work, and gave it up as soon as he had developed his facility in the lighter vein. He studied the music of Haydn and Mozart until he was nicknamed "the little German"; but he imitated their orchestration and fluency rather than the worth of their style.

Rossini wrote his first stage work for Venice, in 1810. This was followed by an *opera buffa* at Bologna, and an *opera seria* at Rome. His career was now a busy one. For the next ten years he brought out no less than thirty operas, in such diverse cities as Rome, Venice, Naples, Milan, and Lisbon. His first work of any value was "Tancredi," given in 1813. During this period he composed also his "Barber of Seville," brought out at Rome, in 1815. This bright comedy, which has done more than any other opera to keep his name alive, was disliked at first, partly because it treated a subject already used by Paisiello. "Otello," produced in 1816, marks the transition from an older recitative style to a smoother and more melodic vein. His "Cenerentola" proved itself another admirable comedy, while "Mosé in Egitto" was afterwards changed into oratorio form.

Rossini's facility in composition is shown by a joke that he played upon a Venetian manager. When the latter gratified an old grudge by forcing the composer to set the poor libretto of "I due Bruschini," Rossini retaliated by putting all kinds of tricks into the score. Thus the second violins began each measure in the overture by tapping on their lamp-shades; the bass was given high passages, and the soprano forced as low as possible; a comical scene was suddenly interrupted by a funeral march; and the words were so arranged in the choruses that a ludicrous jumble of syllables resulted. This opera was naturally retired after one night.

A revolution at Naples in 1820 started Rossini on a trip to Vienna. There, at Prince Metternich's request, he wrote some bright cantatas, and in 1823 produced "Semiramide."

After a short journey to London, he became director of the Théâtre Italien, in Paris. There he revived his old works, and brought out "Il Viaggio a Reims." In 1826 he was named royal composer, with a salary. At Paris Rossini was influenced by the excellent standards in vogue, and he even began to study seriously the works of Beethoven. The result is shown in his "William Tell" (1829) which is written in a far more lofty style than his earlier and more conventional works. It was a worthy member of the series of operas composed by Cherubini, Spontini, and in later days Meyerbeer.

Rossini made a contract to bring out more operas, one every two years at least. But his plans for developing himself in his better style were brought to naught by the revolution of 1830, after which his contract and royal post were abrogated. Then he heard a Meyerbeer work in 1836, and decided not to compete with the new leader. The result was seen in the fact that he composed nothing more for the stage, though he lived until 1868.

Rossini is a clear example of the bad influence of popular taste on a really capable composer. Had he lived in Germany, he would pretty surely have striven to reach the German standards of classicism. But in a country where the public applauded only a tawdry and conventional style of melody, there was no incentive for the composer to develop himself beyond that level. The improvement that Rossini made in Paris shows very definitely that he was capable of higher things than the conventional singing-concerts which form most of his stage works.

Rossini, like Handel, was not above adapting themes from others. Like Handel in another respect, he transferred many pieces from his own early works. In a conversation about his mass, Rossini once began to explain where its numbers had been borrowed; and the list ranged all the way from "Aureliano" to "Semiramide."

The *opera seria*, or tragic opera, was the most conventional affair imaginable. The inanities of this school gave rise to the remark, "Whatever is too silly to be spoken may be sung." In *opera seria* no attention was paid to the principles of dramatic fitness, which Gluck had evolved. While the form was not so rigid as in the days of Handel, it was still a matter of certain conventional solos and ensembles, and a great deal of *bravura* display. The soprano had to have her *scena*, often a mad scene, in which she was allowed to indulge in all kinds of trills, runs, and vocal display. She was almost always in love with the tenor, and pursued by the bass. For some reason the bass singer was usually cast as a villain, who wished to win the soprano's regard, but could think of no better method than persecuting her. Wagner broke through this stereotyped custom, and gave the hero's part to a basso in his "Flying Dutchman."

In comedy, a more natural tone prevailed. The *opera buffa*, for some reason, was unhampered by traditions, and grew into spontaneous excellence. Its dramatic structure was admirable, its music suitable.

Vincenzo Bellini (1801–35) was the son of an organist at Catania, from whom the boy took his first lessons. When he reached the age of eighteen, a patron sent him to Naples, where he studied for several years. He wrote a number of student works, including a symphony and his first opera. He paid attention to both German and Italian models, and was especially interested in Pergolesi. The opera manager Barbaja saw that the young man was really gifted, and at length began to order operas from him. "Il Pirata" (1827) was a great success, though the favorable result was probably due to

Rubini's singing in the chief part. At present, an opera is regarded as an art-work in which the composer must do something worth while, so that a single singer could not now make a poor work succeed. But the Italians of a century ago cared for little beyond smooth melodies well sung.

Of Bellini's dozen or so of operas, three became far better known than the rest. These three were "Norma," "I Puritani," and "La Somnambula." The first is based on a Druidic subject, and has a sufficiently dramatic libretto. Its music is fluent, and not lacking in effects of real breadth. Most famous among its numbers is Norma's great solo of prayer and renunciation, "Casta Diva." "I Puritani" deals with Cromwell's times, although its conventional story of love and jealousy is hardly Puritanical. This work allowed a tremendous success to be made by the so-called "Puritani" quartet of singers, — Grisi, Rubini, Tamburini, and Lablache. For many years they kept the work before the public at Paris. "La Somnambula" treats a Scribe libretto, dealing with complications that result from the sleep-walking of its heroine, Amina. Her final outburst of joy, "Ah, non giunge," is another great favorite with soloists.

Bellini did not enter the field of comic opera, and in his tragedies he did not show the versatility of Rossini. But if he lacked some of the brilliance of his rival, he atoned for it by breadth of effect. His melodies are often tenderly pathetic in style, with much sincerity, and occasionally broad sweeps of feeling. When the standards of the day are kept in mind, it will be seen that Bellini's operas showed considerable tragic solemnity.

Gaetano Donizetti (1797–1848) was born at Bergamo. He received early training from Mayr and Mattei. For a time he entered the army, to avoid being forced into the law. But he soon began to compose operas, and in 1822 his "Zoraide de Granada" procured him an honorable discharge.

The first ten or twelve years of his work were devoted to rather frank imitations of Rossini, without much individuality. By 1830 Donizetti had composed about thirty operas, though none of them showed great merit. But with "Anna Bolena" (1832) his more distinctive period began.

The works by which Donizetti is best known are three tragedies and three comedies. The former are "Lucrezia Borgia," "Lucia di

Lammermoor," and "Linda di Chamounix," while the latter consist of "La Fille du Régiment," "Don Pasquale," and "L' Elisir
d' Amore."

The tragedies have all the faults of their school. While their brilliant solos captivated the audiences of their day, their music is now
seen to have no especial dramatic meaning. These tragedies, like
those of Rossini's earlier styles, show not the faintest approach to
the real dramatic possibilities of opera, as exploited by Gluck. They
are merely groups of singable melodies, with little or no connection
between them and the dramatic situation or the sense of the words.
Their rather disconnected numbers have been likened to a string of
separate pearls; but even the single gems were not of the first water
when compared with those made in Germany.

In the comedies, far better conditions prevail. The music is not
only tuneful, but brightly humorous in character, and well suited to
the needs of the different situations. "La Fille du Régiment" has
for its hero a Tyrolese peasant, named Tonio, who enters the regiment to win the love of its pretty *vivandière*, Marie. Adopted by the
regiment when a foundling, Marie finds that she is the daughter of a
marquise, who carries her home; but Tonio, becoming colonel, traces
Marie, and finally wins her. "Don Pasquale" deals with an old man
of that name who wishes to cut off his nephew's expectations by
making a second marriage. The nephew, Ernest, persuades his
sweetheart Norina to try to captivate the elderly wooer. She charms
him at first, but after a mock marriage she pretends to turn shrew-
ish and extravagant. Don Pasquale is made to hate the idea of marriage before he is told that the wedding was not real. "L' Elisir
d' Amore" treats the story of a love potion bought from a conjuror
by the villager Nemorino. With the aid of this, and various events,
he succeeds in winning his sweetheart, in spite of the fascinations of
a visiting sergeant.

The vivacity and charm of the music in these comedies wins high
praise even now. No allowance need be made in their favor because
of changing standards; they hold their own to-day with scarcely less
vigor than when they were first produced. While the tragedies of
the Italian school seem thin and inartistic, the comedies are still
models in their particular line.

A number of composers were active at the beginning of Rossini's career. While none of them were geniuses, they often scored great local successes in various Italian cities.

Giuseppe Mosca brought out his first opera at Rome in 1791. He is said to have invented an effective method of handling crescendos, which Rossini afterward borrowed. His brother Luigi was another opera composer.

Vittorio Trento won considerable attention in London, between 1797 and 1804. His greatest success was "The Assassins."

Vincenzo Federici was active at Milan and Turin. He followed the style of Cimarosa.

Vincenzo Lavigna wrote several successful operas for Milan, and taught Verdi during the latter's youth.

Stefano Pavesi won success with "I Baccanali," "Ser Marc' Antonio," and "La Donna Bianca."

Giovanni Tadolini divided his time between Italy and Paris, composing operas, songs, and romances.

Pietro Generali, a pupil of Durante, devoted himself to comic operas at Rome. He is classed as the forerunner of Rossini.

Less directly in line with the Rossini school were Paer and Mayr, mentioned elsewhere.

Francesco Morlacchi, composer of sacred works as well as operas, adopted a more Germanic style while choirmaster at Dresden. He too wrote a "Barber of Seville."

Italian composers seem to find opera their most congenial method of expression. Proceeding onward through the nineteenth century, their number increases to large proportions. A partial list includes Carlo Conti ("L' Olympiade"), Antonio Coppola ("Nina"), Lauro Rossi ("Il Domino Nero"), Errico Petrella, Alberto Mazzucato, Teodulo Mabellini ("Rolla"), Alessandro Nini, Achille Peri, and Carlo Pedrotti, who won success with comedies.

Saverio Mercadante survived the Rossini group by many years, but did not rise beyond the limits of its style in tragedy. His successes began with "Elisa e Claudio," in 1821, and included his *magnum opus*, "Il Giuramento," in 1837. He lived until 1870, and composed funeral music for nearly all of his earlier contemporaries.

Giovanni Pacini was a Sicilian by birth. He entered the operatic field in 1813. His best work was "Saffo," produced at Naples in 1840; but he wrote more than three dozen operas after that.

Those who began activity toward the middle of the century included Francesco Chiaromonte, Antonio Cagnoni, the double-bass virtuoso Bottesini, Francesco Schira, Giorgio Miceli, Carlotta Ferrari, and the still later Pietro Platania and Filippo Marchetti. Greece was represented by Spiro Samara and his successor Theophilus Sakellarines.

The two brothers Luigi and Federico Ricci wrote together at times, and made a great success with their joint work "Crispino e la Comare," given at Venice in 1850.

Antonio Carlos Gomez, the Brazilian, was a member of this school, though coming a little after it in point of time. From 1870 on he won attention with his "Il Guarany," "Salvator Rosa," and "Maria Tudor."

Contemporary with Gomez was Amilcare Ponchielli, who studied and composed at Milan. His best work is "La Gioconda," a tale of the love and self-sacrifice of a poor street singer. This holds its place in the repertoire to-day.

Arrigo Boïto, born in 1842, has won fame as an admirable librettist for Verdi. In 1868 Boïto finished his own excellent opera, "Mefistofele." Coming after Gounod's "Faust," it differs from that work in treating both parts of Goethe's great poem. The first scene shows the Prologue in Heaven, with Mephistopheles gaining the Lord's permission to tempt Faust. Then comes the first act, on a square in Frankfort, and in Faust's laboratory. The second act includes the garden scene and the Witches' Sabbath on the Brocken. The third act consists of the prison scene, with Faust returning to find his Marguerite dying. The fourth act shows the Classical Sabbath, on the banks of the Peneus. An epilogue shows Faust in his laboratory, and brings in his ultimate salvation through the happiness he found in working for others.

The music to this great work places it in a more modern category than the date of its completion would indicate. While the majority of Italian composers still followed Rossini or the early Verdi, Boïto blazed a new path for himself, and based his work on the true principles of modern opera. When given with adequate forces, "Mefistofele" is tremendously effective. The choruses of the Cherubim, and the voice of the Lord from behind the clouds, give the prologue a surprising majesty. The first act includes Mephisto's great solo "Son lo spirito." The garden scene is pleasing enough, the witches' revel wildly effective, and the prison duet really beautiful. In the fourth act Helen of Troy has a powerful and dramatic solo; while the epilogue, with its struggle between the powers of good and evil, sustains the dramatic interest well. Boïto has not yet produced a successor to this work, though his "Nero" has been announced many times.

The real Italian leader, however, was Giuseppe Verdi. He was born at Le Roncole, on October 10, 1813, the same year that saw Wagner's birth. Verdi's love for music was displayed at an early age. When a seven-year-old choir-boy, he became so absorbed in listening to the organ that he forgot to hand the holy water to the priest. A kindly musician, Cavaletti, repaired an old spinet, which he gave to Verdi's father because the youngster played so well.

After studying with the local organist, Verdi went to the town of Busseto, where other friends helped him. He was aided especially by the rich merchant Barezzi, who enabled him to study with Provesi and afterward sent the young man to the Milan Conservatory.

There a surprise was in store; for Verdi was rejected by the Milan teacher, Basily. There are several anecdotes telling how he revenged himself afterward by outdoing the conservatory students in fugal and canonic writing. These, however, are probably false; for even in his great "Manzoni Requiem," Verdi rather avoided counterpoint. Verdi studied with Lavigna, and was certainly earnest and diligent enough; for we soon find the merchant-patron allowing his daughter to marry the young composer, before the latter had made a name for himself.

Verdi's first opera, "Oberto di San Bonifacio," was produced at Milan in 1839. This succeeded so well that the manager, Merelli, gave Verdi a contract for three more operas. The first of these was the comedy "Un Giorno di Regno." While he was at work upon it, his wife and his two children died. Under these circumstances he was hardly in the mood for comedy; and it is not surprising to read that the work failed. Verdi was so utterly cast down that he thought of giving up composition; but Merelli finally persuaded him to continue.

The composer's next work was "Nabucco," another success. The soprano who had the chief part, Giuseppina Strepponi, afterward became Verdi's second wife, and lived until 1898.

Other works which Verdi composed at this period include "I Lombardi," "Ernani," "I Due Foscari," "Giovanna d' Arco," "Macbeth," "I Masnadieri," "Luisa Miller," and several more. "Ernani" has lasted better than the others. Based on Victor Hugo's play, it treats a story of romantic power with sufficiently popular music. At this time Verdi understood nothing higher than the style of melodic tragedy introduced by Rossini; but his melodies, even though not aimed to echo the sense of the words, were much stronger than those of Rossini.

"Un Ballo in Maschera," which belongs to a later period, shows how lightly the libretto of an opera was regarded. Verdi's early librettists, Solera and Piave, were veritable slaves, at the beck of composer or manager. In their hands "Macbeth" became so commonplace that Shakespeare would hardly have recognized it. But in the "Ballo in Maschera" (Masked Ball) the incongruities increased at every turn. The libretto dealt with the assassination of a king at the masquerade. When the authorities forbade this as too revolutionary, Verdi made the scribe change the king into the Duke of Mantua. This was not enough to satisfy the police; so Verdi next made a radical change by altering the victim into the "Governor of Boston." One hardly imagines the old Boston Puritans giving masked balls. When the tenor Mario found the costume of the ruler too plain, he altered it into that of a Spanish cavalier.

Verdi at one time attained a peculiar political significance, because of the letters of his name. They stood for "Vittorio Emanuele, Re d' Italia"; and the young patriots who shouted "Viva Verdi" were in reality cheering the idea of a united Italy.

In 1849 Verdi entered upon a new period in his growth. To this belong "Rigoletto," "Il Trovatore," and "La Traviata."

"Rigoletto," the first of the three, has a plot dealing with the intrigues of the Duke of Mantua. His court jester, Rigoletto, has aided him in an amorous adventure, and the friends of the victim revenge themselves by bringing Rigoletto's daughter Gilda to the duke. The jester then hires an assassin, who lures the duke to a lonely house. But the assassin's sister, falling in love with the duke, persuades her brother to substitute another victim in order to earn Rigoletto's money. To cure Gilda of her love for the duke, Rigoletto brings her to see that ruler's attentions to Maddalena. Gilda, fear-ing for the duke's life, rushes in to save him. The assassin then stabs her, and sews the body in a sack, which he gives to her father. The latter opens the sack just in time to receive Gilda's dying blessing.

While the music to this gory tragedy is largely in the old style of Rossini and the early Verdi, it shows traces of growing strength. Rigoletto's fury when the courtiers steal his daughter, and Gilda's love for the duke, are portrayed with the beginnings of real dramatic ability and musical fitness. The opera contains a great quartet, which combines the most diverse emotions into a powerful ensemble. But in its day its most popular number was the light love-song "La donna e mobile." This will show that Verdi's growth was not evoked by Italian taste.

"Il Trovatore," produced at Rome in 1853, is another sanguinary affair. The wicked Count di Luna loves Leonora, but she is in love with the Troubadour Manrico. The count besieges the lovers in their castle, and imprisons Manrico with his supposed mother, the gypsy Azucena. The count threatens to kill his prisoners if Leonora does not agree to marry him. To save their lives, she apparently consents. She tells Manrico of her bargain, but he declines liberty at such a price. She has poisoned herself in the mean time. When Manrico is executed, Azucena tells the count that Manrico was really his long-lost brother, whom she had stolen in revenge for persecution. She is then condemned to be burned.

The music to this sad affair is fluent, and in some places even tawdry; but as a whole, the score shows a wonderful power over melodic expression. Most popular is the well-known "Miserere," sung by Leonora, some hidden monks, and Manrico in his cell. The "Anvil Chorus" of the gypsies is another famous number. Manrico's duet with Azucena is another favorite. There are many effective solo songs, such as the count's aria "Il balen," and Manrico's "Di quella pira." The latter shows that the melodic school of opera is not without its expressive power. On the printed page, this song seems at first sight little better than the conventional melodies of Rossini. But its character is such that the singer can put a tremendous amount of expression into it. This is true in a lesser degree of the entire opera. Verdi was at last awake to dramatic possibilities, though in this work he still clung to the old melodic idiom in expressing them.

"La Traviata" was founded on Dumas' "Camille," with the heroine named Violetta and her lover Alfredo. She leaves him because his father says she will injure his prospects; and he thinks her false. After a meeting at a Paris ball, he learns the truth, but only in time to find her dying. The most famous selections from the score of this work are Violetta's expressive "Ah, fors e lui," and the father's description of home in "Di Provenza il mar." At the first performance, the size of the soprano made the opera a failure; for when the three-hundred-pound singer Donatelli stated that she was dying of consumption, the audience burst into laughter.

Meanwhile Wagner's doctrines had been gradually becoming known, even in Italy. Verdi always disclaimed being influenced by Wagner, but this assertion, though true in the letter, is not true in the spirit. Verdi may not have tried to imitate Wagner's style, but the German master led him to write operas that were far more like the German music-dramas than his earlier works.

"Don Carlos" and "La Forza del Destino" showed Verdi's new tendency; but it reached a much greater perfection with "Aïda," given at Cairo in 1871.

"Aïda," on a plot provided by the Egyptian Khedive, who ordered the work, deals with a story laid in ancient Egypt. At the court, Aïda, a beautiful Ethiopian hostage, falls in love with the officer Rhadames, who returns her love. Rhadames is appointed leader of the force that is to fight the Ethiopian king, whose daughter is Aïda, though her captors do not know of the relationship. The Princess Amneris, who herself loves Rhadames, discovers Aïda's feelings by questioning her. Rhadames brings back the Ethiopian king, Amonasro, as a captive; and he warns Aïda not to betray his identity. On the island of Philæ, Aïda, forced by her father, learns from Rhadames the route of the next expedition. Amonasro then discloses himself, and tries to persuade Rhadames to flee with him and Aïda. While Rhadames is hesitating, the high priest of a near-by temple, brought by Amneris, discovers the trio. Amonasro escapes, but Rhadames is held for judgment. Amneris offers him freedom in exchange for love, but he refuses. He is sealed up in a subterranean vault, into which Aïda has made her way to die with him.

The music of "Aïda" is so fresh, varied, and forceful that the opera is still one of the best drawing cards in the entire repertoire.

CHERUBINI

VERDI

In this work Verdi deserted the simplicity of Italian tunes, and produced a work whose rich harmonies and really expressive melodies were far above anything he had done before. To catalogue the musical excellences of this opera would almost mean giving a description of the entire score; but a few of the chief numbers may be mentioned. In the first act, Rhadames' aria "Celeste Aïda," the chorus of acclamation when he is made leader, Aïda's tragic "Ritorna vincitor," when her lover goes to fight her father, and the consecration service in the temple, are all admirable. The temple scene is based on a real Egyptian melody. In the second act come the dance of the slave-boys before Amneris, her dialogue with Aïda, and in a separate scene the return of the victorious army, the last being one of the most stately scenes in the realm of opera. The third act includes Aïda's foreboding lament, her duet with Rhadames, and the climax of their discovery with Amonasro. The fourth act contains some impressive priests' music, well contrasted with the agitation of Amneris, and in the death scene some fervid snatches of duet, in admirable contrast with the temple service going on above the doomed lovers' heads.

For sixteen years Verdi rested upon his well-earned laurels. Then he produced the tragedy "Otello." Boïto wrote the libretto, and added to it a chain of choruses sung by the Cyprus fishermen bearing gifts to Desdemona, and a sardonic "Credo" of Iago that even Shakespearians admire. While this is not so popular as "Aïda," its music is intensely powerful, and shaped with an eye for tragic effects. Verdi set his own music to the song "Willow," mentioned by Desdemona; but the old English tune, which still exists, would have been more directly expressive.

Six years later, in 1893, Verdi brought out his last opera, "Falstaff," at Milan. Again Boïto was the librettist. This time the play was altered only by the introduction of Falstaff's dissertation on honor, taken from "Henry IV." The libretto as a whole comes from "The Merry Wives of Windsor." Falstaff is made to meet his misadventures, both at Ford's house and at Herne's Oak, in a vein of light sarcasm set to the most delightfully chattering music. As in the play, all ends happily, with Fenton's betrothal to "Sweet Anne Page."

XIX

CHERUBINI AND FRENCH OPERA

LUIGI CARLO ZENOBIO SALVATORE MARIA CHERUBINI, whose name became as famous as it was extensive, was born at Florence in 1760. He was at first trained by his father, a harpsichord player at a local theatre; and afterwards he took a thorough course with Sarti. His life divides itself naturally into three periods, — first, a short career in the conventional Italian style; second, the leadership of opera composition at Paris; and last, a number of years as composer of sacred music and director of the Paris Conservatoire. His lofty style gave point to the saying that he was an Italian who composed German music in France.

In his first period, Cherubini mastered counterpoint, and became familiar with the style and spirit of the old Italian church music.

After a sojourn in London, the young composer made Paris his home, and soon came under the classic spell of Gluck's later operas. Cherubini himself composed an "Ifigenie in Aulide," which was given at Turin in 1788 with much success.

His first Parisian triumph, "Demophon," proved that he had definitely discarded the light Italian style, and adopted something more strongly dramatic. Like Rossini, he was inspired by the traditions of the Parisian stage; but he soon rose to greater heights than Rossini ever reached.

His next French success, "Lodoïska," was brought out in 1791. This work gained for its composer an international reputation. It also cast into the shade the light melodious trifles that were beginning to appear in Paris. In later years, the more superficial works of Boieldieu and Auber became typical of Parisian taste. It is on record that when the former had won plaudits with his "Caliph of Bagdad," Cherubini said to him, "Are you not ashamed to enjoy such an undeserved success?" Boieldieu then studied with Cherubini with good results. In all his career Cherubini was a rather caustic and captious individual, more feared than loved; but he used his critical tongue in defense of a high standard of artistic principle. The libretto of "Lodoïska" was rather weak. It dealt with the efforts of the heroine's lover to rescue her from a powerful rival's castle, and ended with an attack by Tartars that brought about the desired result.

Three years later came "Elisa"; but a far more important work appeared after another three years, in the shape of "Médée." Its dignity and classic power rendered it a masterpiece. It was not popular at first, because it had a rather poor libretto, which placed the interest chiefly with the title rôle, and because its music was rather too harmonic to suit the masses. But it soon grew into popularity.

Cherubini's best-known opera was "Les Deux Journées," given in 1800. This work deals with the fortunes of the Deputy Armand, who has incurred the hatred of Mazarin. The Paris gates are guarded, but Armand escapes in a cask of the water-carrier Mikeli, whose son he had helped on a previous occasion. Once outside, Armand is captured while defending his wife; but a pardon from the queen makes everything end happily. This opera is known in Germany as "The Water-Carrier."

The style of the music to this work, as was true of most of Cherubini's French productions, united a lofty dignity with rare charm of melody and expression. His works, with those of Gluck and others, are often referred to as "classical" opera; but an equally good term, in Cherubini's case at least, would be "symphonic" opera. His scores show the worthiness in material and the skill in its handling that we associate with the great orchestral masters of Germany. Cherubini's overtures, by which he is still known on concert programmes, have all the dignity and power that we expect from the symphonic writers. Especially excellent are the overtures to "Les Deux Journées" and to "Anacréon," which followed the earlier success in three years.

Cherubini was often at odds with Napoleon, who perhaps did not appreciate his music, and in any case did not approve of his independent and arbitrary ways. Cherubini finally found it wise to leave Paris for a time. He went to Vienna, and in 1806 brought out at that capital his last great operatic success, "Faniska." This took Germany by storm; and Beethoven and Haydn praised the work highly.

It is probable that Cherubini served as a model for Beethoven, and helped the German master to develop the strength of expression that he showed in the later part of his second period. But soon Napoleon came thundering at the gates of Vienna, and Cherubini had to move again.

When the Bourbons returned to power, Cherubini was once more in favor at Paris. But his operatic career was over. As Royal Choirmaster and head of the Conservatoire, he devoted himself to sacred music. His works in this field include many admirable short compositions; but his fame rests chiefly on his larger productions, consisting of eleven masses and two superb requiems. He could compose in the pure manner of the Palestrina school, and also show a command of later harmonic expression and dramatic instrumentation. He blended the old with the new in most admirable fashion.

As director of the Conservatoire, he remained active for many years, — in fact, almost down to his death, in 1842. He ruled with a strong hand. His arbitrary decisions led him into several mistakes; for he rejected Liszt and Rubinstein, and sneered at Berlioz. But these were radicals, while he was a conservative. He showed a mastery of his own field by writing an admirable treatise on counterpoint.

Ritter wrote of Cherubini's operas, "They will remain for the earnest student a classic source of exquisite artistic enjoyment, and serve as models of a perfect mastery over the deepest resources and means that the rich field of musical art presents." Fétis said of "Les deux Journées," "There is a copiousness of melody . . . but such is the richness of the accompanying harmony, and the brilliant coloring of the instrumentation . . . that the merit of the melody was not appreciated at its just value." Mendelssohn wrote of "Les Abencerrages," one of the operas, that he could not sufficiently praise "the sparkling fire, the clever, original phrasing, and the unusual delicacy and refinement of the work."

Étienne Nicholas Méhul (1763–1817) was of French birth, and came under Gluck's influence. He played the organ when ten years old, and took up sacred composition soon after. Later on he went to Paris. In spite of the disturbed state of the Revolutionary politics, he soon began to make headway as an opera composer, starting in

1791. He produced nearly three dozen operas, of which "Stratonice," "Adrien," "Uthal," and "Joseph" were the best. "Uthal" was the work that dispensed with violins, and gave the violas prominence to emphasize the sombre nature of its Ossianic subject. Méhul's effects were often broadly impressive. He had not the commanding genius of a Cherubini, but he showed much of Gluck's loftiness of style.

Jean François LeSueur (1760–1837) was at first a choir-boy at Amiens. For many years he devoted his attention to church music, into which he planned to introduce dramatic effects. His first opera was given at Paris in 1793. Less advanced than Méhul or Cherubini, he still sought diligently for new effects. The best of his operas were "Les Bardes" and "La Caverne." His innovations foreshadowed in some degree those of Berlioz, who studied with him.

Jadin, Solié, and Gaveaux were other opera composers of this period.

Cherubini's successor in opera was Gasparo Spontini (1774–1851). Spontini was another Italian who made his career in Paris. But he, too, preceded his Parisian period by Italian works of less importance. He was not rated highly when he first came to Paris; but his one-act opera "Milton" made the critics concede that it showed beauty and feeling. In 1807 came "La Vestale," which scored a tremendous success, and won the special prize offered by Napoleon. This was followed by "Fernando Cortez," produced in 1809 and remodelled later. Both works showed a broad style and much sympathetic expression. Spontini was active as a conductor, and introduced into Paris Mozart's "Don Giovanni," Haydn's symphonies, and other German masterpieces. He became court composer to Louis XVIII, writing many "occasional" stage works for his royal master. In 1819 he produced another opera, "Olympie." He regarded this as his best work, but it made its way rather slowly. In later years Spontini was called to Berlin; but the German romanticism soon drew attention away from him. He tried to regain popularity with "Nurmahal" and "Alcidor," but the librettos of these works were poor. He showed a flash of his earlier grandeur in "Agnes von Hohenstaufen"; but after that he relapsed into obscurity. His genius was lofty, but he lacked variety of style and lightness of touch.

As already recorded, Rossini's "William Tell" belongs to the school of Parisian grand opera.

Another composer who participated in grand opera by a single work was Daniel François Esprit Auber (1784–1871). He was a pupil of Cherubini, whose influence is shown in Auber's early masses and operas. By 1820 Auber became known in connection with opéra comique, which was really his life-work. He associated himself with Eugene Scribe, and set the latter's bright librettos during a period of forty years. But in 1828 he made a successful entry into the Spontini field of historical grand opera, by the production of "Masaniello," sometimes known as "La Muette de Portici." The heroine, Fenella, is dumb. She has been betrayed by Duke Alphonso; but when her brother Masaniello leads a successful rising, she generously causes him to spare the duke and his betrothed, Elvira. Meanwhile the defeated party assemble fresh forces, and overcome the people; whereupon Masaniello, after a fit of madness, is killed by his own comrades, and Fenella kills herself on Vesuvius. The music to this opera has many bold and original effects, in spite of some conventional passages. Auber's light operas include "Le Maçon," "Fra Diavolo," "Le Cheval de Bronze," and "Les Diamants de la Couronne."

François Adrien Boieldieu (1775–1834) preceded Auber, and was a pioneer in his style of light opera. Boieldieu secured Parisian recognition as early as 1795. In 1800 he became a piano teacher at the Conservatoire. He learned much from Cherubini and Méhul, his advance showing in "Ma Tante Aurore," produced in 1803. His best works include "Jean de Paris" (1812), "Le Petit Chaperon Rouge" (1818), and his masterpiece "La Dame Blanche" (1825). The last-named opera is based on scenes from Scott's "Monastery" and "Guy Mannering."

Henri Montan Berton composed nearly fifty operas, and taught composition at the Conservatoire. His best works were "Le Délire," "Aline," and "Françoise de Foix." He was a bitter opponent of Rossini.

Nicolo Isouard, popularly known as Nicolo, was equally active in opera. His most popular works were "Cendrillon," "Joconde," and "Jeannot et Colin." His little melodies were simple enough, but not without artless pathos; and concert singers still delve into his works for unfamiliar but graceful selections. He was rather less careful than Boieldieu; and jealousy of the latter may have been an incentive to the dissipation that ended his career.

Luc de Persuis secured a hearing for his operas and ballets partly because he was a friend of LeSueur.

Rodolphe Kreutzer, the violinist, produced operas of a somewhat earlier date, bringing out a "Lodoïska" in 1791.

Charles Simon Catel displayed much elegance of style, but his music was considered too learned for opera.

Giuseppe Blangini and Giuseppe Catrufo were Italians who worked at Paris. The latter's "Félicie" won some attention.

Michele Carafa was another transplanted Italian. He composed "Le Solitaire," and a setting of "Masaniello" that preceded Auber's.

Contemporary with this school of opera were the Portuguese Marcos Antonio Portogallo, composer of "Fernando in Messico," and the Spaniard Ramon Carnicer, whose best work was "Colombo."

Louis Joseph Ferdinand Hérold (1791–1833) is best known by "Marie" (1826), "Zampa" (1831), and "Le Pré aux Clercs" (1832). He showed some richness of inspiration, and gave to the French ballet its vivid warmth of expression. His last two great works won him almost as much renown as Weber attained. In "Zampa," a pirate of that name captures a Sicilian merchant, falls in love with the prisoner's daughter, gives him freedom at the price of her hand, and displaces her lover; but at the wedding feast the statue of a young girl whom he had betrayed claims Zampa, and drags him off to the infernal regions. "Le Pré aux Clercs" has its scene laid in Navarre, and is full of intrigues and conspiracies.

Adolphe Adam (1803–56) represented light opera in a later generation. He was best known by "Le Postilion de Longjumeau." His style marks a decline toward triviality, though he made some conscientious efforts to enter the field of grand opera.

Albert Grisar was of Belgian origin. His works were poetic in a way, but very light.

Florimond Ronger, Alexandre Lecocq, Émile Jonas, and Jacques Offenbach brought the school to a still lighter, though brighter, level. By their time opéra comique had retraced its steps and become almost like grand opera. In fact, even its name was changed, and it became known as the "drame lyrique." Offenbach's fantastic opera "The

Tales of Hoffmann" was of a higher type than his other works. It makes the bizarre German writer Hoffmann the hero of some of his own stories, each of which is presented in an act. Hoffmann is pursued by an evil principle that always makes his love end unfortunately. Finally the muse offers to console him with fame; but he has been drinking, and is too comatose to accept.

Félicien David, also of a later generation, became known by "La Perle du Brésil," "Herculaneum," and "Lalla Rookh." But he achieved most fame by his symphonic ode "Le Désert," which was a pioneer work in using a real Oriental style and suggestion.

Grand opera was continued in the preceding generation by Jacques Fromental Halévy (1799–1862). A pupil of Berton and Cherubini, he followed Hérold at first, but soon worked on original lines. His greatest operatic success came in 1835, with the tragedy "La Juive" and the comedy "L'Éclair." In "La Juive," the disguised Prince Leopold pays attentions to Rachel, supposed daughter of the rich Jew Eleazar. She penetrates the disguise; and as the prince is married, she denounces him. The cardinal at the court then excommunicates Leopold, and he, with Rachel and Eleazar, is thrown into prison. The wronged princess touches Rachel's heart, so that to save the prince she retracts her accusation. Then she is thrown into a vat of boiling oil; and Eleazar explains that Rachel was the cardinal's own daughter, saved from a fire during infancy.

The last of the foreigners to dominate French grand opera was Giacomo Meyerbeer, whose name was originally Jakob Beer. He was born of Jewish parents at Berlin, in 1791, and soon became a child prodigy. After studying with Abt Vogler, who gave him long-winded dissertations on the fugue, Meyerbeer started his operatic career with "Jephthah's Vow," almost an oratorio, and "Abimelech." Then the young man set out for Italy, where he won attention in spite of Rossini's fame. His "Crociato in Egitto," written for Venice in 1824, was a premonition of future triumphs. Soon Meyerbeer made Paris his home, and did not disdain to take a thorough course of study with French masters.

In 1831, "Robert le Diable," his first great success, aroused tremendous enthusiasm. In this work Meyerbeer first displayed his mastery of instrumental effects, and his dramatic power. The scene is laid in Sicily, to which the daredevil Robert of Normandy has come in order to compete for the hand of the duke's daughter Isabella. Robert's foster-sister Alice tries to keep him in proper paths, but an evil spirit, personified as Bertram, constantly leads him astray. Bertram is really Robert's demon father. Bertram causes Robert to lose everything at the gaming-table, and then incites him to gain magic power by plucking a cypress branch near his mother's tomb at midnight. He does this, among orgies of the spirits of faithless nuns. Robert's power now enables him to enter Isabella's room, with the purpose of carrying her off; but her pleading makes him change his evil purpose. Bertram has only a certain time to gain control of Robert; and Alice thwarts him. The clock strikes midnight; Bertram descends to the infernal regions; while Alice, Isabella, and Robert sing a trio of deliverance.

"Les Huguenots," produced in 1836, has a much more sensible libretto. In this work, Marguerite de Valois tries to reconcile the warring sects by betrothing the Huguenot Raoul de Nangis and the Catholic Valentine, daughter of Count St. Bris. Valentine goes to the house of De Nevers to break off her former engagement to him; but Raoul, seeing her, places a wrong construction on the visit. He breaks his troth, and challenges St. Bris, who in revenge plots Raoul's death. Valentine warns Raoul's servant, Marcel, and Raoul learns that he owes her his life. But the news comes too late, as Valentine has been given again to De Nevers. Raoul and Valentine, during a final farewell, overhear the plans of the St. Bartholomew massacre. In modern versions, the work ends here, with Raoul rushing to the fray. In the complete opera, Valentine comes to Raoul after De Nevers is killed in the fighting; the lovers are united by the faithful servant-minister of Raoul; and the trio are shot down.

In this work Meyerbeer's successful qualities show at their best. Marcel's powerful battle-song, "Piff paff," is a favorite number; while the "Rataplan" of the soldiers, the "Benediction of the Poignards," and Raoul's intensely dramatic fourth-act duet with Valentine, are scenes of tremendous power. Meyerbeer was theatrical in the extreme; but he had no high ideals, and instead of trying to reach a certain standard, he wrote down to his public.

"Le Prophète" (1843) deals with John of Leyden, who is forced to give up his sweetheart to a rival. John turns Anabaptist, and is proclaimed a new Messiah; but his sweetheart's suicide and his betrayal by friends lead him to end all by blowing up the palace where he resides. This work is rather confused in its libretto, but the music contains some scenes of gorgeous pageantry. Most effective is the lofty "Coronation March."

The overture and incidental music to "Struensee" came in 1846.

"L'Africaine," Meyerbeer's last grand opera, was delayed in production until after the composer's death, in 1864. It deals with Vasco de Gama, his sweetheart Inez, a rival official named Don Pedro who tries to steal Vasco's new discoveries, a treacherous slave Nelusko, who wrecks the explorers, and a generous African queen, Selika, who loves Vasco, but returns him to his own sweetheart. The music to this work is less grandiose than that of the preceding operas. Its suavity is in some degree a reaction toward Rossini's methods.

Meyerbeer made two trials of opéra comique. "L'Étoile du Nord" is a story of Peter the Great and his companion Catherine, afterwards Empress of Russia. "Dinorah," or "The Pardon at Ploërmel," deals with the fortunes of two Breton peasants, Hoel and Dinorah, whose adventures centre about buried treasure. Neither work was a great success.

It has become the fashion to abuse Meyerbeer because of his theatrical superficiality. But it must be remembered that he existed before the Wagnerian standards made grand opera a real art-work. In spite of excesses and concessions to public taste, Meyerbeer showed a breadth of conception, a dramatic power, and a mastery of scoring, that kept some of his works on the operatic stage until within a very few years of the present. Schumann accused him of "going over to the circus," but if he did so, he carried out his action successfully.

XX

BERLIOZ AND OTHER FRENCHMEN

FRENCH composers have made their reputation in opera, for the most part. But Berlioz was an exception to this rule; and he won his way into the ranks of the leaders by his great orchestral works.

Hector Berlioz was born at Côte-Saint-André, near Lyons, in 1803. His father was a doctor, and expected the son to follow in his footsteps. By 1822 the boy was sent to a medical school in Paris; but he soon began devoting his time to the study of scores, particularly those of Gluck and Beethoven. In a short time there came a definite breach between father and son, the young man clinging to music. As a result, he was thrown upon his own resources; and he sang in a theatre chorus to gain a livelihood.

His conservatory studies were pursued under LeSueur, who was almost the only teacher not antagonistic to him. Berlioz began to show his radical tendencies at the start; and Cherubini, on looking at some of the pupil's work, dismissed it with an equivalent of the slang phrase "Nix verstay." He was called unfit to compete for the *Prix de Rome*, though after many attempts he reached that goal with his cantata "Sardanapale." His "Messe Solennelle," the over-tures "Waverley" and "Les Francs Juges," and an opera were among his previous attempts at fame.

In the mean while he had seen a beautiful Irish actress, named Harriet Smithson, and fallen deeply in love with her. As a token of his feelings, he produced the "Symphonie Fantastique." This notable work consists of five movements, picturing episodes in the life of an artist. In the first movement he sees his ideal, and falls in love with her; and the fair one is typified by a definite theme. But his love is unrequited, and he seeks various scenes to help him forget her. The second movement is a ballroom picture, with fragments of dance music suggesting themselves, and being woven about the theme of the loved one. The third movement, "In the Fields," is a pleasing rustic scene, with a dialogue between a shepherd and a shepherdess portrayed by English horn and oboe. A thunderstorm arises; and after it passes, a tragedy is suggested when the inquiring strains of the shepherd meet with no response except distant thunder. Meanwhile the artist, in jealousy, kills his sweetheart; and the fourth movement depicts his march to execution. Most composers would have ended the work here; but Berlioz, always fond of morbid subjects, added a fifth movement showing the murderer's reception in the infernal regions. There the *Dies Iræ* is parodied, and the theme of the loved one turned into a ribald waltz.

Another outcome of the composer's feelings may be seen in the "Romeo and Juliet" symphony, which is built on a similar large plan, and carried out in the programme style.

The composer's devotion finally proved acceptable to Miss Smithson; but unfortunately it could not be said that they lived happily ever after. An accident compelled her to leave the stage. Matters grew more and more strained in the household, until a dispute about the composer's tours caused a separation. He supported her, however, until her death. A second marriage, with Mlle. Recio, was quieter in its results; but disagreements came even here. She was a singer, and kept demanding prominent parts in her husband's works, even when she must have known that the rôles were beyond her powers. After her death, her mother helped Berlioz considerably.

At one time Berlioz took up writing as a stop-gap. He has left many criticisms and memoirs, which are marked by an excellent literary style.

Other great works by Berlioz include the monodrama "Lelio," and the overtures "King Lear," "Rob Roy," and "The Corsair." These were followed by another important programme symphony, "Harold in Italy," based on parts of Byron's "Childe Harold." By this time the composer's financial condition began to mend. A Requiem brought him four thousand francs from the Government. Paganini, hearing one of his symphonies, presented him with twenty thousand francs. Beside these amounts, he got ten thousand more for his "Symphonie Funèbre et Triomphale." His foreign trips, in Germany, Austria, and Russia, were continuous triumphs. Even Mendelssohn, the conservative, gave his works a full chance to be heard; though Berlioz said afterward that Mendelssohn's musical judgment was "an abyss of superficiality."

Berlioz used Hungarian gypsy effects to some extent in his great cantata "Le Damnation de Faust."

In opera, his "Béatrice et Bénédict," a setting of "Much Ado about Nothing," won a favorable reception at Baden. An earlier opera, "Benvenuto Cellini," was also a fair success. But his last and most important stage work, "The Trojans," consisting of "The Taking of Troy" and "The Trojans at Carthage," received little appreciation, and had only a short run in Paris. Toward its end, the composer's friends endeavored to cheer him up by saying, "See the people come!" He replied, gloomily, "That's all very well, but I'm going, myself."

Berlioz was often attacked for his radical tendencies; but the authors of these attacks were often too abusive, and too slow in recognizing the composer's greatness. He turned the tables on them very neatly, however, by producing "L'Enfance du Christ," which he pretended he had discovered among old manuscripts. In this cantata he wrote in a simple, melodious style. The critics at once began to praise it; and some said it was a pity that Berlioz could not model his works on such a style. Then he disclosed his authorship of the work, and discomfited his enemies.

Berlioz died in 1869, after a life of varied activities.

The chief point of novelty in his compositions was their tremendous largeness of effect. Wagner said of him, "He ciphers with notes"; and there is a certain calculating quality in his works. But in spite of this, they are often grandly powerful. If their dramatic effects are often highly sensational, their style will be found to fit their subjects. His harmonies were sometimes commonplace; but his orchestration was always strong, and often strikingly original. His symphonies are not classical works, like those of Beethoven. Instead of following old lines, they blazed a path toward new methods. Berlioz was the first of several composers to lay the foundations for the modern programme school.

Charles François Gounod (1818–93) was led into music by three events, — a French performance of "Der Freischütz," the singing of Malibran, and a hearing of "Don Giovanni." His first teacher was his mother. At the conservatory he came under Paer, LeSueur, and Halévy. When twenty-one, he gained the *Grand Prix* by his cantata "Fernand." His Roman stay was marked by the composition of masses. On his return he spent some years in theological study, but finally reverted to a musical career.

His "Messe Solennelle," the "Redemption," the "Mors et Vita," and other sacred works evidently reflect the atmosphere of his studies. He tried the symphonic field also, though with little success.

His operatic career began with "Sapho," which showed some musical richness, but was undramatic. Next came "Ulysse," in which an attempt at an antique style caused some monotony. "La Nonne Sanglante" was based on a story by Lewis entitled "The Monk." This was followed by a setting of "Le Médecin malgré lui," which was effective enough in a way, but without any real comic spirit.

"Faust," brought out in 1859, has been the composer's greatest success, and one of the most constant triumphs in the annals of opera. It deals with the first part of Goethe's tragedy, and the Germans sometimes call it "Margarethe." In its first act, Faust's thoughts of suicide are interrupted by charming choruses from outside; and when Mephistopheles rises at his spell, he agrees to sell his soul for pleasure, after being shown a vision of Marguerite. The next act shows a *kermesse* in a public place. Here Faust meets Marguerite, and Mephisto entertains the crowd, until his drawing flames from a spigot along with wine makes them look askance at him. The next scene shows Marguerite's garden, with Mephisto placing jewels by the flowers of her boyish admirer Siebel, and keeping the duenna Martha out of the way while Faust makes successful love to Marguerite. In the fourth act, soldiers return, including Marguerite's brother Valentine. A mocking serenade arouses Valentine's ire, and in a duel Faust is treacherously aided by Mephistopheles, who kills Valentine and takes Faust away in flight. A church scene shows the now desperate Marguerite unable to escape from remorse, personified by Mephistopheles. In the last act she is shown in prison, having become insane and killed the child of her betrayal. Faust returns to save her, but she dies, and in spite of Mephisto's attempt to claim her soul, it is shown in a vision ascending to heaven.

The music of "Faust" still charms thousands at each hearing. It has a beautiful overture, which modern composers would do well to equal if they could. The first act contains charming choruses. In the second act, Mephisto's "Golden Calf" song, the waltz, and the popular exorcism of the evil spirit, are all highly interesting in different ways. Siebel's "Le parlate d'amor," "The King of Thule," the "Jewel Song," and the love duets are effective parts of the charming garden scene, which was held to be a weak spot in the work before its success proved the falsity of this assumption. The "Soldiers' Chorus," if frankly popular, is also strongly effective, and warms the most hypercritical aloofness into real enthusiasm. The church music is full of power and dignity. The final act is short, but its grand trio forms an effective vocal climax.

"La Reine de Saba" did not fulfill expectations; but "Mireille" was successful in a new direction. The story is a Provençal idyl based on a work of the poet Mistral. Mireille loves Vincent, but her rich father objects to him, preferring the herdsman Ourrias. On a pilgrimage to a church at Crau, Mireille suffers from a sunstroke. Her father then tries to propitiate her by withdrawing his opposition to Vincent; whereupon she speedily recovers. The music to this pastoral story has a charming warmth of expression and coloring, the shepherd's song in the third act being especially suggestive of fragrant meadow flowers.

"Philémon et Baucis" is another pleasing work, in two acts.

"La Colombe" was not a great success, while the later "Cinq Mars" proved hasty, and "Polyeucte" mediocre. But "Roméo et Juliette" was another triumph for the composer. Its music has not the manifold beauties of the "Faust" score; but it contains many popular numbers, such as the waltz song, Mercutio's "Queen Mab" song, and the impressive measures of Friar Laurence.

Georges Bizet (1838–75) was one of the many great composers who were cut off in their fourth decade. The manifold beauties of his "Carmen" and the "Arlésienne" music show that he had a great career before him when his untimely death overtook him.

He won the *Prix de Rome*, and in his sojourn there he brought forth the overture "La Chasse d'Ossian" and the stage works "Don Procopio" and "La Guzla de l'Émir." Another early work was "Docteur Miracle." "Vasco de Gama," which followed, was more ambitious. "Les Pêcheurs de Perles" and "Djamileh" were attractive examples of Oriental coloring, somewhat in the style of David's "Le Désert." These operas, and "La Jolie Fille de Perth," met with some success, but were not markedly popular.

The music to Daudet's "L'Arlésienne" has met with a better fate. In this, Bizet showed all the warmth of expression found in Gounod's "Mireille," combined with a remarkable vigor and directness of expression. The many contrasted numbers have been made into two remarkably attractive suites, which contain some beautiful saxophone passages, a charming adagietto, a broad intermezzo, two dainty minuets, a rollicking farandole, and other numbers.

The opera "Carmen," Bizet's greatest success, is founded on Mérimée's story of that name, altered and made spicy for stage purposes. Carmen is a captivating but wild gypsy, who stabs a companion and is arrested by the soldiers. She beguiles one of them, Don José, to loosen her bonds so that she can escape. In return, she dances for him and entertains him at Lillas Pastia's inn. She keeps him beyond his trumpet recall, saves him from the officers who wish to seize him as a deserter, and takes him to the retreat of her smuggler friends. There she grows tired of Don José, for whom her feeling must have been only a passing fancy; and she finds that she really loves Escamillo, the Toreador who swaggered so impressively at the inn. Meanwhile Micaela, who loved Don José in his native village, comes to take him away to his mother's death-bed. He returns to find Carmen approaching the Seville bull-ring, where Escamillo is to fight; and when he finds that she has cast him off, he stabs her to death.

The music to "Carmen" is one long succession of attractive numbers. The overture, consisting in part of the march to the bull-fight, is brilliant and spirited. The first act contains Carmen's sensuously beautiful "Habanera," her graceful "Seguedilla," some charming phrases in connection with Micaela, a pleasing soldiers' chorus, a burlesque by whistling street gamins, and a humorous scene of confusion when the girls all try to give the captain their version of Carmen's deed. The second act contains some spirited dance music, Escamillo's famous "Toreador" song, Carmen's graceful dance for Don José (interwoven with the trumpet recall), and a dainty smugglers' quintet. The third act has a fortune-telling scene, some bright smugglers' music, and a smoothly melodious scena for Micaela; while the fourth act gives a strong contrast between the glamour of the march and the tragedy of Carmen's death. In all these numbers there is a most satisfying directness of expression, and every theme seems pregnant with its proper significance. In this opera Bizet used a guiding motive in a somewhat Wagnerian manner. There is a phrase of portentous significance that is heard when Carmen throws a rose at Don José; and the phrase recurs later to typify evil or tragedy. Because of this use of a motive, Bizet has been called "the halfway-house between Offenbach and Wagner." At first this was meant as a reproach, since Wagner was then unpopular in Paris; but now it would be a compliment. "Carmen," like "Faust," has been a perennial success; yet the critics attacked it at first. Their malignity did much to bring about Bizet's untimely death. Bizet wrote some beautiful songs, an overture to Sardou's "Patrie," the suites "Roma" and "Jeux d'Enfants." The last is well liked, but his fame rests chiefly on "Carmen" and the "Arlésienne" music.

Charles Ambroise Thomas (1811–96) had a long career in opera, but did not equal either Gounod or Bizet. He produced his first work, "La Double Échelle," in 1837, competing with Auber and Hérold in the days when Meyerbeer's career was scarcely more than begun. Thomas composed a number of such works, and several ballets. More romantic in style was a later group of operas, including "Le Songe d'une Nuit d'Été," "Raymond," and "Psyche." But his greatest success came with "Mignon," produced in 1866. Later operas included "Hamlet" and "Françoise de Rimini," along with a ballet, "The Tempest."

"Mignon" is based on Goethe's "Wilhelm Meister." The heroine, Mignon, has been stolen by gypsies, and is sought by her father, Lothario. She is rescued and protected by Wilhelm Meister, with whom she falls in love. But Wilhelm is captivated by the actress Filina, whom he meets at a castle fête. Mignon is about to drown herself, but Lothario saves her. Sympathizing with her in his half-crazed way, he sets fire to the castle. Mignon is saved from the fire by Wilhelm. He then takes her to Italy, and at Lothario's castle her identity is discovered, and her love returned.

The music of this work is graceful rather than powerful; but it is fresh and natural. Mignon's song "Kennst du das Land," her Styrienne, Filina's dashing polonaise, and a dainty gavotte are the most popular numbers in the score.

Antoine Clapisson, Georges Bousquet, Louis Maillart, Jean Gautier, François Bazin, Henri Reber, Victor Massé, Aristide Hignard, and Ferdinand Poise were among those who worked in French opera at or after the middle of the last century. Friedrich von Flotow, who lived at Paris, is best known by his comedy "Martha," which contains some sentimentality, but much liveliness and charm also.

Félicien David's operas have been mentioned already. His successor in the Academy, Louis Ernest Reyer, showed a similar fondness for Oriental coloring. Reyer's "Sigurd" treated the same subject as Wagner's "Siegfried," while his "Salammbo" was based on Flaubert's story of old Carthaginian times. Gaston Salvayre, another opera composer, is usually classed with Reyer.

Léon Gastinel and Louis Deffès composed operas, but became known in the orchestral field also. Victorin de Joncières did the same at a later date. Edmond Membrée and Auguste Morel kept more strictly to opera.

Léo Délibes (1836–91) became well known through his ballets, such as "La Source," "Coppelia," and "Sylvia." The music to these pantomines is varied and effective, showing a warm richness well suited to the demands of the form. In opera, his most noted work is "Lakmé." In that composition, Lakmé, daughter of a Hindu priest, is loved by an English officer, Gerald. Her father discovers the affair, and finds out who Gerald is by making Lakmé sing in the market-place until he betrays himself. The priest then stabs Gerald; but Lakmé saves him, and nurses him back to health in a forest retreat. In the end he returns to his people; while Lakmé, deserted, poisons herself. The music is full of the charm of delicacy. Lakmé's duet with her slave, her "Bell" song in the market-place, the Oriental ballet music, and her slumber song over the sleeping Gerald are among the best passages in the score. This work wins success by its grace, in spite of the fact that it does not strive for the wildly dramatic scoring of recent decades. Another excellent Délibes opera is "Le Roi l'a dit."

With Délibes may be classed Ernest Guiraud, whose "Piccolino" is a dainty comedy.

Benjamin Godard was a devotee of Schumann. He composed several symphonies, and a number of operas, of which "La Vivandière" was the most successful. He wrote also many chamber works, and a number of songs and piano pieces, of which "Florian's Song" and the piano solo "Au Matin" are widely known.

LISZT

BERLIOZ

Édouard Lalo entered the operatic field with the strong but som-bre "Roi d'Ys." He is better known by his instrumental works, which include a Spanish symphony, a Spanish rhapsodie for violin and orchestra, and the suite "Namouna."

Johann Georg Kastner was a friend of Berlioz, and aided the lat-ter in instrumental research. He composed symphonies, overtures, operas, and smaller works. Reber and David continued the French orchestral school, with Louis Lacombe, who composed the dramatic symphonies "Manfred" and "Arva."

The French organists deserve especial mention for building up a high type of organ music. Many of them worked in the orchestral field also. Thus Alexandre Guilmant composed a number of sym-phonies for organ and orchestra, besides writing organ sonatas and other works. He and his school have done much to keep alive the spirit of counterpoint. With Guilmant may be classed Charles Widor, Antoine Batiste, M. P. Hamel, the Belgian Mailly, Leon Boëllmann, and the somewhat earlier Lefébure-Wély.

Theodore Dubois was an organist who worked along many lines. He composed various oratorios, such as "Les Sept Paroles de Christ," and "Paradise Lost." Beside these he wrote several cantatas, a few operas, some orchestral works, and a number of smaller pieces. His style is solid, but rather too conservative to admit of any marked success.

XXI

LISZT AND HIS CIRCLE

FRANZ LISZT was born in 1811, at the small Hungarian town of Raiding. His father, a steward on one of the Esterhazy estates, was a gifted musical amateur, and trained the child so well that the latter was able to perform in public when nine years old. His precocity aroused the interest of a group of noblemen, who subscribed a liberal sum for his education. The story goes that Beethoven heard the young Liszt, and exclaimed, "He will make my music understood by posterity." Liszt studied under Czerny and others at Vienna, with later lessons at Paris. His early ambition lay in the direction of opera, and his operetta "Don Sanche" was produced in 1825.

On the death of his father he began to make a living by means of piano playing, and soon grew famous in this field. He became a well-known member of the Parisian clique that included Hugo, Lamartine, George Sand, Chopin, Berlioz, and other celebrities. In 1834 he met the Countess d'Agoult (known in literature as Daniel Stern), with whom he became intimately connected. In 1836 came an old-fashioned piano contest with Thalberg, in which Liszt was plainly the victor.

In 1839, Liszt began his long piano tours, in which he spoke of a single concert as "piano recitals." He fully realized his ambition to become the Paganini of the piano; and his tremendous technique has remained unequalled. His profits increased greatly; and he was once able to give substantial relief to flood-sufferers in Pesth, as well as adding $10,000 to a Beethoven monument fund. In the mean time he revived his childish memories of Hungarian music, and echoed it in his piano rhapsodies.

Liszt was one of the first to assert the dignity of the musician's position. Beethoven had shown independence, but it was the exception in the epoch when such masters as Mozart and Haydn had to put up with various slights. The occasion arose when one of Liszt's princess friends asked if he had done good business on his last trip.

Liszt replied, "Madame, I am in music, not business." Perhaps this was straining a point; but Liszt's later career certainly added new lustre to the occupation of the musician.

Liszt's piano pieces contain a large number of transcriptions. These show the utmost variety, ranging from old vocal works of Arcadelt to the art-songs of Schubert and the operas of Rossini, or from the organ fugues of Bach to the symphonies of Beethoven and the glowing orchestral scores of Wagner. His original piano compositions include the rhapsodies and other national music; but beside these they comprise many piano works of tremendous breadth and striking power, such as the great single-movement sonata. Liszt developed a style that has been called the orchestration of the piano. In his larger keyboard compositions, and in the transcriptions also, one may find broad sweeps of tone; melodies supported by the richest and most complicated harmonies; or striking antiphonal effects, like those one might hear when parts of an orchestra respond to one another. Such works as the "Sermon to the Birds," or "St. Francis walking on the Water," bring out keyboard possibilities that were utterly unsuspected by Liszt's predecessors. A number of his pieces are grouped together in the sets entitled "Années de Pélerinage."

In 1849, Liszt was offered a court post at Weimar, which he accepted. In that city began the most famous period of his career. His teaching gathered around him a circle of the greatest pianists in the world, who looked up to him as disciples do to a master. Not every one who was recommended found himself able to enter the charmed circle. Many an overpraised young maiden, sent to play for him, was met by the scarcely veiled rebuff, "Marry soon, dear child." Once a poorly equipped male student heard him mutter, "This before me, who have so often heard Tausig!" But if the student proved able enough to be accepted, he entered into a veritable fairyland of art. Often the lessons terminated in social gatherings, where the leaders performed, or discussed new works. Frequently Liszt himself would play, ostensibly to show how certain passages were to be taken. Liszt was not absolutely infallible, and once he struck a wrong note in some cross-hand work; but he atoned for this by dazzling his hearers with a series of the most brilliant pieces. He was able to read at sight with remarkable facility, and would even play a piano version of new scores set before him.

Liszt used his position as orchestral leader to bring out many new works. Raff, Schubert, Schumann, Lassen, Cornelius, Rubinstein, and Wagner were among those whom Liszt helped into publicity.

Liszt's larger compositions date mostly from his Weimar stay. They include his great Faust symphony, two famous piano concertos, and about a dozen important symphonic poems. Liszt really developed the latter form; and such examples as "Les Preludes," "Tasso," "Die Ideale," "Mazeppa," and others of the group, prove that except for Richard Strauss his work in this field remains unequalled. Liszt's symphonic poems show a most strongly expressive style, a massive handling of the orchestral forces, and a great amount of real musical beauty. They made their way very slowly, and only in the most recent years has Liszt's greatness as an orchestral composer been fairly recognized. Wagner, who was Liszt's son-in-law, once called attention to a passage he had borrowed from Liszt, by saying, at a rehearsal, "Now, papa, here comes one of your themes." "Very good," replied Liszt. "The public will hear it now, at any rate."

Disagreements over Liszt's progressive policy caused him to give up his Weimar post; and he settled in Rome. There, after a broken engagement to marry the Princess of Sayn-Wittgenstein, he began to study for the Church, and gained the title of Abbé. He had already produced the "Graner Mass" and three psalm settings; but in Rome he devoted himself still more to religious music. His later works include the oratorios "St. Elizabeth," "Christus," and the unfinished "Stanislaus," as well as the "Hungarian Coronation Mass" and a requiem. An organ mass was of later date. Other works by Liszt included the symphonic poem "From the Cradle to the Grave," and the cantatas "Die Glocken," "St. Cecilia," and "Die Kreuzesstationen." Liszt divided his time in later years between Rome, Weimar, and Pesth. His influence as teacher and leader was still kept up, and he devoted many efforts to the furthering of Wagner's cause. He died in 1886, at a Bayreuth festival.

While Wagner brought opera to a new orchestral standard, Liszt did the same with concert works. His symphonic poems are very definitely written for modern instead of classical orchestra. These two men, with Berlioz, who modernized the programme symphony, brought the large orchestra into existence, and illustrated its possibilities.

Karl Goldmark, born at Keszthely, Hungary, in 1830, was not a Liszt pupil, but belongs, nevertheless, to the school of modern romanticism. For a time Goldmark supported himself as a violinist in theatre orchestras; and in 1855 he made composition his life-work.

His first decided success was the "Sakuntala" Overture, — a richly colored work, based on the East Indian story of a nymph who is wooed by a king, forgotten, because of magic spells, and finally remembered once more. Similarly rich in color are the overtures "Penthesilea" and "In the Spring"; while the one to "Prometheus Bound" is more severe and classic in style. Goldmark's other orchestral works include various concertos; but he was best known on the programmes of three decades ago by his "Rustic Wedding" Symphony. This composition, which some consider a suite, consists of a wedding march with variations, a bridal song, a serenade and garden scene, and a dance-like finale. Like the concertos, it is rather simply orchestrated in comparison with the works of Richard Strauss, or even of Liszt. A second symphony, an orchestral scherzo, and chamber music are other compositions by the same composer.

Goldmark achieved his greatest reputation in opera. His first success, "The Queen of Sheba," carried its audiences by storm. Once, while the composer was travelling to take charge of a performance of the work, he was drawn into a conversation with a lady. Thinking to please her, he introduced himself as "the composer of the 'Queen of Sheba.'" "Oh, indeed," replied the lady. "I hope the queen pays you well." The work certainly did pay; and the anecdote gave Goldmark the nickname of "Court Composer to the Queen of Sheba." The story of the work is based on the weakness of Assad, who is so bewitched by the queen, at Solomon's court, that he deserts his betrothed, Sulamith. The music shows a richness that is well suited to gorgeous Oriental effects.

"Merlin" is another opera of rich coloring and sumptuous effects. It deals with Viviane's attempts to entrap Merlin; but finally, when she succeeds in getting him into the power of her demon-master, she finds that she loves him, and sacrifices herself to save him.

"Heimchen am Herd" is a setting of Dickens's "Cricket on the Hearth." It is based on the simple but refreshingly melodious style introduced by Humperdinck in his "Hänsel und Gretel."

"Die Kriegsgefangene" treats an episode of the Trojan War, and brings in Achilles' victory over Hector and his love for Briseis.

"Götz von Berlichingen," "Der Fremdling," and "The Winter's Tale" are still later operas by Goldmark; while he recently summed up his memories in the overture "Aus meiner Jugendzeit." His career, reaching practically to the present, has been full of honor and crowned by many successes. He died in 1915.

Joseph Joachim Raff was born at Württemburg in 1822. He was at first a school-teacher, but studied music privately. When he was twenty-one, Mendelssohn helped him to publish some piano pieces and begin a musical career. Two years later, Liszt took the young man along on a tour. Raff then settled in Cologne, as critic and composer. He aimed to take free lessons from Mendelssohn, to get commissions from a Vienna publisher, and to have his opera "King Alfred" given at Stuttgart. But Mendelssohn died; the publisher Mechetti died just before making an agreement with Raff; and the Stuttgart manager declined the opera. Von Bülow then helped him to put other works before the public. In 1851 he became Liszt's assistant at Weimar, and heard his opera performed at last.

Raff was very poor in his younger days. He could not afford a good metronome; and the broken-down one that he used caused his works to seem too rapid when played with more accurate metronomes. He wrote a great deal, and often published rather mediocre pieces in an effort to keep the wolf from the door. Once he was arrested for debt; but Liszt and Dr. William Mason saw to it that he was comfortable. With the pens, ink, and music-paper that they provided, and the good food that they insisted upon, he was really more comfortable than in his own frugal quarters.

In 1856, Raff moved to Wiesbaden; and soon after this he married. In 1863 his first symphony, "The Fatherland," won the prize in a Vienna competition. Another opera, "Dame Kobold," was performed at Weimar. Raff soon became famous through other symphonies, such as "Im Walde" and "Lenore." During his last years he was director of a conservatory in Frankfurt, and taught a number of Americans, including MacDowell. He died in 1882.

His works include eleven symphonies, four suites, nine overtures, an effective piano concerto, a violin concerto, an oratorio, several cantatas, some chamber music, and many smaller pieces. They are

almost all remarkably melodious. Raff resembles Schubert rather
than his benefactor Liszt, and shows little leaning toward modernism. In many cases Raff's melodies are ineffably sweet and charming, and their harmonies delightful. There has been considerable
dispute over Raff's position. Many hold that the too melodious
character of his works places him far down among the second-raters,
But one may remember the couplet,

> "And if his art as artifice you score,
> Where have you seen such artifice before?"

Admitting that Raff's works are extremely melodic in character, we
cannot gainsay the fact that their melody is of the best. His well-
known cavatina is but one of many instances that will prove the
point.

Peter Cornelius (1824–74) was born at Mainz. After some years
of youthful training, he joined the Weimar circle, and heard his
"Barber of Bagdad" given. That opera has for hero Noureddin,
who loves the daughter of the Cadi, and visits her. He takes with
him the loquacious and irresponsible barber, Abu Hassan, who remains outside. Hearing a chance outcry, Hassan at once imagines
Noureddin is being attacked; and he gathers a band to invade the
place. To escape from the Cadi's anger, Noureddin hides in a chest.
Finally the disturbance brings the Caliph on the scene; and Noureddin, rescued in a half-smothered state, is presented with the hand
of his adored Margiana. The music of this rather mixed work shows
decided power, and not a little skill in humorous orchestration. The
interlude of the muezzin call, and the hurly-burly of the last scene,
will stand comparison with the later Wagner. In fact, this rollicking work had a direct influence upon Wagner's "Meistersinger."
Cornelius composed also "Der Cid" and "Gunlod."

Eduard Lassen (1830–1904) was born at Copenhagen, and studied
at Brussels. Liszt brought out one of his operas, "Landgraf Ludwigs
Brautfahrt," in 1858. When Liszt gave up the control at Weimar,
Lassen succeeded him. Lassen composed two other operas —
"Frauenlob" and "Le Captif." He wrote also symphonies, overtures, cantatas, much incidental music, and very beautiful songs,
such as "It was a dream."

Hans von Bronsart, born at Berlin in 1830, was a Liszt piano pupil.
He composed a symphony, the choral symphony "In the Alps," and

other orchestral works. His wife, Ingeborg (Stark) von Bronsart, was another piano pupil of Liszt. She composed several operas and many piano works.

To the Weimar circle belongs also Alexander Ritter (1833–96). He composed two comic operas and several symphonic poems, but is better known because it was his influence that made Richard Strauss adopt the programme style of composition.

Leopold Damrosch (1832–85) was a famous violinist, who composed violin concertos, a symphony, various cantatas, and other works. Before his death he exerted considerable influence upon music in America.

Felix Draeseke, born at Coburg in 1835, became known through overtures, symphonies, operas, and chamber music. In his later life he became unusually conservative.

Hans Guido von Bülow (1830–94) came under Liszt's influence at Weimar and Wagner's at Zurich. He married Liszt's daughter Cosima, who was afterwards divorced and married to Wagner. Von Bülow was a famous pianist, and a thorough conductor. It was his orchestra, at Meiningen, that once started a programme without any conductor when he was unavoidably late. He toured America twice. His programmes were always chosen with a view to improving popular taste. His own compositions include a few orchestral works, some concert pieces for piano, and many transcriptions. He had a very caustic wit, and some of his remarks are quoted elsewhere in this volume. Once a chance acquaintance from some previous meeting stopped him on the street, and said, "I'll bet you don't remember me." Von Bülow instantly retorted, "You've won your bet," and passed on. Again, in rehearsing his orchestra, he once said to the trumpeter, "That passage is *forte*." The trumpeter then blew his hardest; whereupon the leader repeated, "I said *forte*." Then the trumpeter made a mighty effort, and nearly blew his head off; whereupon the leader explained, "I said *forte*, and you have been blowing *fortissimo* all the time."

Klindworth and Tausig were other pupils of Liszt who became better known by their arrangements than by their compositions.

Leschetizky, the great piano teacher, was known also as a piano composer, in a brilliant but rather showy style. Once Brahms, passing him as he worked at his desk, thought to tease him, and said,

"Little things!" "That may be," answered Leschetizky, "but they are ten times more popular than yours." Time has reversed this verdict, for Leschetizky's works seldom figure on contemporary programmes.

Among the violin virtuosos of this time, Ferdinand David (1810–73) has been mentioned as an early leader. His compositions include two symphonies, five concertos, an opera, much chamber music, and many smaller pieces, especially for his instrument.

Joseph Joachim (1831–1907) was David's successor for a time. He also played for five years under Liszt, at Weimar. Afterwards he became prominent as a teacher in Berlin. He composed little, being better known as a performer.

In France, Delphin Alard exerted a great influence on violin playing. He combined Paganini's brilliance with the German solidity. He composed many original works, and arranged much.

In Belgium, De Bériot was the pioneer of a national violin school, composing concertos, trios, variations, études, etc.

Henri Vieuxtemps (1820–81) took the leadership in the next generation. He composed concertos, fantasias, a suite, and other works.

Among other violinist-composers, Ole Bull, Eduard Remenyi, and Henri Wieniawski deserve especial mention. Bull was rather given to the display of a trick violinist. Remenyi showed his Hungarian blood in some spirited works, while Wieniawski, a Pole, composed a number of interesting and brilliant pieces, besides touring America with Rubinstein.

Among composers for the 'cello, Georg Goltermann and David Popper deserve mention, along with Servais, the great virtuoso performer.

Contrabass music is represented by some of the works of Bottesini and Dragonetti; but it seems more like a curiosity than an actual concert or solo repertoire.

XXII

FROM GLINKA TO TSCHAIKOVSKY

MUSIC in Russia has been a popular affair from time immemorial. In the old pagan days, minstrels of all sorts were common. When the land came under Byzantine influence, the native music met with official opposition, but was never entirely rooted out. When Russia became an empire under the Romanoffs, its folk-music flourished again. Poets shaped into literary form the epics of its old legendary cycles, and created innumerable subjects suitable for musical settings. In the eighteenth century, foreign composers, and some native musicians, began to give some attention to these; while in the nineteenth, an important Russian school came into existence.

Francesco Araja (1700–67) was the first foreigner to bring Russian opera into being; and during his stay at St. Petersburg, he set several native subjects. Galuppi, Sarti, Paisiello, Cimarosa, and the Venetian Cavos were other prominent foreigners. Cavos treated the subject of Ivan Susanina, which Glinka used later for his great popular success. Early native musicians included Fomin, Matinsky, Paskievitch, Beresovsky, Bortniansky, Verstovsky, Alabiev, and the Titov brothers. Verstovsky won some success with "Askold's Tomb," but none of these men was gifted enough to found a national school. Bortniansky, famous for his Russian church music, confined his operatic ventures to Italian and French texts.

Michael Ivanovitch Glinka (1804–57) was born of a noble family at St. Petersburg. Brought up in pleasant social surroundings, he showed an intense devotion to music, but at first was little more than an amateur. He began to compose short songs and pieces for a lady friend. His family gave him a musical training, but thought his gifts merely a social asset. It took a foreign trip to develop his latent powers. He enjoyed Italian opera at Milan, but soon found that its idiom was not suited to express his Russian nationalism. It was in Berlin that he obtained real benefit, in studying with Siegfried Dehn. That teacher, seeing that Glinka was both gifted and impatient of drudgery, wisely condensed his instruction into five months, and gave the pupil the chief points of harmony, counterpoint, fugue, and orchestration. This was so beneficial that Stassov said, "Glinka left us a *dilettante*, and returned a *maestro*." He would have continued his studies, but the death of his father recalled him to Russia.

Glinka wrote some instrumental pieces and a number of smaller works, but is best known by his two operas, "Life for the Czar" and "Russlan and Ludmilla." The former work, brought out in 1836, is considered the foundation of the Russian national school. It did for Russia what Weber's "Der Freischütz" did for Germany, by ideal- izing the native folk-music into an artistic composition. Where earlier Russians had merely incorporated folk-songs, sometimes leaving the simple accompaniments unaltered, Glinka brought the resources of the trained composer into action, and gave the music real strength without injuring its characteristic flavor. His use of a melody that he had heard on the lips of a cab-driver caused his opera to be called "Musique des cochers," but the reproach is un- just.

The plot of this work is laid in the seventeenth century, when Russia was largely in the hands of the Poles. The conquerors decide to seize the newly elected czar, Michael Romanoff. On their march they order the peasant Ivan Susanina to guide them. But the latter, too loyal to betray his ruler, secretly sends his son to warn the czar, and leads the Poles astray, though he knows he is thus meeting death. The music is full of Russian touches, even including church modes.

Glinka's incidental music to "Prince Kholomsky" was followed by his second opera. This work, "Russlan and Ludmilla," is based on a legend, in which Russlan, the favored one of three suitors, is to wed Ludmilla, daughter of Prince Svietozar. Meanwhile the wicked wizard Chernomor, seeing Ludmilla, falls in love with her, and car- ries her off from the wedding feast. The three suitors are sent to rescue her, and naturally Russlan succeeds. One of his rivals tries to gain the credit, by throwing the pair into a magic slumber; but Russlan awakes in time to unmask the pretender. The music to this opera is of more solid and learned style than Glinka's earlier work. It caused much discussion, Stassov praising it while Serov called it a retrogression.

Alexander Sergeivitch Dargomiszky (1813–69) gained some instruction from the exercise-books that Glinka had filled when under Dehn's tuition, though he was already proficient in orchestration. His first opera, "Esmeralda," was rather light and trivial in style, though it pleased the public. "The Triumph of Bacchus" was rejected, and remained unknown for many years. "The Roussalka" (1856) met with a better fate, though at first it was too advanced to find much favor with a public that still craved Italian opera. The Roussalki, or water-nymphs who lie in wait for the traveller, are maidens who have been betrayed and have drowned themselves. In the story (written by Pushkin) a young prince falls in love with the miller's daughter Natasha. She accepts his devotion; but when she learns that he has betrayed her, to marry in his own rank, she drowns herself, becoming a Roussalka. The prince marries, but does not live happily. Some years later he is at the mill, which he visits out of remorse. The spirit of Natasha's child appears to him. While he hesitates, the miller, now crazed, pushes him into the water. The music to this opera is national in spirit, but is bright or dramatic where Glinka's scores were more simply lyrical.

Dargomiszky's last opera, "The Stone Guest," is based on the same subject as "Don Giovanni," though using Pushkin's version. It was unfinished at the composer's death, and Rimsky-Korsakoff filled in the orchestration. In this work, which is somewhat declamatory, words and music are welded in close union. The national Russians admired it so much that Balakirev spoke of it as "The Gospel."

Alexander Nicholaievitch Serov (1820–71) became famous in criticism at first, defending Spontini and the historical opera in a way that foreshadowed Wagnerian principles. In later days Serov and Wagner became quite intimate, and apparently formed a "mutual admiration society." Serov was over forty before he tried to clinch his hold on the public by composing an opera; and he had to learn many of the technicalities of composition. Under the circumstances, the strength of his work, "Judith," is remarkable. It is not subtle, but handles gorgeous scenes in a broad, almost Wagnerian manner.

Serov's second work, "Rogneda," was written frankly to fit the public taste; and it succeeded in its object. Its sensational stage effects still hold the Russian public. A third work, "The Power of Evil," was a compromise between Wagner's methods and Russian nationalism; and it lacked the strength of either school.

Alexis Lvoff (1799–1871) composed a youthful opera, and three later ones, but was not especially a pioneer. He wrote violin works also, but became best known by his Russian National Hymn.

Anton Gregorovitch Rubinstein (1830–94) was born in Bessarabia, but was brought up at Moscow. He was of Jewish descent, though his father joined the Orthodox Russian Church. He studied piano with his mother, and later with Villoing, who was with him in Paris when he was refused admission to the Conservatoire. Later on he and his brother were taken to Berlin, where he studied with Dehn. In 1848 he made St. Petersburg his home, and began composing operas. Within a few years he made a European tour to exploit his works, with such success that he was afterwards created court-musician to the czar and head of the Musical Society. In 1862 he started the great St. Petersburg Conservatory, which he directed for many years.

Rubinstein's fame as a performer is mentioned in the chapter "Some Famous Pianists," later in this volume. On his American tours, he kept to a high standard of art, giving the best of programmes. Once, at Buffalo, where he was billed to play with a band, the local manager placed a couple of cheap waltzes on the list of pieces. When Rubinstein saw this, he refused to appear until the waltzes had been crossed off every programme. Even then he regretted that he was not independent enough to show the manager what he thought of the occasion. He proved that his anger was genuine by declining a later offer of a hundred thousand dollars for another American tour.

Rubinstein's orchestral works include six symphonies, three overtures, a symphonic poem, three character-pieces, a suite, five piano concertos, and some fantasias for piano and orchestra. Of these, the best known is probably the "Ocean Symphony," produced in 1868. This has a remarkably effective first movement, but after that the interest gradually tapers off. Nevertheless, Rubinstein kept adding to the work until he had brought it up to seven movements, — possibly typical of the "seven seas." Another successful work was the "Dramatic Symphony," produced seven years later. The concertos are still played by famous pianists, the later ones rivalling the symphonies in popularity.

Rubinstein composed quite a large amount of chamber music. Most pleasing to the public is a string quartet containing the so-called "Music of the Spheres," — a very expressive and saccharine slow movement.

Rubinstein's orchestral and chamber music shows some command of orchestration, and a richness of musical effect arising in many cases from his use of Oriental flavors. His works are often grandiose, but they do not always show real inspiration or sustained power.

Rubinstein's songs are among his best compositions. In these there is no need for lengthy expression, and in their brief space the composer has often given us lyrics of unflagging inspiration. His dramatic strength is shown in "The Asra"; his melodic richness appears in "The Dream"; while "Golden at my feet" is a much-admired example of Orientalism.

The piano works include a couple of sonatas; but the shorter pieces are much better known. Rubinstein himself made many of these familiar to his audiences; but they have held their place after his death. The well-known "Melody in F" verges a little toward the commonplace; but his barcarolles, romances, and other works of the sort are still in evidence on concert programmes.

Rubinstein devoted much attention to the opera. His first dramatic effort, "Dmitri Donskoi," met with only a fair reception; while "Tom the Fool" aroused so little enthusiasm that the composer withdrew it. Other early works were "Hadji-Abrek" and "The Siberian Hunters," each in one act. As Rubinstein had thus failed in Russian opera, he devoted his attention to Germany. There he brought out his "Kinder der Heide"; and the same country applauded his "Feramors." His next efforts were in the field of sacred opera, and resulted in "The Tower of Babel," "The Maccabees," and "Paradise Lost," some of which resembled cantatas. Returning to the secular field, he next completed his best opera, "The Demon," which was brought out at St. Petersburg. This work, based on a poem by Lermontov, portrays a species of Russian "Faust." Its hero is a mortal, with certain demoniac tendencies, who wishes to find consolation in love. He pursues Tamara, the object of his affections, even into the convent where she has taken

RUBINSTEIN

TSCHAIKOVSKY

refuge. Defying her good angel, he enters her cell; but after this Tamara is called to death, and saved, like Marguerite.

Rubinstein's Biblical operas include also "Artaxerxes," "Joseph," and "The Shulamite"; but the best of them were his later works entitled "Moses" and "Christus." His later secular operas consisted of "Nero," a spectacular work that grew popular in Germany; "The Merchant Kalashnikov," dealing with a brave trader whose jealousy of his wife leads him to defy the Imperial body-guard, the Opritchniki; "Der Papagei," a comic opera; and "Gorioushka," another Russian subject. But "The Demon" and "Feramors" remain his best known stage works. The ballet-music from these two operas is deservedly popular.

Rubinstein was eclectic rather than national. He did not believe in limiting his music to the purely Russian appeal of native folksongs. But on the other hand he did not recognize the value of nationalism. He was greatly opposed to Wagner, and feared that the latter's influence on opera would be totally bad. Rubinstein summed up his own position, both racially and musically, by saying, "The Christians call me a Jew, the Jews, a Christian; the Russians called me a German, the Germans, a Russian."

Nicholas Rubinstein (1835–81), Anton's younger brother, was a good musician in his own right. He was an excellent pianist, an able conductor, and a composer of concert and salon music. He founded and directed the Moscow Conservatory.

Peter Ilyitch Tschaikovsky (1840–93) became Russia's greatest composer. His father's mining business took the family to distant places, where there was little art; but a music-box brought the boy much pleasure. School in St. Petersburg was a harsh contrast to the pleasant family life, and laid the foundation of the composer's nervous troubles. Later on Peter was set to studying law, for which he felt an utter distaste. His dislike of mathematics was shown by the fact that he once boasted of having solved a problem unaided; but this did not occur until his fifth year of legal study. This quality showed also in his dislike of Bach and the intellectual side of music. His own works, great as they are, lean too much on emotional effects, in spite of the strength showed by the fugue in his first suite.

After the death of Tschaikovsky's mother, which shocked him greatly, he graduated from his studies and became an official in the

Ministry of Justice. He never worked hard at this post, however. He acquired the habit of chewing paper when at all abstracted. Once, while taking a state document to a certain office, he met a friend in the corridor; and that friend's conversation proved so interesting that Tschaikovsky bit up most of the document before remembering his errand. Fortunately he was able to make another copy from memory.

At this time he had various music teachers, but none of them suspected his future greatness. He received no valuable instruction until the conservatory started. Then he was thoroughly grounded in harmony and counterpoint, and studied form with Zaremba and orchestration with Anton Rubinstein.

Tschaikovsky's tastes were very variable. At that period he placed Wagner far below Serov, and said that piano and orchestra did not blend. Now Serov is known as a "second-rater," while Wagner's leadership is acknowledged; and Tschaikovsky's own piano concertos are among the very best. At this time, too, he showed his own radical tendencies in an overture entitled "The Storm," which caused a real storm when the conservatory people saw it.

Tschaikovsky fell deeply in love with the singer Désirée Artôt, but did not marry her after all, perhaps not wishing to be the male attendant of a travelling star. It would have been better for him if he had made this union; for his own marriage, occurring later, was most unfortunate. A lady whom he had met during girlhood addressed a series of love-letters to him. He informed the lady (Antonina Milyukova) that he had nothing beyond friendship to offer; but she was persistent, and finally the composer feared he might ruin her life if he refused her. They were married in 1877, but the union soon proved unhappy. Tschaikovsky, who was very nervous, would probably have been driven into a premature grave if an early separation had not taken place.

Another woman was of far more beneficial influence on his career. This was Nadeshda Filaretovna von Meck, the wife of a rich engineer. Much moved by Tschaikovsky's music, she gave him the generous sum of six thousand roubles annually, to allow him to compose unhampered by financial cares. She made it a condition that they should never meet; and even when attending the same concert, they passed each other as strangers. But they corresponded, and the composer sent her frequent accounts of his musical activity.

A stay at Clarens, on Lake Geneva, was followed by a trip to Italy and various other places. In Vienna he found Wagner's "Ring" rather tiresome, and came to dislike the works of Brahms. The latter feeling was natural enough, for the intellectual Brahms and the emotional Tschaikovsky were certainly opposites in music.

Back in Russia, Tschaikovsky settled at Maidanovo, where the quiet country life gave him rest. Here he took long walks, which often brought him musical inspiration. The last few years of his life were full of travel. In 1891 he even made an American tour, receiving much appreciation, but meeting many annoyances also from ill-bred hotel employees. He died of cholera, brought about by his drinking a glass of unfiltered water at a St. Petersburg restaurant.

Tschaikovsky's music marks him as a leader in orchestration, and in the best effects of the programme school. His great symphonic poems show a most powerful mastery over the instruments and their combinations.

In Russia, Tschaikovsky is known as a prolific opera composer. His first attempts, however, met with misfortune that was not undeserved. "The Voyevode" was performed, but cut up afterwards into separate numbers. "Undine" was rejected, and its music too was dissected for use in later works. "Mandragora" had a weak libretto. The composer's first success was "The Opritchniki." This received fourteen performances in a year; but Cui called it the work of a schoolboy, ignorant of the needs of lyric drama.

"Vakula the Smith," which won prizes in competition, has for its hero the son of a witch, who brings for his sweetheart the shoes of the empress, demanded as a pledge of love, by tricking and using the demon who is smitten with his mother. The subject is decidedly bizarre, but has its moments of humor as well as dramatic power, and is set to good music.

"Eugene Onyegin," Tschaikovsky's best opera, treats a story by Pushkin. Eugene's friend Lensky, loving a girl named Olga, presents him to her family. Her sister Tatiana falls in love with the stranger, but he sees in her only a country nobody, and ignores her little advances. Later in life he finds her transformed by marriage into the brilliant Princess Gremin. He then feels her spell, and pleads his love; but in spite of her early longing for him she is able to refuse his advances and leave him in despair. The music shows much beauty of feeling, Tatiana's scenes being especially tender.

"Joan of Arc" was a weak blend of Italian and Meyerbeer effects. "Mazeppa" prompted Cui to say that Tschaikovsky had succeeded in producing something worse even than "Joan of Arc." "The Sorceress" was undramatic, the composer showing a tendency to make his score consist of complete musical forms. The later one-act "Iolanthe" was prolix, though occasionally expressive. But "The Queen of Spades" proved another success. This work is based on a Pushkin story of a young gambler who is told of three successful cards by the spirit of a dead countess. He wins on two of them, but the third changes to the queen of spades, on which he loses everything. A love story with the daughter of the countess is added in the libretto.

Tschaikovsky's incidental music to "The Snow Maiden" is very good, — much better, in fact, than that to "Hamlet."

He composed three ballets, "The Lake of Swans," "The Sleeping Beauty," and "Casse-Noisette." All of them show much musical beauty. In the last, the stage manager called for the music in definite amounts, — sixty-four bars of soft music, eight bars of tinkling music as a Christmas-tree lights up, twenty-four bars of lively music for the children's entrance, and so on; but this did not seem to hamper the composer's inspiration.

Tschaikovsky's orchestral works are really much greater than his operas, and are known through the civilized world. Of his six symphonies, the first is called "Winter Dreams." The second was national enough to win praise from Cui, who disliked the composer's cosmopolitan ideas. The third is more conventional, being based on western European models. The fourth, beginning a much greater group, depicts man's troubles with fate, but ends in popular festivity. The fifth, coming some years later, is a strongly effective work, with very characteristic national themes that recur in the different movements. The sixth, the "Symphonie Pathétique," is marked by the most astonishing expressive power. Its first movement contrasts rugged work with a sad-sweet theme typical of tender memories. Its second movement, in ¾ time, shows an undertone of unrest. The third movement culminates in a stirring march, suggestive of glory;

but the fourth, really the slow movement, brings deep gloom for the close, suggesting death.

"Manfred" is practically a programme symphony. Its first movement shows the hero in the Alps, calling upon Astarte in vain, and pleading for oblivion. A fantastic *scherzo* depicts the Spirit of the Alps appearing in the rainbow of a waterfall. An *adagio* typifies the Swiss pastoral life and scenes. The finale is wildly infernal, depicting the caves of Arimanes; and it ends by suggesting Manfred's death. A German critic stated that while Schumann portrayed Manfred's passion, Tschaikovsky depicted his agony.

The first of the symphonic poems, entitled "Fate," was not successful.

"Romeo and Juliet" proved more effective. It has an opening theme suggesting Friar Laurence, and two main parts, typifying the feud and the lovers.

"The Tempest" is less successful, though it has many grand moments, and an effective storm.

"Hamlet" was another Shakespearian affair, condensed to form part of the incidental music.

"The Voyevode" is independent of the opera, but resembles it in not being very great.

Best of the symphonic poems is "Francesca da Rimini." In this the composer rises to tremendous power. Its central section portrays Francesca's narrative, while the first and last part depict the inferno. The wandering of lost souls is shown by an *andante lugubre*, which is followed by a whirlwind of infernal suggestion.

Tschaikovsky's overtures are good, but less important. The first piano concerto is grandly effective, even though Nicholas Rubinstein abused it once. A second concerto is also well liked; while a third is made of posthumous movements. The violin concerto is another standard work. This was the composition that aroused Hanslick's ire in Germany, and made that conservative critic remark that such music was actually malodorous (in fact, he used a more vulgar word). The variations for 'cello and orchestra form still another well-known work. A "Pezzo Capriccioso" and a "Fantaisie de Concert" also exist. Of the orchestral suites, his first begins with the fugue already mentioned.

Tschaikovsky's chamber music is strongly expressive. It consists of three string quartets, a sextet, and a piano trio. His piano works and songs are also attractive, but not well known in America.

Tschaikovsky ranks with the foremost masters. His handling of the modern orchestra, combined with the strongly emotional character of his themes, make his work as important in its way as that of Liszt or Berlioz. His music does not always wear well, for it lacks the underlying intellect of Bach or Brahms; but its glories are most marked, in spite of all criticism.

XXIII

WAGNER AND HIS REFORMS

WILHELM RICHARD WAGNER was born at Leipsic on May 22, 1813. After he became well-known, he omitted the "Wilhelm" permanently. His mother, widowed before his birth, married the actor and artist Ludwig Geyer, the family moving soon to Dresden. Some have thought that Geyer was really Wagner's father, though the evidence seems against the idea. The little Richard was a spirited, warm-hearted boy, with a taste for reading fairy tales. He showed no musical aptitude at first. Geyer, on hearing him pick out a tune that his sister had played, asked himself, "Has he, perhaps, a talent for music?" But Geyer died before having his question answered. It was not until 1827 that a hearing of Beethoven's symphonies and Weber's operas aroused Richard's love of music. His studies with Theodor Weinlig, at Leipsic, resulted in the composition of sonatas, overtures, and even a symphony in C; but these works were nearly all pedantic and uninspired.

Wagner's first libretto, written in his school days, consisted of a tragic affair in which all the characters were killed, and the last act carried on with their ghosts. His first opera was "The Fairies," which he finished at Würzburg in 1834. In that work a prince, who has married a fairy and lost her, goes through various trials in order to regain her. At Magdeburg he completed "Das Liebesverbot," a setting of "Measure for Measure" in the Rossini style. A further position brought him to Riga, where his conducting showed him the really commonplace nature of the Italian opera of that epoch. His next work, "Rienzi," was based on the sumptuous style that Meyerbeer used. The libretto shows at first the Orsini-Colonna brawls; Adrian Colonna's love for Rienzi's sister Irene; and the popular revolt under Rienzi. In the second act the nobles are pardoned, but try to kill Rienzi at the feast of reconciliation. In the third act they rebel, are defeated again, and several, including old Colonna, put to death. In the fourth act Adrian, out of revenge for his kinsman, foments popular revolt; Rienzi, in an impassioned speech, regains the people's allegiance; but the Pope's messengers excommunicate him, whereupon he is deserted. In the fifth act, after a vain attempt to regain his influence, Rienzi retreats to the palace; Adrian joins him, out of love for Irene; and the trio perish when the people burn the palace. This work succeeded, and Wagner could have become rich and famous by continuing in its school; but his artistic ideal drove him to seek higher things.

Wagner the artist and Wagner the man were two widely different beings. In art he sought for the noblest standards; but in life he was often mean and petty. He made the financial loans of his friends minister to his needs; and he seemed to take it for granted that he could be permitted to draw inspiration from woman's love, no matter where he found it. In Magdeburg he married Wilhelmina (Minna) Planer. She was a young actress who gave up her career for him, and helped him in the most practical ways, and by the most patient drudgery. This was especially true at Paris, where the pair went on leaving Riga. The voyage suggested a sea-subject to Wagner, and in Paris we find him beginning "The Flying Dutchman," which first showed something like his later style. Some songs and other works were of little pecuniary aid, and probably Minna's care and sacrifices were all that saved him from starvation. Wagner once said that he could not be a "Meister Bach," doing drudgery in a small post. He recognized his own genius; but he made this an excuse for sponging on his friends, instead of working until he earned enough to let him carry out his ideas. But his later musical plans were so titanic that they could not have materialized without the help of some wealthy patron.

A return to Dresden as Kapellmeister brought some happy years for Wagner, and for Minna too. She wrote afterward that his "Tannhäuser" and "Lohengrin" were composed in her presence, and while he was cherished by her care. She has been accused of not understanding Wagner's real greatness, and not giving him the spiritual companionship that was necessary for the development of his highest ideas; but the women who did give him such spiritual uplift might have been too busy to do so if they had been obliged to look after his physical needs as patiently and as well as Minna did. This marriage, and the subsequent separation, was not a case of the man outgrowing the woman intellectually. Something of that situation was present; but there was also the fact that Wagner made inordinate demands on other women's love, and expected Minna to shut her eyes to such amatory proceedings and keep up his home.

Wagner's wandering affection, if not actual infidelity, was plainly shown in his relations with the Wesendonck couple. He had become involved in the Revolution of 1848 (a proceeding to which the practical Minna naturally objected), and was forced to flee. Making Zurich his home, he brought Minna there also. Mathilde Wesendonck and Wagner grew so interested in each other that she persuaded her husband, Otto, to give Wagner a house next door to her own. Then arose a most fervid love intercourse between the composer and his benefactor's wife. Mathilde told much or all of this to her husband, who no doubt disliked the situation, but forbore to make a scandal. Minna, however, was kept in the dark, and received an unpleasant surprise when she found one of her husband's love-letters to Mathilde. In an artistic way, this platonic influence (if, indeed, it was nothing more) was a source of inspiration to Wagner in composing his "Tristan and Isolde," — in which, incidentally, a passionate love and a forbearing husband are portrayed. But Minna naturally found it hard to accept such a situation while living on the Wesendoncks' bounty. Yet she was still with Wagner when he went to Paris in 1860 and witnessed the public hostility to his "Tannhäuser" in 1861. But his irritability and selfishness soon caused such trouble that when the pair returned to Germany they separated. They remained apart except for a short time at Biebrich, and Wagner had several "affairs" with pretty women acquaintances whom he chose as housekeepers. In Wagner's relations with women, however, he was always fondest of those who appreciated the real greatness of his works. He was much influenced by external conditions, desiring physical comfort as well as protecting and adoring love. He would have his study perfumed, for instance, or would furnish it in keeping with the atmosphere of the work upon which he was busy. As a man, Wagner was indeed no devout "Meister Bach," nor yet a humanity-loving Beethoven. The greatness of his work is sufficient excuse for many meannesses, if they were really necessary adjuncts to the creation of such work. His trust in the financial help of his friends undoubtedly left him free to devote his efforts to art;

but one cannot help feeling that a better treatment of Minna would not have interfered with his creative ability. She died in 1866. Except for a Russian trip, Wagner had for two years been carrying on an affair with Cosima, daughter of Liszt and wife of Von Bülow. After Minna's death, he settled at Triebschen, near Lucerne, and Cosima soon joined him there. Four years later, Von Bülow divorced his wife, and Wagner married her. Wagner died in 1883, and she has survived him for several decades, being alive in 1915. She gave him the spiritual companionship that he desired.

Meanwhile Wagner had planned, and in part completed, the great works that were to make his name famous. His two subjects "Barbarossa" and "Wieland the Smith" were not used. But "The Young Siegfried," which he started in 1851, gradually grew into the great Trilogy (with prologue) that we know as "The Ring of the Nibelungen." The text was printed in 1853. "The Rheingold" was finished in 1854, and "The Valkyrie" by the end of the same year. The latter was scored by April, 1856. Then "The Ring" was laid aside for "Tristan," which was completed in 1859. "Die Meistersinger" was planned in 1862, though not finished until 1867. "Siegfried" was composed in 1869, and scored in 1871; while "Die Götterdämmerung" was composed in 1870, and the scoring finished in 1874. "Parsifal," the "stage-consecration-play," was composed in 1878–79, and scored in 1882. The composer died at Venice on February 13, 1883.

In one respect, at least, that of the criticisms he received, Wagner was fully justified in complaining. The public at first failed to appreciate the greatness of his music. Even composers were not able to do it full justice. It was called, after one of his pamphlets, "The Music of the Future"; and under this title it was subjected to all kinds of ridicule and abuse. Even after it had made its way with the public, officials often intrigued against it. Judith Gautier, in "Wagner at Home," describes a "Rheingold" performance at Munich, in which, after the rehearsals had been correct, the final representation was spoiled deliberately, by a manipulation of lights that kept them sedulously away from the rainbow bridge to Walhalla, and by other similar tricks.

In the last four decades the greatness of Wagner has been recognized. Even those who most disliked the man were reduced to

WAGNER CARICATURED AS ATTACKING THE HUMAN EAR

amazed silence by the revelation of his music. Its titanic strength, its glowing beauty, and its marvellous richness of orchestration almost obliterate the older schools of opera. The music of the future has become the music of the present; and radicals of the Satie-Schoenberg type are even trying to make it the music of the past. Yet once a Ruskin could speak of the glorious score of "Die Meistersinger" as "rotten, baboon-headed stuff."

When Wagner published the text of his Trilogy, he outlined a plan for its production similar to that which was carried out later at Bayreuth. He admitted that such an affair would demand princely aid. At the time Wagner despaired of ever finding such aid; but it was not long in coming. On March 23, 1864, Wagner fled to Mariafeld to avoid his creditors. On May 3 of the same year, Ludwig II, the new king of Bavaria, sent messengers offering his patronage to the hidden composer. By the aid of Ludwig, many of Wagner's dreams were made into realities. The composer lived in Munich for a while, just before settling in Triebschen.

Wagner kept working for the foundation of a national theatre, or opera house, where his own compositions and other good operas could be given. King Ludwig helped somewhat, but the sum needed was very great. Finally Wagner's persistent efforts made the plan possible; and in 1876 the Wagnerian opera house at Bayreuth was opened. There regular Wagner cycles have until now been given. Wagner's later years were passed in the Villa Wahnfried, which he built as a home at Bayreuth.

In person, Wagner was energetic and brilliant. His conversation was fascinating. Henry T. Finck quotes Sir Hubert Herkomer, who painted Wagner's portrait, to the effect that "You lose your identity when in his [Wagner's] presence; you are sadly inclined to forget that there is something else in the world beside Wagner and his music. You are under an influence that sets every nerve at its highest key. He has been able to make people frantic with enthusiasm."

Taking up Wagner's operas in about their order, one may repeat that "Rienzi," comparable to Meyerbeer's works, represents no theories. The germ of these is first found in "The Flying Dutchman." That opera opens in a rocky cove, where the skipper Daland and the Flying Dutchman, Vanderdecken, take refuge from a storm. Vanderdecken is the sailor who boasted that he would finish a voyage in spite of Heaven itself, for which blasphemy he was doomed to sail forever. Release will come only if a maiden loves him enough to sacrifice herself; and once in seven years he may land to seek her. Failure has made him gloomy; but by showing his wealth he obtains Daland's permission to woo the latter's daughter Senta. The second act shows Senta among a merry group of girls busy at their spinning-wheels. But she stands apart, gazing at a picture of Vanderdecken. When teased about her sadness, she tells his story, and says she would willingly save him. Her admirer Erik cannot alter this mood. When Daland brings in the real Dutchman, she is amazed; but soon she plights her troth to him. The third act shows the seamen making merry by the harbor. The Dutchman's sailors, however, do not join. When challenged, their boat glows in a supernatural light, and they sing a weird song taunting their captain with his many failures in love. Senta appears with Erik. The latter again pleads his love. The Dutchman, hearing this, thinks Senta false to him and sets sail to depart. She tries to reach his ship. He tells every one of his identity, so that she may be held back; but she plunges into the sea after him, redeeming him by her sacrifice.

The music shows a rugged vigor well suited to its subject. This strength, combined with a rich harmonic and melodic beauty, is characteristic of all Wagner's later work. Especially attractive are the spinning chorus, Senta's dramatic ballad, the tender theme that portrays her, the sombre figure typifying the Dutchman, and the rollicking sailors' music. The work shows a tendency toward Melos, — the continuous melodic recitative that Wagner afterwards used, instead of single numbers.

"Tannhäuser" shows the minstrel knight of that name revelling in pleasure in the Mount of Venus. But her charms pall, and he returns to the upper world. In a pastoral valley, he hears the chant of passing pilgrims. Landgrave Herrmann, hunting, finds him, and brings him to the tournament of song at his castle. There Wolfram von Eschenbach, Walther von der Vogelweide, and others compete, as they did in actual history. Elisabeth is to award the prize. In his song, Tannhäuser, incited by memory, sings of Venus, and shocks the assemblage. He realizes his sin, and departs to obtain the Pope's forgiveness. Elisabeth, who loves him, awaits his return, and watches the passing pilgrims for him. Then Wolfram sings of his own hopeless love for her. The Pope has told Tannhäuser that "sooner should his dead staff put forth leaves than the knight be forgiven." The latter, returning, attempts to seek Venus again. A funeral procession passes with the body of Elisabeth, who has died broken-hearted. Tannhäuser sinks in death by her bier, while a band of pilgrims bring the Pope's staff, which has blossomed in token of the knight's pardon.

The Pilgrims' Chorus, the brilliant Venusberg music, the songs in the contest, Elisabeth's " Greeting to the Hall," the knights' march, and Wolfram's song of devotion are some of the musical gems in the score.

In "Lohengrin," Elsa of Brabant is charged with the murder of her young brother, Prince Gottfried, who has really been bewitched by the sorceress Ortrud. The latter's husband Telramund is ready to appear against Elsa in ordeal of battle; but no one will fight for her. While the herald calls for her defender, Elsa recites a dream of a knight in shining armor who would come as her champion in a boat drawn by a swan. Meanwhile those at the back of the stage see something approaching. It is really Lohengrin, on the river Scheldt, and Elsa's dream becomes a fact. Lohengrin wins the fight. He begs Elsa to be his bride, but tells her also that he cannot remain with her unless she will refrain from asking his name. The next act shows the outside of the palace, in which a wedding feast is taking place. Ortrud and Telramund, discredited, are hiding outside. Elsa appears on a balcony, and Ortrud wins her pity by pretended humility. Day dawns, and the bridal procession comes to the church. It is startled first by Telramund's emerging from hiding, and again by Ortrud's claiming precedence over Elsa and taunting her with ignorance of the bridegroom's name. In the third act, the bridal chorus greets Elsa and Lohengrin in their apartment. When left alone, the pair express their love; but Elsa's suspicions are aroused, and she asks Lohengrin's name. Telramund breaks in to kill Lohengrin, but drops dead at sight of the latter's magic sword. The scene then changes to the ground by the river Scheldt. Lohengrin explains that he is a Knight of the Holy Grail, who can remain on earth only if unknown. Elsa is disconsolate; but in parting Lohengrin finds himself able to disenchant her brother Gottfried, who was really the swan.

The music to this work, strangely enough, was at first attacked as unmelodic. But its melodies have a rich harmonic support that was evidently too novel for the critics. The Bridal Chorus is now known everywhere. The Prelude is a shimmering web of tonal richness. The work is one long stream of musical beauty; but especially attractive are Elsa's dream, her balcony soliloquy, the processional music, Lohengrin's love-song ("Dost thou not breathe with me") and his farewell.

The Trilogy consists of "The Rheingold," "The Valkyrie," "Siegfried," and "The Twilight of the Gods." Its story is partly told in various versions of the Nibelungenlied. These, with "Tristan," "The Mastersingers," and "Parsifal," are called music-dramas instead of operas. In these Wagner developed his theories with some fulness. In the first place, he insisted that a libretto should be poetic, and worthy. He held also that the composer should write his own librettos. Wagner did this so well that "The Mastersingers" is now a textbook in the German schools. In "The Ring" he wrote in a brief, strong fashion pregnant with expression, and well suited to musical setting. He insisted on the continuous style that he called Melos. He held that the music should always reflect and intensify the spirit of the words or situation; and this idea he carried out faithfully. He summed it up well in the words, "Music is Truth." He used also guiding motives, especially in "The Ring." These are short, pregnant phrases that illustrate some personage or event, and may be used afterwards to suggest that character or event. As will be seen, the use of these motives enables an orchestra literally to tell a story in tones. He discarded ensembles as being unnatural. But back of all theories was Wagner's own musical inspiration. His compositions showed the possibilities of the rich modern orchestra as applied to opera. Liszt handled the instruments equally well, but in certain operatic scenes Wagner's genius went far beyond that of Liszt. Wagner learned from Beethoven, though his idiom is vastly different. Wagner may rank with Beethoven and Bach in leadership.

"The Rheingold" opens in the depths of the Rhine, with the three Rhine Daughters playing as they guard the gold. Alberich, king of the Nibelungs (subterranean Dwarfs), enters suddenly. At first he is charmed by the maidens; but on learning that he who renounces love can win the gold, he turns from them and takes the treasure. From it he makes afterwards a magic ring and a helmet of invisibility (Tarnhelm). A second scene shows the Gods ready to enter Walhalla. The Giants Fafner and Fasolt, who have built it, demand as pay Freia, Goddess of youth and love. Loge, the Fire-God, sent to find a ransom for her, brings news of the gold, which the Giants will accept; and Wotan, the All-Father, decides that the Gods must get it. A scene in Niffelheim shows the Dwarfs at work, slaves to the spell of the ring. The Gods ask Alberich to prove his power of transformation (due to the Tarnhelm); and when he turns to a toad, they clutch him and carry him back to their mountain. There they force Alberich to bring up the gold; but he lays on it a curse that shall cause misfortune to all who possess it until it is returned. The Giants claim the hoard and release Freia. The curse shows its first effect when the Giant Fafner kills his brother Fasolt, to own the gold alone. Then Donner (Thor) smites a rock, and a rainbow bridge appears, over which the Gods march to their new abode.

Before "Die Walküre" begins, Wotan has detailed the nine Valkyries, daughters of himself and Erda (Earth) to bring to Walhalla all heroes slain in battle. In the guise of a man he is father to the Volsung twins, Siegmund and Sieglinde; and he hopes that Siegmund will kill Fafner, now changed into a dragon, and restore the gold. When "Die Walküre" opens, Siegmund, driven by a storm, takes refuge in a forest hut, where he finds Sieglinde, wife of Hunding. The pair are attracted to each other. Hunding enters, and welcomes the stranger; but Siegmund's recital shows that he is an unsuspected enemy of Hunding's tribe. The latter tells him to prepare for battle on the morrow. Left alone by the hearth, Siegmund cries for a sword that his father once promised him for the time of direst need. Sieglinde then appears, saying that she has drugged Hunding, and showing a sword-hilt in a tree-trunk. None could draw the sword; but now Siegmund does so, and the pair flee together. In the next scene, a rocky fastness, Wotan tells Brunhilde, bravest of the Valkyries, to help Siegmund in the approaching fight. But Fricka, his consort, appearing at the moment, demands Siegmund's punishment for making Sieglinde false to her marriage vow; and Wotan has to consent. Brunhilde, won by the bravery and devotion of Siegmund, who now appears with Sieglinde, decides to attempt to save him.

But in the fight, Hunding is allowed by Wotan to kill Siegmund; though Wotan then kills Hunding. The third act shows a gathering of the Valkyries, with Brunhilde coming to escape from her father, who is angered at her disobedience. The two are left alone, and Wotan is pacified, but even against his will he must punish Brunhilde. He puts her into a magic sleep, and makes her the prize of the first man who finds her; but at her request he surrounds her with a magic ring of fire, through which none but the bravest man can penetrate.

Before "Siegfried," Sieglinde has died, and Siegfried, Siegmund's child, is brought up by the Dwarf Mime, who hopes the young man will weld Siegmund's sword and slay Fafner with it.

"Siegfried" opens with Mime at work over his forge, and the boisterous Siegfried being told the story of his birth. After Mime has a dialogue with Wotan, Siegfried forges the sword successfully. The second act shows a forest glade, where Siegfried muses on the sylvan beauty. The dragon appears, and Siegfried kills him. A taste of the blood, which has spattered on Siegfried's hand, enables him to read any one's thoughts. Learning thus that Mime will try to kill him and take the gold, he kills Mime. Guided by the birds' songs, he goes to seek Brunhilde. In the third act, Wotan tries to bar the way, but his spear is broken by Siegfried's sword. Siegfried pierces the ring of fire, and wins Brunhilde's love.

A prologue in "Die Götterdämmerung" shows the Norns, or Fates, spinning the thread of the Gods until it breaks. Siegfried now exchanges his ring for Brunhilde's horse Grane, and starts in search of adventures. After an orchestral interlude, the Hall of the Gibichungs, on the Rhine, is seen. There Siegfried finds Gunther and his sister Gutrune with their half-brother Hagen, son of Alberich. Hagen, who knows of the ring, wishes to get it. He gives Siegfried a magic potion that makes the latter forget Brunhilde and love Gutrune. Then he suggests that Siegfried shall get the ring and bring Brunhilde to be Gunther's bride, which is done by Siegfried in Gunther's form. In the second act, Brunhilde is overcome on seeing Siegfried wearing her ring and marrying Gutrune. She accuses him of treachery; but the potion has made him forget the past. Gunther, thinking himself betrayed, joins Hagen in plotting Siegfried's death. In the third act, in a forest, the Rhine Daughters beg Siegfried to give them the ring; but he refuses, in spite of their warning. Hagen restores Siegfried's memory by a second potion; and when he has told of Brunhilde, Hagen stabs him in the back, — his one vulnerable spot. Another scene shows Gutrune at the castle. Hagen says Siegfried has been killed by a boar. He claims the ring, and stabs Gunther in order to get it. But as he reaches for it Siegfried's dead hand is raised in warning. Brunhilde, having learned the truth from the Rhine Daughters, immolates herself on Siegfried's funeral pyre. As Hagen tries to get the ring from the ashes, the Rhine rises and engulfs him, the maidens thus recovering the ring. Meanwhile a glow in the sky is seen; Walhalla is in flames, the old Gods perish, and humanity rules on earth.

The music of this great epic is best understood by a close knowledge of the words. Without that, some passages seem tedious. But even to one who knows little of the librettos, the scores contain many orchestral passages of great beauty. Such are the entrance into Walhalla, the Ride of the Valkyries, the Magic Fire music, the Forest Rustling, and the Rhine Journey. But all the music is strongly effective, and suits the words remarkably well. In "The Rheingold" are the rhythmic, steady pulsation of the river, the Rhine Daughters' attractive calls, the odd rhythm of the Dwarfs' hammers, and the heavy footsteps of the Giants, beside the various motives of the Gods and the Walhalla music. In "Die Walküre" are the storm, the love-song of Siegmund, the Wotan-Fricka scene, Siegmund's brave protection of Sieglinde, the fight in the darkness, and the wonderful scenes of the Valkyries and the Magic Fire. In "Siegfried" are that hero's forging of the sword, the murmurs of the forest, the fight with the dragon, and the great duet at the close. In "Die Götterdämmerung" the guiding motives are built up into grand climaxes. The use of these motives may be shown by Siegfried's funeral march, which practically tells the story of his life in tones. Another famous example of their use is in the first act of "Die Walküre." Siegmund, alone by the hearth of his enemy, is lost in musing. The motives show that he barely thinks of the storm; he remembers Sieglinde and her kindness instead. Soon he grows agitated, and finally calls for the sword. The firelight then flares up and reflects on the sword hilt in the trunk of the tree about which the hut is built; while in the orchestra the sword motive is interwoven with the motive of Wotan's compact, showing the audience that the promise of the sword will be kept.

"Tristan and Isolde" opens on shipboard. King Mark had chosen as his bride the subjugated Irish princess Isolde, and had sent Tristan to be her escort. Isolde wishes to die; and she summons Tristan (whom she hates because he did not woo her for himself on a former occasion) to drink a fatal draught with her. But her servant, Brangaene, substitutes a love-potion for the fatal draught, and the pair feel its effects. In the second act, at King Mark's castle, Tristan meets Isolde secretly, and they sing of their love. But his enemy, Melot, brings the king on the scene, and wounds Tristan, who is taken away by his squire Kurwenal. The third act shows Tristan sick and delirious at his castle in Brittany. A shepherd signals that a ship is approaching. Isolde enters. Tristan dies, and she sings his elegy and dies of love, just as Mark's men, from a second ship, force their way in. Mark has learned of the potion, and is ready to pardon the pair; but he comes too late.

The music of this work is intense in character. To some it seems monotonous, while others regard it as the very essence of Wagner's theories. If the text is followed closely, the music will be found to illustrate it perfectly.

"The Mastersingers of Nuremberg" opens in a church, with the knight Walther von Stolzing and Eva, daughter of the goldsmith Pogner, falling in love at first sight. Learning that her hand is to be the prize in a mastersinging contest, Walther wishes to enter the masters' guild. The apprentice David, under orders from Eva's maid Magdalena, tells him of their intricate rules. He discards these, however; and he sings to the masters, who have gathered, a trial song that is free, though poetic enough. A pedantic rival, Beckmesser, counts him as failing; and only Hans Sachs appreciates his poetic gifts. The opera is in some sense autobiographical, and Walther represents Wagner, whose genius was not recognized by those who clung to old standards. The second act shows the narrow street between Pogner's house and the cobbler shop of Sachs. Eva and Walther try to elope, but Sachs, working in the open air, prevents them by his presence. Beckmesser comes to serenade Eva, but his ludicrous music reaches Magdalena, who has sat at the window to personate Eva while she met Walther. Beckmesser pretends to

Sachs that he is trying out a song, and lets Sachs mark any mistakes with hammer-strokes on his cobbler's last. Much comedy results, for Sachs interrupts Beckmesser when the latter thinks he has won attention from the figure in Pogner's window. David, seeing Beckmesser serenading Magdalena, grows angry, and starts to beat him; while the people are brought out by the disturbance, and a general riot results. Eva meanwhile enters her home, and Sachs pushes Walther into his shop. The third act shows Sachs in his room, meditating. Walther appears with a song he has dreamed, and Sachs helps him to shape it according to rule, writing it out as Walther sings it. They go into another room, and Beckmesser enters. Seeing the manuscript, Beckmesser accuses Sachs of intending to compete; but Sachs, foreseeing a method of helping Walther, lets Beckmesser take and use the song. Eva then enters to have a shoe mended, and Walther greets her; while Magdalena and David appear, ready for the festival. The scene changes to a meadow by the Pegnitz, where the contest is to take place. It is a festal day, and the guilds march in one by one, the mastersingers coming last. Beckmesser then tries to palm off as his own the song Sachs had given him; but as Sachs had foreseen, he blunders woefully over it. Angered by the people's laughter, Beckmesser says the song is by Sachs. The latter then explains, and gains for Walther a new chance to sing before the masters. This time Walther wins the contest. At first he wants nothing to do with the masters, but Sachs persuades him to respect their honesty, and all ends happily.

The music is a perennial delight. The long Prelude foreshadows the story of the work, suggesting with inimitable humor the debate over Walther's first song. The church chorale, the lively apprentices' music, the meeting of the masters, Pogner's address offering Eva as prize, Walther's trial song, the musing of Sachs in the second act, Beckmesser's ludicrous serenade, the riot music, the call of the belated and timid watchman, Sachs's monologue in his room, the great quintet before the departure for the festival, the lively entrances of the guilds, and the prize song, are all strong points in the score; but in reality every note of the music is delightfully effective.

"Parsifal" deals with that knight's healing of Amfortas. The latter, King of the Grail Knights, had been allured by Kundry into the garden of her magician-master Klingsor, and had dropped the holy spear, with which Klingsor had wounded him. He can be cured only by a touch of the spear. The first scene is a rustic glade, where the innocent Parsifal slays one of the sacred swans, thinking no evil of it. The knight Gurnemanz takes him to the Grail castle, the scenery moving by in a panorama until the pair enter the castle hall. There the Grail service is held, but Parsifal does not understand it. Gurnemanz had hoped to find in him the "guileless fool" who was to heal Amfortas. The second act shows Klingsor's magic garden and its flower maidens. Parsifal, who has entered, is tempted by Kundry; but at her kiss he recoils, and gains the understanding that he had not possessed before. His resistance to temptation overcomes Klingsor; he recovers the holy spear, and the garden sinks into ashes. The third act takes place on Good Friday. Parsifal is baptized by Gurnemanz, and anointed by Kundry, the latter being now freed from Klingsor's spell, and duly penitent. Again the scenery moves until the Grail castle is reached. This time Parsifal knows what to do, and heals Amfortas with the spear, being afterwards made king himself.

The music is sometimes a little spun-out, but it has many great beauties. These include the joyous Parsifal motive, the Grail service, the attractive song of the flower maidens, Kundry's sensuous appeal, the "Good Friday" spell, and the final service.

Wagner composed a few other works, such as his dramatic "Faust" overture and several marches. Of the latter, the "Kaisermarsch" was for Germany, and the "Centennial March" for the Philadelphia Exposition. But his operatic marches, such as the one in "Tannhäuser," are much worthier affairs. The "Siegfried Idyl," planned as a surprise for his wife Cosima at Triebschen, is full of beauty. It uses motives from the music-drama, but treats them in a new way.

XXIV

BRAHMS AND THE SYMPHONISTS

JOHANNES BRAHMS was born at Hamburg in 1833. Son of a contrabass player, the boy soon learned the rudiments of music, though his father's opposition made him work in secret at first. He practised composing exercises and variations by himself for a time; but under Marxsen his studies became systematic and thorough. When fourteen, Brahms appeared publicly as pianist and composer; but he wisely withdrew from the career of a prodigy and studied quietly for some years more. He earned a precarious living by arranging marches and dance music, or playing at dances himself.

At this time he went on a tour with the violinist Remenyi. Once they were to play the "Kreutzer Sonata" of Beethoven. The piano proved too low for the needed violin brilliance; so Brahms transposed the entire piece a semitone upward, from memory, and played it with accuracy and spirit, in spite of Remenyi's misgivings. Joachim, who was in the audience, was so astounded by this feat that he gave Brahms letters to Liszt and to Schumann. The tour ended suddenly at Hanover, where the police remembered that Remenyi's brother (and probably he himself too) had been active in the uprisings of 1848. But the pair went to Weimar, and gave a performance which Liszt heard. Remenyi introduced his companion at Liszt's house, where the latter played Brahms's Scherzo (Op. 4) from an almost illegible manuscript. A little later, Liszt played his own sonata; but when he looked around for approbation, he found that Brahms, worn out from travel, was sleeping peacefully.

Brahms made a much better impression on Schumann. Walking from Göttingen to Düsseldorf (he was too poor at the moment to ride), he was warmly welcomed on his arrival, and entertained for some time. He captivated the local musicians by a performance of Schumann's "Carnival"; and Schumann responded by writing up Brahms most favorably in his magazine. The article calls Brahms the coming hero of music, speaks of his piano sonatas as "veiled symphonies," and praises his other early works.

One result of this praise was an appearance at the Leipsic Gewand-haus. There Brahms met with a foretaste of the adverse criticism that was to follow him for some time. In spite of the praise of Schumann and Joachim, one critic wrote, "Brahms will never become a star of the first magnitude"; and another wished him "speedy deliverance from his over-enthusiastic patrons." But attention was drawn to the young man, and the publishers soon began to print his works.

Brahms was a devoted friend to the Schumanns during the elder composer's illness; and in later life Brahms cherished the greatest admiration for Mme. Clara Schumann.

Soon after this Dietrich described Brahms as having a depth of seriousness, but an underlying vein of quiet humor also. Brahms never married, though at Dietrich's house he met a lady whom he said he would have liked to marry. Poverty prevented him at first, and afterwards he considered it too late. His life was orderly and well-balanced, exhibiting all the virtues of the Germanic character, in refreshing contrast to Wagner.

Much of Brahms's later life was passed in Vienna. He was fond of long walks, and would often settle down for a time at any near-by place that seemed quiet and suitable for composition. In these trips, and in his summer vacations, he showed an extreme fondness for children. He would often carry sweetmeats for them. Once an English lady, wishing to see Brahms when he stopped at the hotel where she was staying, found him on all-fours, giving a horseback ride to three juvenile friends.

Brahms was at first described as "rather delicate, slim-looking, and with a beardless face of ideal expression." He remarked of himself, "I suppose I did look something like a candidate for the ministry in those days." But he grew afterwards to really Teutonic breadth of stature. He was athletic enough, and used to be fond of diving when off on vacations with Henschel or other friends. In mountain-climbing, however, he would soon be out of breath; though he often concealed his state by getting his comrades to pause and examine the view.

Brahms was much averse to writing letters. An English publisher once wished permission to bring out the composer's new works at the same time that they appeared in Germany; but Brahms declined, because he would then have to write two letters about each work, instead of one. A lady friend once sent him some embroidered slippers, and was wise enough to include a card of thanks, all written out ready for the composer's signature. Brahms's dislike for formality kept him out of England, which he regarded as a place where one had to live in a dress suit and white tie. He was of a retiring disposition with strangers, and disliked the adulation of gushing admirers; but among his friends he was usually the life of the party.

Brahms was at one time very fond of reading fairy tales. He never wrote an opera, though he thought of "King Hirsch" as a subject for one.

His modesty was shown once at a restaurant gathering. The best wine had been ordered, and some one praised it by saying that it was "the Brahms among vintages." Instantly the composer retorted, "Then order me a bottle of Bach at once."

In 1896 Clara Schumann died. Brahms missed the train that was to take him to her funeral; and he was so angered by this event that his feelings may have brought on the illness that proved fatal to him. He was told by his doctor that a determination to live would help him; but he made light of his disease at first. It was an affection of the liver, which had carried off his father before him; and he died of it on April 3, 1897.

The music of Brahms belongs to the classical school that Beethoven represented. Von Bülow spoke of the three great B's in music, — Bach, Beethoven, and Brahms. Von Bülow may have been prejudiced in favor of the letter that was his own initial; but his grouping of the composers was fair enough. Just as Reinken, on hearing Bach, rejoiced that the greatness of counterpoint had not perished from the earth, so do present-day audiences, after listening to the Brahms symphonies, feel glad that he kept alive the classical style of pure music, as exemplified by Beethoven. The music of Brahms has a good deal of intellectuality about it. There is nothing in it resembling the plaintive sweetness of Grieg, or the wild emotion of Tschaikovsky. But it shows a vein of underlying feeling that is intense enough. If Brahms leaned towards intellectuality, he still balanced this quality with enough emotion to make his works a lasting monument of greatness. He belongs with the very few foremost masters. Those who do not appreciate him are those who have not learned (either by study or experience) that form is the true logic of music. So great a writer as Finck has called Brahms's work "musical small-talk, meaningless twaddle," and rated the composer as "a great dressmaker; a musical Worth." But the "dressmaking," the balancing of structure, and development of figures, are really points of value in music, and not a cause for reproach. More difficult to understand is Runciman's claim that Brahms "had not the intellect of an antelope," and "had not a great matter to utter." Time has shown the true value of Brahms, who stood for all that was best in classicism.

The orchestral works of Brahms include four symphonies, two overtures, a beautiful set of variations on a Haydn theme, a set of Hungarian dances, a serenade, and another serenade for smaller orchestra. With these works belong also two piano concertos, a standard violin concerto, and a double concerto for violin and 'cello. Of these works, the symphonies are heard oftenest. The first one, in C minor, is the one that Von Bülow called the "tenth," not exactly because it was fit to succeed the nine of Beethoven, but because it came tenth in a list of great symphonies that he was making. The music is deeply earnest and austerely noble. The second symphony is more playful. The third has many moments of beauty, while the fourth is sometimes odd and novel in flavor.

The chamber music of Brahms displays the same earnestness and underlying feeling that the orchestral works show. It consists of two string sextets, two string quintets, three string quartets, a quintet for clarinet and strings, three piano-violin sonatas, two 'cello sonatas, three piano trios, three piano quartets, a piano quintet, a trio for piano, violin, and horn, another with clarinet in place of horn, and two clarinet sonatas. The piano quintet and the sextets are especially great.

The piano solos by Brahms include sonatas, rhapsodies, variations, études, and other pieces. He wrote also an excellent sonata and other works for four hands, besides two organ compositions. In all these, both chamber and solo works, he is at his best. He does not give the artist much chance for technical display. The pieces are hard enough for the performer, but it is a self-abnegatory sort of difficulty, in which he has to present form or emotion without showiness.

Brahms composed many fairly large choral works, sometimes with orchestra. Best of these is the great "German Requiem," not a liturgical requiem, but a noble oratorio treating of death and consolation. He wrote this just after his mother's death, and undoubtedly had her in mind. Another great work is the "Ode of Destiny," for chorus and orchestra. "Nänie" and the "Song of the Fates" are other famous choral-orchestral compositions. The list is completed by motets, psalm, and many choruses.

Brahms composed over two hundred solo songs. In many of these his style of unobtrusive emotion and depth is shown to the best advantage. Such a case is found in the "Sapphic Ode," — apparently simple, but in reality most poignant in expression. Nearly all the songs are vocal gems; but some of the part-songs show an over-refinement of style, and a too great repression that results in commonplaceness. The chamber and orchestral works avoid this defect, for they offer the composer many parts instead of a single melodic voice, and allow him to give to his music the contrapuntal suggestion that makes for strength and permanence.

On the whole, then, Brahms is the composer who leans most toward intellectual effects. These are not dry and uninspired, as some critics assert. His effects are contemplative where those of a Beethoven were dramatic; but they have their full share of feeling, in spite of the occasional quietness of style. The appreciation of Brahms is still growing; and the next generation will probably admit that Von Bülow's ranking him with Beethoven was practically justified. In the wild chaos of modern radicalism, Brahms stands as a model of all that is sane and well-balanced in music. If others do not follow his lead, it is because they do not possess his genius. The impressionistic style is easy to adopt, and the student can soon learn to compose in the programme school by throwing together his masses of orchestral color. But it is much harder to write music that unites the logic of form with the persuasiveness of expressive beauty, and yet does not borrow interest from any outside story. Brahms did this, but no one seems to have inherited his mantle of leadership.

Anton Bruckner (1825–96) was in some respects a rival of Brahms. Without desiring it, Brahms was held up as a model for Wagner by the latter's enemies. Brahms himself could appreciate Wagner's freedom of style, but at first the critics could not. When Bruckner began to become known by his symphonies, their involved character and their use of the full modern orchestra tempted Wagner's partisans to claim him as a symphonist of the Wagnerian school. That Wagner looked askance at all such rivalry is shown by his statement that he intended his style only for opera. But that did not prevent the upholders of both sides from making rivals out of Brahms and Bruckner, with much consequent bickering.

Bruckner was born at Ansfelden, in Upper Austria. His father and grandfather were school-teachers, his mother an innkeeper's daughter. He was the oldest of twelve children. As the teachers were expected to be musicians, Anton found his father ready to teach him. At twelve he was sent to a relative, Weiss. When his father died, his mother and the family moved to St. Florian's, where Anton became a choir-boy. There he continued his studies.

As a school-teacher in Windhag, he was so poor as to be literally half-starved. Kronstorf proved even worse; but he was soon transferred to Steyr, where there was a good organ and sufficient pay. After that he taught at St. Florian, practising ten hours a day on the organ and three on the piano. Later on he became organist at Linz, and finally he went to Vienna, where he became a conservatory teacher.

His great mastery of counterpoint was shown in a theoretical examination, when Herbeck and others gave him a subject on which he was to extemporize a fugue. Herbeck made the subject long and hard; but Bruckner handled it with such mastery that Herbeck exclaimed, "He should examine us instead." In spite of his skill, Bruckner studied with Sechter. This teacher was not the best one, for Bruckner was often diffuse, and Sechter did not correct the tendency.

Owing to the Brahms-Bruckner rivalry, the critic Hanslick became a virulent enemy of Bruckner, slashing at his works, and even opposing his appointment as counterpoint teacher. So much did this injustice rankle that when Bruckner was presented to the Emperor, and asked to name a favor, he replied naïvely, "Won't you please make Mr. Hanslick stop writing about me?" Von Bülow, the Herzogenbergs, and other friends of Brahms were also unable to appreciate Bruckner's greatness.

BRAHMS

BRUCKNER

In person, Bruckner was full of odd mannerisms, and showed a sly peasant humor that betrayed his humble origin. But he was tremendously sincere in his music. Once he said to a friend, "I think that if Beethoven were alive, and I should go to him with my seventh symphony, and say, 'Here, Mr. Van Beethoven, this is not so bad as certain gentlemen would make out,' . . . I think he would take me by the hand, and say, 'My dear Bruckner, never mind, I had no better luck.' Then I'd say to him, 'Excuse me for going beyond you in freedom of form, but I think a true artist should make his own forms, and stick to them.'"

Bruckner composed three masses, a requiem, a "Te Deum" for voices, orchestra, and organ, a "Tantum Ergo," and other sacred works; but he is best known by his nine symphonies. Weingartner says that Bruckner was too much given to the invention of ideas, and too little to their development, while Brahms showed the reverse fault. Bruckner's symphonies are often long, and not always perfectly balanced. But they are earnest to the point of absolute austerity, and their intensity impresses the hearer in spite of any faults of construction. The seventh and eighth symphonies are full of grand effects. The ninth is unfinished, being without a finale. It is dedicated to God. The large plan and serious intent of these works places Bruckner among the masters.

Max Bruch, born in 1838 at Cologne, has been active in many fields. He composed three symphonies, but these are seldom heard now. A better fate awaited his four violin concertos, as they are favorites with the soloists, especially the beautiful work in G minor. His oratorio, "Moses," and the operas "Lorelei" and "Hermione," are comparatively little known; but in the field of the epic cantata he achieved constant success. The martial "Frithjof" and the striking "Odysseus" are works in this form that are most wonderfully impressive. "Arminius" is less so, though it is the composer's favorite. Other works of the same sort are "Achilleus," "The Song of the Bell," and "Damajanti." Such male choruses as "Salamis," "Leonidas," and the "Normannenzug" deserve especial mention for similar virile qualities.

Herman Goetz (1840–76) composed a symphony which has remained in the repertoire for some time. He became known also by an operatic setting of "The Taming of the Shrew."

August Klughardt (1847–1902) composed five symphonies, the symphonic poem "Leonore," several overtures, and four operas.

Josef Rheinberger (1837–1902) produced a Florentine symphony, three overtures, the tone-picture "Wallenstein," two operas, a mass, and much chamber music. He excelled in counterpoint. As a teacher, he had many American pupils.

Friedrich Gernsheim, born in 1839, has been known as conductor, teacher, and composer. He wrote four symphonies, of which the first and last have been most frequently given. His choral-orchestral works include "Die nordische Sommernacht" and "Der Nornen Wiegenlied." His male choruses, such as "Salamis" and the "Wächterlied," are well known. A recent composition is the "Overture to a Drama," which handles modern effects with classic dignity.

Gustav Satter, born in 1832, has composed symphonies, overtures, an opera, and the tone-picture "Washington."

Ferdinand Thieriot, born in 1838, has composed orchestral fantasies, manuscript symphonies, and the opera "Renata."

Georg Riemenschneider, born in 1848, is another conservative composer for orchestra.

Hans Koessler has produced a symphony, a violin concerto, a cantata, and smaller works; but he became best known through his symphonic variations, in which he endeavored to picture Brahms in various phases of life.

Wilhelm Berger, born in Boston, though living in Germany, is another conservative. His "Todtentanz" scored a fair success.

Georg Henschel, for a long time intimate with Brahms, composed some instrumental music, as well as an oratorio, a requiem, and small operas. But he became most famous by his singing and his early leadership of the Boston Symphony Orchestra.

Paul Caro composed four symphonies, as well as symphonic poems and operas.

Ignaz Brüll (1846–1907) composed a symphony, serenades, concertos, and overtures, but was most widely known by his operas, such as "The Fiery Cross" and "The Heart of Stone."

Other German symphonists include Albert Thierfelder, Karl Grammann, Max Zenger, Bernard Scholz, Heinrich Hofmann, Richard Heuberger, Arnold Krug, Otto Kurth, and Richard Metzdorff. Many of these men composed operas also. Other opera composers of the time before Wagner grew popular were Karl Götze, Theodor Hentschel, Edmund Kretschmer, Victor Nessler, Karl Perfall, Richard Perger, Franz Poenitz, Georg Rauchenecker, and Hans Sommer. Kretschmer's "Folkunger" and "Henry the Lion" have received much praise, while Nessler's "Trompeter von Säkkingen" is in a lyric style that made it very popular.

While Bruckner kept the symphony still classic in style, Gustav Mahler (1860–1911) tried to make it dramatic. Like his predecessor, he composed nine large symphonies. Some of these have passages or movements with solo voices or chorus. An instance is found in his second symphony, "Ein Sommermorgentraum," which contains an effective alto solo. His fourth symphony ends with a celestial chorus. Mahler's early works included an incomplete opera, "The Argonauts," a second opera, "Rübezahl," and the choral work "Das klagende Lied." A later choral work of some importance is "Das Lied von der Erde." Mahler composed also many beautiful songs, some with orchestral accompaniment.

The merits and defects of Mahler's orchestral work are well shown by his fifth symphony. That work exhibits sufficient power and variety of style, and a strong handling of the modern instrumental forces. But it is too dramatic, too full of exaggerated contrasts, which suggest a programme where none is given to the auditor. Mahler has been called the successor of Bruckner; but he fell below the earlier master in not really succeeding in the school of pure music. Few of Mahler's symphonies have any programme; but all of them seem like programme works.

XXV

GRIEG AND THE NORTHERN COUNTRIES

EDWARD HAGERUP GRIEG (1843–1907) was the only Scandinavian composer to win a place among the world's great musical masters. Born at Bergen, he benefited by the musical atmosphere of his home, and was well taught by his mother. Ole Bull was so impressed by Grieg's early attempts at composition that he persuaded the boy's parents to send him to Leipsic for study. This was done, and the course completed, in spite of illness. Grieg then worked under Gade for a while; but in Copenhagen he met Rikard Noordraak, whose national principles drew Grieg's attention to the beauty of the Norwegian folk-music. Grieg returned afterward to Norway, where he settled in Christiania, married a charming and cultivated wife, and devoted himself to composition. A later change of residence brought him to a villa near Bergen, where his retired life could not prevent him from receiving many honors, and drawing a government pension. Occasionally he made little tours, where he proved calm and forceful as a conductor, but rather nervous as a pianist.

In composition, Grieg became devoted to a style that echoed the Norwegian folk-music. That music is full of the most expressive and plaintive effects, as may be shown by such songs as "Astri, my Astri," or "The Herder's Call." The richness of melodic and harmonic beauty in Grieg's works of course goes beyond the popular style, but is nevertheless a very definite idealization of it. Grieg's melodies are lyrical, and full of a sweetness that is never commonplace, but always remarkable for its joyous enthusiasm or plaintive sadness. There is in his works a melting tenderness, a warmth of sentiment that seems perennially charming. His harmonic effects are responsible for much of this, as they are not only fresh and novel, but full of feeling and pathos also.

Grieg's compositions may be divided into three classes. These consist of his larger works, the smaller works that are essentially his own, and the many pieces directly inspired by the Norwegian folk-music.

Best known in the first class is the "Peer Gynt" music, which the composer arranged in two concert suites. The melodic beauty of the "Morning Mood," the intense gloom of "Aase's Death," the rhythm of "Anitra's Dance," and the suggestive oddity of "In the Mountain King's Halls" are known to nearly all concert-goers. The second suite is less familiar, but contains "Solvejg's Song," which is a gem of pathetic appeal. His other orchestral works include the impressive Autumn overture, a worthy and dignified piano concerto, the melodrama "Bergliot," and the "Sigurd Jorsalfar" suite, as well as some Norwegian dances. The elegiac melodies, the Norwegian themes, and the Holberg suite are all for strings. These works show all of Grieg's rich fulness of lyrical expression; and the same is true of the large choral works, such as "Olaf Trygvason."

The second group may be said to include Grieg's three beautiful violin sonatas, in F, G, and C minor. Of these the first is the favorite. Many of Grieg's piano works belong here, among them the "Humoresken" and a part of the "Lyric Pieces." Here, too, must be classed the many beautiful songs that Grieg composed. These songs show a most wonderful freshness of inspiration. Such lyrics as "Die Prinzessin," "Sonnenuntergang," "Waldwanderung," "Haakons Wiegenlied," or "The First Primrose," show a most surprising and novel beauty of style. Grieg had something new and interesting to say in music at a time when inspiration seemed at a discount elsewhere.

More directly inspired by the Norwegian music are the "Hallings," "Spring Dances," and similar numbers, both in the "Lyric Pieces" and elsewhere. Some of these, like the "Slätter," Op. 72, were modelled on the actual performances of peasant musicians.

Grieg has been compared with Chopin, since both emphasized emotion, and both drew inspiration from national sources. But while Chopin sometimes grew morbid, Grieg never did. Grieg's music is plaintively expressive rather than intensely passionate. But it loses nothing by this, as its charming originality leaves the auditor refreshed instead of exhausted.

Among Norwegian musicians, Ludwig Lindemann did pioneer work in collecting the folk-music. Waldemar Thrane produced the first native opera. Ole Bull composed a violin concerto and other large works, but wrote also in the national style. Torgeir Audunson was a native genius who refused to take music-lessons. Halfdan Kjerulf's songs were early favorites in many nations. Rikard Noordraak died very young, but became known by his national songs. Edmund Neupert, Adolf Terschak, and Christian Cappelen deserve mention also. Erik Meyer-Helmund (born at St. Petersburg) composed some successful songs and an opera. Among the women, Agathe Backer-Gröndahl is known by her expressive vocal works. Peer Winge and Peer Lasson are also successful song composers.

Johann Severin Svendsen (1840–1911) was less distinctively national in style. He studied in Germany, toured Europe as a violinist, married an American wife, and settled in Denmark. His "Rhapsodies Norvégiennes," like his "Carnival at Paris," give a very much diluted nationalism. His symphonies, his "Zorahayda" music, and his "Sigurd Slembe" overture show similar qualities, being good music, but not distinctively national or overwhelmingly original.

Christian Sinding, born in 1856, has shown himself the greatest of the Norwegians after Grieg. He has entered the orchestral field with a symphony, a "Rondo Infinito," the "Episodes Chevaleresques," a piano concerto, and two violin concertos. A recent work of much merit is his opera, "The Holy Mountain." He writes with modern orchestral control. He has composed songs, but he is most widely known by his many excellent piano pieces, of which the "Rustle of Spring" is a favorite. Sinding has been so fond of weaving rapid tonal embroideries about his themes that the musical copyists united in charging him more than the regular rates.

Johann Selmer, born in 1844, composed several orchestral tone-pictures, and many vocal works.

Otto Winter-Hjelm, born in 1837, wrote two symphonies based on German models, but became more popular by his songs and other short works.

Ole Olsen, born in 1850, has composed a symphony, incidental music, the symphonic poem "Asgardsreien," the opera "Stig Hvide," and much piano music. His birthplace was Hammerfest, the most northerly city in the world.

Sigurd Lie and Eyvind Alnaes are more recent orchestral composers in Norway. Thomas Tellefsen, of Norwegian descent, has written successful chamber music. Gerhard Schjelderup represents the modern radicals, having produced orchestral works and music dramas that are full of modern dissonances.

The Swedish folk-music was collected by Geijer, Afzelius, Drake, and Arvidson. Ivor Hallström was a pioneer in Swedish opera, though Häffner, Dupuy, Randel, and Johann Ahlström had worked in the same field. Olaf Ahlström composed effective chamber music, while Von Kapfelmann wrote part songs.

Franz Berwald (1796–1868) composed a "Symphonie Sérieuse" and other works that were admired by Liszt. His other compositions consisted of chamber music, a large cantata, and six operas. Berwald's uncle was an earlier composer, and a pupil of Abt Vogler.

Otto Lindblad wrote vocal works, including national and student songs. Gunnar Wennerburg became known in the same field; while Josephson composed oratorios. Adolf Lindblad (1801–78) wrote many songs, which were often sung by his pupil Jenny Lind; but he composed also a symphony and an opera. Albert Rubenson was another orchestral composer.

August Södermann (1832–76) worked in a national style, but gained a reputation throughout Europe. His compositions include a mass, an overture, incidental music, and many operettas.

Ludvig Norman (1831–85) was another orchestral composer, writing three symphonies, some overtures, and much chamber music.

Anders Hallén, born in 1846, is the leader of a new Swedish school. His operas include "Harold," "Hexfallan," "Waldemar's Treasure," and other stage works. His symphonic poems and Swedish rhapsodies are well known abroad. He has composed also several important choral works, as well as many beautiful songs.

Emil Sjögren, born in 1853, has written admirable chamber music, good organ pieces, and many striking songs, such as "Der Vogt von Tenneburg." In his larger works he is very expressive, but sometimes too bizarre in his novelty of style. His piano cycles, such as "Auf der Wanderschaft," "Erotikon," and the "Noveletten," are deservedly popular.

Wilhelm Stenhammar, born in 1871, is of a younger generation. His operas are unsuccessful Wagnerian attempts. His large orchestral cantatas, however, fare much better. His string quartets, piano works, and songs are also well received. His compositions show a delightfully fresh enthusiasm, and a warm richness of harmonic beauty.

Wilhelm Peterson-Berger, born in 1867, is an operatic leader, having produced "Sveagaldrar," "Fortune," and the later music-drama "Ran." His operatic lyrics, like his songs, are sometimes pensive, but generally marked by a sunny warmth of feeling.

Hugo Alfvén, born in 1872, has composed three fairly successful symphonies, besides a Swedish rhapsody, a symphonic poem, and many smaller works.

Tor Aulin, born in 1866, is famous as a violinist, and has composed three violin concertos and four idyls of much musical worth.

Erik Akerberg has produced orchestral and choral works. Gustav Hägg has tried the orchestral forms, but is best known by his organ music. Jacob Hägg composed a "Northern Symphony" and other works. Fritz and Anton Hartvigson were pianists as well as composers. Johann Nordqvist is an orchestral writer of an older generation. Widéen has produced excellent male choruses. Lindegren was a composer of chamber music. Bror Beekman has worked in the violin field. Liliefors, Vletbad, Erikssohn, and Lundberg have composed for the piano. Elfrida Andrée leads the women, with Valborg Aulin, Helen Munktell, and Alice Tégner deserving mention.

In Denmark, Gade's prominence obscured both Johann Hartmann and his gifted son Emil, though both had written good symphonies and popular operas. After Gade's death, a new generation succeeded them.

Siegfried Saloman wrote operas for Copenhagen, beginning in 1832. Henrik Rung produced eight dramatic works, beginning in 1847. Alfred Tofft was another Danish opera composer. Jörgen Malling was still another Copenhagen writer of operas. Presben Nodermann became known by his "King Magnus."

In more recent years, Ludvig Schytté (1850–1909) composed several operas, including "The Mameluke," "The Swallow," "Hero," and the burlesque "Circus-Damen," as well as the pantomime "Atelderspuck."

Eduard Lassen (1830–1904) has been mentioned in connection with Liszt.

A recent Danish opera composer is August Enna, born in 1861. He was handicapped at first by poverty, and once indulged in the melodramatic act of burning some of his manuscripts for warmth. His early "Village Tale" won a little notice; but "Areta" was refused, and "Aglaia" sacrificed as fuel. An orchestral suite and a symphony won some attention and a little money, enabling the composer to travel. On his tour he wrote much of "The Witch," his first great triumph. This work was accepted by an opera manager, but laid aside, and rescued from oblivion only when Svendsen happened to look at the score and admire its beauties. It is based on Fitger's drama of the same name. Its success was marked. Since that time Enna has held a leading position in Denmark. His later operas include "Cleopatra," "Aucassin and Nicolette," "Lamia," "The Little Match-Girl," and several other Andersen subjects.

In the orchestral field, Simon Paulli was an early composer who outlived Gade. The Helsted family, consisting of Hermann, Karl, and Adolph, were active in Danish music, the first composing ballets, while the other two wrote symphonies and various large works. Lange-Müller is a more recent symphonic and operatic composer. Joachim Andersen is a flute composer who has also entered the symphonic field. Victor Bendix, a Gade pupil, has composed several symphonies, including the "Felsensteigung" and the "Sommer-klänge aus Südrussland." Asgar Hamerik, who taught for a time in Baltimore, has written six symphonies, some operas, and other large works. Otto Malling has composed orchestral and chamber music. Emil Hornemann has written a number of overtures; Fini Henriques is known by incidental music, as well as piano pieces; August Hyllested is another orchestral composer who has taught in America; August Winding has written a violin concerto; while Karl Nielsen is becoming known as an important symphonist. In the smaller forms, Attrup, a Gade pupil, has composed organ works; while Johann Nebelong and Asgar Juul have produced piano works and songs. Thorvald Otterstroem is a visitor to America who has composed good chamber works.

The first well-known Finnish composer was Bernhard Crusell (1775–1838), who lived in Sweden and Germany and composed the opera "Die Kleine Sklavin." But the real founder of the Finnish school was Fredrik Pacius (1809–91), a German by birth who spent his life in Finland and composed national songs and operas. Filip von Schantz, who lived until 1865, produced songs, choruses, and cantatas. Carl Wasenius was active at Åbo, the former capital. Karl Collan, son-in-law of Pacius, composed very popular choral marches. Conrad Greve, of Åbo, wrote incidental music. Möhring devoted his efforts to male choruses, while Ingelius, Ehrstrom, and Linsén composed well-known songs. Richard Faltin, the successor of Pacius as a teacher, produced cantatas, vocal works, and piano pieces. Martin Wegelius became known by the overture to "Daniel Hjort," and by his critical essays. Robert Kajanus founded and led the Philharmonic Orchestra at Helsingfors, the capital, and composed symphonic poems on subjects from the Finnish national epic, the Kalevala. This epic has much literary interest, and may have inspired the methods used by Longfellow in his "Hiawatha." Armas Järnefelt, born in 1869, wrote orchestral suites and the symphonic poem "Korsholm," and united lyric beauty with rich instrumentation. Ernest Mielck, known as "the Finnish Schubert," died when only twenty-two, after composing a beautiful symphony and other orchestral works. Oskar Merikanto has produced an opera, "The Maid of Pohja." Ilmari Krohn has written instrumental works and motets, besides teaching and publishing essays. Erik Melartin is a song-writer; Emil Genetz awakened much enthusiasm by his male choruses, such as "Heraa Suomi" (Awake, Finland "); while Selim Palmgren is known by songs and piano pieces of much brilliancy.

But the leader of the Finnish school, and the only Finnish composer to win a government pension for musical excellence, is Jean Sibelius. He was intended for the legal profession, but his violin lessons led him to adopt a musical career. He studied with Wegelius in Finland, and with Becker and Goldmark in Berlin and Vienna. He has composed four symphonies at the present writing. His symphonic poems "The Swan of Tuonela" and "Lemminkainen" are based on Kalevala subjects. "Islossningen," "Sandels," and "Snöfrid" demand choruses, while "Kullervo" employs soloists as well. His suites, "Carelia" and "King Christian IV," are earnest works, the Elegy in the latter being especially impressive. His "Finlandia," an orchestral work based on Finnish tunes, aroused such patriotic feeling that the Russians, after depriving Finland of self-government, forbade the performance of the work. His other compositions include cantatas, vocal ballads, songs, piano pieces, string quartets, and additional chamber music.

A comparison of the first and fourth symphonies of Sibelius shows that he has progressed toward attempts at broad effects, but become a little vague in the process. His first symphony is in fairly strict form, with a large-voiced slow movement and an oddly attractive scherzo. In the fourth, however, he seems to strive after the broadest effects of a Bruckner; but he becomes more impressionistic in style. Yet in spite of its vagueness, the latter work is effective enough, and promises well for the composer's future.

XXVI

STRAUSS AND RECENT GERMANS

RICHARD STRAUSS was born at Munich on June 11, 1864. His father, Franz, was first horn player in the court orchestra. On one occasion Franz found certain Wagnerian horn passages too difficult; but he did not know then that his son would one day compose music even more intricate than Wagner's. Richard's mother was a daughter of the brewer Pschorr.

The child's precocity, aided by the musical atmosphere of his home, resulted in a readiness for piano lessons at four, and the beginning of composition at six. Songs and piano pieces were even followed by an orchestral overture. The child's handwriting was still immature, so the mother had to inscribe the words of the songs in order to get them into their proper space.

During his Gymnasium course (at the age of eleven), young Richard began taking lessons in musical theory and composition. An "Electra" chorus, several songs, an overture, and a string quartet came soon after this period. These were all in classical form and style. The same is true of a violin concerto, a horn concerto, and the F-minor Symphony. The latter work was intended to be in the Brahms style, but it is not so deeply earnest as the Brahms symphonies. Piano works of these years, such as the "Mood-Pictures," Op. 9, show much beauty, and are somewhat in Schumann's style. This group includes the delicate and ethereal "Träumerei." Another early choral work is the "Wanderers Sturmlied," Op. 14, for six voices and orchestra.

Soon after this, Strauss gained Von Bülow's esteem, and was appointed assistant conductor at Meiningen. This came about after Von Bülow heard Strauss conduct, without rehearsal, his "Serenade," Op. 7, for thirteen wind instruments. Strauss afterward became chief conductor.

It was at this time that Strauss met Alexander Ritter, who persuaded the young composer to abandon classical forms and styles in passages, and by a love-duet and other sweet music. The hero's battlefield is shown as a fierce orchestral struggle. The hero's works of peace, which form the fifth section, bring in themes from the composer's earlier works, — as many as twenty-three reminiscences, one writer claims. The final section shows the hero's apotheosis. This work is grand in conception, but the thematic material is sometimes commonplace.

The "Domestic Symphony" is a long one-movement work. It is said to depict a day in the composer's home, which is apparently very noisy. There are themes for father, mother, and child, while the advent of other relatives is suspected here and there. Strauss once told the present writer that the work is supposed to depict the passing of night and the succeeding morning, in the latter of which is a fugue portraying the education of the child. But he has given different versions of the symphony at different times. The music is often broadly effective; but it does not gain much from the nature of its subject.

The programme school, which seems to have won first place in contemporary music, permits some variety of treatment. Music can depict emotions successfully, but is at a disadvantage when trying to describe actual scenes or events. A programme subject that indicates contrasts in emotion is therefore more fitted to permit the writing of great music. Liszt's "Tasso, Lamento e Trionfo," has been cited as an example. In the music of Strauss, "Death and Transfiguration" affords a similar effective contrast without forcing the music to depend on trivial details. But "Don Quixote" brings in the objective realism which is hard to portray accurately by musical means. To illustrate this, the reader may listen to short programme pieces (piano solos are most convenient) without knowing their names. He will find that the music is almost always capable of many explanations, and does not of necessity suggest its subject. Strauss claims that programme music will ultimately become much more definitely suggestive and accurate; but this idea, like his claim that all composers really use mental programmes in writing music, is definitely incorrect. What may be called subjective programme music, dealing with emotions rather than events, has more possibilities and more value than objective programme music.

Strauss has composed several operas. "Guntram," the first, is a story of a knight belonging, like Lohengrin, to a mystic order. Guntram rescues Freihild, who is drowning herself to escape a hateful marriage. Her father honors him, but is angered by his praises of peace and meekness. He attacks Guntram, the latter killing him in self-defense. Though Guntram is held blameless, he knows that rivalry in love was his real motive; and he is forced to renounce Freihild.

"Feuersnoth" is based on an old Oudenarde legend. Diemut, the Burgomaster's daughter, is loved by the stranger Kunrad. She resents a kiss given too publicly, and revenges herself by enticing him into a basket, hauling him halfway up to her window, and leaving him there. In his turn he casts a spell that puts out all the fires and lights in town; and she renews her allegiance before he relents. In the legend the girl was made the only source of renewing the fire, so that her pride was abased by exposure to the touch and the eyes of the multitude. This opera has some richly orchestrated music, though it is not often performed. It has an autobiographical passage in the text, in which puns on Wagner (cartwright) and Strauss (bouquet) show that he, like Wagner, objected to the critics who had maligned him at first. But where Wagner's "Meistersinger" passages are artistic, the personal allusions of Strauss are too openly conceited.

His later operatic style has been exemplified by "Salome," "Elektra," "Der Rosenkavalier," and "Ariadne auf Naxos." "Salome" is an intensely dramatic one-act affair. "Elektra," based on Hofmannsthal's version of the subject, is terrifically strong, and the orchestra almost drowns the singers' voices. "Der Rosenkavalier" is somewhat in the style of "The Marriage of Figaro," though scored for full modern orchestra; but it lacks sincerity in a way, and is not rated highly. "Ariadne" is a two-act setting of "Le Bourgeois Gentilhomme," one act being devoted to M. Jourdain's entertainment of the marquise, while the second consists of the play "Ariadne," given for her amusement. It is scored for only thirty-six instruments, but each one is given important work in a solo style.

The songs of Strauss are polished gems of perfection. Sometimes they seem fragmentary at first, but on repeated hearing they all show a most perfect unity. While his orchestral themes are sometimes commonplace, in spite of the grand uses to which he puts them, his songs show a most striking melodic beauty. They are more modulatory than the earlier *Lieder;* but their modulations are guided by a master hand. Such examples as the serenely beautiful "Traum durch die Dämmerung," the sparkling "Serenade," or the short but expressive "Morgen," prove their composer a master of lyric beauty; while the tragic "Steinklopfers Lied" shows him gifted also with dramatic power.

In estimating Strauss, one is strongly reminded of the lines, —

> " O, it is excellent
> To have a giant's strength; but it is tyrannous
> To use it like a giant."

He has the intellectual grasp and power that are needed in handling the complex modern orchestra. In the battle of his "Hero's Life," for example, are chords spread on thirty orchestral staffs, and containing as many as forty-six notes each. His mastery of instrumentation is greater even than Wagner's. But in real inspiration he falls behind the Bayreuth master. He has the sure touch of a master, but his utterances are sometimes commonplace. In certain cases his music becomes so bizarre, so fully devoted to the programme style as an end rather than a means, that one cannot help wishing him less of an extremist. None of his later works seem so well-balanced, or so properly unified, as his comparatively early "Death and Transfiguration." He has the methods and the surety of genius, but he does not always show its inspiration.

Siegmund von Hausegger, born at Graz in 1872, gave up a lawyer's career to become a composer of symphonic poems and other works. While still in school, he wrote a mass. His orchestral ballad "Odinsmeeresritt," and the operas "Helfried" and "Zinnober," were other early compositions. He showed his first flash of genius in the "Dionysiac Fantasie" for orchestra.

His "Barbarossa," a second success, is a three-movement work based on the legend that Barbarossa sleeps under the Kyffhäuser mountain, ready to awake in time of Germany's need. The first movement portrays the distress of the people. Next comes a weird, shadowy picture of the emperor sleeping in his mountain retreat. The last movement shows his awakening and triumph.

"Wieland the Smith," a later work, is in four movements. Wieland is that gifted smith who makes swords so sharp that they can cut off a head and yet leave it in place. In the first movement the celestial maid Swanhilda appears. Wieland loves her, but she is terrified at first by earthly passion, and retires to her lofty abode. The second movement shows Wieland's despair. The third movement depicts him forging a pair of wings, which he completes successfully. In the fourth movement he departs aloft with Swanhilda, leaving the dull world for the realms of eternal sunlight.

Hausegger has written other works, including songs with orchestra. He is prominent as a conductor. His music shows a most richly melodious character, that makes it remarkably attractive. "Barbarossa," for example, has many charming passages, though it is rather long-drawn-out.

Strauss and others consider Jean Louis Nicodé (born in 1853) a pioneer in the programme school. Nicodé taught piano at first, and became a conductor. His works include the "Carnival Pictures," "Maria Stuart," a "Jubilee March," a violin concerto, a set of symphonic variations, and choral-orchestral compositions, such as "Das Meer" and "Gloria," a romantic "Sturm und Sonnen-lied." They show some largeness of structure, and an interesting style.

Felix Weingartner, born in 1863, has been active in many fields, and is known as a gifted conductor. After study with Mayer, who taught Strauss, Weingartner spent some years as conductor in small theatres. In a letter to the present writer, he complains of the hard conditions in these minor posts. "I became acquainted with their wretchedness," he writes. "The salary was small, — 150 marks [$37.50] a month, for seven months and a half. . . . In Dantzic there were only four or five first violins, two contrabasses, third-rate singers, a miserable chorus, and no chance for proper rehearsals, as the directors insisted upon an extensive repertoire."

Weingartner's first opera, "Sakuntala," was given by Liszt at Weimar. Later operas by him were "Malawika" and "Genesius." His "Orestes" is a group of three one-act dramas on subjects from Æschylus. His symphonic poems include "King Lear" and "The Elysian Fields," the latter being inspired by a Böcklin picture. He has also written symphonies, of which the third, with organ, is full of broad effects. His chamber music includes three string quartets and a sextet. He has composed also many beautiful songs, and a number of piano pieces. His larger works show a strong handling of the orchestra, and a commendable freedom of style without radical harmonic excesses.

Max Reger, born in 1873, mingles classical learning with experiments in abstruse styles. His string quartets show the very intricate and jumbled harmonic effects that constitute modern radicalism. He has composed a very beautiful set of variations, with fugue, on a theme by Hiller; but his "Suite in Old Style" shows less direct inspiration. He has written many organ works.

But the wildest radical in modern Germany is Arnold Schoenberg, born in 1874. His earlier compositions, including the large vocal-orchestral "Gurrelieder," were fairly direct in style. In recent years, however, he has employed wildly dissonant harmonies in a most surprising way. His works seem at first sight nothing more than chaotic masses of fragments. His piano pieces have made audiences think that he must have written them as a joke. But in spite of their jumbled character, they show a marked dramatic force, even though they are too radical for those who appreciate the more orderly work of Strauss. The "Five Orchestral Pieces" form another much-discussed and much-abused work. Like the piano pieces, they are for the most part almost too wildly radical to be classed as music. But some of them, especially the first one, entitled "Presentiments," show a dramatic power of utterance that prevents Schoenberg from being disregarded.

A list of those who have composed recent symphonies will include Herman Bischoff, Gustav Brecher, Hugo Daffner, Paul Ertel, the conductors Max Fiedler and Emil Paur, Georg Fitelberg, Gustav Kord, Julius Major, Josef Reiter, August Scharrer, Paul Scheinpflug, Ernst Seyffardt, and Ewald Straesser. Many of these men have composed symphonic poems also. Other orchestral writers are Carl Bleyle, Ernst Boehe, Walther Braunfels, Joseph Foerster, Oskar Fried, Richard Gabriel, Karl Kampf, Siegfried Karg-Ehlert (known also by organ works), the boy-prodigy Erich Wolfgang Korngold (a symphonietta, a pantomime "Der Schneemann," chamber music, and shorter pieces), Gerhard von Keussler, the earlier Julius Kniese, Theodor Kroyer, Walter Lampe, Richard Mandl, Franz Mayerhoff, Heinrich Noren, Siegfried Ochs, Bernhard Paumgartner, Ferdinand Pfohl, George Washington Pittrich, Max Puchat, Felix von Rath, Rudolf Roesel, Hugo Rueter, Hans Schaub,

Bernhard Sekles, Georg Schumann, Thomas Stamm, Rudi Stephan, Otto Taubmann, Amadeus Wandelt, Hermann Wetzler, and the conductor Hans Winderstein. This list does not claim absolute completeness, for orchestral composers in Germany are as thick as blackberries in August. But it is representative enough. Beside these men, a number of the opera composers have written symphonies and other orchestral works. Best known among these are Eugen D'Albert, Waldemar von Baussnern, Leo Blech, August Bungert, Otto Dorn, Josef Erb, Alban Foerster, Robert Fuchs, Paul Geisler, Theodor Gerlach, Albert Gorter, Waldemar Kämpfert, Hugo Kaun, Friedrich Klose, Josef Krug-Waldsee, Friedrich Koch, Arthur Koennemann, Georg Kramm, Franz Mikorey, Leopold Reichwein, August Reuss, Bernhard Schuster, the older Robert Schwalm, Ludwig Thuille, Fritz Volbach, Richard Wetz, Hugo Wolf, Felix Woyrsch, and Heinrich Zoellner. Among those who have paid attention to other forms, Max von Erdmannsdörfer and Reinhold Herman have composed cantatas, Hugo Roehr has produced an oratorio, Robert Kahn and Stephan Krehl are known for their chamber music, Heinrich Gebhard is a piano composer, while Henning von Koss, Alexander von Fielitz, and Hans Heumann have won notice by their songs.

In opera, Engelbert Humperdinck, born in 1854, is the most successful of the contemporary Germans. Studying architecture at first, he took up music at Hiller's suggestion. His works include a Moorish rhapsodie for orchestra, the choral ballad "Die Wallfahrt nach Kevlaar," and many musical plays arranged for his juvenile relatives. The latter include "Dornröschen," "The Kings' Children," "Saint-Cyr," and "Die Sieben Geislein." From these came also his first great success, "Hänsel and Gretel"; while a later opera, "The Kings' Children," is elaborated from the earlier musical play of the same name.

"Hänsel and Gretel," brought out in 1893, is based on one of Grimm's fairy tales. It opens with the two children dancing and making merry instead of working. Finally they upset the cream-jug. Their stepmother, catching them, sends them out to gather berries on the Ilsenstein, to make up the deficit in food. Left alone, she bewails the family's poverty. The father, Peter, returns in a rollicking humor, having sold his brooms and other wares to good profit, and being now laden with supplies. But he grows anxious when he hears where the children have gone, for a witch inhabits the Ilsenstein. The next scene shows the children at play in the forest. They eat some of their berries, crown one another with garlands, and imitate the cuckoo. But at length they realize that they have lost their way. Darkness comes on, the Sandman makes them sleepy, and they lie down to slumber. First, however, they say their prayer asking the angels to guard them; and in answer to their simple faith, after they fall asleep the heavenly hosts do in reality descend to watch over them. In the morning, after the dew-fairy wakes them, the scene changes suddenly to the witch's gingerbread hut. She finds the two children, and casts spells over them. Gretel is set to work, while Hänsel, whom the witch plans to eat first, is fattened in a cage. After a ride on a broomstick, in true magic fashion, the witch prepares her fire and brings Hänsel toward it. But the children push the witch into her own oven. While they are rejoicing over their deliverance, the oven blows up, and some painted figures about the house turn into real children. Taking the witch's wand, Gretel disenchants them so that they can move freely. Peter and his wife then find their children, safe after all; and a chorus of happiness ends the work.

The music to this opera is straightforward and melodious, with a richly beautiful harmonic accompaniment. Its direct attractiveness and its idealization of folk-song effects pointed a moral for those who were trying to imitate only the more bombastic side of Wagner's works.

"The King's Children" begins with a witch berating the goose-girl who serves her. A youth finds the girl later, and loves her. Although he is in rags, he is really a king's son, and carries a crown with him. The town of Hellabrun sends to the witch to find who will be its next ruler, as its king has just died; but she will say only that whoever enters the town gates next day at noon should rule. The second act shows a square in the town. The king's son seeks work, and other by-play occurs. At noon, when all have gathered, the gates are opened, and it is the goose-girl who enters, followed by the minstrel (Spielmann) who had been with those visiting the witch. She greets the king's son, and tells him she has come to join him on the throne; but the people will not accept them. The third act shows the forest again, with the minstrel living in the hut of the witch, whom the people had killed in anger at her supposed mockery. Messengers come to ask him to return; and a child begs him to find the king's son and the goose-girl again. While he is away, the pair return to the hut, famished after their wanderings; but the people refuse them food, and they retreat to the hillside to die. The minstrel finds them too late, and sings a very striking lament over their bodies. The music is keenly expressive and richly melodious. The plot is really an allegory meant to show that true nobility of soul is not recognized by the common herd.

A very successful opera, which has been translated into many languages, is "Der Evangelimann," by Wilhelm Kienzl. Its plot is based on self-sacrifice. Mathias and Johannes, two brothers, both love the same girl, Martha. She prefers Mathias; and Johannes, in anger, sets fire to the barn where the lovers are meeting, and denounces Mathias as the incendiary. Martha's effort to save her lover prove futile; he accepts his fate, and is imprisoned for twenty years. After the term is up, Mathias finds Johannes dying, and forgives him. Kienzl, born in 1857, has composed other operas, such as "Urvasi," "Heilmar der Narr," "Don Quixote," and the recent "Kuhreigen," or "Ranz des Vaches," based on the actions of the Swiss guard at Paris during the French Revolution.

Eugen D'Albert, born in 1864, is famous as a pianist. He has composed piano concertos, a 'cello concerto, overtures, and a symphony. But opera has been his chief work, and he has set a dozen or more dramatic subjects. "The Ruby" is based on Hebbel's version of an Oriental story, in which a Caliph's daughter is magically imprisoned in the gem, and duly freed by her lover. "Ghismonda" treats the love of a low-born man for a princess. When discovered, he dies rather than reveal her secret; but she makes his chivalry known. "Gernot" is a fairy opera with much delicate music. "Die Abreise" shows the reconciliation of a married couple, who had drifted apart, but were brought together through the unwelcome attentions of a third party. "Cain" is a one-act version, somewhat altered, of the Biblical story. "Der Improvisator" is a setting of Hugo's "Angelo." "Tiefland," the best of D'Albert's works, treats a Spanish story of true love that baffles the intrigues of a dissolute lowland Alcalde.

Cyrill Kistler, born in 1848, was once looked upon as a possible successor to Wagner. His "Kunihild," which was well received, has for heroine Kunihild, who lives in a magic castle, and is won by Sigun, but loses him through the enmity of his brothers. Kistler composed also "Eulenspiegel," the legendary "Baldur's Death," the comedy "Im Honigmond," and "Der Vogt von Mühlstein." His style is sometimes too heavy-handed.

Max Schillings has produced the symphonic fantasias "Meergruss" and "Im Morgen," and a dignified prologue to "Œdipus." Of his operas, "Ingwelde" treats a viking story. Its heroine is carried from her home, her kidnapper is killed by his brother, and when she returns, that brother kills her husband also, after which the pair, who love each other, set out in a boat and immolate themselves together. "Der Pfeifertag" is an attempt at the old-time atmosphere of "Die Meistersinger." The plot includes various adventures on "Piper's Day," with the guild resenting an excessive toll; but it is rather confused.

August Bungert went to Grecian mythology for his subjects, and composed a hexalogy consisting of "Achilles," "Clytemnestra," "Circe," "Nausicaa," "Odysseus' Return," and "Odysseus' Death." The plots are admirably arranged, but the music is hardly great enough for such beautiful subjects. Bungert wrote also a comic opera, the "Tasso" Overture, and a symphonic poem.

Hugo Wolf (1860–1903) composed an opera, "Der Corregidor," and partly finished another, "Manuel Venegas." The former is based on a Spanish libretto, and apparently aims to duplicate the success of "Carmen"; but its story is intricate, and its music not strongly dramatic. His symphonic poem "Penthesilea" is a worthy work; but he is best known by his many songs. These are real artworks, and continue the excellence of the German *Lied* with something of the variety and force shown by the Strauss songs.

Siegfried Wagner, born at Triebschen in 1869, has attempted to carry on German opera, but with more persistence than success. His subjects are good enough, consisting mostly of German legendary lore; but his music is never great. His operas include "Der Bärenhäuter," "Herzog Wildfang," "Der Kobold," "Bruder Lustig," "The Kingdom of Black Swans," and others of the sort. But he is better known as a conductor.

Ludwig Thuille (1861–1907) was much praised by Strauss. Thuille composed overtures and chamber works that are well known. His operas consist of the unsuccessful "Theuerdank," the fairy play "Gugeline," and "Lobetanz," given recently in New York.

Leo Blech, born in 1871, is credited with three symphonic poems and several operas. The latter include the village picture "Das war ich," the legendary "Aschenbrödel," the dramatic "Alpenkönig," and the bright comic opera "Versiegelt."

Heinrich Zoellner, born in 1854, shows American influence in his cantata "Columbus" and his choral work "Onaway, awake." He has composed also several symphonies. His operas include "Der Ueberfall," "Frithjof," and "The Sunken Bell."

Hugo Kaun's American stay resulted in "Minnehaha" and other symphonic poems. Born in 1863, he now lives abroad. He has composed a "Fatherland Symphony," choral works, and the opera "Der Pietist."

Emanuel Móor, of Czech extraction, has composed a symphony, two concertos, and three operas.

Among operas that have been highly praised are Friedrich Klose's "Ilsebill," Paul von Klenau's "Sulamith," Julius Bittner's "Der Musikant," Arnold Mendelssohn's "Elsi," Hans Pfitzner's "Die Rose vom Liebesgarten," Max von Oberleithner's "Aphrodite," Max Vogrich's "Buddha," and Waltershausen's "Oberst Chabert." Other opera composers, not mentioned in connection with orchestral works, are Robert Erben, Ivan Knorr, Gustav Kulenkampf, Reinhold Becker, Max Marschalk, Karl Pottgiesser, Eugen von Volborth, Ignaz Waghalter, and Hector von Woikowsky-Biedau.

XXVII

FRANCK AND MODERN FRANCE

César Auguste Franck (1822–90) was a native of Liège, but lived in Paris. After Conservatory study in both places, he became organist at the Ste. Clotilde Church, and divided his time between organ-playing, teaching, and composing. As teacher in the Paris Conservatoire and elsewhere, he influenced many of the later French composers.

Franck's first success was the Biblical eclogue "Ruth." More famous now is "The Beatitudes," a broadly planned musical setting of the Sermon on the Mount. The poor, the weak, and the sufferers cry out in anguish; but they are comforted by the voice of Christ. Satan then tries to stir up dissension; but he is silenced when the sacred voice speaks again. The work is in eight sections, and shows dramatic force, sympathetic feeling, and real inspiration. Later oratorios by Franck include "Rebecca" and "The Redemption."

In the orchestral field, Franck followed a set of symphonic variations by his great symphony in D minor. The latter is a three-movement work of strong and impressive character. Franck's many symphonic poems include "Psyche," which contains solos, duets, and even a chorus; "Les Éolides," based on a poem by Leconte de Lisle, that gives homage to the breezes, the daughters of Æolus; "Les Djinns," depicting the spirits of the Orient that wander about in search of mischief; and "Le Chasseur Maudit," portraying the fate of the fabled Count of the Rhine, who started a sacrilegious hunt on a Sunday, and was forced in punishment to hunt forever, driven by flames and pursued by demons.

Franck's chief opera, "Hulda," deals with a viking subject, and seems to show in its story the influence of "Tristan and Isolde." Hulda is a maiden who is loved by her captor, Gudleik, but prefers Eyolf. She stirs up a duel, in which Gudleik falls. For a time she is satisfied; but when Eyolf returns to a former sweetheart, Swanhilda, Hulda arouses Gudleik's brothers to avenge his death. She leads

Eyolf into an ambush, where he is killed. While the victors debate whether such a gentle maid as Hulda should not be put out of this cruel world, Eyolf's men appear, and she casts herself into the sea to escape their vengeance.

"Le Valet de Ferme" was an earlier opera that did not met with great success. "Ghisella" was left unfinished, and too fragmentary for performance.

Franck composed some excellent chamber music, and a number of shorter works. His organ pieces are naturally well suited to their instrument. His "Prelude, Aria et Finale," and similar compositions for piano, are widely known.

Franck's work is rather modulatory. In his shorter pieces he shows an interesting style, though his modulations are not handled with the freshness possessed by a Strauss. In the orchestral works, Franck's manner is dignified and lofty, and often strongly dramatic. His organ compositions show much solid learning.

Franck's simple faith and devout earnestness won him much respect; and Ropartz wrote of him, "He stands out from his contemporaries as one of another age. They are scoffers, he was a believer; they vaunt themselves, he worked in silence; they seek glory, he let it seek him. . . . They shrink from nothing, — concession, compromise, meanness even; he performed his mission faithfully, and without counting the cost, leaving us the noblest example of uprightness."

Charles Camille Saint-Saëns, born at Paris in 1835, represents a more conservative school. His musical activity began at sixteen, when he produced his first symphony. Soon afterward he became a church organist; and his later improvisations at the Madeleine made him famous. He has been active also as a piano teacher and a public performer, though most of his later years have been spent in composition.

His orchestral works include four symphonies, two suites, and five piano concertos, of which the one in G minor, with clean-cut *andante*, graceful *allegretto*, and brilliant *presto*, is a prime favorite. For voices in addition he wrote a Christmas oratorio, two masses, the ode "La Lyre et la Harpe," and many orchestral ballads. His songs with piano are often Oriental in character. His piano and organ solos are also successful. His four symphonic poems seem rather

RIMSKY-KORSAKOV   DVOŘÁK

FRANCK

thinly scored in comparison with contemporary works, but they were once highly prized. They consist of "La Jeunesse d'Hercule," "Le Rouet d'Omphale," "Phaëton," and the "Danse Macabre." The last one, cited in later chapters on "Instruments," depicts the skeletons emerging from their graves at midnight, and dancing to the music of Death's violin until dawn.

In opera, Saint-Saëns found it hard to get a hearing at first; for his symphonic style and his great learning brought him under the atrocious suspicion of being a Wagnerian. His one-act "Princesse Jaune" did not appear until 1872, and "Le Timbre d'Argent" was delayed even beyond that year. But "Samson et Dalila," produced by Liszt at Weimar in 1877, assured its composer's reputation. This beautiful work shows the Jews among the Philistines, with Samson attaining their leadership. He is captivated by Dalila, whom he meets as she emerges from the temple. In the second act, at her home, the high priest exhorts her to betray Samson; and the ensuing love-scene shows her success. A scene showing Samson blind, chained, and grinding a mill is followed by a gathering in the temple, which he finally overthrows. The first act has some charming choruses. The second act includes Dalila's great solo, "Amour, viens aider ma faiblesse," and the beautiful love-scene "Mon cœur s'ouvre à ta voix." In the third act are the rhythmic and doleful mill music, the temple service, some excellent canonic work, Dalila's taunting of Samson (with a parody of the love-theme), and the final catastrophe.

Later works by the same composer include "The Deluge" (practically a cantata), "Étienne Marcel," "Henry VIII," "Proserpine," "Ascanio," the old-fashioned "Phryne," "Déjanire," "Les Barbares," and "Hélène."

Jules-Émile-Fréderic Massenet (1842–1912) was another conservative. After taking the *Prix de Rome* with the cantata "David Rizzio," he won a name by dramatic oratorios of the sacred opera type, such as "Marie Madeleine" and "Éve," followed later by "La Vierge" and "La Terre Promise." For orchestra Massenet composed a number of suites. Some of these treat Neapolitan, Alsatian, and Hungarian subjects; but the best is the "Scènes Pittoresques," depicting "Noon in the Village," "The Angelus," and other phases of rural French life. Massenet's songs are often charmingly piquant, and usually full of sentiment.

Massenet started his operatic career with "La Grand' Tante" and "Don César de Bazan." "Le Roi de Lahore," which followed, was spectacular. It dealt with the love of Alim for the Hindu Princess Sita, who is coveted also by the powerful Scindia. In jealousy, Scindia strikes Alim dead. The latter, in the Oriental paradise, begs Indra that he may return to earth. He is accorded permission, but must die (permanently) when Sita's life ends. Scindia's pursuit grows so importunate that Sita kills herself. The scene in the Indian heaven is gorgeously set and staged.

"Hérodiade" was another success, but it was thrown in the shade by "Manon." The latter work, founded on Prévost's novel, shows that fair but frail beauty leaving her lover for a rich admirer, passing through various vicissitudes, being reconciled to the former, and finally dying in his arms.

"Le Cid" proved rather weak, as Massenet's style was sentimental rather than dramatic. "Esclarmonde," however, scored another success. It shows the beautiful Byzantine sorceress of that name winning the knight Roland, losing him through his lack of caution, and recovering him when he gains her as prize in a tourney. The prize idea, and the condition that Roland will lose his love unless he keeps their relation secret, seem reminiscent of Wagner's librettos.

"Werther" is based on Goethe's novel of that name. "Le Mage" treated an Oriental subject. The very successful "Thaïs" depicts the conversion of an Alexandrian courtesan, who becomes truly devout and saint-like, while the monk who converted her falls a prey to feelings of earthly love for her. "La Navarraise" is a one-act military affair (belonging to the *verismo* school of realism), in which the heroine kills a hostile leader to earn a reward, but is suspected by her lover of having obtained the money in a way less creditable to her honor. "Le Portrait de Manon" is a one-act love idyl. "Cendrillon" treats a fairy subject. "Griselidis" shows that legendary bride's fidelity, which is unshaken by many attempts to prove her inconstant. "Roma" and "Don Quixote" are later works, but neither of them made a success equal to that of "The Jongleur of Notre-Dame." This delightful mediæval story shows a poor, half-starved Jongleur entertaining a crowd. A monk reviles his calling; and the sight of a donkey laden with food makes him willing to give it up, and enter the monastery. Inside, he becomes the butt of all except the cook; for they can all do something in honor of the Virgin, while he knows nothing suitable to offer her. Struck by a sudden idea, he thinks he will entertain her; and he does his tricks before her statue. The monks find him, and are shocked at what they think blasphemy; but the statue comes to life, thanks him, and calls him to her side in heaven. This opera was written for male voices only, but changed afterwards at Mary Garden's request, the juggler's part being arranged for female voice.

Vincent d'Indy, born in 1852, is a leader of the new school that the Franck pupils developed. In a letter to the present writer, he mentioned Franck's teaching as "worthy and beneficent direction." A trip to Germany in 1872 enabled D'Indy to meet Liszt; and the young man became a devout Wagnerian.

His first success was the "Piccolomini" Overture, which became a part of the later "Wallenstein" Triptych. "La Chevauchée du Cid" and "Le Chant de la Cloche" are vocal-orchestral works. The overture to "Antony and Cleopatra," and the "Jean Hunyadi" Symphony, were followed by the symphonic poem "La Forêt Enchantée." This work, based on an Uhland poem, depicts the knight Harald riding through the woods, until his companions are lost, and he himself thrown into a magic sleep. "Saugefleurie" is another symphonic poem, treating a story by De Bonnières. "Istar," the set of variations treating an old Assyrian legend, shows that heroine seeking her lover in the abode of death. Her procedure is marked by successive sacrifices of her garments, to pacify the warders; and the work depicts this by reversing the usual form, and having the variations grow simpler, with the theme at the end. Of D'Indy's two symphonies, the first is more successful. It is based on a Cevennes air; and the pure, sad melody is treated in a way that is earnest, if somewhat ascetic. Other orchestral works by the composer include the "Karadec" suite and incidental music to Mendes' "Médée."

In opera, D'Indy's early one-act comedy, "Attendez-moi sous l'Orme," has been frequently given. "Fervaal" is based on a Druidic plot, in which the hero, loved by Guilhen, daughter of his Saracen conqueror, renounces everything in a vain attempt to restore the Druids' power. "The Stranger" has a more symbolical plot. It treats of a silent, patient stranger who meets persecution in a fishing-village, but is loved by Vita. André, who is betrothed to Vita, loses her love through his readiness to earn money by ferreting out poor smugglers. The others think Vita foolish; but she knows and loves the stranger's forgiving ways. From the shore a boat is seen in distress. No one will try to aid it; but finally the stranger does so. Vita rushes along with him. The pair reach the ship, but are engulfed with it. The plot extols self-sacrifice by contrasting it with selfish financial shrewdness.

Achille Claude Debussy (1862–1918) was the leader of the movement known as modernism. His work has been aptly termed musical stippling. In his operas, and orchestral compositions similar to "The Afternoon of a Faun," he gains his effects by a succession of more or less detached chords, instead of by flowing harmonic progressions of the usual sort. His ear was exceedingly delicate, the result showing in the continual softness of his orchestral pieces. A climax in his works would be lost in the noise of a Strauss or a Scriabine. His use of chords in fugitive dissonances is much admired by many; but they are always the ones who have been the laggards in appreciating the less fragmentary style of classic and romantic composers. To one who does not sense harmonic relations, Debussy's music will show merely its exquisite delicacy. But to those who are definitely moved by a perception of orderly harmonic progression, the more radical work of Debussy and other modernists seems too fragmentary to be pleasing. Certain French critics have called the modernistic productions "cerebral music"; and the term is fair enough, since those who enjoy them feel a mental appreciation of their delicacy rather than any emotional uplift such as a theme of related harmonies will produce. Thus we may not say that Debussy's more extreme compositions are bad, but that their appeal is not that of earlier music. His little *genre* pictures sometimes seem like miniatures, so excessive is their refinement.

To win the *Prix de Rome*, Debussy laid aside his new style, and produced the expressive opera-cantata "The Prodigal Son." In this he showed himself a master of conservative music; but his own aural delicacy soon led him into strange paths. "La Demoiselle Élue" and "Chimène" are two early lyric scenes. For orchestra, the vague and elusive Prelude to Mallarmé's "Afternoon of a Faun" was followed by the "Nocturnes," consisting of "Nuages" and "Fêtes."

Still later came the group named "Images," which consists of "Iberia" (in separate and well-contrasted movements), the "Gigue Triste," and the "Rondes de Printemps." An earlier piece, remodelled, is known as "Printemps." A recent work by Debussy is the ballet "Les Jeux," which contains pantomime based on tennis and other games. "La Mer" is a beautiful three-movement sketch.

In opera, his chief work is "Pelléas et Mélisande," based on the Maeterlinck play of that name. The vague, shadowy music follows the situation accurately enough. The plot shows the finding of the timid Mélisande by the old king Golaud, and their marriage; the subsequent love between her and his younger brother Pelléas; the latter's death at the jealous Golaud's hands; and the anguish of Mélisande, who sinks silently to the grave. A later work, which seems more like a set of detached scenes, is "The Martyrdom of Saint Sebastian."

Debussy's many songs and piano pieces are often full of beauty. Their vague charm has been likened to a subtle perfume, which pervades the air but defies analysis. Some of them are too chaotic for the conservatives; but many of them are comprehensible and attractive to all hearers. Debussy and his partisans have been rather outspoken against some of the classics. They consider Beethoven lacking in taste, in spite of his genius; and they fail to appreciate Schumann's music. This is due to their placing too much emphasis on delicate effects.

Erik Satie has been rated by some as a predecessor of Debussy. Satie's piano works, such as the "Morceaux en Forme de la Poire," show a decidedly bizarre character.

Ernesto Fanelli is another pioneer in the modern French style. His tone-poem "Thebes," unknown for many years, aroused much appreciation when finally performed. He lived in poverty and obscurity until accidentally discovered by Pierné.

Gabriel Urbain Fauré is classed with Debussy. Fauré's songs, and his opera "Pénélope," show much refinement of style.

Maurice Ravel is another of the modernists. He has composed the comic opera "L'Heure Espagnole," the ballets "Ma Mère l'Oye" and "Daphnis and Chloe," a Spanish rhapsody, the "Scheherazade" Overture, a string quartet, and many piano works and songs. His orchestral suite "Ma Mère l'Oye" ("Mother Goose") is

made from a set of piano pieces. Its five movements show a most
delightfully piquant orchestration, although the thematic material
consists of the bitter-sweet progressions that characterize the modern French school.

Louis Aubert is a younger member of the modernist group. His
opera "La Forêt Bleue" has an attractive plot, and some humorous
moments, but is set in an altogether dissonant and unattractive
style.

Florent Schmitt is another master of dissonance, but he writes in a
more effective and forcible style. He has composed a symphonic
study on Poe's "Haunted Palace," the symphonic poem "En Été,"
the "Combat des Raksasas," two rhapsodies, the ballet "La Tragé-
die de Salôme," vocal-orchestral settings of psalms, chamber works,
and smaller pieces.

Alexis Emmanuel Chabrier (1841–94) wrote in vigorous style,
but with more conservative harmonies. His early operas include
"L'Étoile" and "L'Éducation manquée." His "Gwendoline" is
strongly dramatic. That heroine is the daughter of the ancient
British king Armel. She dreams that a Dane carries her over the
sea. The people laugh at her fears; but their mirth soon changes
to dismay, for the Danes, under Harald, have really come. Gwendoline saves her father and captivates Harald, but Armel plots
to kill the invaders at the wedding. Gwendoline warns Harald, but
he disregards her words. His men are massacred, and he is beaten
down; whereupon she snatches his knife, stabs herself, and joins her
death-song to his. The score is virile and forceful, and the work is
the best French attempt at the dramatic Wagnerian vein. A later
opera, "Le Roi malgré Lui," was lighter and more humorous in
style. Other works by Chabrier include the orchestral "España,"
the "Marche Joyeuse," music to Mendes' "Femme de Tabarin,"
the choral "Sulamite," some piano pieces, and a few oddly humorous songs.

Gustave Charpentier, born in 1860, has some socialistic ideas, and
has taken great interest in the Montmartre laborers. This shows in
his cantata, "La Couronnement de la Muse," and in his best opera,
"Louise." The heroine of that opera is a poor working-girl, who
loves the poet Julien, but is prevented from marrying him by her
parents, who think him too wild. A street scene and a workroom

scene show Julien taking Louise away to a life of free love. They live very happily for a time. Then her mother brings her home, alleging that her father is sick; and the pair try to coerce her. She finally leaves them, while the father curses Paris and its baleful influence. The plot is somewhat confused in its moral, but the underlying idea is a protest against the hard conditions of a working-girl's life. The music is realistic, even including street cries at times. "Julien," in certain ways a sequel to "Louise," has a very weak plot. Charpentier's other works include the suite "Impressions d'Italie" and the cantata "La Vie du Poète." He writes his own librettos.

Alfred Bruneau, born in 1857, won an early success with "L'Attaque du Moulin," treating a story of the Franco-Prussian War. Since then he has set many allegorical subjects from Zola's works; but their music is rather heavy-handed.

Ernest Chausson (1855–99) might have become very great if his career had not been cut short by a fatal bicycle accident. His chief work is the opera "Le Roi Arthus." Other compositions include the symphonic poem "Viviane," the tone-pictures "Solitude dans les Bois" and "Soir de Fête," a poem for violin and orchestra, some chamber music, and various songs. His style is most charmingly expressive, and his harmonies richly attractive.

Gabriel Pierné, born in 1863, is best known by his interesting cantata "The Children's Crusade." Other vocal-orchestral works by him are "The Children at Bethlehem" and the oratorio "St. Francis of Assisi."

Paul Dukas, born in 1865, won fame in the orchestral field by his scherzo entitled "L'Apprenti Sorcier." This illustrates Goethe's ballad of the sorcerer's apprentice, who made a broom bring buckets of water constantly, but forgot how to stop it. The composition is strongly effective in style, and full of humorous touches. His opera "Ariane et Barbe-Bleue" presents Bluebeard's earlier wives as spiritless creatures, while Ariane is more independent and progressive, and leads them to freedom. Other works by Dukas are a symphony, overtures to "King Lear" and "Götz von Berlichingen," the ballet "Le Péri," a piano sonata, and smaller pieces.

Henri Duparc has been active in the field of oratorio. Guy de Ropartz has devoted himself to orchestral and chamber music. Pierre de Bréville has written in all these styles, and composed a mass also. Arthur Coquard is known in opera. René de Boisdeffre has produced a symphony, an oratorio, and other large compositions. Louis Bourgault-Ducoudray composed operas and orchestral works, and became an authority on folk-music. Among the women Augusta Holmes (of Irish descent) wrote large symphonic odes and an opera; Cécile Chaminade has produced ambitious compositions like the lyric symphony "Calirrhoe," but is better known by her dainty piano pieces and songs; while Gabriella Ferrari has become known in orchestral and operatic work.

Operas that have received some notice in France and elsewhere are "Elaine," by Herman Bemberg; Camille Erlanger's "Polish Jew" and "Aphrodite"; "La Cabrera," by Gabriel Dupont; "Monna Vanna," by Henri Février; Reynaldo Hahn's "Nausicaa"; "La Habanera," by Raoul Laparra; Fernand LeBorne's "Girondins"; "Le Chemineau," by Xavier Leroux; "Daria," by Georges Marty; Charles Lefebvre's "Judith"; and "Quo Vadis," by Jean Nouguès. Other French opera composers are Félix Fourdrain, Philippe Gaubert, André Gedalge, Georges Hue, Baron Frédéric d'Erlanger, Eugène d'Harcourt, Charles Lenepveu, Jules Mazellier, André Messager, Edmond Missa, Max d'Ollone, Georges Palicot, Émile Pessard, Henri Rabaud, Samuel Rousseau, Gustave Samazeuilh, Émile Paladilhe, Charles Silver, Antoine Simon, and Paul Vidal. Composers who have kept more solely to the orchestral field are the conductors Camille Chevillard and Édouard Colonne, Henri-Paul Büsser, Roger Ducasse, Paul Ladmirault, Jean Lemaire, Alberic Magnard (killed in the war in 1914), Albert Roussel, Georges Sporck, Charles Tournemire, Richard Vinée, G. Witkowsky, and André Wormser. Gustave Sandré has composed chamber works; Gabriel Grovlez writes for piano; and Jean Baptiste Faure is known by "Palm Branches" and other songs. Nearly all of these men are alive and active at the present writing.

XXVIII

THE RUSSIAN SCHOOL

WHILE Dargomiszky and Serov were building up Russian opera, and Rubinstein and Tschaikovsky were developing into cosmopolitan composers, a more distinctively national school was founded, through the exertions of Mily Alexeievitch Balakirev (1837–1910). He was born at Nijni-Novgorod; and there, after his return from the Kazan University, he was taught and helped by the cultivated Alexander Oulibishev. At twenty he settled in St. Petersburg, becoming known as a pianist. He grew to be a friend of Glinka, whose music he admired. But it was with César Cui that he began the intimate discussions that led to the idea of nationalism for which he and his circle worked. He founded the Free Music School, and organized concerts that were useful in making known the compositions of his set. He was active also in collecting the Russian folk-music.

Balakirev's compositions are not numerous, but they show excellent workmanship. He wrote a symphony, overtures on Russian, Czech, and Spanish themes, the symphonic poem "Russia," incidental music to "King Lear," and the symphonic poem "Tamara." The last production is based on a legend of the Caucasus. Tamara was a beautiful but cruel princess, who lived in a tower over the river Tarek. When any cavalier arrived, there would be a night of revelry; but in the morning the river would receive his corpse. Balakirev composed a number of finely wrought songs, and several piano works, including the difficult Oriental "Islamey."

César Antonovitch Cui, the historian and writer of the national group, was born at Vilna in 1835, his father being a French soldier who settled in Russia after Napoleon's defeat. Like his father, he followed a military career, graduating from the Engineers' School and becoming a professor of fortification in the Military School. In music, he became a pupil of Moniuszko, but gained much real benefit from the advice of Balakirev. His first opera was the one-act "Mandarin's Son," a light work in the style of Auber. More ambitious was "The Prisoner of the Caucasus," based on a Pushkin poem. His real reputation began with "William Ratcliff," produced in 1869. But Cui had criticised others so unsparingly that it was now time for him to receive his own medicine. The work was freely attacked at first, though it gained more success later on. It does not correspond to Cui's written principles, but seems midway between lyric and dramatic opera. Tschaikovsky calls the music too deliberate, and not spontaneous enough. "Angelo" is based on a Victor Hugo play, dealing with the same subject that Ponchielli used in "La Gioconda." This is Cui's most representative work; and he confirmed that estimate himself in a note sent to the present writer some years ago. "The Saracen" is based on the Dumas book entitled "Charles VII chez ses Grands Vasseaux," and contains good love-scenes between that king and Agnes Sorel. "Le Filibustier" is a comedy on a Richepin libretto. "Mam'selle Fifi" is a one-act work on a Maupassant story, while "A Feast in Time of Plague" is another single-act work. "The Captain's Daughter" treats another Pushkin subject. Cui wrote also symphonies, orchestral scherzos, choruses, songs, and piano pieces. His style is not very distinctive or individual.

Alexander Porphyrievitch Borodin (1834–87) was another of the Balakirev group, which comprised five famous names. Borodin was descended from the princes of Imeretia, who in turn claimed King David as one of their ancestors. Like many Russian composers, Borodin had a profession, and he became well known in medicine and chemistry. He was also active in furthering education for women. He considered music an avocation merely, and would not at first publish any works. Yet he wrote several when quite young, producing a flute-and-piano piece at thirteen, and a string sextet soon after. In 1862 he joined Balakirev's circle, and began to compose in earnest. His first symphony met with a pleasing reception. He followed this by numerous songs, including "La Princesse Endormie," "La Vieille Chanson," and others of interest. These are often rather sombre in color, and Borodin showed himself a master of gloom and dissonance. At this time he composed one act of "Mlada," a composite work by himself, Cui, Moussorgsky, and Rimsky-Korsakov. This idea of coöperation was also adopted by younger men, who paid homage to the publisher Belaieff by producing movements of a string quartet on the notes B, La, F. Borodin wrote a second symphony, and part of a third, which was finished by Glazounov. He composed other orchestral pieces, two original quartets, and some piano music. His "Steppenskizze" was the first new-Russian work to become known in America. It is an orchestral composition depicting the loneliness of the Steppes, the passing of a caravan with its varied noises and weird songs, and the return of silence and loneliness.

But Borodin's most important work was his single opera, "Prince Igor." This is based on an old Russian epic, dealing with Igor's expedition against the Polovtsi. A prologue show the prince and his son Vladimir leading their army away, in spite of the portent of an eclipse; while the Princess Yaroslavna is left to rule with her brother, Prince Galitsky. The first act shows Galitsky's misrule, and his efforts to undermine her influence; but at the news of Igor's defeat, the people renew their loyalty to her. The second and third acts take place in the enemy's camp. The noble leader, Konchak, has a daughter, with whom Vladimir falls in love. A banquet to the captive serves to introduce dances, choruses, and great scenic effects. By the aid of another captive, Ovlour, who plies the guards with drink, Igor escapes; but the leader's daughter holds Vladimir back, and is afterwards married to him. In the last act the lamenting Yaroslavna sees Igor return. The music of this opera shows much clear melody, and many strong scenes. The composer wrote it piecemeal, working only when he was unable to give his medical lectures. It was left unfinished; but the obliging Rimsky-Korsakov put in the orchestration, while Glazounov, who had heard Borodin go over the work at the piano, wrote the overture from memory.

Modest Petrovitch Moussorgsky (1839–81) was decidedly the "bad boy" of the national group. He was trained in military science, but drifted about from one post to another, and finally gave up government work. In music, too, he was little amenable to discipline, though he atoned for this by displaying marked originality. His life showed the savage excesses so often found among the Slavs; but his music expressed their strong passions and deep emotions. Meeting Borodin in 1862, he attached himself to the associates, and imbibed their principles. He lacked the simple routine that comes from training; but the formless style of his music did not obscure its striking and original character. He has been called a born poet, expressing his great passions in a medium that he had not mastered. His rugged strength is evident in many compositions, for piano or orchestra as well as for the stage. His orchestral "Intermezzo" and "Night on Calvary" show this quality. His Hebrew choruses, such as "The Defeat of Sennacherib," are also strong works. His piano pieces include the "Tableaux d'une Exposition," while his songs contain many forceful numbers. But he is best known by his operas. His early works in this form include some "Œdipus" music, a setting of "Salammbo," "The Match-Maker," and the comic scenes entitled "The Fair at Soroschini." But his "Boris Godunov" and "Khovantchina" are of greater power.

"Boris Godunov" is founded on a Pushkin drama. Boris, having killed the Czarevitch Dimitri, has his men incite the populace to offer him the crown. A coronation scene follows. The next act shows Gregory and other monks, with Gregory planning to pretend that he is Dimitri, the rightful ruler, whom Boris had killed. The Poles support his claim. Another act shows Boris in his family; but the news of the "False Demetrius" begins to drive him mad. In the last act, the people follow the pretender, while Boris is left deserted, his madness ending in death.

"Khovantchina" is based on the existence of the "Old Believers," who followed early and incorrect Scriptural versions with fanaticism. The story brings out the contrast between them and the newer, more civilized Russians. Prince Khovantsky and his Streltsy (archers) represent the old ideas, and finally immolate themselves rather than surrender.

Nicolai Andreievitch Rimsky-Korsakov (1844–1908) was by all odds the greatest of the nationalists, even though Moussorgsky sometimes excelled him in savage power. Like his compeers, he took up government work, graduating from the naval school and serving for a time at sea. In later years he had the rank of admiral, and was in charge of the marine bands. But he made music his life-work. While on a voyage, begun in 1863, he wrote a symphony, said to be the first work in that form by a Russian. In the autumn of 1865 he joined Balakirev's circle, composing soon afterward the symphonic picture "Sadko," the programme symphony "Antar," and his first opera, "The Maid of Pskov." Accepting a post in the St. Petersburg

Conservatory, he gained a broader appreciation, and outgrew some of the nationalists' narrow ideas. Yet he held to the best of their tenets, and cannot be said to have left their school. In one summer he wrote sixty-four fugues, and an amazing number of contrapuntal exercises, some of which he sent to Tschaikovsky. He also studied Bach, though continuing to write on modern lines. But however freely he composed, such strict work must certainly have had its effect in enabling him to surpass his comrades.

The programme symphony "Antar" depicts a man full of hatred, who retires to the ruins of Palmyra. Rescuing a gazelle from a monster, he finds that the former is really a fairy; and she grants him three wishes. The second movement portrays revenge; the third movement depicts power; while the fourth illustrates love, the fairy reappearing for him. But his life depends upon this love; and when finally he begins to tire of her, and to gaze longingly at the horizon, he falls dead.

"Scheherazade" is a programme symphony depicting four episodes from the "Arabian Nights."

The composer's other orchestral works include a symphonietta on Russian themes, an overture on folk-tunes, another on "The Russian Easter," a Serb Fantasie, a Spanish Caprice, and a Fairy Legend. His piano works include fugues, a suite, and other pieces; while a concerto, dedicated to Liszt, is a worthy affair. Songs, choruses, and a cantata swell a list that is completed by over a dozen operas.

Rimsky-Korsakov's first opera, "The Maid of Pskov" (sometimes known as "Ivan the Terrible"), is based on a drama by Mey. Ivan conquers Novgorod, but spares Pskov because the alleged daughter of its prince is really his own natural child. A later opera, "Vera Scheloga," shows Ivan's love for the mother, who bore that name.

"A May Night," treating a tale of Gogol, is a comedy of village love and intrigue.

"The Snow Maiden," based on a poem by Ostrovsky, embodies the Slav legend of spring. This maiden is the daughter of King Frost and the Fairy Spring. Attracted by a shepherd, she longs for mortal life, and her parents reluctantly grant her wish. The shepherd ignores her and falls in love with Kupava, whose former sweetheart now pursues the snow maiden with attentions. But she cannot yet love like a mortal. When she obtains this ability, by a wish that her mother grants, she returns her lover's ardor; but in that moment a ray of sunlight falls upon her, and she melts away.

"Mlada," first done in collaboration, was also completed by the composer alone. It is based on a ninth-century historical episode.

"Christmas-Eve Revels" treats the story of Vakula the Smith.

"Mozart and Salieri" is practically a short dramatic scene.

"Sadko," based on an epic of the Novgorod set, shows that individual trying to catch goldfish on a wager, and charming the Sea-King with his Gussla music. Afterward he sets sail with ships and goods, and is thrown overboard as a Jonah when a storm arises. He has adventures at the bottom of the sea, where the Sea-King wishes one of his daughters to marry the newcomer. His Gussla playing shakes the sea and earth, and is only stopped when the instrument is smashed. Ultimately he returns to home and hearth.

"The Czar's Betrothed," again based on a Mey drama, shows Griaznoi in love with Martha, who is betrothed to Lykov. Griaznoi gets a potion which he thinks will insure her love. The Czar Ivan sees her, and chooses her as his bride. Griaznoi gives her the potion, but a rival has changed it for one that makes her insane and ugly. The rival finally confesses, and Griaznoi stabs her, quitting the scene after imploring Martha's pardon. This is one of the composer's very best works, the score showing a charming fluency united with a most interesting handling of folk-music. The beautiful overture is widely popular.

"The Czar Saltan" treats that monarch's meeting with three sisters, his marriage to the youngest, and the jealousy of the other two. It is brilliantly orchestrated, using folk-melodies and guiding motives.

"Servilia" deals with Christianity in ancient Rome.

"The Immortal Kastchei" tells of a wizard of that name, whose daughter redeems herself by letting fall a tear, which happens to contain the wizard's fate. The action deals also with the rescue of the Czarevna from his power. When this was first performed, the composer had been dropped from the Conservatory; and his friends made the opera a pretext for giving him ovations and good-will.

"Pan Voyevode" is the story of a Polish noble who parts lovers to get the girl for himself. At the wedding feast, he takes poison meant for her.

"The Invisible City" is a legendary affair. The heroine, Fevronia, is captured at her wedding by Tartars; but they are scared off by a reflection of the invisible city seen in a lake. Fevronia is then called by the prince who loved her, and joins him in the lasting happiness of death.

"The Golden Cock" is a bird that crows whenever danger threatens. It is given to King Dodon by an astrologer. Its crowing causes him to send his sons to meet the trouble, and later to follow himself. The danger turns out to be a beautiful woman, the Queen of Shemakha, who fascinates the king, although his sons had quarrelled over her and killed each other. She laughs at him, but finally becomes his bride, and proves heartless.

The leader of a later generation is Alexander Constantinovitch Glazounov, who was born at St. Petersburg in 1865. He studied with Rimsky-Korsakov, and at eighteen wrote a symphony, which was given by Liszt at Weimar. Since then Glazounov has produced seven similar works, his sixth symphony being especially melodious and pleasing. He composed also several symphonic poems, which echo the joy of spring, the charm of the forest, the spell of the sea, the attraction of the Orient, or the majesty of the historic Kremlin. Another of these treats the story of Stenka Rasine, the Volga pirate who carried off a princess. Glazounov produced a Triumphal March for our Chicago Exposition, and a Coronation Cantata for the Czar. Other orchestral works by him are the Greek and Carnival Overtures, the "Middle Ages" suite, and the glowing "Overture Solennelle." His opus numbers, nearly 100, include many other large compositions, such as suites or orchestral cantatas. His chamber works and smaller pieces show much melodic charm. He has not tried opera, but his ballets, such as "Raymonda" and "The Seasons," hold the stage well. "Raymonda" is the story of a Crusader's wife who remains faithful in his absence in spite of a rival's attentions. A recent work by Glazounov is some strong incidental music to the sacred drama "The King of the Jews."

Anton Stepanovitch Arensky (1861–1906) was another "Rimsky" pupil. While teaching in Moscow, Arensky produced the opera "A Dream on the Volga." He composed also the one-act "Raphael," and the ballet "A Night in Egypt"; but his best work was the opera "Nal and Damajanti." This treats of a mythical king who loses his sweetheart and his lands while gambling, under the influence of a wicked god, but regains them later.

Sergei Rachmaninov, born in 1873 at Novgorod, is known by his picturesque preludes and other works for piano. He has composed a few operas, including "Aleko" and "The Miser Knight." His symphonic poem "The Isle of the Dead," illustrating a Boecklin painting, is an admirable picture of gloom. His other works include a symphony, the cantata "Spring," two piano concertos, and some chamber music.

Sergei Taneiev (1856–1915) composed four symphonies, a few overtures, string quartets, and several choruses; but he became best known through his "Oresteia," a lofty operatic trilogy, in eight scenes, based on the works of Æschylus. Alexander Taneiev, his nephew, is another orchestral composer in Russia.

Ippolitov-Ivanov, active in Moscow, used Hebrew melodies in his opera "Ruth," and put much tender expression into his "Assya." His other productions include suites and choruses.

Michael Ivanov composed incidental music, a symphony, a triumphal overture, the ballet "The Vestal," and the operas "Sabawa" and "The Feast of Potemkin."

Edward Napravnik, a Bohemian living at St. Petersburg, wrote the operas "Nijni-Novgorod," "Harold," "Doubrovsky," and "Francesca."

Paul Blaramberg's operas consist of "The Mummers," "The Roussalka-Maiden," "Mary of Burgundy," "Toushino," and "The Wave."

Alexander Gretschaninov composed the opera "Dobrynia" and some incidental music.

Vladimir Rebikov has produced "In the Storm" and "The Christmas Tree," as well as the so-called *mimodrame* "Genius and Death."

Nicolai Soloviev composed several operas of somewhat restrained character, as well as an overture and the symphonic poem "Russians and Mongols."

Sergei Vassilenko's "City of Kitezh" treats the subject already described as "The Invisible City."

Operas of some success in Russia are Kazatchenko's "Prince Serebriani" and "Pan Sotnik"; Korestchenko's "Belshazzar's Feast," "The Angel of Death," and "The Ice Palace"; and Kochetov's

"Terrible Revenge." Other Russian opera composers include Lissenko, Famintzin, Ilyinski, Kashperov, Lischin, Malashkin, Sokalski, Zemlinsky, Schaefer, Schenk, Glière, Youri von Arnold, and Baron Vietinghov. Glière is known also by some excellent chamber and orchestral works. Kalinnikov died before finishing "The Year 1812," but left symphonies, symphonic pictures, and a suite.

In the instrumental field, Alexander Scriabine has caused much discussion by his radicalism. Even in his lesser works he shows a leaning toward strange harmonies. In his later symphonies (practically symphonic poems), such as "Prometheus," he builds up a new system by making chords out of a succession of fourths. He handles the orchestra with power; but all except the radicals are tempted to speak of it as noise. He has written piano concertos and other piano works.

Another Russian radical is Igor Stravinsky, who is less heavy-handed, but equally bizarre in his harmonies. He is fond of the ballet, having composed in that form "The Bird of Fire," "Petroushka," "The Sacrifice of Spring," and "The Nightingale." He has also written orchestral pieces, such as the tone-picture "Fireworks."

Paul Juon is another recent composer of orchestral and chamber music, including a symphony. Nicolai Sokolov is responsible for an orchestral *Elegie* and incidental music. Alexander Kopylov has composed a symphony and chamber music. Constantin Antipov is known by orchestral melodies and piano music. Henry Pachulski has produced an orchestral suite, in addition to piano music. Anatole Liadov, who died in 1915, was another orchestral and piano composer. Joseph Wihtol has devoted much attention to Lett melodies, which show in his "Lhigo Festival" and other works. Nicolai Stcherbatchev wrote orchestral idyls and piano pieces. Sergei Liapounov's works include a concerto, a symphony, and an "Overture Solennelle." Other orchestral composers are George Konius, Nicholas Medtner, Michael Asantchevski, Nicholas Kasanli, George Galitzin, Michael Kolatchevski, Alexander Koptiaiev, Ivan Pomasanski, Vladimir Puchalski, Ivan Popoff, Edward Schuett, Nicholas Tcherepnin, Nicholas Tutkovsky, Sergei Vassilenko, and the Zaremba brothers. Many of the foregoing have become known by compositions in the shorter forms; while others who have worked in these are Alphéraki, Amani, Grodsky, Blumenfeld, Artsiboutchev, Gabrilovitch, Karganov, Kastalski, Pogojev, and Warlamov. Victor Ewald and Alexander Winkler have written chamber music, while Emil Mlynarski has composed violin works.

XXIX

OTHER EUROPEAN NATIONS

In the last four decades, Italy has done much to put herself abreast of other musical nations. She has no genius of the first rank, as Strauss is the only living man who could by any courtesy be included in that class. But she has revived her traditions of operatic supremacy, and has also produced a small but earnest group of orchestral composers.

The *verismo* (realistic) school of opera was founded by Mascagni. Born in 1863, he was the son of a baker, and was destined for the law. He studied piano and other musical subjects in secret. When fourteen he was discovered at this work, and locked up by his father; but an uncle rescued him, and a friend aided him to take lessons at Milan. He became leader of small operatic troupes, until "Rustic Chivalry" won him a comfortable prize from the Sonzogno firm, and an international reputation. Since then he has composed many other operas, — "L' Amico Fritz," "I Rantzau," "Ratcliff," "Silvano," "Iris," "Le Maschere," "Isabeau," etc. But none of these was successful; and "Le Maschere" was even hissed because of its reminiscences of Puccini.

"Rustic Chivalry" has for its heroine Santuzza, betrayed and deserted by Turiddu. She tells Alfio of an intrigue that Turiddu is carrying on with Alfio's wife Lola. The two then meet, and Turiddu is killed. The music is endowed with a vivid strength that seemed a revelation in Italy. While German composers were making heavy imitations of the inimitable Wagner, this work led to a school that was wholly successful, and well suited to modern needs of rapidity in action. Its one-act length, after the size of Wagner's works, made it seem like a short story in comparison with a novel. Some of the best points in the music are Turiddu's "Siciliana" (sung from behind the curtain as part of the prelude), the broad and noble church service ("Regina Cœli"), Lola's solo "My King of Roses," and the lively "Brindisi," or drinking-chorus. The sugary intermezzo has become widely known.

Ruggiero Leoncavallo, born in 1858, began by composing "Chatterton," at first a failure, but well received afterward. He produced also an ambitious trilogy "Crepusculum," dealing with the Medici. But he did not become widely known until he wrote "I Pagliacci" ("The Strolling Players"), in imitation of Mascagni's style. This opera became famous in many lands. Like Mascagni, Leoncavallo has failed in later works, such as "Bohême," "Trilby," "Zaza," and "Roland of Berlin." For the last of these he was chosen composer by the German Kaiser, who wrote the libretto.

"I Pagliacci," with an excellent libretto by the composer himself, opens with the arrival of the strolling players at a village. Tonio, the clown, overhears Nedda, the leader's wife, planning elopement with the villager Silvio. As Nedda had repulsed Tonio's former advances, he now revenges himself by bringing the leader, Canio, on the scene, but preventing him from identifying the interloper. The second act shows the play within the play, given before the villagers. This is based on a plot much similar to what has happened; and when Canio asks Nedda the name of her unknown lover, his passion becomes real instead of mimic. At last he stabs her. Silvio, rushing from the audience, meets a similar fate. The music is much stronger than that of "Rustic Chivalry," though in the same school. The prologue (for baritone), the chorus of the first act, Canio's intensely strong lament after seeing Nedda's perfidy, and the dramatic close of the play are the chief points in a score that is often strongly dramatic.

The *verismo* school is not merely realistic, but is devoted to a tragic sort of realism that is found in the somewhat crude and elemental lives of the lower classes. Love, jealousy, and revenge are its chief assets. But its strength of expression has made it important in contemporary opera. Other composers of the school are Giordano ("Siberia," "Mala Vita," and "Mme. Sans-Gêne"), Spinelli ("A Basso Porto"), Tasca ("A Santa Lucia"), Coronaro ("Festa a Marina"), and Cesare Rossi ("Nadeya"). Italo Montemezzi chose a higher subject in his "Love of Three Kings," which treats of a girl who was betrothed to a mediæval prince, but forced into a marriage with his conqueror. She still loves the prince, and the suspicions of her husband's blind father lead to discovery and tragedy. Cilea's "Arlesiana" and "Adriana Lecouvreur" are in older style.

Orefice produced the sacred opera "Moses," and arranged the *pasticcio* "Chopin" on that master's melodies. Other Italian opera composers, of various tendencies, are the conductor Mancinelli ("Ero e Leandre"), Catalani ("la Wally"), Buongiorno ("Das Mädchenherz" and "Michelangelo e Rolla," both excellent), Zandonai ("Conchita" and "Francesca da Rimini"), Camussi, winner of prizes, Smareglia, Afferni, Cagnoni, Falchi, Frontini, and Floridia, the last-named having written orchestral works also. Three other men, however, deserve separate mention.

Baron Alberto Franchetti, born in 1850, studied at Munich, and understood the best German standards. This influence shows in the excellence of his works. His dramatic legend "Asrale" has been followed by several operas, — "Cristoforo Colombo," "Fior d'Alpe," the comic "Il Signor di Pourceaugnac," and "La Figlia di Jorio." But his greatest success is the much-discussed "Germania." This work shows the uprising of Germany against Napoleon. Enmities are forgotten in the union of patriots; and the work ends with a strong scene showing the battle-field of Leipsic and Napoleon's retreat. This opera is not popular with the masses, but cultivated audiences grow enthusiastic over it.

Ermanno Wolf-Ferrari, born in 1876, is the son of a German father and an Italian mother, and was sent to Munich for study. His orchestral cantata, setting parts of Dante's "Vita Nuova," is a most pleasingly beautiful work. His operas include "La Sulamite," "Cenerentola," "The Four Ruffians," "Le Donne Curiose," "The Secret of Suzanne," "The Jewels of the Madonna," and "L'Amore Medico." The last treats a Molière subject. "Le Donne Curiose" is a bright comedy showing the women's effort to find out what their husbands really do when away at the club. "Suzanne's Secret" is her smoking of cigarettes, the odor of which causes her to be suspected of having entertained a lover clandestinely. "The Jewels of the Madonna" is a strong tragedy. Gennaro loves his adopted sister Maliella, though at first she believes herself his real sister. Her lowly origin shows in her behavior at the festival of the Madonna (a real Naples holiday), where she sings a wild "Cannetella" and is impressed by the coarse love-making of the brigand Rafaello. In the second act, in her home garden, Gennaro tells her of her birth, and his love; but she repulses him, saying that she would not love him if he were brave enough to steal for her the jewels on the Madonna's statue. She listens with delight to a serenade by Rafaello; but Gennaro does actually bring the jewels. She puts them on, and is lost in ecstasy. The third act, however, shows her fleeing from Gennaro, and coming to Rafaello's retreat. He is shocked by her sacrilege in wearing the jewels, and casts her off. She rushes away to plunge into the sea; while Gennaro, coming after her, stabs himself because of remorse. The overture consists simply of three pistol-shots; but the festival scenes of the first act are carried out in a large style. The lyrics are smoothly attractive, and the climax duly tragic, though the brigands' revels before it are too much spun out.

The chief figure in recent Italian opera is Giacomo Puccini. Born in 1858, of a musical family, he soon attracted attention; and Verdi named the young man as his probable successor.

"Le Villi," produced by Puccini in 1884, was really the origin of the short operas. The Villi, or Wilis, are spirits of betrothed but deserted maidens; and they seek to lure their betrayers to death. The scene is laid in a Black Forest village, where Robert loves Anna. Learning of an inheritance, he goes to Mainz, where he forgets Anna and starts an intrigue. She dies broken-hearted. When Robert returns he is caught in the Wilis' dance, and whirled about until he falls lifeless.

"Edgar," appearing in 1889, has a hero who loves a beautiful gypsy. Tiring of her, he leaves her mountain retreat and becomes a soldier. Returning home, he is charmed by a village maiden who has loved him from the first; but his happiness is short, for the vengeful gypsy stabs her rival. This Italianized "Carmen" was not a great success.

"Manon Lescaut," founded on Prévost's novel, has some strong scenes. In the first act Manon flees with Des Grieux rather than enter a convent. In the second act, she leaves him; and when she returns, her rich protector revenges himself by having her consigned to prison. The third act shows the embarkation of female convicts for America, the monotonous roll-call making an impressive background to the impassioned dialogue. The last act is a long love-scene, ending in Manon's death.

"La Bohême," based on Murger's "Vie de Bohême," shows the

four gifted but poverty-stricken associates in their attic of the Latin Quarter. Rodolfo, the poet, falls in love with Mimi. At the café of the second act, Musetta returns to her faithful Marcel. The third act brings jealousies and quarrels; while in the last act Mimi returns to die in Rodolfo's arms. The music has a haunting sweetness, and the plot seems to give the touch of nature that makes the whole world kin.

"Tosca," based on Sardou's play, shows that heroine's love for Mario, and the latter's troubles resulting from his protection of a political refugee. Scarpia, the wicked official in control, has Mario arrested, and tortures him to make Tosca minister to his (Scarpia's) pleasure. When Tosca pretends to yield, he writes an order for Mario's execution, which he alleges is to be only pretended. Meanwhile, Tosca secretes a knife, and when Scarpia comes to her she stabs him. She then (Act III) goes to tell Mario that his execution will be only pretence; but the treacherous Scarpia had directed his soldiers to fire real cartridges, after all. Mario is killed, and Tosca throws herself from the battlements to escape capture for having stabbed Scarpia. The score is realistic, and follows the sense of the words faithfully, even if it is hardly definite enough to stand alone, as Wagner's music does. Tosca's lament in Act II ("Vissi d'arte") is an effective solo number.

"Madama Butterfly" has a Japanese heroine. An American official, amusing himself with her, goes through a Japanese marriage ceremony, which she naturally considers binding. Left alone, she is shown later living with her son and a maid, and animated by a touching faith in the return of her husband. The consul tries to show her a letter from the absent one, but finally does not dare to do so; and only on the officer's return does she see that he has rated her merely as a pastime, and married a girl of his own nation. Then she kills herself.

"The Girl of the Golden West" is based on the Belasco play of that name, in which Minnie, beloved by all in the Western camp, falls in love with an admirer who comes as a stranger. When he proves to be the highwayman whom all are hunting, she protects him. When he is captured later, she saves him from being lynched, and departs with him to start life anew elsewhere. The music contains two Indian songs, one of which (that of the homesick miner) seems hardly in place.

The leader among the new Italian orchestral composers was Giovanni Sgambati (1843–1914). He produced symphonies, chamber works, overtures, a piano concerto, and many lesser pieces of various sorts. His early efforts met with encouragement from Wagner.

Other Italian orchestral composers include Giuseppe Martucci, Eugenio di Pirani, Edgardo Del Valle de Paz, Ettore Pinelli, Silvio Lazzari, the American-known Martin Roeder, Luigi Torchi the critic, the late violinist Antonio Bazzini, the pianist Luigi Romaniello, the Sicilian Antonio Scontrino, Leone Sinigaglia, the mass composer Alessandro Busi, and Amilcare Zanella.

Ferrucio Busoni has become a modernist, after writing admirable fugues in his youth. His music to "Turandot" has been called by one critic the best example of modernism yet produced.

Marco Enrico Bossi, born in 1861, is known as an organist and teacher. His one-act opera "Paquita" took a prize. He has composed also a symphonic poem, an overture, an organ concerto (given at our Chicago Fair), the dramatic oratorio "Christus," the cantata "Paradise Lost," and many other works. He is a leader in the orchestral field, and is intensely modern.

Don Lorenzo Perosi has been especially successful in composing oratorios and other works for the Catholic service. Born in 1872, he has been very active. His trilogy "The Passion of Christ" (the Last Supper, the Sermon on the Mount, and the Crucifixion) made him known through Italy. Later works of his include the two-part "Moses," "The Transfiguration," "The Annunciation," and "The Raising of Lazarus." Perosi's brother Marziano has composed an opera, "The Last Days of Pompeii."

Simonetti is an excellent Italian violin composer.

Italy had almost no concert halls in 1850; and even the churches were content to use operatic airs with sacred words. In the sixties, an orchestral concert organized by Pinelli earned fourteen *lire*, from which sixty performers were to be paid. Sgambati produced a Beethoven symphony in Rome, but had to pay for it himself. Such absurd conditions are now relegated to the past; and Italy has regained some musical influence.

Spanish composers are greatly devoted to the Zarzuela, which is a national form of light but pleasing and brilliant comic opera. Among those who have worked recently in this form are Larrocha, Arrieta,

Del Campo, Inzenga, Casadesus, Marques, Fernandez, Hernando, Oudrid, Valverde, Vives, Nogueras, Noguerra, and Caballero, as well as many of the orchestral composers. The latter include Manén, Pedrell (the trilogy "Patria, Fides, Amor"), the gifted Granados, various members of the Albeniz family (Isaac writing the opera "Pepita Ximenes"), the violinist Arbos, Breton y Hernandez, Pablo Hernandez, Jimenez, Millet, Morales, Nicolau, Saldoni, and the sacred composer Vilanova.

Portugal is represented by the opera composers Arneiro and Machado; while Ettore Panizza was born at Buenos Ayres.

Switzerland has a real leader in Hans Huber. Born in 1852, he studied with the classicists, but soon began to handle the modern orchestra. His works include the operas "Kudrun," "Weltfrüh-ling," and "Der Simplicius"; a concerto for violin, and two for piano; beautiful choral orchestral works, such as "Pandora" and the "Nordseebilder"; and three great symphonies. One of the latter is entitled "William Tell"; while another is inspired by a group of Boecklin paintings.

Other Swiss composers include Émile Jacques-Dalcroze, who has recently become devoted to the subject of rhythmic gymnastics. Gustave Doret is a protégé of Saint-Saëns; and his "Hymne à la Beauté" is passionately effective.

Among the Swiss orchestral composers are Karl and Walter Courvoisier, Albert Fuchs, Friedrich Hegar, Lothar Kempter, Josef Lauber, Pierre Maurice, Louis Nicole, Richard Alder, Othmar Schoeck, and Hermann Suter. Still other men, working in various forms, are Rudolf Ganz, known in America as a pianist, the choral composer Georg Haeser, Fritz Niggli, Richard Franck, Edward Combe, and A. Denereaz.

Bohemian popular music began with the introduction of Christianity, in the ninth century. The religious style was cherished for a long time, even down to the period of Gluck's teacher Cernohorsky. During the classical epoch Bohemia produced Pokorny, Pichl, Kalliwoda, Tomaschek, the Dusseks, and others; but none of these was of great importance. František Skraup (1801–62) was an operatic pioneer; but he was soon superseded by Smetana.

Friedrich Smetana (1824–84) has been called the Bohemian Beethoven; but beyond the fact that he became deaf, he showed little resemblance to the German master. Composers like Smetana, his successor Dvořák, Huber, and even Raff, are rated a little below the highest standard. They have produced much good music, but they do not quite reach the high level of the greatest masters.

Smetana married the pianist Katharin Kolar, and with her help founded a music school. He was active also as a conductor; but composition was really his life-work. While visiting Liszt he heard Herbeck assert that the Czechs were not original, but merely reproductive; and he determined to disprove this. He succeeded admirably, though the world is not yet as familiar as it should be with his operas.

Smetana's instrumental works include a Festival Overture, a Triumph Symphony, and many symphonic poems. The latter were begun by "Richard III," which was followed by "Wallenstein's Camp" and "Hakon Jarl." Best known, however, is the cycle of six such works known as "My Country." This consists of "Vysehrad," in which the minstrel Lumir is pictured as evoking the past glories of that fortress; "Vltava," the Moldau, comes next, and is a favorite concert number; "Sarka" treats of the legendary Amazon of that name; "Bohemia's Groves and Meadows" is the fourth in the group; "Tabor" depicts the camp of the Hussite soldiers; and "Blanik" is the mountain where they are supposed to sleep, in readiness to awake at their country's need.

Smetana's first opera, "The Brandenburgers in Bohemia," earned for him the reproach of trying to make Bohemian music Wagnerian. Nettled by this, he produced the bright comedy "The Bartered Bride," which is not only original in style, but remarkably attractive. When it was brought to foreign notice, at an 1892 fair in Vienna, the critics asked, "How is it possible that such a genius has been unknown so long?" A return to the serious and tragic vein resulted in "Dalibor," another success. "Two Widows," "The Kiss," and "The Secret" are lighter in style; while "Libusa" and "The Devil's Wall" are strongly dramatic. In passing, one may state that the composer's name should be accented on the first syllable.

Antonin Dvořák (1841–1904) showed an early love for music. At twelve he planned to surprise his relatives with an orchestral polka; and as he forgot to allow for the transposing instruments, the result was even more surprising than he expected. He supported himself for a time in Prague, and at length won the government aid for needy geniuses by some early compositions. He stated that he spent his time in "hard study, occasional composition, much revision, a great deal of thinking, and little eating." After his marriage he sometimes said that he ate less and thought more than ever.

An early opera, "König und Köhler," was attacked as being ultra-Wagnerian. Rewritten in a simpler and more national style, it made a success, although its composer ridiculed his unintelligent public. His later operas, such as "Wanda," "Selma Sedlak," "The Jacobins," "Kate and the Devil" and "Armida," are almost all national in style. "Dimitri" treats of the false Demetrius that Moussorgsky made so famous.

Dvořák's overtures ("Huszitska," "Carnival," and "Nature," and others) are given occasionally on concert programmes. His "Stabat Mater," well received in London, led to an English stay, and the composition of the successful cantata "The Spectre's Bride." A later cantata, "Saint Ludmilla," was a comparative failure; and this fact may have inspired Dvořák's remark, "The English do not love music; they respect it."

His American sojourn inspired him to produce the beautiful "New World Symphony," the greatest of his works in that form. He used the negro songs as the true American folk-music, and made themes that echoed their styles effectively. The negro music is not all devoted to the smooth vein employed by Stephen C. Foster. It is plaintively expressive at times, lively at others, and in certain examples weirdly impressive. Dvořák used all these styles, and produced a master-work.

Zdenko Fibich (1850–1900) was another Bohemian leader. His operas receive almost as much attention as those of Smetana. His work in melodrama (the trilogy "Hippodamia") has been mentioned elsewhere.

Emil Nikolaus, Freiherr von Rezniček, works at Vienna. He, like many others, was destined for law, but deserted it for music. He became known by his operas, — "Die Jungfrau von Orleans," "Satanella," "Emerich Fortunat," the vivacious "Donna Diana," and "Till Eulenspiegel." His early orchestral works, such as his overtures and the "Tragic Symphony," were fairly conservative; but his later symphonic poems, "Schlemihl" and "Der Sieger," place him among the modern programme radicals. He handles the full orches-tra with admirable control and skill.

Among Bohemian composers, Josef Suk, son-in-law of Dvořák, produced the "Fairy Tale" Suite. Josef Mraczek has composed an opera, "The Dream," and the radical orchestral humoresque entitled "Max and Moritz," which depicts the adventures of two bad boys well known in German literature. Heinrich Kaan-Albest has composed several ballets and the symphonic poem "Sakuntala." Josef Nesvera, a writer of masses, won a success with his opera "Perdita." Other Bohemian opera composers are Hrimaly, Jiranek, Kadletz, Kovařovic, Malat, Navratil, Ostrcil, Prochazka, Prokop, Reuter, Rozkosny, Sebor, Trneček, and Skuhersky. Of these, Jiranek, Navratil, and Trneček have entered the orchestral field. Still other Bohemian orchestral composers include Abert, Laska, Nedbal, Novaček, Novak, and Pribik.

Hungary has its school of native opera, brought into being by the Dopplers, and Franz Erkel. The latter's "Hunyadi Laszlo" is very popular. Other Hungarian opera composers include his son George Erkel, Andreas Bartay, Farkas, Hubay, Jarno, Mihalovitch, Poldini, Rekay, Sztojanovics, Szabados, and Count Geza Zichy, the one-armed pianist. Some of these have produced orchestral works also. Erwin Lendvai has composed a radical symphony. Ernst von Dohnanyi has gained much renown by overtures, concertos, a symphony, and the pantomime "Pierrette's Veil." Mihalovitch has won fame by symphonies and orchestral ballads. Other Hungarian orchestral composers include Bartok, Buttikay, Korbay, Szekely, and Vavrinecz. Horvath and Joseffy have produced piano music, while Nachez and Remenyi composed for the violin.

Roumania is represented by Georges Enesco in the orchestral field, Theodor Flondor in opera, and Franz Kneisel in the violin world.

Xaver and Philipp Scharwenka, well known in Berlin, are of Polish origin. The former has written the opera "Mataswintha," a symphony, and three piano concertos; while the latter is credited with choral cantatas, symphonies, a suite, an overture, and many lesser works.

Moritz Moszkowski is another German composer of Polish descent. His compositions include an opera, "Boabdil," the symphonic poem "Joan of Arc," two orchestral suites, a piano concerto

PADEREWSKI

and many smaller works. He seems able to assume many styles, as his piano cycle "Aus aller Herren Länder" will show. He is full of humor, and states as other accomplishments that he can "play billiards, chess, dominoes, and violin, and can ride, imitate canary birds, and relate jokes in the Saxon dialect."

Paderewski is widely known as a composer because of his minuet and other pieces. He has written the gypsy opera "Manru," a long symphony, and a piano concerto, the last of which wins success when he takes the solo part.

Other Polish opera composers include Gavronski, Jarecki, Kazynski, Koczalski, Melcer, Mignard, Moniuszko, Opienski, Rozycki, and Stalkowsky. Polish orchestral composers include Karlwicz, Maszynski, Novoviejski, Statkowsky, Novakovski, Dobrzynski, De Kontski, Chopin's pupil Mikuli, Soltys, Zelenski, Kurpinski, and Zientarski.

In Belgium, a recent leader was Peter Benoit (1834–1901). He composed operas and other works, but was best known by his great cantatas. These include "Oorlog" ("War"), "Lucifer," "De Schelde," "De Rhyn," "Prometheus," and a Rubens cantata. They have been described as "great decorative pictures in tone, suggesting vistas of grand palaces, armies in battle array, rich fields of grain, mystic visions of the spirit world, or gorgeous triumphal marches."

Paul Gilson, born in 1865, is another Belgian leader. His symphonic sketches entitled "La Mer" made him well known. These picture sunrise at sea, the rollicking music of the sailors, a love-scene with departure, and a tempest. The cantata "Francesca da Rimini" is another strong work by Gilson. The lovers are condemned by Minos, and taunted by demons in the Inferno. Francesca's prayer finally wins pity for her; but she will not accept mercy without Paolo, and decides to stay with him. Other works by Gilson include the oratorio "Moses," the operas "Princess Sunshine," "The Adventurers," and "The Demon," incidental music, orchestral works with declamation, overtures, fantasies, suites, and many other compositions.

Guillaume Lekeu (1870–94) showed much promise in his brief career. He produced symphonic poems, chamber works, and lesser pieces, often tinged with gloom, but usually very effective.

Edgar Tinel's chief composition is the oratorio "Franciscus." This is a three-part work showing Francis of Assisi as young nobleman, as monk, and as saint in heaven. Tinel's "Saint Godelive" is another successful oratorio. He has written also orchestral pieces and cantatas.

Jan Blockx (1851–1912) produced orchestral works of various sorts, but was best known by the ballet "Milenka" and by his operas. Of the latter, "The Princess of the Inn" meets with most success. Its heroine, Reinilde, loves Merlyn, and refuses Marcus; whereupon Marcus plans to ruin Merlyn, by means of Rita, an innkeeper's daughter. Rita's discarded lover Rabo becomes jealous, and kills Merlyn. Reinilde is then ready to kill Rita, but decides that a life of remorse will be a greater punishment for her. Other Blockx operas are the one-act "Iels Vergeten," the opéra-comique "Maître Martin," "La Fiancée de la Mer," and "Thyl Uylenspiegel."

Among Belgian operatic composers, Keurvels has produced "Paris," "Rolla," and "Hamlet"; Wambach has composed "Nathans Parabel," as well as oratorios and a symphonic poem; the works of Dupuis include "Moina" and "Cour d'Ognon"; Vleeshouwer is a Blockx pupil; Van Duyse is credited with seven operas; Waelput's "Stella" is better known than his four symphonies; Raway's "Neon" and "Freya" are ambitious works; Van den Eeden's "Rhena" has been well received; Juliet Folville, a leader among the women, has composed "Atala" and many orchestral works; Émile Mathieu has written incidental music as well as operas; while other active opera composers include Callaerts, Daneau, Kaiser, Lebrun, Neuville, Pâque, Radoux, Rasse, Ratez, Van der Meulen, and Verhulst. Other Belgians deserving mention in various fields are Gevaert, organist and teacher; Huberti, an oratorio composer; Lenaerts, who has composed cantatas; and in general orchestral work, Mailly, Mestdagh, Ryelandt, Ruefer, Thiebaut, Tilman, Vreuls, and Wouters.

In Holland, Richard Hol was for many years a leader, famous for his national hymn and for symphonies, cantatas, and other compositions. Julius Roentgen also composed orchestral works. Van't Kruis has been very active in producing overtures and symphonies. Other Dutch orchestral composers are Averkamp, Coenen,

De Haan, Diepenbrock, Kes, Van der Linden, the conductor Mengelberg, Cornelia van Osterzee, Van der Pals, Scaefer, Smulders, the pianist Stavenhagen, Zweers, Berlijn, and the Brandt-Buys family. In opera, Gottfried Mann witnessed the performance of his charming "Melaenis"; Van Milligen produced "Brinio" and "Darthula"; Schey wrote "The Eagle's Nest"; while Wagenaar, Grellinger, and Cora Dopper have also composed stage works.

England, like Italy, was for some time in a state of decadence. The ballad operas of Balfe, Wallace, Benedict, and Costa were very conventional in style, even in comparison with Bishop's earlier works; and the English songs were sentimental and "mushy." Five men led a renaissance from this musical "slough of despond." They were Stanford, Parry, Mackenzie, Cowen, and Goring Thomas.

Charles Villiers Stanford, born in 1852, has composed symphonies and similar works, as well as two oratorios. In opera his chief success came with "Shamus O'Brien," though his "Canterbury Pilgrims" is a laudable attempt to revive the atmosphere of early days in England. His Irish Symphony, based on folk-music, is decidedly characteristic.

Charles Hubert Hastings Parry, born in 1848, has composed symphonies and overtures, but is best known by his oratorios, such as "Judith," "Job," and "King Saul." In these he often shows a lofty and exalted style, and "brings all heaven before our eyes," according to one enthusiastic critic.

Alexander Campbell Mackenzie, born in 1847, includes among his works oratorios, such as "The Rose of Sharon" and "Bethlehem"; cantatas, including "Sayid" and "The Cotter's Saturday Night"; operas, especially "Colomba" and "The Troubadour"; and many orchestral works. He is of Scotch birth, while Stanford is Irish.

Frederic Hymen Cowen, born in 1852, is known by six symphonies, among which the Scandinavian, Idyllic, and Welsh are the best. He has won fame also with his cantatas, such as "The Sleeping Beauty," "St. John's Eve," "The Water Lily," and "The Veil." He has composed also two oratorios and four operas.

Arthur Goring Thomas (1850–92) won success with his opera "Esmeralda," though a later work, "Nadeshda," was poorly received. Of his cantatas, "The Swan and the Skylark" and "The Sun Worshippers" are the most popular.

With these five men worked a number of others, such as the MacFarren brothers, Sir Frederick Bridge (known as the "Westminster Bridge," because he is organist in Westminster Abbey), Parratt, Barnett, Lloyd, Corder, Cusins, and Williams. On the whole, the school had worthy aims, but lacked deep inspiration. Ernest Newman once said that men of the Bridge-Mackenzie type could no more hatch out a new school than a hen could hatch hard-boiled eggs. This is too severe a criticism, but its point is correct.

English hymnology received an impetus from Wesley, whose work was carried forward excellently by Stainer, Barnby, Webb, and others.

Sir Edward Elgar, born in 1857, is the leader of a newer and less academic style. The story goes that when he was sent to school, and asked by a teacher what his name was, he replied, "Edward Elgar." "Add the sir," demanded the pedagogue, wishing to instil principles of respect; whereupon the boy replied, "Sir Edward Elgar." But he has now attained knighthood in reality, an honor won by the value of his works.

In childhood he delighted in his father's organ-playing at Worcester. He was largely self-taught in music, and for practice in composition he wrote a symphony with Mozart's G-minor work as a model, making his themes and other divisions of the same size as Mozart's. Of instruction books he once said, "I have read them, and I still live." But he approved of Mozart's "Thorough-Bass School."

His early cantata, "The Black Knight," was given at a Worcester festival. Other cantatas, written as an outcome of the first one, were "The Light of Life," "Caractacus," and "Sir Olaf." His Enigma variations for orchestra, each describing a friend, form a very attractive work, and earned him recognition in London. The first of his oratorios, "The Dream of Gerontius," won him international fame. Later compositions in this form by him are "The Apostles" and "The Kingdom." Other vocal works of Elgar's are, "Scenes from the Bavarian Highlands," "The Banner of Saint George," "Lux Christi," and a Te Deum. For orchestra he has written several overtures ("Froissart," "In the South," and "Cockaigne"), some effective "Pomp and Circumstance" marches, incidental music to "Diarmid and Grania," a Coronation March, and the Sea

Pictures, for solo voice with orchestra. In recent years he has gone over to the radicals. His two symphonies are rather abstruse, though the finale of the second is very impressive. His violin concerto is full of difficulties.

Joseph Holbrooke, born in 1878, is another radical. His opera, "The Children of Don," is to be made the first of a Trilogy. For orchestra, sometimes with voices, he has written "The Raven," "The Skeleton in Armor," "Ulalume," the bizarre but effective "Queen Mab," and a Poe Symphony. His works are not sufficiently tuneful for real success.

Frederick Delius, born in 1863, is another modernist. His "Brigg Fair" introduces old English melodies; but his other works, such as "Appalachia," "The Dance of Life," "A Mass of Life" (with voices), "Sea Drift," "Paris," and "The Song of the High Hills," are fragmentary and bizarre in their harmonies.

Cyril Meir Scott, born in 1879, is one of the few composers who can handle modern effects in an interesting way. His harmonies are novel, and intricate enough; but he builds them into works that have beauty and coherence. He is known in America by some of his interesting piano pieces. But he has composed in the larger forms too, producing a symphony, a piano concerto, three overtures, and some effective chamber music.

Another radical who has done good work is Granville Bantock, born in 1868. His early efforts resulted in the one-act operas "Caedmar" and "The Pearl of Iran," as well as a vast setting of Southey's poem, "The Curse of Kehama," in twenty-four orchestral numbers. He composed also a cantata, "The Fire-Worshippers," and the overtures "Saul" and "The Pierrot of the Minute." The latter is rather fragmentary. Recently he has tried to develop a symphonic form for voices alone, his "Atalanta in Calydon" having four movements and dividing the vocal forces into twelve groups.

With Bantock have been associated William Wallace, composer of a Creation Symphony, a choral symphony, six symphonic poems, the opera "Brassolis," and other works; Erskine Allon, whose orchestral ballad "Annie of Lochroyan," cantata "The Oak of Geismar," and overture "The Maid of Colonsay" have made his early death a subject for great regret; Reginald Steggall, who has composed several *scenas*; Stanley Hawley, who has become known by his melodramas; and Arthur Hinton, whose "Triumph of Cæsar," "Endymion" suite, and piano concerto are effective works.

Samuel Coleridge-Taylor (1875–1912) was the son of a full-blooded negro physician of West Africa and an English mother. His works are expressive and impassioned in style. His cantata "Hiawatha," in several parts, shows much beauty. Other vocal-orchestral works by him are an oratorio, "The Atonement," the cantata "Endymion's Dream," and "A Tale of Old Japan." His orchestral works consist of a Solemn Prelude, the Herod music, and other numbers. He composed also effective songs, piano pieces, and violin works.

Sir Arthur Seymour Sullivan (1842–1900) was a conservative in style. Known on several continents by his successful light operas, he excelled also in a more serious vein, with such works as the ora-torios "The Prodigal Son," "The Martyr of Antioch," and "The Golden Legend," the cantata "Kenilworth," a Te Deum, some overtures, much incidental music, the opera "Ivanhoe," and a sym-phony. His songs are widely known, "The Lost Chord" being an especially broad and effective solo.

With Sullivan may be classed the opera composers Alfred Cellier and Edward Solomon; but Edward German (really German Ed-ward Jones) is now better known than either. He has composed two symphonies, but has won his greatest recognition by incidental music to various Shakespearian and other plays. His dances from the "Henry VIII" music are widely popular. He finished Sullivan's "Emerald Isle," and composed "The Rival Poets" and "Merrie England." He has employed the folk-song style with marked success.

The English folk-music is direct and lively in style, being mostly in major. The Scotch folk-songs, with their use of the pentatonic scale, are even more attractive. The Welsh songs are much like the Scotch, and the Irish often have odd but impressive harmonies. While Russian folk-songs show the greatest variety of style and mode, those of Great Britain are attractive also.

The English orchestral composers are now very numerous. Many of the following should have special mention, if space would permit. A list of the chief names includes Arthur Somervell, Frederick Cliffe, Arthur Hervey, Robert Bridges, Herbert Bunning, Samuel

Liddle, Algernon Ashton, Charles Macpherson, Charles Stuart Macpherson, Alan Grey, the Scotchman Hamish MacCunn, Allan Macbeth, Alick Maclean, Henry Coward, Walford Davies, the Irish-born Michael Esposito, Isidore de Lara (known in opera), Eaton Faning, Balfour Gardiner, Percy Grainger, Hamilton Harty, Gustave von Holst, Oliver King, Norman O'Neill, Percy Pitt, Ebenezer Prout (an excellent author), Roger Quilter, Donald Francis Tovey, and among the women Alice Mary Smith, Ethel Smyth (operas "Der Wald" and "The Wreckers"), Agnes Zimmermann, Rosalind Ellicott, and Marie Wurm.

A number of English composers have become famous by their songs. Among these are Hatton, Hullah, Watson, Maybrick (writing as Stephen Adams), Oliver King, Bruno Huhn, Molloy, Gaul, and Marzials, the songs of the last-named being especially dainty. Among the women, Liza Lehmann, Frances Allitsen, Guy d'Harde-lot (Mrs. Rhodes), and Maud Valerie White have done artistic work, while Hope Temple and Teresa del Riego adopt a more popular standard. In the same class are the Anglo-Italians Tosti, Mattei, and Pinsuti. The Aptommas brothers and Parish-Alvars have earned notice by their harp music.

On the whole, England is now successful in disproving Rubinstein's assertion that it was the most unmusical nation on earth.

XXX

AMERICA

THE musical life of the American colonies came from small beginnings. Virginia had its Cavalier songs, but did not develop them into an original school; while Massachusetts was at first devoted solely to psalms, even hymns being barred at first. Its early scholars published the "Bay Psalm Book," and disputed learnedly over who should be allowed to sing. When hymns came into use, they were at first "lined out," each line being read before it was sung, since not all the church-goers possessed books. This sometimes produced rather strange effects, as in the hymn which began, —

"The Lord will come, and he will not"

and continued, —

"Keep silence, but speak out."

In the eighteenth century, concerts began in such centres as Boston, New York, Philadelphia, and Charleston. These are well described by Oscar G. Sonneck in his "Early Concert Life in America."

The first American composer was probably Francis Hopkinson (1737–91). He graduated at Princeton, and in 1759 began a collection into which he put several original songs. In a much later set, dedicated to Washington, he definitely claims the honor of being the first American composer. His only rival was James Lyon, the minister, who graduated at the same college, composed commencement odes, and published the hymn collection "Urania" in 1761. William Billings (1746–1800), of Boston, was a composer of somewhat more advanced style. He was a tanner's apprentice at first, but he soon began chalking musical exercises on the sides of leather. By 1770 he published an original collection, "The New England Psalm Singer," which established his reputation. In later years he worked at "fugue-tunes"; and while his fugal effects were very flimsy, his preface showed that he understood the nature and beauty of counterpoint. Billings was the man who was asked whether snoring was vocal or instrumental music; but history does not give his reply. Other hymn composers, of later date, were Oliver Holden, Samuel Holyoke, Jacob Kimball, Henry Kemble Oliver, Daniel Read, and Lowell Mason. In more recent years, William Bradbury composed hymns and cantatas; the evangelist Ira D. Sankey wrote many hymn-tunes; and Hart Pease Danks produced hymns as well as the familiar "Silver threads among the gold."

In the early part of the nineteenth century came the development of orchestras and singing societies, as well as the advent of opera troupes. William Henry Fry (1813–64) composed the opera "Leonora" in 1845, though it was not given until 1858. In 1863 he finished another opera, "Notre Dame de Paris." George F. Bristow (1825–98) composed "Rip van Winkle" in 1855. Both men wrote instrumental works, which were performed by Jullien on an American trip.

The national songs of America are largely borrowed. The melody of "Yankee Doodle" came from English sources, and was adapted by Dr. Shuckburgh to his words satirizing the Colonials in the Old French War. It was at first a British tune, and not taken by the colonies until near the end of the Revolution. "America" is borrowed directly from "God save the king," a tune that is used in many countries. "Hail, Columbia " is original, but not a source for pride. It was first known as "The President's March." The melody of "The Star-Spangled Banner" is taken from an old English drinking-song, "To Anacreon in Heaven," which explains its awkwardly large compass and bold outbursts. The Civil War, however, brought forth good native songs. "Glory Hallelujah" was originally a Southern camp-meeting hymn, known as "Say, brothers, will you meet us." It was adopted by the soldiers at Fort Warren, Boston, with words made up to tease one of their members, named John Brown. When these men marched to the front, they sang the song on their way, and made it instantly popular. Two years later, Julia Ward Howe wrote new words for it. If the North got its best war-song from the South, it paid the debt fully; for "Dixie" was a Northern affair, composed by Dan Emmett as a minstrel's "walk-around" in New York. George F. Root wrote "The Battle-Cry of Freedom" and other war-time successes; while Henry Clay Work produced the ever-popular "Marching through Georgia." H. L. Schreiner and A. E. Blackmar wrote Southern war-songs of decided spirit. Stephen Collins Foster's songs show the plantation style. After the war, the growing musical atmosphere in our larger cities, especially New York, Boston, Cincinnati, and Chicago, resulted in the development of composers whose work is more ambitious in style, and more in line with the great European models. Valuable influence was exerted by the pianist William Mason and the conductor Theodore Thomas.

A leader among American orchestral composers was John Knowles Paine (1839–1906). Born at Portland, Maine, he studied in Berlin, and became known in both Germany and America by his organ concerts. In 1862 he became head of the music department at Harvard College, where he worked until his death. In 1867 his Mass in D won a Berlin success. This was followed by the American production of his oratorio "St. Peter," a work of much skill and also much difficulty. Paine's first symphony, in C-minor, was performed by Thomas; but his second, the "Spring" Symphony, proved a greater success. At the Philadelphia Exposition of 1876, his "Centennial Hymn" showed more inspiration than Wagner's blatant "Centennial March." Paine's symphonic poem "The Tempest" proved to be another interesting work. His music to the "Œdipus Tyrannus" of Sophocles was lofty, dignified, and thoroughly effective. This was the best American composition of its time. Paine wrote also such vocal-orchestral works as "Phœbus, arise," "The Nativity," the "Song of Promise," and the "Columbus March and Hymn." Another symphonic poem by him was "An Island Fantasy," composed after a painting of the Isles of Shoals by J. Appleton Brown. The music to "The Birds" of Aristophanes was good, though hardly equal to "Œdipus." Paine composed an opera, "Azara," based on the old Trouvère story of "Aucassin et Nicolette." It contains much beautiful music, but is not essentially dramatic, as the composer's forte was a more conservative style.

Edward Alexander MacDowell (1861–1908) was held to be America's best composer. He studied in Germany, and taught at Darmstadt. In later years he was in charge of the music department at Columbia College. MacDowell's music is earnest, impassioned, and expressive. His studies with Raff resulted in giving him a command of melodic utterance. He was not a strict classicist, but put into the

CONVERSE   PAINE   HADLEY

MACDOWELL

CHADWICK   FOOTE   PARKER

old forms the freedom that modern standards allow. His two great piano concertos have been frequently played by Mme. Carreño. The same is true of his sonatas, which are remarkably effective works in the modern free form. The first of these is the dramatic "sonata tragica"; the second is the "sonata eroica," inscribed with the words "Flos regum Arthurus"; the third, dedicated to Grieg, has been called by Huneker "An epic of rainbow and thunder"; while the later Keltic Sonata bears witness to its composer's Scotch ancestry. MacDowell's orchestral works include the symphonic poems "Hamlet," "Ophelia," and the beautiful "Lancelot and Elaine"; the Indian Suite, based on real Indian melodies; "The Saracens," "The Lovely Alda," two fragments of the "Song of Roland," and a later suite, often given in Germany, consisting of "In a Haunted Forest," "Summer Idyl," "In October," "The Shepherdess's Song," and "Forest Spirits." The Indian Suite naturally shows the composer's own orchestral use of the themes. There has been much discussion as to whether Indian or negro music is the real folk-music of the United States. The latter carries off the palm, for two reasons. In the first place, Indian music is not known to many people, and consequently does not have the wide appeal of true folk-music; and in the second place, it is merely unison melody, so that in instrumental use it derives its character from the individual composer's harmonies. Arthur Farwell has used Indian melodies effectively for piano, but the harmonies are his own; while the very beautiful chords of Charles Wakefield Cadman would undoubtedly sound strange to the Indians whose songs he uses as melodies. MacDowell wrote "An Indian Lodge" for piano, but it is no more folk-music than his other piano works, — the "Woodland Sketches," the "Sea Pieces," or the earlier and more classical piano suites. MacDowell is known also by many beautiful songs, varying in style from the emotion of "Thy Beaming Eyes" to the sombre force of "The Eagle." Especially effective are the Eight Songs (Op. 47), containing "The Sea," which shows a noble breadth of effect, and the delicate "Midsummer Lullaby."

George Whitfield Chadwick, born at Lowell, Massachusetts, in 1854, studied with his elder brother at first. He began composition while a pupil at the Lawrence High School; and some of the dances he produced then were used later in his successful musical comedy

"Tabasco." Studies at the New England Conservatory resulted in the composition of orchestral works and piano trios. Chadwick's father wished him to begin a business career; but the young man made music his life-work by starting out as music teacher in a Michigan college. There he earned money enough for serious study at Leipsic, under Reinecke and Jadassohn. Since his return, he has been teacher and musical director at the New England Conservatory. His "Rip Van Winkle" Overture and two string quartets date from his German student days, and received much praise. His "Melpomene" Overture unites classic dignity with tragic power in a way that deserves the highest recognition. "Thalia" is an overture to the muse of comedy, while "Euterpe" is a later offering to the muse of dancing. The "Adonais" Overture is another work of nobly expressive character. Chadwick has written three symphonies, the second of which made use of plantation effects long before Dvořák came to America to work in the same field. Chadwick has sometimes used this flavor in his chamber works, of which a piano quintet and a later string quartet deserve mention. His "Judith" is an ambitious sacred opera, though so far it has been given only in oratorio form. "Phœnix Expirans," "The Lily Nymph," and "Noel" are successful cantatas. Later orchestral works include a Symphonietta (containing the wildly American "Vagrom Ballad"), a Suite Symphonique, the symphonic poem "Cleopatra," and a later one, "Aphrodite." The last-named, inspired by a beautiful head of the goddess that is now in the Boston Art Museum, portrays scenes that might have taken place before the statue when it stood in its temple. The music suggests sacred dances; a storm at sea; the thank-offerings of rescued mariners; temple services; moonlit solitude; and other appropriate ideas. Chadwick's many songs contain such gems as "Allah," "Sorais' Song," the "Song from the Persian," and the "Bedouin Love-Song." His "Tam o' Shanter," a symphonic sketch in Scottish style, was performed with success in 1915.

Horatio Parker, born at Auburndale, Massachusetts, in 1863, did not become interested in music until the age of fourteen. Then he began asking many questions about it, and devoted himself to study with Chadwick, and with Rheinberger at Munich. On his return he became musical director in various schools, teacher in the

National Conservatory, and finally head of the music department at Yale. His early works include piano pieces, songs, chamber music, several overtures, and a number of cantatas. His "Hora Novissima" achieved an international reputation. This is an oratorio treating a mediæval Latin poem by Bernard de Morlaix. Its contrapuntal structure and lofty atmosphere make it an absolute masterpiece, of which even a Bach might have been proud. This work resulted in an English order for the Hereford Festival of 1900, for which the composer wrote "A Wanderer's Psalm." A later oratorio of lofty dignity is "St. Christopher." Still more recent is "Morwen and the Grail," a mystic oratorio with rather modulatory music. Parker has written also an organ concerto and lesser organ pieces of much worth. He has entered the field of American opera too, winning a prize with his "Mona," and another with "Fairyland."

The libretto of "Mona," by Brian Hooker, is on an old British subject. Quintus, son of the Roman governor, has been brought up among the Britons as Gwynn. He loves Mona, the last descendant of Boadicea. Caradoc, the bard, urges rebellion, aided by Mona's foster-brother Gloom. Gwynn, whose Roman origin is unknown to the others, works for peace, and thereby gets himself disliked. He follows Mona as she spreads messages of revolt, and saves her life; while at the same time he tells his father that he can avert the war. He wins Mona's love, but she distrusts him when he tries to make her give up the revolt. He is kept prisoner by her Britons while a battle is fought. Gwynn then tells Mona of his parentage. She disbelieves his story, and kills him; but when taken captive she finds with vain regret that he told the truth. The score of "Mona" is scholarly, earnest, and masterly in its orchestration and choral numbers. It errs by being rather too unmelodic, and not always dramatic; but it is still a great work.

Arthur Foote, born at Salem in 1853, is entirely an American product. His overture "In the Mountains" is a dignified composition. More interesting, however, are his suites, that in D-minor being for orchestra, while an earlier work, in D-major, is for strings. In these he shows a union of the classical spirit with real inspiration. His four character pieces, based on verses from "Omar Khayyam," are more in the pictorial style of programme music. His chamber works, which are highly prized, include a piano quintet, a string quartet, a piano trio, and an excellent violin sonata. Another work, for orchestra, is the effective symphonic prologue to Dante's story of Francesca da Rimini. Foote's cantatas, such as "The Skeleton in Armor" and "The Wreck of the Hesperus," are made of worthy music, but the words are sometimes spun out, and repeated too much. His songs include many favorites, such as the "Irish Folk-Song," or "When icicles hang by the wall."

Henry Kimball Hadley, born at Somerville, Massachusetts, in 1871, studied with Chadwick in Boston and Mandycewski in Vienna. The four movements of his "Youth and Life" symphony seem to typify aspiration, sorrow, high spirits, and triumph. "The Seasons" is another symphony, dividing naturally into four movements. A still later symphony, "North, East, South, and West," boxes the compass in excellent fashion, portraying the ruggedness of the North, the mystery of the Orient, the lively jollity of the South, and the victorious spirit of the golden West. Hadley's overtures include "Hector and Andromache," "In Bohemia," and "Herod." His ballet music has been arranged in suites. He produced the opera "Safie" in Germany; while "The Atonement of Pan," composed for the "high jinks" of the San Francisco Bohemian Club, is practically another opera. He has produced chamber music of real value, and a number of artistic songs; but he seems to prefer the larger forms. "Lelewala" is an early cantata that brings in Niagara. "Merlin and Vivian" is a lyric work of dramatic tendencies, for solo voices, chorus, and orchestra. "The Fate of Princess Kiyo" is another cantata, this time for women's voices. Most advanced, however, are his symphonic poems, consisting of "Salome" and "The Culprit Fay." In the former, the largest modern orchestra is handled with Strauss-like control and power of expression. The latter is based on a poem by Joseph Rodman Drake, aimed to show that American rivers and scenes should have their poetic legends. The culprit fay, disgraced by the glance of a mortal maiden's eye, regains his status by voyaging in a mussel-shell boat to obtain the glistening drop of water from a leaping sturgeon and the spark from a falling star. After a successful return, he joins the fairy dance that ends with cock-crow. In the music, Hadley has given many effective suggestions, such as the grace of the fairies, the culprit's troubles, the immensity of sea and sky, the joyful return, and the final dance.

Frederick Shepard Converse, born at Newton, Massachusetts, in 1871, is another orchestral and operatic leader. Two of his symphonic poems, "The Festival of Pan" and "Endymion's Narrative," are inspired by the poetry of Keats. Both are effective enough, but rather contemplative in style. More dramatic is "Ormazd," which depicts the conflict between the followers of that beneficent deity and the forces of the wicked Ahriman. "Night and Day" and "The Mystic Trumpeter" were inspired by Walt Whitman's poems. Other instrumental works by Converse are an early symphony, given while he studied with Rheinberger at Munich; the concert overture "Youth"; a violin concerto; and two string quartets. He has composed also the oratorio "Job," the baritone ballad "La Belle Dame Sans Merci," and incidental music to Percy Mackaye's "Joan of Arc." But he is known most widely by his operas, "The Pipe of Desire" and "The Sacrifice." He is now working at "Beauty and the Beast."

"The Pipe of Desire" begins with revels of the Elves, who decide that their favorite peasant Iolan shall be allowed to see them, in spite of the warnings of the Old One, their king. The latter plays his sacred pipe, and thus forces even Iolan to dance; but in revenge Iolan seizes the pipe. The peasant will not give it back until its notes have shown him a vision of his desire, — a fertile farm, and a comfortable home in which wife and children await him. He calls his beloved, Naoia, to come to him. Because of the pipe's power, she has to obey; but the journey is so long that she dies in the arms of Iolan, who is thus punished for attempting to obtain supernatural power. The delicate, contemplative style of the music is almost too refined for stage success.

"The Sacrifice" deals with the renunciation of an American captain (Burton) who loves a Spanish girl (Chonita) during the taking of California by the United States. The plot is based on a story by Lieut. H. A. Wise. Chonita in reality loves Bernal, her countryman. The first act contains an impressive Indian prophecy, an attractive song by Chonita, and an impassioned love-duet. The second act, in the interior of a mission building, begins with a spirited soldiers' chorus and a piquant dance of gypsy and Mexican girls. When the chapel empties, Chonita enters, and sings a melodious prayer. Bernal, who is really outlawed, is discovered in disguise; he tries to kill Burton, but Chonita throws herself between the men, and is wounded. The third act shows Chonita recovering, and Burton planning to free Bernal for her. When some Mexicans arrange a surprise, he lets himself be killed, so that Bernal's freedom will be assured. The work has much virility, but moves slowly at times.

An earlier American opera composer was Frederic Grant Gleason (1848–1903). His works include the cantata "The Culprit Fay," the orchestral compositions "Edris" and "The Song of Life," and the operas "Otho Visconti" and "Montezuma."

Victor Herbert, born at Dublin in 1859, has made himself thoroughly American. He has composed symphonic poems, a 'cello concerto, a suite romantique, and many light operas as well as the grand opera "Natoma." Even in his light operas he usually includes some serious number, such as the Bridal Chorus in "The Red Mill." He has been a well-known 'cello player.

"Natoma" is based on an Indian subject. Natoma is the servant of Barbara, who is loved by Paul Merrill, whom she prefers, and by Alvarado; while the half-breed Castro admires Natoma, who loves Merrill hopelessly. When the unwelcome suitors are refused, Castro arranges for Alvarado to kidnap Barbara. The second act shows a festival, under cover of which Alvarado is to act; but Natoma, dancing the dagger dance with Castro, rushes by him and stabs Alvarado, seeking sanctuary in a church. Here (Act III) Natoma's vengeful ideas are calmed down, and she becomes a nun. The score contains both Indian and Spanish color, with brilliant festival effects in the second act. A shorter opera by Herbert is the one-act "Madeleine."

With Herbert in light opera belong Reginald de Koven, whose "Robin Hood" and "Maid Marian" are worthy works. Here, too, should be mentioned John Philip Sousa, writer of marches and the opera "El Capitan."

Walter Johannes Damrosch, son of Leopold Damrosch, wrote a "Manila Te Deum." In opera his "Scarlet Letter" was earnest, but not inspired. "The Senator" is a successful musical comedy. His latest effort is "Cyrano," which is set with a fair share of humor.

Frank Damrosch, brother of Walter, is active in school music.

Louis Adolph Coerne, born at Newark, New Jersey, in 1870, lived and studied abroad, though finishing under Paine. He has been active as organist and director. At Harvard he produced a violin and 'cello concerto, an orchestral fantasia, and several anthems. Other early works by him are a string suite, an organ concerto with strings, horns, and harps, the interesting ballet "Evadne," and the symphonic poem "Hiawatha." Later orchestral works are a Requiem, the tone-poem "Liebesfrühling," the tone-picture "George Washington," and several large cantatas. In opera, his "Woman of Marblehead" was well received in America, while his later "Zenobia" was favorably mentioned in Germany. His style is richly expressive, as may be seen from his song "The Sea." In this a broad melody is supported by changing harmonies that glow with kaleidoscopic beauty.

Charles Wakefield Cadman, born at Johnstown, Pennsylvania, in 1881, has devoted himself to Indian melodies. His forthcoming opera, "Daoma," is to be based on about forty native themes, chiefly Omaha, but partly Iroquois and Pawnee. Most interesting among his shorter works are the "Four American Indian Songs." The melodies, played in unison as an introduction in some instances, are kept intact in the songs; but the glowing beauty of the harmonies is of course the work of the composer. Of his other compositions, "Three Songs to Odysseus" is a vocal set deserving special praise. Still other cycles are the Japanese "Sayonara" and a recent group of South Sea Island songs.

Arthur Finley Nevin, born in 1871, has composed several suites, and the Indian opera "Poia," performed abroad.

His older brother, Ethelbert Nevin (1862–1901), is known because of the beauty of his short works. His song "The Rosary" and his piano piece "Narcissus" are national favorites, and show that it is often better to excel in small forms than to obtain only mediocre results in the large ones.

George Balch Nevin, born in 1859, is related to the preceding two men. He has become known through his cantatas and sacred songs. His son, Gordon Balch Nevin, has produced good organ works.

Paul Allen has composed several operas for Italy, which seems only a fair return for the many Italian operas brought here.

Harvey Worthington Loomis, born at Brooklyn in 1865, has hundreds of works in manuscript, besides having published many compositions. An early piano concerto was the result of study with Dvořák. He has composed several cantatas, such as "The Fairy Hill," for children. He has been active in the field of melodrama, writing backgrounds (which he sometimes calls "Musical Symbolism") for "Sandalphon" and other poems. His many pantomimes include such diverse subjects as "The Enchanted Fountain," "Her Revenge," and "In Old New Amsterdam." "The Maid of Athens" and "The Burglar's Bride" are burlesque operas. His "Tragedy of Death," partly vocal and partly melodramatic, is a striking work. It shows a mother's efforts to save her child before Death can take it from the Garden of Souls to Heaven; while Undines and Fates participate with effective choruses. In piano works and songs, Loomis shows a remarkable originality. His hunt for novelty is sometimes too restless, but his work is always interesting.

J. Remington Fairlamb (1837–1908) left his opera "Leonella" in manuscript. He studied at Paris; was consul at Zurich under Lincoln; and received a medal from the King of Württemberg for a Te Deum with double chorus and orchestra. He wrote sacred music, and parts of later operas.

Other composers who have operas in manuscript are Arthur Bird, Harry Rowe Shelley, Alexander Hull, Johann H. Beck, E. F. Schneider, W. H. Neidlinger, Jules Jordan, Gaston Borch, and W. Franke-Harling. The last four have written songs. Hull has composed a manuscript symphony, and has published "Java" for full orchestra and piano. He has under way the operas "Paolo and Francesca" and "Merlin and Vivien." His songs and piano works show very interesting effects of modernism, his harmonies being novel and attractive. Bird has composed the comic opera "Daphne," the ballet "Rübezahl," a symphony, and three suites. Homer Moore, of St. Louis, has planned an American operatic trilogy, — "The New World," "The Pilgrims," and "The Puritans."

Charles Martin Loeffler, born at Mülhausen in 1861, is now an American citizen. His works are radically modern, being full of the quickly-changing harmonic effects that have been called "musical stippling," and that make the works of Debussy so chaotic to conservative ears. Loeffler's works include a suite and a divertimento for violin and orchestra, a 'cello concerto, and the orchestral tone-poems, "The Death of Tintagiles," "La Villanelle du Diable," "La Bonne Chanson," and "A Pagan Poem." "The Death of Tintagiles" is admirably expressive, and "La Bonne Chanson" a work of infinite sweetness.

Another composer of foreign birth is Gustav Strube, born at Ballenstedt in 1867. He became known as violinist and conductor in Boston. His works include overtures ("The Maid of Orleans" and "Puck"), symphonies (the second being a strong work), a set of orchestral variations, two violin concertos, a 'cello concerto, chamber music, and the symphonic poems, "Longing," "Fantastic Dance," "Echo et Narcisse" and "Die Lorelei." He uses the intricate harmonic style of the modernists; but his work is direct and virile, where that of Debussy is often shadowy and vague.

Another foreigner active in Boston is André Maquarre, a Belgian by birth. He is first flutist in the Symphony Orchestra. He has composed operas, but is known in America by orchestral works, such as "Sur les Falaises."

Otto Urack, 'cellist in the Boston orchestra until recalled by the European war in 1914, composed a melodious symphony.

Bruno Oscar Klein (1858–1911) was a German who composed the opera "Kenilworth" and smaller works.

Pietro Tirindelli is another foreign-born operatic composer.

Louis Maas (1852–1889), born at Wiesbaden, was inspired by America to write concertos, overtures, suites, and the symphony "On the Prairies."

Rudolf Friml, born in Prague but living in New York, has composed several ballets, a number of operas (including "The Firefly"), various songs, and instrumental pieces of novel and pleasing character.

Other foreigners who have composed orchestral music in America are W. C. Seeboeck, Fritz Stahlberg, the Chicago conductor Frederick Stock, Arthur Hartmann (who came to America when two months old), Anton Hegner, the Dane Carl Busch, the Dutchman John A. Broekhoven, and the Englishman Horace Wadham Nicholl. Other men deserving mention for various compositions are Carl Baermann, Richard Pohlig, Will C. Macfarlane, Arthur Claassen,

Henry Eichheim, Nicholas J. Elsenheimer, Louis Victor Saar, Frederick Brandeis, Robert Goldbeck, Richard Hoffman, Karl Müller, Sebastian Bach Mills, P. A. Schnecker, Otto Floersheim, Julius Eichberg, and Emilio Agramonte.

Otis Bardwell Boise, of Ohio, who lived abroad and in Baltimore, produced a symphony, two overtures, and a piano concerto.

Another American choosing to live abroad is George Templeton Strong, born at New York in 1855. Of his symphonies, the "Sintram," No. 2, has been highly praised. He has written also cantatas, such as "The Haunted Mill," and symphonic poems.

Howard A. Brockway, born at Brooklyn in 1870, keeps his symphonies in manuscript. He is known by his excellent "Sylvan Suite" for orchestra, an orchestral Ballade, and many violin works, including some that are practically concertos.

Edgar Stillman Kelley, born in Wisconsin in 1857, studied in Chicago and in Germany. His setting of "Puritania" is remarkably pleasing, and better than the usual light opera work. His "Macbeth" music, made over into a suite, is more earnest and dramatic; while the incidental music to "Ben Hur" adds much to that striking play. In songs, such as "Eldorado" and "Israfel," Kelley has shown marked melodic gifts; while his "Lady picking Mulberries" is a successful adoption of the Chinese style. During a recent stay abroad he earned very favorable notices with his piano quintet, Op. 20, and string quartet, Op. 25. A later work is his "New England" Symphony, the movements of which illustrate appropriate quotations from the "Log of the Mayflower." "Christmas Eve with Alice" is a set of dainty orchestral pictures.

Dudley Buck (1839–1900) belonged to an earlier generation, and composed before modernism had gained its hold. His works include the opera "Deseret," orchestral pieces, cantatas such as "The Voyage of Columbus" and "The Light of Asia," and a set of five sacred cantatas known as "The Christian Year." His style, naturally, was conservative..

William W. Gilchrist, born in 1846, is another of the pioneers. His psalms, cantatas, and "Song of Thanksgiving" have orchestral accompaniment.

Ernest R. Kroeger, born at St. Louis in 1862, has produced a symphony, the symphonic poem "Sardanapalus," a "Hiawatha" overture on Indian themes, a "Thanatopsis" overture, chamber music, piano pieces, and songs. His recent "Masque of Dead Florentines" is a large work portraying famous characters of the past.

Frank Van der Stucken, born in Texas in 1858, is of Belgian extraction. His symphonic prologue "William Ratcliffe" and his "Pax Triumphans" are written for the fullest modern orchestra.

Adolph Martin Foerster, born at Pittsburg in 1849, has composed the orchestral picture "Thusnelda, " a Dedication March, two string quartets, some good violin music, and many smaller works.

Rossetter Gleason Cole, born at Clyde, Michigan, in 1866, has composed an orchestral Ballade with 'cello, and many lesser works; but he is best known by his melodrama "King Robert of Sicily."

Charles Crozat Converse, born at Warren, Massachusetts, in 1832, produced an American overture and many sacred works.

Harry Rowe Shelley, born at New Haven in 1858, is widely known by such songs as "The Minstrel Boy" and "Love's Sorrow." He has written a manuscript opera, "Leila," the symphonic poem "The Crusaders," a strong cantata "The Inheritance Divine," a "Baden-Baden" suite, and two spirited symphonies.

Carl V. Lachmund, born at Boonville, Missouri, in 1857, is best known by his Japanese Overture.

Henry Schoenefeld, born at Milwaukee in 1857, won a success with his "Characteristic Suite." His overture "In the Sunny South" uses plantation themes. Another, "The American Flag," illustrates a poem by Drake. His other works include a violin concerto, a piano concerto, and his famous "Rural Symphony."

James Cutler Dunn Parker, born at Boston in 1828, composed an oratorio, "The Life of Man," and other sacred works.

George E. Whiting, born at Holliston, Massachusetts, in 1842, is a gifted organist and organ writer; but he has composed also a symphony, an overture, a piano concerto, and a one-act opera. His cantatas, including "The Tale of the Viking," "Henry of Navarre," and "The March of the Monks of Bangor," are works of tremendous virility. He has also a gift for charming melody.

Arthur B. Whiting, his nephew, born at Cambridge, Massachusetts, in 1861, has composed a concerto and a fantasia for piano and orchestra, both of which are bold and striking. His concert overture and chamber music are also praiseworthy. But he is best known by his songs, such as the cycle "Floriana" and the "Barrack-Room Ballads."

Rubin Goldmark, nephew of the European Goldmark, was born at New York in 1872. For orchestra he has written a theme and variations, a "Hiawatha" overture, and the symphonic poem "Samson and Dalila." His string quartet won a prize; while an earlier piano trio caused Dvořák to say, "There are now two Goldmarks."

Henry Holden Huss, born at Newark in 1862, seems to favor H as an initial; for he married Hildegard Hoffmann. He has produced a piano concerto, a violin concerto, songs with orchestra, chamber music, and lesser pieces.

Edwin Grasse, the blind violinist, was born at New York in 1884. He has composed a symphony, a suite, and many violin works.

Another violinist-composer is Eugene Gruenberg, known in Boston as a teacher. He, too, has composed a symphony.

Arthur Farwell, born at St. Paul in 1872, is devoted to Indian melodies. They even figure in his "Cornell" overture, side by side with college songs. They are more in place in his other orchestral pictures, such as "The Domain of Hurahan," "Dawn," and the "Navajo War Dance." His songs vary in style; but his piano pieces are almost always based on Indian themes.

Among other American orchestral composers (taken in alphabetical order, to avoid disputes over precedence), John Carver Alden has written a piano concerto. Maurice Arnold is responsible for overtures and "Plantation Dances." Percy Lee Atherton has composed a tone-poem entitled "Noon in the Forest," and several symphonic movements. Homer W. Bartlett has produced a violin Concertstück and shorter pieces. Johann H. Beck, of Cleveland, numbers among his works the manuscript music-drama "Salammbo" and several overtures. John Spencer Camp, of Hartford, is responsible for cantatas as well as orchestral works. Philip Greeley Clapp has written the tone-poem "Norge" and a symphony, very learned, but too dissonant. Hugh A. Clarke presides over the music department at the University of Pennsylvania. H. Clough-Leighter has composed an orchestral cantata, and many fluent songs. Arthur M. Curry has produced the symphony "Atala," based on Chateaubriand's tragedy. Henry M. Dunham has composed for organ and orchestra.

Henry F. Gilbert has written a Comedy Overture and other works based on negro themes. A. J. Goodrich is known as a theorist. William E. Haesche, of New Haven, has composed a symphony, a "Wald-Idyll," and the symphonic poem "Frithjof." Edward B. Hill has set pantomimes. Ernest Hutcheson, the pianist, is credited with a piano concerto and the tone-poem "Merlin and Vivien." Harry Patterson Hopkins is a symphonist. Nathaniel Irving Hyatt is the composer of an "Enoch Arden" overture. Carl V. Lachmund's Japanese Overture was praised by Theodore Thomas. Daniel Gregory Mason wrote orchestral music of much interest for the impressive Cape Cod Pageant. Homer Norris has composed cantatas and an overture. Arne Oldberg, in charge of music at the Northwestern University, numbers among his works symphonies, concertos, and dignified chamber music. Nathaniel Clifford Page is known for his incidental music. E. A. Parsons has composed a piano concerto. Henry Bickford Pasmore is responsible for a march, an overture, a mass, and some beautiful songs. John Nelson Pattison wrote the "Niagara" symphony, for orchestra and military band. Smith Newell Penfield is an overture composer. Ellsworth C. Phelps has produced a "Hiawatha" symphony and the sacred opera "David." John Powell, of Richmond, is known by a violin concerto. Silas G. Pratt has worked industriously in the largest forms, composing programme symphonies and suites, and having his operas "Zenobia" and "Lucille" given with success in Chicago. Cornelius Ruebner, music professor at Columbia College, has entered the symphonic field. Ernest Schelling, the pianist, made clever use of "Dixie" and "The Suwanee River" in his fantasie for piano and orchestra. Edward Faber Schneider, of Omaha, has written an Autumn Symphony. Arthur Shepherd has composed the prize-winning Overture Joyeuse, "The Nuptials of Attila," and the large cantata entitled "The City in the Sea," all of which show an interesting handling of modern harmonic complexity. David Stanley Smith includes among his many orchestral works a symphony and the symphonic sketch "Prince Hal." Albert Augustus Stanley has composed a symphony entitled "The Soul's Awakening," and the symphonic poem "Attis." Humphrey J. Stewart has produced the suite "California Scenes." Frank Taft has won success with a "Marche Symphonique." Richard Henry Warren is an organist as well as an orchestral composer.

Mortimer Wilson is well known in Atlanta. In addition to these, many others are entering the field as graduates from our foremost musical conservatories.

Among the women, Mrs. H. H. A. Beach is the leader of the natives. Her Gaelic Symphony is built on broad lines, while her mass with orchestra is another large work. She has published "The Rose of Avontown" and other cantatas, and is well known through her piano works and expressive songs.

Mme. Helen Hopekirk's piano concerto and *Concertstück* are of unusual value; and show rare musicianship. Her violin sonata is another worthy work. Her "Iona Memories," for piano, and many of her songs also, bear witness to her Scottish birth.

Mrs. Clara Kathleen Rogers (Clara Doria) is another orchestral composer of foreign birth.

Margaret Ruthven Lang has heard two of her three overtures performed. Her published works consist chiefly of piano pieces and songs, the latter including "My Lady Jacqueminot," "Eros," "Ghosts," "Prelude," "Tryste Noel," "Northward," and similar lyric gems.

Among other American women, Helen Hood has composed worthy chamber music. Edith Noyes Porter has worked in the same field, with occasional orchestral excursions. Mabel Daniels has composed a Ballade for baritone and orchestra, and won prizes with her solo songs. Laura Sedgwick Collins is another who has essayed the classical forms. Marguerite Melville is still another composer of chamber music. Fannie Dillon is said to have large works in manuscript. Julia Rivé-King and Fannie Bloomfield Zeisler have written piano works. Mrs. Mary Carr Moore, composer of songs, has in manuscript the opera "Narcissa," dealing with the adventures of Narcissa Prentiss, who married Marcus Whitman, went with him to the Pacific Coast on missionary work, and was massacred there by Indians. Mary Turner Salter has written many remarkably interesting songs, of much musical value, a recent success being the tragic "Cry of Rachel." Gena Branscombe's songs, such as the cycle "A Lute of Jade," show unusual poetic beauty. Patty Stair, the pianist, has excelled in both humorous and serious songs. The lyrics of Harriet Ware and Lola Carrier Worrell have been frequently heard at American recitals. Mary Knight Wood's songs are freshly spontaneous, her "Ashes of Roses" being a popular favorite. Mrs. C. W. Krogmann and Mrs. L. E. Orth have composed songs and piano pieces of much teaching value; while Mrs. Jessie L. Gaynor excels in songs for children. Other women deserving mention are Mrs. Clara A. Korn, Harriet P. Sawyer, Fanny Knowlton, Eleanor Freer, Natalie Curtis (who made the best collection of Indian tunes), Gertrude Sans-Souci, Fay Foster, and Fanny M. Spencer, composer of hymns.

The late Benjamin Cutter produced, among other works, an admirable mass. James H. Rogers, Frederick R. Burton, Nathan H. Allen, Charles Fonteyn Manney, James C. Macy, Gerrit Smith, and C. Whitney Coombs have become noted in the cantata field, besides composing shorter pieces. Willard J. Baltzell has produced some chamber music. Louis Campbell-Tipton writes advanced violin works in the Debussy vein. John Alden Carpenter has composed a good violin sonata, in addition to serious and humorous songs. Others who have written for the violin are Theodore Spiering, Ernest O. Hiler, and Benjamin P. Whelpley. Organ composers include John Hyatt Brewer, George A. Burdett, W. H. Dayas, Henry M. Dunham, Percy Goetschius, Charles A. Havens, the late Frank Lynes, John P. Marshall, Sumner Salter, Everett E. Truette, Samuel P. Warren, Mortimer Wiske, and R. Huntington Woodman, many of whom have worked in other fields also. A. Lilienthal has received much praise for his chamber music. A. W. Kramer excels in the short forms. Charles F. Dennée has worked in the field of musical comedy. Philo Adams Otis is known through his excellent church music.

Wilson G. Smith deserves special mention for his "Hommages" to various masters, and other piano works. Noble Kreider is a rising piano composer of great power. Herman P. Chelius has published a grand Prelude and Fugue, and is finishing a set of piano tone-pictures. Frederick Ayres is another fugal writer. The piano composers include also the late Albert Pease, Francis Hendriks, Frank LaForge, Albert Ross Parsons, the Canadian Calixa Lavallée, Alvah Glover Salmon, J. Frank Brackett, and the radical John Beach.

Clayton Johns is best known for his very attractive songs, such as "I cannot help loving thee." Sidney Homer has produced the intense "Prospice" and many later works of remarkable strength.

Other American song composers, in alphabetical order, are James C. Bartlett, the late Fred Field Bullard of "Stein Song" fame, Charles H. Dana, William H. Dana, L. R. Dressler, William Arms Fisher, Hallett Gilberté, Victor Harris, Frank S. Hastings, Rupert Hughes, Herbert Johnson, William Spencer Johnson, John A. Loud, H. C. MacDougall, A. A. Mack, Malcolm D. McMillan, George L. Osgood, H. R. Palmer, Winthrop L. Rogers, Walter Morse Rummel, Arthur Ryder, Lily Strickland, Arthur W. Thayer, Everett H. Titcomb, Stephen Townsend, R. S. Willis, and G. D. Wilson. Other names deserving mention in an American list, for various reasons, are F. Addison Porter, Brainard, Dial, Alexander Russell, Carl Engel, Benjamin Lambord, Henry Waller, William Schuyler, Chester Ide, Caroline Walker, and William McCoy, many of whom have had works published by the patriotic Wa-Wan Press.

While the first edition of the present book was in press, John Alden Carpenter entered the orchestral field with a large work entitled "Adventures in a Perambulator." It pictures the impressions of an infant, and is divided into six movements for full modern orchestra. "En Voiture" forms a rather dignified introduction, with rhythmic suggestions of the moving perambulator. "The Policeman" is shown chatting with the nurse and stalking about with heavy steps. "The Hurdy-Gurdy" is suggested most humorously by two xylophones against the orchestra, and they revel in popular tunes until reprimanded by the ponderous policeman. "The Lake" is a most charming picture of rippling wavelets, and forms an admirable contrast to the preceding bits of humor. "Dogs" are heard barking on various instruments; and "Dreams" bring a quieter conclusion. The score shows a wonderful mastery of orchestral technique, and full measure of inspiration. This one work has placed Carpenter in the front rank of American composers.

PART III
MUSICAL FORM

XXXI

MELODY AND APPRECIATION

THE average non-musical auditor is generally ready enough to enjoy a tune; but when classical music is given, he does not enter into the spirit of the occasion. A taste for good music comes largely from listening to it; so that even the non-musician should be patient with the classics, and not condemn them all at once. Time will teach him that Mark Twain's remark about Wagner is of general scope, and that classical music, as well as Wagner's, is not as bad as it sounds.

The elements entering into musical appreciation are first of all a perception of pitch. This would seem to be something common to every one; yet it is not necessarily so. Even among great intellects there is sometimes a lack of the simplest musical comprehension; and such men as Tennyson and Charles Lamb were tone-deaf.

Granting an appreciation of tone, the three chief elements found in music are rhythm, melody, and harmony.

The first of these, rhythm, is present in a marked degree in the so-called popular music. The prevalence of rag-time, with its varying accent and emphasis, testifies to a widespread appreciation of rhythm.

One of the chief defects of popular music, in comparison with classical, is its extreme simplicity. It appeals to the cultivated musician much as a problem in arithmetic would appeal to the student of quaternions. The rhythm of almost all popular music is absurdly simple. It does not follow that good music must necessarily have a complex rhythm; but the simplicity of the popular song, even allowing for the rag-time variations, is the simplicity of weakness and ignorance, not that of true art. If a composer uses straightforward effects, he does so because they suit his theme; as, for example, in Dvořák's "Humoreske." But the popular composer (?) plods ahead in total ignorance of anything better, and produces works like the college-song atrocity known as "Mrs. Cragin's Daughter."

One of the chief points that the student must note, and try to appreciate, is the variety of rhythmic effect to be found in good music. He will very seldom come across the plain unvarnished see-saw that pervades popular music.

Daniel Gregory Mason illustrates this point by citing poetry. He rightly states that without metre music would be formless; but on the other hand he is just as correct in protesting against the monotonous *dum, dum, dum* that arises from having the rhythm too lacking in change. Variety of effect is desired; and at the same time this variety should not prevent a larger sense of unity from characterizing an entire work. In poetry, Keats is cited as an example of the avoidance of monotony; and the point is well brought out by the following lines: —

> "A thing of beauty is a joy for ever.
> Its loveliness increases; it will never
> Pass into nothingness; but still will keep
> A bower quiet for us, and a sleep
> Full of sweet dreams, and health, and quiet breathing."

The delicate rhythm of these lines, and their skilful avoidance of anything monotonous in accent, is plainly evident. Mason illustrates the same point in music by citing the original and the final state of the opening melody in the slow movement of Beethoven's fifth symphony. An examination will show that the finished work has much more variety.

A glance at the first line of this music, which is the original idea that Beethoven wrote down, will show that it is fairly regular. Two notes on the third beat of the measure begin both halves of the melody, and a note on the first beat, followed by one on the second, end them in each case. More than this, the second half is practically the same as the first half, except for the fact that it is given a tone higher.

Looking at the theme in its final shape, we may notice much greater variety of rhythm. There is slightly less resemblance between the two whole measures in each half-theme; then the second half is made to begin with three notes instead of two; while the ending of the second half, still on the first two beats of the measure, is made to consist of three notes that seem to shift the accent along to the second beat. All these changes in a theme of only four bars show that Beethoven was a careful worker; but they also indicate that the best music has variety of rhythm as well as a large unity pervading the whole. The little changes add to the variety, while leaving enough regularity to make the theme still very swingy.

The music of the great composers is rhythmic enough, and many examples of their work might be cited to prove this. One could tap his feet to the accents of Beethoven's Seventh Symphony, or nearly all of Wagner's Prelude to "The Mastersingers," or the final chorus of Bach's "St. Matthew Passion." Even the second movement of Tschaikovsky's "Pathetic Symphony," which has the unusual number of five beats to each measure, is made rhythmically attractive by the skill of its composer; while the march in the third movement is compelling in its swinginess. There is no lack of rhythm in the classics, when once the listener has shaken himself free from the too simple and monotonous effects of commonplace music.

Taking up the question of melody, the student will find its appreciation governed by somewhat similar rules. Much of the popular article, and even a great deal of fairly good music, has its melody divided off in phrases that suit the conventional rhythm of equal parts. While this division is often useful, it should not be the only one, any more than a succession of eight-syllabled lines in iambic tetrameter (known as "long metre" in the hymn-books) should be the only kind of poetry to receive widespread attention.

In place of melody, good music sometimes consists rather of what might be called melodiousness. It is tuneful and melodic, but not limited by being forced to suit a commonplace rhythm. Instead of coming in cut-and-dried lengths, like so much macaroni, it is given to us in suitable and pleasing variety.

As an example, the reader may look again at the final form of the

Beethoven theme printed above. It is not exactly a tune, but it is tuneful. It is not cast in any cut-and-dried shape; for after the four opening bars cited above we find added rhythmic variations that allow the melody to take a free and attractive shape.

Many passages in classical music show a marked melodic character, in addition to a clear rhythm. Such passages are very much in place. The good composer does not strive to make his music needlessly ugly or involved. Melody forms a valuable part of his assets. What he does do is to use melodic passages in balance against others, or in contrast with them. There may be in one part of a piece a tender melody, and in another a set of fiery chords, or sombre phrases, or rushing themes of unrest. A good example of such contrast is found in the "Funeral March" by Chopin, in which the gloomy and powerful chords of the march are put in contrast with the smooth, song-like section that forms the middle part of the work. Composers, then, do not often follow any one simple style of melody, but aim to use more than one style, and bring out in their works the beauty that comes from variety, and the strength of structure that depends upon artistic balance and contrast.

The listener must, therefore, educate himself to see the beauty of different kinds of music. To quote a few examples on the spur of the moment, he will find a bright and dainty opening theme in the finale of Beethoven's first symphony; an infinitely beautiful serenity in the passage beginning the second symphony of Brahms; a half-pathetic happiness in the second theme of the first movement in Schubert's "Unfinished" Symphony; a wild, almost savage gloom in the first rapid theme of Tschaikovsky's fifth symphony; or intense chords that seem to have very little melody at the start of Brahms' first symphony.

For variety, one may inspect such a song as Schubert's "Wanderer." It begins with an almost forbidding style, when the wanderer mentions the hard conditions of "flood and field." Then comes a tenderly pathetic passage of regret at his many trials and few bits of happiness. This is followed by a brightly rhythmic melody as the traveller remembers with joy his own home-land; but it ends in sudden suggestion of doubt when he cries, "O land, where art thou?" Then once more is heard the theme of regret. After this comes a ghostly suggestion of an answer to his eternal question of

"Whither"; and an expressively pathetic final phrase with the words that happiness is wherever he does not go.

The melodies used by the great composers are sometimes "chopped off in definite lengths"; but they are usually blended into a work in more plastic fashion. The themes do not need to come to a sharp end on the keynote, like so many separate bits of mosaic, each a single entity even though put in juxtaposition to make a design. The melodies that a composer employs, along with the unmelodic passages that he may choose for contrast, can be blended into one another as smoothly as the colors unite to form the many-hued spectrum or the rainbow. If one tries to follow up some of the themes mentioned in the last paragraph but one, he will find that they melt into the movements where they occur in very close-knit fashion for the most part. The Beethoven theme is the most nearly separate of all, though too short to stand alone. In the Brahms second symphony, the melody is balanced in two parts of two phrases each, but instead of having any suggestion of ending, it is echoed and prolonged until some mysterious chords replace it. The Schubert theme is interrupted angrily in its first appearance, but allowed to finish to a partial cadence (or close) later on in the work. Such uniting and blending of melodies into a larger unity pervading an entire movement or work enables composers to build up long pieces, in which they may actually shape their material into quite definite designs, — either the known forms that have been accepted by common consent, or the freer individual designs that modern composers have agreed to permit. Recent writers have invented a long word for this building up of a musical structure. They call it architectonics. As implied above, certain methods of construction have been accepted as artistic, and used by the great composers. These will be described in later chapters, along with the principles governing the freer and more recent schools.

The composer has other resources than the mere creating or repeating of melodies and themes. The process known as development allows him to use the material of a melody in new ways, building up a musical structure by the design-like imitation of a subject or motive. This imitation may be strict or free, as he chooses; but so long as the material is recognizable as being derived from the original theme, he may feel sure that his work will appeal to the

hearer's intellectual sense of fitness. Such development may take
the entire theme for treatment, or a single phrase, or even a simple
figure. The figure is the shortest recognizable bit of music. It may
consist of as few as two notes; and such a two-noted figure may be
found on the second and third beats of nearly every measure in
Schuett's "Rêverie," filling out the melodic pauses. Beethoven's
ninth symphony begins with a two-noted iambic figure; and the
scherzo of the same work contains a three-noted dactylic figure.
For musical treatment or development, a figure should usually be
longer than this, though it is quite possible for a composer to work
up two-note effects.

Still another method of treating melodies is by contrapuntal
imitation, which has been previously mentioned. This consists of
allowing a theme, or subject, or even a figure, to be used in part-
music, appearing first in one voice and then in another, and making a tonal design by its well-balanced and orderly recurrences.
Such work will be treated in the chapter on "Contrapuntal
Forms."

Harmony is the science of chords and chord-progressions. Here,
perhaps, the taste of the non-musician is more lacking than in other
ways, and less amenable to training. The comparative monotony of
harmony in popular music is evident when one considers how much
of it consists simply of the "three chords" learned on the banjo
and other similar instruments. These are the tonic, on the first
scale-degree; the dominant, on the fifth; and the subdominant, on
the fourth.[1] Here again the good composer will show his ability
by using even these chords in a more tasteful and artistic fashion
than is found in the work of the hack writer who grinds out popular
trash. Incidentally, the author does not mean to imply that all
popular music is trash; but some of it is, and the public is seldom
able to know the difference. Examples of simple chord-work from
the classics may be found in the first rapid theme of Beethoven's
seventh symphony; the choruses behind the scenes in the first act
of Gounod's "Faust"; or the opening theme in the finale of the
first Brahms symphony. The hearer, then, must learn to discrimi-
nate between artistic and inartistic harmony, and to judge whether

[1] For information about chords, scales, etc., see the chapter on "How to read
music," in Part V of this volume.

the chords of a piece are brought out in pleasing succession or merely thrown together carelessly and without plan.

There are different styles of harmony, and the hearer should learn to appreciate them. Just why certain harmonies produce certain effects on the brain is a deep psychological question that has not yet been thoroughly answered. Association has something to do with the judging of music as a whole; but it does not account for everything. The more rapid rhythms are brighter than the slow ones, and high-pitched notes more cheerful than low ones. In harmony, however, no such clear rule is found. The appreciation of harmony consists in a perception of the relationship between successive chords. This relationship may be kept simple, or smoothed into delicate adjustment, or even made abstruse. A musical example will show the difference between the first two styles. The opening vocal phrase of Bach's song, "O heart ever faithful," has the same notes as the first line of Jensen's "Murmuring breeze"; but the Bach work has simple and direct harmonies (the three chords again), while the Jensen lyric varies the tonic chord by chromatic alterations. There is a marked variety in the rhythm of the two voice parts and accompaniments; but even allowing for that, there is a noticeable difference in the harmony too.

Changes of chords may be slight or abrupt. In the first case, nearly all the notes of one chord are held for the next; while in the second, there is very little connection. As long as the hearer is able to perceive the relationship, whether it is close or distant, he will continue to appreciate the music in a greater or less degree; but when the chord-sequence passes beyond the range of his perceptive powers, it will become a chaos of unrelated sounds, a mass of unmeaning discord. Some of the more involved classics have this effect on the listener who has not cultivated his sense of harmony; but after he educates himself by continued hearing of good works, he begins to find order emerging from the apparent harmonic chaos. There is therefore only one real way for the student to develop his taste for good harmony; he must put himself in a musical atmosphere, and listen to the best pieces until he learns to appreciate them. This growth in appreciation is something that follows naturally on the frequent hearing of good music; and even the great composers have not been exempt from its improving influence, as a comparison of their youthful productions with their more mature ones will show.

As stated above, melody, harmony, and rhythm are more or less inextricably blended into one organic whole. Especially is this true of melody and harmony; so that a melody will usually suggest to the musician the harmonies that might go with it.

One limitation of popular music is noticeable in our own country, if not in certain others; that consists in the too continuous use of the major mode. There is much beauty in the minor mode. Sometimes it is devoted to effects of sadness and pathos, while at other times it is made to show the most delicate grace. The opening theme of Mendelssohn's "Hebrides" overture is of the latter character, and has been cited as a perfect reflection of its subject. The underlying rhythm of the low notes gives the large pulsation of the waves; while little rippling figures above, surging to different heights, give a perfect suggestion of the wavelets that chase one another on the surface of the larger billows. In Mendelssohn's Scotch Symphony the minor mode of the first and last movements is made to show a most wonderful variety of effects. The training in appreciation of this mode is a necessary part of every auditor's education.

It will be seen from all these considerations that the composer has a far vaster field to work in than the manufacture of conventional popular music. The great composer may handle many styles of melody, balancing one against another in actual design; he may vary melodic work by contrasting it with wholly different styles, such as development or contrapuntal imitation; and he may give to his entire work a variety and originality of harmony that can make it glow with ever-changing beauty. It stands to reason that the only way to learn to appreciate good music is to hear it. But if the listener knows what to look for, his task will surely be made easier; and this section is planned as a guide for him.

XXXII

FIGURES AND PHRASES

THE French have an apt saying that "Architecture is frozen music." This presupposes a perception of the fact that music, in its plastic way, is subject to the laws of form. In this chapter the student will find a description of the smallest elements that enter into musical form — figures and phrases.

The figure being the shortest recognizable musical unit, we are very seldom able to associate it with completeness. Figures are the smallest units in the musical story, where phrases are clauses, and periods made up of phrases correspond to whole sentences. But while the writer can make no permissible use of the repetition of a word, the composer, like the painter, may build his design by duplicating his motive, or making it the basis of a larger idea. The comparison of periods with sentences must also be supplemented by the statement that expression in music is much more concise and intense than in literature.

The musical figure, when used to build up a phrase, or a theme, or even a long section of development, may be treated and varied in certain different ways, which do not prevent its remaining recognizable in the musical design. These ways may be enumerated as follows: —

1. *By transposition.* The figure may reappear intact on a new scale degree, with the same sized intervals of time and of location on the staff. Sometimes a transposed figure has intervals unchanged in actual size, but an alteration may come through the different relative position of the semitones in a scale. Thus a figure G-E-D-C may be transposed to become A-F-E-D, with slightly different intervals, or C-A-G-F, with no change. The use of continual and regular transpositions, causing the repeat of a figure in changing locations, is called a sequence.

2. *By expansion.* The intervals of a figure may be increased more than would result from any altered scale position. Usually

the outer notes of a figure (upper and lower) are the ones to be altered. Even a two-note figure may be altered in this way. For example, in Liza Lehmann's song "The Cuckoo," that bird calls in notes a third apart; but once or twice, for purposes of harmony, the interval is changed into a fourth.

3. *By contraction.* As a reverse of the preceding method, the intervals of a figure may be made smaller.

4. *By augmentation.* A figure may be given in notes of larger value than before.

5. *By diminution.* A figure may be given in notes of smaller value.

6. *By repetition.* Certain notes of the figure may be repeated in the necessary number of smaller notes.

7. *By omission.* Part of a figure may be given instead of the whole. For example, in the allegretto of the second Brahms symphony there is a very rhythmic figure,

which gradually trails off into nothingness by the repetition of the C alone, on the second beat of two or three measures, while the accompaniment softens and dies away.

8. *By change of order.* The sequence of the notes may be altered. This is not a common procedure, as it is apt to make the figure unrecognizable.

9. *By reversion.* A figure may be played through backwards.

10. *By inversion, or contrary motion.* A figure may be inverted, having its upward intervals changed to downward ones, and *vice versa.* An example of inversion with reversion and contraction is found in the finale of the first Brahms symphony, where the figure

becomes

11. *By elaboration.* A figure may be made more intricate by the addition of new notes.

12. *By simplification.* This is the reverse of the preceding.

13. *By ornamentation.* Turns, trills, and other embellishments may be put into the figure.

14. *By rhythmic imitation.* The rhythm of a figure may be imitated on a single note, or by an instrument of no pitch, like the bass

drum or triangle. The latter starts a theme in Liszt's E-flat piano concerto by giving its rhythm.

15. *By rhythmic alteration.* This might come under repetition, or elaboration, or simplification, but may be classed as a separate method. Thus in the Brahms allegretto mentioned above,

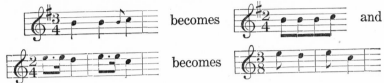

As already shown by example, combinations of any of the foregoing processes may be employed.

It is by means of some or all of these devices that a composer creates the musical structure known as development, in which the figures of one or more themes are used in various ways to build up an impressive tonal edifice. But figure treatment has many more uses than this. It may be called upon for the creation of the themes themselves, though not all melodies show figure repetition. Figures may also be interwoven into the accompaniment of themes.

The student may now get a clearer understanding of figure treatment by inspection of certain works.

First of all let him take the opening movement of Beethoven's fifth symphony. The writer has that work in the Litolff edition, arranged for piano solo by Winkler, but the number of bars will be the same in any good edition.

The first two bars show the figure on which much of this movement is based. It is a virile figure, having been explained by Beethoven as the knocking of Fate at the door, — although on another occasion he claimed that he had heard this rhythm pounded out when a belated and intoxicated reveller had returned home to seek admission. The figure runs thus: —

In later use the last note is sometimes held for its full value, and sometimes made an eighth-note to permit of a recurrence of the figure immediately after.

In bars 3–5, the figure is repeated, transposed downward. In bars 6–9 three occurrences of the figure, the second contracted, and the last two transposed, make the first phrase of the chief theme.

Bars 10–13 are similarly formed, the figure being now expanded in the first case, as well as contracted in the second. Bars 14–19 show first an altered figure, the third note being now between the second and fourth in pitch, and then an inversion of the altered figure; the alteration appearing three times and the inversion twice. The next two bars have a chord each, ending the first theme with what is known as a half-cadence, — a close on the dominant chord instead of the tonic. In bars 21–24 the figure is repeated separately, as at first. Then for two groups of four bars each it appears (in various positions) in three downward recurrences, the last one contracted, and one inverted and expanded occurrence. From bar 33 to bar 44 it is worked into a long upward progression, the third note of the inverted figure being altered, and the later measures of this group showing a sequence. Bars 44–56 show three four-measure groups of downward progressions. A repetition of the figure, from bar 59, serves to usher in a second theme, starting in bar 63. This is not built of the original figure at all; but we see the latter forcing its way into the accompaniment, and not letting itself be forgotten. It appears in the left-hand part in bars 65, 69, 73, 77, 81, 84, 86, 88, 90 and 92. Its rhythm is slightly suggested by the running passage from bar 95 to bar 110. In the latter bar it comes back unmistakably, and from then on is used to build up the close of the first section, which is marked for repeat after bar 124.

In the first movement of a symphony, the exposition of the themes should be followed by a section of development. This is found to be the case here, though the four-note figure has been used so constantly that almost all the movement seems to be a development of it. Bars 125–128 announce the figure (first transposed, then contracted also) as a sort of introduction to this section. The figure is then employed in various ways. For a time the chief theme is suggested; then in bar 141 a downward progression begins, still built of the figure material; while from bar 159 to bar 167 inclusive the figure is imitated in altered shape, without repeated notes; and from there on to bar 179 the figure is rhythmically imitated in chords, with more or less change. From that point on other material predominates, but in bar 240 the figure is introduced prominently once more, and reiterated as a signal for the end of the development and the beginning of the usual restatement of the original themes.

The restatement, or recapitulation, or reprise, begins clearly on the second beat of bar 248. This section is much like the first part of the work. It runs to the first beat in bar 374. Here the work might have ended, but it keeps on, in the form of a long coda, or musical postscript.

The coda starts with rhythmic imitation of the four-note figure, in loud chords, at first with changing harmonies and alterations in the bass. This stops to allow a faint, questioning inversion of the figure, unaccompanied, in bar 387; but the question is answered only by more of the savage chords. Then follow various versions of the other thematic material, until in bar 469 the rhythm of the original figure interrupts insistently, and finally brings the work to its closing phrase.

The movement is over five hundred measures long. At least three fourths of this famous classic will be found to consist of the four-note figure, in its original or altered shapes. It will thus be clear that figure treatment may be made into a most valuable asset by the composer. It need not hamper his inspiration; and this Beethoven movement happens to be rated as one of the most powerful and dramatic works in the whole musical repertoire.

The reader who wishes to investigate this subject further is referred to the first movement of Beethoven's sixth symphony, known as the "Pastoral Symphony." The first four bars of that work show a complete musical phrase; and the figures that make up nearly all the rest of the movement are simply different parts of this passage, treated with the usual variety of method to which a composer is entitled.

Longer than the figure is the phrase, or simple musical thought. The first four bars in the "Pastoral Symphony" form a phrase, giving the effect of a single idea, but being too long to be classed as a figure. This is followed by another phrase, finishing on the first beat of the sixteenth measure.

The beginner will recognize phrases best by assuming that they correspond to double lines of poetry in songs. This is not always the case, but it is generally true of short songs. Take, for instance, the familiar "Drink to me only with thine eyes." The stanzas in this are eight lines long, and two lines go to the formation of each musical phrase. The phrase of the first two lines is repeated for the next two; the third pair has a new phrase; but the fourth pair uses the original phrase once again.

The composer may balance phrases in instrumental compositions if he desires. He may follow one phrase of conventional length with another of the same length, or he may make the second phrase much longer than the first, which must be kept fairly short. He is not compelled to write in the style of balanced phrases unless he chooses; but if he does adopt this style, he may produce attractive works in it.

A section made out of two such balanced phrases is known to musicians as a period. It is sometimes called a theme, but that term has other applications, so that the word period is adopted in this work, for the sake of clearness.

Periods may vary from the simplest to the most complex. The first half of "Drink to me only with thine eyes," or of "The Last Rose of Summer," shows a period in which both phrases are alike. Not much different is the first half of "Annie Laurie," in which the second phrase is the same as the first except for an alteration of the final note, which brings an effect of completeness. In "My Old Kentucky Home," the second phrase is changed only slightly more. A little more difference is found between the first two phrases of "Yankee Doodle." Most well-known songs show this resemblance between their first and second phrase. In piano music, the resemblance need not be so close; and we may find in Mendelssohn's "Hunting Song," after the obviously separate introduction, a four-bar phrase followed by a second phrase that lasts through twenty bars. Incidentally, phrases used in forming periods are almost never less than four bars in length, and often longer.

Any piece may have an introduction, varying in length or scope. In the "Hunting Song" it is a little prelude-like phrase of less than five bars; while in Beethoven's "Sonata Pathétique" it is a large section, forming a complete contrast with the rapid themes that follow it.

Any piece may also have a coda, or musical postscript bringing it to a close (and sometimes a climax) after the demands of the form have already been satisfied. The coda is free in shape, but establishes the key of the piece to which it belongs, and brings it to a clear ending.

The very short introductions to some of Mendelssohn's "Songs without Words," sounding like piano phrases before the start of an actual song, are sometimes spoken of as preludes. When they recur at the end of such a piece, they are then called postludes. Both are found in the piece known as "Consolation."

It will be seen by referring to the songs cited that more than one period is used ordinarily. It is possible to have a piece consist of a single period. The German folk-song known as "The Broken Ring," or sometimes as "The Mill in the Valley," is a single-period form. Its second phrase is lengthened by repetition in a somewhat altered form; and the song consists of only two phrases. A certain piano prelude by Scriabine shows a single-period structure; but it is lengthened by an introduction and a coda.

Most of the songs cited end with a phrase from the first part. "Annie Laurie" is an exception, having its second period independent of the material of the first; but such instances are comparatively rare in popular songs.

The songs mentioned show a two-period form; but more than two periods may be used in some cases, or the two may be differently arranged. It is also permissible for a composer to balance a period at certain times by a passage of contrasted style. The ordinary period has two phrases, called antecedent and consequent, the second one seeming to answer and complete the first. But music does not need to be confined to this structure; and a period may sometimes be followed by a free episode. The forms in common use are described in the next chapter.

XXXIII

THE SONG–FORMS

COMPOSERS have a very prevalent habit of repeating themselves as much as possible. They write a theme, and alternate it with other music, but often insist on bringing back the original theme again, partly to give a finished and balanced effect to their work. They are very fond of doing this in the song-forms; the rondos are named from the procedure; and even in the freer sonata form the themes are followed by a development of their material, which in turn is succeeded by a repeat of the themes.

The shortest song-form in common use consists of two periods, each having a first phrase, known as the antecedent, and a second phrase, known as the consequent. In the two-period independent form, the phrases of the second period are made of wholly new material. In the two-period form with partial return, the consequent of the second period is derived from a phrase of the first, with no change or only slight alterations. The partial-return form is much more popular than the independent form, because of the tendency shown by composers to end as they began. Even when they use the two independent periods, they may suggest the original section by employing some of its material in a coda.

The best single volume for the study of the song-forms is the collection of Mendelssohn's "Songs without Words." In these, an example of the two-part independent form is seen in no. 6, the first Venetian Gondola Song. As its title would imply, it is soothingly rhythmic, being in 6/8 time. An introduction defines the rhythm. The first period begins on the last beat of the seventh measure. Its antecedent is four measures long, while the consequent is prolonged to six measures, and ends on a cadence in the dominant key. A longer section of new material follows, having an antecedent of eight measures and a consequent of nine. The piece could end at that point; but the composer, following the prevalent impulse of letting some of the opening material return, added a coda based on the phrases of the first period.

The periods of a song-form are sometimes very clean-cut, and easy to recognize; but the good composers often blend them into one another to some extent. Introductions and codas relieve any plainness of design at the beginning or end; while between any two periods there may always be a little passage linking them together. This is called a transition passage when introducing new material, or a returning passage when it is followed by matter previously given.

The three-part song-forms consist of a period, a contrasting section, and a return of the first period, either unchanged, or partly altered, or even partly suppressed. The contrasting section may be either a second period (called a countertheme) or a bit of free writing known as an episode. Theorists hold that a countertheme must have antecedent, consequent, and a full cadence, or close. The episodes are sometimes much like counterthemes (as in Chaminade's "Scarf Dance"), but sometimes very free; so that the present writer has suggested classifying them under the two heads of episode and free episode. An introduction may begin any piece, and a coda finish it. We may also find transition or returning passages.

In the two-period forms, either or both periods could be repeated separately if desired. In the three-part form, the first part (period) may be repeated by itself, the second and third parts may be repeated together, or both repeats made if desired.

When the first period returns to form the third section, it may be repeated unchanged. Usually, however, some change is necessary to bring a cadence in the key of the piece; and for this purpose, or else simply at the composer's wish, the consequent may be altered, the antecedent being generally kept intact. If only a single phrase returns, instead of the original two-phrased period, then the piece is in three-division form with abbreviated return.

Looking at Mendelssohn's "Consolation," the ninth "Song without Words," we find a prelude of two and a half measures, used again as a postlude. Then follows an eight-bar period, with four-bar antecedent and consequent, the period ending in the first half of measure 11. A six-bar episode follows, rather free because consisting of only one phrase and having no cadence. Then comes a return of the original period, with antecedent the same but consequent altered. It will be seen that the last note of the period and the first note of the postlude are played at the same time. This is one of several little devices for making a piece unified in effect. Such overlapping is called compression.

The "Funeral March," no. 27, is another three-part song-form. A prelude of four bars precedes the first period, which begins at the end of the fourth full measure. This period has four-bar phrases for antecedent and consequent. It is then repeated, being written out with fuller harmony than at first. An episode follows, with two four-bar phrases, but no cadence, and four extra measures giving the rhythm and style of the prelude. These serve as a returning passage to bring back the original period, now set with still broader harmony, and prolonged four measures by a delayed cadence. Four measures of postlude follow, echoing the rhythm of the prelude.

Variety is shown also by the "Spinning Song," no. 34. An introduction of almost two bars is followed by a period of two four-bar phrases, ending in the dominant. A nineteen-bar episode is followed by a return of the period, this time with an altered consequent of eight bars, ending in the proper key. Episode and return of period are repeated, but now the episode is in minor instead of major, for variety. A sixteen-bar coda ends the piece.

The use of a countertheme is shown in "The Return," no. 41 of the set. It has a four-bar prelude and postlude, starting with a repeated octave figure that is skilfully echoed in the main body of the work. The first period, beginning with three occurrences of the same eighth-note chord, consists of two four-bar phrases, ending in the dominant key. The countertheme, beginning with the third chord in the twelfth full measure, is also built of two four-bar phrases, ending with a cadence in the relative minor of the dominant. The first period returns, with its consequent altered and extended to seven measures in length.

The abbreviated three-division form may be illustrated by no. 19, called "On the Seashore." The first period begins in the last half of the third bar, and has a four-bar antecedent followed by a four-bar consequent. After a thirteen-bar episode, the return shows only a single phrase instead of a two-phrased period. This phrase is lengthened to six bars, but it is indubitably not a period.

A similar abbreviated return is found in Schuett's "Rêverie." In that piece, cited for its constant use of a two-noted figure, an eight-bar antecedent and a consequent of the same length are replaced, in the return, by a single ten-measure phrase using the same material.

A summary of the song-forms will give the following table: —

Two-division independent form. A period, followed by another period made of independent material. Either period may be repeated by itself.

Two-division form with partial return. A period, followed by another period having a new antecedent, but the consequent repeated or derived from a phrase in the first period. Either period may be repeated by itself.

Three-division form with countertheme. A period, followed by another period of new material, which is in turn succeeded by a recurrence of the first period, at times with altered consequent. The first period may be repeated alone if desired, or the second and third parts repeated together, or both repeats made if required. In rare examples a countertheme may be repeated alone.

Three-division form with episode. The same as the preceding, but instead of a countertheme (having antecedent, consequent, and cadence) there is an episode, lacking some or all of these points, and being in a more or less free style.

Three-division abbreviated form. The same as either of the two preceding forms, but having the return of the first period altered into a single phrase instead of a complete period.

Larger pieces are made from these simple song-forms by uniting them in a three-division cycle, just as the single periods of a three-division song-form are grouped. In other words, many pieces are made on the plan of a complete song-form followed by another complete song-form, which in turn is followed by a recurrence of the first song-form, either wholly or in part. Such a piece is known as a song-form with trio, and the second song-form is called the trio. In the old days, when groups of similar instruments appeared in alternating selections, it was often really a trio. Thus in some of Lully's music we find three flutes giving a piece in contrast to the more constant violin work. The name has been kept, and has come to be used for a contrasting section of song-form. The trio is generally marked by a change of key, usually being in the subdominant, though sometimes it is in the dominant.

Either the first song-form or the trio may be of several shapes. But it manifestly would not do to have a single-period form for both the song-form and the trio, as that would result in a simple three-part song-form. The single-period form is more often found in the trio than in the first section, though it is not very frequent in either case.

Song-form with trio is probably the most familiar of all the forms to the general public. About all the popular dances and marches are written in this form. As a rule, such pieces show rather long antecedents and consequents. The waltz is apt to have each phrase consist of sixteen measures instead of the usual eight. A very little training should enable even the non-musical reader to analyze the popular examples of the form, and pick out the periods, or recognize the trio, with fair certainty.

In song-form with trio, as always, there may be introduction or coda or both. There may also be transition or returning passages at any desired point.

If the first song-form does not return as a whole after the trio, the piece is described as a song-form and trio with abbreviated return. The abbreviation may be made to avoid monotony if the periods are too long or too similar. Another device to give variety is found in Scharwenka's "Polish Dance" and Meyer-Helmund's "Dance." In both works, when the return of the first song-form is nearly over, a bit of the trio is interpolated before the close of the piece.

In the old gavottes, the trio was often of musette-like character, having a drone-bass effect as of bagpipes. This style of trio may be found in the Meyer-Helmund "Dance," where it is in admirable contrast with the rest of the piece.

Schubert's first Military March may be cited as a clear example of song-form with trio. The opening song-form begins with a fanfare-like introduction of six measures. The first period, which follows, consists of sixteen bars in two equal phrases. It is repeated. After its second ending come four bars of fanfare suggestion as transition. Then a countertheme follows, with a four-bar antecedent and a twelve-bar consequent, ending in a perfect cadence on the dominant. This brings a return of the first period, with consequent very slightly altered. Countertheme and return are repeated together. The trio, which follows, consists of an opening period with eight-bar antecedent and ten-bar consequent, followed by a second period of two eight-bar phrases. The first period is repeated. The second is also repeated, with a postscript of eight bars that seem like a returning passage, though ordinarily such a passage would occur after the repeat instead of in it. The first song-form is then replayed. In passing, any repeats in the first song-form of such a piece are to be disregarded when the song-form returns after the trio.

So many minuets are in this shape that some teachers speak of it as minuet form instead of song-form with trio. The latter title is better, as some might think the former term would apply only to minuets.

Schumann included in his first symphony a scherzo movement with two trios. The term scherzo applies to a style, and not a form, meaning playfully or jestingly; but this movement is really a song-form with two trios. The song-form at the beginning is of three-division form. The first period has sixteen bars in two equal phrases. The countertheme has two seven-bar phrases with a bar of linking-material between them and a bar of returning passage at the end. This is followed by the return of the first period, now given richer harmony, but otherwise unchanged.

The first trio is not perfectly regular, though clear at the start. It begins with a period of two similar fifteen-bar phrases, each followed by a bar's rest to fill out the rhythm. Its style of echoing chords is continued for two more phrases, each eight bars long; but we cannot call this a period, as more new material follows. It has to be considered as part of an episode. The first period of the trio does not return clearly. Its harmonies are suggested, and a long new consequent attached to the altered antecedent. The second and third part of this trio are repeated together.

The first song-form then returns. While its parts were repeated in the original appearance, the repeats are now omitted, to avoid monotony.

The second trio begins with an eight-bar phrase, repeated to form its own consequent. Again the succeeding material is episodical in spite of its clear phrases, because there are too many sections here to make a song-form unless we call this part an episode. Again the return is not suggested clearly, being one of style rather than form. An extra phrase after the second repeat is evidently a returning passage.

The song-form of the beginning comes back. It is now given without repeat, and without return after the countertheme, which now leads directly into the coda.

Contrasts of style as well as material make this movement very attractive. The first song-form is strong and rhythmic; the first trio a dainty web of echoing chords; and the second trio in brisk, running style.

Examples of song-form with two trios are found in Mendelssohn's works; and the student will find pleasure in analyzing for himself the familiar "Wedding March" and the "Priests' March" from "Athalie," which are both in this form.

XXXIV

THE RONDOS

THE rondos resemble the song-forms in certain ways. They consist of a chief theme, or main section, which alternates with one or more other sections. The main section, however, is not necessarily a single period. It may be a complete song-form in itself, or may be entirely free in shape. In the old rondos of Haydn and Mozart, and even in those of Beethoven, the themes are usually clean-cut, and each section is in some fairly definite form. Even when this is the case, the rondo differs from the song-forms, for in rondos the first section, or chief theme, is emphasized and made more prominent than in song-forms, all the other sections being brought into definite contrast with it. But in many cases the rondo shows more freedom of shape than the song-forms. When this characteristic is found, it will be seen that a rondo may have its sections blended into a much more unified whole than can be obtained from the song-forms.

The so-called first rondo consists of a main section, a side section, and a return of the main section. The side section and main section may be repeated together, just like the second and third parts of a three-division song-form; and in this case the shape is called first rondo extended by repeats. A coda may always occur at the end of a rondo, or an introduction at the beginning; and the unified character of the rondo often makes transition and returning passages practicable.

As an example of first rondo, the slow movement of Beethoven's first piano sonata (Op. 2, no. 1) may be inspected by the student. It shows a fairly clear structure. The first sixteen measures form a first section. New material makes a clear side section. Then the first section returns, quite clearly, and is prolonged into a coda. Some analysts have called this movement a song-form; but the evidence seems contrary to their verdict. The first sixteen bars seem more like a two-period form than a single period; and if the

two-period structure is admitted, then the side section is too episodical to be a trio.

A clear example of first rondo form may be found in the
adagio movement of Mozart's sonata in D, no. 15 in the Litolff
collection.

Clementi's Rondo in the key of F is another very clear example.
The piece is divided into two well-marked sections, both in a free,
running style. After the second section is finished, a D.C. mark
brings the return of the first section.

Any section of a rondo may be repeated by itself. Sometimes
the first theme is repeated on its first appearance; but that is
scarcely necessary, as its recurrence in the form will insure its receiving sufficient attention.

The first rondo may often approach very near to the three-division song-form. "Anitra's Dance," from Grieg's "Peer Gynt"
suite, and Poldini's "Poupée Valsante," have been chosen to illustrate this point.

In "Anitra's Dance," the first section, coming after a brief introduction, is a sixteen-bar period, repeated. The side section may
with perfect propriety be called a long episode. The first period
returns in due order, and the episode is repeated with the return
of theme. The general unity of style in the piece suggests the
rondo idea, even though the divisions are not unlike those of the
song-form. Incidentally, the student will note that the returned
theme has a prolonged antecedent, instead of an altered consequent,
to make it end in the proper key. This is a very unusual procedure.

In Poldini's "Dancing Doll," the same structure is apparent, —
a short introduction, a single period repeated, an episodical side
section, and a return of theme, the last two divisions being repeated
together. This work has a long coda, based on the thematic material already used. This coda is rather too large for a simple song-
form, and its use of the earlier material gives the piece a rondo
suggestion.

Chopin's Nocturne in G, Op. 37, no. 2, is an example of the first
rondo extended by recurrences, if not literal repeats. The first section, of about two pages in the usual editions, is not in periodic
shape, but is based almost wholly on the material of the first three
or four measures. The side section, *sostenuto*, is of song-like charac-

ter, and more definite period structure. The first section returns, somewhat shortened. The second section is again heard. Then comes a still briefer suggestion of the first section, followed by a phrase of the second as coda. The successive shortenings are not called for by the rules of strict form, but the composer makes use of them to avoid monotony. Such shortenings may be found in the scherzo of Schumann's first symphony; while in the scherzo of his fourth symphony, the final appearance of the first-period material is suppressed, to make way for a long transition to the following movement.

The allegretto of Brahms's second symphony may be taken as another example of first rondo extended by recurrence of side section and chief theme. The first theme occurs in triple rhythm. Then a chattering eighth-note suggestion of the theme leads into new material, thus forming a side section, which is in even rhythm. The chattering version then leads back to the second entrance of the first theme, now shortened and varied. Then comes the side section material again, altered into rapid triple rhythm. The chattering figures, also in triple time, lead to a final resumption of the first section, which is followed by a short coda. The student will find this movement an admirable example of the variety that may be given to thematic material. Where a lesser composer would have repeated his themes almost intact, Brahms used altered rhythms, new keys, and unexpected modulations with the most consummate skill, keeping his effects fresh and interesting without obscuring the main lines of the form.

The second rondo consists of main section, first side section, main section again, second side section (new material), and main section for the third time. It will be seen that when the chief theme occurs a number of times, it should be made of interesting material, or it will become monotonous. In the second rondo, this defect may be avoided by having the sections fairly long, and the side sections in strong contrast with the chief theme.

It will be noted that the structure of the second rondo (A-B-A-C-A) has no parallel among the song-forms. When the sections of such a rondo consist of single periods, some teachers speak of the shape as the five-part song-form. But of course some of the rondo sections may be longer than a single period, in which case there is no disagreement about the name. In the five-part song-form, the simplest second rondo, all sections are of about equal importance.

An example of this five-part single-period structure may be found in Moszkowski's Spanish Dance, Op. 12, no. 1. The others of this set are song-forms with trio, but in the first dance the five-period arrangement is clearly present. Other examples are found in the final movements of Mozart's first two piano sonatas (Litolff edition).

Beethoven's "Für Elise" is a clear example of second rondo. In this piece the first section consists of a short three-division song-form. Then follow in order the first side theme, the first return, the second side theme, and the final return of theme. There are returning passages after the side themes.

The slow movement of Beethoven's "Sonata Pathétique" is another very clear example of second rondo. The student should find no difficulty in noticing its divisions.

Grieg's "Norwegian Bridal Procession" is again in single-period divisions, with the first side section repeated.

Mozart's Rondo in A-minor illustrates the use of embellishments.

An unusual structure is found in Berthold Tours' Gavotte Moderne. Such a dance is usually a song-form with trio. The trio is found in proper shape in this piece; but instead of the song-form at the start, there is a little rondo. This consists of an eight-bar theme, an eight-bar episode, a four-bar partial return of the theme, a second side theme of nine measures, and a full return of theme. Rondo with trio is not a recognized form. The musician will say that it does not exist; just as the farmer, on seeing a giraffe for the first time, refused to believe his eyes, and exclaimed, "There ain't no such animal." But composers often rise superior to rules, and produce many unusual forms.

The so-called third rondo is like the second, with an additional return of the first side section and the main section, to finish the work. This is not frequently used.

The old rondo, as exemplified by C. P. E. Bach, and others of his period, consisted of a chief theme that occurred a number of times, in contrast with any convenient number of side themes. In this connection, the use of the term rondo instead of five-part song-form is justified by the early composers, who always gave such works the former title.

Anything that cannot be classed elsewhere is apparently put among the rondos, if possible. Thus Mozart's "Alla Turca" movement seems at first sight to be much like a song-form and trio. But an extra theme is added, both after the song-form and the trio, which makes the piece a somewhat irregular first rondo.

Another sort of rondo is illustrated by Sinding's "Rustle of Spring." It will be seen on examination that this is based wholly on two periods. They are given first with the melody in the left hand, and a running embroidery of tones in the right. Then they appear as massive chords for the right hand. Then they return as at first, in the left hand. Even if it is admitted that the periods of a two-part song-form may sometimes be repeated together instead of separately, there are too many repeats in the Sinding piece to allow it to be classed as a song-form. The work is called a rondo on two themes. It does not follow that all rondos on two themes are like this one in shape; but all such pieces will be made up of a treatment of two themes, or sections, that cannot well be classified with the more usual rondos. The rondo on three themes exists also.

In all rondos, the chief idea is a recurrence of one main theme or section, with one or more side sections in contrast with it. While some rondos show a periodic structure, there are also rondos in which the sections are of freer style, and blended into one another so as to give a more unified effect than would be possible in the song-forms.

XXXV

THE SONATA–ALLEGRO FORM

THE works of Domenico Scarlatti, Galuppi, Paradisi, Kuhnau, and C. P. E. Bach brought about a gradual development of the sonata, until it took shape in the hands in Haydn and Mozart. The distinctive quality of the sonata consists in the shape of its first movement; and as this first movement is generally an allegro, the shape is mentioned here as sonata-allegro form. The sonata consists of various movements, whose contrasts of style admit of much artistic excellence. The same excellence is found in the form used in the first movement.

The sonata-allegro form is first of all divided into three main parts. These are the exposition, or first playing of the themes used; the development, or building up of a tonal structure from the material in the themes; and the recapitulation, or return of themes. If desired, a middle part, of new material, may be substituted for the development; but composers do not usually make this substitution without some good reason.

The themes used in a sonata may be much freer than those of a song-form. It is this variety of material in sonata themes that makes the piano sonatas of Beethoven so great. There is practically no limit to the power and expression that the composer may put into such themes.

The principle of contrast is introduced in the exposition; for the themes, three in number, may be of different styles. In general, the chief theme, or first theme, is expected to be bold and resolute in character, while the second theme should be more lyrical and tender. Between the two is a short tributary passage, of modulatory character. After the second theme comes a short closing theme, usually of brilliant style. The exposition is always marked for repeat, so that the themes may be clearly suggested to the hearer; but the modern tendency is to do away with many repeats. In piano sonatas the exposition is still usually given twice, though in symphonies the repeat is optional with the conductor.

The development admits of artistic possibilities of a different sort. In that section the material of the themes may be worked up into the most striking and beautiful tonal designs.

The recapitulation, or reprise, gives the movement the balance that comes from any return of theme after other material has been used. Here there may be some variety, not only in the tributary passage, but to some extent in the themes themselves.

Development and recapitulation were repeated together in the old sonatas.

The so-called modern sonata, or free sonata, does not respect the divisions or key-schedules of sonata-allegro form; but it should still reflect the earnest spirit of the sonata, which balances intellectual and emotional effects in artistic fashion.

The schedule of divisions and keys for the sonata-allegro form in any major key is as follows: —

1. Chief theme, in the tonic key, generally ending in a cadence. After this comes the tributary passage, modulating finally into the dominant, and usually ending with a half cadence in that key. (A half cadence consists of the tonic chord followed by the dominant.)

2. Second theme, or side theme, in the dominant key, ending in a full cadence.

3. One or more short closing themes, each ending in a full cadence.

4. Development of themes. Sometimes the end of the development will be marked by a fairly clear returning passage. The development may be modulatory.

5. Return of chief theme, in tonic key. Tributary passage this time must end in the tonic key.

6. Second theme, in tonic key.

7. Closing theme or themes, in tonic key.

The movement may have an introduction or a coda. It may also have transition or returning passages wherever needed, as at the end of the exposition.

In the return of themes, they need not always begin on their proper key; but if not, they must modulate to it soon after starting.

The sonata-allegro form in minor has the added possibility of contrast between the minor and major modes. The divisions are as before, but the schedule of keys is different. The structure is as follows: —

1. Chief theme, in the tonic minor. Tributary passage, leading to a half cadence in the relative major.

2. Second theme, in the relative major.

3. Closing theme or themes, in the relative major.

4. Development, free in style and key.

5. Return of chief theme, in tonic minor.

6. Return of side theme, in tonic minor or major.

7. Closing theme or themes, in tonic minor.

If there is a coda, division 7 may be in the tonic major, allowing the coda to establish the tonic minor key.

Another form of sonata allegro in minor allows divisions 2 and 3 to occur in the dominant minor, instead of the relative major. In the return, divisions 6 and 7 will then occur in the tonic minor.

To illustrate the sonata allegro in major, the Mozart Sonata in F (no. 3 in the Litolff collection), may be analyzed here: —

Chief theme, in F, measures 1–22. Tributary, here a theme, leading from D-minor to a half cadence in C, measures 22–40.

Second theme, in C, measures 41–86. From measure 56 some tributary modulation appears, but the ending is on the proper key.

Closing theme in C, measures 86–93. All three themes repeated.

Middle part, of new material, in different keys, ending on the dominant seventh chord of F, measures 94–132.

Recapitulation. Chief theme, in F, measures 133–154. Side theme, ending this time in F, measures 154–176.

Second theme, now in F, measures 177–222. Tributary work begins at measure 192.

Closing theme, now in F, measures 222–229.

The first movement of Haydn's Sonata in D (no. 7 in "Ten Celebrated Sonatas") is analyzed here as another example of the form in major: —

Chief theme, an 8-bar period, ending in a full cadence. Tributary, 8 bars ending with a half cadence in the tonic.

Second theme, 19 measures long, in A.

Closing theme, a little over five bars, in A.

Development, 20 measures.

Return of chief theme, in D, somewhat altered and extended. Tributary passage altered to 6 measures.

Second theme, much as before, but now in D.

Closing theme as before, but now in D.

As a clear example of the sonata allegro in the usual minor form, the opening movement of Beethoven's first sonata (Op. 2, no. 1) is now analyzed: —

Chief theme, in F-minor, measures 1–8. Tributary, with half cadence in A-flat-major, measures 8–20.

Second theme, in A-flat-major, measures 20–41.

Closing theme, in A-flat-major, measures 41–48. All repeated.

Development, founded largely on the main figure of the chief theme, and modulatory, measures 49–93. Returning passage, measures 93–100.

Return of chief theme, F-minor, measures 101–108. Tributary passage, with modulations altered, measures 108–119.

Second theme, now in F-minor, measures 119–140.

Closing theme, extended, now in F-minor, measures 140–152.

The first movement of Beethoven's "Sonata Pathétique" is an excellent example of Beethoven's union of form with expressive power. Knowing his love of liberty and his high conception of humanity, this movement seems almost like a tone-picture of man's struggle with adversity.

The introduction that begins the work is gloomy and tragic in the extreme. Then come the themes, powerful enough to suggest almost any sort of effort or combat. The seventeen-bar chief theme and the twenty-three-bar tributary are literally full of fight. The thirty-eight bars of the side theme are less tumultuous, but the long thirty-three-bar closing theme soon grows combative again. Struggle, sadness, and renewed effort are what the themes seem to typify. A returning passage leads to the repeat, and a transition passage to the development. When the latter begins, four measures of the sad introduction are heard. Then renewed struggle is suggested by the development, starting with the opening figure of the chief theme. The recapitulation follows, with a transition to the coda. The latter begins with the introduction figure, which is here made suggestive of utter weakness by the omission of an accented chord. Just at the finish, however, the true Beethoven spirit of defiance shows itself; and the movement ends with one more rush of the chief-theme figure, like a last command to fight on, even against fate itself.

The finale of Beethoven's first piano sonata (Op. 2, no. 1) is a good example of the sonata-allegro form with the themes appearing in the dominant minor instead of the relative major. The movement being in F-minor, the second and closing themes appear first in C-minor, and return later in F-minor. Such constant minor effects would be apt to produce monotony if unrelieved; so Beethoven put in a middle part instead of a development, and wrote it fluently in major for purposes of contrast. After it ends, a returning passage leads to the recapitulation.

The sonatas of Mozart and Haydn show clearness of form, and a light but pleasing cheerfulness. Those of Beethoven have much more dramatic power. Weber's sonatas were highly prized, but are not often heard now. Liszt's sonata, and those of MacDowell, are free in form, and in the modern style. The last five sonatas of Beethoven, too, are free in shape. They are tremendously broad piano rhapsodies in style and spirit, and have been aptly spoken of as "veiled symphonies." But while the later Beethoven and the modern radicals dispensed with strict form, it must not be forgotten that their genius entitled them to liberty of thought and expression. The student of to-day will do well to study form thoroughly, and appreciate all its possibilities. He should be able to master form before he discards it, if he wishes to excel in composition.

XXXVI

OTHER SONATA MOVEMENTS

THE piano sonata, and the orchestral forms that are built on the same lines, consist usually of three or four movements, the latter being the more common number in a large work. The first movement is generally in sonata-allegro form, and somewhat intellectual in character. The second movement is often a slow, expressive affair, lyrical and emotional in character. The third movement is often light and playful, or at least animated in style, — a minuet in the Haydn-Mozart works, or a scherzo in more recent compositions. The fourth movement, or finale, is usually brilliant. All these movements except the first may be in any one of several different forms. Sometimes it is rather a puzzle to find for the finale material that will make it a worthy conclusion to a work without causing any repetition of form or style.

The first movement itself may be free in style. This is unusual, but examples are readily found, as is shown by Beethoven's so-called "Moonlight Sonata." This work, entitled "Sonata quasi una Fantasia," has a free, fantasia-like movement at the beginning. Its bright allegretto and rushing finale suggest that the opening fantasia corresponds to the slow movement, and that the sonata is really written without any first movement.

The second and third movements may sometimes change places.

In a three-movement work, the scherzo movement is suppressed, the slow movement thus coming between two quick ones.

The slow movement of a sonata, symphony, etc., may be in one of many forms. It may use one of the song-forms, with or without trio; it may be a first or second rondo; it may be a theme, perhaps andante, with variations; it may be a sonata-allegro form again; or it may be a sonata rondo, or sonatina, or sonatina rondo.

Of these different shapes, the song-forms, rondos, and sonata form have been described already. A song-form is found in the slow movement of Mendelssohn's violin concerto. The slow movements of a Beethoven and a Mozart sonata have been cited previously as first rondos. The slow movement of Beethoven's "Sonata Pathétique" has been mentioned as a second rondo. The 5/4 movement of Tschaikovsky's "Symphonie Pathétique" is an example of a large song-form with trio; and minuets are regularly in this form. The slow movement of Beethoven's first symphony is an illustration of the use of sonata allegro.

The so-called sonata rondo varies the sonata-allegro form by the principle of the rondo, i.e., the frequent appearance of the chief theme. There is usually no repeat in a sonata rondo. The theme appears twice more than in sonata form, — once at the end of the exposition, and once at the end of the recapitulation. The divisions of the sonata rondo are therefore chief theme, second theme, closing theme, chief theme, development, chief theme, second theme, closing theme, and chief theme. An example of the sonata rondo may be found in the finale of Beethoven's "Sonata Pathétique."

The sonatina form is a short, primitive sonata allegro. It begins with two themes, a chief theme and a side theme, contrasted and joined like those of the sonata allegro, but rather lighter in style. Usually there is no development. The recapitulation consists of the two themes, this time both in the tonic key. The sonatina may have two or three movements. Clementi wrote a number of works in this form, which the student may inspect for purposes of analysis. The sonatina form may be used for a sonata movement.

The sonatina rondo consists of theme, second theme in the proper related key, theme, second theme in the tonic, and theme again. This form also may be used in a sonata movement.

Variations of a theme have been a favorite form with the great composers. Beethoven, Brahms, Elgar, Reger, Tschaikovsky, and others have made a separate work of this form, the Brahms variations on a Haydn theme being especially beautiful. Beethoven used variations in the finale of his "Eroica Symphony," in the slow movement of his piano sonata (Op. 14, no. 2), and in the slow movement of his "Kreutzer Sonata" for violin and piano. Variations enable a composer to show his mastery over different styles of writing. There is always danger of their growing into a mere technical display; and the composer must guard against this fault.

The minuet movement of the old symphonies was regularly in

the shape of song-form with trio. The minuet in Beethoven's first symphony is a case in point. Beethoven substituted the scherzo for the minuet, and in his later symphonies made it very brusque and strong. In the scherzo the dance-like character of the themes is absent, the treatment is fairly free, and development is permissible. But many scherzo movements keep to the song-form and trio structure. Schumann has been quoted as using the song-form with two trios in the scherzo of his first symphony. The scherzo is now treated as an independent piano piece, and works in this form by Kullak and Chopin may be investigated by the student.

Brahms replaced the scherzo by the intermezzo. This is still much like a song-form with trio. The first part generally consists of two themes, as in the song-form. A trio follows, in contrasted style. The earlier themes do not return as a whole, but are replaced by a coda containing reminiscences of them.

The minuet is properly in 3/4 rhythm; but the scherzo and intermezzo may be in any suitable rhythm, although most scherzos are in 3/4 rhythm.

The finale is usually a brilliant movement. Yet every rule has exceptions, and we find Tschaikovsky ending his "Symphonie Pathétique" with a very mournful slow movement. But this is only one of the cases that prove the rule.

In the time of Haydn and Mozart, the finale was often a light, jovial movement in rondo form. Even Beethoven followed the earlier custom in the finale of his first symphony. This style of ending was evidently taken from the old suite, which closed with a rollicking gigue, or jig.

In Beethoven's second symphony he ended the work with more power; while in his third, he used variations that were built up into a grand climax. The fifth symphony finale is another tremendously powerful movement, before which the rondos of Haydn and Mozart may hide their diminished heads. The finale of Beethoven's seventh symphony is a riot of speed and liveliness. The eighth closes more conventionally, but the ninth again ends powerfully, having variations that bring in the choral work described in a previous chapter.

Besides variations, the sonata form is sometimes used in the finale, or even the sonata rondo, as already illustrated. The finale of Beethoven's sonata Op. 7 is a sonata rondo. The finales of Op. 2, no. 1, and of the fifth symphony, are in sonata form. The sonatas Op. 109 and Op. 111 end with variations. The sonata Op. 106, known as the "Grand Sonata," closes with a fugue. The fugue was sometimes used as a finale by Haydn and Mozart, while Lachner employed it in his suite Op. 113.

The full possibilities of the sonata form should now be apparent to the reader. The complete sonata consists of four movements which show the utmost variety of style, and allow the composer to make the most artistic contrasts.

In the first movement, the themes themselves are of varying character, allowing the composer to balance them in excellent fashion. The exposition is then put in contrast with the development, in which the thematic material may be woven and interwoven to form an exquisite design, or worked up to a grand climax.

Against this movement, usually somewhat intellectual in character, is placed the lyrical and expressive emotion of the slow movement. Here feeling is paramount, and simplicity is often the keynote.

Following this comes the scherzo or its equivalent, — again a complete change in style. Now everything is playful and light, or else bizarre or brusque in effect.

The finale brings still another change. In some degree it is a reversion to the style of the first movement. But as a general rule the finale is made dashing and brilliant, while the first movement was more earnest and serious.

In all the later movements, the composer has such choice of form that he should be able to give the fullest expression to his musical ideas. Even in the first movement, there is sufficient freedom within the form for him to develop his thoughts unhampered. The variety and artistic possibilities of the sonata and symphony have resulted in music of the utmost value, — music that comes as a revelation to the cultivated hearer, and appeals to his highest emotions in a language that is said to begin where speech ends.

XXXVII

THE ORCHESTRAL FORMS

As already intimated, the symphony is an orchestral sonata, usually in four movements. Occasionally these movements are different from those of the sonata, and national dances may be used. Thus Tschaikovsky introduced the brilliant Russian Kamarinskaia, while Dvořák employed the melancholy Dumka and the wild Furiant. Berlioz and Tschaikovsky tried a waltz movement in a symphony; but the waltz is rather too informal for the best effects. Rubinstein's "Ocean Symphony" contains seven movements.

The concerto is generally a three-movement orchestral sonata, with the scherzo omitted. Sometimes concerto movements merge into one another with no pause between them. This is true occasionally of the symphony also. Toward the close of the first movement in a concerto, and sometimes in the last movement, occurs what is known as a *cadenza*. This is an unaccompanied passage for the solo instrument. It is usually brilliant in character, giving the soloist a chance to display his technique. Sometimes the cadenza is written by the composer. More often, however, it is left to the performer. He may sometimes use a cadenza of his own, or one written by anybody, even when the composer has made his own cadenza. A number of cadenzas in great works have been published separately by famous performers. The place for the cadenza is indicated in the score by a hold on a dominant or 6/4 tonic chord. The performer ends the cadenza by a long-sustained trill, on a note that will allow the conductor to make the orchestra enter in proper harmony, — usually the dominant degree.

Concertos may be written for more than one instrument of the same kind, or even for instruments of several kinds, with orchestra. The best concertos do not resemble instrumental solos with accompaniment, but are really orchestral works with one or more threads of solo music interwoven into their texture. Beethoven, who thought naturally for orchestra, wrote concertos that fulfilled this requirement admirably. Schubert avoided the concerto, and even in his symphonies it often seems as if the musical ideas were thinly disguised songs. Schumann's massive chord-style was pianistic enough, but not unsuited for orchestral use also; and his piano concerto shows the proper balance, even though his instrumentation is often poor. Chopin, on the other hand, was more exclusively devoted to an expressive melodic style. As a result, his concertos seem like piano solos with incidental orchestral accompaniment.

Symphonies and concertos can be built on a far grander scale than piano sonatas. In the first place, the variety of orchestral coloring is very great. A piano piece in comparison with an orchestral work has been likened to a black-and-white drawing beside an oil painting; and the comparison is certainly just. In piano work, too, the number of notes is limited to the ability that can be shown by a single pair of hands; while in the orchestra a chord may consist of many notes. This increases the possibilities of dramatic effect. In orchestral music, too, development is carried to a greater extent than in piano music.

Chamber music is very often written in sonata form. The term "chamber music" is derived from the Italian words *musica di camera*, in contradistinction to *musica di chiesa*, or church music. It was played at first only in the chambers of wealthy amateurs. All music for combinations of instruments smaller than an orchestra is called chamber music. The most common form is the string quartet, consisting of a first and second violin, a viola, and a 'cello. Piano quartets, with piano, violin, viola, and 'cello, are fairly numerous; and piano trios, with violin, 'cello, and piano, are still more so. Many sonatas have been written for single instruments with piano. The piano quintet adds the keyboard to the instruments of the string quartet. Various combinations for strings and woodwind have been employed; while even the brass instruments are used occasionally. In chamber music the grandeur of the orchestra is absent; but this is atoned for by a clear and interesting leading of the parts. Thus a string quartet may be a work of consummate skill, in spite of its often having an apparently simple effect.

Overtures are often written in sonata-allegro form. In such cases there is usually no repeat of the exposition. Some overtures have little development, the chief interest lying in the well-contrasted themes.

One of the earliest styles of this form was known as the French overture. In fact the word overture comes directly from the French, and means an opening piece. Lully and others of his time developed an overture consisting of a slow movement followed without pause by a quick one. The slow section was a fairly short introduction, while the rapid part was often a fugue. Handel used this form in the overture to his "Messiah." Sometimes the French composers followed the rapid section with a moderately slow dance movement, which was held to be part of the form.

The classical overture has the sonata-allegro shape, with no repeat of the exposition. Mozart's opera overtures, such as those to "Don Giovanni," "The Marriage of Figaro," etc., are in this form. Weber used the form, slightly modified, in his "Freischütz," "Euryanthe," and "Oberon" overtures, and at the same time chose the themes from the music of the operas that followed.

The dramatic overture aims to give a suggestion or an epitome of the opera that follows it. Such overtures were not restricted in form. They were originated by Gluck, who sometimes kept them separate, but generally allowed them to lead directly into the opera. At times they approached the sonata-allegro form in shape. Beethoven adopted the dramatic overture with evident preference for it, and his "Leonora no. 3," for the opera "Fidelio," is an excellent example. Beethoven always kept the overture as a separate piece. Beethoven's other overtures, too, are really dramatic, though the one to "Egmont" approaches the classical overture in form.

The concert overture resembles the classical overture in following the sonata-allegro form. It derives its name from the fact that it is not attached to any opera or play, but is a separate composition intended for concert performance. Mendelssohn brought this form into prominence, his "Hebrides" and "Sea-Calm and Prosperous Voyage" overtures being unconnected with any dramatic work.

The medley overture, used by Hérold, Auber, and others, has no definite form, but is merely a string of melodies drawn from the opera that is to follow it. The tunes and sections are put together without any regard for definite form; but the composer usually sees to it that they are well contrasted and arranged to make a climax whenever possible.

The Wagnerian Prelude, or *Vorspiel*, is an outgrowth of the dramatic overture. But Wagner's preludes are so varied in form and effect that they deserve a separate classification. Sometimes, as in the "Meistersinger" Prelude, he foreshadowed the plot of the opera itself; while on other occasions, as in the Prelude to "Lohengrin," he limited himself to a simpler suggestion, — the coming and going of the Holy Grail. The *Vorspiel* leads directly into the opera that follows it.

Liszt and others have developed the symphony along the lines of programme music, and even invented a new form, the symphonic poem, to satisfy their desires and enable them to devote themselves wholly to programme effects. As stated in a previous chapter, programme music is music that tries to portray definite scenes or events. Very often the title is a sufficient clue. Thus in Liszt's "Faust" Symphony, the first movement typifies Faust, the second, Marguerite, and the third, Mephistopheles.

The symphonic poem is a free orchestral form. There are no laws governing its shape, except those of good taste, — or those of public taste, one might better say. Yet composers generally choose poetic subjects, so that they are enabled to write expressive or dramatic music. In the symphonic poem, form thus becomes an individual matter. Yet the general laws hold good still. There must be sufficient balance, contrast, and growth toward a climax. There must also be good music. Very many works by contemporary composers are heard once or twice, and then laid aside as uninteresting. In all the modern struggle for suggestive tonal effects, inspiration has not yet been made unnecessary by mere skill. Talent, or genius, is still a *desideratum*.

Liszt chose excellent subjects for his symphonic poems,—subjects that enabled him to give free rein to his creative ability. His most glorious work, "Les Preludes," illustrates a sentence of Lamartine, which shows that the varied phases of life, such as love, happiness, or glory, are all a prelude to eternity. In "Tasso, Lamento e Trionfo," the strong contrast between the two parts of the work is brought into notice at once by the title. The "Battle of the Huns," after a painting by Kaulbach, is another suggestive subject.

Richard Strauss has gone farthest afield in programme music; and he claims that the time will come when music can give a detailed description of such a definite subject as a man at a meal, and show when he takes up or puts down his knife or fork. But the fact still remains that Strauss himself is best in those subjects that bring the emphasis on emotion rather than events. The yearning memories and the great apotheosis in "Death and Transfiguration" are of higher artistic value than the attempts to show Don Quixote in an upsetting boat, or on an imaginary trip through the air.

Composers have used the variation form to some extent in programme music. Strauss's "Don Quixote" is still the most prominent example. Elgar, however, indulged in a more private style of programme music by portraying various friends in his "Enigma" variations. D'Indy's "Istar" is another large programme work in the variation form. In this composition the variations are complex at first, while the theme comes at the end. This unusual procedure is suited to its subject, as Istar is forced to disrobe in order to reach her lover in the Halls of Death.

The symphony itself has been used in programme music ever since the time of Beethoven's "Pastoral." Raff wrote a number of programme symphonies, including those entitled "Lenore" and "Im Walde." Goldmark's "Rustic Wedding" Symphony was very familiar a generation ago. Rimsky-Korsakov's "Antar" and "Scheherazade" are both called symphonies, though they tell very definite stories.

The growth of the programme school has resulted in a strongly dramatic style, that has threatened to obliterate the quieter vein of classicism. Attention was given to this subject in the chapter on Brahms and Bruckner, in which it was shown that Bruckner wrote pure music that was more closely related to the modern programme effects than that of Brahms. In Mahler's symphonies the dramatic style is far more in evidence. They are full of such strong contrasts and discordant intensity that they seem like programme music with the programme left out. They are symphonies in name, but symphonic poems in fact.

The suite, or "set" of pieces, is now an orchestral form in several movements; but the individual movements have more freedom and informality than those of the symphony. Some composers made the suite into a definite form, while others arranged suites from the incidental music they had written for some play or ballet. Lachner worked purposely in the suite form, writing eight examples of it. Most famous among Lachner's suites is the one containing his well-known march and an orchestral fugue. In such suites the form of the first movement may sometimes approach the sonata allegro; but the style is not necessarily as elevated as in symphony. The other movements may have any of the forms enumerated in the preceding chapter.

Of the suites built up from incidental or other music, Grieg's two "Peer Gynt" suites and Bizet's two "Arlésienne" suites are the best known. There is no attempt at sonata-allegro form in these works. Bizet's two compositions, taken from music to Daudet's play, begin in frankly melodious fashion; while the first Grieg work opens with a tone-picture of a "Morning Mood" that certainly suggests sunrise and the growing light of day. Another well-known suite is the "Nutcracker," by Tschaikovsky, taken from one of his ballets.

The divertimento is somewhat like the suite, but even more light and informal in character. Tschaikovsky made it a single suite movement.

The serenade was formerly held to be a piece or set of pieces playable in the evening. It thus became somewhat like the divertimento. Volkmann's Serenade for string orchestra is an example.

The old suite, composed of dances and similar movements, will be described in the following chapter.

In all these works the composers took care to give the proper balance between the styles of the different movements.

XXXVIII

DANCES AND PIANO STYLES

DANCING has existed from the earliest times; and it probably originated, among prehistoric races, from pantomime intended to be descriptive of hunting or martial scenes. Many of the early religions adopted dancing as part of their ceremonial; but in historic times it has always been an independent art as well.

Circular dances are found to have existed among the old sun-worshippers. The Biblical dance about the Golden Calf, or that around the bull Apis, show the same character. A similar round formation existed in the German "Reigen" of early mediæval times, which survive in children's games, such as "Little Sally Waters" and others of the sort.

The Grecian dances and the Roman pantomime, described in an earlier chapter, had little effect on mediæval dancing. The art received scant encouragement during the dark ages; but the Troubadours and Minnesingers brought in their train a revival of dancing as well as of song. In Germany, a quick dance was often followed by a slow one, while a later return of the quick movement brought about a first rondo effect. In France, the French overture developed from a slow dance followed by a rapid one. There were various religious dances, of more or less influence on the popular branch of the art. The Flagellants had a penitential dance, which they employed in times of plague or other calamity.

The stately Saraband arose directly from the dance of the Spanish altar-boys on Holy Thursday. It was a slow dance in triple rhythm.

A dance that is now not clearly understood is the English Morris Dance. Some claim that the title comes from *Morisco*, and indicates a Moorish origin, if not a relation to the Spanish Fandango. In England it was merged into an old pantomime celebrating Robin Hood. The Morris Dance could be made to progress from place to place; and Will Kempe once danced it from London to Norwich.

In modern times, Edward German composed a very pleasing Morris Dance in his music to "Henry VIII."

The Hornpipe, once cherished by sailors, was originally an English shepherds' dance, the horn being really a shepherd's pipe, as shown by the name English horn. The Hornpipe was a lively dance in even rhythm.

Another rustic dance in England was the Hay, or Hey. This was a circular arrangement, much used at May-Day gatherings. When Shakespeare makes Titania say, "Come, now, a roundel and a fairy song," the roundel refers to the circular Hay. Sometimes words were sung to it.

In "Much Ado about Nothing," Beatrice remarks that "Wooing, wedding, and repenting is a Scottish jig, a measure, and a cinque-pace." The jig, in various nations, was a lively 6/8 or 12/8 movement. It was often called "Gigue," from the German word *Geige*, meaning fiddle; and that instrument was well suited to the rapid style of the dance. The Gigue was typical of the lover's haste. The Measure, derived from "Passo-Mezzo," or medium step, was more quiet and regular. When Lochinvar exclaims, "Now tread we a Measure," he refers to this dance, and not to a bar of music. Its even course typifies quiet married life, according to Beatrice. The Cinque-Pace (*cinque-pas*) was an irregular five-step affair, aptly illustrating the break-up of domestic harmony.

Somewhat slower varieties of the Gigue were known as the Loure and the Canary.

The Gaillard was a more graceful dance, though still fairly lively. In Italy and France it was known, from its Roman origin, as the Romanesca; and Liszt's piano arrangement of this old singing-dance will show the graceful style of its music. In even rhythm, it flows along smoothly at first, but hurries before the close. Evidently the Gaillard demanded some agility; for an old English letter says, "Our Galliardes are so curious that thei are not for my daunsyng, for thei are so full of trickes and tournes, that he which hath no more but the plaine Singuepace is no better accumpted of than a verie bomgler."

The Tordion, or Tourdion, was much like the Gaillard, but slower and smoother.

Another dance mentioned by Shakespeare is the Dump. But the words "Play me some merry dump" are paradoxical, since the Dump was a dance of sad and doleful character. It was probably derived from the Bohemian Dumka, the elegiac movement that Dvořák used in his symphonies.

The Allemande was of German origin. It was a fairly cheerful movement, like an Allegretto, in 4/4 rhythm. Some have thought that the Allemande was not really a dance.

The Courante was a rapid dance in triple rhythm, with the running effect that its name implied.

The Bourrée was a fairly rapid dance in 4/4 time, with considerable liveliness of style. It had its origin in Auvergne.

Somewhat like the Bourrée, but slower, was the Gavotte. This was named from the Gavots, or inhabitants of Gap, near the Pyrenees. It is in 4/4 time, with a suggestion of syncopation owing to its beginning on the third beat of the measure. Its pleasing character is brought about by skipping intervals and short, crisp phrases. The trio of the Gavotte was often in the style of the musette, with drone-bass effects.

The Rigaudon was another fairly rapid dance, sometimes also sung by the performers. It was invented by Rigaud, the dancing master of Louis XIII. The old song-dances were sometimes called Ballets, from the Italian word *ballare*, to dance.

The French Volte may well have been the precursor of our waltz, the name signifying merely a turn. Thoinot Arbeau wrote of it, "You may pursue it thus through many turnings, whirling now to the right and now to the left." Later, he added, "You shall return your partner to her seat, where, do what she may, she will find her shaken-up brain full of swimmings and whirlings; while you will probably not be much better off." Then came the familiar complaint, "I beg you to consider if it be decorous for a young girl to straddle and stride."

The Passepied, corrupted into Paspy, was another fairly rapid French dance in triple time. Like the Gavotte, it had several strains and reprises.

The Minuet was of a slower type. Its graceful 3/4 music was to be taken at a decorous pace, though the symphonic Minuets were fairly quick.

The Branle, or Brawl, was another slow dance, given by pairs in imitation of a leading couple.

The Pavane was also slow and stately, but in even rhythm.

The Chaconne was another slow and dignified dance. It was usually in triple rhythm, though examples in even rhythm have been found. It is best known now through Bach's famous Chaconne for violin alone.

The Passacaglia was a slow dance in triple rhythm, much like the Chaconne, but more often in minor. It was given with much exaggeration and bombast, the couples succeeding one another in a fashion that is now found in the cake-walk. Some derive the name from *pasar calle*, which is Spanish for walking along the street; but others trace it to *passo gallo*, or rooster step.

The old suite was composed of several of these early dances. The usual succession was Allemande, Courante, Saraband, and Gigue, which suggests the general style of a symphony with the slow movement coming third. But many other movements were permissible. Between the Saraband and the Gigue, Intermezzi were sometimes introduced. These were usually dances of moderate pace, like the Gavotte or Minuet, which would be in sufficient contrast with the slow tempo preceding them and the rapid tempo that followed. The middle movements could be varied. If this was done by means of slight embellishments, the variation was known as "Les Agréments," while a more decided alteration was called a Double. Certain movements that were not dances often entered the suite. A fugue was permissible. Often it came after a Toccata, a brilliant piece full of technical display. Less ambitious than the Toccata was the Toccatina. The Air was a simple melody, while the Burlesca was playful in style. Somewhat like the Burlesca was the Scherzo, not to be confused with the symphonic movement of the same name. The suite could begin with a prelude, known under the various names of Intrada, Preambule, Fantasia, Overture, or even Sinfonia. The last word was often applied to any interlude, such as the Symphony in Bach's "Christmas Oratorio," or the Pastoral Symphony in Handel's "Messiah." In Bach's B-minor Suite is a charming movement entitled "Badinerie," which consists of some delightfully chattering flute work against an orchestral background. The Partita was an early name for the suite itself.

In more recent times, Germany has given to music the Ländler, or country dance of waltz type. The waltz itself was developed in

Germany, a cotillion being still known as a German, while the dance itself was the Deutsche. The waltz has been developed into a piano form, not suitable for dancing, by Chopin, Rubinstein, and others. The waltz is written in 3/4 time, but played as if composed in 6/4 rhythm instead.

Spain has been devoted to the dance for many centuries. Most popular in that country is the Fandango, a 3/4 or 3/8 affair accompanied by castanets. Local varieties of this are the Malaguena, Rondena, Granadina, and Murciana. The Andalusian Cachucha is another dance in triple rhythm, this time fairly rapid. Still another dance of the same sort is the Jota. The Bolero is a dance of moderate pace, in 3/4 rhythm, accompanied by castanets in certain alternations of large and small notes. Sometimes the Bolero contains a Tirana, which is a passage of gentle 6/8 melody. The Seguedilla is more rapid, and in 6/8 rhythm. Other national Spanish dances of this sort are the Jaleo and Guaracha. The Spanish gypsies use an attractive 3/8 dance called the Polo Gitano. The Habañera (Havanaise), adopted by Spain from Cuba, is in moderate tempo, and usually in triple rhythm, though the one in Bizet's opera "Carmen" shows even rhythm, with frequent triplets.

Italy has given music the Tarantella, a swift, running dance in 6/8 rhythm. It is said that this dance was named from the tarantula, as its fiery style would incite people to the exertion of rapid dancing that was held necessary in curing that spider's bite; but the Italian tarantula was evidently not the tropical one. The Saltarello is an Italian dance of similar style, but containing more skips than the Tarantella. Mendelssohn ended his Italian Symphony with a Saltarello. The Furlana, or Forlane, is a rapid 6/8 affair of Venetian origin, much used by the gondoliers. Ponchielli employed it in "La Gioconda," and Wolf-Ferrari did the same in "The Jewels of the Madonna." The Siciliano was a pastoral Sicilian dance, or dance-song, of gentle and soothing character, in slow 6/8 or 12/8 rhythm.

Among the dances of Provence, the Farandole is best known, because of Bizet's use of it in his "Arlésienne" music. It is a lively, rapid dance, sometimes in 4/4 rhythm, but occasionally in 6/8. The Française denotes a graceful French dance in 3/4 rhythm. The Galop is a very quick dance, generally 2/4, though other rhythms are sometimes used.

Among Slavic dances, the Cracovienne (Krakowiak) is a Polish dance in 2/4 rhythm. The Varsovienne is in moderate 3/4 rhythm. The Polacca is similar to this, but somewhat quicker. This must not be confused with the Polka, which is the Bohemian Pulka, a rapid dance in even rhythm. Raff and Rubinstein composed polkas, but the dance does not offer many musical possibilities. The Mazurka (Masurek) is a Polish dance in triple rhythm and rather capricious style. It has frequent accents on the second beat of the measure, which the dancers emphasize by a kick. The Polka Mazurka is about the same in style, though slower, and with the unexpected accents on the third beat. The Polka Redowa is faster, and has no unusual accents. The Redowa itself sometimes alternates 3/4 and 2/4 measures. The Czardas, or Csardas, is a fiery Hungarian dance. Most stately of all is the Polonaise, originally a dignified dance-parade in which the Poles marched before their leader, John Sobieski, when he was given the Polish crown. Chopin made excellent use of both Polonaise and Mazurka.

Norway offers the Springdans (3/4) and the Halling (2/4), both illustrated in the shorter works of Grieg. The latter is a boisterous affair for men only, at which the performers try to kick the low rafters of the barn or other building where they dance.

Russia has many folk-dances. The one exerting most influence on music is the lively dance for men known as the Kamarinskaia, which Tschaikovsky made into a symphonic movement.

Scotland is suggested by the Schottische, or "Scotch Dance." This is a slow dance in even rhythm, having a number of short notes in each bar, to which the performers take three moderate steps and two quick ones. The Reel is a very animated affair, in rapid even rhythm. The Strathspey is somewhat slower, and has what is known as the Scotch snap, — a sixteenth note followed by a dotted eighth note. The Contra-Dance, or Country Dance, known in England and other lands, is a rustic affair, much used in former centuries, and somewhat resembling our Virginia Reel; for the dancers were placed in opposite rows, and made to go through certain figures accompanied by rapid four-bar or eight-bar phrases in the music. The Quickstep was a sort of march in very rapid 6/8 rhythm. The Quadrille was originally a French dance, consisting of five movements, which were entitled *La Pantalon, La Poule,*

L'Été, La Trenise (or *La Pastorelle*), and *La Finale*. These names were to some extent descriptive of the music, which was naturally in five divisions, either 6/8 or 2/4.

Among modern dances, the Two-Step, and the Brazilian Maxixe as well, are in fairly rapid 6/8 rhythm. A 4/4 rhythm may be used, but does not fit the dance so well. The Tango, coming from the Argentine Republic, is in 4/4 rhythm, consisting largely of eighth-notes.

The March, which is practically a dance, has been popular with many composers because of its stirring or martial character. It can be in 4/4, or rapid 6/8 rhythm; but a lofty processional effect is attained by the use of 12/8 rhythm. The Coronation March in Meyerbeer's opera "Le Prophète" is an excellent example of the last sort. An added adjective often shows the character of a March, — as Wedding March, Funeral March, etc.

The Ballet, brought into recent prominence by the admirable work of the Russian dancers, is simply a pantomime set to music. The Ballet may have several acts, and be as long as a moderate-sized opera. Adam's "Giselle" and Delibes's "Coppélia" and other similar works are well known as French examples; while in Russia, Tschaikovsky, Glazounoff, and the more radical Stravinsky have given much attention to the form. Naturally no set laws govern the Ballet, which is a series of dances in varying styles and rhythms. Single ballet scenes were often introduced in certain old operas; but these did not usually have any special meaning, whereas in the complete Ballet each dance helps to illustrate or unfold the plot.

A number of short musical titles, usually employed for piano pieces, and representing styles rather than forms, may be given here.

The Fantasia is a work in free form, which may treat various themes or figures, but does so in a free, fanciful way.

The Capriccio is a work of much the same character. But while the Fantasia is generally earnest in style, the Capriccio should be lighter, more "capricious," and even bizarre. Both may be cast in various musical forms, but should not let the form hamper their qualities of style.

The Rhapsodie is another free composition, of impassioned and intense character. Liszt used it to show the wild power of the Hungarian gypsy music. Many of the actual gypsy pieces show a two-part structure, the first part, or Lassan, being slow and very melancholy, while the last part, the Friska, is wild and fiery.

The Prelude is a short piece in free form written to precede another piece. Thus a Prelude precedes each Fugue in Bach's "Well-tempered Clavichord." Chopin treated the Prelude as a separate form, and its free, impassioned style suited his genius well.

The Rêverie is a dreamy, tender composition, often in one of the song-forms.

The Romanza is a piece expressing romantic feeling, if not aiming at an actual story. It may be written in one of the song-forms or rondos, but is usually free in style.

The Poème is similar to the Romanza.

The Légende carries with it a suggestion of legendary romance, or supernatural mystery. Wieniawski's Légende for violin and piano is an admirable example.

The Ballade is another work in poetic and emotional style, with some degree of narrative suggestion. Chopin's Ballades are good examples.

The Italian term Ballata sometimes means Ballade, but is more often a dance-song or dance-like piece.

The Novelette, a title well used by Schumann, is a piece composed of sections so striking and characteristic that they seem to tell a story.

The Novellozza carries with it a humorous suggestion. Godard's Novellozza is an admirable illustration.

The Cabaletta is a pleasingly melodious piece, of fairly simple style, with an accompaniment of triplets or other notes that will suggest a galloping horse.

The Nocturne is a piece in emotional style representing the poetic feelings aroused by evening or night. Field was a pioneer in this form, but Chopin's Nocturnes soon drew attention away from those of the earlier composer.

The Berceuse is a cradle-song, generally with a lulling 6/8 rhythm. Chopin's Berceuse is an example.

The Serenade is an evening song of melodious character, suggesting a love-song. Both Serenade and Nocturne once referred simply to music for evening use.

The Aubade is a morning song. Liszt's transcription of Schubert's "Hark, hark, the lark" is an instrumental example.

The Pastorale is a piece of rustic suggestion.

The Barcarolle is an Italian boat-song, suggested in instrumental music. It is generally in swingy 6/8 rhythm.

The Gondoliera is similar to the Barcarolle, but carries a definite suggestion of Venetian effects.

The Cavatina is a smooth, attractive melody in vocal music, and in piano music must keep the same style. Raff's expressive Cavatina for piano and violin is an excellent illustration.

The Elegie, or Dirge, is a melodious piece of sad or mournful style.

The Song Without Words is a short melodious piece of song-like character, composed definitely in one of the song-forms.

The Moment Musical is a short piece of melodious style.

The Bagatelle, meaning "trifle," is a short and simple piece.

The Albumblatt, or Album Leaf, is a short piece of improvisational character, such as one might write in an album.

The Impromptu is another piece of marked improvisational style.

The Étude is primarily a technical study, but may be made of interesting music. Chopin's Études are examples in point, being studies in the sense that a painter's sketches are studies.

The Intermezzo is a short piece in free style, generally found between others.

The Entr'acte is a piece to be played between the acts of an opera. Sometimes such a piece is known also as an Intermezzo; but the latter may occur at other places, as the Intermezzo in Mascagni's "Rustic Chivalry" will show.

The Potpourri is a medley in which various fragments of a musical work are strung together in continuous shape. Potpourris from the famous operas are the most common examples.

The Pasticcio is a medley of another sort, made up of various single pieces. In an operatic pasticcio, words are set to melodies already existing separately. The Pasticcio may be based on works of more than one composer. Orefice's opera "Chopin" is an example of the Pasticcio. In that work, Orefice took various Chopin pieces, and blended them into an opera by adding suitable words.

XXXIX

THE VOCAL FORMS

THE larger forms enumerated in the preceding chapters are not used in vocal music. Vocal rondos exist, in second rondo form; but they are never very intricate in construction. Many songs are written in the song-forms, while some show the shape of song-form with trio; but vocal music has forms and styles of its own.

Alessandro Scarlatti developed the *da capo* aria, and used it in his operas. This is practically a vocal song-form with trio, consisting of a section, an alternating section, and the repeat of the first section. An example of this shape is found in the solo "He was despised," from Handel's "Messiah." Sometimes there is only a partial return.

Opera at first gave an important place to recitative, which is musical declamation much resembling speech, though always with a definite pitch. As early as Handel's time there were two varieties, — *recitativo secco*, with no support except occasional chords, and *recitativo stromentato*, with a much fuller and more varied accompaniment. Both kinds are present in "Comfort ye," the opening number of "The Messiah." The accompanied recitative comes first, the change appearing with the words, "The voice of him that crieth."

The songs of Handel's time were classed in five varieties, — *aria di bravura, aria di portamento, aria di mezzo carattere, aria parlante,* and *aria cantabile*.

The first of these, the *aria di bravura*, was aimed to display vocal technique. The old solos of this sort, such as Handel's "Ev'ry valley" or "Why do the nations so furiously rage" (in "The Messiah"), make great demands on a singer's ability to give rapid roulades in clean-cut style. These arias are full of beautiful music, wherein they are superior to the meaningless brilliance of certain showy scenes in Italian opera. The *aria di bravura* was usually given to a female voice, "Rejoice greatly" being a good example in "The Messiah."

The *aria di mezzo carattere*, as its name implies, was of more ordinary character and style. Haydn's "With verdure clad" may be taken as an illustration.

The *aria cantabile* was a song of marked smoothness. "He shall feed his flock," from "The Messiah," will serve as an example.

The *aria di portamento* called for frequent use of the vocal portamento, which is a sweep of the voice toward the note coming next, before the time of the note given is entirely finished. The song "Jerusalem," from Mendelssohn's "Saint Paul," shows something of this character, though it is *cantabile* in style.

The *aria parlante* was more in a spoken style, though less abrupt than recitative. Its character may be shown by a more modern song, — Rubinstein's "The Asra."

The style of singing in Mozart's time was smooth, light, and fluent. The Rossini operas again called for brilliant execution, but their solos did not show much musical depth or harmonic variety. Gluck had revived recitative in his works; and after the Italian vogue grew less, Wagner introduced a sort of melodic recitative, which he called Melos. In the mean time Schubert and the Lied composers had written works that called for a more dramatic and expressive style of singing than the Mozart lyrics necessitated. The German Lied exists in a variety of styles, but all of them show a close union of the music with the words, and an attempt to express in tones the real inwardness of the poem. The French *chanson*, and to some extent the Italian *canzone*, placed more emphasis upon daintiness and grace in the melody.

The art-song is a song in which music is set to the entire poem; while in the strophe form the music is repeated for each stanza. The art form is usually much more artistic. Many beautiful strophe songs exist; but in that style of composition there are two possible defects. The music may become monotonous on repetition; or the character of the melody and accompaniment may fit only certain stanzas, and be unsuited to others.

The *scena* is a vocal composition of some size, in which the composer is expected to use a variety of styles. The *scena* will contain some recitative work; a smooth aria-section, known here as a *cavatina;* and an aria or other portion devoted to more brilliant effects. A *scena* may be either part of an opera, or a wholly separate composition. Mendelssohn's "Infelice" is an independent *scena*.

The hymn is a song or part-song, with accompaniment, set to the words of some sacred poem. Hymns are divided into phrases corresponding with the lines of the poem. For four-line stanzas, most hymns are in the single-period form, antecedent and consequent each extending for two lines. Eight-line settings of hymns are usually in the two-period form, sometimes independent, and sometimes with partial return. The metre of hymns is shown by letters or numbers. S.M., or short metre, describes an iambic hymn with four-line stanzas, each of which consists of six, six, eight, and six syllables respectively in the lines. C.M., or common metre, has four iambic lines containing respectively eight, six, eight, and six syllables. L.M., or long metre, consists wholly of eight-syllabled iambic lines. The letter D after any of the above signifies double-length stanzas, and calls for an eight-line tune. Other metres are almost always shown by figures. A single figure will do if all the lines are equal; as, for instance, 7s, signifying seven-syllabled (trochaic) lines. If the lines are not all equal, it is customary to give the number of syllables in each line; as, for instance, 8:7:8:7, in which (trochaic) lines of eight and seven syllables are alternated. In some cases the letters P.M. are used to signify peculiar metre.

The anthem is a part-song set to sacred words, with accompaniment. Anthems are usually much more ambitious and varied in style than hymns. They are often sung by a choir, which will take all the parts; whereas a hymn, if sung by a congregation, is usually given wholly in the soprano part, as a unison melody.

Chants and canticles form a part of various church services.

The canticles or other music in plain-song, or plain-chant, make use of the Gregorian modes.

In the time of the contrapuntal schools, music was almost entirely vocal. Counterpoint, in its simplest significance, means part-writing.

Among the contrapuntal forms used for voice, the motet was a sacred part-song. It has been derived from *motus*, or movement, and from *mot*, meaning the sacred Word.

The madrigal was the chief rival of the motet. The name has been derived from *madre*, meaning mother, and explained as designating a song in praise of the Virgin; but this definition is not final, since madrigals treated secular subjects also. In the madrigal, the melody, or *cantus*, was usually divided among the various parts, instead of being kept to one voice. A true madrigal was always sung without accompaniment. The term is often misapplied.

The chorales of Luther's time and later were very strong and rugged in character. They often contained suggestions of the harmonic style, and a more definite melodic structure than was common in their time.

But the most important vocal form of the contrapuntal period was the mass. The composers' fondness for masses, and their use of popular tunes in them, has been mentioned already. Masses are written by modern composers also; but these are usually less strictly contrapuntal than the older works.

The chief divisions of the mass are the Kyrie ("Lord, have mercy"); the Gloria (containing also the "Qui tollis," "Quoniam," and "Cum Sancto Spirito"); the Credo (having as subdivisions "Et incarnatus," "Et resurrexit," and "Amen"); the Sanctus; the Benedictus; the Agnus Dei; and the Dona nobis. The varying emotions of the Latin words used in these divisions enable composers to treat the form with due variety and contrast of style.

The Requiem mass is generally shorter. It omits the Gloria, and contains instead a "Requiem æternam," "Lux æterna," and "Dies iræ." The last division is a thirteenth-century poem describing the Day of Judgment.

The Stabat Mater is another mediæval Latin poem, depicting the sufferings of the Virgin Mary at the Cross.

Horatio Parker made an admirable setting of the early Latin poem entitled "Hora Novissima." This work is really an oratorio.

Shorter Latin poems that are often set include "Veni Creator," "O Salutaris," and "Ave Maria."

The oratorio is a large sacred work using Biblical text and treating the various phases of some Biblical subject or event. Such a work consists of solos, *ensembles* of more than one voice, choruses, and even instrumental interludes. Two styles of oratorio are used, being known as the epic and the dramatic. In the former the singers merely narrate the text in its vocal guise; but in the latter style, each singer represents a certain character. Handel's "Messiah" is epic, while his "Samson" is dramatic. Mendelssohn combined the two styles in his "Saint Paul" and "Elijah."

The Passion is an oratorio dealing with the martyrdom of Christ. The best example is the "Saint Matthew Passion," by Bach.

The cantata is a vocal work somewhat similar to the oratorio in general aspect, but treating a secular subject. Cantatas are usually shorter than oratorios, though not necessarily so; and they are generally less contrapuntal. Sacred cantatas exist, treating religious subjects in a brief or informal manner.

The traditions of Handel and Mendelssohn have made England the home of oratorio and cantata. In Germany the epic cantatas of Max Bruch, such as "Frithjof," "Odysseus," and "Arminius," deserve especial mention.

The English composer Granville Bantock has recently endeavored to found a new form, consisting of separate movements for voices alone. His "Atalanta in Calydon" divides the voices into several groups, and treats the various groups much as an orchestral work would treat its individual instrumental parts. The composition is in four sections, and the contrasts of style are much like those of the symphonic movements.

Strictly speaking, melodrama is not a vocal form. It is music set as an accompaniment to spoken words, and demands a reader instead of a singer. Schumann's melodrama passages in "Manfred" add excellent orchestral music to parts of Byron's poem; while the "Enoch Arden" of Richard Strauss places a striking piano accompaniment against Tennyson's words. The Bohemian composer Fibich has set an entire trilogy, "Hippodamia," in this fashion. Melodrama is one of the few forms that have not yet received the attention they deserve.

The Singspiel, with music either as a setting for the important parts of a drama or as a diversion in the unimportant parts, has been described already, in connection with early opera.

The opera itself is too free in style to be called a definite form; but the different schools of opera show various distinctive characteristics. Peri, and the Florentines who helped him, meant opera to be declamatory, with the music heightening the effect of the action. But opera grew away from that ideal, and by the time of Handel, it was practically a singing-concert, with a conventional thread of mythological plot. Mozart made opera fluent and life-like, but even before his time Gluck had revived the idea of having operatic music illustrate and echo the text. Gluck still kept the structure of separate operatic numbers. The Rossini school then caused public taste to welcome a revival of the singing-concert idea, this time with less musical worth than was shown in Handel's day. Wagner brought about another reversal of public taste; and his great music-dramas showed the world that music of a most advanced type could be made to support and intensify the text in wonderful fashion. Wagner was the first to discard the idea of separate numbers in opera, and cast his music in the form of a plastic whole instead of a set of loosely-joined parts. His continuous melodic recitative has been mentioned already. He was also the first to make prominent operatic use of *Leitmotiven*, or guiding motives. As stated in the chapter on Wagner, these short, impressive phrases, each one typical of some character or event, enable the composer to make his music remarkably suggestive, and sometimes actually tell a story in tones. More recent composers have not made such successful use of guiding motives; but they do not possess the genius which Wagner brought to the creation and use of these musical figures. Contemporary opera aims to be strongly dramatic, and usually employs the continuous style.

XL

THE CONTRAPUNTAL FORMS

WHEN the layman learns that counterpoint is simply part-writing, he takes the statement lightly. The student, however, who has been through a course in the heart-breaking rules that govern the leading of the parts, appreciates the fact that counterpoint is an important branch of music. The composer finds a knowledge of counterpoint almost indispensable; and the reader will remember that Schubert planned a thorough course in this branch just before his untimely death.

While composers in the harmonic style make use of counterpoint in a passing way, and allow suggestions of it to strengthen their works, there are also certain contrapuntal forms that are wholly independent of the harmonic style. Counterpoint is the science of combining melodies, instead of supporting a melody by chords.

Counterpoint is classified into five different varieties. In the first order, the different parts show note against note. In counterpoint of the second order, two (or sometimes three) notes of discant (accompanying part) are used for each one in the cantus firmus (fixed theme). The third order shows four notes against one. The fourth variety consists of syncopated counterpoint, in which each note of the discant begins when a note of the cantus is half done. The fifth variety, florid counterpoint, makes use of all the preceding kinds in a single composition.

Good examples of counterpoint as used in harmonic works may be found in the last part of the first section of the slow movement in Beethoven's Seventh Symphony, and also in the latter part of Wagner's "Tannhäuser" March, where fairly rapid and regular bass notes are used against the return of the first theme, in chords. Counterpoint of the third order is suggested by both examples.

When two voices, or parts, are written in counterpoint, it is possible for the composer to make them of such a nature that they can be transposed as a whole with reference to each other, and made to exchange positions. One part may be transposed an octave while the other stays in its original position; or the same result can be reached by having one part move up a fifth while the other is transposed down by a fourth; or one may move up and the other down an octave. Such an inversion of parts is called double counterpoint.

In the cases suggested, the change in relative position would always be in octaves; and the transposition is spoken of as double counterpoint at the octave. But other intervals may be used instead of the octave. Double counterpoint at the tenth is frequently found in the old works.

Double counterpoint may be accompanied by one or more free parts in other voices.

Triple counterpoint would consist of three parts inverted in any order. This is much harder to write than double counterpoint. Even higher orders than triple counterpoint may exist.

Imitation is often used in counterpoint. That consists of the employment of the same figure or figures in more than one part, at different times.

One part may be made to serve as its own accompaniment, by having the same material start in a second voice after it has already begun in the first. As stated earlier in this work, such a use of a theme or melody for its own accompaniment is called a canon. The second part usually begins one or two measures after the first has begun. The second part may start at any desired interval from the first, making a canon at that interval. If the parts begin an octave apart, a canon at the octave results. In Jadassohn's Pianoforte Album (Op. 32), are a number of canons, some of which are at the seventh, or other intervals. A canon at the unison may exist, the second part starting the theme on the same note with which it began. An example of such procedure is found in Marzials's duet in canon entitled "Friendship." In this the voices take the same melody, one voice beginning a measure later than the other. But if one voice is male and one female, the song becomes a canon at the octave.

The old puzzle canons were described in the chapter on the contrapuntal schools. The melody of a crab canon, it will be remembered, is accompanied by the same melody sung backwards. This canon was sometimes known as the canon *per recte et retro*. It may also be restated that the phrase "Out of light, darkness," or *vice versa*, meant that the white (hollow) notes of a melody were to be used in accompaniment as black (solid) notes, having a different time value, or *vice versa*.

The study of the contrapuntal forms is one that usually arouses the pupil's enthusiasm. Only a few illustrations and analyses can be given here; but by the understanding of these the student should be enabled to continue by himself, and analyze all the music that he studies.

If the student will look at the second of Bach's Fifteen Two-Part Inventions, he will find examples of various points mentioned in the foregoing paragraphs. In the first place, the ten opening measures form a canon. The lower voice uses the same material as the upper voice does, at an interval of an octave downward. By having the lower voice start two measures after the upper one, a canon is made in which the lower voice uses eight measures of the material found in the upper voice. Then there is a change. One part moves down an eleventh, and the other up a fifth, making double counterpoint at the octave (really the double octave). The material is then started by the lower part, while now it is the upper part that enters two measures later with the canonic accompaniment, after filling in free material for these two measures. When the second canon ends, two measures of modulatory character are found, with the lower part in the first one becoming the upper part in the second. The next four measures show similar contrapuntal changes; and after them the piece closes.

An inspection of other Inventions in the set will show that such pieces are not all cast in the same mould. The Invention may be defined as a short contrapuntal piece, somewhat in the informal style of an improvisation, but always aimed to show ingenuity.

Most varied and interesting of all the contrapuntal forms is the fugue. The name comes from the Latin word *fuga*, meaning a flight; and different voices take up the fugal themes successively, in a manner that makes the term appropriate enough. The fugue is built up from one or two thematic ideas, which are woven and interwoven into an intricate and beautiful tonal design.

The fugue consists of material of three sorts, — exposition, strettos, and episodes. The exposition comes first, after which strettos and episodes alternate with one another.

The exposition consists of the introduction of the theme chosen for the fugue in all the different voices used. The theme enters at first in one voice, and is known as the subject. After that a second voice takes up the theme, transposed a fifth upward or a fourth downward. In this transposed position, the theme is known as the answer. Meanwhile the first voice goes on, very often using a second theme known as the countersubject. After this a third voice takes the theme, now on some octave from its original pitch, and known again as the subject. Meanwhile the second voice, having finished the answer, takes up the countersubject in a transposed position; while the first voice, having finished the countersubject, becomes a free part for the time being. This procedure is continued until subject or answer has appeared in all the voices, and the countersubject in all but one. The odd-numbered appearances of the theme are always subject, and always begin on the same scale-degree; while the even-numbered appearances are always the answer, and always start on the fifth scale-degree (or some octave of it) from that on which the subject begins. The word theme is not used in connection with the fugue, — at least not in America; but it is employed here for convenience in explanation. The countersubject, it may be stated, is sometimes shorter than the subject.

A schedule is given below, showing the manner in which the parts are employed in one arrangement of the exposition in a four-voiced fugue. In this arrangement the voices start from the lowest part upward.

				Answer
Soprano	. . . . . .	. . . .	Subject	Countersubject
Alto	. . . . . .	. . . .	Countersubject	Free part
Tenor	. . . . . .	Answer	Free part	Free part
Bass	Subject	Countersubject		

There are several other successions in which the voices may enter with good effect. The most usual of these, in addition to the one given, are alto-tenor-bass-soprano and soprano-alto-tenor-bass. A fugue may have any moderate number of voices, four being most usual. Sometimes it has only two; while Bach, in his "Art of Fugue," composed one with six voices.

Episodes are passages in free style. They may be wholly independent, but very often their material is derived from the subject, or countersubject, or both.

Strettos are canons made by the appearance of subject or answer in different voices, starting at different times. Such canons may occasionally use the theme in more than two voices, thus making a canon of more than two parts. At the end of the fifth fugue in volume II of the "Well-tempered Clavichord" there is a stretto which runs through four voices.

Other treatments of subject and answer are called repercussions.

The exposition leads into a first episode, which ends in a passing cadence. After this the first stretto appears. Then come other episodes, followed in each case by other strettos, until finally the fugue ends with what is called the coda-episode. In a strict fugue, the number of strettos and episodes is arranged by rule, and their keys determined in the same way. There may be also a counter-exposition, giving answer and subject in a reversed succession of voices, just after the first episode.

Fugues may be classified in a number of ways: —

1. A fugue is known by the number of voices that it uses; as, for instance, a four-voiced fugue, a three-voiced fugue, etc.

2. A fugue may have more than one subject, a single fugue having one, a double fugue two in succession, etc.

3. When the answer uses exactly the same intervals as the subject, the fugue is called a real fugue; but if the intervals are at all altered in the answer, to keep it in the key, or "tone," the fugue is known as a tonal fugue.

4. Fugues may sometimes be classed by the scales they use; as diatonic fugues, without accidentals; chromatic fugues, with a subject wholly chromatic; or even fugues named after one of the Gregorian tones when such a scale is employed.

5. Fugues are classified also by any treatment given to the answer. This may be augmented, inverted, or otherwise changed, giving rise to augmented, inverted, or other fugues.

6. Fugues are classed as strict or free, according to whether they do or do not follow the key-schedule and number of strettos and episodes prescribed by the rules for a strict fugue. These rules are seldom respected now, but they may be found in the text-books on fugal composition.

A free fugue is by no means necessarily simpler than a strict one. The fugues in the "Well-tempered Clavichord" are very free for the most part; but at the same time they show the greatest originality, and the most marked contrapuntal skill. In some of them the countersubject is worked up along with the subject; in others there is no real countersubject; while still others are composed of double or triple counterpoint instead of strettos and episodes. But every one of them is almost wholly derived by contrapuntal transformations of the material in its exposition.

A fughetta is a very short fugue, consisting of an exposition and a few episodes.

A fugato passage is a passage that suggests fugal treatment.

For a clear example of fugue, the reader may look at no. 7 in volume II of the "Well-tempered Clavichord." It is found to be a four-voiced fugue, with a single subject; it is a tonal fugue, because the answer deviates once from the intervals of the subject; it is not an augmented, inverted, or otherwise altered fugue; and lastly, it is a free fugue.

The parts enter from the lowest upward. The subject lasts for six bars, and ends on the first note of the next bar, the answer beginning while this final note of the subject is sounded. The answer starts with a fourth instead of a fifth, but follows the subject in all its later intervals. In spite of a similarity in the accompaniment to the subject or answer, there is no real countersubject. The answer does not overlap when it ends, and there is even a brief interlude, in measure 13, before the subject enters in the alto voice. The same interlude recurs before the soprano voice enters with the answer. When the exposition ends, on the first beat of bar 25, the first episode continues it to a cadence three measures later. There is no pause at this cadence, however; and in bar 28 the tenor voice starts the answer, with its first note shortened so that it fills only the last half of the measure. In bar 29 the subject enters in the bass part, making a stretto. In bar 31 the upper two voices stop, giving this stretto full prominence. In measure 35, the alto starts the answer, while the soprano begins the subject in the next measure, forming another stretto. From bar 42 onward an episode is found, fairly free in shape, but conforming to the general style of the preceding work. In bar 51 the subject reappears in a repercussion, taken by the tenor voice in the subdominant key. After this, in bar 57, the answer begins in the soprano; while the subject, entering in the bass part in the next measure, forms another stretto. This stretto is the final one; and it is made majestically prominent by the use of the two outside voices, while the two middle voices add strength by their accompaniment. The subject ends on the first beat of bar 64, and the coda-episode then closes the work. Thus this fugue is chiefly made of three complete canons.

Sometimes a climax is brought about, near the end of a fugue, by the use of what is known as an organ point, or pedal point. This is a long-sustained note in the bass, over which the other parts proceed continuously.

In fugue no. 5 of the above-mentioned volume a different structure is found. This is a four-voiced, single, and free fugue; but examination shows that it is real instead of tonal. The subject consists of the first nine notes, and ends on the first half of the third beat in the second measure. The exposition is consequently very short, and the fugue is found to consist chiefly of strettos and episodes. Strettos will be found in bars 14, 21 (three voices), 27, 33, and 44. The episodes, it will be noted, are made up chiefly of the subject material. Sometimes the subject or answer appears in a single part during these episodes; but more often they are built largely or wholly of a figure taken directly from the last four notes of the subject. The student will find it an interesting exercise to mark with pencil every appearance of this figure.

The final stretto of this fugue has been cited already as going through all four voices; but it merits still closer attention. Examination will show that the theme enters successively in the soprano, alto, tenor, and bass voices; that the time-interval between one appearance and the next is always the same; and that the scale-degree difference between one appearance and the next is also kept the same. The scale-interval between successive appearances of the theme is always a third, though an extra octave is added between the alto and tenor parts. Such a stretto, in which the time-intervals and the scale-degree differences are kept equal while the theme appears in all voices in succession, is called a *stretto maestrale*, or masterly stretto. In the example cited, it occupies less than three measures; and this will serve to illustrate the fact that a seemingly simple contrapuntal passage may show the most varied and intricate beauty to those who have learned to appreciate it. The clean-cut musical logic of the fugue is well worth understanding; and whoever learns to follow it will soon come under its spell.

With the aid of these chapters on musical form, the student should be enabled to do his own analysis in all but the most exceptional cases. He will also notice a newer and deeper charm in music, and a far more interesting structural design than the outsider can possibly suspect. He will see balance and variety in the song-forms; symmetry and well-judged contrast in the rondos; strong thematic effects and great climaxes of development in the sonatas; and tonal designs and derivations of the most amazing skill in contrapuntal pieces. With this knowledge, he will find the beauty of good music enhanced a hundred-fold.

PART IV
THE INSTRUMENTS

XLI

THE PIANO AND ITS PREDECESSORS

THE old Assyrian relics show pictures of the instrument that ultimately became our piano. It was a very primitive form of stringed instrument, with the strings running over a flat support. When such an instrument was hung about the neck and played with a quill, it was called a psaltery; and under this title it became popular in mediæval as well as ancient times. Similar to the psaltery, but played by striking the strings with a hammer, was the Arabian dulcimer. This instrument, with a compass of four octaves, two below and two above middle C, undoubtedly attracted the attention of pilgrims and crusaders, who brought it back with them to Europe. There it received the German name of Hackbrett, or chopping-board, from the hammering motion needed to play it; while the psaltery became the Schweinskopf, or pig's head, from its shape.

Perhaps the earliest application of keys to an instrument came in the shape of the light clavicytherium, in which the strings of the kithara were set in motion by quills on the keys. Little is known about the actual origin of keyed instruments; but by the end of the fifteenth century there were two main kinds in existence. One family consisted of the spinet type, which applied the psaltery principle of plucking the strings. The other variety, represented only by the clavichord, was more like the dulcimer. But where the dulcimer hammer made the strings vibrate through their whole length, just as the piano hammer does to-day, the clavichord key had what is known as a tangent, or tongue, which pressed directly against the string and stayed there, forming one end of the vibrating part. The clavichord tone, formed by the stroke of the tangent at one end of the part that would vibrate, was necessarily soft. By alternating light and heavy pressure on the key, the performer could make the tangent loosen or tighten the string. This recurrent alteration of the tension produced the vibrato effect of the violin, by slight pitch variations, but gave in addition a varying power of tone, greatest when the string was tightest. This tremolo effect (Bebung) made the clavichord very expressive. Beethoven tried to imitate it on the piano by alternately pressing and releasing the soft pedal; but he did not succeed. The clavichord tone, though soft, is of an infinitely appealing sweetness.

In the spinet-harpsichord type, the keys were provided with quills, or jacks, which plucked the string in passing as each key was played. The jacks were sometimes made of leather instead of quill.

The smallest instrument of this type was known as the octavina, and consisted of a single octave of keys in a small box. The virginals, which wholly superseded the older clavicytherium, was still box-like in shape, but had four octaves. It could give music of some worth; and the English virginal school of composers, who flourished in and after the Elizabethan age, wrote pieces of astonishing breadth and value for this little instrument. The name virginals came from the fact that the instrument was a favorite with young girls. As the quill passed over its string to pluck it, a scraping noise was usually audible; and this made the historian Burney describe the tone as "a scratch with a sound at the end of it."

The name spinet is derived either from *spina*, a thorn, in suggestion of the pointed quills, or from Spinetti, a Venetian maker. The spinet was sometimes square, but more often harp-shaped, like our grand pianos. While the virginals was a mere box set on a table, the spinet had legs of its own. Its longer strings gave a fuller tone, though still somewhat light.

The early harpsichords had a compass of less than five octaves. But the instrument grew, until we find such makers as the Ruckers or Taskin producing harpsichords with two large keyboards and half-a-dozen pedals. The double harpsichord had two strings (and two quills) for each tone. The second keyboard had jacks of different material from the first, to obtain a different tone-quality. The various pedals could make one quill effective instead of two, or couple the two manuals together, or cause the sounding of any note with the octave above or below. Thus the harpsichord had a great variety of effects, and was a worthy instrument, even though its tone was somewhat tin-panny.

There was an upright spinet called the clavicytherium, which must not be confused with the earlier instrument of that name.

The piano (German, *clavier;* French, *pianoforte;* Italian, *pianoforte*) differs from all these instruments in going back to the hammer idea used in the dulcimer. Such a hammer-action was first brought out by the Italian Cristofori, at Padua in 1711. Similar inventions were claimed by the Frenchman Marius, the German Schroeter, and the Englishman Wood; but Cristofori deserves the real credit.

The early pianos had two strings to a note where ours have three. As a result of this, the old term calling for soft pedal was *una corda,* or one string, the other being thrown out of action by the soft pedal. Now we should say *due corde,* as two strings are left in action when the soft pedal takes one out. On the old pianos, *due corde* signified a release of the soft pedal. At present this is called for by the words *tre corde.*

The piano did not at once displace the older instruments. This was especially true of the clavichord, on which the soft, tender tones were wholly different from the piano quality. Bach kept to the clavichord, while the harpsichord continued to hold its own even in Mozart's time. It was Beethoven who turned the scale definitely in favor of the piano; for his broad and massive effects were too strong for the harpsichord.

The piano of to-day may be grand, square, or upright in shape, though the square pianos are not now manufactured. The upper notes have three strings to a tone, the lowest notes having one and some other low notes two. The deepest strings are wound with copper wire, to make them heavy enough to be strung tightly without getting too high a pitch. The tension increases as the pitch of the strings rises. To hold all this pull, modern pianos are provided with metal frames. One end of each wire is fastened around a pin, which may be turned by a "piano-hammer," causing a tightening or loosening of the (wire) strings. The other end of each string goes over a bridge that rests upon the sounding-board, which is of spruce front and maple back. When a piano key is played, it works as a lever, and throws up a felt-covered hammer against the strings. There is a complicated "action" governing the hammer, which allows it to fall back a little after it hits the strings. When the key is played, it also raises off the strings a felt damper, so that the hammer stroke causes free vibrations. When the key is released, this damper drops back upon the strings and stops the tone. The key itself moves in a way governed by oval pins that extend into felt-lined cavities on its under side.

The damper pedal of the piano, often miscalled the loud pedal, operates by moving all the dampers up off the strings. The highest notes have no dampers, as their tones are made short by the extreme tightness of the wires. But all except these have dampers. When the dampers are lifted off the strings, the tones will not only last until they die away of themselves, but will make some of the other strings vibrate in sympathy with them. Low notes will last longer than high ones when the damper pedal is used.

The soft pedal operates in different ways, according to the style of piano used. In grand pianos, it shifts the action to one side, so that the hammers strike only two strings out of three. In upright pianos, it usually moves the hammers so near to the wires that their stroke lacks the power obtained by a long swing. In the square piano, the soft pedal sometimes muffles the tone by making tongues of soft leather or felt come between the hammer and the strings. In all cases the object is to soften the tone.

Some pianos have a sostenuto pedal, which will hold notes only if it is put into use after they have been played. The performer may thus strike a note or chord that he wishes to sustain, and then put down the sostenuto pedal, after which the tone will last, even though he releases the keys and uses his hands elsewhere.

Other instruments have bass damper pedals, which will sustain all the lower tones of the piano, but none of the higher ones.

It will be seen from the mechanism of the piano that after a note has been played, and the hammer has dropped back from the strings, the player can in no way influence the quality of the tone. Yet it is not unusual for great artists to be seen wiggling their fingers on the key, as if they expected in some mysterious way to make the tone expressive by such procedure. There are differences in the quality of tones, but these are caused by the varying degrees of strength with which the key is struck in the first place.

There are at present two main methods of piano practice, — that of finger-strength, represented by Leschetizky, and that of weight, represented by Breithaupt. There is little doubt of the correctness of the finger-strength method. Those who study by it are easily able to help their performance by weight of hand and arm; but those who neglect to develop their fingers sufficiently will never do great work. The weight school, however, is not without its finger exercises.

The good pianist is known by his all-round musicianship. He does not merely depend on the technique necessary to dazzle an audience, but he shows also an expressive power that is properly used in the interpretation of great works. If he is lacking in the expressive qualities, and depends too much on technique and mechanical ability, he is called a virtuoso. In so far as it means lack of expressive power, the term is a reproach; but some pianists have sufficient musicianly feeling, and are called virtuosos only because they have such remarkable technique that it attracts more notice than the other qualities.

The technical points for an auditor to look for in piano playing may be easily enumerated. They have to do with finger dexterity, or with the use of the wrist, forearm, or upper arm and shoulder.

The finger-skill is by far the most noticeable point in a good pianist's work. If his rapid passages, trills, and other embellishments are clear, even, and well controlled as well as fast, then he has mastered the technical side of his art. If the pianist's hands are visible, it may be of interest to see how he holds his fingers. Most performers incline rather to the flat than to the high-arched finger position, though the artist will vary his hand-position for different effects. The skill with which a pianist makes rapid skips of some length is another point worth watching. This will involve control of hand and forearm as well as fingers.

Octave passages are played by a rapid fluttering swing of the wrist, which is guided by the forearm. Clearness and rapidity in these is made a special point of practice. The same procedure may be used in playing light, rapid chords. For heavy chords, however, the full-arm stroke is used. The weight-players make it a point to have the knuckles well bent to take the weight of an arm stroke; but this is a natural position, which the players of the finger-school adopt of themselves.

Technique is properly used as a means to the end of artistic expression. In the matter of power, every great pianist is more than sufficiently equipped. In other words, he is able to pound the piano so forcibly that even the best instrument will give forth only a blur of noise. The artistic effects are obtained by control and variation of power, not by abuse of it.

The same is true of speed. The pianist does not usually play a piece as fast as he can, but takes the pace suited to the work, and gives it expression by changes of speed as well as of power. By using the proper accelerations and retards, and the most effective changes of pace, as well as proper accents and balance of force, the pianist may bring much out of a piece, and make it notably expressive. The hearer may always ask himself questions on these points. Does the performer make the right contrasts of speed and power, or are they minimized or exaggerated too much? Does he bring out the melody and form of a piece properly? Or is it over-emphasized, or left obscure? Variations in power, variations in speed, and the proper use of control and contrast, are what the hearer must train himself to notice and estimate. He will then be able to tell whether a performance is quiet or passionate, repressed or exaggerated, well-balanced or eccentric. He can also tell whether the pianist is striving to interpret a piece logically, or trying to display his own powers at the expense of the composer's meaning. The use or abuse of the pedal is another point worthy of attention.

The nature of the piece played is often a guide, as different schools of piano music require different treatment. Thus the early sonatas of Scarlatti, and the music of Couperin, Rameau, and others of their sort, demand a light ease of control and more than usual directness in style. The Mozart pieces admit of more expression, though still direct and straightforward. With Beethoven's great sonatas the dramatic element plays a more prominent part. In connection with these there has been much discussion over the fitness or unfitness of rubato. That is a change of pace within the measure or phrase, a prolonging of certain notes at the expense of others for the sake of expression. Paderewski claims that Beethoven's works should have rubato; but the young pianist will do well to use it in very moderate quantities. Modern works of the Liszt type may be given the fullest degree of dramatic expression.

Works of contrapuntal character demand a special treatment of their own. They are based on a system of part-writing, in which each part, or voice, has its own importance. In harmonic (homophonic) music, there is one chief melody, supported by an accompaniment of chords. In strict counterpoint, such as is found in the fugue, each voice has its own melodic line, and the voices blend with each other, like colored strands twisted to form a variegated rope. There are many pieces that come between the two extremes, and have some contrapuntal (polyphonic, or many-voiced) effects while being mostly harmonic in style, or *vice versa*.

In polyphonic music, such as the fugues of Bach, Mendelssohn, and others, the pianist must bring out each part. Instead of having a single melody to be made prominent against a background of chords and harmonies, he now has several melodies, which must be balanced against each other in such a way that the important parts of all are brought out. This is hard work, and its success marks the true musician.

But in spite of general rules, there is still much latitude in the rendering of a piece. We may, therefore, judge the pianist by his own individual work. If he plays with control and variety of speed and power, brings out his themes expressively without "tearing them to tatters," and balances section against section, or voice against voice, in proper fashion, expressing the very best effects of which a piece is capable, then we may feel sure that he is a great artist.[1]

The use of electricity to vibrate wires has been embodied in an instrument known as the choralcelo. This looks like a double upright piano. Electric magnets, controlled by properly interrupted currents, attract and release the wires, thus making them vibrate at the desired rates. The result is a very pure and pleasing tone quality, of flute-like or organ-like character. The choralcelo has also an ordinary piano action, which may be used by itself or in combination with the electrically produced tones. Recent improvements in the instrument include the use of bars, plates, and chains of various sizes, which give many pleasing tone-colors.

---

[1] For an estimate of the work of certain players, see the chapter "Some Famous Pianists," in this work.

XLII

THE ORGAN

THE organ (German, *Orgel;* French, *orgue;* Italian, *organo*) has been called the king of instruments; but if the title is correct, it has had a much longer reign than usually falls to the lot of royalty.

"The just designs of Greece," which the poet Collins seemed to think superior to "Cecilia's mingled world of sound," had no place for the organ, unless we accept as a primitive organ the syrinx, or set of Pan-pipes. That the organ sometimes took such a small form is shown by the regals of Monteverde's seventeenth-century orchestra, which was a tiny portable organ somewhat resembling the syrinx. The larger stationary organ of Monteverde's day was known as the positive; and this term is still kept to describe the choir organ in France and Germany.

Rome had a somewhat mysterious water-organ, worked by hydraulic pressure. Its construction is not now known, in spite of references to it by Vitruvius and others.

The Eastern Empire kept the organ, though with human instead of hydraulic motor power. In the eighth century, the Byzantine Emperor sent an organ as a present to King Pepin of France. These early organs were noisy affairs, without the selective power that comes with the use of stops; and when a note was played, all the pipes of that pitch gave their tone together. It is on record that a lady at Charlemagne's court was driven crazy by hearing the organ unexpectedly for the first time. A century or more later, the organ at Winchester, England, was described by the monk Wulstan as having "a noise like thunder."

The idea of stops grew up gradually in the middle ages. Stops depend on the simple principle of having two operations necessary, instead of one, to let the air into an organ pipe. Pressing down a key must be preceded by a drawing out, or other adjustment, of the stop. Each stop operates a bar, known as a slider, which keeps its set of pipes closed until certain holes in the slider are brought directly under the corresponding pipe openings. After one or more sets of pipes are prepared for use by the stop-adjustment, the pressing down of a key will sound only the pipe of the desired pitch in each set that has been prepared for use by the stops. While the key is intended to let air into all pipes of a given pitch, the stops admit the air only to those pipes where its action is desired, and exclude the air from all other pipes controlled by the key.

From the sixteenth century onward, the organ has grown continually in size. The small forms, with pipe-ranks parallel to the keys and just behind them, were developed into larger sizes, in which some of the pipes were set off at a distance, and controlled from a roller-board that operated with strings or wires. The mechanical organ developed first, but now there are pneumatic and electric organs also.

The mechanical organ is operated by systems of rods and levers. Pressing down the key pushes up a "sticker," or push-rod; this works a lever, or "back-fall"; the back-fall, either directly or by means of the roller-board, pulls down a "tracker," or pull-rod under the pipe to be used; the tracker, in its turn, drags with it a "pull-down," or wire that passes up into the wind-chest; and lastly, this pull-down moves a "pallet," or valve, the motion of the pallet opening the pipe and letting the air rush into it to make it sound.

In the pneumatic organs, each key is provided with an air-tube extending to the wind-chest. This tube contains air under pressure when not in use. When the key is played, some air is released from the tube. The pallet is so arranged and connected that when the air pressure in the tube is lowered, an opposing air-pressure over-balances it, and forces the pallet to open.

In electric organs, each key is provided with wires. When the key is played, an electric contact is formed, and the current causes a release in the wind-chest, that allows the pallet to open. The electric organs thus resemble the pneumatic ones, except that the long part of the air-tube outside the wind-chest is here replaced by wire, and the release effected by the key electrically instead of pneumatically.

The largest organs have five different keyboards, known (from the lowest up) as the great, swell, choir, solo, and echo organs. There is a pedal board also, played by the feet. Each manual (keyboard), and the pedal board too, has a number of different sets of pipes connected to it, each set shown by a stop. Organ pipes come in various sizes. In the first place, any set of pipes must range from large to small to give the scale, halving the length always giving an octave higher, and so on. But on the organ a set is also designated by the length of pipe connected with the key known as great C, two octaves below the middle C of the piano. An open pipe about eight feet long will give this note. Any series of pipes sounding the pitch of the note played is called, from this, an eight-foot series; and tones that sound the pitch of the key played are called eight-foot tones. This is thus a designation for those pipes that sound the pitch of the key played, even though the pipes above great C are shorter than eight feet, and those sounding below it are longer. The other figures used to designate sets of organ pipes enable us to compare them with the eight-foot sets, or stops. Thus a sixteen-foot stop is one whose pipes may be twice as large, for the same pitch, as those of an eight-foot set; at any rate, the sixteen-foot set must sound an octave deeper, for any given key, than the eight-foot set. There are thirty-two-foot sets of pipes, that sound an octave deeper yet for a given key. It will thus be seen that one key on the organ, unlike one on the piano, may give several different tones. The eight-foot stops are called foundations, and the sixteen-foot stops doubles, while stops smaller than eight feet are known as mutations. Of these smaller stops, the four-foot sounds an octave above the key played, and the two-foot two octaves above it. The interval of a fifth is used also, a stop of five and a third feet giving a fifth above the foundations, while one of two and two thirds feet gives an octave and a fifth (the twelfth) above the foundations. There are also stops of ten and two thirds feet, giving the fifth above the doubles; but these are used chiefly for the pedals. Sets of two or three ranks of very small pipes, sounding together, are called furniture or mixture. They are used in combination with heavy tones, to brighten them. The doubles and foundations are often played together, with enough mutation and mixture to get the desired effect. The fifth is never used alone, but is combined with other stops to brighten them.

It will be seen on reflection that a single large organ will have a great number of pipes. Each of the five manuals, as well as the pedals, will have many stops; and each stop represents a set of pipes usually containing one for each key. The organ at the town building in Sydney, like the still larger one recently erected at Liverpool, has about ten thousand pipes.

Pipes may be open or closed, the latter being stopped at one end and sounding an octave deeper than open pipes of the same length. Pipes may be wide or narrow in proportion to their length, the narrow ones giving the more brilliant tone. Pipes may be made of wood or of metal. Finally, they may be provided with reed mouthpieces, or simply have air-openings instead, being known as flue-pipes. The organ builder combines all these possibilities so as to produce the maximum variety in tone-color. Incidentally, his instrument has to be "voiced" to the church or hall where it is set up. This consists in trying out all the tones, and making them even wherever necessary. If this were not done, certain pipes in a rank, or stop, which are reënforced when their wave-length happens to fit the building, would sound too loud.

Stainer, in his book on the organ, gives a classification of the stops that is quoted here for reference. His table is still useful, though descriptions of other stops may be found in the works of Hopkins and Rimbault, or Audsley.

MANUAL FLUE STOPS

16-ft.
- Double stopped diapason or bourdon...Soft and sweet.
- Double gamba or contra gamba.......Reedy, generally soft.
- Double (open) diapason metal.........Full rich tone.

8-ft.
- Stopped diapason.
- Lieblich gedackt.
- Clarinet flute.
- Rohrflöte. ....Soft and sweet.
- Hohlflöte.
- Harmonic flute. ....Sweet, but fuller-toned.
- Salicional or salicet.
- Dulciana.
- Keraulophon. ....Soft and reedy.
- Gamba or viol da gamba.............Very reedy.
- Gemshorn.
- Spitzflöte.
- Viol d'amour. ....Thin and delicate.
- Small open diapason.................More powerful.
- Large open diapason...............Full and rich.
- Bell diapason...................
- Flute à pavillon..................Very rich, full, and very reedy.
- Gamba (full-toned) or bell gamba....

4-ft.
- Flute.
- Waldflöte.
- Flute d'amour. ....Sweet and bright.
- Salicet flute.
- Gemshorn.
- Geigenprincipal. ....Reedy and very bright.
- Spitzflöte.
- Principal or octave.................Full-toned.

2-ft.
- Piccolo.
- Flageolet. } ....Very bright, but "fluty."
- Spitzflöte. }
- Gemshorn. } ....:....Very bright, almost shrill.
- Fifteenth or super-octave............Bright and full-toned.

5⅓-ft. Quint, full-tone; adds breadth and dignity in combination.

2⅔-ft. Twelfth, full-tone; adds richness in combination.

Compound
- Echo cornet.......................Soft in combination.
- Sesquialtera.......................Adds fullness.
- Furniture........................... "   "
- Mixture........................... "   brilliancy.
- Sharp mixture..................... "   "

MANUAL REED STOPS

16-ft.
- Tenoroon or contra oboe. }
- Double bassoon. } .... { Soft and rich; generally on the swell organ.
- Double trumpet. }
- Trombone. } ....Full-toned and rich.
- Contra posaune. }

8-ft.
- Oboe (orchestral). }
- Clarinet. }
- Corno di bassetto. } .... { Of special quality of tone; generally used independently as solo stops.
- Cor Anglais. }
- Vox humana. }
- Hautboy, soft and sweet; used on Swell as foundation stop.
- Horn. }
- Cornopean. } ....Full and rich on swell.
- Trumpet. }
- Posaune. }
- Tromba. } ....Loud and rich.
- Harmonic trumpet. } .... { Very loud and brilliant on high wind pressure.
- Tuba mirabilis. }

4-ft.
- Octave hautboy....................Bright.
- Clarion..........................Very bright.

PEDAL FLUE STOPS

32-ft.
- Sub-bass, double stopped diapason, or contra bourdon. Very soft, little used except in combination.
- Double diapason. Rich and full, lowest notes used in combination.

16-ft.
- Bourdon (16-ft. tone. }
- Violone. } ....Soft and most useful.
- Open diapason......................Full and heavy.

8-ft.
- Stopped flute (8-ft.) }
- Violoncello. } .... { Sweet and soft; generally useful.
- Principal or octave .... { Full-toned; most useful to strengthen bass.

4-ft. Fifteenth or super-octave............Adds brightness.

10⅔-ft. Quint, produces a very heavy tone in combination.

5⅓-ft. Twelfth............................Adds brightness.

PEDAL REED STOPS

32-ft.
- Contra fagotto .... { Soft, but useful only in combination.
- Contra posaune. }
- Contre bombarde. } .... { Most useful addition to full power.

16-ft.	Fagotto or bassoon.................	Soft and frequently useful.
	Trombone. ⎱	Add weight to a forte combina-
	Posaune. ⎰	tion.
	Bombard. ⎱	
	Ophicleide. ⎰	Of great power and grandeur.
8-ft.	Bassoon.........................	Soft and useful.
	Clarion or trumpet...............	Gives brilliancy to a forte com-
		bination.
4-ft.	Octave clarion......................	Adds brilliancy.

The compound stops vary a good deal on different organs, but
they are always used for the same purpose, — to reënforce the
higher overtones of a note when brilliancy is desired. The tremu-
lant is a device, used with certain pipes, which interrupts the wind
flow at regular intervals of time. Another sort of tremolo is obtained by having two ranks of salicional (salcional) or dulciana
pipes, one rank being slightly flatter than the other; in which case
the vibrations of the two ranks will coïncide a certain number of
times per minute, causing a beat, or increase in tone volume, each
time they coincide. Such combinations of ranks are given new
names, like vox angelica, unda maris, etc.

The pipes of the swell organ are enclosed in a box, with shutters.
These may be partly opened by pressing a pedal, so that the player
can cause swells and subsidences as he opens or closes the box.
Sometimes other pipes than those joined to the swell manual are
given a second swell box.

But the chief variations in power come from the performer's use
of different stops, which are not all equally strong. The art of using
the proper stops is known as registration. At times the composer
marks his registration pretty fully, but often it is left to the deci-
sion of the performer. The latter is sometimes hard put to it to
change the stops without interrupting the flow of a piece. To aid
him in this, modern organs are often supplied with combination
pistons, so arranged that the player can group several stops together under the control of one piston.

Experience is the best guide for the combination of stops, for the
reason that different organs may differ greatly in effect. But there
are certain main principles of combination that are given in the
organ handbooks. Thus the softer bourdons and diapasons, perhaps stopped, form the basis of soft notes, with some smooth stop
added to make them blend well. These will be mostly eight-foot

tones on the manuals, and sixteen-foot on the pedals. An open diapason increases the tone, while the addition of other eight-foot and four-foot stops brings fair power. For loud notes, the doubles are used to add the lower octave, while still more foundations, mutations, and mixtures are thrown in.

The auditor, then, will look most of all for quality of tone when hearing the instrument. If he can see the player manipulate the stops, so much the better; but he can hear changes of any importance in the tone. He will find himself able, with very few trials, to tell whether the deep sixteen-foot stops are present or absent; and he may even learn to detect the presence and probable amount of mutation stops. There are not many special points of finger-technique for him to watch; the performer's touch must simply be clear enough, and quick enough, to get a clean-cut entrance of the wind into the pipes; while he plays the pedals with a heel-and-toe movement that does not challenge attention. But if the player handles his registration properly, he will give broad effects and build up grand climaxes that fully justify the organ's claim to a regal title.

XLIII

THE human voice (German, *Stimme;* French, *voix;* Italian, *voce*) is an instrument of the same type as the oboe or bassoon. These instruments have what is known as a double-reed mouthpiece; and in similar fashion the throat is provided with two membranes called the vocal cords, which swing toward and away from each other when producing a tone, and let out successive air-puffs of the requisite number per second for the pitch of the note sung.

The lungs and the muscles controlling them supply the necessary air. When we breathe with an open throat, the air current is exhaled without impediment. But when the vocal cords are in action, closing the throat except for the release of air-puffs, the muscles controlling the lungs may be in definite action, forcing the air out if a tone of any volume is to be obtained.

The muscles governing the lungs act in three ways. The diaphragm, a broad flat-arched muscle at the base of the lungs, contracts downward to inhale air, and relaxes upward to let the air be exhaled, or even pushes upward in making a tone. The rib-muscles may expand the lungs by enlarging the chest circumference. Still another sort of inhalation may be made by lifting the chest and elongating the lungs upward by means of the shoulders. There is a great deal of discussion as to what is the best method of breathing for singers; but many of them are now agreed that an enlargement of the lower ribs, helped by a slight back-expansion and raising of the shoulder-blades, is the proper method of inhalation. The student may train his back in breathing by inhaling in a sitting position, leaning forward until the face almost touches the knees. After the inhalation, the burden of action in tone-producing is shifted to the diaphragm, which controls the tone best during exhalation. Breathing by the diaphragm is the most wholesome procedure in ordinary life; but the singer must train for special results.

The larynx, which may be felt as the Adam's-apple, is the

apparatus at the top of the wind-pipe (trachea) that acts as vibrating mouthpiece in producing a tone. The larynx consists of several cartilages, united by muscles and covered by membranes, the whole being suspended from the hyoid, or tongue, bone.

Lowest of all is the cricoid cartilage, named from the Greek to show its resemblance to a signet-ring. This is joined to the top of the windpipe by a circular ligament. The widest (highest) part is in the back.

The thyroid cartilage is much larger. It rests on top of the cricoid, and forms the main part of the Adam's-apple. It is not a complete ring, but is shaped much like two square shields facing diagonally forward. The back ends are joined by the thyro-hyoid membrane. From the back ends rise rod-like projections connecting the cartilage to the hyoid bone. At the upper front part of this cartilage is the flexible tongue known as the epiglottis. When we swallow food, the epiglottis bends back to let the food pass over it, across the top of the larynx, to the gullet, or œsophagus, which is behind the windpipe.

On top of the high back part of the cricoid cartilage are two little hillocks known as the arytenoid cartilages. On top of these are the two very small Santorini cartilages, and beside the arytenoids are the two tiny Wrisberg cartilages.

The vocal cords are membranes, one on each side of the larynx, looking not unlike the halves of a drum membrane, with an open slit or passage, called the glottis, extending from front to back. When the cords are loose, this slit is more like a round hole. The front end of the cords is attached to the thyroid cartilage, and the back ends are united to the arytenoid cartilages, one to each. When the cords are tightened by the muscles governing the cartilages, the slit becomes narrow enough to make the air escape in the intermittent puffs needed to produce a tone. The cords are smooth membranes of grayish-white color, though inflammation may make them red or cover them with lumpy nodules.

Above the vocal cords are two so-called false vocal cords, and between the two pairs are recesses known as the Morgagni pockets. The use of the false cords and pockets is not clearly understood. Some think they direct the tone upward through the throat. Others believe that they make the tone-quality soft and rich. Still others think that the false cords actually take part in tone-production, and replace the real ones when the latter are out of condition. The false cords are red folds of the mucous membrane, and secrete enough moisture to keep the true cords from getting dry and hard.

The cavity above the larynx, formed by the nose and mouth coming together, is known as the pharynx. The cavities of the nose and mouth act as resonating chambers. The shape of the mouth is subject to alteration, while that of the nose remains practically constant. Nasal tones have good penetrating power. Alteration of the shape of the mouth, by means of tongue movements, causes a change in the tone-quality which enables us to distinguish between different vowels. The "oo" sound, as in "food," has the fewest overtones. A gradual opening of the lips will make the mouth correspond to a conical rather than a cylindrical tube, giving more overtones and a brighter quality. As we open the lips we pass through the vowel sounds found in the words "foot," "fun," "not," and "awe"; while with the sound of "ah" the mouth should be fully open. A further emphasis of the conical shape is then made by gradually closing the back of the mouth-cavity, by raising the tongue. We pass through the sounds of the vowels in "mat" and "met," until with the sound in "meet" the passage between the tongue and the roof of the mouth is at its narrowest.

The presence of overtones in different proportion is also shown by the fact that each voice has its own quality. If two voices produced tones having the same proportion of overtones in union with the fundamental tone, they would sound alike.

The action of the throat should not be self-conscious. The singer knows what pitch he wishes to get, and he strikes it without thinking of working the crico-thyroid muscles or stretching the vocal cords. Yet there is evidently a very accurate relation between idea and act, for the vocal cords at once adopt the tension necessary to produce the required pitch. This tension may be obtained in two ways, however, and the singer knows which one he is going to use.

The so-called chest register (better named chest quality) is obtained when the vocal cords vibrate at full length along their straight edges, which are thus held tight to narrow the opening known as the glottis, or "chink of the glottis." In this method of singing, increased tones mean increased tension. As the pitch rises, the

Adam's-apple, which carries the front ends of the cords, rises also, and takes a stiffer and stiffer position, demanding more and more muscular effort. To sing high notes in the chest register (with chest quality) is very fatiguing. The chest notes in a man's voice have the fulness and quality obtained in ordinary shouting.

If the singer uses the so-called head register, he will obtain a tone of much smoother quality. To get such head tones, the throat must be left lax, and the nose open. Such tones are often developed by humming through the nose. In these, the authorities tell us, the vocal cords vibrate more in a lateral direction, like a pin that is stuck in a wall and twanged. The head register requires none of the fatiguing stiffening of the throat that is needed for chest notes. It has a much smoother quality of tone, being almost like the falsetto voice in character. In reality, the falsetto is simply a very high part of the head register. The head tones have nothing of the gruff character of the shout, but have the smoother, lighter quality of a whine.

The good singer will use the head tones as much as the nature of his voice permits. With men, this blending of a maximum of head quality with the tone may be done at all pitches, but more especially in the high ones. Sir Morell Mackenzie said that sopranos use a maximum of chest register, while contraltos depend much more on head quality for their high notes. But this statement is many years old, and probably the sopranos now make a much greater use of the head register than formerly.

Oertel studied head tones by means of an instrument called the stroboscope, connected with the laryngoscope. The latter is an arrangement of mirrors enabling an observer to see into the throat. The former is based on the idea of a revolving plate with a hole in it, permitting vision only when the hole reaches a certain spot in its path of revolution. If the stroboscope revolves, for example, 250 times a second, and the vocal cords under the laryngoscope are vibrating 251 times a second, then each revolution of the stroboscope will show the cords in a position slightly advanced from that seen previously. In this way a sort of moving picture is obtained showing the vocal cords in action *apparently* at the rate of one vibration per second. By using this, Oertel found that in head tones the vocal cords were divided into segments lengthwise, the segments vibrating laterally.

In the later sections on tubular instruments, it is shown that the length of the vibrating air-column producing a tone varies inversely as the pitch. The vocal cords are controlled by muscles, while the mouthpieces of reed instruments are not. We may therefore make the vocal cords give any rate of vibration that they can, and the length of the vibrating air-column will vary in accordance with their rate. But where the air-wave in a clarinet, for instance, is four times the length of the tube, that of a vocal tone may be many more times the length from vocal cords to lips. Yet there is some shortening of the air-column in the throat as the pitch is raised. With chest tones, the thyroid cartilage shortens the air-space by rising as the pitch rises; and chest-singers often throw the head back for high notes. For head tones, there seems to be a lowering of the upper part of the larynx toward the cords, producing the sensation of "drinking in" the tone.

All this no doubt leads to rather abstruse considerations. There is, however, much room for further investigation of the larynx in action; and the reader may not find it amiss to have these hints of what the investigator's problems are like.

From the hearer's point of view, too, the above items may be of value. He can watch what method of breathing a singer adopts, or tell whether he or she blends head and chest tones skilfully.

Voices are classified in many ways. Taking them in general divisions from the bottom up, we have the *basso profundo*, the *basso cantante*, the baritone, the *tenore robusto*, the (lyric) *tenore di grazia*, the contralto, the mezzo-soprano, and the full soprano.

The voice of the *basso profundo* is full and deep, while that of the *basso cantante* is smoother and more fluent. Similarly, the *tenore robusto* has a voice of heroic proportions, while the lyric tenor (*tenore di grazia*) has less strength, but more smoothness and sweetness of tone. The saccharine quality of the lyric tenor's tones is apt to grow monotonous; and it caused Von Bülow to remark that "Tenor is not a voice, but a disease." The true contralto (alto) voice, too, is broad and strong in quality, while that of a mezzo-soprano with almost the same range is more lyrical. Sopranos have the same division, the strong voices being suited to the dramatic school, while the more fluent and smooth voices of the so-called coloratura sopranos can be managed with the most brilliant flexibility. The last-named voices are those that are displayed in the runs, embellishments, and rapid passages of the conventional mad-scenes in Italian opera of the Rossini or Donizetti school.

Men's voices sing music in the G clef an octave lower than it is written.

Vocal execution is a matter in which the singer must keep up constant practice. In the piano field, Rubinstein is alleged to have said, "If I neglect practice one day, I know it; two days, my friends know it; and three days, the public knows it." Something of the sort is true of the singer also.

The singer must not only practise execution, but he must develop tone quality as well. Where the pianist cannot vary his tone-color, the singer can modify his tones noticeably by practice. A good voice is in part a natural gift; but it may be much improved, and in some cases singers have attained success without it. Thus Ludwig Wüllner, renowned for his rendering of German art-songs, obtains his effects by his mastery of technical management, and advertises himself as "the singer without a voice."

When judging of a singer, the listener may first of all note the quality of his voice. If the performer is a man, the voice may be of either lyric or robust style; if a woman, her tones may be broadly dramatic, or may have the pure, clear quality of the "voix blanche," the clean-cut, somewhat cold tone-color shown by certain colorature singers.

Breathing and breath management are worthy of notice. Does the singer breathe naturally, with only the slightest pause, and no apparent effort? Or does he make hard work of it? Also, does he pause for breath at the proper times, or does he let his inhalations divide the phrases wrongly? In some songs, there is little chance for the vocalist to go astray. In the old Handel airs, however, such as "Ev'ry valley," in "The Messiah," there are long roulades, in which any misjudgment would receive its full share of prominence.

The quality of tone is kept at its best if the tone is given proper resonance by the nose, and more especially by the mouth. We hear many teachers tell their pupils to "focus the tone on the teeth." This does not mean that the teeth have any share in the tone, but that the student is to let the tone resound clearly and not be smothered by the mouth or throat.

The tremolo is a fault that depends on breath management. If a singer has good control of the muscles governing his lungs, he should not be troubled with any objectionable tremolo.

Inaccuracy in pitch may come from the singer's inability to hear certain notes mentally. It is apt to show itself on long-held notes of very high or very low position in a singer's range. A singer need not be blamed greatly for an infrequent lapse on a single note; but if such carelessness grows to be a habit, it is naturally an important defect.

The attack of a tone is the way in which a singer begins it. This should be even and clean-cut, unless other effects are used purposely. If a singer is heard to "feel" for a tone lightly and searchingly, instead of starting it cleanly at full power, his audience will soon grow tired of him. The singer often experiences a temptation to slide up to a high note with a "scoop"; but he must resist this feeling. The only permissible case of such sliding is the *portamento*, in which a singer ends a note by carrying it rapidly up (or down) to the pitch of the next, before pronouncing the syllable that goes with the second note. *Portamento* work should not be over-used, or it will grow wearisome in its effect. The release of a tone, like the attack, should be clean-cut and sudden. The proper tone, according to Santley, is started full, held evenly, and released cleanly, forming what he calls a "rectangle of sound."

After these technical points are noted, there comes the subject of musical expression. The singer, like the pianist, has many gradations of speed and power, — almost an infinite variety in the case of the voice. These, under his management, constitute his rendering of a song; and if they are employed with due regard for balance, contrast, and unity of the entire effect, they mark the singer as an artist. The singer has one admirable guide that the pianist lacks, — the sense of the words. These usually give him the general outline of the effects he desires, his practice merely refining the details. Yet even here there is room for judgment. Thus an opera singer will often exaggerate the effect of recital songs, and try to make them too dramatic, — a fault usually avoided successfully by the concert artist. It will be seen that the song-singer and the opera-singer have different standards; and an artist who changes from one field to the other, even temporarily, should remember this fact.

XLIV

THE VIOLIN

While the piano demands the maximum amount of effort from the performer, the violin (German, *Geige;* French, *violon;* Italian, *violino*) is the instrument that is capable of the greatest variety of expression. Like the human voice, it may echo every emotion.

The origin of the violin, as already intimated, is shrouded in mystery. The rebab of Arabia, the ravonastron of India, the early Welsh harp known as the crwth, or even the primitive instruments of Africa, may have played their part in its development. Greilsamer, a French authority, now claims that it may have come from the kithara, because of the expansion of one of the latter's sides to a violin-like body in certain early mediæval specimens.

The term fiddle, also viol, is derived from the Latin *fidicula,* meaning a stringed instrument. The early viols, which came into general use in the time of the Jongleurs, were flatter in shape than the present violin. Their tone was different, being less incisive and brilliant, but more calmly sweet and plaintive. Viols of various sizes remained in use some time after the violin had developed. When the early sixteenth-century music is revived for modern ears, the viols are often used in place of violins, and with very pleasing effect if heard with harpsichord, for example.

Gasparo da Salo and the Amati family were pioneers in violin-making, the former living in the Tyrol and the latter in Cremona. Andrea Amati, the pioneer in the Cremona manufacture, was born in 1520. His two sons Antonio and Geronimo continued the work, but it was brought to greater perfection by the latter's son Nicolo. The last-named was the teacher of the greatest of violin-makers, Antonio Stradivarius (1650–1737). Another famous family of violin-makers was that of Guarnerius, of whom Joseph (1683–1745), called Del Jesu, is known through having one of his instruments used by the great Paganini. Other famous violin-makers were the Magginis, the Ruggieris, the Guadagninis, the Cerutis, and Storioni.

The violins of these men are valued for their excellence of tone. This comes in part from age, or rather continued use; because the constant vibration of the violin-box makes it give tones of constantly increasing fulness and purity. But age is not the only quality, else all the old instruments would be equally good. There were secrets in the making and using of the varnish, the seasoning of the wood, and so on. These points, or others of the sort, are still open to discovery, and modern makers sometimes produce unusual results. Thus a famous New York firm, which exhibited some of its new violins at a Vienna fair, was refused the prize, at first, on the ground that its instruments were too good to be really new.

The chief parts of a violin are the body and neck, made of maple or pine; a thin wooden bridge of maple, supporting the strings; an ebony bar into which the strings are knotted beyond the bridge; an ebony finger-board over which they run; a peg-box, in which the ends of the strings are wrapped around pegs that are used for tuning; and the four strings themselves. The strings are called catgut; but in the instrumental field, at least, the cat is innocent, as the strings come from the sheep or the goat when not artificially made. The deepest string is wound with wire. With the violin comes a bow of horsehair, and a metal or wooden clamp (the mute, or sordino). The bow is drawn over the strings to set them in motion, whereupon the vibrations are transferred by the bridge to the body of the instrument, which acts as a sounding-board, and vibrates in sympathy with the string, but much more powerfully. The mute is stuck on the bridge in clothespin-fashion when in use, and diminishes the volume of tone by letting less powerful vibrations reach the sounding-box. The muted tone is peculiarly sweet as well as soft. When the mute is to be put on or taken off, the composer always puts some rests into the player's part, so that he may have time to dig the mute from his vest pocket and adjust it on the bridge, or to reverse the process.

The violin strings are tuned in fifths, to G, D, A, and E in ascending order, beginning with the G just below middle C. Since making a string shorter causes it to give a higher tone, the player may get tones of higher pitch than that of the whole string (open string) by pressing his finger on it, at different distances from the peg-box; in which case the part of the string between the bridge

and the player's finger is what vibrates and gives the tone. In principle it is simple, but in practice the procedure is varied and difficult. The violinist's left hand, which is used to finger the strings,
is trained to a most delicate perfection of activity, — a perfection
that is injured by the slightest bruise, so that the performer may
not indulge in anything so violent as baseball, for instance. The use
of the bow, too, demands a perfect adjustment of arm, wrist, hand,
and fingers. So it must have been a very ignorant man who said,
when asked if he could play the violin, "I don't know; I never tried."

The violinist, when playing, supports the neck of his instrument
in the hollow between the thumb and first finger of his left hand.
This brings his four fingers over the strings in such a way that any
one of them may press the string against the finger-board, known
as "stopping" the string. When the hand is nearest to the peg-
box, it is in what is called the first position. By moving in toward
the body of the violin, so that each finger gives a note one tone
higher than before, it reaches the second position. In ordinary
playing, six positions are used. For the upper positions, or for any
note still higher on the E-string, the fingers must do some reaching,
as the body of the instrument prevents the hand from moving in
as a whole. In Beethoven's time the compass of the violin was
considered to be one tone over three octaves. Since then the composers have called for still higher notes from it; and Wagner, in
the music depicting the Holy Grail in the prelude to "Lohengrin,"
demanded unusually high tones, whose thin, clear quality, blended
with flute notes, gave an excellent picture of celestial bliss.

In this case Wagner used what are known as harmonics, besides
employing the ordinary tones. Harmonics, known also as overtones or upper partials, are formed when a string of the violin is
made to vibrate in fractional parts instead of in one large swing
along its entire length. To produce such an effect, the player
touches the string lightly at a certain point instead of pressing it
down firmly. If he touches the string in the middle, it vibrates in
halves, sounding an octave higher than if it vibrated as a whole.
If touched one-third of its length from the peg-box end, it vibrates
in thirds, giving a still higher tone; and the pitch may be still further raised by making the string divide into fourths, fifths, etc.

The playing of harmonics is one of the points in which a good performer shows his skill. He must be perfectly accurate in finger-ing, as the slightest deviation from the exact location will cause a series of meaningless squeaks. The so-called artificial, or stopped, harmonics are derived from a stopped tone, in which one finger presses the string down in the ordinary way while another makes this shortened length of string divide into fractional parts. The use of thin strings aids greatly in the production of these tones; and Paganini, the most famous technical master of the violin that the world has known, could in this manner make the string subdivide into as many as twelve parts. Most concert violinists do not go above eight or nine.

The hearer can soon learn to distinguish the thin, piping, "flageo-let-tone" quality of the harmonics; and if he is near enough to see the player's fingers, he may note the light touch on the string needed to produce them.

The most common style of the violin is a smooth legato, melodic and expressive, in which the composer uses a slur to show which notes are to be played in a single bow-stroke, and sometimes indi-cates whether it is the up or down stroke.

Among other technical points to be watched for, the most com-mon is double-stopping, or the playing of two strings at once. On ordinary violins the bow cannot touch three strings at once, al-though the performer may alternate notes on two adjacent strings so quickly that he seems to be playing in three or four part har-mony. He may also sweep his bow over three or four strings in very rapid succession, giving a chord of three or four notes in the harp-like style known as arpeggio. It is said that Ole Bull had a special violin bridge made, with its top more nearly flat than usual, so that by bearing on heavily with the bow he could touch three strings at once. But usually such chord effects, as seen in the great Chaconne for solo violin by Bach, are made by the arpeggio-sweep, and only one or two of the notes really sustained for any time.

In orchestral music, where there are two groups of violins, the same effect is obtained by dividing the forces as much as desired. Thus Wagner, in the "Forest-Rustling" in "Siegfried," divided his first violins into three parts, with a solo violin besides, while the second violins played in four parts, and the lower strings were also divided. This gave a many-voiced effect that represented very successfully the rustlings and murmurings of the forest. Such procedure (*divisi*) is common now with all the orchestral instruments, and produces a much broader or more massive tone than the older method of scoring for unison parts.

The violin tremolo, which is so often heard in our melodramas when the villain is about to kill the heroine, or some other blood-curdling event takes place, is produced on a single tone by swinging the bow rapidly to and fro on the string. This effect was originated by Monteverde in the seventeenth century; though if he had known to what base uses it would come, he might have refrained from inventing it.

The vibrato is used to give a series of apparent swells and subsidences to a single smooth tone. It is caused in reality by slight regular changes in pitch, for in producing it the player sways his hand rhythmically and more or less rapidly while keeping his finger on the string.

Staccato notes, which are short and quick, may be produced by the stopping of the bow on the string, in which case the tone ceases at once. Such a staccato is called "détachée," or "martellato."

Another staccato is produced by letting the bow drop on the string and rebound quickly by its own elasticity. This is known as the "flying staccato" or "arco saltando."

When the string is lightly brushed and the bow lifted off it between each tone, the so-called "spiccato" is produced.

The violin strings may be plucked, like those of a guitar. This procedure, known as "pizzicato," may be used for guitar-like accompaniments, but it has a mysterious and striking effect that is valuable for its own sake also. Skilful solo players will sometimes give pieces that demand pizzicato effects in combination with bowing; and while a tone of the usual sort is going on, they will be seen to pluck a string also with one of the free fingers of the left hand. The pizzicato, like the tremolo, was invented by Monteverde.

A tone produced by tapping the string with the back of the bow is called "col legno," meaning "with the wood." This effect is too light for solo use, and is rare even in orchestral work.

The mute, or sordino, has been mentioned above. The muted tone is too smoothly sweet for lengthy use, but in short passages it makes a good contrast to the more brilliant tones of the unmuted strings.

Trills are produced by a rapid alternation of two notes, the lower one being held, or consisting of an open tone, while the upper one is played and released very quickly.

The glissando is the effect produced when a finger is slid along the string while the bow is playing on it. This procedure and others are often burlesqued in vaudeville, but when properly used are decidedly effective.

Embellishments of various sorts, such as turns, trills, mordents, and rapid runs, are much used in violin music. The player's left hand is continually in action, and a close watch of its nimble fingers will show a constant overcoming of difficulties that are not all recognized as such by the ear alone.

The violin is capable of expressing every emotion, from the deepest pathos to the wildest gayety or the utmost frenzy. Its use as a solo instrument is widespread, and it plays the most important part in the orchestra. It lends itself to the expression of every shade of feeling, and while many instruments have only one or two distinctive tone-colors, the violin possesses them all.

A very great deal of this expressive power depends on the performer's use of the bow. This is a matter of life-long attention from the student's earliest days. The fingers stop the strings to get the correct pitch; but it is always the infinite variety in the speed and pressure of the bow that brings out the tone-quality. The broad and beautiful notes of an Ysaye or a Kreisler depend wholly upon the correct and artistic use of the bow.

In the orchestra, the first of the violin players, known as the "Concertmeister," ranks next to the conductor himself, and should be able to replace the latter if necessary. He is always a performer of high merit, and best able to play the solo passages that abound in modern scores.

Sometimes special tunings of the violin are used. Thus Saint-Saëns, in his "Danse Macabre," depicting the skeletons dancing at midnight, had a solo violin tuned with its upper string a semitone flat. This gave a peculiarly weird effect when Death began to tune up his violin for the skeletons' dance. Paganini would often tune all his strings a semitone too high, and finger the pieces a semitone lower than they were written, combining the correct pitch with the brilliance obtained from tight strings. Many others have used special effects in tuning.

When the layman attends a violin recital, he will be able to notice many of the points enumerated here. He will almost surely see much double-stopping, many harmonics, pizzicato passages, and other bits of technical display. These he may follow in part with the eye, by watching the fingers of the player's left hand. But the artist's chief glory is to be judged by the ear. If he shows breadth and purity of tone, true expressive power, real delicacy of feeling, and an emotional warmth that is well marked without being unduly exaggerated, then he is truly great.

XLV

OTHER BOWED INSTRUMENTS

THE viola (German, *Bratsche;* French, *alto;* Italian, *viola*) is exactly similar to the violin, except that it is one fifth larger, and has heavier strings. It is tuned a fifth below the violin, its strings thus giving C, G, D, and A, the deepest tone being an octave below middle C on the piano. Its two lowest strings are wired.

The viola is played in a manner similar to that used for the violin, except for the greater stretches in fingering, due to the greater length of the strings. All the technical points of violin execution are possible on the viola, but owing to the veiled quality of its high tones its music is confined to the first five positions, giving the viola a compass of about three octaves.

The dull, mournful tone-color of the viola comes from the fact that its strings are thick. Its increased length over the violin would make its tones only a third below those of the violin if the same thickness of string were used. The extra depth is attained by increasing the thickness of the strings, which always makes the tone lose brilliancy. Thus the viola gets a tone-color of brooding melancholy. If over-used, it becomes tiresome. When Méhul aimed to portray the lofty melancholy of the Ossianic poetry in his "Uthal," he tried the experiment (at Napoleon's request) of leaving out violins and making the viola the chief instrument of the string group. The result was decidedly too successful; for the tone-color of the piece became so monotonous that Grétry, after listening to the end, exclaimed, "I'd give a hundred francs to hear a violin."

Among more recent composers, Mendelssohn has used the viola beautifully in the slow movement of his Italian Symphony; while Berlioz employed the instrument admirably to personify the dreamy and contemplative hero in his "Childe Harold" Symphony. In the second movement of that work it has some delicate tones which are played very near the bridge, — a style known as *sul ponticello.*

The viola plays the third part in the string quartet, which con-sists of a first and second violin, a viola, and a violoncello. This does not mean that it is always below the two violins in pitch, for the string quartet depends upon interest and variety in the leading of its four parts, and sometimes the viola may be playing the highest note of a chord. In orchestral work the viola has much the same duty. It is often called upon for its special tone-color, but usually it is found playing in four-part harmony with the first and second violins and the violoncellos. In the eighteenth century its rôle was more humble, and it was often compelled to follow the bass viol. Yet Gluck gave a strong example of its power in his "Iphigenie en Tauride." In that work Orestes, pursued by the Furies, sinks down overcome in prison; but the gloomy muttering of the violas shows that his rest is due not to peace of mind, but to exhaustion.

The *viola d'amore* is not really a viola, but belongs to the old viol type, and is nearly obsolete now. It had seven catgut strings and seven steel strings vibrating in sympathy with them. Its sweet tones are called for in the music of Bach's time, but are very infre-quently demanded in later works. Loeffler, however, used them in his "Mort de Tintagiles."

An attempt has been made to substitute for the present viola an instrument with brighter tone. A German musician named Ritter brought out a large affair, which he called the *viola alta*, but which the musical world now knows as the Ritter viola. It is half as large again as the ordinary viola. For this reason its tones are brilliant and resonant, as its size gives the required depth in pitch without the need of having the strings thickened. Orchestras have not adopted it, because it is too large; and only men with very long arms can play it. As a whole, music is the most conservative of the arts; and even a successful innovation is not adopted for many years.

The violoncello, or 'cello (German, *Violoncell;* French, *violoncelle;* Italian, *violoncello*), takes the fourth part among the strings, both in the quartet of solo instruments and in the orchestra. Of course in the latter case any instrument may be used for a solo or *obbligato* passage, whenever a composer desires to make its tone-color promi-nent; but in *tutti* passages, when all the instruments play together, it takes the low notes of the string group. The name should never

1. MANDOLIN; 2. LUTE; 3. VIOLA D'AMORE; 4. VIOLIN; 5. BANJO; 6. VIOLA;
7. VIOLONCELLO; 8. GUITAR; 9. HARP; 10. CONTRABASS

be spelled "violincello." The term is derived, not from the violin, but from the violone, the old Italian name for double-bass. Here again there is a slight lack of accuracy, for the violone is of the flat viol type, while the 'cello has the more rounded violin form. In England the 'cello is sometimes called the bass viol.

The strings of the 'cello are an octave deeper than those of the viola, the two lower ones in each case being wound with wire. But while the viola tone is dull from thick strings, the 'cello is so much larger that its deep pitch is obtained by length of string, without disproportionate increase in size. The instrument is so large that its body is rested on the floor during performance, instead of on the player's arm. In fingering, a large stretch is needed to produce the necessary changes in pitch. Various positions are used, as with the violin; but while the very high positions are difficult on the violin, because the fingers are crowded together, they are easy on the 'cello, because the large stretch needed in the lower positions diminishes to a comfortable size. The compass of the 'cello is therefore extensive, being nearly four octaves. The 'cello player will sometimes use his thumb to stop a string.

The early Puritans seem to have possessed a decided predilection for the 'cello. Just why they chose this instrument for participation in their religious services is hard to see; for they regarded the violin as a device of the evil one, and looked askance at nearly all music except congregational singing. When Thomas Brattle imported an organ, in the early years of the eighteenth century, he wished to give it to a Puritan church. He quoted Scripture, telling the elders to " play skilfully and with a loud noise"; but even with this sage advice they would not accept the gift, and he passed it on to an Episcopal church. Yet the Puritans adopted the 'cello in their services, sometimes even paying the player as much as $70 a year.

Owing to the length and comparative thinness of its strings, the 'cello has as much variety of expression as the violin; but its utterance is of a deeper and more masculine sort. Great composers often indulge in the device of writing an antiphonal dialogue between two different instruments; and the violin and 'cello form a pair well suited for this procedure. An excellent example of such a dialogue between them is found in the slow movement of Beethoven's Eighth Symphony. Beethoven usually obtained the maximum of effect from the instruments he used, and made them speak out in their most characteristic tones.

In solo execution, all the technical points of the violin are practicable on the 'cello. There are, however, certain limitations. Thus double-stopping is regulated by the size of the instrument, and intervals practicable on the violin or viola are often impossible on the 'cello. Arpeggio chords for the 'cello must be written with due regard for the size of the human hand, and generally include at least one open string. Tremolo, vibrato, and glissando effects are easily obtained. The mute can play its part. Arco saltando and other devices of bowing are perfectly applicable. The pizzicato is excellent, as the long strings of the 'cello give a full tone when plucked. Harmonics of good quality may be played, especially on the upper string, where they resemble muted violin tones in effect. Artificial harmonics on the 'cello are limited by the performer's reach. They are not often called for, though Verdi used them very effectively in the Nile scene of "Aïda."

The 'cello is a favorite instrument in orchestral expression. Cherubini wrote three real parts for his 'cellos in the opening scene of his opera "Faniska." Rossini called for five solo 'cellos in the "William Tell" Overture, though the passage is now generally arranged for one. The 'cello is very effective with the voice, as in the song "Be thou faithful unto death," from Mendelssohn's oratorio "Saint Paul."

'Cello playing was of slow growth, as the old six-stringed *viol da gamba* was hard to displace. But the more powerful 'cello tone blended better with the violins, and the instrument came into use in the time of Corelli and Tartini, while Haydn and others placed it in the string quartet. The French player Duport introduced chromatic fingering, — an important step forward. So well did Duport play the 'cello that Voltaire said to him, "You make me believe in miracles; for you can create a nightingale out of an ox." At this time it was customary for players to display their ability by performing difficult violin pieces, such as Tartini's "Trille du Diable," on the 'cello. But the most wonderful master of the instrument was by all odds Adrien François Servais, who lived until 1866. His compositions are tremendously difficult, like those of Paganini for the violin.

The contrabass, or double-bass, or double-bass viol (German, *Kontrabass;* French, *contre basse;* Italian, *contrabasso*), formerly known in Italy as the violone, is the largest of the bowed instruments. Its size, which is its most striking feature, was emphasized by the old English custom of giving trios with one such instrument; the travelling performer would play on it, and add a second part with his voice, while a third part came from the voice of a boy concealed in the instrument. The English contrabasses used to have three strings, but those now in large orchestras have four. They are tuned in fourths to the notes, E, A, D, and G, the first being the lowest E on the piano. The compass runs nearly to middle C. By common consent, contrabass music is written an octave higher than the actual pitch, to avoid the use of many extra lines below the staff (leger lines). It therefore sounds an octave lower than it is written.

Special tunings are sometimes demanded. Thus Berlioz advises that half the contrabasses be tuned differently from the rest. Wagner, at the beginning of his "Rheingold," has the contrabass players tune their lowest strings to E-flat, which is held as a sustained bass for wavy harmonies that represent the flowing of the river. Beethoven went even further down, and called for a low C, — a fact which led the German Karl Otho to bring out a five-stringed contrabass with C for its lowest tone. The thickness of the strings necessitates great strength to stop them; and double-stopping is almost impossible unless one of the tones comes from an open string. In orchestral work, of course, the contrabasses may be divided into parts, as at the beginning of Tschaikovsky's "Pathetic Symphony."

The tone-color of the contrabass is heavy, gruff, ponderous. It takes the bass part in the orchestra, but it may be used in solo passages with telling significance. It may also be used to burlesque the effects of lighter instruments. In swift passages it can never be entirely clear; for its long, heavy strings are slow to cease vibrating. Yet Mendelssohn, in his setting of the 114th Psalm, has the contrabass play sixteenth-notes at a metronome mark of 116 for a quarter-note, giving a rate of 464 notes per minute in the playing. Another hard nut for the contrabass player to crack is the accompaniment to Mozart's song "Per questa bella mano," in which the chord effects and high notes suggest that the music might have been played two octaves lower than written.

Solo playing on the contrabass would seem at first sight to have all the delicacy that an elephant would display while dancing. The contrabass harmonics are of little value; the mute produces no change in quality; the repeated notes and tremolo are effective enough, and the pizzicato excellently strong; but the tone-quality seems too heavy for solo work. Yet there have been great solo performers on the contrabass, such as Dragonetti or Bottesini. Dragonetti possessed a fine instrument, upon which he could obtain many striking effects. It was with this contrabass that he imitated the approach of a thunderstorm, scaring the monks of San Giustina, near Padua, until they came out of their cells in the dead of night.

The pizzicato has been well used by Weber, in the overture to "Der Freischütz," in which piece it gives a strikingly sombre effect just after the opening horn quartet. Rossini, in the overture to "William Tell," divides the contrabasses to obtain effects of pizzicato and bowing combined. Another famous use of the contrabass pizzicato is found in the Symphonie Fantastique of Berlioz, where the hero, after being led by jealousy to murder his sweetheart, is marched to execution. Bach used the contrabass well in "Ye lightnings, ye thunders," and Gluck employed it in glissando passages to imitate the barking of Cerebus in "Orpheus." But Beethoven, who brought out most wonderfully the possibilities of his instruments, was the first to make the contrabass important in the orchestra. At the end of his Fourth Symphony is a rapid contrabass passage that demands all the players' skill.

When this work first came out, Weber, often at odds with the more serious and irascible Beethoven, wrote a satire on the contrabass passage, which was printed in a musical periodical. He pictured a concert hall, in which this symphony had just been performed. After the departure of the musicians, the instruments came to life, and began to hold an indignation meeting against the merciless composer who forced them to do such hard work. When the smaller instruments had aired their grievances, the contrabass arose gravely, and said, "Your troubles may be real enough; but what do you think of mine? Instead of letting me proceed in a quiet and orderly manner, as befits my dignity, this intolerable composer makes me jump and skip about in the craziest way, just as if I were a giddy young violin." At this the instruments burst into cries of anger, causing such an uproar that the janitor heard the disturbance and came into the hall. On realizing the trouble, he ordered the instruments to stop their noise instantly, or he would get Mr. Beethoven to write another symphony. At this the tumult was hushed, for all the instruments grew mute with terror.

Beethoven's reply to adverse criticism usually consisted of equal parts of personal abuse and profanity. But he remained true to his ideals of art, and he used the contrabass prominently again in the Scherzo of his Fifth Symphony. In the Sixth, or Pastoral, Symphony, he pictured thunder by having the contrabass play groups of four notes against groups of five on the 'cello. Orchestral thunderstorms are very popular, and in all of them the contrabass plays an important part.

But if Beethoven gave the contrabass a share in the hard work, he atoned by giving it some wonderfully impressive passages in the Ninth Symphony. Beethoven was a lover of liberty, a dreamer of human brotherhood. His Heroic Symphony (the third) was dedicated to Napoleon at first, being made impersonal only after Napoleon showed self-seeking tendencies by taking the imperial throne. The Ninth Symphony is really a picture of the millennium to come, in contrast with the strife and tumult of the world. Beethoven introduced into his finale the words of Schiller's "Ode to Joy," and used the contrabasses as a transition from the instrumental to the vocal part.

The earlier movements of this work have their share of beauty, but it is made to seem transient and temporary. The fourth movement opens tragically, as if with a cry of agony and anguish at human misery. Then comes a dialogue between the contrabasses and the rest of the orchestra. Phrases from the earlier movements return, as if to suggest some remedy for the turmoil; but in vain. They are interrupted, in turn, by passages of solemn dignity on the contrabass, which seem like a voice rebuking the world for its impotent passions. Even the tender theme of the slow movement seems unacceptable, and dies away into silence. Then the contrabasses enter with the melody that is to be used later with the words, and their broad, full tones give it with wonderfully impressive effect.

The contrabass, then, may be used for the most part as a humble drudge, giving the bass parts of the orchestral music. But it has capabilities, and the great composer will sometimes give it passages that are of the utmost importance and significance.

XLVI

PLUCKED–STRING INSTRUMENTS

OF those instruments whose strings are plucked instead of being rubbed by a bow, the most important by far is the harp (German, *Harfe;* French, *harpe;* Italian, *arpa*). It undoubtedly originated from the twanging bow-string of early savages; and the nanga, a modern form of negro harp, is practically a bow with five strings instead of one. Nearly all the ancient races had harps of some form; and as the harp was the best instrument known in old times, its use was ascribed to celestial beings as well as mortals. The ancient harps varied in size and number of strings; but as they lacked the vertical pillar that makes our harp a triangle, they must have been hard to keep in tune. The Hebrew harp, or Kinnor, was probably copied from the Egyptian instrument ; while the Greek word kithara has been translated indifferently as harp, lyre, lute, or guitar.

The Irish claim to have originated the harp. Undoubtedly the oriental harps were earlier, though the Roman legions brought the Irish harp back from Britain. Its use in the Apulian city of Arpi may have given the instrument its name, though Max Müller claims a Teutonic origin for the term. The ancient races of the east gave the instrument various names, while the Germanic tribes knew it under its present appellation.

The old Irish harp, in its largest form, had three rows of strings, two outer rows of twenty-nine each giving diatonic tones, while the middle row of twenty gave the chromatic intervals. The instrument existed in other forms, and as late as 1608 we find Monteverde calling for a "double harp," evidently with two rows of strings. The triple form lasted until nearly 1800.

The old laws of Wales mention the use of the harp as one of three points that distinguished the freeman from the slave; and pretenders were often discovered by their unskilful use of it. Only the king, his musicians, and the gentlemen of the realm could own a harp; and slaves were forbidden even to touch the instrument. The harp was exempt from seizure for debt, as its loss was presumed to mean degradation to the ranks of the slaves. The Welsh musical festivals, or Eistedfodds, were originally very important affairs, participated in by those who had reached the rank of chief minstrel. Candidates had to pass a three-years' initiation, and other periods of practice for higher degrees.

The Anglo-Saxons cherished the harp, and respected the wandering minstrel. As early as the year 495, when Colgrin was besieged in York, his brother went through the hostile camp disguised as a minstrel to get the information that enabled him to relieve the place. A similar story is told of King Alfred, who disguised himself as a harper to enter the Danish camp. At festivals it was customary for the guests to sing and play in turn. Once the poet Caedmon, who had neglected music for more purely intellectual accomplishments, found himself unable to play when his turn came in such a gathering; whereupon he rose from the table and went home to hide his shame.

The Minnesingers of Germany made frequent use of the harp, instead of the guitar that the Troubadours sometimes favored. The effect may be seen in Wagner's "Tannhäuser," in which the contestants indulge in a tournament of song.

In England the lute and viol gradually replaced the harp, while the spinet and virginals, which were smaller forms of the harpsichord, drove it still further into obscurity. Yet in 1720 Handel called for harp music in his oratorio "Esther," the parts being performed by two Welsh harpists.

The invention of pedals for the harp has been ascribed to Hochbrucker in 1720, and Paul Velter, in 1730. The modern concert harp, however, is the work of Sebastian Erard, who perfected it in 1810. This has what are known as double-action pedals. The harp is tuned in the scale of C-flat when its strings are open. There are seven pedals, one for each note of the scale. Pressing a pedal halfway down will cause a set of metal pins on revolving discs to clamp all the strings giving that note, and raise the pitch a semitone by shortening the length of the string. Thus for the key of C all the pedals would be depressed half-way; while for A-flat, as an instance, the pedals for C, F, and G would be pressed down, the others not.

By pressing a pedal down to its full capacity, the player brings into action a second set of discs, shortening the strings still more, and causing sharps to sound instead of natural tones. The harp pedals, unlike those of the piano, are used simply to regulate pitch; and it was a very ignorant critic who once wrote of a harpist's having over-used the pedals.

The harp strings are vertical, running from the curved neck to the slanting sound-board, while the third side of the harp is formed by a vertical pillar. An eighth pedal is sometimes used to close holes in the sound-box, reversing the principle of the swell box for organ pipes; but this extra pedal is of little value, and is frequently omitted. To aid the performer, the C-strings of the harp are colored red, and the F-strings blue. Harp music is written for two hands, on the two staffs used for piano music. Flat keys sound best, because then most of the strings are open, vibrating at full length. Thus Prout, in his cantata "Alfred," has F-sharp for the key of the piece, but writes the harp part in G-flat. Gounod was not so careful, and in "Faust" there is a long harp passage in B that would have sounded better in C-flat. Wagner made inordinate demands on his harpists, both in the Magic Fire music and in the entrance of the gods into Valhalla, the latter scene being in the "Rheingold." As the little finger is not used, harp chords should contain not more than four notes for one hand.

Chord-effects are excellent upon the harp. Quick sweeps of broken chords in succession are known as arpeggio, or "harp-like," even when used on other instruments. The harpist gives these by alternating his hands.

With the exception of chromatic passages, nearly everything suitable for the piano will sound well on the harp. Harmonics, also, are practicable except on the highest and lowest strings. The first harmonic, an octave above the full-string pitch, is the only one used. It is obtained by touching the string lightly in the middle with the ball of the hand and plucking with the thumb or first finger. An abrupt staccato may be obtained from about the same position, the string being plucked and the tone quickly stopped by heavy pressure of the hand. All tones may be ended by laying the open palm on the strings; and this point gave Longfellow the idea of a beautiful simile in his "Golden Legend": —

"Time hath laid his hand upon my heart,
    Gently, not smiting it,
But as the harper lays his open palm
    Upon the strings, to deaden their vibration."

If the harp strings are plucked near the end instead of the middle, a more twangy tone, with more overtones, is the result. Harp trills are possible, but not much used. The harp glissando is a sweep along the strings. The tremolo, or repetition of a single note, is obtained by tuning two adjacent strings to the same pitch, except for the notes D, G, and A. In similar fashion a harp may be tuned so that a sweep of its strings will give the chord of minor thirds instead of a scale. The harp has the fullest and richest tone of all the plucked-string instruments, and is well suited to accompany the voice.

Bach did not use the early harp, and Handel gave it very few trials. Beethoven employed it only once, in "Prometheus." Weber would not use the improved harp in any of his operas; but Spohr wrote much for it. This may have been a matter of domestic as well as musical harmony; for he married the harpist Dorette Scheidler, and wrote many sonatas for harp and violin, in which she took the former instrument while he played the latter. Berlioz, in his Childe Harold Symphony, produced bell effects by combining harp and horn or harp and flute. Across the channel, Cowen used much harp work to add local color to his Welsh Symphony.

To-day the harp has given way to the more popular piano; but in Erard's time it held its own. Once its popularity was threatened by the guitar, when a troupe of Spanish players toured England; but Erard was equal to the occasion. He bought a large number of guitars, and presented them, with a printed method, to clerks, shop girls, and so on. When the fashionable people saw the new instrument in the hands of such humble folk, they at once gave up their newly-formed plans of learning it, and continued to buy Erard harps.

In 1898 the French firm of Pleyel, Wolff & Co. brought out a chromatic harp. Its strings are arranged in two sets, chromatic and diatonic; and they slant so as to cross each other in the middle. This instrument has good tones, as its strings are always open, and need no pedals; but it has not become very popular as yet.

The guitar is not considered to belong to the orchestra. Sometimes it is used for special effects, as in the accompaniment of Alma-viva's air in Rossini's "Barber of Seville"; but the great composers call for it never. Paganini, who once gave up the violin for the guitar while he was guest of a certain noble lady, wrote quartets for strings with guitar; but these works have not made any great impression. The guitar tones are rather too soft for combination or orchestral work; so they are used chiefly in solos or to accompany the voice.

The guitar has six strings, of which three are usually catgut and the others (the lower three) made of silk wound with fine wire. They are tuned in fourths with one third, giving the notes E, A, D, G, B, and E in ascending order. The lowest E as written is the one just below middle C, but the guitar is a transposing instrument, and sounds an octave deeper than the written part. For sharp keys the strings may be tuned to E, B, E, G-sharp, B, and E. On the neck are frets (little horizontal ridges), to show where the strings are to be pressed. The fingering is done by the left hand; the little finger rests on the face of the instrument, while the other three fingers take the upper strings and the thumb the lower ones. The strings are plucked by the thumb and fingers of the right hand, and may be played either in the chord style or in more open, running fashion. The tones of the instrument are dreamy and melancholy in charac-ter. The guitar, like the mandolin and banjo, is too often devoted to commonplace music; but there is a good guitar repertoire, and the gifted Spanish performers can make the instrument remarkably expressive. The bandurria is an extra large Spanish guitar. The Hawaiian ukulele is a small instrument of guitar-like shape and tone quality.

The mandolin comes in several forms, but the most usual one has four pairs of strings, tuned like the violin strings. The lowest pair are catgut covered with silver wire, the next two copper, the third pair steel, and the upper ones catgut. They are played by a pick, or plectrum. The mandolin can give chords, but is more effective in rapid melodic work. Its tones are thin and tangy in quality, but original and striking enough in effect. Composers call for it occa-sionally, and Mozart used it in "Don Giovanni" to accompany that amorous hero's serenade, though nowadays the violin pizzicato is used instead.

This passage figured in an anecdote of Joachim, the great violinist. He was to play it once at Leipsic; but just before he began, some one, probably a conservatory pupil, managed to get some split peas into the sounding-box of the instrument. Instead of the usual dainty pizzicato runs, the soloist produced an unexpected series of sudden rattlings. This illustrated the fact that the tone of the instrument is caused by the vibrations of the sounding-box, and not the strings alone; but probably the artist was too surprised at the time to care much about acoustical principles.

The banjo is essentially an American product. Some derive it from the *bandore*, and others from the Senegambian *bania*, but whereever the name came from, the instrument was perfected in the United States. It carries a negro suggestion, but is more used in reality by white men than by negroes. It consists of a flat tambourine-like parchment sound-board (if the term board is permissible), held by a flat hollow cylinder of metal; a long neck, with frets; and five strings. The latter are tuned upward from the A just below middle C, and give, in ascending order, the notes A, E, G-sharp, B, and E. The "Bass-tuned-to-B" style is the same except that the lowest string is raised a tone. Six-stringed banjos exist, but are not common. The banjo quality is rather tin-panny. The instrument has not entered the orchestra.

The Russian balalaika is a three-stringed affair with a triangular wooden sound-box. This instrument comes in various sizes. It is not powerful in solo work; but bands composed of balalaikas have an excellent effect. Its tone resembles that of the guitar.

The lute is now obsolete, but was an important instrument two or three centuries ago. Sometimes it had a large pear-shaped body, and as many as thirteen or more pairs of strings. As each pair had to be tuned into unison, as with the mandolin to-day, Mattheson claimed that if a lute-player lived to the age of eighty, he must have spent sixty years of his life in tuning his instrument. Elizabethan England had some gifted lute composers, such as Dowland and Ford. The lute gave rise to systems of musical writing known as tablatures, which represented the music by some characters other than the usual staff notation. For the lute, the tablatures consisted of numbers showing where the strings were to be fingered. The lute music was light in character, but very dainty and attractive.

The zither is really a successor of the lute. It consists of a rectangular sounding-board, lying flat on a table or other support, with thirty horizontal strings. The lower ones are played with a pick on a ring worn on the performer's thumb, while the upper ones are plucked. The zither is much used in Switzerland.

XLVII

FLUTE AND PICCOLO

THE great antiquity of the flute, and its prominence in Roman music, has been already described. It must be kept in mind, however, that the term flute, as used by the ancients, often included instruments with reed mouthpieces of various sorts, like our oboes, clarinets, etc.

In old times some of the flutes were held straight out from the mouth, and played by direct blowing into the tube. This type was known as the flute-a-bec, and afterwards called beak flute from its resemblance to a bird's beak. Sometimes such a flute would branch into two tubes, in which case one may have played a drone-bass accompaniment.

The use of the flute in the Grecian games has been already mentioned. Flute-playing was considered part of the necessary education of the rich Greek youths. Great flute-players grew very popular, and the account of their rivalries reads very much like the story of opera singers' disagreements in our own day. At one time Alcibiades checked the growing popularity of the flute somewhat, refusing to play the instrument because he feared that the large mouthpiece would spoil the shape of his mouth. His prestige was so great that he altered the fashion for a time; but some unknown flute-maker obviated the difficulty by producing a flute with a smaller mouthpiece than usual. Flutes were much prized, the most ornate ones selling for sums as great as three thousand dollars. The salaries of the best professional players were also very large. One of them, Nichomachus, earned by his playing enough money to buy an immense collection of jewels. Even theatrical flute-players were well paid, receiving more from the choregus (director) than all the members of the chorus. This must have been a comfortable salary; for the Athenians had a proverb stating that the way to ruin a man was to have him made a choregus.

Egypt had its flute music also. In the year 280 B.C., Ptolemy

Philadelphus gave a great festival at Alexandria, with singers, kithara players, and flutists, amounting to six hundred in all. A century later, Ptolemy Physcon was a great patron of flute music. He evidently had his full share of "temperament"; for on marrying his brother's wife he killed the latter's son, and after a later marriage with his niece (then his step-daughter) he despatched all the family. Probably he regarded music as a solace for family troubles. After another century came Ptolemy Auletes, father of Cleopatra, his surname of "flute-lover" showing his fondness for that instrument.

In Rome, flutes were used on almost every public occasion. They were employed at funerals, but the ostentation and luxury of these events grew so great that a law was passed limiting the number of flute-players to ten at each funeral. The flute was used also as a pitch-pipe; many great orators, including Caius Gracchus, would have a slave stand behind them, while they spoke, and sound a flute at intervals to give them the proper pitch for their declamatory efforts.

In mediæval times the flute was rather overshadowed in importance by the harps and viols of the Troubadours. But it continued in use nevertheless, in both the straight and the traverse form. The latter, in which the tube is held sidewise, became known gradually as the German flute. The old English beak flute was known as the recorders, and is mentioned by Shakespeare in "Hamlet." The recorder type of flute had a large hole in the tube, covered with thin bladder, giving it a distinctive tone-color. In the time of Henry VII it was described as producing the best effects in the middle register, " but manifold fingering and stops bringeth high notes from its clear tones."

Another royal devotee of the flute was Frederick the Great. In 1728, while still crown prince, he heard the famous flute-player Quantz at Berlin, and was so captivated that he arranged immediately to have the great performer visit him periodically and teach him the flute. The old king, Frederick I, was a narrow martinet who cared nothing for art, so the lessons were taken under difficulties. Once the king threatened that if the lessons were not stopped he would break the flute over his son's head and hang the teacher. It is pretty sure that he would have done this; for once, when the prince ran away from his father's harsh rule, the latter had him con-

demned to death as a deserter, and spared him only at the interces-
sion of the English ambassador. It was therefore with no little fear
that the royal pupil and his teacher saw the old king approach during a later lesson. All that saved the situation was a friendly chim-
ney, up which Quantz was forced to crawl. But better days were in
store, and when the prince became king he made Quantz the court
composer. Frederick was a good musician and composer himself,
writing operas and playing the flute with much taste. For accom-
panist he had another famous protegé, — Carl Philip Emanuel
Bach, a son of the great John Sebastian Bach.

The old form of concert flute (German, *Flöte;* French, *flûte;* Italian, *flauto*) was a slightly tapered tube, with a large hole near one
end serving as mouthpiece, and six finger-holes near the other end.
With the finger-holes closed, the flute sounds D above middle C.
As the tone is produced by the vibration of the air-column in the
tube, the opening of the finger-holes, beginning farthest from the
mouthpiece, will continually shorten the column of air, and give
higher tones. The six holes are so located as to sound the diatonic
scale of D. There are also keys which may be pressed, resulting in
the formation of sharps and flats. Two extra keys give the D-flat
and C below the lowest D. By increasing the force of blowing, the
player can make the air-column divide into halves, giving a new
scale an octave higher than the first one; and still harder blowing
causes a further subdivision, and higher notes yet. The compass of
the flute is rated at three octaves. The action of the flute and other
wind instruments is described in detail in the chapter on "Acoustics."

On the old flute it was rather hard for the player to manage all
the holes and keys. To do away with such difficulties, Theobald
Boehm improved the flute, in 1832, by a new system of rings and
levers, in combination with keys, which brought the fingering into
much smaller space than before. The Boehm flute has a cylindrical
tube.

When Boehm took his improved instrument to show to Rossini,
he found that composer shaving. While waiting in the anteroom,
Boehm started to demonstrate the worth of his invention by playing all sorts of trills, runs, and roulades, including many that were
impossible on the older instrument. Rossini listened with growing
wonder, and at last rushed in with the soap still on his face. "You

can't play that," cried the composer, "it's impossible." "But I am playing it," replied the inventor. From that moment Rossini became an ardent devotee of the new flute.

The technical points of flute-playing have reference to both blowing and fingering. The tone-color varies according to the register, or pitch, the lowest octave being dull and soft, the middle register sweet and full, and the highest notes shrill and piercing. In general, flute tones express a melancholy sweetness that is noticeably characteristic of the instrument. Gluck used flutes excellently in portraying the calm and passionless joy of the Elysian Fields.

A staccato on the flute is given by the mouth, and not the fingers. If the player wishes a full and abrupt effect, he interrupts his breath by pronouncing the letter T. To obtain a slightly less marked effect, he will use the sound of K. Often he will alternate the two, as if pronouncing the words "ticker" or "tucker." This effect is called double-tonguing; and the use of still another consonant results in triple-tonguing.

The fingering is called into execution by the many rapid runs and trills found in flute music. A striking instance of such musical agility is found in the aria "Sweet bird, that shun'st the noise of folly," from Handel's "Il Penseroso." In this number both voice and flute give alternate imitations of a feathered warbler indulging in all sorts of runs, trills, and *fioriture*.

The flute is in constant service in the orchestra, taking the melody for the wood-wind group just as the violin does for the strings. Often it is combined with the violin for this purpose. The lower wood-wind instruments have for some time consisted of the oboe, the clarinet, and the bassoon, while more recently the group has grown to include the English horn, contrabassoon, and bass clarinet. The flute is the highest of these, and is surpassed in pitch only by the piccolo, which is a half-sized flute used chiefly for special effects.

The flute has often served to picture birds, and Beethoven used it in his Pastoral Symphony to represent the nightingale. Mozart was not fond of the instrument, although he wrote a concerto for harp and flute, and the well-known opera "The Magic Flute." Scarlatti detested wind instruments, saying that they were never in tune. Cherubini disliked the instrument very much, and said, "The only thing worse than a flute is two flutes." Mendelssohn, on the other hand, admired the smooth flute tones very greatly. In his Reformation Symphony, when he wished to form a gradual climax on the chorale "Ein feste Burg ist unser Gott," he started by giving the melody to the flutes alone, — an effect that was really too soft, although the later climax of course brought full power. Among solo flute composers, the name of Kuhlau is so prominent that he has been called "The Beethoven of the Flute." A more recent flute devotee was the poet Sidney Lanier, who made the rather too partisan prophecy that the time would come when orchestras would have as many flutes as violins. Two flutes were enough for the early classical composers, but now three, and even four, are used in the standard orchestras.

There are at present no flutes of lower compass than the one here described. The *flauto d'amore*, which sounded a minor third lower than our flute, is now obsolete. Massenet had a bass flute made, a fourth lower than ours, but it is not in common use. It is probable that this deep instrument in the flute family will be a success, for the soft, smooth quality of its tone sounds well in the low notes. It is sometimes called the alto flute.

There is a flute, rarely used, which is a semitone higher than the ordinary flute. This is called the D-flat flute, from the pitch of its lowest note. There is also an instrument with E-flat for its lowest note. This is called the tierce flute, and its crystalline tones were well used by Gade in "The Crusaders." In keeping the fingering the same on all three kinds of flute, the pitch will vary; and in order to make the pitch the same when different flutes are used, the fingering must be varied. Thus the fingering for C would give E-flat on the E-flat flute; and in order to make this flute actually *sound* the C, the fingering for the A below would have to be used. Thus if an instrument transposes up any interval for a certain fingering, its part must be written at that same interval below where it is to sound, in order to prevent alterations in fingering. This point will be more fully treated in connection with the clarinets.

The piccolo (German, *kleine Flöte;* French, *petite flûte;* Italian, *ottavina*), sometimes classed as a separate instrument, is really a half-size flute, giving tones an octave above those of the flute. Its full Italian name, *flauto piccolo,* means simply "little flute." It is a transposing instrument, sounding an octave higher than the written part. In the orchestra, the piccolo is sometimes interchangeable with one of the flutes, the flute-player using the smaller instrument for a time. As the piccolo transposes up an octave, he fingers it exactly the same as he would a flute part. Large modern orchestras have a separate player for the piccolo. The compass of the piccolo is nearly three octaves. It begins with D instead of C (an octave above the lowest flute D), and extends up to the highest B on the piano. Any tone above that is too piercingly shrill to be useful.

As the last sentence suggests, the piccolo is the shrillest of the orchestral instruments. Its keenly brilliant tone-color is almost always called for in picturing wild, frenzied merriment or infernal revelry. Like the flute, it has three distinct registers. Its lower octave is too weak and hollow for orchestral use; its second octave is bright and joyous; while its upper notes have the piercing quality that gives the infernal suggestion to this "imp of the orchestra." The high notes may also give a martial effect, as in Meyerbeer's "Huguenots" and in the cadence of Beethoven's "Egmont" Overture. Gluck, in his "Iphigenie in Tauris," pictured the frenzy of the barbarous Scythians by using piccolo with violin, tambourine, and cymbals. Beethoven made rising notes on the piccolo portray the wind in the storm of his Pastoral Symphony. But it can have softer uses, as in the aria "Ye pretty warbling choirs," from Handel's "Acis and Galatea."

Usually one piccolo is more than enough for its purpose. But Weber, by using two a third apart, produced an inimitably diabolic sneer in Caspar's drinking-song, from "Der Freischütz." Spontini, in his "Fernando Cortez," used two piccolos, with almost everything else that would make a noise, to picture the march of the Mexicans. Berlioz, who was very fond of exaggerated infernal pictures, called for three piccolos in the third part of his "Faust," and even added the shrill tones of an E-flat clarinet.

There are two transposing piccolos, giving still higher tones; but these are restricted to military bands.

The flageolet is a small and shrill survival of the old straight-flute type. It is not used in the orchestra, though Mozart, in his "Entführung aus dem Serail," called for a flageolet in G, sounding a twelfth higher than written.

The tiny and innocent appearance of the flageolet once misled a non-musical minister who used it to illustrate his point. He was speaking of building a character thoroughly in its smallest details, and mentioned the orchestra as an example. "During a certain rehearsal," he said, "the director suddenly rapped on his desk to demand a halt, and said, 'Flageolet, you were silent.' In the midst of all the mingled sounds, he had noticed the absence of one tiny flageolet." Unfortunately for his illustration, that one little instrument could make more noise than almost all the others together; and none but a deaf man could fail to note the difference between its presence and absence in the music.

XLVIII

OBOE AND ENGLISH HORN

THE oboe family is distinguished by having a mouthpiece consisting of two small tongues of reed. Such reed mouthpieces are of
great antiquity, being represented in the sculpture and painting
of ancient Egypt. Early specimens have been found with straws
beside them, probably for making the mouthpiece. The oboe, as
well as the clarinet, was mentioned by mediæval authors as the
schalmei, chalumeau, shawm, etc. There was also a family of old
oboes called bombardi, or pommers.

The double reed used to-day consists of two thin slips of cane,
with a narrow air passage between them. They are fastened by silk
thread to the thin brass tube (called staple) that fits into the end
of the main tube. The English horn, bassoon, and contrabassoon
have similar mouthpieces of larger size. These are deeper instruments; so that while the flute type has only a soprano range, the
double-reed type has a much larger and deeper compass.

The name oboe (German, *Oboe;* French, *hautbois;* Italian, *oboe*)
comes from the French term "hautbois," or high wooden instrument. The oboe has a conical tube expanding away from the mouthpiece, which results in brightness of tone and increased strength
for the overtones. The natural oboe scale is that of D, reaching up
two octaves and a minor third from the D above middle C. It has
extra keys to close holes so that it reaches to the B below middle C;
and the French instruments go a semitone lower. The second octave is produced from the octave harmonic, obtained by increased
strength of blowing. The highest notes are obtained by cross-fingering, producing still higher harmonics. The oboe can give trills,
runs, and rapid passages, but these grow more difficult as the key
of the piece is farther removed from D. This does not refer to distance in the scale, but to the number of sharps or flats called for.

The lowest notes of the oboe are rather harsh and nasal in
quality. The middle register, which is the best, has a reedy and

penetrating quality, still somewhat nasal; while the highest notes are thin and more piercing. As the oboe resembles a shepherd's pipe, it is admirably suited to portray effects of pastoral simplicity. It is also used to picture rustic merriment. Still another effect, arising from the artless simplicity of its tones, is that of pathos and grief. The older oboe, retained in some foreign orchestras, is fuller and more nasal; but the lighter tone of our instrument is amply effective, and has been aptly likened to a silver thread in the orchestral web of sound.

Unlike most wind instruments, the oboe demands less than the natural amount of breath. The player, therefore, has too little work for his lungs; and in long passages he must pause to exhale before taking breath to start again. The older composers often wrote long oboe passages, which the performer has to divide into sections. Schumann once made the same error; and in the second of his three Romances for oboe and piano there is a passage of eighty-four bars without a rest.

There is not much solo music for the oboe. In addition to the Schumann pieces, there are six concertos for it by Handel; one by Mozart, now lost; another by Kalliwoda; and a four-movement trio by Beethoven for two oboes and an English horn. Among recent composers, Arthur Foote has produced a set of three pieces for oboe and piano.

In orchestral music the situation is different, and the incisive tone of the oboe makes it a favorite. The scores of Handel are full of striking passages for it, and in his time it came near being a rival to the violin. The old composers, in fact, had many more wind instruments than we use, and sometimes there were nearly as many oboes as violins. With Haydn the oboe is more of a solo instrument, in light and playful melodies. It is often used antiphonally with the bassoon in the musette-like trios found in his symphonies; but it is employed also in "The Seasons" to represent the crowing of the cock. Saint-Saëns used it in similar fashion in his "Danse Macabre," where the dance of the riotous skeletons comes to an abrupt end at dawn. Mozart employed the oboe freely, and in his Twelfth Mass (providing he wrote that work) there is a famous solo passage for it. Gluck used the oboe effectively in his operas to represent pathos.

1. BASSOON; 2. OBOE; 3. BASS CLARINET; 4. BASSET HORN; 5. CLARINET;
6. OLD FLUTE ; 7. SAXOPHONE ; 8. ENGLISH HORN; 9. BOEHM FLUTE

But it was Beethoven who brought out most fully the capabilities of his instruments; and we find him employing the oboe freely. Its effect of sadness is prominently used in the funeral march of the Heroic Symphony, and cleverly abandoned for 'cellos before it could become monotonous. In the Scherzo of the Pastoral Symphony the oboe plays a large part in the rustic gayety that pictures a village festival. In the opera "Fidelio," the oboe is employed prominently when the hero, Florestan, awaits death by starvation, — a rather distant fate, to judge by the size of many opera singers. Among other instances, the "Egmont" music contains an effective oboe passage, this time in the florid style.

Among very many later examples, Raff lets the oboe take the theme almost alone in the finale of his fourth symphony. Most striking, however, is the dialogue between oboe and English horn in the Symphonie Fantastique of Berlioz. This represents a conversation between a shepherd and a shepherdess in the fields, and leads into one of the many orchestral thunder-storms. After the storm, the English horn resumes, as if inquiring; but there is no reply from the oboe, its absence giving a striking suggestion of tragedy.

The oboe tone quality is very frequently injured by tuning, or any alteration in pitch. It was used, therefore, to give the pitch for the rest of the orchestra to adopt. The custom has continued from Handel's time to the present; although the clarinet, which was not at first in the orchestra, is even harder to tune. Another difficulty with wood-wind instruments results from the fact that the pitch alters as they expand with the heat of the player's breath. When an orchestra is ready to tune, the oboe gives a long-held A. The stringed instruments are soon set at the proper pitch, but the clarinet player will continue to tootle away. He is not doing this for exercise, but to warm the tube of his instrument so that it will not vary in pitch later on.

The oboe is not now a transposing instrument, but transposing oboes have existed in the past. In Handel's "Flavio" there is a song in B-flat-minor, for which the oboe part is in A-minor, suggesting an oboe a semitone higher than usual; but such an instrument is not found elsewhere. The old oboe d'amore, much used by Bach, was a minor third deeper than our oboe. Another old form was the oboe di caccia, a fifth (sometimes a sixth) below our instrument. This was in use as late as Haydn's day, and we even find Rossini calling for it in his "William Tell" Overture, to imitate the alpine horn when giving the "Ranz des Vaches," though this passage is now given by the English horn.

The English horn (German, *Englisches Horn;* French, *cor anglais;* Italian, *corno inglese*) is simply an oboe half as large again as the smaller instrument; and in consequence of its size, its pitch is a fifth lower. When the oboe player had to take the English horn also, the music for the latter was written a fifth higher than it was to sound, so that the oboe fingering could be used, while the size of the instrument gave the low pitch desired. Thus for a piece in D the English horn part would be written a fifth higher, in A, but would sound in D. At present a separate man is needed in large orchestras for the English horn, so the part could be written in the proper key and played by him accordingly; but the custom of using the transposition has not yet been changed.

The English horn is not really a horn, but is named from the old shepherd's pipe used in England and known as the hornpipe. This is mentioned by Chaucer, in his "Romaunt of the Rose," in the lines, —

"Controve he wolde, and foule fayle,
With hornpipes of Cornewaile."

The word "controve" means to compose, and has the same root as "Trouvère." Some claim that the instrument was the "cornpipe," made from cornstalks, just as the chalumeau was named from the Latin *calamus*, a reed. But the corn may also come from the Latin *cornu*, a horn, as is the case with the word cornet.

The natural scale of the English horn is that of G-major, starting just below middle C. It has extra keys which extend its compass downward to E. Its upward limit is the B-flat two and a half octaves higher. The lowest scale of G comes from the natural tones; the next scale is produced from the first overtone, obtained by harder blowing; while the highest notes are obtained by cross-fingering, — opening the holes near the mouthpiece, and stopping others, to obtain still shorter vibrating air-columns.

The tone quality of the English horn is quieter and more solid than that of the oboe. In place of the oboe's appealing pathos we have here a dreamy melancholy. The middle and lower register is especially full, rich, and sonorous. The earlier masters used this instrument very little. It is now admitted to Bach's music, but only to replace the oboe di caccia. Haydn and Mozart called for it a very few times. Beethoven may have used it in the trio with two oboes, but more probably called for an oboe di caccia. Schubert, Weber, and Mendelssohn did not write for it at all. It would have been most appropriate after the storm in the Pastoral Symphony, instead of the clarinet-horn combination that Beethoven used. Schumann avoided the English horn for the most part, but he gave it one prominent passage in his "Manfred," where that hero hears a shepherd's pipe in the Alps. The "pipes in the liberal air," about which the hero pauses to moralize, are well represented by the English horn. Cowen used the instrument excellently in his Scandinavian Symphony, where it depicts the loneliness of the impressive fiords. The French composers showed more appreciation of the instrument, and Meyerbeer gave it due prominence in the fourth act of his "Huguenots." Wagner understood its use in pastoral scenes, and in "Tannhäuser," when the hero emerges from the Mountain of Venus, he finds an excellent English horn player tending sheep in the fields near by. An expressive English horn theme is found in the slow movement of Dvořák's beautiful "New World" Symphony. In modern orchestras the English horn is regarded as indispensable. Sibelius uses it most admirably in his "Swan of Tuonela," a mythical bird that sings mournfully while floating on the River of Death.

There have been attempts to make double-bass oboes, deeper than the English horn; but these have not yet been successful. A small oboe in E-flat, found in some bands, is a minor third higher than the ordinary instrument.

The musette is an instrument somewhat like a bagpipe, but with two pipes where the latter has three. It has the very penetrating quality of the small double-reed instruments. The bagpipe, which has two tubes giving a drone-bass while the third, or chanter, plays the melody, has been found in many forms, such as the ordinary Highland bagpipe, the old German *Sackpfeife*, the French *cornemuse*, the *bignou* of Brittany, the Calabrian *zumpogna*, and the old Irish bagpipe, all blown by the mouth; while the French *musette*, the

Lowland bagpipe, and some other forms, were blown by the bellows.

The Heckelphone, made by the German Heckel, is practically a baritone oboe, nearly an octave lower than the ordinary oboe. Its double reed is between those of the English horn and the bassoon in size. The Heckelclarind, invented by the same maker, has the single reed of the clarinets. It was intended for the English horn solo in the third act of "Tristan." The tarogato is another conical wooden pipe with clarinet reed, and has been used for the same purpose.

XLIX

THE bassoon (German, *Fagott;* French, *basson;* Italian, *fagotto*) is probably an instrument of great antiquity. Its name suggests an instrument taking a bass part, just as tenoroon has been used for one taking the tenor part. But the Arabians had an instrument named *besuin*, while the Egyptian term for a deep-toned pipe was *zummarah-bi-soan*. The use of the term *busaine* or *buisine*, in mediæval manuscripts, points to an Oriental origin for the instrument. Its Italian name, *fagotto*, comes from its fancied resemblance to a bundle of sticks, also called *fagotto*. The Grecians probably had instruments of this type; for the sombre effect of their "Nome of Kradias," or march to execution, had just the sort of impressive gloom that the bassoon could give.

The present bassoon is the work of Afranio, canon of Ferrara, in 1540. It consists of a tapering tube, doubled upon itself, and provided with a brass crook to hold its rather large mouthpiece. Like that of the oboe, this consists of two pieces of reed. The bassoon scale is singularly hard to play, but all efforts to obviate this seem to have injured the tone-color.

The natural scale of the bassoon is that of G-major; but it has a number of extra keys that enable it to reach down to the B-flat over two octaves below middle C. Its compass extends up to the A-flat above middle C, giving it a range of nearly three octaves. The lower register forms a good bass to the wood-wind quartet, which in later classical times consisted of flutes, oboes, clarinets, and bassoons. The middle register of the bassoon is dull and hollow, while the upper tones have a penetrating power that is not unlike a cry of agony. The tone-color of the bassoon is sometimes impressively sombre; but it is well suited to grotesque effects also, and has been called "the clown of the orchestra."

As the music of the bassoon is written in either bass or tenor clef, it may be well to enumerate the clefs here. Taken in order, from the highest to the lowest, they alter the pitch of any written note by thirds. The highest clef is the so-called French violin clef, placing the G above middle C on the lowest line of the staff. This clef is not used now. The usual G-clef puts this G on the second line of the staff, with middle C on the first line below. Then there is a set of C-clefs, placing middle C on the various lines of the staff. With C on the lowest line we have the soprano clef; on the second, the mezzo-soprano; on the third, the alto; and on the fourth, the tenor. The baritone clef brings the F below middle C on the third line of the staff; while the bass clef puts this F on the next line above that, next to the top line. The G-clef and the bass clef are used in piano music, but for orchestral work some of the others are called for, notably the alto and tenor clefs. Any change of clefs has for its object the keeping of the notes on or near the staff, so that there will be no need for many extra lines (leger lines) above or below the staff. The C-clefs were often employed in old vocal music.

Rapid passages on the bassoon sound best in its natural key of G, or in closely related keys. Trills are practicable, though not on every note. Staccato notes have a good effect, as in the allegro of Beethoven's Fourth Symphony. But in general the tone-color of the instrument is so striking that the composer need only write passages of straightforward character for it, without making it do technical tricks.

In Cambert's "Pomone," given at Paris in 1671, we find the bassoon used merely as a bass instrument. But the introduction of still lower instruments, and the improvement in the bassoon's upper (vox humana) notes, has left it free for special effects.

Handel used the bassoon little, though in his "Saul" he gave it effective phrases when the Witch of Endor raised the ghost of Samuel. Bach sometimes let it do a little more than reinforce the bass part. But it did not come into its own until the time of Haydn, who used its expressive upper notes very freely. Mozart employed its comic effects in the G-minor symphony, by making it imitate a violin figure.

Beethoven showed unusual fondness for the bassoon, and it was really his favorite instrument. He called for it continually, and evidently understood its tone-color absolutely. In the first movement of his Eighth Symphony it is used with exquisite humor; but its most comical effects are shown in the scherzo of the Pastoral (sixth) Symphony. In this is a picture of village revelry, in which a rustic band takes part. The bassoon player of the band is inspired by the occasion, and perhaps by something more definitely exhilarating. He is depicted as having seen better days, being now condemned to play on an instrument which has only three keys left. These keys give F, C, and F in descending order; and the bassoonist comes in heavily with them every time they are needed, and even indulges in them once or twice when they could be spared.

The humor of the great composers would form a book in itself, and not the least important part of it would be that dealing with the comical effects they have produced with the instruments. Thus Mozart once wrote a "Musikalischer Spass," or musical joke, in which he pictured a young composer struggling to write an ambitious piece. The weak character of the themes, and the flimsy attempts at development, are duly portrayed; and at the end, when the neophyte tries to introduce the complex form of a fugue, he is soon tangled up, and has to cover his retreat with a blare of noise.

Where Beethoven used the bassoon in rather grotesque fashion, Mendelssohn handled it more daintily. The latter composer gave the bassoon many bits of inimitable humor in his "Midsummer Night's Dream" music. Most noticeable among them are the quaint clowns' march for two bassoons a third apart; the imitation of a rustic band in the funeral march, with the bassoon making a ludicrous cadence by itself on a low note; and, in the overture, the braying of the transformed Bottom.

Wagner's sense of humor wins unbounded admiration, and in his "Mastersingers of Nuremberg" it is worthy to rank with that of a Shakespeare or an Aristophanes. The libretto, which he wrote, is such a superb comedy that it has become a textbook in the German schools. But the score, too, is full of delightful passages, such as the tapping of Sachs's hammer while he listens to Beckmesser, the confusion of themes in the riot scene, the discordant horn of the watchmen, the painful attempts of the beaten Beckmesser to sit down, or the latter's fearful and wonderful efforts to recollect the melody of the prize song. But the wood-wind's share of fun comes in the long prelude. Here the story of the opera is foreshadowed, and the music shows how the narrow masters fail at first to recognize the freer genius of the hero, Walther, who tries to enter their guild in order to win a bride. After Walther's first song has been suggested, the masters' theme reasserts itself. It is given to the wood-wind group, and made to sound inimitably fussy and self-conceited. Fragments of Walther's trial-song recur, but are constantly interrupted by bits of the masters' theme, until there is practically a free fight in the orchestra, calmed only by the appearance of Walther's second trial-song, which the masters ultimately crown with a prize. In all this the bassoon plays a most prominent part.

The French composers used the bassoon freely, Cherubini writing a great solo for it in his "Médée." Meyerbeer, in "Robert le Diable," used the hollow middle register with blood-curdling effect in the scene where the hero plucks a branch of cypress from his mother's grave, amid the ghosts of faithless nuns. Berlioz, with his usual wholesale tendencies, called for seven bassoons in his "Damnation de Faust." But he showed that he knew the instrument by his use of it in the fourth movement of his "Symphonie Fantastique," where it gives a wonderful picture of the insistent footsteps of the crowd surging about the victim on his way to the scaffold. Ambroise Thomas employed the bassoon to represent Caliban in his ballet "The Tempest," and our own Professor John K. Paine did the same in his symphonic poem on that subject. A more recent French composer to use the bassoon with infinite humor is Paul Dukas. In his "Apprenti Sorcier," picturing the magician's pupil who made a broom produce a torrent of water but forgot how to shut it off, various skips and passages on the bassoon lend an inimitably comic flavor to the rushing of the water and the growing apprehensions of the unlucky apprentice.

There is a smaller size of bassoon, known as the basson quinte because it sounds a fifth higher than the ordinary instrument. It is used as a transposing instrument, and therefore must be written a fifth lower than desired, to allow of the same fingering as the usual instrument. It is not used in the orchestra, and is not of great importance, since its upper register is much like the tone of the English horn.

The contrabassoon (double bassoon) is a still larger and deeper instrument of the double-reed family. It has a tapering tube about sixteen feet long, and gives an octave below the bassoon, just as the contrabass sounds an octave below the 'cello. The contrabassoon can reach as low as the lowest D on the piano, while some contrabassoons even reach the B-flat below that. It is therefore the deepest instrument of the orchestra. Its compass extends up about two octaves from the lowest D; it can give some higher notes, but these are better obtained on the bassoon. The contrabassoon is a transposing instrument, sounding an octave deeper than the written part.

The contrabassoon forms a broad and effective bass for the wood-wind group, sounding like the tone of a deep-voiced organ pipe. Rapid passages are not suited to an instrument of this large size, though Beethoven wrote some quick phrases for it in his Ninth Symphony. It was first used by Handel at the coronation of George II, in 1727. Haydn employed it well in "The Creation," to represent footsteps at the phrase, "By heavy beasts the ground is trod." Mozart and Spohr used it in nonets for wind instruments. Beethoven, in the grave-digging scene of "Fidelio," called for it in combination with two bassoons; and when one of the trio of players was absent from a rehearsal, Beethoven grew very angry with Prince Lobkowitz, one of his patrons, for suggesting mildly that perhaps two performers would do. Beethoven was often irascible, but the value of his music amply excused his temper.

Some decades ago a Frenchman named Sarrus adapted reed mouthpieces to brass tubes. His instruments have not entered the orchestra, though they are much used in military bands, where they are very effective. One of them, the sarrusophone, has a double-reed mouthpiece, and the same system of keys as that used on the wood-wind instruments. Like all the instruments described in this and the preceding chapter, it may be classed as a member of the oboe family. It sometimes replaces the contrabassoon.

L

THE CLARINETS

WHILE the instruments of the oboe family have two bits of reed in their mouthpieces, the clarinets have only one. This is a broad strip, narrowing at the top to a very sharp edge. It is attached to the mouthpiece of the instrument by two metallic bands provided with screws. The player presses the end of the reed against his lower lip while performing, and the vibrations of the reed cause the air-column in the tube to vibrate also, and produce the tone.

The early instruments known as shawms, and probably some of the old Greek *auloi*, were of this type. But the clarinet as we know it is due to Johann Christopher Denner, of Nuremburg, who perfected it in 1690. This instrument was improved by Stadler, of Vienna, and by Sax, of Paris; but it is not suited for the Boehm system of keys. The main part of its tube is cylindrical, which has some effect; but the size of the reed is really responsible. While the flute and oboe act like open pipes, the clarinet behaves like a stopped pipe, closed at one end. One result is a deeper pitch, the clarinet sounding an octave below a flute of the same size; while another effect is found in the fact that stopped pipes do not give the odd-numbered harmonics. This point is explained in the chapter on "Acoustics." The first harmonic, an octave above the normal tone in pitch, is used to get a second octave scale in the flute or oboe; but it does not exist on the clarinet. The over-blowing in the latter case causes the air-column to vibrate in thirds instead of halves, giving a rise in pitch of a twelfth instead of an octave. Thus a fingering based on octaves must be supplemented in some way.

The clarinet (German, *Klarinette;* French, *clarinette;* Italian, *clarino*) has six finger-holes, played by three fingers on each hand. These give the scale of G major, a fifth below that of the flute. There are extra keys to close holes at the end away from the mouthpiece, thus lengthening the air-column and lowering the compass to the E below middle C. The usual keys for sharps and flats are present, completing a scale from G to F-sharp. By overblowing the lowest E, the B a twelfth above it is produced; but between the F-sharp and the B are four semitones which must be obtained by special devices. One of these is produced by lifting the thumb off an extra finger-hole, while the other three are provided for by keys which open holes near the mouthpiece. The fingering begins again at the twelfth instead of the octave, while the highest tones are produced by cross-fingering.

The compass of the clarinet is from E below middle C to the C three octaves above it. This compass is divided into four registers, though some authorities speak of only three. The natural scale, sometimes including the "medium" notes with special keys, is called the chalumeau register, after the obsolete instrument of that name. It has a rich, full, and somewhat reedy tone. The acute register is the scale which the keys obtain from the harmonic of the twelfth; while the upper register includes the highest notes.

With its many registers, the clarinet is also capable of many gradations in power of tone. This makes it the most expressive of the wood-wind group. Owing to the complex fingering, it is hard to play the C clarinet in keys containing many sharps or flats. Many trills are practicable, but in certain signatures some of these become impossible, as the finger would have to skip from key to key. Rapid passages in the medium register are impracticable because of the fingering; while passages that cross and recross the "break," or change in pressure of blowing, can never be played at all swiftly. In these changes there is always danger that the tone may break into harsh noises, called "couacs."

To obviate these difficulties, the clarinet is made in several pitches. The one already described is called the clarinet in C. For flat keys there is a B-flat clarinet, sounding a tone lower; and for sharp keys an A clarinet, a minor third lower. As the Germans speak of our B-flat as B (our B being called H), German scores will call for the B clarinet, meaning what we know as the B-flat instrument.

The two lower clarinets are transposing instruments. The same fingering that gives C on the C clarinet would give B-flat and A on the two lower instruments. So, to keep the fingering the same, the part for the B-flat clarinet is written a tone above where the instrument will make it sound, and for the A clarinet a minor third above. The same player will use these different instruments in different pieces; so that here, at least, the transposition is still of use to the player. But modern performers could dispense with it; and many efforts are now being made to do away with such transpositions, and have all parts written as they sound, even though the player has to alter his fingering. At present, if a piece in D calls for the A clarinet the part must be written in F (and fingered for F) to sound in D. For a piece in E, the A clarinet would be fingered as if for G, thus making the player figure for only one sharp, whereas four sharps would be necessary if the C clarinet were used. But if the clarinet part were written in E and meant to sound there, the player, using the A clarinet, could play it just as easily, as he would know instantly that he would need the G fingering anyway.

It will be seen from all this that orchestral keys, unlike those on the piano, are limited by the nature of certain instruments. The keys with few sharps or flats are most practicable. Of course other considerations guide the composer, such as bringing out the best registers of certain instruments; but he ought not to call for such keys as G-flat, or D-flat, or B, for example. Some of Liszt's Hungarian Rhapsodies, when taken from the piano and scored for orchestra, are purposely transposed, to make the instrumental work easier.

Composers favor the B-flat clarinet, and after that the A clarinet, because both of them have a sweeter and richer tone than the instrument in C. The tone-color of the clarinet is weird and sombre in the chalumeau register, and full and clear in the second scale.

The clarinet, like the oboe, is influenced by heat, and the player must blow into the tube to warm it up before he starts. The process of tuning an orchestra is not the most agreeable in the world, although a Chinese dignitary once applauded it and preferred it to the later numbers that he heard. The oboe, as already stated, gives the pitch by sounding a prolonged and repeated A. The string players then get their A-strings to this pitch, after which they tune the others in a series of empty fifths and fourths that would shock a harmony teacher. Then the clarinetists begin "tootling" on their instruments, to warm up the tubes and adjust them to the pitch. The other wood-wind instruments do the same, while grunts from the tubas and other brass instruments add to the varied mixture of tone.

Handel once tried to obviate this disturbance by having the instruments tuned beforehand. But while the audience was coming in, some practical joker got at the orchestra and put a number of instruments out of tune. In due time the players took their places; but when the leader gave the signal for the opening chord, there was a grand crash. The composer tumbled over a few instruments in his hurry to find out who would do "such a vicked thing," but he never discovered the joker.

The clarinet was the last instrument to enter the classical orchestra. Handel left an incomplete work for two clarinets and a horn, while Johann Christian Bach, son of the great Bach, used the clarinet in 1763 in his "Orione." Gluck employed the old chalumeau in his early scores, and Haydn wrote some clarinet passages in his oratorios; but Mozart was the first to bring out its chief possibilities. One of his three last and greatest symphonies, the one in E-flat, is often called the clarinet symphony, from the prominence he gave to the instrument when writing it. The clarinets now used in Handel's "Messiah" were introduced into the score by Mozart. Beethoven was very fond of the clarinet. In the Pastoral Symphony it imitates the call of the yellow-hammer; in the first movement of that work it has a difficult passage that includes the break; while after the thunderstorm it is combined with horns to give the shepherd's call. Weber made wonderful use of the clarinet's ghostly chalumeau effects in the supernatural scenes of "Der Freischütz." Mendelssohn employed it admirably in the Scotch Symphony. The clarinet is an integral part of the modern orchestra. It has a solo repertoire, and Spohr wrote a concerto for clarinet and orchestra.

Still other clarinets exist. Thus Mozart, in his "Idomeneo," called for a clarinet in B, transposing a semitone, and very useful in keys with many sharps. It is not in use now, however. Clarinets which transpose upward are found in the keys of D, E-flat, F, and A-flat. Wagner and Cherubini have used the instrument in D. That in E-flat is too shrill for orchestral use; but Berlioz, the great experimenter, called for it in his "Symphonie Fantastique." In that gory work, a lover has killed his sweetheart in a fit of jealousy. He is marched to execution, and beheaded by the full orchestra;

but he is not allowed to rest even then. An extra movement shows his reception into the infernal regions. In this movement the E-flat clarinet aids the piccolo in making the revels truly satanic. The F clarinet, still more piercing, was formerly employed by German military bands; while that in A-flat, the shrillest instrument in existence, is used in Austria.

Tenor clarinets exist, which transpose a fifth and a sixth downward, but the former is practically the same as the basset horn. The basset horn thus bear the same relation to the C clarinet as the English horn does to the oboe. The basset horn is a transposing instrument, with a compass beginning an octave below middle C. It is less brilliant than the clarinet, but has a sombre richness of tone well suited to religious or funereal subjects. Mozart used it well in his Requiem, in which the only reed instruments are two basset horns and two bassoons. He employed it also in the temple scene of "The Magic Flute."

The bass clarinet is a still larger and deeper instrument of this family. It has a crook for the mouthpiece and a large bell at the other end. The usual form sounds an octave below the B-flat clarinet. It is treated as a transposing instrument, sounding a ninth lower than written. A bass clarinet in C exists, and Wagner called for a deeper one in A. The compass of the B-flat instrument ranges from the D, nearly two octaves below middle C, to the F an octave and a half above that C. The highest notes are seldom used. The lower register, corresponding to the chalumeau of the clarinet, is the best. It is excellent in combination, and may be made to have either the weird quality of the chalumeau or the solemn effect of an organ pipe. It has been well used by Meyerbeer in his "Huguenots" and it even takes the melody for a time in the coronation march from his "Prophète."

In recent years a Parisian maker named Besson has produced a clarinet an octave deeper than the preceding, known as the pedal clarinet. This instrument can reach the lowest D on the piano.

Like the double reed, the clarinet reed has been adapted to brass tubes. The resulting instruments are known as saxophones, from the name of their inventor, Adolphe Sax. The saxophones come in several sizes, and resemble the clarinets in appearance. The saxophones have tapering tubes, and. unlike the clarinets, can produce all the overtones. The fingering, therefore, resembles that of the oboe. There are in all twelve varieties of saxophone, in the six classes of sopranino, soprano, alto, tenor, baritone, and bass. All the instruments except the one in C are transposing. They are much used in the French military bands, but have not entered the orchestra. Gevaert describes the saxophone color as "a voice rich and penetrating, the rather veiled quality of which partakes at once of the 'cello, the English horn, and the clarinet, with more fulness of tone." Thus it would almost seem to be an orchestra in itself. Bizet, in his ever-beautiful "Arlésienne" music, wrote a charming melody for the alto saxophone in E-flat. with orchestra; but up to the present very few have followed this lead.

LI

HORNS, TRUMPETS, AND CORNETS

THE wood-wind group of instruments derive their tone from the vibration of reeds, even the flute being considered to have an air-reed, or space of compressed air near the blow-hole acting like a reed. In the brass instruments there is no such device. The player presses his lips against a brass mouthpiece, and blows through a narrow opening between them. If his lips are loose, no tone will result; but if he stiffens them, they vibrate regularly, and transmit their vibrations to the air column in the tube. By increasing the stiffness of the lips, the player can make them vibrate more quickly, and cause the air-column to subdivide, giving overtones. While only a few such overtones are used in the wood-wind group (obtained by increased force of blowing), a much larger number of overtones can be produced on the brass instruments. In the so-called natural instruments, such as the bugle or the Waldhorn (forest horn), these overtones (harmonics) are the only notes that can be obtained. On the valve instruments there are valves (keys) which act by throwing in extra sections of tubing and lowering the pitch. Still other brass instruments, such as the trombone and slide trumpet, are made with inner and outer tubes, so that the length of tube used can be altered by pulling or pushing, as with a telescope. The mouthpiece of the brass instruments is a metal cup, or cone, against which the lips are pressed.

The simplest brass instrument is the natural horn, or Waldhorn. This is merely a tube with a mouthpiece. Horns of this sort have been known from ancient times. They were much used for military signals, and in the middle ages for hunting calls. The simplest horn of to-day, the post-horn, consists of a mouthpiece and a straight tube. The hunting-horn was bent in a single curve at first, and later on in a threefold circle, so that it could be hung on the shoulder. Louis XV, with his master of the hunt, systematized the horn-calls, giving a meaning to each, and making some of them quite intricate.

1. VALVE TROMBONE; 2. SLIDE TROMBONE; 3. TRUMPET; 4. SERPENT; 5. HORN;
6. BASS TUBA; 7. CORNET; 8. OPHICLEIDE

The horn (German, *Horn;* French, *cor;* Italian, *corno*) was used as an orchestral instrument by Scarlatti, Bach, and Handel, while Gossec introduced it in Paris. It seems strange to think that the horn was opposed at first; for now its smooth tones are highly prized among the orchestral colors. Yet when it first entered the orchestra, it was considered coarse and vulgar, and unfit to mingle with the more delicate violins and oboes.

The natural horn, without keys or valves, is an expanding tube, curved upon itself, having a tapering mouthpiece at the narrow end, and a large bell, or expanded opening, at the other end. When the player puts his lips firmly against the mouthpiece and blows to make them vibrate, he produces only the harmonic series, without ever being able to get the fundamental note from which the harmonics are derived. Thus a tube eight feet long should give the C two octaves below middle C; but the eight-foot horn (C-alto) starts with the C only one octave below middle C, which is the first harmonic of its series. This series consists of the following notes, in ascending order: C, G, C, E, G, B-flat, C, D, E, F-sharp, G, and so on in decreasing intervals. It may be stated in passing that the bugle cannot sound even the first harmonic with any good effect, but begins with the second. Thus its tones have intervals corresponding to the notes G, C, E, and G in ascending order.

The lack of intermediate notes in the lower register of the natural horn prevents the solo player from getting any real melody. But as horns exist in many keys, orchestral composers could call for horns in several keys, and combine them into chords. The C-alto horn, little used now, is the highest of the family, and is written as it sounds. The lower horns, transposing downward in accordance with their pitch, are in B-flat alto, A, A-flat, G, F, E, E-flat, D, C, and B-flat basso, the last transposing downward a major ninth. The natural horns are provided with crooks of various sizes, or in rare cases a slide, which may alter the length of the tube and enable the player to get all keys.

The lowest horn is eighteen feet long. As longer tubes give more overtones, it follows that the compass of the lower horns is greater than that of the higher ones. But the low notes sound best on the shorter instruments. The natural tones are best on the horns in

F, E, and E-flat. Extreme intervals are not easy on the horn, as they imply a sudden and great change in force of blowing and stiffness of lips. Trills are practicable only in the high register, the compass of these horns being nearly three octaves.

The beauty of the horn tones is seen in nearly every orchestral piece. Among the most famous examples is the great horn passage in the scherzo of Beethoven's "Heroic Symphony." In the finale of Schubert's C-major symphony these instruments come in softly, like "horns of elf-land, faintly blowing," and gradually swell into the richest of harmonies. The horn quartet in "Der Freischütz" is another well-known example; and still another is found in the third movement of Mendelssohn's Italian Symphony.

The performer must influence the tones of the horn by inserting his hand into the bell, more or less deeply, and relaxing his lips. The lowest open note can thus be lowered by several semitones, the new notes being called factitious, or artificial. The upper harmonics are similarly treated, and for deep insertions the tone is called stopped, or muted. Such tones have a veiled quality, but when blown loudly become very harsh and ugly. Muted horn tones are freely used to picture evil, as when Faust is asked to sign the contract with Mephistopheles, in Gounod's opera, or when Siegfried is killed, in the second act of Wagner's "Götterdämmerung." Massenet found a clever use for muted horns when he let them represent the cracked village bell in the Angelus movement of his "Scènes Pittoresques."

The valve horn now replaces the natural form, and gives tones that are almost as good, though some difference is caused by the valves, or ventils. These are three in number. The first valve throws into use enough extra tubing to lower the pitch a tone; the second will lower the pitch a semitone, and the third, a tone and a half. The first two played together give about the same result as the third, but are sometimes used in preference, as the third is played by a weak finger. The largest interval between two horn tones is the fifth between the first and second harmonics. Again taking the C horn as an illustration, this interval will be from the lowest C to the G above it. Now on the valve horn the second valve will lower the G to F-sharp; the first will lower it to F; the third (or the first and second), to E; the second and third to E-flat; the first and third to D; and all three valves together will lower the G to D-flat. This, it will be seen, makes the complete scale possible upon the horn. As each of these altered pitches has its own series of harmonics, it becomes possible for the player to produce high notes in several different ways.

Although all tones in its compass are possible on the valve horn, which can thus modulate freely, it is still advisable for the composer to keep to the natural tones as much as possible, as they sound best. But since the horn in F has about the best quality, composers will often call for it, even when the piece is not in F, and write its part in the requisite key. If the horn part written in C sounds in F on the F horn, then, for example, if a piece is in A, the part for the F horn must be written in E.

The post-horn is a straight tube four feet in length, usually in the key of C or B-flat, giving the first five harmonics. The bugle gives the same number of harmonics, though in both instruments the lowest one, being dull in quality, is not used.

The trumpet was widely known in ancient times, playing its part in the fall of Jericho, and even in the Trojan War. The Roman lituus was a curved affair coming from Oscan models, while the tuba was of Etruscan origin. Trumpets were martial and royal instruments through the middle ages, and the trumpeters' guild became important and influential. This guild existed down to the nineteenth century, when we find the Duke of Saxe-Weimar having to pass an examination for admission, under just the same rules that applied to the humblest aspirant.

The trumpet (German, *Trompete;* French, *trompette;* Italian, *tromba*) differs from the horn in having its tube cylindrical, except near the bell, or enlarged open end. Its mouthpiece is a hemispherical cup instead of a cone, and its shape nearly oblong. The trumpet in C is eight feet long, like the C-alto horn. Its lowest note is the first harmonic, but the real trumpet quality begins with the second. As with the horns, crooks of different length may be inserted to vary the key, while the music is written in C. There are trumpets transposing upward in F, E, E-flat, and D, that in C sounding as written and the one in B-flat transposing a tone downward. The trumpet compass, like that of the horn, is rated at three octaves, but it rarely extends over two and a half.

In Monteverde's time we find two kinds of trumpet, — the clarino (clarion), a small, high instrument, and the tromba, larger and deeper. The music of Bach and Handel shows this distinction, the so-called "Clarinbläser" taking the upper parts, while the "Principalbläser" gave the lower notes. The "Clarinbläser" had a shallow mouthpiece, by the aid of which they could give the most brilliant passages. In the classical period of Haydn, Mozart, and Beethoven, the trumpet was less prominent. Wagner employed it well in some of his operas, though it has not regained its old-time brilliance. The trumpet, like the horn, is provided with a mute, a pear-shaped affair that can be held in the bell in place of the performer's fist. Muted trumpets are not much used, though Wagner had them imitate the tiny trumpets of the toy-makers' guild in "Die Meistersinger." The usual color of the trumpet is bold and martial, and its ringing fanfares can be heard easily through the tones of an entire orchestra.

The older composers were fond of writing duets for voice and trumpet. Such a duet, for bass, is "The trumpet shall sound," in Handel's "Messiah." Another instance is the song "Let the bright seraphim," this time for soprano. The trumpet does not always win in such a comparison. Thus the great basso Lablache could dominate an entire orchestra with his voice. The famous tenor Farinelli once out-sang a trumpet, and held his tones much longer than those the trumpeter could give. Mrs. Billington, the famous English soprano, so exceeded the trumpet in volume of tone that once a conductor and trumpeter almost came to blows because of the latter's inability to balance her voice.

The natural trumpet has been modified by slides and by valves. Thomas Harper, a famous English trumpeter of the eighteenth century, used the slide trumpet, in which the tube has a double joint so that it can be elongated slightly, like the trombone, though drawn toward the player. The slide can be used to correct certain harmonics that are out of pitch with our scale, such as the sixth and the tenth, which would be the B-flat and the F-sharp in the series from C, given above. The valve trumpet has three valves, similar to those of the horn. The old florid passages can be readily played with the aid of the valves, but the natural (open) tones are still the best in quality. Wagner has used a bass trumpet, a valve instrument an

octave deeper than the usual form; but its tones lack the nobility of
the higher trumpets.

The cornet, known also as the cornet-a-pistons, is a tapering brass
tube a little over four feet in length, and with a bore that is noticeably wide in proportion. Its natural key is B-flat, though crooks
may be used to set it in A, A-flat, or G. It is treated like the transposing instruments of the wood-wind, having its part written in C
when the key in which it is set is used. The small size of the cornet
makes it sound an octave higher than the trumpet in the same key.
Thus when the trumpet and cornet play the same scale, the cornet
is giving lower harmonics, based on a higher fundamental note, than
that of the trumpet. From this it follows that there will be fewer
changes of blowing on the cornet, and more notes, in a given scale,
derived from a single harmonic. This is the cause of the great
fluency shown by the cornet in comparison with the trumpet. The
cornetist can give rapid passages, trills, and other embellishments
with great ease.

The tone-color of the cornet is below that of the trumpet in value.
Where the trumpet tones are bold and clear, those of the cornet
sound blatant and vulgar, although the skilful cornetist will make
its notes sound fairly agreeable. Cornets are so much easier to play
than trumpets that many small orchestras make this substitution;
but when a really good conductor comes along, he will insist on
banishing the cornet and recalling the trumpet. The tone-color of
the cornet is due in part to the width of its tube, and in part to its
mouthpiece, which is a deeper cup than that of the trumpet. Sometimes the performers put a cornet mouthpiece on a trumpet tube.
The cornet has been used brilliantly in Italian opera. The French
composers have at times employed the instrument for its own color;
but it has never been really accepted in the orchestra. Berlioz,
with his usual fondness for novelty, tried cornets and trumpets in
combination. He claimed that this gave a good effect, but later
composers have not agreed with him. Meanwhile the fluent character of the cornet makes it a favorite at popular concerts, where it
has no real rival.

LII

TROMBONES AND TUBAS

THE trombone, like the trumpet, is of ancient origin. The principle of the slide, or elongation of tubes within tubes, has been ascribed to Tyrtaeus, in 685 B.C., and even to the mythical Osiris. Such slides have not been found in ancient relics, but the early writers describe them. Arcadius, writing in A.D. 200, used as a simile the contrivance that could make the *aulos* elongate. Another ancient passage, attributed to Apuleius, states that when the channels (canales) of the trumpet (tuba) are moved in or out by the right hand, different musical sounds are produced.

At the close of the middle ages, trombones were well known in Germany, Hans Menschel being a celebrated trombone maker in 1520. A century later, Praetorius gave pictures of trombones in sizes corresponding to the alto, tenor, bass, and contrabass instrument. Bach used these various sizes, as well as a still smaller soprano trombone. The soprano trombone stood in B-flat, its first harmonic being a tone below middle C. This, like the other forms, was sometimes used to reënforce the voice part in concerted music. The alto trombone was a fourth lower, in F. The tenor trombone, the one usually employed now, is a fifth lower yet, in B-flat, with its first harmonic a ninth below middle C; while the bass trombone is in G, F, or E-flat. Wagner called for a contrabass trombone, an octave below the tenor form. With the use of the slide, it can get down to the lowest E on our pianos; and this tonal growl is found in the opera of "Siegfried."

The name trombone (German, *Posaune;* French, *trombone;* Italian, *trombone*) comes from *tromba,* and means a large trumpet, just as violone means a large viol. The old English name of sackbut is said to have been derived from the Moorish word *sacabuche,* meaning pump; and this term is decidedly expressive in suggesting the player's motions as he draws the slide in or out. This slide is entirely separate from the rest of the instrument. It is a long tube doubled on itself in the form of a narrow U. Both ends of the U fit over tubes, one of these carrying the mouthpiece while the other continues the instrument to the bell. The sliding U can be made to lengthen the tube. When nearest the performer, it is in the first position; and he can move it away through six other positions, each higher one lowering the pitch a semitone. He can also give any intermediate tone, or correct the pitch of the sixth harmonic, or create glissando effects.

The trombone most used in orchestral work is the tenor instrument. Its tube is about nine feet long, giving the B-flat a ninth below middle C as its first harmonic. The trombone compass is smaller than that of the horn, running up only two octaves from its first harmonic, although solo players sometimes go higher. Like the valve instruments, the slide trombone can give high notes in more than one way. Thus, for example, the B-flat just below middle C could be either the third harmonic from the first position, or the fourth harmonic from the fifth position.

But while the trombone cannot go so high in proportion as the horn, it can give its fundamental note, an octave below the first harmonic, which is impossible on the smaller brass instruments. Theoretically, each of the seven positions has its own fundamental, or pedal tone. The French maker Sax devised a piston to produce the notes between the lowest harmonic and the highest pedal tone, but it is not much used. On the tenor trombone, the pedal tones may be obtained in reality only from the first four positions. But these few tones are considered quite valuable, having a gruff and ponderous quality that is very striking, and well repays the performer for the rather difficult task of mastering them. Pedal tones on the bass trombone are unusually fierce in character.

The orchestras of the present generally contain three tenor trombones, though when they are used in three separate parts, the names given to them are somewhat misleading. The trombone parts are written as they sound. The parts for the smaller instruments were in various clefs, but the tenor trombone alone may have its music in the alto, tenor, or bass clef. The bass trombone, with its music in the bass clef, is called for only when its lowest tones are desired. It is hard to play, as it demands much breath from the player. Composers therefore employ it for only a few notes at a time, with frequent rests.

The use of the slide makes fairly rapid passages possible on the trombone, especially if they lie largely in one harmonic series, and can be blown without much change of position. Passages that demand the same harmonic in different positions, or that do not have any abrupt change in blowing, are limited in speed only by the strength of the performer's arm as he moves the slide. Rapid execution may be used by a solo player to dazzle an audience; but in orchestral work the trombone is treated more slowly.

The trombone is a most important instrument in picturing heroic emotions, as its tones in orchestral work may be made grand and noble. It may portray almost every broad emotion, from sacred calm to the wildest strains of martial glory. It has also a portentous and threatening quality, and its sombre tones are thus excellently fitted for tragic effects also.

The threatening color of the trombone has been well used by Gluck to accompany the chorus of the Furies in his "Iphigenie in Tauris." In his "Alceste," also, they give a wrathful chord in response to Alceste's defiance of the powers of death. Mozart obtained a similar effect in "Don Giovanni," where that hero's ribald invitation to the statue of his victim to sup with him brings an unexpected acceptance, amid trombone chords of solemn warning. The impressive quality of the trombones is present also in the religious service of "The Magic Flute." Beethoven knew something of the instrument, but did not use it in his earlier works. It entered the symphonic orchestra when he wrote his Fifth Symphony; but here, as in the Sixth, it does not play an important part. When Beethoven's career was nearly over, in 1823, he put many eager questions to a visiting trombone player, inquiring especially about the use of the instrument in high passages. His resultant knowledge is shown in the Ninth Symphony, and in a letter that he wrote afterwards to his publisher Schott. Having occasion to make a complaint in the letter, he ended it with a few lines of half-humorous abuse, and added to his signature a trombone trill, with the word *minacciando* (threateningly), on a bit of staff scored for the sixteen-foot bass instrument. Mendelssohn admired the trombone very much, reserving it for the most solemn occasions. Schubert obtained good effects by using soft trombone tones against the strings. The wholesale Berlioz, in picturing the Day of Judgment in his Requiem, called for four extra groups of brasses, including trombones. His score required a complete band of strings, four flutes, two oboes, four clarinets, eight bassoons, an English horn, twelve brass horns, four cornets, sixteen tenor trombones, two tubas, four ophicleides, twelve trumpets, sixteen kettledrums, two bass drums, three pairs of cymbals, and a gong, — certainly enough instruments to represent the crack of doom. Trombone chords make an admirably triumphant effect in Liszt's "Tasso."

A valve trombone exists, which has no slide, but obtains its scale by means of ventils, or pistons, similar to those used on the other brass instruments. This is easier to play than the slide form, and admits of more rapid execution. But this advantage is more than offset by its inferiority of tone-color. For this reason most orchestras do not use it; and it is found chiefly in military bands.

The modern tuba (German, *Tube;* French, *tuba;* Italian, *tuba*), like the trombone, exists in many sizes. There are six of these, — soprano, alto, tenor, baritone, bass, and contrabass. The smaller members of this family are not found in the orchestra, but take part in military bands, especially in France, under the name of sax-horns. The tenor tuba, and a small-bored baritone instrument, are called alt-horns. The two lowest instruments are known as tubas, and used in modern orchestral scores.

The bass tuba, or bombardon, is the usual form employed. It consists of a rather wide tapering brass tube, curved in a fairly short and rounded oblong, and provided with a mouthpiece like that of the trombone. It has the usual pistons, or valves, but is provided with an extra one that lowers the pitch a fourth. The four pistons thus enable the player to produce a scale of an octave below any given open tone on the instrument. Sometimes a combination of pistons will throw a tone off its proper pitch, but as the tuba is played with comparatively loose lips, the performer can correct such tones by regulating his blowing. In passing, it may be said of valves that as a general rule they injure tone quality somewhat by making the air-column pass through too many curves, each piston lengthening the tube by making the air go through a short additional curved section of tube.

The bass tuba can give the lowest E-flat on the piano, and stands in the key of that note. Its deeper tones are full, and somewhat forcible, almost brutal, in quality. Its compass extends upward about two and a half octaves. A form of tenor tuba, known as the euphonium, sounds a fifth higher, in the key of B-flat, and is in unison with the tenor trombone. Its notes are weaker than those of bombardon. The contrabass tuba is an octave lower than the euphonium, and gives gruff, heavy notes. Wagner gave an impetus to the use of tubas, calling for five in his Trilogy. Here the two bass tubas are in F instead of E-flat. The tuba has been used as bass for three trombones in four-part harmony. It often takes the bass part of the brass group, sometimes in unison with the deeper trombones; and it has even been employed as a bass for strings.

The tuba has not the smooth quality of the trombone, but its gruff harshness can be made very effective. Wagner employed this tone-color in the first act of "Die Walküre," to picture the fierce character of Hunding. The weary Siegmund, driven by storm and pursuit, has taken refuge in Hunding's forest hut. Soon the footsteps of the returning warrior are heard outside; and just as he enters the door, the four tubas play the short, pregnant motive that represents him in the music. The effect of these tubas by themselves is impressively savage. In "Siegfried," when the hero has found the lair of the dragon, that redoubtable monster utters many dragonine curses on the tubas, before meeting a well-merited death.

The group of keyed bugles was at one time much in evidence, but is not now found in the orchestra. Its most prominent member was the ophicleide, used until recent years, but now superseded by the tuba. The name ophicleide is derived from two Greek words meaning key and serpent, which describe the instrument appropriately, as it had a curved form and was provided with keys. Alto ophicleides exist, but their quality was unpleasant, and their pitch inaccurate. Bass ophicleides in C and in B-flat were frequently employed, while a contrabass form, still deeper, demanded excessive lung power. The ophicleide tone is powerful and obtrusive, and does not blend well with other instruments, which is one reason why it has given way to the tubas. But it is often found in old scores. In fairly recent times Schumann used it in his "Paradise and the Peri"; but its most famous employment is in Mendelssohn's "Midsummer Night's Dream" music, where it gives a comical picture of the snores produced by Bottom the weaver in his drunken slumber.

The serpent, now entirely obsolete, was a wooden tube a trifle over eight feet long, provided with keys. The old cornetto was a smaller member of the serpent family, and not, as the unwary might think, a cornet. The serpent is named from its shape. It was sparingly used by Beethoven and Mendelssohn, and Wagner admitted it only to his earlier scores. Its tone was powerful, but very rough; so that Handel, on hearing it for the first time, said that he held it too unattractive to have been the serpent that seduced Eve.

LIII

INSTRUMENTS OF PERCUSSION

THE preceding instruments have been more or less suited to melodic work, and have been played by bowing, plucking, or blowing. Besides these there are a large number of instruments which are simply struck with a drumstick, hammer, or similar object, and which are mostly incapable of melody. Instruments that are struck are known as percussion instruments, and sometimes alluded to in an orchestra as the battery. The instruments of percussion may be further divided into those that have a definite pitch and those that do not.

By far the most important are the kettledrums (German, *Pauken;* French, *timbales;* Italian, *timpani*). These consist of hollow hemispheres of copper, supported on tripods, and covered with a parchment called the head. This head is attached to the body of the drum by a metal ring, in which are screws that may be used to tighten or loosen it. The kettledrum, or simply drum, as it is often called in the orchestra, has a definite pitch, in spite of its drum-like character; and the screws are used to tune it.

Not only does the kettledrum have pitch, but a skilful player can make its tone vary in quality also. Two pairs of drumsticks come with it, one pair of wood and the other with tips of fairly soft sponge. Sometimes a third pair, tipped with leather, is used; while Strauss once called for birch rods. These different kinds of stick give different sorts of tone; and the performer can also vary the tone by striking at different places. A stroke near the side gives the sharpest and brightest tone, while one in the middle is duller. The usual spot chosen is about halfway between these two. The drum may also be muffled, for which purpose it is covered by a piece of cloth, which will deaden and shorten the tone.

In the orchestra are at least two kettledrums, of different sizes and pitches, played by one performer. The larger drum can be tuned to any note of the fifth between F and C, an octave below

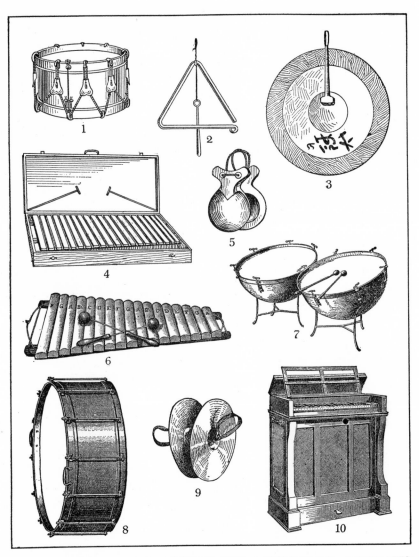

1. SNARE DRUM; 2. TRIANGLE; 3. CHINESE GONG; 4. GLOCKENSPIEL; 5. CASTANETS;
6. XYLOPHONE; 7. KETTLEDRUMS; 8. BASS DRUM; 9. CYMBALS; 10. CELESTA

middle C. The smaller drum can be tuned to any note from the B-flat of the large drum to the F next above it. The notes of the drums are now written as played, except for the fact that no accidentals are used. Thus a drum part in B-flat would use the note B-natural, though "timpani in B♭" or some such phrase would be written at the beginning of the score.

For a long time the drums were tuned to the tonic and dominant of the key used in a piece, and employed merely for rhythm or noise. Thus Haydn, in his "Surprise Symphony," creates the surprise by having a forcible drum-stroke come at the close of a soft passage. The drums can give fairly long tones, or be stopped off short, and are also capable of sustained rolls, or trills. When more than two drums are used, they can give an actual melodic phrase; and this can be done even with two notes, as shown in the first symphony by Sibelius. In that work a much-used figure is repeated accurately by two drums.

Beethoven made the kettledrum more important than his predecessors did, sometimes using it on other degrees than the tonic or dominant. Mendelssohn also gave it various tunings. In his time the orchestral composers began to use three drums, the third being often tuned to the subdominant, or fourth note of the scale, the dominant being the fifth. The thunderstorm in the "Symphonie Fantastique" of Berlioz is one of the most famous uses of the instrument. Wagner, who led the way to our complex modern orchestration, gave the kettledrum a new employment by using it to emphasize suspense or dread. In a moment of sudden orchestral silence, he makes the drums give soft, irregular strokes that intensify the emotion, and seem almost like anxious heartbeats. This device is found in "Lohengrin," where Telramund drops dead at the sight of the holy sword of the knightly hero; in "The Flying Dutchman," when Senta is suddenly confronted by that unfortunate mariner; and in "Die Götterdämmerung," when Siegfried is killed. Another striking solo phrase for the kettledrum is found in "Die Walküre," where it echoes the rhythm of the Hunding motive. The most extensive use of this instrument was made by Berlioz, who called for sixteen kettle-drums and ten drummers in his Requiem.

The famous kettledrummer Pfundt tried to introduce an instrument that could be tuned mechanically, by a rod that moved a system of levers; but it has not proven a success. Pfundt also pub-lished a kettledrum method. He became able to produce remark-ably fine tones. Once, however, he created an unusual effect. He was very miserly, and dunned a fellow-performer unmercifully for the return of a small loan. The latter finally brought the money in pennies, and spread them secretly around the rim of the drum; so that Pfundt's first stroke was followed by an unexpected shower of coppers.

The kettledrummer has few notes and long rests in orchestral music. He should count these, but in practice he either knows the music, or has a bit of it written out to give him the cue, or gets the signal from the conductor. There is a story that the kettledrummer of Richter's Vienna orchestra could count automatically, which en-abled him to go out for refreshment in long pauses and return on time; but it sounds a little apocryphal. There is no real solo reper-toire for the instrument. Yet the English drummer Gordon Cleather wrote a concerto for kettledrums, and rapped it out in front of the orchestra on six drums of various pitch. The German composer Tausch wrote a similar work calling for five drums.

Paderewski has perfected an affair that he calls the tonitruone, which he has used in some of his works to imitate thunder. But the new instrument has not replaced the kettledrum for this purpose.

The subject of storms suggests the wind machine, used by Richard Strauss in his "Don Quixote." This contrivance, borrowed from the theatre, consists of a simple sheet of canvas held against a re-volving cylinder. As the cylinder increases in speed, the realistic sound grows higher in pitch, and *vice versa*. It is used in the passage representing Don Quixote's blindfold flight in the air.

The bass drum (German, *grosse Trommel;* French, *grosse caisse;* Italian, *gran cassa*) has not the definite pitch of the kettledrum. Bass drums are used for their aid in a rhythmic capacity. They are played with different sticks, one small and one large; while the French have a stick called the *mailloche*, which is held in the middle by the player and has a knob on each end. A roll on the bass drum may also be given with the kettledrum sticks. Berlioz, Verdi, and others have tried to obtain definite pitch on the bass drum, but without success.

The ordinary drum, known also as the snare-drum or side-drum

(German, *kleine Trommel;* French, *tambour;* Italian, *tamburo*), can be suitably used for martial scenes. It can give both single taps and long rolls, and can aid in working up great climaxes, such as the scene of the benediction of the poniards in Meyerbeer's "Huguenots." An oddly dull and rattling sound can be produced by playing with the drum-head somewhat loosened.

A medium-sized drum exists, known as the tenor drum. The tambourine (Basque drum) is practically a very flat drum with one end open. It is struck by the hand, though the performer may vary this effect by rubbing it with his thumb. It has bits of metal attached, which give a jingling noise when it is struck. The tambourine is used in connection with Spanish or gypsy effects, while Berlioz employed it also in his Roman Carnival Overture and his "Childe Harold" Symphony.

Bells (German, *Glocken;* French, *cloches;* Italian, *campane*) are used, when desired, as instruments of definite pitch. Wagner, in his "Parsifal," has a striking four-toned bell figure, but in this case the sounds come from steel bars struck by hammers. Some composers have used a piano note from behind the scenes to give bell effects. Tschaikovsky's overture "1812," which celebrates the Russian victory over Napoleon, was first given at an outdoor festival, with real cathedral bells joining in the jubilant finale. Long steel tubes are often used for bell notes. An actual bell may be used in some cases; but the tone of a large bell is not always pure.

The Glockenspiel, or carillon, is a set of flat steel plates, giving a series of sweet, bell-like tones when struck with a mallet. The bell-harmonica, in which musical glasses are struck, has a somewhat similar tone. The Glockenspiel can give entire melodies, though each of its strips can only sound a single pitch. Mozart used its saccharine tones in his "Magic Flute"; and Wagner called for them in the slumber scene of "Die Walküre," as well as at the entrance of the toy-makers' guild in "Die Meistersinger." The usual compass of the Glockenspiel is about two octaves, beginning an octave above middle C, but written an octave lower than it sounds.

The celesta is a modern bell instrument, looking much like an upright piano with the upper four (formerly five) piano octaves. Its keys are played by hand, causing the hammers, inside the instrument, to strike steel plates placed over wooden resonators.

Tschaikovsky employed the celesta with good effect in his "Casse-Noisette" music. The dulcitone, or typophone, is somewhat like the celesta, but less powerful.

The gong, or tam-tam, is sometimes heard with the orchestra. Like many large bells, it does not produce a pure tone, but gives a note that is blended with a mixture of so-called "by-tones." Its sharp and noticeable effect has been employed in representing any sudden catastrophe. Soft strokes on the gong produce a weird result. Meyerbeer has called for them in "Robert le Diable," to go with the rising of the ghostly nuns; and Rossini used them in "Semiramide," when the tomb of Ninus opens to show that monarch's spirit.

Still another bell-like tone comes from the triangle (German, *Triangel;* French, *triangle;* Italian, *triangolo*). This is a small steel bar bent into triangular shape, which is held on a string and played by a pencil-like rod from the inside. Its high, tinkling note has no very definite pitch. It is used whenever a tinkling effect is desired, and sometimes merely to mark rhythm. Its proper place is in rather light music, though it is found in scores of Haydn, Beethoven, and Schumann. Weber used it to add color to the gypsy scenes in his "Preciosa." Its most important occurrence to date is in Liszt's piano concerto in E-flat, where it starts a theme by announcing its rhythm in solo notes.

Cymbals (German, *Becken;* French, *cymbales;* Italian, *piatti*) consist of a pair of round metallic plates, made of copper and tin, to be clashed together by the performer. They are of Oriental origin, coming from either Turkey or Arabia. Sometimes they are played by the bass drummer, with one of the pair of plates tied to his instrument; but a better tone is produced if they are held in the hands and struck against each other slantingly. Their notes are often considered the same as those of the bass drum, which are with a double stem when the cymbals are desired also. The loud tones of the cymbals do not last very long, but they may be stopped abruptly if the plates are held against the performer's coat. Such loud strokes give an excellent suggestion of combat, or of wild revelry. Wagner used them thus in the Venus scenes of "Tannhäuser." In the same place he produced a mysterious tremolo effect by having the two plates rattled together softly. Elsewhere he has created new effects by a single stroke, and a drum-roll also, on a hanging cymbal. The cymbals give no definite pitch, as their vibrations are too irregular. In the "Symphonie Fantastique," the last note (if it can be called a note) is a drumstick stroke on a hanging cymbal.

Castanets, or castagnettes, are bits of ebony or boxwood, to be clicked together by hand. These, like the tambourines, are much used for Spanish or gypsy music, or in tropical dances. They are employed for such suggestions by the composers, though they rarely appear in the concert orchestra. They figure excellently in the dance-scene of the second act in Bizet's beautiful "Carmen."

The xylophone resembles the Glockenspiel, but has its plates made of wood instead of steel. The xylophone can thus play melodies; but its tone-color is not exactly musical. Its first important passage in the orchestra is found in the "Danse Macabre" of Saint-Saëns, already mentioned for several of its instrumental devices. In this piece, which represents the skeletons dancing to the fiddle of Death, the xylophone is used to represent the bones of the skeletons knocking together. Rezniček called for a xylophone in his "Schlemihl," to aid in picturing revelry.

With the exception of the kettledrum, the percussion instruments are not held to be a regular part of the orchestra. But all large orchestras have them, as they are called for in very many modern works. In the old days, when musical beauty was its own excuse for being, they were not especially needed. But at present, when almost every composer is trying to write programme music, and picture some definite scene or event, they have nearly all come into constant use.

PART V
SPECIAL TOPICS

LIV

SOME FAMOUS PIANISTS

NEARLY two centuries ago, in a large German city, a certain man sat playing industriously at a harpsichord, while a second man listened from a concealed nook. There came from the performer's fingers a series of beautiful works, in many-voiced and orderly succession; but the hidden hearer did not seem pleased, and after a time he took a secret but hurried departure.

The player was Bach; the listener, Marchand. Bach's works do not usually drive their hearers away. But Marchand was to have met Bach in a contest in harpsichord playing; and after hearing his rival, Marchand knew that he could not hold his own in such an unequal competition.

Yet Marchand was rated highly in his native France. Once he had boasted that he could add an embellishment to every note. The many turns, trills, and other *fioriture* of the eighteenth-century music came into being because the clavichord and harpsichord could not sustain their tones for any length of time. Any long-held note needed to be prolonged by some embellishment, to prevent a period of silence before the next note. But embellishments were used also because of their decorative effect.

Before Bach's time, the thumb was not generally used in playing, and scales were given by letting the fingers overpass one another. When the thumb came in, it was first marked by an O, and later by an X, the fingers being numbered 1, 2, 3, and 4.

Carl Philipp Emanuel Bach, son of the great John Sebastian, was a master of expression, as is shown by his book on "The True Art of Playing the Clavier,"—the term clavier was used to designate all keyboard instruments; but his brother, Johann Christian Bach, who settled in London, was the real piano devotee of the family.

Handel, like Bach, was a masterly player. Handel used to conduct his own operas from the keyboard of a harpsichord, as custom then dictated.

Domenico Scarlatti was the pioneer in the early Italian school, introducing many new effects. One of these was cross-hand work. When he grew old and fat, and unable to reach across easily, he dropped the cross-hand work from his compositions. Scarlatti met Handel at Venice, in one of the usual competitions. A draw resulted at the harpsichord, but Handel was awarded the victory at the organ. It is said that after this event Scarlatti would cross himself whenever he heard Handel's name mentioned.

Muzio Clementi was a leader among the early pianists, his "Gradus ad Parnassum" being still considered a valuable training in technique for the student.

Mozart was a child prodigy in piano playing as well as composing, and traveled about with his sister, under paternal care, giving concerts when only six years old. When he reached the age of twenty, one critic said of him, "Mozart plays with great power, and reads whatever is put before him; but that is all that can be said. Beecke is far greater." Later on, however, Rieder speaks of Mozart's bold flights of fancy, "heavenly harmonies," and skill in improvisation. Mozart and Clementi indulged in one of the usual competitions, after which the latter set to work to unite Mozart's "singing touch" with his own technical skill.

A concert given by Mozart at Mantua shows that genius was expected to display itself in many ways. The programme included a symphony of his own; a piano concerto to be read by him at sight; a sonata to which he should add variations, with repeat in a new key; the words of a song, which he should sing, improvising both melody and accompaniment; themes given by the audience, upon which he would make a sonata and a fugue; a trio for which he would improvise the violin part; and another of his symphonies.

Franz Duschek was a Viennese pianist of the Mozart school. Another was Anton Eberl, who imitated Mozart's style of composition so well that his works were sometimes said to be by Mozart.

Another of this school was Johann Nepomuk Hummel, who studied with Mozart when young. Hummel once visited John Field in St. Petersburg. As his name was not announced, he pretended to be merely a humble stranger, anxious to hear the great Field. The latter played for a time, and then thought of having some amusement by making his visitor play. Field expected the strumming and stumbling of some fourth-rater; but instead, he heard a most brilliant performance, which made him cry out, "You must be Hummel." Field played in a rather suave fashion, well suited to the smooth style of his own nocturnes.

Beethoven displayed the breadth of the Clementi school. He showed passionate strength, and made technique a means to an end. Beethoven improvised wonderfully, and the passing nature of his extemporizations must be a great loss to art.

Daniel Steibelt was a precocious virtuoso. His later show-pieces have caused him to be called a charlatan, but he had real technique. Once he challenged Beethoven to a contest; but he ran away after hearing the great composer play.

Johann Ladislaus Dussek was the first to sit sidewise on the stage. He introduced the harmonica, or set of musical glasses invented by Benjamin Franklin.

Johann Baptist Cramer was Beethoven's favorite, — perhaps because he devoted himself to Beethoven's works. Cramer showed enough spirit at first, but when he grew older his work was called "dry, wooden, harsh, and without cantilena."

Joseph Woelfl, another rival of Beethoven, had very large hands. He, too, could extemporize readily; and once, when a passing band disturbed his tempo, he changed the rhythm to suit that of the band, and kept with it until it was out of hearing. Czerny spoke of "Woelfl, distinguished for bravura playing; Gelinek, popular because of his brilliant and elegant execution; and Lipansky, a great sight reader, renowned for his playing of the Bach fugues."

Czerny was a good pianist, but better known as a teacher, as his much-used "Velocity School" would indicate. Among his pupils were Liszt, Thalberg, and Queen Victoria.

Ferdinand Ries, Beethoven's pupil, adopted his master's powerful methods of expression. The critics often spoke of his romantic fire, but his emphatic manner led one of them to call him "a woodchopper at the piano." Ries composed sonatas and concertos, and wrote interesting reminiscences of Beethoven.

Francesco Pollini was a Mozart pupil who became prominent in Italy.

Kalkbrenner was another child prodigy, and grew up into a brilliant, if rather mechanical, performer. The Englishman Cipriani

Potter excelled him in expressive power. Kalkbrenner invented a guide-bar to support the wrist, but it was not of great use. Mechanical aids to the hand have never seemed really effective. Schumann tried to strengthen his fourth fingers by a pulley-and-weight system, but only succeeded in injuring his hand. This was the world's gain, as it drove him into composition. Few pianists excel in this field, though Liszt and Rubinstein managed to do so. Usually the pianist is too busy to compose well, while the composer does not play enough to be a great pianist. The latter case is illustrated by Schubert, who has been mentioned as breaking down. several times in one of his own fantasias.

Ignaz Moscheles, who lived until 1870, was held foremost in his day. He was precise, exact, and vigorous in his playing, with accurate attention to rhythm and accent. These qualities were well suited to the more important classics, which he favored. He could not appreciate the nuances of the romantic school, as exemplified by Chopin and Liszt. Mendelssohn was one of his pupils and admirers.

Chopin's playing was essentially soft and delicate. Even in his moments of fiery ardor, his *fortissimo* was less than that of Moscheles, and much less than Liszt's. A critic called Chopin's performance light and airy, and said that his fingers "seemed to glide sidewise, as if all technique were a *glissando*." Chopin was naturally a master of the *rubato* that his works demand, — an expressive retarding or hurrying of the melody over an accompaniment that goes on steadily. In playing, as well as by his compositions, he fairly earned the title of "the Poet of the Piano."

Stephen Heller was another performer of excessive refinement. He was too sensitively organized to be a steady success in public, but when in proper mood he played with much grace and vivacity. Like nearly all the pianists, he composed for his instrument, producing works that show much sentiment and poetry.

Adolf Henselt was a pianist of phenomenal power and expression. His legato was remarkably good, and he composed special studies to develop a large reach in this style. His other works include a concerto, many excellent études, and some attractive solo pieces. He was always nervous at concerts, and retired from public playing in later life. When appearing with an orchestra, he would rush on at the last instant; and once he caused great amusement by forgetting to leave his cigar behind. Henselt was a great Bach player, and used to practise that master's fugues with the piano strings muffled by quills. When young, he despaired of success on hearing Thalberg's "singing tone"; but he soon set to work and acquired it himself.

Alexander Dreyschock's repertoire was limited mostly to his own works, and these showed display rather than depth. He excelled in handling tremendously difficult passages in thirds, sixths, or octaves. He became very proficient in works for the left hand alone.

Sigismund Thalberg was another who devoted himself largely to his own works. In his case, however, the compositions were expressive enough. He inclined somewhat to the light type known as salon music, but he excelled in both melodic and brilliant passages. He could embroider accompaniment about a melody with such skill that it seemed as if he must have three hands. He became an idol of the matinee girls. His "Art du Chant appliqué au Piano" is a valuable method even now.

The greatest of all pianists was undoubtedly Franz Liszt. His own works have become standards of difficult piano execution. "In comparison with Liszt," wrote Tausig, "we other artists are all blockheads." A French critic said, "Thalberg is the first pianist, but Liszt is the *only* one." His wild power shocked the conservatives; and we find Mendelssohn calling his performances "a heathen scandal, in both the glorious and the objectionable sense of the term." On the other hand, Rubinstein said, "Liszt plays like a god, Thalberg like a grocer." Rubinstein knew of Liszt's prowess by experience. When the Russian showed Liszt his manuscript Fantasie for two pianos, the latter suggested that they play it at a certain social gathering. After the guests were assembled, Liszt looked over the manuscript casually for a few moments. When the performance began, the crowd was divided equally about the two artists; but before it ended, every one present was watching Liszt, and Rubinstein found himself left alone. On another occasion Grieg brought a new violin sonata to Liszt, and was astonished by hearing him read it off at once, adding the violin part to the piano accompaniment, and bringing it out with the most exquisite balance.

Liszt's style has been aptly termed the orchestration of the piano. It is well shown by some of his song transcriptions for piano, which have broad sweeps of melody combined with great antiphonal effects for accompaniment. His original works, too, show the greatness of the new style, whether in the broadly powerful sonata or the more delicate "Sermon to the Birds."

Liszt was a great admirer of Paganini, and did for piano what Paganini did for violin, — that is, wrote pieces of such brilliance and difficulty that his successors have sometimes been hardly able to master them. Liszt's hands were not unduly large, but the rapidity of his skips made some of his hearers think that he had an unheard-of reach. In 1839, Liszt employed the words "piano recitals" as a new title for his solo concerts.

As stated in a preceding chapter, Liszt always made it a point to uphold the dignity of the musician's position. But the day had gone by when it was possible for geniuses to receive the indignities that were heaped upon Mozart. When Princess Metternich asked Liszt if he had done well on a certain tour, and he replied, "Madame, I am in music, not business," the remark was not nearly so bold as if it had been made six or seven decades earlier. The French Revolution and the disturbances of 1848 had helped individual freedom. Beethoven was far more independent in reality; and when some one talked during a duet given by him and Ries at Count Browne's house, he stopped abruptly, and said, "I play no more for such hogs."

Henri Herz was one of the first great pianists to tour America. He played his own works for the most part, which were superficially brilliant. Once, at Baltimore, he expressed a willingness to improvise upon themes given by the audience; but trouble arose, for several dozen people tried to give him their favorite theme by whistling, singing, or shouting it. In New Orleans he arranged a piece for eight pianos and sixteen performers. When one of the players did not appear in time for the concert, he impressed the services of a lady from one of the boxes. She said she could not play, but he told her that she would only need to go through the motions. But he forgot a certain passage where all parts had a rest; and the audience was pleasantly surprised by seeing her continue in dumb show while the other players were silent.

Gottschalk was more successful in meeting a similar difficulty at San Francisco. One of his fourteen performers fell ill, and was replaced by an insistent substitute who could not play at all well. In order to avoid trouble, Gottschalk had the hammers removed from the substitute's piano just before the concert. Gottschalk played in a romantic style well suited to his own works, which were mostly exotic tone-pictures of peculiar charm, such as "Le Bananier," "La Savane," and so on.

But the greatest pianist to tour America was Rubinstein. He was a player of leonine temperament, and showed the most tremendous emotional power. He was not always accurate; and when a lady auditor once began to cover him with gushing adulation, he remarked, "Madame, I could give another concert with the notes I left out." When he forgot parts of his selections, he would sometimes proceed to improvise until he could get back to a later section of the piece in question. He made various tours with the violinist Wieniawski. Once, in Boston, the pair drew a very small audience; and on being asked if they would return for another concert, Wieniawski replied, "We fear that if we did so we should get out of the habit of playing in public." But they returned after all, and had the pleasure of appearing before a much larger audience. Rubinstein's brother Nicolai was a great pianist also, as well as a conductor and composer.

Theodor Leschetizky, known as a world-famous teacher, was associated with Rubinstein at first, and toured Europe before settling in Vienna. He played his own pieces, among others.

Hans von Bülow was a pupil of Liszt who became renowned partly by playing his master's works; but his taste was eclectic, and he could excel in all schools. His technique was admirable, and his remarkable memory was of great service to him. He arranged his programmes in a way that almost always helped to improve popular knowledge and taste. It is an interesting physiological fact that he was unmusical during childhood, his musical taste appearing at the age of nine, after he had received a severe blow on the head. This blow, it was afterwards found, resulted in some sort of lesion on his brain, which must have had the effect of making it sensitive to vibrations. It would be hasty to adopt a rule that unmusical people should be knocked on the head; but in this case the blow seemingly changed its victim into a music-lover.

Carl Tausig, the son of a pianist, was Liszt's best pupil, and gained

such astonishing control over the keyboard that he actually out-
shone his master in certain cases. Tausig was a thorough musician
in the best sense of the word, endowed with a sympathetic touch,
passionate power of expression, and real artistic balance. His technique was so remarkable that Liszt once called him "the infallible,
with fingers of brass." When an ambitious young pianist once
played rather poorly for Liszt, the latter exclaimed, "Such playing!
And for me, who have heard Tausig so often!" Cosima, afterwards
Mme. Wagner, said of Tausig, "He has no touch, no individuality;
he is a caricature of Liszt." But this was in Tausig's early student
days, before he matured; and no doubt Cosima was partial to Liszt
because he was her father. Tausig died at the age of thirty.

William Mason deserves mention for his valuable work in raising
the taste of our own country. After study with Moscheles, Dreyschock, and Liszt, he made a well-deserved name by his playing and
teaching.

A curiosity among pianists is Count Geza Zichy, of Hungary.
When seventeen years old, he lost his right arm in a hunting accident. But his love for music did not let this prevent him from becoming a famous pianist. He studied with Liszt until he became
a great artist. The repertoire of music for the left hand is fairly
large; and he increased it by writing a number of left-hand pieces
for his own use.

Those pianists now before the public may well be left to the tender
mercies of the critics. Some of them grow famous as specialists in the
works of one composer, like De Pachmann, who prefers Chopin's
works. Some, like Rosenthal and Godowski, are in the virtuoso
class because of their astounding mastery of technique, although
they may not be lacking in expressive power. Others, like Busoni,
are best in intellectual and classical works. Paderewski's greatness
is shown by the fact that he is not a specialist, but succeeds in all
schools and styles.

Among the women pianists, Clara Schumann won high regard,
not alone for her ability as a performer, but for her service in making
her husband's works known to the public. Ernst Pauer, himself a
great performer, made a list of the twelve greatest pianists at the
middle of last century, and included three women, — Clara Schumann, Mme. Clauss-Szavardy, and Arabella Goddard. Miss God-

dard married her teacher, Davison; which made "Punch" assert that her life's harmony was transposed from G to D, in accordance with her initials. Davison devoted himself to furthering her cause; and a Paris wit declared that whenever a pianist started to cross the channel to England, Davison would appear on the Dover cliffs, and shout, "No more pianists needed here; we have Arabella Goddard."

To-day there are many well-known women pianists. Katharine Goodson, Helen Hopekirk, Olga Samaroff, Antoinette Szumowska, and Germaine Schnitzer are but a few of the most prominent names. The leader of the older generation is Teresa Carreño, noted for her fiery brilliance of expression and her devotion to the works of Mac-Dowell, who studied with her in his younger days.

In bringing this very incomplete list to a close, one may be pardoned for advising the hearer to seek breadth of vision. Not all pianists are alike. Some have one virtue, some another; and if we are taught to give even the devil his due, we should certainly make it our duty to give any pianist full credit for whatever good qualities he may have. The performer may be limited to one school or style; but the listener should make himself able to appreciate the good points of all.

LV

SOME FAMOUS SINGERS

A LITTLE over two centuries ago, a young student of singing went to a famous Italian teacher for lessons. The teacher accepted the pupil, and wrote him out a set of exercises for practice. Although these exercises covered no more than a single page, the pupil was kept at them for a year. At length he mustered up courage enough to ask, "When may I sing?" "Not yet," was the reply, and more work on the exercises followed. In another year the pupil repeated his query, but received the same answer,— "Not yet." Still a third year was spent on the exercise sheet, sung with syllables instead of vowels. Again came the question, "When may I sing?" This time the teacher answered, "You are now the greatest singer in Italy." The teacher was Porpora, the singer Farinelli. Some doubt has been cast upon this anecdote; but it deserves to be true, if only as an example showing students how valuable it is for them to stick to their exercises.

Farinelli sang in the operas of Handel, and made a tremendous success in England. An enthusiastic woman once spoke of "One God, one Church, and one Farinelli." Yet he was not the "only one," though perhaps he was the greatest of his class. Senesino was another favorite in England, and was made the recipient of many attentions and laudatory verses. Caffarelli, too, grew famous. All of these stars belonged to the extinct class of male sopranos, who were prevented, by surgery, from having the usual change of voice during youth. One of them, Bernacchi, founded a famous singing school.

With the adulation that singers of both sexes received, it was no wonder that some of them indulged in rivalries worthy of spoiled children. Even to-day the singers do not all love one another with genuine fervor. In Handel's time, the greatest disagreement came between the two most famous sopranos, Francesca Cuzzoni and Faustina Bordoni. Each of these two supplemented an enthusiastic estimate of her own powers by a low opinion of her rival's; and the matter became so public that the London opera-goers took sides. The two principals actually came to blows, and bore marks of each other's prowess when separated. Cuzzoni finally held the field alone, for Faustina married the composer Hasse.

Cuzzoni was imperious to all, but she met her match in Handel. Once, when he had everything ready for her at a certain rehearsal, she refused to go on. Handel held her out of the window, and threatened to drop her unless she consented to sing. In her position (a very aerial one) she found herself unable to decline, and gave in as gracefully as she could. Such caprices on the part of the singers were only a natural result of great public adulation. Cuzzoni's popularity may be shown by the fact that the dress she wore in "Rodelinda" was adopted as a national uniform of feminine youth and beauty.

Elizabeth Weichsel, better known as Mrs. Billington, is held to have been the greatest singer ever born in England. Like Farinelli, she could out-sing a trumpet and excel the trumpeter in length and power of tone. Sir Joshua Reynolds painted her in the attitude of listening to an angel choir above her; whereupon Handel said, "That is a mistake; you should have painted the angels listening to her."

A singer with an unusual range was Lucrezia Agujari, who lived toward the end of the eighteenth century. She was probably the highest soprano ever known. The ordinary soprano singer can reach the second G above middle C. With that G begins the so-called alt-octave, running up to F-sharp just below the next G. Most high sopranos think they are doing very well if they can reach D or E in alt with a tone of fair quality. Agujari could sing not only the alt octave, but the one above it, the altissimo, as far as F, — the highest F on the piano. Mozart, who heard her, said that these high notes were pure and of good quality.

In the beginning of the nineteenth century, Angelica Catalani was the leader of the colorature singers. She could give embellishments and *fiorituri* with such ease that she often sang ornate solos intended for the violin. Her accuracy in this caused the Parisians to nickname her "L'instrument Catalani.' She had a most marvellous accuracy, and could sing six distinct intervals within the compass of a semitone. She had little artistic conscience, and would stoop to almost anything to catch the public; but her private career was marked by uprightness and generosity.

Henrietta Sontag was another famous singer of the same period. Catalani said of Sontag, "She is first in her style, but her style is not the first." This remark should have been somewhat of a boomerang, for Sontag's style was similar to Catalani's.

Giuditta Pasta was a more admirable artist, if not a greater vocalist. Her voice was originally weak, limited, and unattractive; but hard and faithful work enabled her to obtain a compass of over two octaves and a rich fulness of tone. She never entirely equalized all her notes; but she gave them a dramatic significance far beyond the power of even those who were endowed with better voices. She was the first to introduce real acting into opera, the most conventional gestures having served before her advent.

Mme. Maria Malibran and Mme. Pauline Viardot were both daughters of Manuel Garcia the elder, and sisters of the younger man of that name. All four were famous singers. The father was exceptionally long-lived, dying in the twentieth century at the age of a hundred and one.

The elder Garcia was a very severe disciplinarian, and sometimes would even beat his daughters. The neighbors occasionally heard shrieks issuing from the singer's home; but they shrugged their shoulders and said, "It is only Monsieur Garcia teaching his daughters to sing."

Maria's début was brought about by his severity. When she was seventeen, he was called upon to sing in a certain performance of Rossini's "Otello"; and he insisted on her taking the part of Desdemona. She declined, because little time was left for her to prepare for it; but he made her go on, and threatened that if she did not do her best he would use his weapon, which was a real dagger. Naturally she obeyed; but in the last act, which he gave with great intensity, she had a renewed access of fear. She cried out in terror, "For God's sake, do not kill me"; but the audience thought this only a bit of realistic acting, and applauded her wildly.

Malibran's voice was very intractable, but her father's excellent tuition enabled her to overcome its defects, with the aid of constant practice. She had a very large range, covering both soprano and alto registers; and this enabled her to charm by variety of effect.

Her marriage to M. Malibran, in New York, proved unfortunate, as he merely wished to use her money in paying his debts. After his death she married the violinist De Beriot, with happier results; but her career was soon cut short by a fatal fall from a horse.

While she was undergoing matrimonial misadventures, her father too met with a financial reverse. While travelling in Mexico, he and his family were "held up" by brigands, and relieved of the proceeds of their tour. To add insult to injury, the brigands made the famous tenor sing for them before they would release him.

In spite of Maria's earnest work, Pauline was her father's favorite child. He said once, "Pauline can be guided by a thread of silk, where Maria needs a hand of iron." Pauline's voice, like her sister's, seemed to combine soprano and contralto registers, though the upper notes had to be built out of nothing by hard work. Her singing, like that of her sister, was very dramatic in character. She became known as a teacher and composer. Her musical intelligence was remarkable, and she sang at sight a rôle in an act of "Tristan and Isolde" when the other artists engaged for the work were giving it up as being too difficult.

Mme. Tietjens was another singer of the dramatic type who flourished in the middle of the last century.

Giulietta Grisi was a member of the famous "Puritani" quartet, that made Bellini's opera of that name well known in Paris. The other singers in this remarkable group were Rubini the tenor, Tamburini the baritone, and Lablache, greatest of bassos. Grisi was not commandingly original, but she sang and acted with spirit and ability. She married Mario, the tenor who soon replaced Rubini in the quartet. When the Czar met her with her children, he asked if they were "little Grisettes"; whereupon she replied, "No, sire, little Marionettes." Grisi was delicate as a child, but she became strong later, perhaps largely from the gymnastics of singing; and in a career of over thirty-five years she scarcely ever had to cancel a performance because of illness.

Lablache had the most tremendous of bass voices, and could roar down an entire orchestra. His voice was flexible, too, as well as strong; and once he mimicked a soprano, following faithfully all her trills, turns, and other rapid embellishments.

Jenny Lind is known to Americans by her very profitable trips under the management of the late (and great) Barnum. Lind was another example of the value of hard work. During her youth she overworked her voice; and when she came to Garcia for lessons, she broke down in trying to sing for him. He said, "It would be useless to teach you, for you have no voice left." She persuaded him to try to bring her voice back; but she had to start over at the very beginning, with scales, vocalises, and breathing exercises. In ten months the damage was more than repaired. Her devotion to work is shown by the hours she spent in practising the pronunciation of one German word, — "zerschmettert."

Mendelssohn admired Lind greatly. Expecting her to sing in his "Elijah," he put into the solo "Hear ye, Israel" a high F-sharp, a tone especially resonant in her voice. But she could not come after all, and the prim and precise Caradori-Allan, who replaced her, found the solo "not ladylike." Carlyle wrote of Lind's performance in "La Somnambula," "She seemed to me a very true, clean, genuine little creature, with a voice of extraordinary extent. . . . She sang, acted, etc., with consummate fidelity, but had unfortunately nothing but mere nonsense to sing or act." Carlyle thus showed himself a better critic than most authors, and a refreshing contrast to Ruskin, who spoke of "The Mastersingers" as "baboon-headed stuff."

The name of Adelina Patti brings memories of perennial farewell tours. She gave a concert as recently as 1908, which seems wonderful when one remembers that her début occurred in 1859. Such a long career is amazing, and means that the singer must have taken great care of her health, besides having a strong constitution to begin with. Patti's voice, in its prime, was of the most bird-like clearness and flexibility. She had no very high ideals of art, but as a coloratura singer she charmed two continents for five decades. Her sister Carlotta was more dramatic, but did not have a long career.

The health of singers is a valuable commodity that demands much care. They must avoid catching cold, and keep away from draughts and dampness. Even the moisture of a new house may prove harmful; and the Spaniards have a saying that runs, "Give your newly built house for the first year to your enemy, for the second to your friend, and stay in it yourself only when the third has come." Many singers take excessive care of their diet, though here

ADELINA PATTI

the matter is an individual one. The only general rule places the ban on hotly spiced dishes, and on nuts, which cause huskiness. Add to incessant care the need for constant practice, and it will be seen that the singer's career is not an uninterrupted round of pleasure. He must act on the proverb *Per aspera ad astra;* and in his case it may be taken to mean that a rough voice will not prevent him from becoming one of the stars, if he takes pains enough.

Many singers are helped by certain drinks or foods taken just before performance; and a few of these may be mentioned. In Handel's time a warm drink spiced with fennel was very popular, though tradition does not tell us of what the drink consisted. Here the warmth was probably the most beneficial factor; and a contemporary singer uses in similar fashion a raw egg beaten into hot beef tea. Farinelli would often eat an anchovy, although the Italians as a rule opposed salt fish before singing. Jenny Lind often ate a salt pickle before appearing in concert. Lemon-juice and vinegar have been used by some and abused by others. Cold tea with lemon is another prescription. It was said that Malibran sipped champagne; but in reality she used merely an effervescent powder. A raw egg, either alone or in sherry, is a favorite with many; and the white of the egg undoubtedly soothes the throat. Oysters have been used for a similar purpose.

Toward the end of the last century, Christine Nilsson was held by some to be a rival of Patti. Her voice, however, was of somewhat different quality, being pure and appealing where Patti's was brilliant.

In Patti's early days she found a more formidable rival for popularity in Pauline Lucca, a native of Vienna. After her first engagement, at Olmutz, Lucca's triumphs began, in the shape of serenades and a torchlight procession. After a Prague performance, she was rather startled to see an elderly man walk in and kiss her on both cheeks; but the man was Meyerbeer, who had come to give her a Berlin engagement. Here Lucca and Patti met, and became firm friends. London gave Lucca an ovation, and Berlin decorated her house with flowers; but the climax came in St. Petersburg, where streets were illuminated in her honor, students took out her horses and drew her carriage themselves, the orchestra and audience gave her presents, and even the royal family sent her a gift of jewelry.

Such tributes were fairly earned; for Lucca was endowed with original genius, and had a sympathetic voice that imparted vitality to the tamest rôle. Her expressive voice and impassioned acting made the critics speak of her as "transcendentally human."

Certain singers have grown famous by being identified with a composer. One of these, Sophie Arnould, deserves mention for her singing in Gluck's operas. She displayed a wit and vivacity that captivated our own Franklin. When Piccini was brought to Paris as a rival to Gluck, and both composers set the same libretto, "Iphigenia in Tauris," Arnould helped to make Gluck's work a success. When her rival in the Piccini work showed traces of intoxication, it was she who said, "This is not Iphigenia in Tauris, but Iphigenia in Champagne."

Wilhelmine Schroeder-Devrient was identified with the earlier Wagnerian performances. She was the first to show the possibilities of really dramatic singing, and she always made her voice echo the emotion of the text or situation. In her early years she scored a great success as Leonora in Beethoven's "Fidelio." At first she nearly broke down with stage fright, but the audience, thinking that her emotion belonged to her tragic part, was loud in its applause. She evidently was not again troubled with stage fright. In this opera she has to give the starving Florestan a crust of bread; and once, when he forgot to take it, she had coolness enough to whisper, "What's the matter? Do you want it buttered?" It is well to get past the days of stage fright, but a due amount of nervousness is not at all bad if it keeps the singer eager to do the best possible work.

Lilli Lehmann is now remembered by her Wagnerian rôles; but she excelled also in the smoother style of Mozart and the Italians, and Paris critics gave high praise to her slow *coloratura*. Her Wagnerian career, like that of the De Reszkes, Nordica, and others, showed that Wagner's music did not need to be howled, but could be given with smoothness and good method as well as expressive power.

Some of the many Wagnerian singers who deserve mention are Niemann, Van Dyck, Schott, Winkelmann, Fischer, Scaria, Brandt, Brema, and Ternina. Most devoted of them all, if not absolutely the best singer, was the full-voiced Amalia Materna. Her work at Bayreuth and elsewhere was always intended to further the composer's cause; and her later poverty, caused partly by her generosity to needy relatives, should be a matter of reproach to Wagner's widow.

Singers seem to grow either very rich or very poor. Their large salaries are fairly earned, not merely by excellence in performance, but by the long years of faithful study that precede it. Some are well-balanced enough to strike an average; but too many are either spendthrifts or misers. The spendthrifts, however, do more good than the miserly ones. Once the husband of a close-fisted singer was asked how the pair spent their leisure hours. "We economize in the morning," was the reply, "and then we have a light lunch and go on economizing." Materna was not one of these.

Among the men, the English singers must be given full credit for their excellent pronunciation. Incidentally, we should not attempt opera in English until every member of a cast can manage that language without any foreign accent.

An early school of ballad-singing was well represented by Incledon, whom Thackeray praises highly in "The Newcomes." Braham exemplified the same school at a later date, and found an easy method of getting rid of his salary by trying to manage an opera company of his own. A story of Braham will illustrate the tricks sometimes played by memory. Once he could not remember how to begin "Sally in our alley," a popular favorite that he had sung hundreds of times. Finally he said, "I've forgotten the first line"; whereat nearly the entire audience sang it at him. Such lapses may come from excitement or overwork.

Sims Reeves was another famous ballad-singer, known also in opera. His audiences could not be sure of his appearance until he actually came on the stage; for he would break an engagement if he were not in best form. Another singer who took good care of his voice was Brignoli. Once, when a Boston audience applauded him vociferously, the manager suggested an encore, saying that the public insisted. "What do I care," replied Brignoli; and he pointed to his throat, saying, "This is my capital."

Singers are usually trained from early youth; but they are sometimes discovered later in life. Such a case was that of the cab-driver Wachtel, son of a stable-keeper. Once, at an operatic performance, the tenor was absent as one of his arias became due. When Wachtel

and playing with the most amazing rapidity, correcting the false pitch of the strings by his fingering. The startled Corelli cried out, "Sir, they call me an archangel [Arcangelo]; but you must be an arch-devil."

Giuseppe Torelli belonged to the same period. He helped Corelli to develop the concerto and the concerto grosso, in which a single instrument or a group of instruments was played against a concerted orchestral or other accompaniment. Other Italian composer-performers were Marini, Fontana, Laurenti, and Antonio Veracini; while Germany produced Briegel, Schmelzer, Pesel, Walther, and others. Lully was a violinist when he first won recognition in Paris.

Giuseppe Tartini, who lived until 1770, shared with Corelli the honor of being a violin pioneer. He united Corelli's finished style with more vigor, passion, and daring; and at the same time he developed a far more advanced technique in handling embellishments, rapid passages, and double-stopping. He composed many famous works.

Italy still continued to hold the lead in the number of famous violinists. From the late sixteenth to the late eighteenth century, Italy was preëminent in music, though Bach and Handel had foreshadowed the coming of German supremacy. It was this early excellence of Italy, in contrast to its later sterility, that made Von Bülow say, "Italy was the cradle of music, — and remained the cradle."

The eighteenth century saw Italy's leadership in the violin world upheld by such masters as Vivaldi, Francesco Veracini, Geminiani, Locatelli, Tessarini, and Somis. Vivaldi expanded the concerto to orchestral size. Geminiani wrote an early violin method, based on Corelli's ideas. Veracini was an intense player of the Tartini school. Locatelli was one of the first to use violin tricks and special tunings in public; while Somis served as a link between the Italian and French players. France produced Leclair and Guignon, the latter of whom became unpopular by trying for a musical monopoly. Germany was the home of Pisendel, Johann Graun, Franz Benda, Johann Stamitz, and the Italian Giardini.

Toward the end of the century, the leadership began to pass. Pugnani upheld the broad Corelli school in Italy, while Nardini followed the brilliant Tartini standards. Greater than either was

Pugnani's pupil Viotti, called "the father of modern violin-playing." But Viotti went to Paris, and started a school there. The members of this Paris group were Rodolphe Kreutzer, the German-born artist to whom Beethoven dedicated the "Kreutzer Sonata"; Pierre Rode, of broad and sympathetic tone; and François Baillot, Rode's friend and rival. The works of these men are of great value to-day, and their breadth of tone made them the most artistic players of their time. The more showy technical side had been represented by Pierre Gaviniès, called by Viotti "the French Tartini." Italy had an amazing technical virtuoso in Lolli, of Bergamo. Leopold Mozart may be mentioned among the Germans, though he spent most of his later life in guiding his precocious and famous son. Another German violinist, of slightly later date, was Andreas Romberg, composer of symphonies and other works.

The violin repertoire by this time was of ample proportions. Its value, too, is shown by the frequency with which modern players draw upon the old music for their programmes. Kreisler won a great success with Couperin's "Chanson Louis XIII et Pavane," and followed it by pieces from Pugnani and others of his time, besides the usual Tartini display. Ysaye scored a tremendous triumph with a Vitali Chaconne for violin and organ, and supplemented it by an interesting Vivaldi concerto. The old violin music has nearly as much classical value as the fugues of Bach have in the piano repertoire.

While the Paris school developed expressive power, Italy added to her celebrities the greatest technical master of the violin that the world has ever seen — Nicolo Paganini. He was not merely a virtuoso, for he showed sympathy and pathos in slow work, as well as matchless brilliance in rapid passages. His ups and downs of life, and his strange persecutions, in combination with his marvellous ability and odd personality, make his life read like a romance.

Paganini was born at Genoa in 1782. He was compelled to practise without many periods of rest; and if he had not loved the violin, he might have been turned against it by parental harshness. As it was, he soon began to spend much time and patience in mastering new difficulties of his own invention. This persistence, and faithful practice, were probably responsible for his amazing technique. Yet many thought him possessed of some special secret.

In after life, while he stopped at a certain hotel, a guest peeped in at him to discover this secret; but instead of finding anything unusual, the observer saw only a tall, thin man fingering certain violin chords repeatedly, without using the bow. In his later days, Paganini traded on the reputation that the supposed secret gave him. It is a strange fact that he made his pupil Catarina Colcagno play with astonishing brilliance when she was only fifteen; but his own great knowledge of technique would account for his ability to impart it.

He began to play in public himself at the age of thirteen. Three years later he ran away from home, and developed a taste for dissipation and gambling. He devoted some years to the guitar, in consequence of the preference of a noble lady at whose castle he stayed. The result shows in his quartets for strings and guitar, recently revived. After this he returned to the violin, and began to investigate the use of single strings. This procedure arose in part from his admiration for a certain lady, for whom he wrote and played love-dialogues between the first and fourth strings. His great facility on the G-string was developed at this time. On a certain occasion, the breaking of an E-string during a concert compelled him to play a number of difficult pieces on the remaining three strings.

The persistence with which strange stories followed Paganini was most marked. Even to-day innocent men are sometimes made victims of waves of popular persecution; but among the credulous Italian peasantry of a century ago, almost any story would find believers. The most common idea about Paganini consisted in a certainty that he was aided by the devil; and not a few of his hearers claimed to have seen that satanic individual standing beside the performer and helping him.

Paganini's excellence on the G-string was explained by another story. It was claimed that in a fit of jealousy he had murdered his mistress, in consequence of which he had spent eight years in prison. He was allowed to keep his violin; but the dampness of the cell caused the upper strings to break, finally leaving him only the G-string; and upon this he was compelled to play, if he played at all. The simplest investigation proves this story not only false, but impossible. He lived at home for nearly sixteen years; and with the

PAGANINI

exception of the guitar period, during which he was easily traced, he was constantly before the public. If he committed such a crime before becoming a public performer, he must have done it at the mature age of eight, and had his family and friends agree to pretend that he was at home studying. Yet in spite of its utter lack of possibility, the story persisted.

Paganini's technique was wonderful enough to make the credulous ones believe that he must have had some unusual aid, whether from the devil or from some other obliging spirit. The player's personality helped to sustain the idea of strangeness; for he was tall, thin, and pale, with brusque manners that heightened his cadaverous effect. His technique does not appear superhuman when looked at from the standpoint of present-day virtuoso playing; but it must have seemed tremendously striking in contrast with the lesser attainments of his period. His ability is proved by many anecdotes. One of these relates that the Neapolitan artists, jealous of his fame, engaged the young composer Danna to write a violin piece bristling with unheard-of difficulties; and when Paganini arrived, they asked him to read the piece. Paganini saw the trap they had set; but his ability was so great that the merest glance at the work enabled him to play it with the utmost ease. His proficiency in double-stopping, harmonics, left-hand pizzicato, and G-string work must have been marvellous, to judge from his compositions as well as his press notices. His use of very thin strings probably gave him a mastery over harmonics. A favorite trick of his, already mentioned, was to tune his instrument a semitone sharp, and transpose the music a semitone down, thereby getting the proper pitch of a work, but an unusually brilliant quality of tone.

Paganini has been called ignoble, selfish, self-indulgent, and miserly. These accusations are not devoid of truth; but on one occasion he showed a most excellent and discriminating generosity. It was in Paris, and he was at a concert where a new work was given — a symphony by the young and struggling composer named Berlioz. Paganini was so impressed by the work that he sent to its composer the sum of twenty thousand francs. It is said that self-indulgence, and the use of a quack medicine, brought on his last illness and death, which took place in 1840. His body was refused burial at Nice, and was taken to Parma for interment. His favorite violin, a large Guarnerius, has been kept on exhibition in a showcase, but would probably be in better condition if played upon.

There were other Italian violinists after Paganini, such as Polledro, but none of overwhelming prominence. Music had reached a period of decadence in Italy, and the public could appreciate nothing higher than the conventional works of the Rossini style. Even the Paris school declined, with the death of its leaders; and for a time the sceptre passed to Germany.

Ludwig Spohr, who brought the German school into its leadership, drew away from the sensational style inaugurated by Paganini, and made breadth and expressive power prominent once more. A symphonist of some greatness, an opera composer of romantic tendencies, he wrote a number of violin concertos, and brought that form well along to the large size and prominence that it now displays. His excellence as a composer was somewhat veiled by mannerisms, such as an excessively chromatic style.

He composed a number of works for violin and harp, the latter instrument being played by Dorette Scheidler, whom he married. Spohr died in 1859, which brought the school to within six decades of the present writing.

Other German and Austrian masters were Joseph Mayseder, Joseph Bohm, Johann Kalliwoda, and Wilhelm Molique, while Karl Lipinski was a Pole. Ignaz Schuppanzigh, who preceded Spohr in point of time, was a friend of Beethoven.

A French group of the time included Alexandre Boucher, Antoine Habeneck, Jacques Mazas, and others. But after the German school had flourished, the sceptre passed to Belgium. Charles Auguste de Beriot, the first of the Franco-Belgian school, held the foremost rank in his day, and continued the ornate and brilliant style of Paganini. From the contrast between his work and Spohr's it is still held that the German school is solid where the Belgian is brilliant; but these distinctions no longer exist. Thus Henri Vieuxtemps, the successor of De Beriot in Belgium, was still brilliant, but showed more breadth.

The German school was carried on by Ferdinand David and Joseph Joachim. David was concertmaster in the Gewandhaus Orchestra which Mendelssohn reorganized at Leipsic. Like Vieuxtemps and De Beriot, he became known also as a composer. Joachim was a classicist in the best sense of the word. But by this time violin preëminence was not confined to any single country. France produced Alard and others; Spain offered Sarasate; Hungary gave the world Remenyi; Wieniawski, who toured with Rubinstein, was a Pole; while Ole Bull came from Norway. Sivori was a Genoese of the Paganini school, while Bazzini, of Brescia, united Italian and German methods.

The great violinists were nearly all composers, from Corelli down to Ysaye and Kreisler. Some of the performers limited themselves to display pieces, but by far the larger part were really gifted musicians, and left works of value for their instrument. But with the development of the sonata form, the great composers began to pay due attention to the violin. Haydn was one of the earliest to write string quartets, but since his day nearly all the masters have tried this form. There are many varieties of chamber music. The old Italian *musica di camera* was meant for secular performance, in contrast to the church music of the time. Nowadays we have piano trios, with violin and 'cello; piano quartets, with a viola usually added; piano quintets, with a second violin; sonatas for violin and piano; and various other combinations for strings. The great composers have brought all these to a high standard. The large orchestral concertos, too, are as ambitious as any three-movement symphony. Beethoven, Mendelssohn, Tschaikovsky, Brahms, and Bruch have written great violin concertos; while contemporary composers attempt the form with persistence, if not always with success. There is also a repertoire for the violin alone, the best-known piece of this sort being the famous Chaconne by Bach.

Among the living violinists, Eugene Ysaye held the first place for a long time. His tone is tremendously broad, and therefore in direct contrast to the supposed character of the Belgian school, to which he belongs.

In recent years, Fritz Kreisler has gained a position rivalling that of Ysaye, if not actually overtopping it. Kreisler, too, is most broadly and poignantly expressive. He is an Austrian.

A still more recent star in the violin firmament is the Frenchman Jacques Thibaud. He shows masterly ability, and has won an unusual success in the past few years. His playing of the Bach

Chaconne, which is a standard test for violinists, is said to be unrivalled.

Other great violinists visit us from time to time, but each of the above three has at times been considered *primus inter pares*. This article is not intended as a catalogue, but aims merely to give a general outline of violin development. Many other names might have been mentioned, in the past as well as the present; but there is not space for them here. Those who are alive should not feel slighted by the omission; and those who are dead are not likely to protest.

LVII

ORCHESTRATION

THOUGH made up of different instruments, the orchestra may be regarded as a unit from the point of view of composer, conductor, and audience. The conductor's share in the matter will be treated in a special chapter, but it has seemed worth while to explain here a part of the composer's work, and certain points that the audience may look for when hearing orchestral music.

The orchestra of Bach, although it had many instruments now obsolete, did not give quite the effect of the full modern orchestra, as it lacked many of the deeper instruments, such as the tubas, contrabassoons, and so on. Bach's music, therefore, is not overpowering in effect, but flows along naturally and smoothly. The contrapuntal character of his music (written as if in parts instead of chords) makes this fluent quality particularly noticeable. In some cases the modern instruments replace the obsolete ones.

Handel's and Bach's scores were often merely outlined, or only partially filled out. In this music the composer was often the leader, and sat at the harpsichord, or organ, where he could arrange his own harmonies to suit himself. For modern purposes, some of the old scores have had to be "filled in" by more recent composers. Thus in the case of the oratorio "The Messiah," which is given widely even to-day, there are two such refurbishings, as already stated, — one by Mozart and one by Robert Franz.

The scores of classical and modern times are complete, having been wholly finished by their composers; and from them the student can trace the growth of the orchestra.

The symphonies of Haydn and Mozart led to those of Beethoven, who is the great representative of the classical period. The classical orchestra consisted of first and second violins, violas, 'cellos, contrabasses, flutes, sometimes a piccolo, oboes, clarinets, bassoons, horns, trumpets, sometimes trombones, and kettledrums. With these the composer could give all the effects he desired.

Taking only the nine symphonies of Beethoven, we find such diverse pictures as bird-calls in pastoral surroundings, a thunderstorm, the funeral march of a dead hero, or the noble antiphonal dialogues of the Ninth Symphony. Modern composers have many more instruments; but they do not give greater music, in spite of its growing complexity. Mendelssohn and Schumann continued to use the classical forces with few changes; but after them Berlioz, Liszt, and Wagner developed the larger orchestra. Our having a large orchestra does not show that the smaller one is out of date; for Brahms, in the latter half of the nineteenth century, kept to the classical forces, and showed that they were amply sufficient for the creation of noble music.

The scores of the classical period show the use of simple tone-colors or combinations of color. There is none of the mixed, impressionistic quality that came later. The instruments stand out by themselves, in fairly clear contrast to the "mingled world of sound" in which modern composers work. Among many examples, one may quote the oboe in Beethoven's orchestral funeral march; the contrabass in the finale of his Ninth Symphony; the clarinet in Mozart's clarinet symphony; the horns in the closing theme of the finale of Schubert's C-major symphony; or the impressive clarinet passage before the coda in the finale of Mendelssohn's Scotch Symphony. This use of simple colors in clear fashion characterizes the classical music.

While the classical composers often divided an instrumental part, giving two notes instead of one to a single kind of instrument, they did this mostly in climaxes for full orchestra, and did not keep it up long. But modern composers, using Wagner and Liszt as models, have indulged much more freely in this divided writing, sometimes giving several notes at once to nearly each kind of instrument. The modern orchestra, too, is much larger than that of classical times. Where Beethoven and Brahms would use only twelve or thirteen staffs, the radical of to-day will write on more than twice that number. As stated elsewhere, there is a passage, in the "Heldenleben" of Richard Strauss, where that composer writes on thirty different staffs, and includes as many as forty-six different notes in a single chord.

In such modern mixtures of tone, the instrumental colors are blended in remarkable fashion. If the orchestra is doubled in number of instruments, the number of possible combinations of all or part of these is much more than doubled. The result is that many modern composers have been so busy hunting for new combinations of color that they have forgotten to write interesting music. The parallel between impressionism in music and in art is fairly exact. If an old-school picture is reduced to black-and-white, it shows much more accurate drawing than an impressionist picture would show under the same conditions. Similarly, in music, if a classical work is arranged for piano, it shows good themes and clear development of these themes into tonal structure; while many modern compositions, if so treated, appear dull and chaotic.

The composer's task in writing orchestral music has been greatly increased; but the older geniuses showed themselves gifted enough in their methods. Beethoven would rewrite his music many times, till it came to sparkle with meaning like a perfect gem of thought. The result can be seen by comparing the rather conventional themes in his notebooks with the impressive shape in which they occur in the actual works. For rapidity, Handel set a good record when he wrote his "Messiah" in twenty-three days. Mozart wrote the overture to "Don Giovanni" in a single night, as it was to be given the following evening. Mendelssohn had only two days in which to compose his "Ruy Blas" Overture for a concert performance. Rossini wrote his "Barber of Seville" in eighteen days. Such rapid work bears witness to the fact that gifted composers think out the music in their heads before they put it on paper.

The modern composer has so many more instruments to take care of that he must necessarily work more slowly. He writes out the important instrumental passages first, and then fills in the rest. Even the old composers would put in the string parts first, and then add the others; though Mendelssohn, in writing the "Ruy Blas" Overture, filled in all the instruments for each measure before passing to the next.

The tone-colors which the modern composer can use have been given in connection with each instrument, but they may well be grouped together here. They are as follows: —

Violin. — All emotions.
Viola. — Rather gloomy melancholy.

Violoncello. — All emotions, but with a more masculine effect than those of the violin.

Contrabass. — Ponderous, portentous, or sometimes comical by reason of its heaviness.

Harp. — Celestial or ecstatic effects, or minstrel accompaniment.

Flute. — Gentle melancholy in the lower register; brilliance in the upper.

Piccolo. — Wild, frenzied gayety, or infernal effects; sometimes used for military suggestion.

Oboe. — Rustic gayety; artless innocence; grief and pathos.

English horn. — Dreamy melancholy; suggests shepherd's pipe.

Bassoon. — Earnest and sombre in lower register, or grotesquely comical; weird in middle register, or like a cry of human pain in upper register.

Contrabassoon. — Deep, impressive, like an organ pipe.

Clarinet. — Eloquent and tender in middle register, spectral in lower.

Bass clarinet. — Sombre. (Basset horn the same, with rich tone.)

Horn. — Romantic, suggesting forest scenes and hunting calls, or ugly and repulsive when muted.

Trumpet. — Bold and martial.

Trombone. — Solemn, impressive, or menacing.

Tuba. — Brutal and powerful.

Kettle-drums. — Explosive, rhythmic, or capable of portraying anxiety and suspense.

Other drums. — Military effects.

Cymbals. — Suited to the clash of battle, or wild festivity.

Glockenspiel. — Tinkling sweetness.

Celesta. — Effect of light melodious bells.

Tambourine and Triangle. — Spanish or Gypsy effects, festivity.

With these colors at his disposal, the modern composer is able to create many odd effects and fairly definite suggestions. While the older composers wrote pure music, for the most part, their more recent successors have become largely devoted to programme music, or music that tells a story or portrays an event that must be described on a printed programme. For this the many instrumental colors are indispensable.

When the auditor hears orchestral music of the classical school, he may expect clear structure, logical development of themes, artistic effects of contrast, and well-balanced work without exaggeration. In the radical modern music he may look for more impressionism — more effects of blended colors that are to be taken as a whole, and not analyzed into the simple colors that made them. He may still seek for artistic symmetry and contrast, but in a freer form than before. Much of the modern auditor's time is taken up in looking at his programme to watch for coming events in the orchestra. If he can tell just when Don Quixote encounters the windmills, or when Mraczek's two bad boys of the orchestra, Max and Moritz, are chased for killing poultry, he will feel happy with the happiness of one who solves a puzzle successfully. But that is not true musical enjoyment. The auditor will do well to learn the plot of the piece before he hears it; but even then he should be entitled to look for good music, and not merely follow a string of effects with a view to seeing what they mean. If the composer has not given good music, he has failed in his duty. Two examples from Strauss will prove the point. His "Don Quixote" variations, picturing that hero's adventures, are full of attempts at suggestion, such as the flock of sheep, the air-trip, the upsetting boat, and so on; but the music is not essentially attractive. On the other hand, his "Death and Transfiguration," contrasting the vain struggle against death with the glorious apotheosis beyond, may be analyzed just as literally (one commentator has found two fever-themes), but is performed and applauded frequently because its music is grand.

Some of the instrumental colors may seem a little arbitrary to the beginner; but after he has learned to pick them out as well as a composition will permit, he will see that they have a basis of accuracy. With these the composer must do his best; and if he handles them properly, they will glow upon the ear with all the warmth that the colors of a Titian show in their appeal to the eye.

LVIII

CONDUCTING

THE art of conducting, in the sense of timekeeping, is very ancient. In the theatres of Grecian times, the duty of leading fell upon the *choregus*, who kept the rhythm by tapping an iron shoe on the floor of the stage. In the Middle Ages, accounts show the Emperor Charlemagne beating time, in similar fashion, by tapping with a wooden staff. Even down to the present, the violinist who leads a small orchestra, when not playing himself, will conduct by tapping on his violin with the bow.

This method of tapping was held responsible for the death of Lully, in the seventeenth century. At the performance of one of his works, a *Te Deum*, celebrating the French king's recovery from sickness, the composer, who was conducting, made such frantic flourishes with his cane that once he struck his gouty foot instead of the floor. Inflammation followed, and neglect allowed it to turn into gangrene, which proved fatal. It may thus be said that Lully died of conducting.

In the music of Handel the composer (or conductor) usually presided by sitting at the harpsichord, where he could fill out the harmonies and guide all the effects. Handel won early notice by stepping to this post of honor at a Hamburg opera performance when Keiser, the regular conductor, was absent dodging creditors. Sometimes the organ was used instead of the harpsichord, especially in the sacred works of Bach.

Haydn and Mozart did away with this harpsichord procedure, and the conductors of their works, whoever they were, could pay complete attention to leading the performers. Haydn conducted his own music for Prince Esterhazy, in whose service he remained for many years. It is said that once, when the princely patron thought of disbanding his orchestra, Haydn wrote and led a symphony in which the players were allowed to cease, one by one, putting out their lights and departing from the room, until only the first violinist was left; and soon he, too, ceased his sad strain and disappeared. When the prince inquired the meaning of this procedure, Haydn replied, "This is our sorrowful farewell." Thereupon, it is said, the prince revoked his dismissal, and kept the orchestra. But the story of this "Farewell Symphony" has been doubted.

Beethoven knew the instruments well, but was not really a good conductor. Even when young he was too eccentric in his moods to exercise proper control of his forces. Later on, when he became deaf, he still continued to lead; but the results were so bad that finally the musicians agreed to follow the first violinist, and disregard Beethoven's irregular motions.

Spohr and Weber were admirable conductors, the latter being very brilliant for his time. He was also one of the first to use the baton, which had been introduced by Mosel in 1807. Spohr carried the baton to London, and won much fame there.

Mendelssohn brought conducting toward its present high level. Under his lead the Gewandhaus Orchestra, at Leipsic, won the rank that it still holds to-day. He, too, gained fresh laurels in London. He was rather strict, but he earned respect by his thorough knowledge. His conducting, like his music, was sunny and cheerful, and did not quite reach the real depths of poignant expression. Wagner, who succeeded him in London, found it some work to alter the Mendelssohn traditions.

At about the same time, Berlioz proved himself a model for the French conductors. His leadership made his continual calls for wholesale effects seem rather strange; for any good conductor knows that moderate forces can be guided with more certainty than excessively large ones. Yet when Paris thought of having a permanent festival organization, he suggested four hundred and sixty-seven instruments, with three hundred and sixty voices. Once he led no less than twelve hundred people. He had four chorus-masters, one at each corner of the group of singers; and two assistant conductors, one for the wind instruments and one for the percussion; all six looking toward him and taking their time from his beat. Such large forces give a great volume of tone, but lose in clearness of attack and accuracy of shading. Wagner, with a free hand to choose the orchestra for his Bayreuth opera house, took only a hundred and sixteen men, and had them all concealed in a sunken space in front of the stage.

Wagner was a gifted conductor, and the insight this gave him into the trivial nature of certain Italian operas may have helped in leading him to write better music himself. He was among the first to conduct freely from memory, without using the score. This may sometimes be done by relying on the men a little, and remembering only a general outline, sufficient to enable the leader to give cues to certain instruments at the right time. But Wagner had many scores completely memorized. When he first tried this procedure, with Beethoven's Ninth Symphony, his men were disposed to ridicule him; but he challenged any of them to play a passage from any part, and showed his knowledge by continuing the part after the player ceased.

Von Bülow, as leader of the Meiningen Orchestra, went so far as to have his players memorize their own parts. He was most painstaking in his attention to details of shading, phrasing, and so on. His men became so proficient that once, when he was unavoidably late, they began the programme in his absence, playing the "Tannhäuser" Overture without any conductor, and finishing it successfully just as he came in.

In general, composers make poor conductors. Some of those already mentioned are exceptions; but there are several reasons for the rule. To begin with, composers are seldom broad enough to judge the music of all others properly; and we see Spohr rating the Beethoven symphonies as dull and uninspired. Then, too, many composers lack the needed executive ability. When conducting, they are apt to listen dreamily to the music instead of guiding it. Schumann was especially given to this procedure. It is said of Richter, who became a great conductor, that when he first took up orchestral leadership, he burned all his compositions, and made a cup of coffee over the fire.

Among French conductors, Lamoureux and Colonne grew famous in the latter part of last century. In Germany, Levi and Mottl were followed by Weingartner, Mahler, Nikisch, Strauss, Muck, Fiedler, and others. Mahler was remarkably great, being able to give to a piece a continual flow of *nuances*, that would make old works seem new and come with the force of a revelation. Weingartner is best known in opera, where the Italian Toscanini also deserves mention. Richard Strauss inclines to powerful effects, and Hausegger is another of the same school. In our own country, Theodore Thomas deserved the highest praise for his earnestness in educating public taste.

A conductor plays upon the orchestra just as a pianist plays upon his instrument. Where the latter may give a maximum of ten notes at once, and cause his fingers to give each note the proper emphasis, the former will have anywhere from twelve to thirty different kinds of instruments to look after, and will emphasize the different parts by means of his beat. He is always responsible for the "reading" of the piece, — the shading given to it, the *nuances* of speed, the comparative emphasis placed on the different parts, and so on. Here tradition is sometimes a guide. The classical works, for instance, are to be taken in a fairly straightforward manner, without any attempt at exaggeration of effects. The same is true of the classical piano repertoire, and we find Paderewski causing much argument by playing the Beethoven sonatas with rubato, which means little caprices in the time of a piece. Whenever a conductor tries to "modernize" a Beethoven symphony in this way, he lays himself open to just criticism, although Mahler sometimes did this.

Sir Frederic H. Cowen, in an article on conducting printed in "The Musician's Guide," gives a number of rules for the conductor, which may well be mentioned here.

First of all, the conductor must possess a distinct and reliable beat, so that the players may know definitely what motion he is making, and from this what result he wants.

The conductor must, of course, have a good musical ear, to enable him to single out any tone of the orchestra, for purposes of correction or alteration.

He must have a thorough working knowledge of all the instruments under him. This does not mean that he shall be a star performer on all of them; usually such knowledge of one or two is all that he possesses. But he must know at least how all the instruments are played, and be familiar with their compass, color, and capability in each case. The conductor will find it useful, also, to be a good pianist; while he surely needs a clear voice to give directions, even if not trained as a singer.

He must be able to read an orchestral score, and master its contents quickly. This is a matter that demands training, for the number of staffs and variety of clefs used, to say nothing of the transposing instruments, make a score very complicated. The reader will remember that the viola is written in the alto clef, the trombone sometimes in the tenor clef, and the other deep instruments in various ways, according to the pitch used; while the clarinets not in C, the English horn, the horns not in C, and sometimes other instruments, transpose the written note to various intervals. The conductor must not merely read the notes of a score, but he must be able also to judge what effects will be produced by the instrumental combinations used.

The conductor must understand the music he is leading, and be able to express its intellectual or spiritual meaning.

He must have a full command of light and shade, or variations in speed or dynamic force; he must be able to make his men bring out these variations; and he must be able to phrase artistically. The balancing of phrases and passages in just the proper way makes all the difference between a performance that is merely passable and one that is excellent. The conductor must also have a correct idea of tempo. One conductor will take certain movements slower or faster than another man will do; and naturally one case gives better results than the other. Here again tradition helps with the old works, in which exaggerated speed or slowness is out of place. For the rest, the pace is largely a matter of individual temperament, though of course it is regulated in a general way by a composer's directions. Thus if a composer calls for an adagio, it is necessarily a slow movement; but some conductors will make it slower than others do. The nature of the music is often useful as a guide, showing whether or not there is to be any exaggeration of pace. Sometimes the composer shows the exact pace by using a metronome mark, putting at the beginning the letters "M. M." (Maelzel's metronome) and a figure with a note of definite value. This will show that the value of the note given should occur a certain number of times to the minute, the number being shown by the figure used. Of course this applies only to the average pace, as there will be passages to be taken faster or slower, as the conductor's ideas or the composer's marks demand.

In the performance of a concerto, which is a piece of symphonic style with a solo instrument playing a special part, the conductor must accompany the soloist, taking care to make the orchestra keep with the solo instrument, or come in properly after solo passages. The same is true for songs with orchestral accompaniment.

The conductor should not allow his personal preferences to interfere with his presenting examples of various schools; and he should do his best to give a good rendering of all pieces that he puts on his programme. Incidentally, the making of programmes is no unimportant detail. It would be wrong, for instance, to follow an overpowering modern tone-picture with some simple bit of Mozart or Haydn, which would seem hopelessly tame in comparison. It is wise for the conductor to end with a powerful or triumphant work. He may follow a purely musical symphony by a story-telling piece of the programme school. He has also the chance to make contrasts between the modern masterpieces of rich harmony and the abstruse experimental effects of the more radical group of composers. There is no lack of variety for him; but he must arrange his pieces so that any resulting contrast will seem to improve them. Max Fiedler, lately with the Boston Symphony Orchestra, may be cited as an excellent programme-maker.

The conductor must have such control that he can guide his forces with the utmost accuracy in making them express what he wishes, and in bringing out the thousand little points that make a good performance. He must "play upon them, individually and collectively, and make them into one responsive whole, ready to understand and follow the least sign or movement of his baton."

In addition, he must be a man of executive ability, able to handle quarrelsome players and enforce obedience and discipline without losing respect himself. For performance, he should also have that indefinable quality known as magnetism, which will enable him to inspire enthusiasm in those who work under him.

The young composer who is sometimes allowed to conduct his own works is to be treated leniently. He is present only to elucidate his own musical ideas. The orchestra will carry itself along, by its own momentum, to a fairly successful performance. He is therefore acting in the capacity of musical interpreter rather than conductor.

The permanent conductor may be judged by the audience in

accordance with the points given above. In the first place, does he make good programmes? Does he pick out interesting novelties, and balance them against well-known master-works in such a way as to gain the most pleasing effect? Then, one may ask, is he a good judge of tempo? Does he take the slow movements too slow, and drag even in rapid movements, or *vice versa?* Then comes the all-important question of reading. Are his contrasts in force exaggerated or minimized; does he make his changes in force gradually or abruptly; in speed, also, does he overdo or underdo the contrasts, and does he make changes too radically or not; is his phrasing properly expressive, and sufficiently varied to avoid monotony; does he control his forces well; does he ever indulge in over-exaggerated effects, in an ill-judged attempt to be original; does he bring out important themes clearly; and is the sum total of his effects, the reading of the piece as a whole, spirited and beautiful, or dull and ineffective? These are a few of the main questions that an auditor may ask himself while listening to an orchestral performance. If the conductor is good, if he performs great music with detailed care, sympathetic understanding, and due enthusiasm, then one may truly admit that a symphony concert becomes a real feast of reason and flow of soul.

Opera conductors are not always judged by the high standard of symphonic work; but some of them have reached the first rank, nevertheless, as Weingartner and Toscanini prove. Opera conductors have troubles of their own, as they have to keep players and soloists together, or guide the chorus, besides attending to the instruments.

The points of conducting, and the questions enumerated above, apply to opera conductors, but in a lesser degree than to symphonic leaders. The opera conductor is not too anxious for delicate *nuances*, which are sometimes lost in a large auditorium; but he tries rather to keep the forces together in a rendering that shall be spirited and striking.

On the whole, then, the conductor earns his salary, even when that salary reaches fancy figures. His is the brain that guides the entire orchestra; and his is the ability that leads it to success.

LIX

ACOUSTICS

SOUND is caused by a disturbance of the atmosphere, which then transmits itself outward through the air. This takes place by having each disturbed air-particle push the one beyond it, so that the disturbance travels outward somewhat like a stroke through a line of billiard balls, or an engine's push through a train of loosely coupled cars.

Sound is either tone or noise, the former being distinguished from the latter by consisting of regular vibrations, where noise is irregular. The push of the air-particles causes hearing by strokes on the eardrum, whereupon certain nerves take the sensation to the brain, which records it as sound. The brain also notes the pitch of the sound, which depends on the number of vibrations (impacts) per second. The human brain can hear such vibrations only between the limits of 16 per second and 38,000 per second, — from nearly an octave below the piano to over three octaves above it. Vibrations that are below the lower limit come to the ear as separate puffs, if heard at all; while those above the high limit are totally inaudible. The upper limit varies with different people, so that some can hear tones which others cannot. Certain animals, such as the cat, have a much higher range than mankind.

One may pause here to pay his respects to the question of the supposed relation between color and pitch. Light waves differ wholly from sound waves in being a disturbance of the ether. In sound, the octave above a note has twice as many vibrations as the note itself; and judged by this principle, the visible color-scale, from red to violet, is less than an octave, the violet having more vibrations than the red in about the proportion of 73 to 46. Light waves, too, are incomparably more frequent, and travel much faster, than sound waves. From all this we may draw the conclusion that there is no relation between color and tone. Many musicians have associated the two; but as we may naturally expect, from our conclusion, such association is merely a matter of individual ideas, that have no real basis in fact. Investigation will show that those who associate certain colors with certain tones differ hopelessly among themselves as to which color goes with any given note.

Sound will travel in other conductors than air. It may be conducted through solids, though the vibrations then have to come through the air in the ear-tube to be audible. In water, sound travels nearly four times faster than in air. This fact is applied in the submarine bell signals now being adopted for lightships and other such places. Steamers are equipped with under-water receivers, one on each side, attached to telephone receivers in the pilot-house. When the bell is equally audible through both receivers, then the steamer is pointed directly toward the lightship, and can figure its proper course from that fact.

The speed of sound in air is about 1120 feet per second. It travels a little slower in dry weather than on damp days, but is more clearly audible. It travels quicker through air of low pressure than through high-pressure air. Thus when the barometer has fallen, just before a storm, the ordinary sounds of daily life, such as whistles, cart-rumblings, and so on, will sound much louder than usual.

A sound wave, resulting from an impulse communicated to the air, is of a perfectly definite length for each pitch, and may be figured exactly if we know the pitch. Such a wave will consist of crest and trough, — the impulse of pressure that strikes the ear-drum, and a lower pressure following it, half-way between the pressure-crest in front and the next one coming after it. If a tone has 35 vibrations a second, and sound travels 1120 feet a second, a simple division will show us that the length of each wave, from one pressure-impulse to the next, is 32 feet. Deep tones, with long sound-waves, do not travel any faster than others; but they penetrate farther, as shown by ocean-steamer whistles. The distance to which sound will travel varies greatly with atmospheric conditions. Tyndall showed the existence in the air of what he called acoustic clouds, which aid or hinder the progress of a tone when present. These clouds form and change so quickly that their action may be noticed during the tolling of a bell. Some of the bell-strokes will sound loud and clear, while others, just before or just after them, may be much muffled in comparison. It may be that these differences come from what the aviators call "holes in the air," which are spaces of low pressure between gusts. If many such low-pressure spaces happened to be in the path of a sound, it would appear louder than usual. Under most favorable conditions, sounds can travel to unexpected distances, perhaps aided by reflectors in the shape of real clouds or fog-banks. Thus a ship's crew in the South Atlantic once heard strange bells while at sea; and later information showed that the sounds came from a festival at Rio Janeiro, over 120 miles away.

The laws governing the vibration of stretched strings were formulated by Pythagoras, in about the year B.C. 600. He found that, all other things being equal, the number of vibrations varies inversely as the length of a string. Thus half the length gives twice the vibrations, or an octave above a note; two thirds of the length gives three halves the number of vibrations, or a fifth above the original note; and so on. With all other conditions equal, he found that vibrations vary directly as the square root of the tension applied, and inversely as the square root of the weight of the string. Thus if a pull of 10 pounds on a string permits it to give 50 vibrations a second, a pull of 40 pounds will be needed to get 100 vibrations a second. Also, if a string weighing an ounce vibrates 120 times a second, a string weighing four ounces will vibrate 60 times a second, one weighing nine ounces will vibrate 40 times a second, and so on. Thick or loose strings give an unclear tone, thin, tight strings (also long ones) giving a better result. All these laws are used in stringing a piano, the highest strings being short, thin, and tight, while the lower ones are longer, thicker, and looser. The lowest strings of all are wound with wire, to give them weight enough so that they need not be too loose. The same is true of the G-string of the violin, and certain strings on other instruments. If the requisite depth in pitch were obtained chiefly by looseness of tension, the tone would be poor and weak.

When a string vibrates, it does not merely swing as a whole, but subdivides into fractional parts, which form shorter vibrations superimposed on the main one. These fractional parts, being shorter than the whole string, give higher tones. These tones, as mentioned in connection with certain instruments, are called overtones, or harmonics, or upper partials, and blend with the main or fundamental tone whenever it is sounded. Their presence may be shown by a simple experiment with the piano. If separate pieces of paper are laid on the strings for each note, and any low note then played loudly with the damper pedal held, those upper strings that correspond to the pitch of the overtones (except the irregular sixth one) will begin to vibrate of themselves, and will shake off the papers. The series of overtones, starting from any C as an example, will be, in ascending order, C, G, C, E, G, B-flat, C, D, E, F-sharp, G, A, B-flat, B, C. The F-sharp, the high A, and the first B-flat will be somewhat off pitch from our scale. The first ten of the series are enough for all practical use.

The presence of these overtones in varying amounts is what causes the difference in tone-color between different instruments or voices. In stringed instruments the quality may be varied in accordance with the place where the strings are bowed, plucked, or struck. The nearer to the middle, the hollower the tone will be; the nearer to the end, the brighter the tone. The former case gives few and faint overtones, while the latter makes them more numerous and stronger. If there are too many overtones, the quality will be incisive and "tin-panny," like that of the banjo or of a worn-out piano. An old piano may be altered by having its hammers tipped with new and soft felt, or by having the old felts jabbed with a needle until soft enough. If harp-strings are plucked near the end instead of near the centre, their tone will lose fulness and become too twangy. A plucked string gives the most overtones, especially if plucked by some hard substance like the pick of a mandolin.

The vibration of strings alone is not powerful enough to cause much of a tone. They are therefore strung over bridges, or supports, which carry the vibrations to a sound-box or sounding-board. The mute of the violin, when in use, operates by clamping the bridge and preventing it from vibrating freely, so that the vibrations reaching the sound-box are weaker than usual, and give a softer tone. Power of tone depends upon amplitude of vibration, and the mute lessens this. The sound-box must be open to the air, to allow free vibration. Sounding-boards are of course exposed to the air, and need no holes.

Pythagoras regulated the intervals of the diatonic scale by a fractional system giving what is known as the scale of nature. In this the vibrations of the notes, compared with the keynote, were in the following ratios: —

> Nine to eight for the second degree.
> Five to four for the third degree.
> Four to three for the fourth degree.
> Three to two for the fifth degree.
> Five to three for the sixth degree.
> Fifteen to eight for the seventh degree.
> Two to one for the octave.

By this scale, considering a certain C to have 120 vibrations a second, the scale above it would be D, 135; E, 150; F, 160; G, 180; A, 200; B, 225; and C (the octave), 240 vibrations a second. Sharps and flats were held to be nearer to their notes than at present, and not coinciding, so that A-flat would be higher than G-sharp, for instance, in the ratio of 128 to 125. The ratio between a note and its sharp was as 25 to 24. This scale sounded very sweet and attractive. It lasted, with slight changes, until after A.D. 1700. In this scale the whole-tones are of two different sizes, the ratios being 9 to 8 and 10 to 9. For this reason, it was not possible to modulate into keys with many sharps or flats without making a piece sound out of tune. Willaert had suggested a change, in the sixteenth century; but his idea was not taken up until about 1700, when Werckmeister (1645–1706) suggested a division into twelve equal semitones. As previously stated, Bach liked this idea, and gave it permanence by writing the two volumes of his "Well-Tempered Clavichord," each volume containing a prelude and a fugue in every possible key. The new scale, which is in use to-day, is known as the "tempered scale."

The acoustic principles governing air-columns in tubes are a little more difficult to the beginner than the string laws; but they may be understood by comparing the row of particles in a column to the loosely coupled cars of a long freight train. Tubes like the oboe and flute, and all similar pipes acting like open tubes (such as the brasses), have a wave-length twice the length of the tube. Taking the freight train as an example, suppose the engine gives a push. This push travels down the train, which corresponds to the tube, until it reaches the end. Then the last car tends to leave the train, but is suddenly hauled up short by its coupling. It thus exerts a pull, and the pull travels back up the train toward the engine. When this pull reaches the engine, the engine is pulled in until it bumps the nearest car, and pushes it. The push then travels along the train as before.

If we suppose that the engine, like the vibrating mouthpiece of a tube, cannot move far from one spot, we may imagine that the engine's first push had made it rebound, so that it reached the back end of its space just as its push was transmitted to the farthest car. It then gives a pull at its end, just as the farther car is transforming the push it received into a pull. The engine's pull and the pull from the other end travel along the train until they meet. They even pass each other and continue on, though we can imagine the middle car not moving when equally pulled from opposite sides. The train, then, has two pulls travelling through it in opposite directions, which are transformed into two pushes when they reach the end.

Something similar happens in the tube of an open wind instrument. The reed mouthpiece, or the player's lips, or the imaginary air-reed that is supposed to be formed in a flute, gives a push which travels down the tube to the open air beyond. As the push goes out of the tube, it sends a pull back through the tube, just as the last car did in the case of the train. Meanwhile the reed has vibrated back, and produced the pull at its end, just as the engine did. When the pull from the other end comes back, it finds the reed ready to push again, and start a new vibration.

While the pull goes back through the tube, the original push has had time to travel out through the air a distance equal to the tube's length. As it is this distance away from the bottom of the tube when the next push is given at the top (mouthpiece), it follows that there will be twice the length of the tube between successive pushes. This constitutes the wave-length. Thus we know that if we make a flute of such size as to have a two-foot column of vibrating air, the wave-length will be four feet; and if sound travels 1120 feet a second, there will be in the flute tone 280 such waves, or vibrations, per second.

We also know that the air at the ends of the tube is in motion at constant pressure, while the particles in the middle, like the middle car of the train, are under varying pressure, first higher and then lower than the air, but have no motion. It may be held that the performer's breath travels through the tube, but that goes extremely slowly, not influencing the vibrations; and a flute or other tube will give its tone if a tuning fork of the same pitch is held to its mouthpiece, in which case no air-current passes through.

For stopped tubes, giving an octave deeper for the same size as open tubes, the wave-length is four times the length of the tube. Suppose an impulse of pressure starting along such a tube. Reaching the open end, it gives its push to the air, and goes back along the tube as a pull. At the stopped end, the pull is exerted, but that pull is not now transformed into a push, as it would be if the tube were open at that end. It must travel back to the open end as a pull. When it reaches the open end, this pull is transformed into a push again, but the push goes down the tube and is reflected back by the stopped end before it can push outward to the surrounding air. Thus each pull and push must travel down the tube and back, or twice its length, giving four times the tube length between successive pushes.

The clarinet, it will be remembered, acted like a stopped pipe. To go back to the freight-train simile, we may suppose that the engine is large and unwieldy. When its push has travelled down the train and come back as a pull, the engine, moving only half as readily as in the other supposed case, is itself only ready to exert a pull. It does so, and the pull of the train cannot then be transformed into a push, but must travel to the farther end of the train to make that transformation. When the impulse next comes back, as a push, the engine is now ready to push, and so the push again must travel to the farther end of the train. Thus the engine is strong enough to prevent any change from push to pull, or *vice versa*, occurring at its end of the train. Such changes occur only at the farther end, corresponding to the open end of the tube; and the impulses must travel up and back, or twice the tube length, before being changed. Thus the same change will recur only after the impulse has travelled four times the length of the tube. The engine is always in opposition, and is strong enough to "govern" the train. We say, similarly, that in the clarinet the reed governs the tube, while in the oboe, for instance, the tube governs the reed. In passing, it may be re-stated that the human voice resembles the oboe in principle, the two vocal cords acting like a double-reed mouth-piece.

A few more bits of imagination will enable the student to finish with the subject of tubes. In placing holes and keys on the wood-wind instruments, these holes are placed at the proper distances to make the air-column of the different fractional lengths needed for the pitch of the scale. Thus opening a hole three fifths of the distance from the mouthpiece to the other end would raise the pitch a major sixth; two thirds would raise the pitch a fourth, and so on. As with strings, the vibrations of air-columns vary inversely as their length. To get lower notes than usual, holes near the end of the mouthpiece are closed, lengthening the air-column. The D-flat and C of the flute are instances. The holes for these are left open, and closed when needed; while the other holes are naturally closed, and opened when needed.

The formation of overtones to the exclusion of the fundamental, caused by increased force of blowing, makes the air-column sub-divide into fractional parts. Wherever there is free motion at constant pressure, we may take such a point as a centre of vibration, halfway between the points where there is change of pressure but no motion. In an open tube, such free motion is found at each end. When the air-column divides in half, there will be two changing-pressure points, at one fourth and three fourths the length of the tube; one being at high pressure while the other is at low pressure, and *vice versa*. The constant-pressure-and-free-motion points are at each end, and in the middle of the tube. Similar subdivisions for higher overtones always have free-motion points at each end of the tube, no matter how many more are part way along the tube; and from this we see that all overtones are theoretically possible in open tubes.

If a stopped tube is imagined, it will be seen that the stopped end is always a point of changing pressure and no motion, while the open end is a point of free motion and constant pressure. Now if we suppose a wave-length of half the usual size, giving the octave tone of the first harmonic, this wave-length will be twice the tube length, instead of four times its length. The condition for a wave-length of twice the tube was found to be that the tube must be open at both ends, with the point of no motion but varying pressure in the middle. Since this condition is not true of the stopped tube, which is closed at one end, it follows that the octave harmonic cannot form. Also, any other harmonic that needs to have both ends of the tube open cannot form in a stopped pipe. On the other hand, those harmonics will appear, in a stopped pipe, which have a wave-length of such proportion to the tube that one end may be a no-motion point, with changing pressure, while the other end may be a constant-pressure point, with free motion. A little figuring will show that such distance between points of no motion will be two thirds the tube length, or two fifths, or two sevenths, or any fraction with an odd-numbered denominator. As the change from a point of high pressure to one of low pressure (from crest to trough) is only half a wave-length, it follows that the whole wave-lengths will be four thirds, four fifths, four sevenths, the length of the tube, and so on. As the fundamental wave-length was four times the tube-length, it follows that the harmonics that can form will have wave-lengths one third, one fifth, one seventh, etc., as long as the fundamental wave-length. As the full harmonic series has fractional wave-lengths of one half, one third, one fourth, one fifth, etc., it will be seen that the odd-numbered harmonics are absent from a stopped pipe, only the even-numbered ones forming.

The tone quality of pipes is also influenced by their shape, narrow ones being more brilliant than wide ones, and conical tubes more brilliant than cylindrical ones, because the overtones are present in a larger proportion.

The organ, as stated in a previous chapter, is sometimes provided with a double rank of pipes, instead of a single one, to produce a tremolo effect. For this purpose one set of pipes is slightly flat of the other set. That means that its wave-lengths are slightly longer. As two pipes sound for a key, one from each set, the vibration-puffs from the two, being unequally far apart, will reach the auditor at different intervals, though the interval for each pipe is constant. The idea may be illustrated by imagining two hammers beating, one four times a second and the other five times. Their strokes will coincide once a second. When the vibration-puffs coincide, at regular intervals, they strike the ear with increased force, just as the doubled hammer-stroke would do. Such increases in power, occurring at regular intervals, are known as beats. They may be heard when piano strings get out of tune with one another.

The sound of a tube or pipe, as stated above, is not due to any air-current passing through it, but merely to the pipe's ability to reënforce the vibrations at its mouthpiece. For this reason the pipe may be said to vibrate sympathetically, or in synchronism, with the mouthpiece. Yet a sapient reporter once made a clear blunder in this matter, which he must have manufactured out of whole cloth. In a certain city, a large pipe on one of the well-known organs became out of order, and would not sound. A mouse, it seems, had located a home near the flue mouthpiece of the pipe, and thus interfered with the forming of the vibrations. Here the reporter "got in his fine work," describing the affair at length, and stating that the pipe continued silent until the fullest pressure was put on, after which there was a sudden burst of noise, and the mouse's nest flew out against the ceiling. If the reporter had known the nature of flue-pipe vibrations, he would have seen that they are not due to any strong air-current, and that such an obstruction could not have been blown out in the way that he claimed.

The vibrations of such air-columns are said to synchronize with those formed at the mouthpiece. As already stated, any vibrating object near the mouthpiece will cause a tube to sound, provided that the vibrations are of the same pitch as those that the air-column can give. If they are of any other rate, the tube will not respond. This vibration in sympathy with something else vibrating at the same rate is called synchronism. The sound-boards and sound-boxes of the string instruments are able to synchronize with different tones, thus reënforcing all notes played on such instruments. Those instruments that have a second set of strings, vibrating in sympathy with the first, depend upon this synchronism. The strings corresponding to the overtones of a piano note, whenever the note is held by the damper pedal, will vibrate in sympathy with those overtones. This synchronism is quite a delicate matter, a few vibrations too much or too little causing it to vanish almost wholly.

Objects in a room will often vibrate in synchronism with a certain tone. The writer remembers a vocal duet, heard in private, at which the sounding of a high note caused a gas globe to be shattered into fragments. The heat from a gas flame will sometimes crack such a globe; but in this case the vibrations of the globe, synchronizing with those of the voices, gave the added touch necessary for the smash.

A similar case occurred with a St. Louis organ, built for an exposition. When a performer was playing it, he struck a note synchronizing with the skylight, and causing the latter to break. Immediately the ubiquitous reporter "put in his oar." He stated that the player was in no wise to blame, but that the trouble had evidently been caused by the jarring of some harsh note previously played by some one else. The first part was correct — the player was not at fault; but the synchronism of the skylight was brought out, not by a harsh note, but by an unusually clear and pure tone of exactly the right vibration rate.

Synchronism has even been used in the plot of a recent detective story. One of the mysterious affairs in that story is a large and strongly built harp, which seems to give no tone when its upper strings are touched. The explanation states that these strings sounded above the limits of human hearing, and were used to make similar strings on another such instrument vibrate in synchronism. So far, so good; but this synchronism, used as a means of giving signals, was supposed to carry out of a room, across a courtyard, over a wall, and still beyond that to some one who was hiding outside. As high tones do not carry so far as low ones, the tones in real life would not cause any appreciable effect beyond a very few yards' distance.

That synchronism may produce powerful effects is shown in a number of ways. A regiment marching across a bridge will make it sway dangerously, unless the men are allowed to "break step." Many buildings vibrate noticeably in synchronism with their engines; and once a new cotton mill was found to be so shaky that the engineer could not be permitted to use certain rates of speed. The falling of the walls of Jericho may well be "founded on fact" and due to synchronism; for the trumpet blasts from outside, if of just the right rate, could have made the walls shake until they dropped. A structure will not necessarily respond to a single tone; but any building may possibly do so.

The need for "voicing" an organ depends on synchronism. The wave-lengths of certain notes may be perfect fractional parts of the length or width of the building in which the organ is set up. The air in the room will vibrate in sympathy with such notes, and make them seem stronger than the rest; a result that the maker obviates by weakening the tone of the pipes in question. It is possible to voice a piano to suit the room or hall containing it.

The acoustics of halls is a matter not well understood. In Paris, the hall of the Conservatoire is old, irregular, and badly ventilated; but it is excellent acoustically, and the authorities will allow no improvements, for fear of injuring this excellence. The Trocadero, also in Paris, was built on the idea that sound would be reflected like light; but it proved a failure. Sound travels through the air somewhat as waves progress in the ocean. It will bend around corners and obstacles, and thus differs from light in its action. The excellence of buildings with semi-oval roofs, such as the Salt Lake City Tabernacle, is due to the fact that the sound waves swish along the curves with the impetus that waves show when washing up a sloping beach. The ancients may have known more about acoustics than we do; for the remains of their open-air buildings show seats sloped at an angle that helps the acoustic effect.

Echoes are sometimes a source of trouble. A certain Boston church, when taken over from the builders, was found to have a perfect echo, which naturally rendered preaching impossible in the building. The church members could not remedy the defect. Another set of owners, who bought the edifice at a low figure, finally eliminated the echo by floor and roof alterations, combined with the stringing of wires and the building of a gallery. But the entire proceeding was a "rule-of-thumb" affair, and showed that we still have much to learn about architectural acoustics.

LX

HOW TO READ MUSIC

IN an earlier chapter, the rise of notation was discussed. Here the notation of to-day is described, for the benefit of those who wish to learn to read the notes from the printed page.

The notes on the piano are named by groups of twelve, called octaves. The thirteenth note upward from any given note (counting the given note as one) is called the octave of that note; while the thirteenth note downward from any given note is the octave below it.

On piano and organ keyboards, the groups of twelve adjacent keys consist of five black ones and seven white ones. There is a black key between white ones except for two places in the group. As a result, the five black keys seem grouped in two and in three, with a white key between the black ones in each case.

The white note just below the group of two black keys is known as C. The letters A, B, C, D, E, F, and G are used to name the white keys. The deepest notes are at the left, the highest at the right as one faces the keyboard. Each A is of course the second white note below each C, each D the first white note above the C's, and so on.

Each black key is known either as the sharp of the white key just below it, or the flat of the white key just above it.

For writing or printing these notes, a staff of five parallel lines is used. A sign representing a letter (i.e., a note) is put on one of the lines of this staff, to show the position of the note named. This sign is called a clef. Both the lines and the spaces of the staff are used, so the position of a note on one of these lines or spaces will determine what note it is.

Three clefs are used, signifying the F below middle C of the piano, middle C itself, and the G just above middle C.

On full-sized pianos, the lowest note is A. This A, with the B-flat and B just above it, are known as belonging to what is called the sub-contra octave. The C's, from left to right, are known as contra, great, small, one-line, two-line, three-line, four-line, and five-line. Middle C is the same as one-line C. The eleven keys next above each C are described by the same adjective used for the C. Thus we can locate any note on the piano by its name — great F, three-line D-sharp, two-line A-flat, etc. The so-called international pitch gives two-line C 517.3 vibrations per second, while philosophical pitch gives it 512. Concert pitch is variable, but always high.

The sign for a sharp or a flat is placed before the note, the staff lines and spaces being devoted to the white keys. The sign for a sharp is ♯, and for a flat, ♭. The sign for a double-sharp, sometimes used, is ✻. The sign for a double flat is simply two flats, ♭♭. When any of these signs have been in force and are to be neutralized, a single natural sign is used. The natural sign is ♮. For a single sharp after a double sharp, ♮♯ is used; and for a single flat after a double flat, ♮♭ is used.

Illustrations are now given, on staffs using the three different clefs.

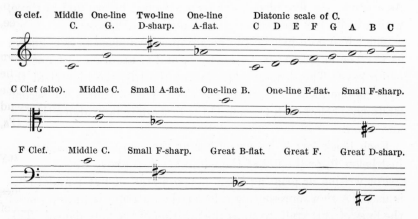

The F clef is now usually fixed in position, though it has been used on the third line of the staff, instead of the fourth. In its regular place it is called the bass clef, while on the third line it is known as the baritone clef. The C clef may be placed on the first (lowest), second, third, or fourth line of the staff, in which case it is known respectively as the soprano, mezzo-soprano, alto, or tenor clef. The G clef always places one-line G on the second line of the staff, though in old music it was sometimes used on the first line, and known as the French violin clef. In piano music, two staffs are usually employed, the upper one, for the right hand, being in the G clef, while the lower one, for the left hand, is in the F clef.

As may be seen from the illustrations, notes that come above or below the staff are notated on short extra lines, or in the spaces made by these lines. The extra lines are known as leger lines.

Sometimes, when several notes in succession occur above the staff, or below it, a change of the clef will save the trouble of writing many extra leger lines. This change may be found fairly often in piano music, where the F clef is sometimes used on the upper staff, or the G clef on the lower, for a short time. The clef in use is always printed at the beginning of each line. The new clef is printed wherever it is desired to come, and when its action is finished, the original clef must be inserted again.

Our octave is made up of twelve equal semitones. The use of these twelve in order forms what is known as the chromatic scale.

Intervals are named in accordance with the number of semitones they contain, or the distance between the two scale-degrees forming the interval. The smallest interval is of course the semitone, coming between E and F or B and C among the white keys, or between any white key and an adjacent black key.

Here a musical rule complicates matters by allowing the intervals to be named from the scale degrees. Thus the interval from C to D-flat is regarded as a minor (small) second; while the interval from C to C-sharp, which is really the same as the preceding one in size, is called an augmented prime, or augmented unison.

Octaves, fifths, and fourths are known as perfect, diminished, or augmented. An octave from D to D, for instance, is a perfect octave; from D below to D-sharp above, an augmented octave; and from D-sharp below to D above, a diminished octave. A fifth from C to G is called perfect, and any other fifth of the same number of semitones is called perfect; from B to F, or C-sharp to G, or C to G-flat, is a diminished fifth. From C to F, E to A, etc., is a perfect fourth; while from F to B, or C to F-sharp, or E to A-sharp, is an augmented fourth. Diminished fourths would be of the same size as major thirds, while augmented fifths would be the same as minor sixths.

Seconds, thirds, sixths, or sevenths are spoken of as major, minor, and sometimes augmented and diminished.

From C upward to B, or any other seventh of that size, is a major seventh; from G upward to F, or any seventh of that size, is a minor seventh; while from C-sharp upward to B-flat, or any seventh of that size, is a diminished seventh. From C to A, G to E, or any sixth of that size, is a major sixth; from C to A-flat, or G-sharp to E, or E to C, or any sixth of that size, is a minor sixth. Theoretically, from C-sharp to A-flat would be a diminished sixth; but this would be the same in size as a perfect fifth. Browning, in "A Toccata of Galuppi," wrote of "Sixths, diminished, sigh on sigh"; but that would be a succession of fifths in reality, and such a progression was strictly forbidden by the harmony teachers. To resume, the interval from C to E, D to F-sharp, or any third of that size, is a major third; while from C to E-flat, D to F, C-sharp to E, or any third of that size, is a minor third. From D to E, G to A, E to F-sharp, or any second of that size, is a major second (whole tone); from E to F, G to A-flat, C-sharp to D, or any second of that size, is a minor second; while from F to G-sharp, or any interval of that size, is an augmented second. Some illustrations are given below.

The so-called major scale, starting with any one of the twelve notes in the octave, consists of the following intervals, in ascending order: — tone, tone, semitone, tone, tone, tone, semitone. The scale of C major is therefore C, D, E, F, G, A, B, C, and consists wholly of white keys. But when we attempt to form a major scale on any note other than C, we find that some black keys must be used to keep the scale-intervals correct. Thus the scale of G major needs F-sharp instead of F; while the scale of F major needs B-flat instead of B. The sharps or flats needed for any given scale (key) are put with the clef at the beginning of each staff, and are known in that place as the signature. The keys needing sharps are G, D, A,

E, B, and F-sharp. The sharps needed number from one to six, in the following order: — F-sharp, C-sharp, G-sharp, D-sharp, A-sharp, and E-sharp, the last being really the note F. The key of G demands F-sharp; the key of D, F-sharp and C-sharp; and so on. The keys needing flats are F, B-flat, E-flat, A-flat, D-flat, and G-flat, the last being the same as F-sharp. The flats needed, in order, are B-flat, E-flat, A-flat, D-flat, G-flat, and C-flat, the last being the same as B. The key of F needs B-flat; the key of B-flat needs B-flat and E-flat; and so on. The keys of C-flat and C-sharp exist, but are rarely used.

Any sharps or flats used elsewhere than in the signature are called accidentals. These remain in force to the end of their measure; they may affect a note held from one measure into the next. Usually an accidental is held to affect any octave of the note altered; but such octave notes should really have the accidentals written in. Accidentals should be used in all cases where any possible doubt might be caused by their absence.

Examples of signatures: —

Each major scale has related to it a minor scale, which keeps the same signature, but begins and ends two scale degrees below the major scale, i.e., a third below, or a sixth above. Thus C major has the scale of A minor as its relative scale, D major has B minor, A-flat major has F minor, and so on.

If a scale is named only by its keynote, the major scale is meant.

There are two varieties of minor scale, the harmonic and the melodic. The harmonic minor has the intervals of tone, semitone, tone, tone, semitone, augmented second, and semitone. The harmonic A minor scale would thus be A, B, C, D, E, F, G-sharp, and A. The melodic minor has different intervals in two cases, according to whether the scale ascends or descends. Its ascending intervals are tone, semitone, tone, tone, tone, tone, and semitone. The melodic scale of A minor, ascending, will therefore consist of A, B, C, D, E, F-sharp, G-sharp, and A. In descending, its notes are A, G, F, E, D,

C, B, and A. The relative minor of any major scale begins on the sixth degree of the latter. Some examples are given below.

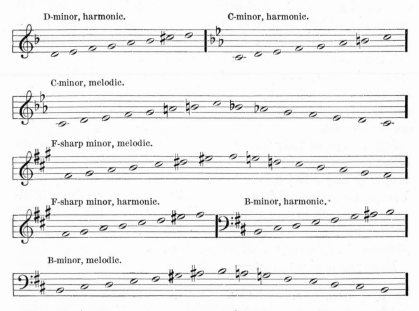

The choice of a key is not made at random. On the piano, high keys are more brilliant, lower ones more solid. In vocal music, the range of the voices must be considered. In the orchestra, many instruments are easiest to play in those keys that have the fewest sharps or flats.

Some musicians associate certain emotions with certain keys. Such ideas are merely individual whims, and no two systems agree.

The major and minor scales are the ones commonly used in our music; but others exist, and are sometimes employed by composers.

The Gregorian scales, or tones, have been described in the section on the evolution of music. They are still employed in the services of the Catholic Church. At times a composer will introduce music written in these scales, to give a religious effect or suggestion.

The Hungarian gypsy scale has been used by Schubert, Liszt, Paderewski, and other composers. This scale is like the harmonic minor, with an additional augmented second and semitone instead of two tones. Its intervals correspond with those of a scale consisting of A, B, C, D-sharp, E, F, G-sharp, and A. Its effects are strongly expressive, in both the sad and the fiery styles that the gypsies use.

The Byzantine scale, little used in our music, has intervals corresponding to a scale on the notes C, D-flat, E, F, G, A-flat, B, and C.

The pentatonic scale has been mentioned in connection with Chinese music.

Some Oriental races have scales that divide the octave into five, six, or seven equal intervals. In the modern French school, Debussy has made frequent use of a whole-tone scale, consisting of intervals like those given by the notes C, D, E, F-sharp, G-sharp, A-sharp, and C. This scale is not used by itself, but its effects are blended with our more usual scales.

The Hindoos have a scale consisting of smaller intervals than ours, such as third-tones, or even quarter-tones. These small intervals are grouped by them into many different modes.

The different notes, or degrees, of our scales are given certain names. In ascending order, these are the tonic, supertonic, mediant, subdominant, dominant, submediant, and leading tone, or subtonic. By means of these it is possible to describe a modulation, or change of key.

Our music is divided by vertical lines (bars, bar-lines) into measures of equal length, or time-value. Our notes are made to signify a definite length of time in the measure, according to whether they are solid, or merely outlined, or provided with stems, or have on the stems little appendages called flags. The smallest notes have most flags. Sometimes such notes of small value are joined together by lines through their stems, called ties; in which case there must be

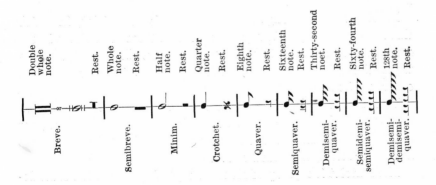

as many lines as there would have been flags on each separate note. Any note may be replaced by a rest, which indicates a pause of a certain duration. The various notes, with their American names above and English names below, are given on page 521. Each note is followed by a rest of the same value as the note. 256th notes have been used, but are uncommon. Beethoven and others have used 128th notes.

So-called "cadenza" notes have no definite value, but are grouped together by joined stems to fill a certain space as a whole. These may be found in the works of Liszt, Chopin, and others. The notes usually fill one or more measures, though it is not always necessary to compress them into exact time. The result is a free running phrase, which the performer may take at any suitable pace. Cadenza notes are always printed in a smaller size than ordinary notes.

Artificial groups may be made by joining an unusual number of notes with a slur, and placing above it a figure equaling the number of notes. This means that such a number of equal notes must be played in the time-value of the place that they occupy in the measure. An artificial group usually occupies some simple fraction of a measure, or of a beat.

The simplest of such groups is one consisting of two artificial notes to replace three normal ones. The two are written in the next larger denomination than the three, and joined by a slur with the figure 2 above it.

The slur, which will be discussed later, is a slightly curved line placed horizontally, or nearly so, above or below the notes that it is intended to influence.

Most common among artificial groups is the triplet, in which three notes are played to replace two. The three are written in the same denomination that the two would have. It is possible for a triplet to consist of two notes, the first having twice the value of the other, or *vice versa*.

By artificial grouping, four notes may be made to replace three.

Any number of notes may be made into an artificial group. But if the number is large, it is customary to write the notes as cadenza notes, with no figure added above.

The sextolet is a group of six notes replacing four of the same denomination. The true sextolet is taken either as one group, with the accent on the first note of the six, or as three groups of two notes, bringing an accent on the first, third, and fifth notes. A sextolet that divides into halves is wrongly written, and should have been made into two triplets. Even the greatest composers have been careless in this matter, and have made this mistake hundreds of times.

Some examples of artificial groupings are given here, in single measures.

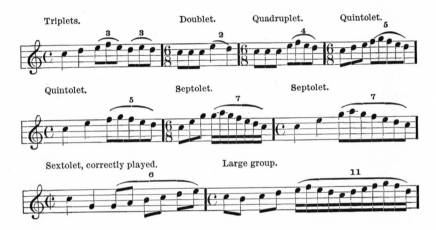

The measure consists of a value that is determined by figures placed at the beginning of a piece, or at any place where a change in value is desired. In the latter case, it is usual to let the figures come just after a double bar line, or an unusually thick line.

The figures are always in the form of a fraction, the upper number showing how many notes of a certain value make up a measure, and the lower number telling what that value is. Thus 4/4 means measures of a value equal to four quarter notes; 3/8 means measures of a value equal to three eighth notes; and so on. The fraction 4/4 is equal to unity, which would be simpler to write; but the former must be used, because it implies accents in certain parts of the measure. The sign $\mathbb{C}$, used to replace 4/4, is not the letter C, but two thirds of a circle. In the old days the monks held triple rhythm perfect, because it suggested the holy Trinity; and they represented it by a circle. Even (double) rhythm was only two thirds of the triple rhythm, and was represented by that much of the complete circle. The 4/4 rhythm is known also as common time. For 2/2 time the sign ≕₵≕ is used, and for 4/2 time ≕₵≕ or ≕₵·₵≕ The ≕₵≕ 2/2 rhythm is called "alla breve," and the 4/2 is sometimes spoken of as "long alla breve."

In even rhythms the measure divides naturally into halves; but in the simplest cases the halves themselves are single beats. When the halves subdivide evenly one might speak of the rhythm as double even rhythm, though this distinction is not made. Even rhythms include 2/1, 2/2, 2/4, 2/8, 4/1, 4/2, 4/4, and 4/8.

Triple rhythms are those in which the measure divides naturally into three beats. They include 3/1, 3/2, 3/4, 3/8, and 3/16.

Compound even rhythms are those in which the measure divides into halves or quarters, and these in turn divide into three parts. Examples of such rhythm are 6/2, 6/4, 6/8, 6/16, 12/4, 12/8, 12/16, and 24/16.

Compound triple rhythms are those in which the measure divides into thirds, and each part subdivides again into thirds. Examples of this are 9/4, 9/8, and 9/16. Even 18/8 has been used, and accented like a 3/4 measure with double triplets.

Peculiar rhythms are those in which the measure divides into five or seven parts. They include 5/2, 5/4, 5/8, 5/16, 7/2, 7/4, 7/8, and 7/16.

At first sight it would seem that the number of beats in a measure would determine its speed, and that the printing of these beats in notes of larger or smaller denominations would denote the pace. As a matter of fact, a 3/8 piece with a slow tempo mark might be slower than a 3/4 piece with a rapid tempo mark; but usually the smaller denominations call for greater speed, and a certain lightness of style.

Complex rhythms occur in certain compositions. These are made by the playing together of measures made up of dissimilar rhythms.

Accents in music are either natural or artificial. The natural accents are those that come at definite times to show the rhythm of the measure. Artificial accents are those that are marked especially, by certain letters or signs.

In the simple even rhythms, with two beats to the measure, the first beat is accented slightly. The same is true when there are three beats in the measure. With four beats, the first receives an accent, and the third another, but slighter, accent. With six beats in the measure, the first receives the chief accent, and the fourth the slighter accent. With five beats in the measure, the first always receives an accent, while the secondary accent may come on the third or the fourth beat, or may be absent altogether. With seven beats, the first is accented, and either the fourth or the fifth receives the secondary accent. With nine beats, the first is accented, while very slight secondary accents come on the fourth and seventh beats. With twelve beats, the measure is divided into four parts, each divided into three. The main accent comes on the first beat, a very slight one on the fourth, a little stronger one (the secondary accent) on the seventh, and the slightest of the accents on the tenth beat. The same holds true when 4/4 measures consist of eighth-note triplets, making twelve equal notes in the measure. In connection with natural accents, it will be readily noticed that most waltzes, though written in 3/4 rhythm, are accented as if two of their measures were really one measure in 6/4 rhythm. Rimsky-Korsakov has used an 11/8 rhythm, and Scriabine a 15/8 rhythm, of which the former is a 4/4 rhythm varied by occasional bars in 3/4 rhythm, while the latter is made of five groups having three beats apiece.

The amount of power to be used in playing a piece is regulated by the use of the letters *p*, *m*, and *f*, which stand for the words *piano* (soft), *mezzo* (medium), and *forte* (strong or loud). The usual scale of dynamic marks, from the softest to the loudest, runs from *pp* to *ff*. It consists of *pp* (*pianissimo*, very soft), *p* (*piano*, soft), *mp* (*mezzo-piano*, moderately soft), *mf* (*mezzo-forte*, moderately loud), *f* (*forte*, loud), and *ff* (*fortissimo*, very loud). For more extreme effects, *ppp* and *fff* have been used. Some composers have gone as far as *ffff*, while Verdi even used *ppppp* in his "Requiem," and Tschaikowsky used both extremes freely in his "Symphonie Pathétique." Such excesses are applicable only to orchestral music, which admits of strong contrasts and delicate shading.

These letter-directions are usually supposed to remain in force until contradicted. But to make assurance doubly sure, or to avoid error, the composer may put after any of them the word *sempre*, meaning always.

An increase in power is called for by the word *crescendo*, or its abbreviation *cresc.*, followed by a long dotted line extending until the desired climax of power is reached. Such a gradual increase in power may be called for also by the use of two lines that start from a single point and diverge gradually to show increasing loudness. For the reverse effect, a gradual softening may be called for by the words *decrescendo* or *diminuendo*, or by the abbreviations *decresc.* or *dim.*, followed by the dotted line of desired length; or the softening may be marked by two lines that start a little distance apart and gradually converge to a single point.

An increase of pace is called for by the words *più mosso*. A gradual increase is called for by the word *accelerando*, or its abbreviation *accel.* A sudden decrease of pace is demanded by the words *meno mosso;* and a gradual decrease by the word *ritardando* or its abbreviation *rit.* A number of the most important terms used in music have been defined in the following chapter, and they may be investigated whenever necessary.

The tempo marks, showing about what general speed is desired, are tabulated here for reference. From the slowest to the fastest, they are *grave*, gravely, heavily; *largo*, largely, broadly; *larghetto*, less broadly; *adagio*, slowly; *andante*, fairly slow-moving; *andantino*, less slow than *andante; moderato*, at a moderate pace; *allegretto*, somewhat lively; *allegro*, lively, fast; *presto*, very fast; and *prestissimo*, faster yet, the most rapid tempo of all. *Andante* and *andantino* are not used in their strict Italian sense.

The artificial accents are those that have to be marked in especially wherever desired. The two signs ∧ and ≻ both call for a loud accent. Either one may be used in a composition; but if both are used at different places in the same piece, then the former calls for a louder accent than the latter. Accent is implied by *staccato*, or by an extra stem on a note. Accent is called for by the letters *sf*, *sfz*, or *fz*, which are abbreviations of the word *sforzando* or *forzando*. The letters *sffz*, coming from the superlative *sforzandissimo*, demand a very loud accent. The letters *fp* call for a loud note, or chord, followed by softness. The letters *sfp* indicate a very loud note followed by softness. The letters *rf* or *rfz*, coming from the word *rinforzando*, mean a fair amount of fulness without excessive loudness. The *tenuto* mark, consisting of a dash above a note, signifies a clinging, expressive accent. The *marcato*, a dash with a dot below it, implies the same sort of accent, but the note is to be slightly separated from these before and after it. The *portamento*, which might better be called the *demi-marcato*, consists of two or more notes under a slur, with dots over each note and beneath the slur. In this case each note is given the clinging accent and slight separation. If only the second of two such slurred notes has a dot over it, the first note receives the clinging accent and is held to its full length, while the second note is lighter and shorter, almost staccato. A famous piano teacher once explained *portamento* to a pupil by saying, "Play the notes as if you were trying to give a legato with one finger."

The word *staccato* implies that a note is to be shortened, and given with a quick release. The staccato effect is most often called for by the use of a dot over each note that is to be so treated. Sometimes a thin vertical wedge is used, instead of the dot. If both dot and wedge are found in the same piece, then the wedge calls for a more abrupt staccato than the dot. Staccato usually implies some degree of accent; and in a few cases the dot has been used to indicate accent without staccato. The opposite of staccato is legato, which means a smooth, well-connected style of playing.

When the rhythm of a piece is altered, and a false rhythm substituted briefly and unexpectedly, the process is known as "syncopation." The odd accenting of some rag-time music is really syncopation, though not all syncopation is rag-time. The result may be reached by several different methods. A long note may be written on the unaccented part of the measure, so that it has to be held over the place where the accent would come. Accents may be placed on the unaccented part of the measure. The accented notes may be made short, while *tenuto* marks are placed over the unaccented notes. Rests may be written on the accented beats of the measure, and notes or chords on the unaccented parts. Short slurs may be used to connect unaccented notes with the accented notes that follow. Finally, notes may be written so that they begin on the second half of a beat, and extend beyond the next accent. In all cases, the syncopation should not be carried on for a long time, for if continued too far the false rhythm will seem to be the true one. Examples of the different methods of obtaining syncopated effects are given on page 528.

The slur is a slightly curved line, placed horizontally (or nearly so) above or below the notes it is intended to affect. The long slur, extending over more than two notes, came originally from violin playing, in which it is used to mark the notes to be played by a single bow-stroke. It was then adopted for vocal music, to show how many syllables were to be sung at a breath. In piano music, the long slur may show either the notes that make up a phrase, or a legato style. It may be used after staccato work, to show a resumption of ordinary playing, even without any marked legato.

The short slur, over two notes, has some especial rules. If the notes are small, the first one is accented and held for its full length, while the second is made lighter and shorter. But if the notes exceed quarter notes in length, the second one must not be shortened. If the second note is longer than the first, the slur should be treated simply as a legato mark. In any rapid passage, a short slur is to receive only a slight accent.

The slur is used also to bind together two notes of the same pitch, in which case the two are played as one. When the slur is used for this purpose, it is called a tie, and placed so that its ends almost touch the notes that are to be joined together.

Any note may be lengthened by half its value if a dot is placed directly after the body of the note. If two dots are used, the note is lengthened by a half and a quarter of its value. Examples of dotted and tied notes are given here.

Two dots in the two middle spaces of the staff, as shown in the margin, are used to indicate the repeat of all or part of what has gone before. The two dots are always placed just before a double bar, which may have extra marks above and below the staff to attract attention. If no previous dots are found, the repeat is to be made from the beginning of the piece. But if other dots are previously found, this time just after a double bar, the repeat is to be made from that point.

Very often there will be what are known as first and second endings for the repeated portion of a piece. These endings are shown by the use of long horizontal lines over the requisite notes, each line being marked with its proper figure. The figure 1 will come first, with its line, which will end with a short vertical line at the repeat dots. In repeating, everything under the line marked 1 is omitted, the player proceeding from just before the figure 1 to just after the repeat dots, where he will find a new ending indicated by the figure 2 and another horizontal line above the staff.

D.C. and *D.S.* mean, "repeat from beginning," or "from the sign."

If a single measure is to be repeated, the sign ·/. is placed in each of the succeeding measures where such repeat is desired. But if any other material intervenes, the original measure must occur again before the repeat sign can be used. In other words, the sign always repeats the last measure previously printed.

A figure filling less than a measure may be marked for repeat by the

following signs:—

The above is often used for what are known as broken chords, in which the notes of a chord are played in succession instead of simultaneously. The last of the above examples is an illustration.

When a note of small value is repeated a number of times, an abbreviation may be made, by which one large note is written to fill all the time value (or as much of it as possible), and signs added to show that small notes of a certain denomination are to be repeated until the value of the large note has been filled. Lines through the note-stem, or under the note if there is no stem, are used as the sign for such repeated notes; and the number of lines corresponds to the number of flags that would be found on the stem of one of the smaller notes. Examples are given here.

The letters *8va* over a staff show that the notes beneath the mark are to be played an octave higher than written. If the letters apply to more than the note over which they occur, they are extended by a dotted line, which stops at the point where the printed pitch is to be resumed. Sometimes this resumption is marked by the word *loco*. The sign *8va bassa* below any note or notes means that they are to be played an octave deeper than written. But the words *con 8va bassa* imply that the notes are to be played as written with the addition of the octave below in each case.

The abbreviation *ped.* is used to signify the pressing of the damper pedal, which raises all the dampers from the strings of a piano, and allows the note played to resound continuously. An asterisk is used to show where the pedal is to be released, and the dampers dropped back upon the strings. In some American editions of music, the duration of the pedal's use is shown by a horizontal line below the music, with short upward vertical lines marking the beginning and ending of the pedal's use. Incidentally, this pedal should not properly be spoken of as the loud pedal. The soft pedal is called for by the words *una corda*, and its use discontinued by the words *tre corde*, as explained under the word *corda* in the chapter on the piano.

Rests and notes should be grouped to follow the beats as closely as possible. With the notes, this may be done by tying the stems so as to show the proper divisions of the measure. In using rests, certain rules are followed. Thus when the first or last half of a measure is filled by two unequal rests, the larger one should come first. Dotted rests are not often used by modern composers, though they are sometimes found. When the first two of three beats are filled by a rest, one sign is usually employed; but for the last two beats in a group of three, two separate rests are required. In a measure of four beats, one rest is used for the first or last two, but two rests are needed for the second and third beat. In orchestral music, rests often cover many measures. Below is given the sign for the four-

4 bars'   2 bars'   7 bars'   23 bars'
rest   rest   rest   rest
                          7   23

bar rest, in connection with the other illustrations. The use of figures to show the number of bars' rest is illustrated also.

Embellishments consist of grace notes, trills, mordents, and turns.

The long grace note is called the *appoggiatura*, from a word meaning "to lean"; and it consists of a note of small body, written before another, and blending or leaning into the note that follows it. The grace notes are not given any time-value in the printed measure, but their time-value is taken from the note against which they are printed. The long grace note is generally written as half the value of the note that it modifies. Some teachers give the long grace note its printed value, shortening the next note by the same amount. But this rule does not always hold. Other musicians say that the time should be divided evenly between a long grace note and the note with which it is printed. This rule, too, is not universal. If the large printed note is followed by another of the same pitch, then the grace note is allowed to take almost the entire time of the note against which it is printed. Before a dotted note the grace note is given two-thirds of the total value. Long grace notes are most usual in vocal music.

The short grace note, or *acciaccatura*, is named (in Italian) from a word meaning "to squash"; and the short grace note is literally squashed into the note after it, against which it is written. The short grace note, as stated above, has no time-value in the printed measure. It is made as short as possible, and its time-value taken from the note following it. Most beginners abstract the time for the short grace note from the preceding note; but this is a mistake. The short grace note is printed as an eighth note, with smaller body than usual, and a diagonal line through the flag and the stem. As the last-mentioned line is the chief difference between long and short grace notes, its presence must be carefully observed. Many misprints have been made in this matter, and the pupil must be on the watch to detect them. The style of the music is often a guide, for the long grace note is slow and languishing, while the short one is crisp and bright. Examples of long and short grace notes are given here, with their proper execution added.

Written   Played   Written   Played   Written   Played

The trill is a rapid and continual alternation of any given note with the note next above it in the scale. The sign for a trill consists of the letters *tr*, followed by a short wavy horizontal line. This is placed over the note to be used in the trill. A separate sign is required for each note that is to be made into a trill. If no other sign is present, the trill alternates the note with the next note above it in the scale used in the piece. But the presence of a sharp or a flat or a natural indicates that the printed note is to be alternated with the sharp, flat, or natural of the upper note. A trill is now generally considered to begin with the printed note, though Von Bülow and others held that it should begin with the upper note. A trill is ended by the occurrence of the printed note, the note below it, and the printed note again, all in rapid tempo. The trill must of course be carried on until it has filled the time-value of the note over which the trill sign is printed.

Trills are usually played with adjacent fingers, though sometimes the thumb and middle finger are used. The pianist Ketten employed a so-called force trill, in which he took the alternate notes with different hands. Liszt used a trick known as the vanishing trill, in which a softening trill is ended by the holding of the two notes, varied by an occasional light stroke on the upper note. This procedure works best when the notes are a semitone apart, in which case the beats between the two tones appear to continue the trill in a most delicate and ethereal fashion.

The mordent, derived from a French word meaning "to bite," is simply a single alternation of notes "bitten" out of a trill. The mordent consists of the printed note, the note above it, and the printed note again, the three notes played quickly, but the last one held, to fill out the proper time-value. The sign for the mordent is ᴧᴧ. As with the trill, if no accidental is present, the upper note is the next one in the scale used in the piece; while a sharp, flat, or natural means that the sharp, flat, or natural of the upper note must be used. The accent may come on the first short note, or on the third note, which is held. The Germans call the former case a *Praller*, or *Pralltrill*, while they name the latter a *Schneller*. Some such distinction should be made in English. The inverted mordent is called for by the same sign, but with a vertical line drawn through it thus, ᴧᴧ. The inverted mordent (which the Germans call simply *Mor-*

dent) consists of the principal note, the note below it, and the principal note again. As before, an accidental is used with the inverted mordent when desired.

The sign for a turn is as here shown, ∿. This sign has different meanings, according to whether it is printed over or after a note, or what the size of the note is, or what relation this size has to the size of the following notes. Examples are given later.

A turn over a long note is played as a rapid triplet before the note, the time-value of the triplet being taken from the first part of the note. The triplet consists of the note above the printed note, the printed note itself, and the note below it. In all turns, trills, and mordents, the largest interval allowed is a whole tone.

A turn over a short note dissolves that note into a quadruplet, consisting of the note above, the printed note, the note below, and the printed note again.

If the short printed note is followed by another of the same pitch, the quadruplet consists of the note itself, the note above, the printed note again, and the note below.

If the short note with a turn over it is at all important, then the quadruplet should be replaced by a quintuplet, consisting of the printed note, the note above, the printed note, the note below, and the printed note again. The same is sometimes true of a turn after a short note, instead of over it.

A turn after a note of ordinary or large value consists of a quick quadruplet played during the last part of the note's time-value. This quadruplet consists of the note above the one given, the printed note, the note below, and the printed note again.

A turn after a long dotted note, or one in 6/8 time, is treated in the same way as the preceding case, the note being held nearly to the end, and the rapid quadruplet finishing the note's time-value.

If a note with a turn after it is followed by another note of the same pitch, then the quadruplet is reduced to a triplet, by having the last appearance of the final note omitted.

A turn after a fairly short dotted note is played by giving the note half its value, putting a triplet into the second half, and playing the note again for the value of the dot. The triplet consists of the note above the printed note, the printed note itself, and the note below it.

But if such a dotted note is followed by another note of the same pitch, then the turn becomes a triplet given in the last part or the total of the dot's value. The triplet, as usual, consists of the note above the printed one, the printed note itself, and the one below it. An inverted turn is called for by the same sign as an ordinary turn, with a short vertical line drawn through it. The inverted turn is the reverse of the ordinary turn, starting with the note below the printed note instead of the one above it.

The intervals of a turn are usually a tone above the printed note and a semitone below it. But with a printed note of the third or seventh degree in the scale, the semitone above and the tone below are used. Turns with whole tones above and below must be indicated by the use of a natural or accidental above or below the turn sign. Such a turn is usually found on the second degree of the scale, as in Schumann's Novelette in F.

The hold, or *fermata,* ⌢ is placed above a note (or chord) to signify that the note (or chord) is to be held for a long time, — usually several beats more than its printed value would indicate.

The sign ⊕ is often used to mark the beginning of a coda, so that the player may repeat a part of a piece and then jump directly to the coda.

In violin music, ⋁ signifies an upward bow-stroke, and ⊓ a downward bow-stroke.

A circle, ○, shows the thumb position in violoncello music.

In organ playing, the registration, or kind of stops to be used, is often marked in by the composer with more or less completeness. The signs used in pedaling are as follows: Λ above note, right toe, Λ below note, left toe. ⊔ above note, right heel. ⊔ below note, left heel. Λ—V, change toes. Λ‿Λ, slide toe to next note.

It has been considered advisable to add a few facts concerning chords.

A chord consists of three or more related tones sounded together. Notes which do not belong to a chord, but happen to be sounded with it, are called non-harmonic tones. These usually occur in positions next to the proper notes of a chord. They are called suspensions when held over from a preceding chord, or passing notes when introduced independently.

A major triad is a three-noted chord consisting of a major third with a minor third above it, such as C, E, and G. The tones of any triad, from below up, are named the root, third, and fifth.

A minor triad has a minor third below and a major third above; as for instance D, F, and A.

A diminished triad consists of two minor thirds, such as B, D, and F.

An augmented triad consists of two major thirds, such as C, E, and G-sharp.

An inversion of a chord occurs when one or more of its notes is transposed an octave. If the root is transposed up an octave, the first inversion is formed; and if both root and third are transposed up an octave, the second inversion is formed. In the first inversion, the upper note is a sixth below the lower one: and the inversion is called the chord of the sixth, or the six-chord. Similarly, the second inversion, having notes a fourth and a sixth above the lowest note, is called the chord of the six-four. Thus if C, E, G in ascending order is the triad used, then E, G, C is the six-chord and G, C, E the six-four chord derived from it.

When the notes of a chord are as close to one another as possible, the chord is said to be in close position. But when any of the notes have between them other notes that might belong to the chord if played, then the chord is in open position; as G, E, C in ascending order.

A seventh chord consists of a triad with an extra third added above it; as G, B, D, F in ascending order. As either a major or a minor third may be added to any one of the triads (except a major third with an augmented triad), it follows that there are several kinds of seventh chords, which are described below.

In Harmony and Thorough-Bass, the chords are described by Roman numerals. The first triad is that of the keynote, and the others are numbered from the scale degrees. Capital letters are used for major triads, small letters for minor triads, and for diminished triads the small letters are used with the addition of a tiny circle, like the mark for thermometer degrees. For an augmented triad, the capital letter is used with a little plus sign at its upper right-hand corner.

The triads of any major scale are therefore I, ii, iii, IV, V, vi, and vii°. Those of the harmonic minor scale are i, ii°, III$^+$, iv, V, VI, and vii°.

The seventh chord is demanded when the figure 7 is placed against the triad numeral. The number 7 without qualification calls for a minor seventh above the root, while 7′, with an apostrophe, calls for the major seventh, and 7° for the diminished seventh. Thus I^7 is the first major triad with a minor third above it, to make the distance from the root a minor seventh. V^7 is the dominant seventh of either a major or a minor scale. IV$^{7′}$ is the fourth major triad with a major third above it. The chord i$^{7\prime}$ is the first minor triad with a major third above it, as A, C, E, G-sharp. The chord vii° is a diminished triad with a major third above it, as B, D, F, and A. The chord vii°$^{7°}$ is a diminished triad with a minor third above it, as B, D, F, and A-flat. The other chords may be figured in similar fashion. The chord vii°$^{7°}$, or any chord composed of three minor thirds, is known as the diminished seventh chord.

All the seventh chords are subject to inversion, having three inversions instead of two. Taking for example the dominant seventh of C, which consists of G, B, D, and F, the inversions are seen to be B-D-F-G, D-F-G-B, and F-G-B-D. From the intervals of the other notes above the lowest note in each case, these chords are called for in harmony study by the figures 6–5–3, 6–4–3, and 6–4–2 respectively.

In four-part counterpoint exercises, each part is expected to have some melodic effect when taken by itself. In such a leading of the voices (as the parts are called) conjunct motion is a proceding by small intervals, while disjunct motion is a proceding by large skips. The melody of "America," for example, is conjunct, while that of "The Star-Spangled Banner" is disjunct. In harmony or counterpoint the bass part may be in disjunct motion, but the other voices should be in conjunct motion for the most part.

Parallel motion results when two or more voices move in the same direction and keep the same interval apart. Similar motion occurs when two or more parts move in the same direction with altering intervals. Oblique motion is found when one part remains stationary while another part moves up or down. Contrary motion consists of the movement of two parts in opposite directions.

This chapter should enable any one to learn to read music by himself if he desires. He will find added information in the ensuing section, which defines certain musical terms. The student need not worry if he sometimes finds a doubtful case; for there are divergent opinions on several of the subjects treated here. But the rules and explanations given here may be taken as a guide for everything except the very few doubtful points that may arise.

LXI

MODERN MUSIC

IN the second and third decades of our century, the trend of music has been very definitely in the direction of modernism. The old harmonies do not seem to suffice. Debussy's whole-tone scale, which appealed to him, led other composers to adopt whatever effects they pleased in using harmony or melody. The result has been in some ways a broadening of the limits of musical expression; but there is now room for so many individual styles that the results are sometimes a little chaotic.

For piano, the modernist works are extremely interesting and effective. They are mostly programme pieces, but the composers treat these with skill and expressive power. Perhaps this is because the piano is a monochrome instrument, and the composers devote the time saved from orchestration to thinking up interesting ideas.

In the orchestral field, however, one may not give such unstinted praise, despite many beautiful works. The variety of instrumental color and the almost infinite possibilities of combination have led some of the modernists to overemphasize tone-color, without giving enough thought to the musical material. The simple expedient of arranging such works for piano will usually show whether the contents are interesting or not. Another action would also indicate how little the musical content matters in the more radical works; for if one could privately erase certain notes of the score and write others in at random, the public, and perhaps even the composer himself, would not realize that any alteration had been made. The more radical of the modern works may therefore be regarded as studies in orchestration, or in new harmonic or melodic effects; but they are not always studies in producing beautiful or well-balanced music. Those that do satisfy the hearer's ideas of musical beauty are the works that are least radical, that depart least from the melodic and harmonic ideas of previous schools.

Certain of the more advanced modernist works seem to show

some analogy to cubism in art. The styles that seemed natural to a Debussy or a Stravinsky have led some, at least, into a deliberate search for odd effects. The more radical music has got to such a point that one could readily compose a modernist piece by sitting at the piano with eyes shut and banging the keyboard at random. If he will have due regard to rhythm and put a cadence at the end, he can have his improvisation taken down by a recording machine, written out, orchestrated, and sold as a modernist piece. It would surely be as good as some of the incoherent orchestral ramblings that are inflicted on concert-goers at times. The works of the extremists sometimes win a hearing through local or national pride; but the great majority of these compositions will be laid aside and forgotten.

The modern use of involved harmonies is naturally the basis of the entire school. From Bach to Brahms, or even to Wagner, seems less of a harmonic change than from Brahms and Wagner to the present. Taking the chords by themselves, it is quite true that the modern tonal combinations, which would have been held discordant in previous times, now do actually appeal to those who compose them. One famous modernist, who has produced successful works, stated that Mozart seemed too utterly simple to have any interest for him. That may be the case with many who make music a profession, and who grow to find the simpler harmonies trite and unexpressive on repetition. Although this idea may be misused as a defense by the extremists, there is still something in it, and music should not stand still. That the involved chords have their appeal to creative musicians is shown also by the case of a leading woman composer, who set the simple folk-songs of her native land with a most intricate modernist accompaniment, unsuited in this particular case, but evidently beautiful to her.

When involved chords are used in a succession of involved and unrelated progressions, the result may or may not sound good. Sometimes other things give a work success, but these are generally programme adjuncts or an actual vocal text. Modernism gives the composer a free hand in creating programme music, and much of this shows great power. It also gives room for many individual styles, from the delicacy of Debussy to the charming oddities of Stravinsky, or the tremendous strength of Prokoviev. In general, the more definite and detailed a programme is, the more chance will the music have to create a favorable effect. When there is little to guide the hearer except a title, the composer runs more risk of failure if he does not make his musical ideas clear. Still more necessary is it for a composer to give something beside tonal puzzles if he attempts to enter the field of pure music. Many of the modernists think themselves equipped to write symphonies — a strange delusion if they wish these works to be compared with those of Beethoven, Schumann, or Brahms. Modern rhapsodies would be a less misleading title, in all but a few cases.

Modernism in its present stage has justified itself by many beautiful compositions. Some of them have grown in appeal on repeated hearings, being first endured, then pitied, then embraced. Others win a more rapid success and show much musical beauty. Modernism may at times have degenerated into something like cubism or vorticism in art, but on the whole it is fairer to speak of it as harmonic impressionism. It may not yet have found its Monet, but it still has given rise to worth-while works, and includes many justly famous composers, as the following pages will show.

In Germany, Strauss no longer holds the lead as a radical, for many have gone beyond him in harmonic complexity; but he is still the leading contemporary composer, and one of the great figures in musical history. In the orchestral field, his chief novelty is the Alpine Symphony. This is a one-movement affair, with the following sections marked in the score: "Night — Sunrise — The Ascent — Entrance into the Forest — Wandering by the Brook — At the Waterfall — Apparition — In Flowery Meadows — On the Mountain Pasture — Lost in the Thicket and Brush — On the Glacier — Moments of Danger — On the Summit — Vision — Elegy — Calm before the Storm — The Thunderstorm — The Descent — Sunset — Night." This is far too large a programme to be properly treated in one movement, or indeed in one concert, as nearly every one of the subjects could have a symphonic poem for itself. So the work cannot help being rather hurried and fragmentary, despite its many exquisite effects.

The composer's recent stage works have been more successful. "Intermezzo," a light comedy with orchestral interludes and parlando effects well intermingled, treats of a court conductor and his wife who go out separately after a quarrel. The wife, returning first, finds a *billet-doux*, which should have gone to another man of the same surname and initials as her husband's, but was missent. Threats of divorce follow, but an explanation finally brings about a reconciliation.

"Die Frau ohne Schatten" is an example of the composer's grander style. An emperor, having caught a white gazelle, sees it turn into a beautiful woman (daughter of the king of the Djinns), whom he marries. If she has no children (they being the "shadows"), the emperor must turn to stone; so she bargains with the dyer's wife Barak for the latter's future babes. But when Barak has performed the needed rites and stands shadowless, the empress, out of pity, renounces the bargain. The latter is then borne off on her nurse's magic mantle, while the dyer and his wife are swept off by a tidal wave. This scene reaches a climax so difficult and exciting that singers call it "The ride to death." In the last act the emperor is shown in his petrified condition; but the tears of the empress finally cause his release.

"Josephslegende" is a very ambitious ballet dealing with the Biblical subject of Joseph and Potiphar's wife. When the latter's temptations meet with no response, she accuses Joseph of having made the advances and has him condemned to torture. But he is rescued by an archangel, after which she strangles herself.

"Schlagobers," or "Whipped Cream," is a ballet depicting in humorous fashion the wild dream of a communicant who has partaken too freely of the Viennese cream puffs that go with the occasion. The climax shows all the dancers made up to represent these puffs, which are beaten into an immense bowl by a gigantic cook.

Franz Schreker is another operatic modernist who uses allegorical plots. "Der ferne Klang" treats of a dreamer who neglects his sweetheart in pursuit of vague ideals until she is driven from bad to worse, and he awakes only when she dies in his arms. "Irrelohe" deals with the evils of uncontrolled love. "Bezeichneten," or "Marked Men," is based on the longing of cripples for normal beauty. "Der Schatzgräber" shows a minstrel, whose lute can unearth buried treasure, torn between baseness and ideality because of his love for a woman who has committed crimes in pursuit of a stolen necklace. "Das Spielwerk und die Prinzessin" treats of a princess who foments evil by a magic chime, but is finally cured of her madness by the more potent magic of love.

Erich Wolfgang Korngold is now known by his opera "The Dead City," in which Paul, a Bruges artist, sees in the dancer Marietta the image of his dead wife Marie. But in a dream, which forms the main part of the work, Marietta's jealousy of Marie and her other unpleasing qualities finally lead Paul to strangle her. On awaking, Paul finds his infatuation cured. "Violanta" deals with a heroine who tries, with her husband's permission, to entrap the royal betrayer of her sister; but she, too, falls in love with the princely gallant, and finally takes the dagger-thrust intended for him. "The Ring of Polycrates" treats the ancient story of that Ægean monarch for whom excessive luck was merely a presage of misfortune.

The extreme radicals are represented in opera by Alban Berg, whose "Wozzek" caused much discussion. Far more successful, as well as more conservative, is Hans Pfitzner's "Palestrina," dealing with that early composer's success in saving music for the church.

Paul Hindemith's one-act "Nusch-Nuschi" has given rise to an orchestral suite. Other operas by him are "Sancta Susanna," the comedy "Mörder, Hoffnung der Frauen," and the longer "Tutti-fantchen Weinachten." His other large works include orchestral numbers, a piano concerto, and a concerto for strings. He has composed much chamber music, as well as songs and ballads. Born in 1895, he is now the leader of the younger Germans. He writes in an odd style, using melody that has all the characteristics of what is now called melody, except that it is wholly unmelodic in effect. Strauss asked him why he wrote atonally when he had so much ability and talent; but Riemann's famous lexicon calls Hindemith "The freshest and most robust of the younger German composers."

Among others, Walter Braunfels is known by incidental music to some of the Aristophanes comedies, as well as by the operas "Princess Brambilla" and "Till Eulenspiegel." Alfred Kaiser's "Stella Maris," "Körner," and "Andreas Hofer" deserve mention, as also Hugo Kaun's "Menandra."

In France, Debussy (d. 1918) produced two effective ballets in his last years. "Fêtes Galantes" depicts an ardent lover evoking Watteau scenes in the vain hope of making a shallow girl respond to his love; while "Khamma" shows a lovely dancer of ancient Egypt, who, on finding her countrymen's prayers to Ammon-Ra unnoticed, sacrifices herself to the god in order to insure victory for her country.

Satie (d. 1925) continued his self-styled "musical symbolism" with works under many odd titles — "Véritables Préludes flasques (pour un Chien)," "The Dreamy Fish," "Airs to make one run," "En Habit de Cheval," etc., some of which were to be played "on yellow velvet," "dry as a cuckoo," "light as an egg," or "like a nightingale with the toothache." But the works may be very effective, as the "Sonneries de la Rose-Croix" will show. "Socrate" adds voices, but is somewhat monotonous. "Parade" and "Rélache" are ballets, and two "Gnossiennes" have been orchestrated.

Fauré has devoted the recent years to a symphony, concertos, and incidental music to "Pelléas et Mélisande," a suite from the last consisting of a prelude, a spinning-wheel scene, and the tragic finale.

Ravel's "Valses Nobles et Sentimentales" have given rise also to a ballet, "Adélaide," dealing with love-rivalry in flower language. "La Valse" is a so-called choregraphic poem — a long title for a light work of Viennese flavor. More interesting is the ballet "L'Enfant et les Sortiléges" (The Child and the Enchantments), in which a naughty child finds tapestry and furniture coming to life to resent his having injured them, and a story-book princess and Old Man Arithmetic with his figures blaming the child for torn pages. In the garden come more reproaches, from animals he has tormented. But when he binds the paw of a fallen squirrel, all agree that he has become his better and kindlier self.

Rabaud, the former Boston Symphony conductor, won some success with his opera "Marouf," dealing with a Cairo cobbler whose pretenses of wealth enable him to marry a princess. When exposed and driven out with his bride, he helps a Djinn, who then makes his stories of wealth come true. Rabaud has written symphonies also, and a "Procession Nocturne," showing Faust envying the happiness of religious paraders on Saint John's Eve.

Pierné has added to his fame by several operas, including "Les Elfes" and "Le Docteur Blanc." "L'An Mil" is a symphonic poem with voices. Among his incidental music, "Ramuntcho" shows interesting Basque effects.

D'Indy's chief recent success is a "Poëme des Rivages," depicting the ocean in four contrasted moods. "De Bello Gallico" is a four-movement symphony inspired by the war.

Florent Schmitt's orchestral "Rêves" combines modern effects with a definite melodic line in most pleasing fashion.

Albert Charles Paul Roussel (1869–) described the impressions of Oriental trips in his "Évocations," consisting of "Les Dieux dans l'Ombre des Cavernes," "La Ville rose," and "Aux Bords du Fleuve Sacré." A symphony and a dance suite are less successful than the symphonic poems, such as "Résurrection," after Tolstoi, "Le Poëme de la Forêt" (including the effective "Faunes et Dryades"), and "Pour un Fête de Printemps." He has worked also in the ballet-opera form, consisting of dance scenes alternating with vocal numbers. "Le Festin de l'Araignée" typifies human passions in the form of spiders; while "Padmavati" is a colorful Oriental story of a queen's love triumphant over wars and death.

Jacques Ibert (1890–) is another modernist landscape painter in tones. His "Escales," or ports of call, describes Palermo in fluent style, Tunis-Nefta in Oriental vein, and Valencia in brilliant fashion. "Noël en Picardie" is another pictorial number. A suite, comprising "Les Bouquetières," "Créoles," and "Les Bavardes," is drawn from the ballet "Les Rencontres." A "Chant de Folie" and the "Ballad of Reading Jail" use voices with orchestra. Ibert's stage works include "Le Poëte et la Fée," "Persée et Andromède," and "La Jardinière de Samos."

Roger Ducasse is now known by the three-act mimordame "Orphée," an orchestral prelude, an "Epithalame," a "Marche Française," and a "Nocturne de Printemps," the "Sarabande" and "Le joli Jeu de Furet" having vocal parts as well.

The conductor André-Caplet has composed "Epiphanie," for voices and orchestra, as well as other sacred works for the same forces.

Marc Delmas (1885–) is known by the stage works "Jean de Calais," "Lais," "Stephanie," "Camille," and "Anne-Marie," as well as the prize-winning lyric drama "Iriam." His orchestral works include "Les deux Routes," "Au Pays Wallon," "Le Bateau ivre," and a "Penthesilea" overture. "Le Masque" and "Cyrca" are his most recent operas.

Adolphe Bouchard has produced the symphonic poem "L'Élan," a Basque fantaisie for piano and orchestra, an Ode with soprano added, and the orchestral "Portia-Juliet-Ophelia."

Roland-Manuel (Roland Alexis Manuel Lévy) is responsible for the opera-pantomime "Isabelle et Pantalon," a ballet "Le Tournei singulier," a symphonic poem "The Harem," and an opera "Le Diable Amoureux."

Lili Boulanger (1893–1918), cut off from a promising career by an untimely death, was still able to produce many large works, such as "Soir sur la Plaine," "Hymne au Soleil," "La Tempête," "Les Sirènes," "D'un Soir Triste," "D'un Matin de Printemps," "Sous Bois," and "Prière Indoue." "Pour les Funérailles d'un Soldat" adds a chorus and baritone solo; while "La Source" has several vocal parts. An opera based on "La Princesse Maleine" was left incomplete.

In the last decade a so-called "Group of Six" has attracted notice, if not notoriety, by its extreme radicalism in word and deed. Darius Milhaud (1892–) is its acknowledged leader, while the others are Arthur Honegger, Georges Auric, Louis Durey, François Poulenc, and Germaine Tailleferre.

Among Milhaud's many stage works, "La Brebis Égarée" shows a wife saved from being misled. "Les Malheurs d'Orphée" is another three-act opera. "Esther de Carpentras" is an opéra-bouffe; while "Les Matelots," a three-act affair lasting only forty-five minutes, is the first of several tabloid operas. Among the composer's ballets, "Le Train Bleu" satirizes Deauville fashions; "La Création du Monde" has a South-Sea Adam and Eve; "L'Homme et son Désir" is allegorical; while "L'Enfant Prodigue" is self-explanatory, and "Salade" is known through a suite, "Le Carnaval d'Aix." Most interesting to Americans, however, is the masked ballet, "Le Bœuf sur le Toit," satirizing prohibition. In an illicit bar the revels of the customers are disturbed by a policeman. The sign "Milk only served" does not satisfy him, and finally the bartender beheads him with an electric fan, to escape detection. The head is placed on a platter, and a shock-headed girl dances before it, *à la* Salôme. The bartender finally reunites the head to the body, with the aid of a bottle of gin, and presents a bill. Milhaud's incidental music to translations of "Agamemnon" and the "Chorephori" shows his search for needless oddity, for the first of its three parts is scored for percussion alone, the second adds orchestra and chorus, and the third is in operatic form.

Honegger won some attention by his locomotive picture "Pacific 231." But though he claimed that it pictured emotions rather than objective details, it shows little more than the simple rhythm of the engine. More successful is the oratoric "Judith," with striking lamentations, a strong incantation scene, and a triumphant chant of victory. "Le Roi David" shows Oriental color, while "Skating Rink" is an effective modern ballet. Honegger's orchestral works include "Horace Victorieux," a "Pastorale d'Été," and the overture to "Aglavaine et Selysette."

Georges Auric has won notice by his ballet "Matelots," which uses some popular songs.

Germaine Tailleferre has produced a ballet "Le Marchand d'Oiseaux," a Ballade, Morceau Symphonique, and concerto for piano and orchestra, "Jeux de plein Air" for orchestra, an "Image" and a Pastorale for smaller forces, and several chamber works. She shows less radicalism and less posing than certain others of the "six," whose compositions and comments sometimes seem to show a lively sense of the value of advertising.

Spain still cherishes the memory of Isaac Albeniz and Enrique Granados. The former planned an Arthurian Trilogy, of which only "Merlin" was completed. The latter became known in New York by a Metropolitan performance of his "Goyescas," as well as by smaller works.

To-day the leader in Spain is Manuel de Falla. His first opera "La Vida Breve" shows a gypsy girl, Salud, betrayed by the wealthy Paco, who is to marry Carmela, of his own class. Salud appears at the marriage feast, but, after vain appeals, falls dead before the assemblage. "El Amor Brujo" (Love the Wizard) is a suite of dance episodes, showing a gypsy girl prevented by the jealous shade of a dead lover from accepting a live one, until the apparition is put to flight by a witch. "El Sombrero de Tres Picos" treats the subject chosen by Wolf for his "Corregidor," and shows that magistrate's misadventures when he tries to make illicit love to a miller's wife. Other works are "Nights in the Gardens of Spain," and a number of effective modernist piano pieces.

In Italy, Puccini produced a successful Triptych of one-act operas, in contrasted styles. "Il Tabarro" (The Cloak) is of the Verismo, or Police-Gazette, school. On a barge in the Seine, Giorgetta, wife of the captain Michele, receives a lover Luigi, and tells him she will light a match when wishing him to come. Michele, after vainly trying to reawaken his wife's love, lights his pipe. This brings Luigi, whom he finally kills and covers with a cloak. When Giorgetta reappears, he uncovers the body and flings her on it.

"Suor Angelica," for female voices only, is a somewhat futile effort to rival Massenet's "Jongleur," with a male cast. Angelica, having taken the veil in penitence, asks after her nameless babe. When a cruel aunt says that it has died, she kills herself; but her prayers have been so effective that the Virgin receives her in Heaven.

"Gianni Schicchi," with a bright and dainty score, shows Donati's heirs asking Schicchi to impersonate the dead man, who had left his money to charity, and make new bequests in their favor, before the death becomes known. But Schicchi bequeaths the money to himself, thereby making his daughter desirable in the eyes of Donati's son, whom she loves.

"La Rondine" is a rather aimless picture of a Paris courtesan giving up a rich banker for love of a student, only to find that his parents naturally object to her.

"Turandot," on which Puccini was at work when he died, unites Occidental melody with real Chinese effects.

Among Mascagni's later works, "Isabeau" is a strung-out version of the Godiva story, with Peeping Tom replaced by Folco, who really loves the lady who had nothing on for the day, but is killed by the populace. "Lodoletta," based on Ouida's "Two Little Wooden Shoes," shows a young girl in love with a gay artist, and freezing to death outside his house. "Parisina" is an unwilling bride who falls in love with a comrade when both are sent on an expedition; whereupon the jealous husband has the pair beheaded, only to learn that he has thus killed his own natural son. "Il Piccolo Marat" seems better, having a good plot and effective ensemble and choral scenes. The "Little Marat" is Orso, tyrant of Nantes during the French Revolution. A nobleman, disguised as a Jacobin, comes to rescue his mother from prison. He falls in love with Orso's good and beautiful niece

Mariella; and with the aid of a carpenter, who turns from coward to hero, he escapes with both mother and sweetheart.

Leoncavallo, too, has failed to equal his early success. His "King Œdipus" is on the well-known classical subject. "Maia" has pretty folk-song effects, despite a tragic plot in which the heroine, led to doubt one lover by the lies of another, sacrifices herself by trying to separate them when they fight. "La Reginetta delle Rose" has a happier ending, Prince Max being captivated by the flower-girl Lillian, imprisoning her by a trick, and marrying her on the pretext that he needs a rose-stem, when his pen breaks, to sign the act of his accession. "Tomasso Chatterton" treats of the unfortunate English poet; while "Gli Zingani" deals with jealousy among the gypsies, the losing suitor killing the bride and her husband by setting fire to their tent.

Montemezzi's new works include "Giovanni Gallurese," in which a dying soldier's horn-call saves his sweetheart from the wicked prisoner who killed him; "Il Nave," showing a mediæval Venetian girl vamping the two brothers who rule the city, to avenge family injuries, and inciting one to kill the other, but finding, when taken on his ship, that his ardor has cooled to the point where he kills her; and "Paolo e Virginia," an undramatic subject, though showing fine tone-pictures of Nature.

Franco Alfano won an international success with "Resurrection," based on Tolstoi's novel of seduction, downfall, prison, and Siberia for the girl. "L'Ombra di Don Giovanni" shows that adventurer winning a girl's love after slaying her brother, and remaining with her to meet death when he could have escaped. "Sakuntala" treats the East Indian legend. Franco's music is fluent, if lightly scored, and illustrates the text very faithfully.

Giordano's "Andrea Chenier" is a love tale of the French Revolution. "Rasputin" shows the charlatan who dominated the Russian court. "Fedora" treats the Sardou play, while "Giove a Pompeii" is a comedy. More successful is "La Cena delle Beffe" (The Jesters' Supper), in which the poet Gianetto incites Neri to wreck a wine-shop, because Neri has bought the poet's sweetheart Ginevra. Neri, in prison, is further tormented by being confronted with the women he has betrayed. When Neri returns home, Gianetto sends Neri's own brother to Ginevra, to receive the sword-thrust meant for the poet.

Zandonai's "Giulietta e Romeo" uses a different version from that treated by Shakespeare. "Melanis" shows a deserted courtesan of ancient Rome killing herself at her lover's wedding. "The Cricket on the Hearth" does not equal Goldmark's setting.

Bossi's "Il Viadante" (The Prophet) shows a wandering seer preaching love and forgiveness, but killed by a mob that suspects him of intrigues.

Wolf-Ferrari's "Gli Amanti Sposi" is a social comedy, in which a marquise keeps her husband's love by pretending to flirt with other men.

Franchetti's "Namiko-San," with a prince's betrothed falling in love with a wandering priest and sacrificing herself to save him, seems to be a futile attempt to emulate the success of "Madama Butterfly."

Busoni's chief success was "Die Brautwahl," based on a Hoffmann tale. Albertine must choose between three suitors, a pedantic Counselor, a Jewish sport, and a dreamy artist. There is a choice by caskets; and Manasse and Leonard, representing evil and good, take a hand in the game. The artist finally wins. The score has many striking numbers. "Doktor Faustus," on a Faust pantomime, was so radical that its performance almost caused fights in the audience. "Arlecchino" seems almost a parody on the stilted conventions of opera.

Francesco Malipiero is an extreme radical known by his orchestral "Pauses of Silence," which are anything but silent between the pauses. Of his two operatic trilogies, that on Goldoni's plays consists of "The Coffee House," "Sieur Todolo Brontolon" (a miser), and "Le Baruffe Chiozzotte," or the gay Chioggians. "L'Orfeïde" includes "La Morte delle Maschere," in which traditional comedy is locked in a cupboard; "Sette Canzoni," the seven songs being taught to the people; and "Orfeo," himself. A symphonic poem is based on the past glories of Venice; while the opera "Canossa" shows Gregory VII bringing the Emperor Henry IV to terms.

Ottorino Respighi seems the present orchestral leader, being not afraid to strive for musical beauty. His opera "Belfagor" shows the troubles of Mephisto in trying to buy a girl from her sweetheart. "Il Re Enzio" has a historical subject, while "Il Scherzo Veneziano" is a ballet. Better known are the orchestral works. "The Fountains of Rome," showing pastoral effects, liveliness, quietude, and sunset as well as plashing water, was so successful that it was followed by "The Pines of Rome," showing children at play, somber effects near a catacomb, moonlight on the Janiculum (with a phonographic record of a real nightingale), and the past glories of the Appian Way. Other worth-while works are a Concerto Gregoriano for violin, a piano concerto in the Mixolydian mode, and the four-movement " Vetrate di Chiesa" (Church Windows), picturing sacred subjects.

Alfredo Casella, pianist and conductor, composed "Il Convento Veneziano," a spirited work in which an abbess, strangely enough, gives a festival for the Grand Turk. "La Jarre" is a Sicilian ballet in which a hunchback mends a large vase with himself inside. Orchestral works include two symphonies, the rhapsody "Italia," "War Pages" (arranged from piano duets), and a Partita with piano.

Ildebrando Pizetti, a successful modernist, is responsible for the operas "Debora e Jaele," "Fedra," and "La Pisanella," the first being most effective. Domenico Monleone tried a "Rustic Chivalry," but is better known by "Il Misterio." Other operas deserving mention are Ezio Camussi's "Dubarry"; Riccitelli's "I Compagnacci," dealing with Savonarola's times; Franco Vittadini's " Nazareth " and "Anima Allegra"; Gabinetti's "Il Nazzareno"; Arrigo Pedrollo's "Maria di Magdala" and "The Man who Laughs"; Francesco Santoliquido's Arabian "Ferhuda," in modernist style; Barilli's Oriental "Emiral"; Mancinelli's "Paolo e Francesca"; Vittorio Gnecchi's effective "Cassandra"; Gino Marinuzzi's powerful "La Jacquerie"; Vincenzo Davico's "Dogaressa"; Lattuada's "Tempest," after Shakespeare; Filiasi's " Manuel Menendez " ; Franco Leoni's " L'Oracolo " ; a tragedy of San Francisco's Chinatown; Seppili's veristic "Nave Rosso"; Pachiarotti's "The Saint"; Emilio Pizzi's "Vendetta"; Renato Virgilio's Sardinian "Jana"; De Sabata's "Macigno," on Apennine feuds; and Giuseppe Mariani's comedy "The Cat and Boots." Sicily is represented by Marcel Donaudy's "Ramuntcho" and "Körner."

In Greece, Spiro Samara followed his "Flora Mirabilis," showing a magic flower woven into a love story, by "Le Martire," in which a Servian wife is sacrificed to her husband's indifference.

Anis Fuleihan used authentic Arabian melodies in his "Arab Fantasia," given in New York.

Ernest Bloch may represent Switzerland, though identified with America also. His Three Jewish Poems (Danse, Rite, and Cortège Funèbre) are well known in the orchestral field. Other works by him are the symphony "Israel," the orchestral "Schelomo," three Psalms, a Concerto Grosso, and a suite for viola and orchestra.

Bohemia is still represented by Reznicek, whose "Ritter Blaubart" is a successful satirical opera. An "Ironical Symphony" is one of his later works, Mraczek has produced the opera "The Glass Slipper," the Hindoo "Ikdar," and incidental music to "Kismet." One of Leos Janacek's operas, "Jenufa," was given in New York. Hans Krasa has composed an effective if rather radical symphony.

In Hungary, Jene Hubay has produced the operas "Anna Karenina," "The Village Butt," and "The Cremona Violin-Maker," as well as the war symphony "1914–1915." Theodor Szanto composed the Chinese opera "Taefun." Bela von Ujj has brought out the tuneful but tragic folk-opera "The Miller and his Child." "The Stronger," by Siegmund Vincze, is a verismo work.

Zoltan Kodaly is a real Hungarian composer, though for a time Paris did not think so. That capital had just been hoaxed by a modernist picture of a sunset, ostensibly by Boronali. After the critics had been told that the work was not a reproduction of a sunset, but a representation of the emotions aroused, and after the connoisseurs had all marveled at it and accepted it on this basis, the exhibitors explained that Boronali was Aliboron, the Ass of La Fontaine's fables — that this animal had been placed with his tail toward the canvas, in proximity to a pot of paint, and that motion had been secured by holding a vegetable at the beast's less dangerous end, until the switching of his tail brought the paint to the canvas. Different colors were used with different vegetables, and the result duly exhibited. It was just after this exposure that some of Kodaly's modernistic works were given at Paris; and the public for a time suspected another hoax and refused to be trapped. But Kodaly to meant his works to be taken seriously.

Bela Bartok is now the modernist leader of Hungary. His "Wood-cut Prince" is a ballet, with a willful princess dancing with an image instead of the true prince, until the former is broken by a fairy and the pair brought together. This work has an effective Tree Dance and Wave Dance. "Knight Bluebeard's Castle" is a strong one-act work. His orchestral pieces cover a wide range, from "Kossuth" to Dance Suites.

Roumania is still best represented by Enesco, whose works include a "Poëme Roumain," three "Rhapsodies Roumaines," a symphony, a suite, a pastoral fantaisie, and a Symphonie Concertante with 'cello. Filip Lazar is known by his orchestral picture "Tziganes," and other instrumental works, including a Divertissement.

The leading figure in modern Poland is Alexander Tansman (1897–). Starting to compose at the age of nine, he heard his Symphonic Serenade for strings given when fifteen. During the ensuing fifteen years he has produced the opera "La Nuit Kurde," the ballets "Le Jardin du Paradis" and "Sextuor," incidental music for "Lysistrata" and "Huon de Bordeaux," a symphonic poem, a symphony, and various other works, large and small. They show strength, control, and expressive power, though modern in style.

Serge Prokoviev seems to be the Russian leader at present. He has tried concertos and symphonies, but his tremendous orchestral vigor is better suited to subjects like his Scythian Suite, or the wild primitive incantation entitled "They are Seven."

"Chout" is a ballet in which a buffoon has his wife play dead and come to life at the touch of a whip, so that he can sell the whip. When the buyers return for vengeance, he hides his wife and disguises as a cook. A rich merchant, selecting a bride, chooses the cook, and takes the supposed female home with him. The cook is let down from a window and ties a white goat in his place. Doffing his disguise, he reënters the house and accuses the merchant of having stolen his cook. The merchant pays for the loss and the money is used in a grand orgy.

"The Love for Three Oranges" shows a melancholy prince who must be made to laugh in order to live. When all else fails, an involuntary somersault by the witch Fata Morgana causes the required mirth. But she, in revenge, condemns him to fall in love with three oranges. Each orange contains an enchanted princess. Two die when the fruit is opened, but by advice of the spectators, who line the sides of the stage, the last princess is saved. Taken home for betrothal, she is transformed by the witch; but the latter finally loses her power, and all ends happily.

Stravinsky's ballets (or rather suites from them) are still prominent on concert programmes. "The Fire-Bird" shows that feathered creature giving a prince one of her magic pinions, by the aid of which he defeats the plans of the wicked wizard Kastchei, and rescues princesses. "Le Rossignol" is the nightingale of Andersen's tale, whose song cured the Emperor of China. "Rites of Spring" shows a pagan people celebrating the return of that season. "Petrouchka" is the unfortunate hero of a puppet-play at a Russian carnival, being ousted from the favor of the ballerina, and finally killed, to appear as a wraith above the booth. Though Stravinsky dislikes opera, "Le Rossignol" was written in that form at first, and "Mavra" is a short opéra-comique on a Pushkin story. "Pulcinella" is a ballet using Pergolesi's themes. "L'Histoire d'un Soldat," the burlesque "Le Renard," and other works have been written for voices with various combinations of instruments. Stravinsky, like Prokovieff, has tried the classical forms (in a piano concerto, sonatas, etc.), but is more at home in a freer style, in which he has done some very graceful things.

Scriabine's three large works, "Prometheus," "Poëme d'Extase," and "Poëme Divin," seem not at all too radical in the present state of modernism, and stand out as really great compositions.

Anatole Liadov is another nationalist, as his researches into folk-songs would indicate. This tendency shows in such witch pictures as "Kikimora" and "Baba-Yaga." Other orchestral works by the composer include "The Enchanted Lake," "Nenia," "From the Apocalypse," a Maeterlinck suite, folk-songs, and a Pushkin polonaise. The ballet "Lella and Adelai" was left unfinished at the composer's death.

Glazounov in Leningrad, and Rachmaninov on various trips, have kept up their standard of work. Liapounov is known for his use of the Ukraine folk-songs. Reinhold Glière has composed symphonies, symphonic poems like "The Sirens" and "Ilia Murometz," chamber works of some value, and many shorter pieces. Karol Szymanowski, coming from Kiev to New York via Berlin, has composed symphonesi, symphonic poems, "Mythes," overtures, and two operas, "Hagith" having been given at Warsaw. Vladimir Dukelsky is a young modernist who has produced overtures, a concerto, and the ballet "Zephyr et Flore," with something of the vigor and variety of effect shown by Prokovieff. Among other Russians, Nicholas Medtner and Lazare Saminsky are deserving of mention.

Sibelius still leads in Finland. His symphonies now number seven, the later ones giving strong and somber effects with simple means. Thus the seventh, in one movement, is described as "enigmatic, puissant, and strangely moving." His later symphonic poems include "A Saga," "A Song of Spring," "Oceanides," and "Night Ride and Sunrise." "Scaramouche" is termed by the composer a "fantastic pantomime."

In Norway, Schjelderup has won a recent success with his symphonic poem "Brand." In Sweden, Peterson-Berger has continued his operatic successes.

In Denmark, the most successful of Enna's later operas is "Gloria Arsena." Georg Holberg won notice with "a Catacomb Wedding." Carl Nielsen forsook his symphonies long enough to produce "Saul and David," as well as the symphonic poem "Pan and Syrinx." Hakon Börresen was successful with "A Royal Guest" and the Greenland love-story "Kaddara." Christian Lahusen has composed ballets, including "The Forest" and "The Wedding of the Shepherdess," as well as incidental music to "The Comedy of Errors."

In Holland, the younger Brandt-Buys has won success with his recent operas, "Mi-Carême" and "The Tailor of Schönau." The 'cellist Jacobus Langendoen has produced variations for 'cello and orchestra on the old Dutch theme "Bergen-op-Zoom."

New names in Belgium are De Jongen, Theodore Ysaye, Bouzerez, and De Boeck. Scharres won much praise with a piano concerto, while the overture to "Herrmann and Dorothea," by Dupuis, met with a similar reception.

In England, where modernism has taken on brilliant and interesting characteristics, Granville Bantock has continued his career with "Dante and Beatrice," "Fifine at the Fair," "Omar Khayyám" with solo voices, and the opera "The Seal Woman," on a Hebrides legend of a wife who comes from the sea and is tempted back into it.

William Wallace has composed many suites, and a prelude to "The Eumenides."

Frederick Delius, a somewhat lonely pioneer for many years, has produced "In a Summer Garden," a "Dance Rhapsody," and "The First Cuckoo" for orchestra; while his operas include "Fennimore and Gerda," on a Danish story, "Koanga," on an episode from Cable's "Grandissimes," "A Village Romeo and Juliet," on a German story, and "Margot la Rouge," dealing with a Parisian subject.

Cyril Scott has entered the operatic field with "The Alchemist," in which a youth obtains his wishes for an hour, but finds that happiness comes from within. Scott has written many orchestral works, including two overtures to that modernist favorite, "Pelléas and Mélisande." His chamber works are interesting, but he is known most widely through his very effective piano pieces, such as "Snowflakes," "Pierrot Lunaire," the cycle "Egypt," the "Chinese Pictures," or the "Impressions from the Jungle Book."

Ralph Vaughan Williams (1872–) is fond of English pictures, such as the Norfolk Rhapsody, "The Lark Ascending," "Harnham Down," "Boldrewood," "In the Fen Country," and a Pastoral Symphony. The same atmosphere shows in his operas, "Hugh the Drover" and "Old King Cole." Best known, however, is the London Symphony, its four movements showing a contrast between quiet streets and crowded traffic (finishing with the notes of "Big Ben"), an evening scherzo with suggestions of "pubs" and hand-organs, the quiet of the river in contrast to a Surrey Side fair, and a military finale.

Arnold Edward Trevor Bax (1883–) prefers Celtic subjects, such as "In the Faëry Hills," "Nympholept," or "Tintagel," adjourned to Cornwall. Other works include "The Garden of Fand," "In

Memoriam," "Spring Fire," and various nature pictures. A recent success is a group of four pieces, consisting of "Pensive Twilight," "Dance in the Sun," "The Mountains of Home," and "The Dances of Wild Irravel."

Gustav Holst has drawn inspiration from India in his two sets of "Hymns from the Rig-Veda" (one with orchestra), the symphonic poems "Indra" and "Savitri," and the music-drama "Sita." "The Perfect Fool" is a symbolic opera. Successful works with voices are "Hecuba's Lament," "The Cloud Messenger," and the "Ode to Death," on Whitman's "Lincoln Hymn." In the "Planet Suite," Mars brings war, Venus peace, Mercury messages, Jupiter gayety, and Saturn old age, while Uranus is a magician, and Neptune a mystic.

Eugene Goossens, master of chromatic effects, has composed the symphonic poem "Perseus" and other orchestral works, the one-act opera "Judith," incidental music, ballets, and chamber music; but he too is best known by his piano pieces, such as the twelve striking numbers of "Kaleidoscope," four "Conceits," including the brilliant "Marionettes," a set of "Nature Poems," and the three Ship Preludes entitled "Tug," "Tramp," and "Liner."

Arthur Bliss produced a Color Symphony, with purple pageantry, red revelry, blue melancholy, and green for hope, spring, and victory. Among other works are a two-piano concerto, and smaller pieces with voices, such as "Rout." Despite a somewhat tedious modernism in many compositions, he has shown much humor in "Conversations," including "The Committee," "In the Wood," "At the Ball," "Soliloquy," and "In the Tube at Oxford Circus."

Lord Berners is a most successful modernist. His opera, "The Coach of the Holy Sacrament," shows a Governor's favorite playing pranks with the vehicle, and finally saving herself by dedicating it to the Bishop's use. But he is best known by his very effective piano pieces, such as the extremely humorous "Funeral March for a Rich Aunt."

Among English opera composers, Rutland Boughton put beautiful music into "Alkestis," "King Arthur," "The Immortal Hour," and the dramatic "Queen of Cornwall." Nicholas Gatty has shown much power in "Greysteel," "The Tempest," and "Duke or Devil." Isidore de Lara followed "Messalina" with the Moorish love-story

"Naïl," the warlike Turkish "Solea," the Corsican picture "Les Trois Masques," and "Amy Robsart." Dame Ethel Smyth has composed "The Boatswain's Mate," on a Jacobs story. Vincent Thomas has produced "Elaine," "Enid," and the underworld "Tale of Alsatia." Other operas worth naming are Herbert Bunning's "Princess Osra," Raymond Roze's "Joan of Arc," Cyril Rootham's Scotch tragedy "The Two Sisters," Philpot's "Nigel" of Roundhead days, and Frederick Barlow's delicate modernist "Sylvie." Orchestral works deserving mention are the overtures and fantaisie with organ by Benjamin Dale, John Ireland's "Forgotten Rite" and Dorian Mass, Frank Bridge's "Dance Rhapsody" and "The Sea," Holbrooke's "The Squook," depicting a fantastic animal, Percy Grainger's modernist treatments of folk-music, Cecil Forsyth's works in classical style, York Bowen's suites, concertos, and "The Lament of Tasso," William Turner Walton's modernist overture "Portsmouth Point," and Ethel Leginska's symphonic poem, "Beyond the Fields we Know," and two pieces on passages from Tagore.

That music in America is not all localized in the United States may be shown by a brief list. Not to mention Canadian composers, such as Oliver King, the southern countries have not been inactive. In Cuba, Eduardo Sanchez Fuentes has set a local legend in "La Doreya," and told of love and disaster in "Il Naufrago" (The Shipwreck). "La Esclava," by J. Mauri, is a folk-opera depicting Spanish misrule. Mexico is represented by Ancieto Ortega's opera "Guatimozin," Ricardo Castro's Aztec "Atizamba," and Morales's "Colombo a San Domingo." In Peru, José Valle-Riestra's fine "Ollanto" adds native instruments to the orchestra and uses Inca melodies in treating the Quichua legend of a chieftain's love for the Inca's daughter. "Atahualpa" is by the same composer. In Brazil, Carlos Gomez, whose "O Guaraney" dealt with a love-story and Indian rivalries under Brazilian rule, has continued with "Marie Tudor" and the less successful "Condor." Francisco Braga produced "Japyra," while Francisco Mignone's "Diamond Contractor" deals with eighteenth-century mining. In the Argentine Republic, Pascual de Rogates's "Huemac" shows a priest leading his people to a "promised land" in Mexico. Other operas are Pablo Berutti's

"La Pampa," Felipe Boreo's "Tucuman," and the latter's one-act "Raquela," using songs and dances of the Pampas. Riccardo Boncioli's "Don Juan de Garay" treats of the leader who founded Buenos Ayres.

In the United States, Hadley has produced symphonic poems, such as "Lucifer" and "The Sea," and many other orchestral works. But he has been active also in the operatic field. "Safie" was followed by "Azora," or "Montezuma's Daughter," the heroine loving Xalca, the pair being intended for a sacrifice by the jealous general Ramatzin, and the arrival of the Spaniards bringing rescue at the last minute. "Cleopatra's Night," on the Gautier story, tells of the young officer who wins that queen's favor, but must be sacrificed on Antony's unexpected return. "Bianca," perhaps the best native opera, is based on the comedy "La Locandiera," made familiar when Duse played that capricious landlady, who teases a woman-hater, and accepts her own aide when he rescues her from quarrels caused by her flirting. "Nancy Brown" is a comic opera, while "The Garden of Allah" is another Oriental affair.

Chadwick's "Padrona" and "Love's Sacrifice" are still in manuscript.

Converse has continued his stage career with "The Immigrants," on a MacKaye play. The rascally agent Scammon tempts Italians to leave their native land, and then makes love to Maria while trying to get her betrothed Giovanni deported. When Scammon fails to tempt her with wealth and tries to tell her that Giovanni is dead, she stabs him, just as Giovanni, rescued by a friend, arrives on the scene. Converse has added to his orchestral list the symphonic poems "Ave atque Vale" and "Euphrosyne," but a more popular work is the amusing "Flivver 10,000,000," which pictures the manufacture of the ten-millionth Ford car and its later adventures, from romances to collisions.

Cadman's "Daoma" shows an Indian lover, betrayed to the enemy by a jealous rival, escaping in time to denounce the traitor, who must then kill himself. "Shanewis," the Robin Woman, is an Indian girl who is sought by a white man who is already betrothed. Later, on the reservation, an Indian suitor kills the white man, leaving both girls disconsolate. "The Sunset Trail" shows a love episode during the removal of a tribe to its reservation. "The Garden of Mystery" treats Hawthorne's story of Rappacini's daughter, brought up so constantly among poisonous plants that her very breath becomes fatal, and an antidote brought by her lover kills her while neutralizing the poison. "The Witch of Salem" shows a jealous girl denouncing her rival, but confessing and freeing her from the gallows. Cadman's work is always charmingly melodious, and his use of Indian themes most skillful and successful.

Arthur Nevin's "Poia" tells of a Blackfoot brave who wins his bride by doing a service to the sun-god, only to have her take the stab that a rival meant for him. "A Daughter of the Forest" shows true love not running smoothly.

Among other Indian operas, Frederick Zech has composed "Wa-Kin-Yan," besides the southern "La Paloma." Francesco de Leone's "Alglala" shows an Indian girl preferring a white man to her native suitor, saving the former in their quarrel, and fleeing with him, only to be brought back and executed by her father, the chief. This work uses Chippewa melodies most excellently. Willard Patton won some notice with his "Pocahontas," while Edith Noyes Greene composed "Waushacum."

De Koven chose an American subject for his "Rip van Winkle," though going abroad for "The Canterbury Pilgrims." Pietro Floridia composed a "Scarlet Letter," but won more success with "Paoletta." Jules Jordan wrote a "Rip van Winkle," as well as "Nisida." John van Broekhoven composed "A Colonial Wedding," on a Puritan subject. W. Franke Harling's "Light from St. Agnes" deals with a Creole story. Julian Edwards wrote "The Patriot," as well as the melodious "King René's Daughter." Earl R. Drake used Longfellow's "Blind Girl of Castel-Cuille," besides composing a ballet. Most wildly Afro-American is George Gershwin's "135th Street," a "jazz opera" on a tragedy of negro jealousy.

Joseph Breil's "The Legend" shows a bandit nobleman trapped by an agent who pretends to love his daughter. The nobleman is shot while escaping, the girl shoots the agent when he is exposed, and soldiers shoot the girl. The plot seems gory, but the music won a Metropolitan performance.

Deems Taylor's opera "The King's Henchman" has been even more warmly received. It shows King Eadgar sending Æthelwold, hitherto a woman-hater, to bring back Ælfrida to be queen. The messenger departs, and the lady, who has gone out to cast spells that would show her her future husband, finds him asleep and awakens him with a kiss. The pair then fall in love, and Æthelwold sends back word that Ælfrida has been overrated. The king then decides to come. Æthelwold tries to have Ælfrida stain her face and hide her beauty; but she, now knowing she should have been queen, decks herself in rich garments and jewels, thus exposing the deception. Æthelwold then kills himself. The composer's other works include the suite "Through the Looking-Glass" and the prize-winning "Sirens."

Ralph Lyford's "Castle Agrazant" shows a crusading husband returning to avenge a persecuted wife. Theodore Stearns's "Snow Bird" is a Tartar beauty loved by a hermit prince, but killed by mistake. Joseph Redding's "Fay-Yen-Fah" treats of the influence of white education on the Chinese mind, with a mingling of musical effects. Ernest Carter's "White Bird" shows a deformed husband, wrongly jealous, making his wife's true friend shoot her in the idea that her scarf was the bird. Simon Buchalter's "Lovers' Knot" lets a disguise produce happy matches. Eleanor Freer composed "The Legend of the Piper." Timothy Mather Spelman's "La Magnifica" is a short love-story of a corrupt southern capital; "The Sea Rovers" is a later opera, while Spelman has composed also a ballet, suites, and ambitious symphonic poems, both sacred and secular. Frank Patterson's "Echo" shows a victory over evil. John Adams Hugo's "Temple Dancer" is an unrepentant Bayadere who gets into trouble. His "Hero of Bysanz" is another Eastern subject. Albert Mildenberg composed "Michael Angelo" and shorter works. William J. McCoy produced "Egypt," as well as shorter "grove plays" for the San Francisco Bohemian Club. Humphrey J. Stewart and Edward Faber Schneider wrote for the same organization, Stewart having produced larger operas also. Henry Bethuel Vincent composed "Esperanza." Thomas Carl Whitmer produced sacred dramas. Other names are Florizel von Reuter, Alexander Hull, Bertram Shapleigh, Henry Bickford Pasmore, and Louis Campbell-Tipton. Alf G. Robyn worked in light opera. Masque composers include George Colburn and Charles L. Seeger; while Howard Talbot, Nathaniel Clifford Page, Frederick Beale, and Paul Bliss deserve mention in operetta.

John Alden Carpenter, a leader among American composers, has devoted much attention to the ballet. His "Birthday of the Infanta" tells the story of the dwarf whose true love for the princess did not save him from ridicule. "Krazy Kat" is a delightful work on Herrman's cartoon characters, with jazz effects, "Catnip Blues," and other humorous gems. The Kat, at first snoring, is awakened by a bill poster, does a dance in imitation of Debussy's "Faun," and dances with Ignatz Mouse in disguise, the latter finally throwing a brick at Kat while Officer Pup is approaching. "Skyscraper" is a so-called choregraphic representation of American life, both business and pleasure, with a background of lofty scenery. Carpenter's "Concertino" for piano and orchestra is another work deserving mention.

Edward Burlingame Hill's "Pan and the Star" shows the close of mythology, in richly inventive music. Among his many orchestral works, from "Lancelot and Elaine" to the New England idyl "Lilacs," his two "Stevensoniana" suites, on poems from the "Child's Garden," deserve especial mention for their rich beauty and sympathetic expression.

Henry Eichheim put real Chinese effects into his ballet "A Chinese Legend," depicting the progress of war and love between a handsome general and the lovely widow of an ugly general whom he has killed in battle. "Oriental Impressions" and the smaller "Malay Mosaic" show Eastern effects in orchestral work, while "The Song of the Bell" is an earlier production.

Emerson Whithorne's "Sooner or Later" seems like a satire on civilization, the first scene being a primitive tribal ritual, the second a typical city with show-girls and a negro White Way ballet, and the third a picture of a mathematical "crystal age" of the future.

Other ballets deserving mention are Julius Mattfeld's "Virgins of the Sun," in which human love causes trouble among the sun-god's celestial daughters; "The Cairn of Koridwen," a setting of the Tristan legend by Charles Tomlinson Griffes; Henry F. Gilbert's "Dance in Place Congo," showing jealousy among the New Orleans levee workers, and using wild African dances; Felix Borowski's Persian "Boudour"; and Bainbridge Crist's dance-drama "Le Pied de la Momie."

Coerne (d. 1922) composed the melodrama "Sakuntala," as well as two violin concertos. Loeffler has produced the interesting "Memories of my Childhood," on Russian village scenes. Kelley has written incidental music to "Prometheus Bound," and the miracle play "Pilgrim's Progress." Van der Stucken produced a "Louisiana" march. Damrosch has written incidental music to several Greek tragedies. Kroeger has continued with the overtures "Atala" and "Pittoresque," the suite "Lalla Rookh," and lesser works. Goldmark's "Negro Rhapsody" and his "Requiem" (on Lincoln's Gettysburg Address) have won favorable notice. Schoenefeld has written a second (Spring) symphony, a festival overture, two rhapsodies, a suite, and many other works, besides having an Indian opera in manuscript. Huss has continued with a "Wald-Idyll." Shelley's later cantatas include "Vexilla Regis," "Death and Life," and "Lochinvar's Ride." Brockway has produced more violin works, the cantata "Sir Oluf," and "Lonesome Tunes," a set of Kentucky mountaineers' songs. Foerster is responsible for the symphonic poem "Sigrid," an Ode to Byron, and two suites. Lachmund has composed a second overture and an Italian suite. Loomis has produced operettas, and the piano set entitled "Lyrics of the Red Man." Arthur Whiting has written a second concerto, and revived music of the harpsichord days in his recitals. Beck's later works include the cantata "Deucalion," and several orchestral pieces. Strong has been very active, a recent success being the humorous choral work "Der Dorfmusikdirektor." Schelling is responsible for symphonies, concertos, and the variations entitled "Impressions of an Artist's Life." David Stanley Smith has been very industrious producing symphonies, overtures, symphonic poems, the oratorio "Saint Bernard," and the manuscript opera "Merrymount."

John Powell shows the effect of his Richmond birth in a "Negro Rhapsody" for orchestra, a "Virginianesque" violin sonata, and the piano suite "In the South." Carl Busch, of Danish birth, composed a symphony, many prize-winning cantatas, and the symphonic poem "Minnehaha's Vision," with Indian themes. Mortimer Wilson shows the Southern influence in his "Country Wedding" suite, "New Orleans" overture, and the piano suites "In Georgia," "Rustica," and "By the Wayside." Henry Albert Lang, of New Orleans, becomes pictorial only in his "Fantastic Dances," his symphonies and chamber works being classical in tendency. Charles Sanford Skilton uses aboriginal themes in two "Indian Dances" for orchestra, three "Indian Scenes" for string quartet, and three "Indian Sketches" for piano. His other works include the overture "Mount Oread," the symphonic poem "A Carolina Legend," the cantatas, "The Witch's Daughter" and "Carmilhan," and various shorter works. Arne Oldberg has won international successes with his symphonies, concertos, variations, the overtures "Festival" and "Paolo and Francesca," the rhapsody "June," and the fantaisie "Night." Edward Ballantine has written an overture, "The Piper," a second symphonic poem, "The Awakening of the Woods," and incidental music to Hagedorn's "Delectable Forest," as well as a humorous setting of "Mary had a little lamb," in the style of ten different composers, from Mozart to Debussy. Camille Zeckwer (d. 1924) won a prize with his beautiful "Jade Butterflies," consisting of "Dance Rhythm," "Silence," "Balance," "Return," and "Motion." His other works included a concerto for piano, a Swedish fantaisie with violin, the opera "Jane and Janetta," and the symphonic poem "Sohrab and Rustum." Leo Sowerby, first to hold an American *Prix de Rome*, has composed a symphony, a "Set of Four," concertos for 'cello and for piano, the symphonic poems "Comes Autumn Time" and "The Sorrows of Mylath," and many lesser works. Blair Fairchild, living in Paris, has composed symphonic poems on Persian subjects, as well as works in classical form. Victor Benham, another exile, is responsible for symphonies, concertos, and string quartets. Other native or adopted symphonists are Sigismund Stojowski, Frederick A. Stock, Daniel Gregory Mason, Frank Edwin Ward, Fred Preston Search, George Eliot Simpson, Roger H. Sessions, Louis Leslie Loth, and with organ Edward Shippen Barnes and Clarence Dickinson. A symphonist in the Roman Church is Ludwig Bonvin, who has composed masses as well as orchestral works. Nicola Montani produced masses and a suite. Pietro A. Yon, John Eliot Trowbridge, and Henry G. Thunder are other mass writers, while Charles W. Douglas has produced Episcopal masses.

Chester E. Ide has composed symphonic poems, suites, and incidental music. Elliott Schenck has done the same, and has in manuscript two operas, "Tess" and "The Children of the Evening Star."

Curry has written overtures and a "Keltic Legend" with chorus. Cecil Burleigh composed "Evangeline," "Mountain Pictures," and violin concertos. Maurice Arnold wrote overtures and "Plantation Dances." W. H. Humiston has a "Southern Fantasy" and a "Twelfth Night" overture. Horace Alden Miller took a Western subject in "The Wickiup." Patrick O'Sullivan has produced a "Fantaisie Irlandaise," with piano, and other large works. Arthur Shepherd continued with a successful Humoresque with piano. A. Walter Kramer has written Sketches, a violin rhapsody, and chamber works. Alexander Steinert won a *Prix de Rome* with his "Southern Night." Philip James is credited with "Aucassin and Nicolette" and an overture. A. W. Lilienthal is responsible for dances and transcriptions, as well as chamber music. Aaron Copland is an ambitious modernist, producing large works. Good overtures have been composed by Samuel Bollinger, Eric Delamarter, Leo R. Lewis, Lindsay Norden, William H. Oetting, Walter Spry, Winthrop Sterling, and Howard R. Thatcher. Heinrich Bellermann and Walter Ruel Cowles have written piano concertos, while Albert Spalding and Arthur Emil Uhe produced violin concertos. Suites have been written by Arthur Olaf Andersen, George Whitfield Andrews, John Hyatt Brewer, Preston Ware Orem, Chalmers Clifton, and Louis Arthur Russell. Other orchestral composers include Stanley R. Avery, William J. Kraft, Frank Stuart Mason, Paul White, Benjamin P. Whelpley, Henry Dike Sleeper, and James P. Dunn.

Nathaniel Dett, leader of the American negro composers, has produced the cantatas "The Death of Moses" and "The Chariot Jubilee," effective songs, including the cycle "The Heart of a Poet," a piano sonata, piano suites such as "The Magnolia" and "In the Bottoms," and many brilliant single numbers besides the famous "Juba Dance." His work shows spirit, intensity, and a beauty that is often exotic.

Other cantata composers include Harry Alexander Matthews, John Sebastian Matthews, Harvey B. Gaul, Frederick Stevenson, Charles Gilbert Spross, Frederick Schlieder, Clifford Demarest, and Will C. Macfarlane.

Composers of chamber music include Albert Stoessel, Walter Stockhoff, the physician Franklin M. Class, William N. Pommer,

W. Humphrey Dayas, Abram Ray Tyler, Clarence G. Hamilton, and Wallingford Riegger.

Among piano composers, Leo Ornstein's "Gargoyles," "Wild Man's Dance," and other works are radical but powerful. Georges Antheil wrote a tame "Jazz Sonata," and a wild "American Symphony," depicting modern life with bassoon, trumpet, trombone, flute, and violin. Among other piano composers, Henry Cowell has tried new effects with elbows and string picking, while Thurlow Lieurance has used Indian subjects and themes.

New names in organ composition are George W. Stebbins, Nicholas Douty, John Winter Thompson, Ralph Lyman Baldwin, Walter C. Gale, Stanley T. Reiff, and Russell King Miller. Peter C. Lutkin and Frederick Maxson have composed part music, while song writers include Robert Braine, A. Buzzi-Peccia, L. R. Dressler, Frank S. Hastings, Charles Huerter, Bernard Rogers, and H. Wintter-Watts.

Among the women, new works include Mrs. Beach's cantata "Sea Fairies," Mme. Hopekirk's piano suite and serenata, Isabella Beaton's scherzo and chamber works, Clara Korn's symphony, concerto, and opera "The Last War," Gena Branscombe's orchestral prelude, Mabel Daniels's orchestral odes, such as "Peace with a Sword," and Fannie Dillon's works. New names among the song composers are Fanny Knowlton, Florence Turner-Maley, Floy Little Bartlett, Harriet P. Sawyer, Anne Stratton, Theodora Dutton, Phyllis Fergus, Ina Rae Seitz, Lalla Ryckoff, Natalie Wollin, Elizabeth Siedoff, Kathleen Manning, Beatrice Fenner, Ruth Rapoport, and the hymn composer Fanny Spencer. Piano composers include Beatrice Hall, Eva Spalding, and Florence Newell Barbour, whose suites and cycles show much charm.

The most important event in the musical world of the past few years is undoubtedly the invention of the radio. Little as wireless telegraphy seemed likely to affect both music and musicians, its most recent manifestation has already had a profound influence on the appreciation of music the world over. The only mechanical invention to be compared to it, in the field of the arts, is that of the printing press, and just as the printing press has developed the art of writing, so the radio will develop the art of music. Both have made it possible for the pleasure of the few to be offered to the many, and both have aroused new intellectual and emotional interests. Whether or not the influence of the radio is entirely good, it is a force to be reckoned with now and in the future.

Musicians are divided in their opinions of the subject. Some, like Kreisler, have set their faces against what they regard as a cheapening of the art to which they have devoted their lives. Others, such as Walter Damrosch, have hailed with enthusiasm the development of a popular interest in their work. What will be the results of broadcasting — on music, on musicians, and on the millions of people who listen in?

The typical family to-day tunes in the radio in the evening, and listens with enjoyment to music which is being played perhaps hundreds of miles away by "jazz" performers, or by the symphony orchestra of a great city; with a turn of the wrist the listeners can regale themselves with the songs of the vaudeville artist, or the arias of the Metropolitan star; another "set," and they hear the violinist or pianist of more or less fame. Whatever type of music it may be, it is music that holds the chief place in the radio programme.

It is for the pleasure of a vast unseen audience that the programme is selected. What will please them? Are they to be entirely satisfied with "jazz," or will they demand something more enduring, compositions of a more permanent worth? In the past few years the best the world has to offer has been given them. Bori, Chaliapin, Jeritza, Garden, Schumann-Heink, Gigli, and Matzenauer; Chemet, Zimbalist, Bauer, and Spalding; the Chicago Opera Company, the Boston Symphony, and the New York Symphony have sung or played to ears that have perhaps never heard good music before.

One of the most interesting of the broadcasting plans was carried out in the winter of 1926 by the New York Symphony Orchestra, with Walter Damrosch conducting. The programme consisted of a brief talk explaining the music to follow, the circumstances of its composition, some information about the composer, and then the performance of the piece by the orchestra. These concerts, at first regarded with some skepticism, were enthusiastically received, and their success fully justified the beliefs of Mr. Damrosch, who explained his point of view. "If New York," he was quoted as saying, "has six million inhabitants, and fifty thousand of them, at a generous estimate, attend orchestral concerts, that means that 5,950,000 still live in Egyptian darkness so far as music is concerned. These millions are human beings with human emotions and aspirations just the same as the fortunate fifty thousand. I can see no reason why the greater part of them should not be made to understand this most beautiful language of the emotions — music. What is true of New York is true of every city, town, and village in our country. Radio offers such opportunities and can reach so far beyond the limits of the concert hall that I am overcome with its marvelous possibilities."

So much for the benefits of the audience; but the interests of the musician must also be safeguarded, and many think that, while inferior performers will be encouraged, the great will suffer. They fear the loss of patronage, and still more the loss of the personal element. There is no doubt that the personality of the artist and the spirit of the audience affect the rendering of the best compositions. This interaction cannot take place over the radio. It is also true that faults in receiving sets and imperfect atmospheric conditions sometimes interfere.

On the other hand, along with the development of the radio, there has been an increase in the number of symphony orchestras in the United States, and at the same time an increased attendance at concerts and operas. There may be a period of adjustment, such as those which have followed all great scientific discoveries, but this temporary disorganization must end by an increase in the general welfare.

Many critics already see an improvement in the musical taste of the public. To the man in the street, the enjoyment of classical music is a new sensation. Now that the works of the great composers are put before him, he is developing an intelligent appreciation of their excellence. Music is no longer a property of the elect, but an intimate part of normal domestic life. It is to be hoped that along with this willingness to listen to the best will go a desire for information about music and its composers, and an interest in the elements of musical composition. Then the pleasure which the radio affords will rest on a firmer and more enduring basis.

The possible effect of the radio on music itself is a highly debatable subject. Broadcasting may bring about the composition of a still greater body of music of the more popular type. It may, on the other hand, provide the talented composer with an audience which will demand his best work, and which will reject music displeasing to an educated taste. The influence of such an attitude on the part of the public would be far-reaching. Certainly it would bring nearer the golden possibility of a musical renaissance.

APPENDIX

APPENDIX

IMPORTANT MUSICAL TERMS

(G and ch in German are guttural. Final n after a vowel in French is very nasal. See index for other terms.)

A (It., ah). By, at, for, etc. In English, A is the sixth note of the scale of C, and the first note of the scale of A minor.

Abbandono (It., ah-bahn-do'-no). With *abandon*, or passionate expression.

A cappella (It., ah kah-pel'-lah). In church style, i.e., unaccompanied.

Accelerando (It., ah-chay-lay-rahn'-do). Accelerating; increasing the speed.

Accent. Emphasis or stress on a certain note or passage.

Acciaccatura (It., aht-tchec-ahk-kah-too'-rah). A short grace note.

Accidentals. Sharps, flats, or natural signs not in the signature.

Adagietto (It., ah-dah-jyet'-to). A tempo somewhat less slow than *adagio*, or a short piece in *adagio* tempo.

Adagio (It., ah-dah'-jio). A slow tempo, slower than *andante*, but not so slow as *largo*.

Ad libitum (Lat.). At will; at the performer's discretion.

Affettivo (It., ahf-fet-tee'-vo). Affecting, pathetic.

Affettuoso (It., ahf-fet-too-o'-zo). With tender expression.

Afflitto (It., ah-fleet'-to). Sorrowfully, mournfully.

Affrettando (It., ahf-fret-tahn'-do). Hurrying, quickening the tempo.

Agevole (It., ah-jay'-vo-leh). Lightly, easily.

Agilita (It., ah-jeel-ee-tah'). Agility, lightness.

Agitato (It., ah-jee-tah'-to). Agitated, restless, hurried.

Agréments (Fr., ah-gray-mong'). Embellishments for spinet or harpsichord.

Ais (Ger., ah-iss'). The A-sharp.

Al (It., ahl). To. Contracts with the definite article to various forms, such as *alla, allo, alle, agli.*

Alcuna (It., ahl-koo'-nah). Some, a little.

Al fine, e poi la coda. (It.², ahl fee'-neh, ay po'-ee lah co'-dah). To the place marked *fine*, and then play the coda.

Alla breve (It., ahl-lah bray'-veh). Originally 4/2 rhythm, each measure being equal to a *breve*, or double note whole. Now usually 2/2 rhythm.

Allargando (It., ahl-lahr-gahn'-do). Growing broad; louder and slower.

Allegretto (It., ahl-lay-gret'-to). Light, cheerful; like *allegro*, but a little less fast.

Allegro (It. and Fr., ahl-lay'-gro). Quick, lively; the usual tempo of the first movement in symphony, sonata, etc.; rapid and cheerful.

Allmählich (Ger., ahl-may'-likh). Gradually, little by little.

Alt (It., ahlt). High; with sopranos, the octave extending from two-line G to three-line F.

Altissimo (It., ahl-tees'-see-mo). Highest; the octave above the alt.

Alto (It., ahl'-to). High; in old days a high part above the tenor; now applied to the lowest female voices. Another name for the viola.

Amabile (It., ah-mah'-bee-leh). Amiable, graceful, gentle.

Amoroso (It., ah-mo-ro'-zo). Tenderly, lovingly.

Ancora (It., ahng-ko'-rah). Again, once more, yet.

Andante (It., ahn-dahn'-teh). A slow, even tempo; literally, " going."

Andantino (It., ahn-dahn-tee'-no). A little less slow than *andante*.

Anhang (Ger., ahn'-hahng). A coda; an appendix.

Animato (It., ah-nee-mah'-to). Animated; with spirit.

Appassionato (It., ah-pahs-sio-nah'-to). Passionate, intense.

Appoggiatura (It., ah-pod-jyah-too'-rah). Leaning note; long grace note.

Arabeske, arabesque. A piece with a noticeable design of tonal embroidery.

Arco (It., ahr'-co). Bow, of violins, etc.

Ardente (It., ahr-den'-teh). Ardent, fiery, vehement.

Arioso. (It., ah-ree-o'-zo). A short piece like an aria, but less symmetrical. For aria, see chapter on " Vocal Forms."

Arpeggio (It., ahr-ped'-jyo). Harp-like. Playing the notes of a chord in swift succession instead of simultaneously.

As (Ger., ahs). The A-flat.

Assai (It., ahs-sah'-ee). Very, extremely, much.

Attacca (It., aht-tahk'-kah). Attack, start, go on, begin the next.

Aubade (Fr., oh-bahd'). A morning song, literally a dawn song.

Ausdruck (Ger., ows'-drook). Expression.

B. The seventh note of the scale of C major. In Germany, B means the note we call B-flat.

Ballet (Fr., bahl-lay'). A pantomime story with musical accompaniment.

Bars. Vertical lines drawn on musical staffs to mark off measures. Now used to denote the measures also.

Basso continuo (It., bahs'-so con-teen'-u-o). The continual or figured bass in old music.

Battuta (It., baht-too'-tah). A beat; a measure. *A battuta*, in strict time.

Beat. A motion with hand or baton to give the tempo; a division of a measure; a throbbing heard when two tones are not quite alike in pitch.

Bel canto (It., bel cahn'-to). A pure and sympathetic *legato*, the opposite of *bravura, coloratur, agilita*, etc.

Bémol (Fr., bay-moll'). Any flat.

Bemolle (It., bay-mol'-leh). Any flat.

Ben, bene (It., bayn, bay'-neh). Well, thoroughly.

Bewegt (Ger., be-vaygt'). Rather fast; with motion.

Bis (Lat.). Twice; to be repeated; continued.

Bogen (Ger., bo'-ghen). Bow, of violins, etc., Also a slur or tie.

Bourdon (Fr., boor-dong'). A set of large stopped organ pipes. A drone bass accompaniment.

Bravura (It., brah-voo'-rah). Spirit, skill, requiring dexterity.

Break. The change between head and chest register, in voices. The change between the fundamental and the harmonic series on clarinets.

Broken chords, broken octaves. Chords or octaves whose notes are played in succession, and not simultaneously.

Buffo (It., boof'-fo). Comic; a singer who takes comic parts.

C. The first note of the scale of C. The sign for common time (4/4) is not really a C, but two thirds of a circle.

Cadence. A close in melody or harmony, ending a period, section, or entire piece, usually on the tonic chord of its key.

Cadenza (It., cah-den′-tsah). An ornamental solo passage introduced near the end of an instrumental piece or song; the *cadenza* may be written by either composer or performer.

Calando (It., cah-lahn′- do). Becoming softer and slower.

Calmato (It., cahl-mah′-to). Tranquil, quiet.

Caloroso (It., cah-lo-ro′-zo). Warm, animated.

Cantabile (It., cahn-tah′-bee-leh). In a singing style, smoothly.

Cantilena (It., cahn-tee-lay′-nah). The melody of a song or piece; a melodious song, piece, or passage.

Capo (It., cah′-po). The beginning, the top, or head.

Capriccioso (It., cah-pree-chyo′-zo). Capriciously, fancifully.

Carita (It., kah-ree′-tah). Feeling, tenderness.

Cembalo (It., chem′-bah-lo). A harpsichord.

Ces (Ger., tsehs). The note C-flat.

Chiarezza (It., kee-ahr-et′-tsah). Clearness, purity, neatness.

Cis (Ger., tsis). The note C-sharp.

Codetta. A short coda or extra concluding passage. For coda, see chapter on " Song-Forms."

Coloratura (It., co-lo-rah-too′-rah). Roulades, embellishments, or ornamental passages in vocal music.

Come (It., co′-meh). As, like, the same as.

Comma. The difference between a major and minor tone in the scale of nature (ratio of 81 to 80).

Comodo (It., co′-mo-do). Quietly, easily, conveniently.

Compass. The range of notes that a voice or instrument can give.

Con (It.). With.

Concert-Meister (Ger., con-tsairt′-my-ster). The chief violinist of an orchestra.

Concerto (It., con-chair′to). A piece of several movements for one or more solo instruments with orchestra (sometimes one solo instrument with piano).

Concertstück (Ger., con-tsairt′-stik). A concert-piece; a concerto.

Continuo (It., con-teen′-oo-o). Constant, continual.

Contralto. Literally, a deeper alto. Often used to mean alto.

Corda (It., cor′-dah). A string. In piano music, *una corda* (one string) means soft pedal, while *tre corde* (three strings) means a cessation of the soft pedal. Sometimes *due corde* (two strings) calls for the soft pedal halfway down, but in old times, when piano notes never had more than two strings apiece, it meant a cessation of the soft pedal.

Crescendo (It., creh-shen′-do). A gradual increase in power.

D. The second note in the scale of C major. Abbreviation for *da* or *dal*.

Da (It., dah). From, by, through, etc. *Dal, dalle*, etc., are the same.

Da capo al segno (It., dah cah′-po ahl say′-nyo). From the beginning to the sign. *Dal segno* means " from the sign."

Deciso (It., day-chee′-zo). Boldly, decidedly.

Decrescendo (It., day-creh-shen′-do). Gradually diminishing the power.

Delicato (It., day-lee-cah'-to). Delicate, smooth.

Des (Ger., dehs). The note D-flat.

Destra (It., dehs'-trah). Right, right-hand.

Détaché (Fr., day-tah-shay'). Detached, staccato, in violin music.

Di (It., dee). Of, with, from, etc.

Diapason. The entire scale or range. A set of organ pipes running through the entire keyboard.

Dièse, dièze (Fr., dee-ez'). Any sharp.

Diluendo (It., dee-loo-en'-do). Dying away into silence.

Diminuendo (It., dee-mee-noo-en'-do). Gradually diminishing in power.

Dis (Ger., dees). The note D-sharp.

Divisi (It., dee-vee'-see). Divided, separated; used when a single group of voices or instruments is to take two or more notes instead of one.

Do (It., do; like " doe "). The syllable applied to the first note of a scale in singing, etc. In the " fixed *Do* " system, *Do* is always C. The French use *Ut* instead of *Do* in instrumental music.

Dolce (It., dol'-cheh). Sweetly.

Dolente (It., doh-len'-teh). Mournful, grieving.

Doloroso (It., dol-o-ro'-zo). Sadly, sorrowfully.

Dopo (It., do'-po). After.

Doppio (It., dop'-pee-o). Double, twofold; sometimes with the octave added.

Double (Fr., doo'-bl). An old term for a variation.

Doucement (Fr., doos-mong'). Sweetly, softly.

Dritta (It., drit'-tah). Right, right-hand.

Droit (Fr., drwah). Right, right-hand.

Duo, due (It., doo'o, doo'-eh). Two.

Duolo (It., doo-o'-lo). Grief, sorrow.

Dur (Ger., door; like " poor "). Major, major key.

E. Third note of the scale of C major. In Italian, *e* or *ed* means " and."

Écossais (Fr., ay-cos-say'). Scotch, in Scotch style.

Einfach (Ger., ine'-fahkh). Simple, plain.

Empfindung (Ger., emp-finnd'-oong). Feeling, emotion, sensitiveness.

Energico (It., en-air'-jee-co). Energetic, forcible.

Ensemble (Fr., ong-som'-bl). Unity, smoothness, literally, " togetherness."

Entr'acte (Fr., ongtr-act'). Music played between the acts.

Erhaben (Ger., air-hah'-ben). Lofty, elevated.

Ernst (Ger., airnst). Earnest, serious.

Eroica (It., air-o'-ee-kah). Heroic.

Erotik (Ger., Nor., air-ot-eek'). A love-song; an amorous composition.

Es (Ger.). The note E-flat.

Espressivo (It., es-pres-see'-vo). Expressive; with expression.

Etta, etto (It.) are diminutive terminations.

Etwas (Ger., et'-vahs). Somewhat; some; a little.

F. The fourth note of the scale of C major. Abbreviation for *forte*.

Fa. The name applied to the fourth note of the scale in singing, etc. In the "fixed Do " system, it is always F.

Facile (It., fah'-chee-leh). Light, easy.

Falsetto. Very high head tones in the male voice.

Feurig (Ger., foy'-righ). Fiery, ardent.

Filar la voce (It., fee'-lahr lah vo'-che). To spin out or prolong a tone with the voice; to let the tone diminish very gradually.

Fine (It., fee'-neh). The end.

Fioriture (It., fee-o-ree-too'-reh). Embellishments in singing.

Fis (Ger., fees). The note F-sharp.

Forte (It., for'-teh). Loud, strong.

Fortissimo (It., for-tees'-see-mo). Very loud. Abbreviated to *ff*.

Forza (It., for'-tsa). Force, power.

Forzando (It., for-tsahn'-do). Forced, accented. See *Sforzando*.

Freudig (Ger., froy'-digh). Joyfully.

Frisch (Ger., frish). Fresh, lively.

Fuoco (It., foo-o'-co). Fire, passion.

Furioso (It., foo-ree-o'-zo). Furious, vehement.

G. Fifth note of the scale of C major. Abbreviation for *gauche*.

Gauche (Fr., gosh ; the *o* as in " go "). Left, left-hand.

Gefühl (Ger., geh-feel'). Feeling, sentiment, expression.

Gehend (Ger., gay'-end). The same as *andante;* literally, " going."

Gentile (It., jen-tee'-leh). Graceful, elegant.

Ges (Ger., ghes; like "guess "). The note G-flat.

Giocoso (It., jyo-ko'-zo). Merry, humorous.

Gis (Ger.; like "geese "). The note G-sharp.

Giusto (It., joos'-to). Exact, in exact time. Sometimes it means moderate, i.e., not excessive.

Glissando (It., glees-sahn'-do). Gliding, sliding. With voice or violin, sliding toward a tone instead of attacking it directly. In piano music, a white-key scale played by dragging a finger or thumb along the keys.

Grave (It., grah'-veh). The slowest musical tempo; very slow and solemn.

Grazia (It., grah'-tsee-ah). Grace, elegance.

Grosso (It., gros'-so). Full, grand, great.

H. Used by the Germans to mean our B-natural. Heel in organ pedaling.

Harmony. The agreement or consonance of sounds uniting into a pleasing whole when heard together. The science and study of chords.

Heftig (Ger., hef'-tigh). Insistent, boisterous, vehement.

Hirtlich (Ger., heert'-likh). Pastoral, rustic.

Homophony. In modern music, a style of melody supported by chords, in contrast to polyphony, which is melody supported by other melodies or parts or voices.

Incidental music. Pieces written to go with a play or drama.

Innig (Ger., in'-nigh). Deep, sincere, earnest.

Inversion. A change of an octave in the pitch of one or more notes in an interval or chord.

Issimo (It., ees'-see-mo) is a superlative termination.

Istesso (It., is-tes'-so). The same.

Janko keyboard. A system of piano keys in several manuals, or ranks, invented by Paul von Janko. This keyboard necessitates only a small stretch for large intervals.

Kapellmeister (Ger., kah-pell'-my-ster). The director of music, at first in a church or chapel, but now in any chorus or orchestra.

Key. The lever that is moved to make the piano action strike the strings. A lever opening or closing a hole in wind instruments. A scale, the key being the first (tonic), note of the scale.

Kräftig (Ger., kref'-tigh). Powerful, strong, energetic.

L. Abbreviation for left, or (Ger.) *linke*, hand.

La. A syllable applied in singing, etc., to the sixth note of the scale.

Lamentoso (It., lah-men-to'-zo). Lamenting, mournful.

Langsam (Ger., lahng'-sahm). Slow. The same as *lento*.

Languendo (It., lang-gwen'-do). Languishing.

Largamente (It., lahr-gah-men'-teh). Broadly, with fulness.

Larghetto (It., lahr-get'-to). A tempo not quite so slow as *largo*.

Largo (It., lahr'-go). A slow, broad tempo, almost as slow as *grave*.

Lebhaft (Ger., layb'-hahft). Lively, quick.

Legatissimo (It., leh-gah-tees'-see-mo). Extremely smooth and fluent.

Legato (It., leh-gah'-to). Smooth, with no pause between notes.

Leggiero (It., led-jyair'-o). Light, delicate.

Leidenschaftlich (Ger., ly'-den-shahft-likh). Passionate.

Lento (It., len'-to). A slow tempo, usually between *adagio* and *andante*.

Licenza (It., lee-chen'-tza). License, freedom of style.

Linke (Ger., ling'-keh). Left, left-hand.

Loco (It., lo'-co). Place. Used to show a return to the pitch of printed notes after an 8va transposition.

Lunga (It., loong'-gah). Long.

Lustig (Ger., loos'-tigh). Merry, gay.

M. Abbreviation for *mano* or *main*, meaning " hand."

M. M. Abbreviation for Maelzel's metronome.

Ma (It., mah). But.

Maestoso (It., mah-es-to'-zo). Majestic, stately.

Maggiore (It., mahd-jyo'-reh). Major.

Main (Fr., like " man " with a nasal sound instead of the *n*). Hand.

Mano (It., mah'-no). Hand.

Marcato (It., mahr-cah'-to). Marked, accented.

Martellato (It., mahr-tel-lah'-to). Strongly marked.

Mässig (Ger., may'-sigh). Moderate, *moderato*.

Meno (It., may'-no). Less.

Messa di voce (may'-sah dee vo'-che). A gradual swelling and subsiding on a single tone in singing.

Mestoso (It., mes-to'-zo). Sadly.

Metronome. A device invented by John Maelzel in 1815, in which a weighted rod, projected upward, swings from side to side in regular time, to mark the beats of the measure. The rate may be varied by a movement of the weight. Figures are placed on the rod, indicating where the weight should be put to obtain any desired number of beats per minute. Composers sometimes mark their pieces with a metronome mark; i.e., a figure and a note of definite value, showing that the piece must be played so as to sound that number of notes of the given value in a minute.

Mezzo (It., med'-zo). The middle, half.

Mi (It., mee). A syllable used for the third note of the scale in singing, etc.

Minacciando (It., meen-aht-chyahn'-do). Threateningly.

Misterioso (It., mis-tair-ee-o'-zo). Mysteriously.

Mit (Ger., mitt). With.

Moderato (It., mod-air-ah'-to). Moderate tempo, between *andantino* and *allegretto*.

Moll (Ger.,). Minor.

Molto (It., mol'-to). Much; extremely; a great deal.

Morendo (It., mo-ren'-do). Dying away gradually.

Mosso (It., mos'-so). Movement, motion, speed.

Moto (It., mo'-to). Motion, movement.

Nachdruck (Ger., nahkh'-drook). Emphasis.

Nicht (Ger., nikht). Not.

Noël (Fr., no-ail'). A Christmas song; derived from **nouvelles**, " tidings."

Non (It.). Not.

Obbligato (It., ob-blee-gah'-to). A passage of such importance that it is obligatory, and cannot be omitted; sometimes a solo passage.

Octave-marks, 8va, *and* **8va bassa.** When *8va* is put over a note, the note is to be played an octave higher. A line extending from the *8va* shows that all notes under the line are to be played an octave higher. *8va bassa*, placed under a note or notes, transposes an octave downward.

Ohne (Ger., o'-neh). Without.

Organ point, see pedal point.

Ossia (It., os'-see-ah). Or.

Ostinato (It., os-tee-nah'-to). Obstinate, continual, unceasing.

Ou (Fr., oo). Or.

P. Abbreviation of piano, meaning " soft." Abbreviation of pedal.

Parlando (It., pahr-lahn'-do). In a speaking or declamatory style.

Partitur (Ger., pahr-tee-toor'). A full score.

Patetico (It., pah-tay'-tee-co). Pathetic.

Pedal point. A sustained pedal or bass note, over which are varying chords and harmonies.

Perdendosi (It., pair-den'-do-zee). Decreasing in power, dying away.

Piacere (It., pee-ah-chair'-eh). Pleasure. *A piacere*, at pleasure, as desired.

Piangendo (It., pee-ahn-jen'-do). Plaintively, sorrowfully.

Pianissimo (It., pee-ahn-ces'-see-mo). Very soft. Abbreviated to *pp*.

Piano (It., pee-ah'-no). Soft. The name " piano," as applied to the instrument, comes from *Gravicembalo con piano e forte*, meaning a keyed instrument with both soft and loud tones.

Più (It., pyoo). More.

Plus (Fr.; like " plea " pronounced with the lips nearly closed). More.

Poco (It., po'-co). Little, a little.

Poco a poco (It.). Little by little.

Poi (It., po'-ee). Then, after that, next.

Polyphony. Music that is composed of parts, or voices, which support one another, in contrast with *homophony*, which is melody supported by chords.

Ponticello (It., pon-tee-chel'-lo). The bridge of a violin or other stringed instrument.

Portamento (It., por-tah-men'-to). The carrying-over of one note into the next, so rapidly that the intermediate notes are not defined. In piano music, two or more notes under a slur, with dots above them; the notes to be played with some emphasis and separated slightly.

Prestissimo (It., pres-tees'-see-mo). Extremely fast; as fast as possible. The quickest tempo in music.

Presto (It., pres'-to). Very rapidly; quicker than any tempo except *prestissimo*.

Primo (It., pree'-mo). Principal, first.

Quadrat (Ger., quad-raht'). The sign for a natural.

R. Abbreviation in English or German for right.

Rallentando (It., rahl-len-tahn'-do). Making the tempo gradually slower.

Re (It., ray). The syllable used in singing, etc., for the second note of the scale.

Recht (Ger., rekht). Right, right-hand.

Registration. The combination of stops in organ playing.

Rinforzando (It., rin-for-tsahn'-do). Reinforced, accented.

Risoluto (It., ree-so-loo'-to). Resolute, bold.

Ritardando (It., ree-tahr-dahn'-do). Retarding, delaying the time gradually.

Ritenuto (It., ree-teh-noo'-to). Retained, kept back; more slowly.

Roulade (Fr., roo-lahd'). A florid vocal phrase.

Rubato (It., roo-bah'-to). A style of playing in which one note may be extended at the expense of another, for purposes of expression.

Sanft (Ger., sahnft). Soft, mild.

Sans (Fr.; " sahn " with a nasal sound instead of the *n*). Without.

Scale. A series of tones, comprised within an octave. The chromatic scale on our pianos consists of twelve equal semitones. By choosing intervals that have sometimes one semitone, and sometimes two (a whole tone), the diatonic scale is made. See chapter on " How to Read Music."

Scherzando (It., skairt-zahn'-do). Jestingly.

Scherzo (It., skairt'-zo). A jest, or play. A piece of lively tempo and jesting style, often in triple rhythm.

Schleppend (Ger., shlep'-pent). Dragging, drawling.

Schnell (Ger., shnell). Quick, rapid.

Sciolto (It., shee-oll'-to). Light, free.

Scotch snap. A sixteenth note followed by a dotted eighth note.

Se (It., say). If.

Segno (It., say'-nyo). A sign.

Segue (It., say'-gweh). It follows; now follows.

Sehr (Ger., sair). Very.

Semplice (It., sem'-plee-cheh). Simple, in a pure style.

Sempre (It., sem'-preh). Always; constantly.

Senza (It., sen'-tsah). Without.

Sforzando (It., sfor-tsahn'-do). Forced, accented. Abbreviated to *Sf.*

Si (It., see). The syllable used to denote the seventh note of the scale.

Signature. The sharps or flats necessary to give the key used for a composition. These are put at the beginning of each staff.

Sino, sin' (It., see′-no). To, toward, as far as.

Smorzando (It., smor-tsahn′-do). Dying away.

Sol (It.). The syllable denoting the fifth note of the scale.

Sopra (It., sop′-rah). Above, over, before.

Sostenuto (It., sos-teh-noo′-to). Sustaining the notes to their full length.

Sotto (It., sot′-to). Under, below.

Spianato (It., spee-ahn-ah′-to). Smooth, even; *legato*.

Spiccato (It., spik-kah′-to). Separated, detached; a semi-staccato for violin obtained by brushing the strings lightly with the bow and lifting it off quickly.

Spirito (It., spee′-ree-to). Spirit, fire, energy.

Staccato (It., stahk-kah′-to). Detached, separate. Notes made as short as possible.

Stesso (It., stes′-so). The same.

Stringendo (It., streen-jen′-do). Hurrying, accelerating the tempo.

Subito (It., soo′-bee-to). Suddenly, immediately.

Sul (It., sool). Upon, near.

Tanto (It., tahn′-to). So much, as much; too much.

Tedesco (It., teh-des′-co). German; in German style.

Temperament. The division of the scale into semitones. We have equal temperament, but before that (in the seventeenth century) musicians used a compromise with the scale of nature, called "mean temperament."

Tempo (It., tem′-po). Time, with regard to speed; the pace at which a composition is to be played.

Tenerezza (It., ten-air-et′-za). Tenderness.

Tenuto (It., teh-noo′-to). Held, sustained for its full time.

Tessitura (It., tes-see-too′-rah). The location of a majority of tones in a piece or song.

Ti. A syllable sometimes used for the seventh note of the scale, in place of *si*, which is too sibilant.

Timbre (Fr., tam′-br). Quality of tone.

Time. Properly used for the rhythm of a piece; i.e., the number of beats in a bar; as 3/4 time, 9/8 time, etc. But it is safer to use the word " rhythm " instead of " time," to avoid confusion with " tempo."

Tonart (Ger., ton′-ahrt). Scale, mode, key.

Toujours (Fr., too-zhoor′). Always.

Tranquillo (It., tran-queel′-lo). Tranquil, calm.

Tremolo (It., treh′-mo-lo). A trembling or quavering; the rapid repetition of a note.

Tristezza (It., trees-tet′-sah). Sadness, pensiveness.

Troppo (It., trop′-po). Too much.

Turca (It., toor′-kah). In Turkish style.

Tutto (It., toot′-to). All, the whole.

Umore (It., oo-mo′-reh). Humor, playfulness.

Un, uno, una (It., oon, oon′-o, oon′-ah). One, a, an.

Ut. The syllable used by the French, in instrumental music, instead of *Do*, to designate the first note of the scale, or C.

Veloce (It., vay-lo'-cheh). Swiftly.

Vibrato (It., vee-brah'-to). Recurrent swells and subsidences in a tone.

Vivace (It., vee-vah'-cheh). A brisk, animated tempo.

Voce (It., vo'-cheh). The voice.

Vorspiel (Ger., for'-speel). A prelude; one of Wagner's preludes, with which he replaced the operatic overture.

Wenig (Ger., vay'-nigh). Little, a little.

Zart (Ger., tsahrt). Gently, tenderly, softly.

Ziemlich (Ger., tseem'-likh). Somewhat, rather.

Zierlich (Ger., tseer'-likh). Graceful, neat.

Zögernd (Ger., tsay'-gernd). Retarding, hesitating.

INDEX

INDEX

INDEX TO SUPPLEMENTARY CHAPTER